PENGUIN BOOKS

THE PENGUIN HISTORY OF MODERN CHINA

'A newsdesk blockbuster, packed with facts and breathless drama' *Independent*

'At times he is the prosecutor, seeking the truth behind sacred planks of Chinese propaganda ... At other moments he has a journalist's eye for telling details ... Fenby finds facts that jolt and surprise' *Daily Telegraph*

'Panoramic narrative ... a wonderful resource' Professor Pamela Crossley in the *Far Eastern Economic Review*

'For an accessible, authoritative, fair, comprehensive and well written account, this would be hard to better' *BBC History*

'Reads like a novel and is never less than thoughtful and compassionate for the fate of a much-abused people' *Herald*

'Vivid ... Fenby excels at weaving the strands of his complex narrative into heroic and more often harrowing tales' *The Times*

'The most compelling and judicious account of China's phoenix years that is currently available ... A journalist's eye for detail, undemanding prose and a thunderous sense of narrative assure Jonathan Fenby of a triumph' *The Times Literary Supplement*

'[Fenby] has identified a gap in the literature on the country that anyone who claims to be informed about the contemporary world needs to at least try to understand ... Readers will relish this book' *The Australian*

ABOUT THE AUTHOR

Jonathan Fenby has edited the *Observer*, the *South China Morning Post* and Reuters World Service as well as holding senior positions at the *Economist*, *Independent* and *Guardian*. His books include *Generalissimo: Chiang Kai-Shek and the China He Lost*, *Dealing with the Dragon: A Year in the New Hong Kong*, *Seventy Wonders of China*, *Dragon Throne*, and *Alliance: How Roosevelt, Stalin and Churchill Won One War and Began Another*. He is currently Editor-in-Chief and China Director of the analytical service *Trusted Sources*. He was made a Commander of the British Empire in 2000 for services to journalism and is a knight of the French Order of Merit.

The Penguin History of Modern China was selected among the 2008 Books of the Year by the *Economist* and the *Financial Times*.

JONATHAN FENBY

The Penguin History of Modern China

The Fall and Rise of a
Great Power, 1850–2009

PENGUIN BOOKS

PENGUIN BOOKS

Published by the Penguin Group
Penguin Books Ltd, 80 Strand, London WC2R ORL, England
Penguin Group (USA) Inc., 375 Hudson Street, New York, New York 10014, USA
Penguin Group (Canada), 90 Eglinton Avenue East, Suite 700, Toronto, Ontario, Canada M4P 2Y3
(a division of Pearson Penguin Canada Inc.)
Penguin Ireland, 25 St Stephen's Green, Dublin 2, Ireland
(a division of Penguin Books Ltd)
Penguin Group (Australia), 250 Camberwell Road, Camberwell, Victoria 3124, Australia
(a division of Pearson Australia Group Pty Ltd)
Penguin Books India Pvt Ltd, 11 Community Centre, Panchsheel Park, New Delhi – 110 017, India
Penguin Group (NZ), 67 Apollo Drive, Rosedale, North Shore 0632, New Zealand
(a division of Pearson New Zealand Ltd)
Penguin Books (South Africa) (Pty) Ltd, 24 Sturdee Avenue, Rosebank, Johannesburg 2196, South Africa

Penguin Books Ltd, Registered Offices: 80 Strand, London WC2R ORL, England

www.penguin.com

First published by Allen Lane 2008
Published in Penguin Books with minor revisions 2009
008

Typeset by Rowland Phototypesetting Ltd, Bury St Edmunds, Suffolk
Printed in Great Britain by Clays Ltd, St Ives plc

A CIP catalogue record for this book is available from the British Library

978-0-141-02009-9

www.greenpenguin.co.uk

ALWAYS LEARNING   **PEARSON**

To Renée, with love again

Contents

PART 3:
Wars Without End

PART 4:
The Rule of Mao

PART 5:
The Age of Deng

PART 6:

Jiang Zemin and Hu Jintao

Acknowledgements

Simon Winder commissioned this book in the first place and has been as enthusiastic and constructive an editor as an author working through 150 years of complex history could wish for. So my first thanks go to him, followed by Christopher Sinclair-Stevenson, who convinced me that this was not too great a mountain to set out to climb.

Robert Ash and Rana Mitter were supportive of the project, and devoted time to reading portions of the manuscript to come up with most helpful suggestions. I am also particularly grateful to Bob Ash for data on social and economic conditions since 1949. Lisa Croll smoothed my way to the invaluable resources of the School of Oriental and African Studies in London: she is sadly missed. I have also benefited along the way from the help and observations of Richard Baum, Jasper Becker, Jean-Philippe Béja, Robert Bickers, Kerry Brown, Robert Elegant, Joseph Fewsmith, Paul French, Isabel Hilton, Christopher Hughes, David Kelly, William Kirby, Willy Lam, Jonathan Mirsky, Richard Pascoe and his colleagues at Nottingham University, Sun Shuyin, Gary Tiedeman, Steve Tsang, Ezra Vogel, Arne Odd Westad, Hans van de Ven, and Xinran and Wei Zhang, as well as from the knowledge and wisdom of the China Pol website.

Mark Handsley copy edited the book expertly, and was long-suffering with last-minute additions. Amanda Russell handled the photographic research with great skill and understanding. Alice Dawson and Richard Duguid at Penguin kept the wheel turning most efficiently. Rebecca Lee showed both dexterity and patience in seeing through the changes to bring the paperback edition up to date for 2009.

This book draws on the extensive body of written work on modern China by historians on four continents, and on discussion and meetings with some of them. I am constantly struck by the breadth and depth of scholarship on China, from detailed monographs to wide surveys of the country and its recent past. While it may be invidious to single out any particular books from those mentioned in the bibliography, I am particularly indebted, in addition to those authors cited above, to works by Lloyd Eastman, Joseph Esherick, Immanuel Hsü, Simon Leys, Roderick MacFarquhar, Evelyn Rawski, Michael Schoenhals, Jonathan Spence and Frederick Teiwes. As indicated in the text, I drew on the *Tiananmen Papers* edited by Andrew Nathan and Perry Link for the events of 1989. Graham Hutchings's *Modern China* was, once more, an invaluable reference point. My colleague Lawrence Brainard provided stimulating insights into the post-reform Chinese economy, while Alexander Monro came up with revealing nuggets and Bo Zhuang was of great assistance in supplying information and improving my display technique. As in previous books, I have also drawn substantially on contemporaneous accounts by journalists and other observers which provide eyewitness material often missing in archival documents and can act as a valuable counterweight to the official line handed down by successive regimes.

As always, I profited from the hospitality of friends who gave me boltholes in which to work, put up with my disrupting social stays and acted as sounding boards – among them, Annie and Thomas Besnier, Anne Boston, Andrew and Sarah Burns, Peter Graham, Ginette Vincendeau and Simon Caulkin, and Lisa and André Villeneuve on the Avenue Wagram. Sara and Erol Arguden were pillars of strength when needed close at hand, as were Alexander and Lianne further away.

The dedication of this book to my wife only dimly reflects her vital role, not only in her comments and close-focus editing but, more basically, in support that gave me the confidence to carry through the project. For that, I owe her an unending debt – provided, of course, that her confidence does not prove misplaced by the result.

Note on Transliteration and Currency

The Pinyin system of transliteration has generally been used in this book with the exception of some names – such as Sun Yat-sen, Chiang Kai-shek, the Soongs or Canton – which are most familiar in the older Wade-Giles system. Earlier transliterations of the names of cities are given in footnotes.

The currency denoted by the $ sign up to 1949 is the Chinese yuan; where US dollars are involved, this is specified. Thereafter, $ = US currency.

List of Illutsrations

Photographic acknowledgements are given in parentheses.

Section One

1. The Dowager Empress Cixi, with the Chief Eunuch.
2. Prince Gong.
3. Li Hongzhang and Gladstone *circa* 1870 at Hawarden Castle, Wales. (Getty Images)
4. John Charles Oswald in his company's tea-tasting room in Fuzhou around 1890. (unknown photographer: Oswald Collection, SOAS (0s05–164))
5. Puyi and his father, Prince Chun. (Getty Images)
6. Manchu commander Jung-lu.
7. Imprisoned boxers in their compound *circa* 1900. (copyright © Bettmann/CORBIS)
8. Coal miners in Shaanxi, early twentieth century. (Father Leone Nanni/PIME MILAN)
9. Women with bound feet. (Father Leone Nanni/PIME MILAN)
10. Yuan Shikai and Chinese generals after inauguration, 1912. (Getty Images)
11. Nationalists meet in a Shanghai drawing room in late 1911.
12. Zhang Xueliang.
13. Li Zongren.
14. Yan Xishan.
15. Feng Yuxiang.
16. Sun Yat-sen and his wife, Soong Qingling, 1916. (Getty Images)
17. Chiang Kai-shek and financier Soong Ziwen. (T.V.Soong)

Section Two

Maps

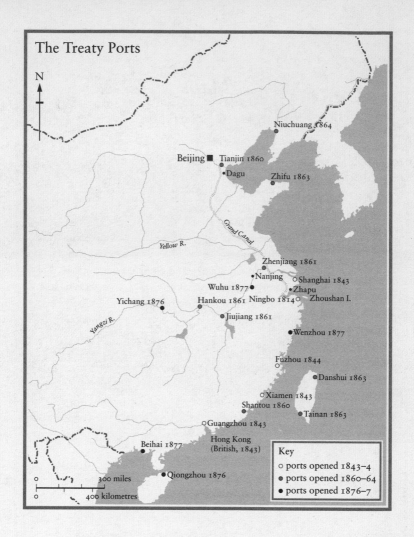

The Treaty Ports

N

Niuchuang 1864

Beijing ■ Tianjin 1860
•Dagu
Zhifu 1863

Grand Canal

Yellow R.

Zhenjiang 1861
•Nanjing ○ Shanghai 1843
Wuhu 1877• •Zhapu
Hankou 1861 Ningbo 1814○ Zhoushan I.
Yichang 1876•
•Jiujiang 1861

Yangzi R.

•Wenzhou 1877

Fuzhou 1844○
•Danshui 1863

○Xiamen 1843
Shantou 1860
•
○Guangzhou 1843
•Tainan 1863

Hong Kong
(British, 1843)
Beihai 1877•

•Qiongzhou 1876

300 miles
400 kilometres

Key
○ ports opened 1843–4
• ports opened 1860–64
• ports opened 1876–7

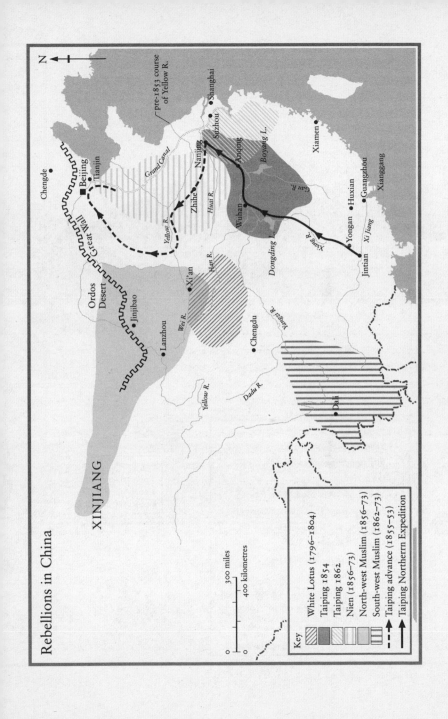

Rebellions in China

Key

White Lotus (1796–1804)
Taiping 1854
Taiping 1862
Nien (1856–73)
North-west Muslim (1856–73)
South-west Muslim (1862–73)
Taiping advance (1855–53)
Taiping Northern Expedition

The Warlord Era

Urumqi (Wulumuqi)

(1)

XINJIANG

QINGHAI

TIBET

Lhasa

Key

(1) Yang Zengxin

(2) fifty competing militarists

(3) Long Yun

(4) Yan Xishan (The Model Governor)

(5) Feng Yuxiang (The Christian General)

(6) Wu Peifu (The Philosopher General)

(7) Guangxi Clique

(8) Chen Jiongming/Kuomintang

(9) Sun Zhuangfang

(10) Zhang Zongchang (The Dogmeat General)

(11) Beijing came under control of Zhang, Wu and Feng at different times

(12) Zhang Zuolin (The Old Marshall) and Zhang Xueliang (The Young Marshall)

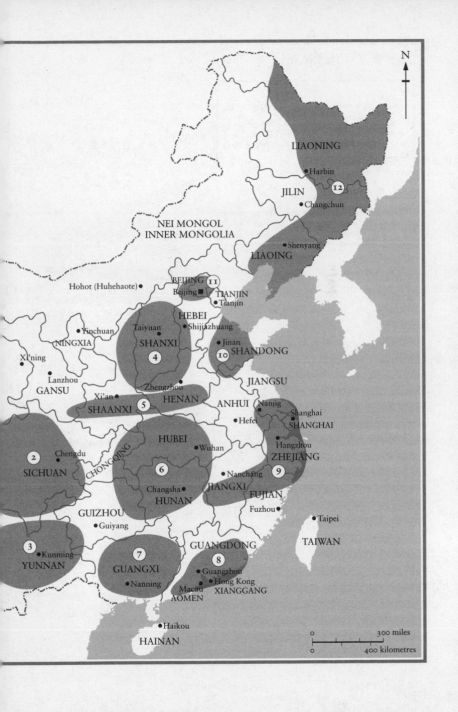

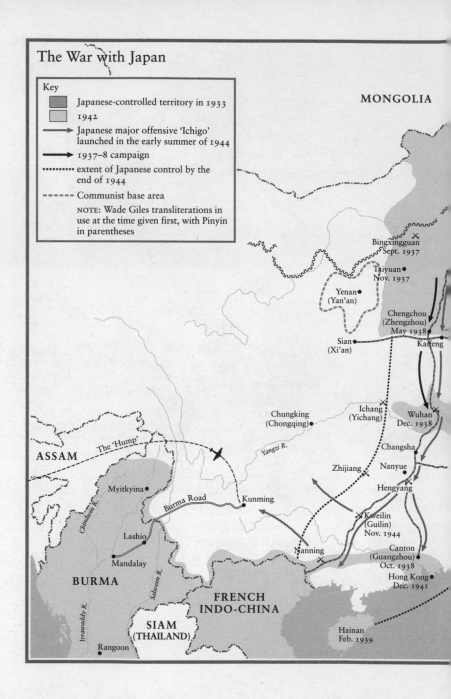

The War with Japan

Key

- Japanese-controlled territory in 1933
- 1942
- Japanese major offensive 'Ichigo' launched in the early summer of 1944
- 1937–8 campaign
- .... extent of Japanese control by the end of 1944
- ------- Communist base area

NOTE: Wade Giles transliterations in use at the time given first, with Pinyin in parentheses

MONGOLIA

Bingxingguan
Sept. 1937

Taiyuan
Nov. 1937

Yenan
(Yan'an)

Chengchou
(Zhengzhou)
May 1938

Kaifeng

Sian
(Xi'an)

Ichang
(Yichang)

Wuhan
Dec. 1938

Chungking
(Chongqing)

Yangzi R.

Changsha

Zhijiang

Nanyue

Hengyang

ASSAM

The 'Hump'

Myitkyina

Burma Road

Kunming

Kweilin
(Guilin)
Nov. 1944

Canton
(Guangzhou)
Oct. 1938

Lashio

Chindwin R.

Nanning

Hong Kong
Dec. 1941

Mandalay

BURMA

Salween R.

FRENCH
INDO-CHINA

Irrawaddy R.

SIAM
(THAILAND)

Hainan
Feb. 1939

Rangoon

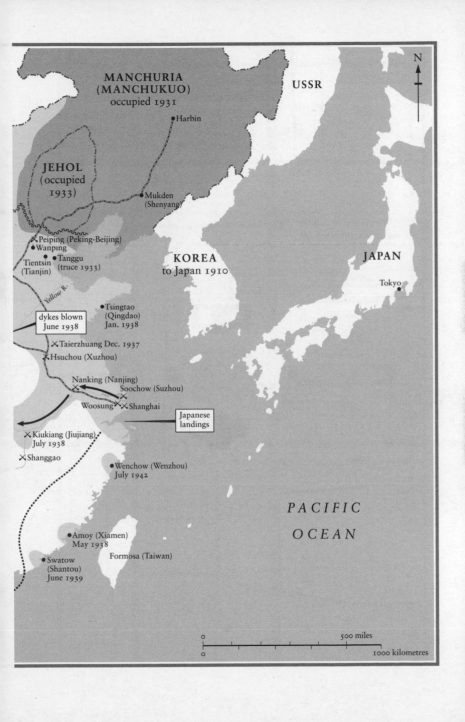

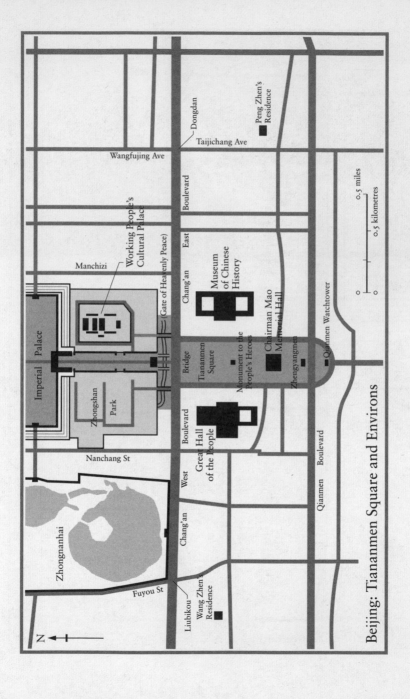

Beijing: Tiananmen Square and Environs

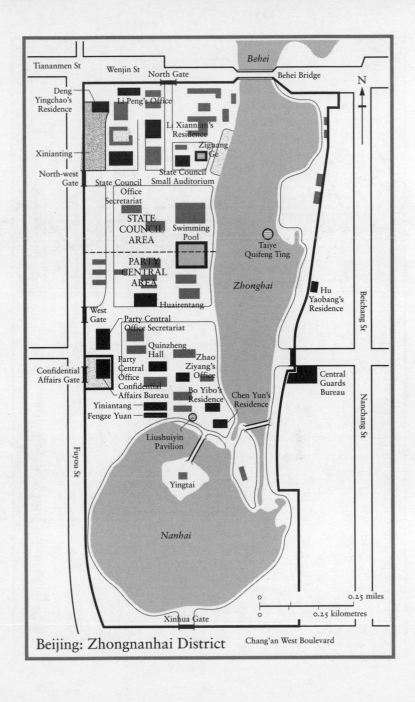

Beijing: Zhongnanhai District

China's Crops and Cultivation Patterns

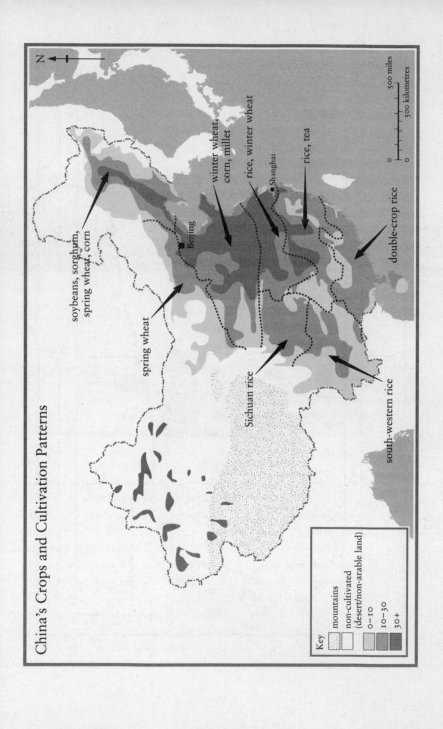

Key

- mountains
- non-cultivated (desert/non-arable land)
- 0–10
- 10–30
- 30+

N

500 miles
500 kilometres

soybeans, sorghum, spring wheat, corn

spring wheat

winter wheat, corn, millet

Beijing

rice, winter wheat

Shanghai

rice, tea

double-crop rice

Sichuan rice

south-western rice

Economic Growth Zones

N

Key

(1) metropolis of 30 million inhabitants being developed

(2) fastest growth under economic reform

SEZ special economic zone

LIAONING

•Harbin

JILIN

•Changchun

NEI MONGOL
INNER MONGOLIA

•Shenyang

LIAOING

major development
for 2008 Olympics

Hohot (Huhehaote)•

BEIJING
Beijing■

TIANJIN
•Tianjin

growth pole

HEBEI

•Shijiazhuang

•Yinchuan

Taiyuan

NINGXIA

SHANXI

•Jinan

SHANDONG

•Lanzhou

Zhengzhou

JIANGSU

growth pole

GANSU

Xi'an•

HENAN

ANHUI

Nanjing

SHAANXI

•Hefei

Shanghai

SHANGHAI

SICHUAN

HUBEI

•Wuhan

Hangzhou•

•Chengdu

CHONGQING

ZHEJIANG town enterprises

(1)

•Nanchang

Changsha•

JIANGXI

FUJIAN

growth pole

HUNAN

Fuzhou•

GUIZHOU

•Guiyang

Xiamen
SEZ

•Taipei

•Kunming

GUANGXI

GUANGDONG

TAIWAN

YUNNAN

(2)

Nanning•

Guangzhou•

•Shantou SEZ

Zhuhai SEZ•

•Shenzhen SEZ

Macau
AOMEN

Hong Kong
XIANGGANG

•Haikou

HAINAN SEZ

0   300 miles

0   400 kilometres

Introduction

In the second half of the nineteenth century, China appeared as the sick man of Asia, rocked by recurrent revolts and huge natural disasters, ruled by an anachronistic imperial system and humiliated by foreign invasions as it declined from the heights it had reached less than a hundred years earlier. Karl Marx saw it as bound to disintegrate when it met the glare of outside light, like 'any mummy carefully preserved in a hermetically sealed coffin'. The first half of the twentieth century was even worse. The republic which replaced the empire stumbled into warlordism and fell under an inefficient dictatorship before suffering fourteen years of invasion by Japan that led to death and destruction on a massive scale. Then came four years of civil war, followed by three decades of erratic, oppressive rule by Mao Zedong with its catalogue of failed experiments, famine and massive purges that killed tens of millions, culminating in the nightmare of the Cultural Revolution.

At the start of the twenty-first century, the People's Republic of China (PRC) is a major global force, booming economically and confident that it holds the keys to a future in which it will rival the United States on the world scene. Spectacular as the impact has been since the start of economic reform in 1978, this is likely to increase even further; if China gets into trouble, the effect will be felt across the globe.

Growth has brought with it major fault lines and imbalances, leading some observers to consider that the process is unsustainable. Too often, policies are inadequate, uncoordinated and poorly implemented. For all its economic expansion, the PRC is still a poor country overall, with a gross domestic product (GDP) less than a quarter of that of the United States – and far smaller in per capita terms. But the speed and scope of its transformation since the country's dynamic forces were unleashed at the end of the 1970s have been blinding and unprecedented, with worldwide impact because it has taken place in the context of globalization.

That makes it easy to forget what went before, in particular the recurrent ordeals the world's most populous nation suffered from the 1850s to the 1970s, during which time more than 100 million of its people died at the hands of their compatriots and leaders. Significantly, if not surprisingly, the grand pageant of China's history at the opening of the Olympic Games in Beijing in 2008 made no mention of the period. Yet this experience forms the essential backdrop to understanding the country's more recent evolution, leaving a heritage that continues to shape China in the new century. That is the subject of this book.

With 1.3 billion inhabitants and an average of 44,000 births a day, the PRC is at the centre of the world stage. It has the third biggest national economy on earth, nuclear weapons and a standing army of 2.2 million troops is the largest in the world – the military budget has been rising officially at 18 per cent a year, though the figure understates real spending. American military capacity and technology remain far superior, but the growth of the PRC's power could jeopardize the strategic hegemony of Washington in Asia. As well as staging a space walk in 2008 and planning to send a man to the moon, Beijing flexed its muscle by shooting down one of its own satellites, a move seen by the Pentagon as a potential threat to America's communications systems. US command of the seas of Asia is confronted by a Chinese programme to build aircraft carriers and modernize its fleet; a PLA submarine popped up in the middle of one major American exercise in 2005. To protect its cargo ships, the PRC sent a naval task force to the Indian Ocean in 2009.

Beijing has a permanent seat on the United Nations Security Council, and a fast-expanding global economic and political presence – in 2007, it offered Africa triple the aid the continent got from the West, and that year's summit of the African Development Bank was held in the most un-African location of Shanghai. PRC companies buy into the five continents. Under Mao, the PRC sought to export revolution; now it spreads 'soft power' through diplomacy and assistance, cultural institutes and festivals. China's history (often fashioned to deliver an approved political message) has hit international cinema screens. At the end of 2007, a 23-year-old Beijing secretary was elected Miss World.

The PRC has no compunction about the regimes it befriends if they can serve its interests, even if other powers shun them as rogue states. Beijing has been Sudan's best ally, the friend of Robert Mugabe's Zimbabwe, and a partner for Iran and North Korea as well as developing close links with Burma, to where a million Chinese have emigrated. The United States, Europe, Japan and others are torn between co-operation and fearing the intentions and clout of the phoenix power.

This is not a country with existential doubts, though the sharp economic downturn that set in at the end of 2008 jolted confidence. Surveys show 80–90 per cent of Chinese positive about their homeland. National pride was boosted by the 2008 Olympics, with some Chinese attributing pro-Tibetan western protests against the Olympic flame to envy of the progress of the People's Republic. With a quarter of the global workforce, mainland China has tilted international economics. Since the launch of economic reform in 1978 more people have been made materially better off in a shorter span of time than ever before in human history. This has produced a social revolution as aspirations and mobility have risen. The number of Chinese travelling abroad each year has increased to more than 35 million, and three quarters of a million Chinese study overseas each year.

The 'socialist market economy' has grown tenfold in three decades, buoyed by cheap labour, cheap capital and high productivity, which is reckoned to have increased by an average of 20 per cent a year from 1996 onwards. In 2008, the PRC was the world's second biggest manufacturer, with 15 per cent of output, just behind 17 per cent for the USA. Beijing has set itself the target of quadrupling per capita GDP by 2020. The huge corporate, personal and state savings pool has poured into fixed asset investment and export industries, giving a relatively poor country an unprecedented place at the centre of the global system.

At the end of 2008, its economy was worth 27.4 trillion yuan – $4 trillion or £2.7 trillion in nominal exchange-rate terms – and, by a World Bank calculation, twice that in purchasing-power parity – i.e. what money actually buys. The first put it behind the European Union, the US and Japan, the second behind only the US. Annual growth in the early twenty-first century ran at 9–10 per cent, jumping to 13 per cent in 2007 on figures revised in early 2009 to take account of the growing service sector. This put China ahead of Germany in the size of its economy. But growth then dropped to single digits in the downturn of 2008. The trade surplus hit record levels, generating reserves of

$1.9 trillion by the end of 2008, going largely into US Treasury and mortgage bonds, thus funding the federal deficit and helping to keep down interest rates, making it easier for Americans to live on credit while aiding the fight against inflation on the other side of the Pacific. China's success brought pressure for Beijing to increase the value of its currency which it did, but at its own pace. Meanwhile, Chinese savings continued to soar in contrast to the spending and indebtedness of the West. By mid-2008, household savings alone reached 20 trillion yuan.

While other nations worry about low growth or an insufficient stock of cash, China had the opposite problem before the impact of the global financial crisis in 2008 slowed down economic expansion as its property market dropped, its main export markets contracted, and the Shanghai stock market slumped. Money has become the great determinant in a country whose leadership professes its faith in the tenets of Marxism–Leninism–Mao Zedong Thought. The father of economic reform, Deng Xiaoping, probably never actually said, 'It is glorious to grow rich', but he recognized that poverty and the lack of incentive for self-improvement were fatal constraints on a country waiting to escape from the shackles of its past.

Thirty years after Deng gained the upper hand in the power struggle that followed the death of Mao Zedong, China has a spearhead private sector and state-owned enterprises that apply market principles, engaging in cut-throat competition and slashing their labour forces by a total of some 60 million workers. There is a middle class estimated at 80 million, mainly living in big cities and defined primarily by its consumption. In 2007 up to 100 people were thought to be US dollar billionaires, though the richest fifty were estimated to have lost a third of their wealth when the stock and property markets slumped in 2008. The five most frequently asked 'what is' questions on the most popular Chinese Internet search engine concern finance. At a Buddhist temple in Shanghai, monks take credit card donations from visitors.

Under economic reform, Communist Party cadres whose provinces or cities produce high growth can expect advancement. They also use their positions to promote their own interests, relying on the fact that 'however poor some places may be, the government will never be poor'. In a list of China's 'powerful people' it produced at the end of 2007, the website of the Southern News group put officials first, ahead of industrial monopolists, real estate developers, stock market manipulators, managers of large multinational companies, and those whose skills are in high demand in sectors such as health care and education. As well as the cadres themselves, a network of family, friends, associates and mistresses spreads the charmed circle, as officials form alliances with business and speculators, arousing resentment among those left out from this flowering of bureaucratic capitalism.[1]

Wealth disparities are spiralling. Rich parents, and some officials, buy their way round the one-child policy by simply paying fines for having a second, third or even fourth child. By 2008, a hundred million trading accounts had been opened on the stock exchanges in Shanghai and Shenzhen. When the market index trebled in value in 2007, company shares were quoted at up to fifty times earnings – in the prosperous eastern city of Wenzhou, the authorities had to issue a formal ban on officials dealing in shares from their desks or leaving the office to visit brokers.

The bubble burst in late 2008 after the headlong increase in property prices in the previous years went into sharp reverse and manufacturers suffered from over-capacity and big inventories. Confidence slumped with a flood of declining economic figures, including the first fall in exports for seven years. (Imports fell even more sharply to maintain the trade surplus.) The regime was suddenly on trial on the economic front. A string of stimulus measures was unveiled, designed to ensure that annual growth did not fall below the 7–8 per cent level required to keep the economic machine running, create at least 10 million jobs a year, and enable industry to modernise.

In its quest for growth, China has waged a relentless campaign to buy up the raw materials needed to fuel growth – hence the friendships with Sudan, Iran and Zimbabwe, along with big deals with the Democratic Republic of the Congo (for copper) and Angola and Venezuela (for oil). It has set out to acquire Western technology and managerial and marketing skills. A Chinese firm took over IBM's personal computer business and turned it into the Lenovo brand. In 2007, Chinese banks bought into leading Wall Street private equity firms and brokerage houses, and acquired stakes in European and African banks, losing a lot of money when financial markets crashed. A $200–300 billion sovereign wealth fund was established by the Chinese state, in part to invest abroad. The Party leader, Hu Jintao, laid out an economic agenda at the 2007 Party Congress of encouraging innovation and private enterprise, looking forward to the growth of global firms that could market 'Chinese brands' – hardly language one might expect from a follower of Marxism–Leninism–Mao Zedong Thought.

The country's small-sized town and village undertakings employ as many people as the whole American labour force. A hundred and fifty million migrants work in factories in the booming coastal areas, and as many again are underemployed in agriculture, providing a potential new stream of workers in manufacturing and services.

Having become the hub of worldwide production and logistics, the PRC makes 80 per cent of the world's best-selling toys, and offers transplant hearts at $150,000 each. A cluster of towns in Zhejiang province, in the east, produces a third of the world's socks, 40 per cent of its ties, and 70 per cent of its cigarette lighters as well as 350 million umbrellas a year and a billion decks of playing cards.

Around the world, prices of everything from energy to timber, iron ore to soya beans, are deeply affected by Chinese demand. In Europe, theft of drain covers and lead from church roofs have been put down to the PRC's hunger for metal. Before the downturn of 2008, the usual up-and-down cycle of shipping rates was punctured by the call for ships to sail to mainland ports with the supplies China needs, and to take out goods. Though its own innovation lags, the PRC has become the greatest assembly shop the world has known, contributing significantly to the profitability of American, Japanese and European firms. The third biggest destination for overseas investment after the US and UK, the mainland attracted $800 billion in foreign money between the start of economic reform in 1978 and 2008. In 2007, 88 per cent of Chinese exports of high-tech goods were from firms owned or invested in by foreign companies. In 2007, for the first time since the 1930s, another country contributed more to global growth than the United States. A Gallup poll in early 2008 reported that 40 per cent of Americans considered the PRC to be the world's leading economic power, while only 33 per cent chose their own country.

The speed and scale of modernization are overwhelming in a nation which was still emerging from the madness of the Cultural Revolution only a generation ago, and where hundreds of millions can remember the uniformity of collectivization and the famine that killed tens of millions around 1960. In 2007, more than 8,000 villages had annual incomes exceeding 100 million yuan. At the start of the economic reform, the big city of Wuhan in central China had no taxis; today it is estimated to have 30,000. In 2008, the PRC had 3,000 television stations, 1.3 million websites, 300 million Internet users, (the highest number of any country) 540 million mobile telephone users, and 137 handsets for every 100 urban inhabitants. Fast food chains proliferate. The showpiece city of Shanghai is Manhattan on steroids; rich young men there complain that development is changing the street pattern so fast that the GPS systems are out of date before they take delivery of their new limousines. Beijing caught up with its major make-over for the 2008 Olympics, sprouting tower blocks, shopping malls, advanced urban transport networks and modernistic buildings, including a futuristic theatre inaugurated by the former President, Jiang Zemin, warbling light operatic airs.

With GDP more than doubling between 2002 and 2008 to 27 trillion, China has become the biggest producer of steel and aluminium, and, among so many other things, provides 60 per cent of the world's vitamin C. Construction reached such a pitch in the early years of the twenty-first century that half the world's cranes were estimated to be at work in the mainland. Huge infrastructure projects were topped by the Three Gorges Dam on the Yangzi, which has been dreamed of since imperial days. Further up-river, planners were turning the once isolated Sichuan city of Chongqing into a metropolis of 30 million people. For foreign companies seeking new markets, the PRC was the last great frontier for everything from luxury goods to airliners, the place they had to be.

China's sheer size and population mean that everything about it tends to be vast. It has always been that way. The huge infrastructure projects of the Communists mirror similar undertakings stretching back to the First Emperor's construction of the first Great Wall, his vast necropolis at Xi'an and myriad other monumental edifices. The present one-party regime has lasted a lot longer than his Qin dynasty, which expired after fourteen years following the death of its founder in 210 BC; but its ability to cope with the potential destabilization confronting it remains an open question for the current generation of leaders.

Major questions hover over the economy three decades after Deng Xiaoping launched the reform process. The trade surplus and a flood of 'hot money' betting on currency appreciation brought a wave of liquidity in 2007–2008 which the inadequate banking and financial system could not contain. Imbalances proliferated. The role played by exports and investment in fixed assets like factories, housing and infrastructure projects was too large, consumption too low and savings which rose to 50 per cent of GDP too big.

Then the impact of the slowdown in western export markets took its toll at the end of 2008 as growth fell below 10 per cent, underlining the way the PRC is now exposed to global forces. This posed a particular issue for China. The shedding of Marxist–Maoist ideology has made material improvement the prime claim to legitimacy for the regime and the Communist Party. So a serious decline could put the whole edifice at risk. But, since political diversity is ruled out and the promotion of 'inner party democracy' is designed to strengthen the CCP and not to challenge it, there is no way another ruling group could take over without bringing the fundamentals of the system into question. Another, linked, core claim of the rulers is that they ensure social harmony. But official figures report up to 70,000 protests by 100 or more people annually. Many are by farmers over expropriation without proper compensation. In Shanghai and Xiamen, middle-class protestors staged demonstrations to block projects threatening their property. In inland towns, riots were set off by factors varying from bus fares to the death of a teenage girl. These are single-issue demonstrations not an organized opposition; still, their scale shows the degree to which people are ready to press complaints. Fear of protests by laid-off workers is very real. Such issues raise a string of interrogations for China, and the world, which are given added force by the heritage dealt with in this book.

The PRC is the only one of the ten major global economies not to be a multi-party democracy. In view of its economic and social transformation, can it continue to be run effectively by a Communist Party whose leader entitled his report to his movement's Congress in 2007 'Hold High the Great Banner of Socialism with Chinese Characteristics and Strive for New Victories in Building a Moderately Prosperous Society in All Respects'? China's history is one of authoritarian regimes – the only partially free multi-party election ever held on the mainland, in 1912, ended in the assassination of the head of the winning party. Is this tradition compatible with the modernity the PRC is now experiencing? Does that point to regime change? Or, with greater material well-being, is stability with Communist characteristics sufficient for most people after the turmoil of the past? Or will it foster pressure for liberty and multi-party elections that would destroy the top-down mode inherited from the past? Whether the regime can cope with the challenges confronting it – politically, economically and socially – is a prime global question for the early twenty-first century.

As heir to the Mandate of Heaven, the Communist Party, whose leadership resides for the most part in an old imperial estate beside the Forbidden City, is intent on not sharing power with anyone. In contradiction of Marx's vision of the state withering away, the last major power claiming his inheritance cleaves to its apparatus, backed by a huge police machine. Though people enjoy far more individual freedom than was the case in the first three decades of the People's Republic, organized dissent is stamped on and individual human rights activists are persecuted. For the Olympics, three sites were set aside for protests, but all applications to demonstrate were turned down. Petitioners who go to Beijing to seek redress for their complaints risk being locked up. In late 2008, protestors in Shandong province were reported to have been sent to a mental hospital while the publication in the US of a call for democracy by 300 Chinese intellectuals was swiftly followed by the detention of one of its prominent signatories. The Falung Gong spiritual movement is seen by the regime as a visceral threat, a re-birth of the secret sects that dot Chinese history. The media are strictly controlled. Websites which step out of line are closed down, while the 'Great Firewall of China', manned by 30,000 cyber guards, seeks to block access to critical services.

Though Hu Jintao and his colleagues appear in public in smart black suits and smile for the cameras, the tradition of using violence to settle disputes is deeply ingrained. The massacre in Beijing in June 1989 is part of living history, even if the regime cannot bring itself to do anything but parrot the Party line on the event. The People's Liberation Army (PLA) is an important political force, as the Revolutionary Army was under the republic and the modernized forces were in the late imperial period. Like militias of the past, the People's Armed Police (PAP) forms a paramilitary force which has often been estimated to be a million strong, though a white paper in 2006 put its numbers at 660,000. At local level, some authorities and business people use thuggish gangs to supplement the police, just as 'bullies' working for landlords under the republic and 'yamen runners' (from the name for their offices) under the empire imposed the exactions of their masters. In 2004, 40,000 unqualified police were sacked or transferred, but violence and self-seeking by the security forces remain a feature of the Chinese landscape.

As in the past, official and family links predominate; many of the country's richest citizens rely on them for their fortunes. The sons and daughters of earlier Communist leaders, known as 'princelings', prosper in business and politics, constituting 40 per cent of the Politburo in 2009. In the absence of objective rules or an independent legal system, with vague property rights, fallible contracts and frequent sharp practice, the way ahead is to 'learn the tricks of the trade and work hard', as a businessman puts it. Though the Party, like its predecessors, preaches morality, nobody takes much notice, from senior figures exploiting their posts for profit to overseers using slave labour in brick kilns. In 2007, officals were reported by the state auditor to have embezzled the equivalent of $7 billion, including disaster relief funds.[2]

In this supposedly socialist nation, the wealth gap is greater than that in Europe or the United States. The pressure of work in factories has given rise to a new term – 'overwork deaths'. Migrants in sweatshops labour for twelve or more hours a day, sometimes locked in, with fatal results when fires break out. Household income in provinces such as Guizhou and Gansu, which have been little touched by economic expansion, is one sixth of that in prosperous coastal zones.

There is massive ecological degradation. In 2007, the PRC passed the United States as the biggest emitter of greenhouse gases (though in per capita terms it remains far behind). Air pollution causes more than 400,000 premature deaths a year. The official plan to urbanize half the population by 2020 means a huge increase in energy demand – in 2007, a new coal-fired power station was opened on average every week, most spewing out brown coal fumes. The city of Linfen in Shanxi was named by the World Bank in 2006 as having the worst air quality on earth. The Asian Development Bank forecasts that a fifteenfold increase in the number of cars will triple CO_2 emissions by 2040. The government regularly announces anti-pollution campaigns and lays down targets, but – given China's reliance on polluting industries like coal, cement and steel for its expansion and the cost of clean technology – growth usually wins out; the spraying of a barren mountainface in the southwest with green paint might stand as an ironic example of the limits of environmental campaigning. At the end of 2007, a government plan was announced to move 4 million people from the area of the Three Gorges

Dam, in addition to the more than one million already relocated, to avoid what was described officially as a potential environmental catastrophe from China's most highly touted project. Limited improvement in air and water quality in 2008 was attributed to the economic slowdown.[3]

With 22 per cent of the world's population and 7 per cent of its arable land, China faces a constant battle to meet the food security levels laid down by a government fearful of becoming dependent on imports. But a million hectares are lost to agriculture each year. Urbanization eats up land. Desertification is spreading at the rate of 2,000 square miles a year. Ten per cent of fields are estimated to be polluted. In addition to its own growing mountains of urban waste, China has become a destination for global rubbish, though economic downturn of 2008–9 cut a swathe through Beijing's army of 160,000 collectors of waste for recycling as packaging. Water is dangerously short in the north; hundreds of urban centres draw their drinking supplies from rivers into which raw sewage pours and rural supplies are hit by diversion to factories. In April 2007, 10 per cent of the longest river, the Yangzi, was reported to be in critical condition, and 30 per cent of its main tributaries seriously polluted.[4]

The number of people living in absolute poverty has been slashed, still stands at 76 million by international measurement standards. The PRC ranked only eighty-first worldwide in the United Nations Human Development Report in 2006. The previous year, just seven of its thirty-one provinces recorded consumption spending above the national average. Lack of education leaves 110 million people aged over fifteen illiterate. The pension system is a black hole. A demographic crisis is looming as the one-child policy cuts the number of young people while life expectancy rises – the number of people aged over 65 is expected to go from 100 million in 2005 to as many as 329 million in 2050, or from 7.6 to 23.6 per cent of the total population. A major gender imbalance has emerged from the preference for male children and abortions of female foetuses. The absence of health provision means that three quarters of rural dwellers cannot afford care. Epidemics such as the outbreaks of the SARS respiratory disease or bird flu are cloaked by official secrecy. At least 700,000 people were infected with HIV as of the end of 2007.[5]

Abolition of agricultural taxes has lifted a burden on farmers, but means that local authorities lack the revenue to provide services. The 750 million people living in the countryside have been left behind economically. Land belongs to the state, though a scheme was launched in 2008 to allow them to rent out leased land to boost their incomes. Expropriation of agricultural plots for development reduces the growing area.

Regulation is weak or non-existent. In 2007, a quarter of the toys produced in China were reckoned to be unsafe, some covered with lead paint, leading to an international outcry. The former head of the food and drug administration was executed that year for accepting bribes to issue retail licenses for unsafe medicines. A survey of 450,000 food companies found that 60 per cent did not have quality control facilities. Then, in 2008, tens of thousands of babies were affected by tainted milk powder that had been treated with a chemical to increase its apparent protein content, which had been widely used in other food products. Commercial piracy is rampant – 80 per cent of software in use in the PRC is estimated to be counterfeited. 'We're not living in a moral society, and sure as hell not in a moral age,' argued a software pirate who sold Windows for 10 per cent of the Microsoft price.*[6]

Though growth has magnified these challenges, and introduced new ones, many are legacies from the past, or reflect historical patterns. Autocracy, persecution of dissent, a self-protective, self-serving elite, use of force, absence of the rule of law or external accountability, corruption and cronyism, provincial disparities, the imposition of arbitrary fees and rents by local officials, lack of welfare, limited concern for the environment, a thin layer of wealth on top of an ocean of relative poverty – all go back to the imperial era. As a result, China in the early twenty-first century is, at one and the same time, very new and quite old.

The 'princeling' offspring of first-generation CCP leaders constitute an aristocracy that could have existed at an imperial court. Ritual and precedence still play a central role, at Party congresses and in the carefully orchestrated rankings of the leadership from the Standing Committee of the Politburo downwards. The Communists do not admit doctrinal error any more than the emperors did, claiming their own Marxist–Leninist–Maoist Mandate of Heaven and operating as much like a secret

---

* In a piquant episode in late 2007, a court in eastern China fined the French engineering group Schneider the equivalent of $45 million for infringing patents held by a local firm at its local factory.

society as a ruling party. Any individual who presumes to resist its wisdom must be wrong, or a traitor.

As under the imperial dynasties, nationalism is equated with Sino-centrism which asserts the supremacy of the system practised in the Middle Kingdom. China's special place in the world remains a tablet of the law. Sovereignty is paramount, enshrined in Beijing's insistence that nations should not interfere in one another's affairs. This has the advantage of closing off international debate over its own repression and its continuing rule over territories conquered by force, and is calculated to please other governments which do not want to be held to account.

Mao Zedong and Deng Xiaoping have the status of hallowed ancestors, with constant references to their teachings. On the 110th anniversary of the Great Helmsman's birth, the Party chief, Hu Jintao, delivered a 10,000-character speech to extol the achievements of the founder of the PRC; before speaking, Hu went to the Memorial Hall beside Tiananmen Square to bow three times to a statue of the man responsible for the deaths of many tens of millions. At local level, traditional power structures stretch through provinces to towns and villages, even if they are exercised today by Communist cadres and business people, rather than imperial magistrates and gentry landowners.

As Party secretary, head of state and chair of the Military Affairs Commission, the supreme leader is the equivalent of a dynastic ruler, either imposing himself (Mao, Deng) or operating through factions and coalition-building (their successors). In the first decades of Communist rule, old men clung to power like emperors who carried on into their dotage, but were still able to command events. Mao and Deng were both in their mid-seventies when they launched, respectively, the Cultural Revolution and economic reform. The twenty-five-member Politburo ushered in at the 2007 Party Congress contained just one woman, and the Standing Committee none. Thrusting younger politicians in China tend to reach the top at an age at which they would be contemplating retirement in the West.

In a tradition stretching back to the First Emperor, history is subordinated to the requirements of the ruling power. In 1999, a professor was arrested and charged with stealing state secrets when he dared to research the Cultural Revolution. A re-examination of the massacre of demonstrators in Beijing in 1989 remains off-limits. An academic who suggested taking into consideration the excess of the Boxers in their rising of 1900 was censured. In the spring of 2006, senior officials handling the publishing industry issued instructions at a private meeting that 'reports on important historic events and persons must strictly follow' Communist Party directives. 'Abide by the propaganda discipline, stand in the same line as the central government and the people,' it urged.[7]

Internationally, the history of half a century of war and bloody invasion colours relations with Japan, even if both sides appear to recognize the need to move on. Along China's north-eastern border, the legacy of the Korean War is perpetuated in the division of the peninsula and Beijing's uneasy relationship with Pyongyang. Despite talk of the emerging economic power of 'Chindia', links with the other major Asian country continue to be edgy, bedevilled by frontier disputes in the Himalayas. The key contact, with the United States, is affected by the history of trade and missionaries, the fractious alliance in the Second World War, Washington's refusal to intervene to save the Nationalists from the Communists in 1949, the long Cold War enmity and then the burgeoning links after Richard Nixon's trip to meet Mao in Beijing in 1972. Each country needs the other, but on either side of the Pacific are those who see a threat which has to be confronted.

Since the earliest days of the empire, and despite periods of dislocation, China has been a unitary state. But the strength of its regions and their different characteristics mean that, at times, it more resembles a federation. Recently, the decentralization of economic reform has perpetuated the centuries-old tug of war between the centre and the provinces. Senior CCP officials are not posted to their home regions, to avoid their constructing local power bases, just as the magistrates of imperial days were stationed away from their native areas to prevent the development of a feudal system. Despite repeated efforts by Beijing to control expansion, provinces went on opening steel mills, cement plants, infrastructure schemes and coal mines in pursuit of growth. Notwithstanding Hu Jintao's aim of a 'harmonious society', officials staged 131,000 land grabs in 2006 from farmers. Decentralization and a long tradition of provincial power mean that networks of influence have to be taken into account by officials of the central power – as a saying goes, 'A mighty dragon cannot overpower a snake in its lair.'[8]

Hu is anxious to rejuvenate the Communist Party, but a conundrum cannot be evaded. Only 11 per cent of its 73 million members are in the industrial proletariat. Nineteen per cent are retired people. The five-yearly Party Congress of 2007, which gave Hu another five years at the top, was dominated by political managers – workers and farmers got hardly a look-in. As under the empire, China is led by an elite that seeks to co-opt the best and brightest and thus head them off from opposition. Old ways may be swept aside in theory, but they live on in practice, though business now offers a highly attractive alternative route ahead.

'Face' still counts in political, social and business relationships. The old calendar was abandoned after the fall of the empire, but, a century later, everybody takes an extended holiday at lunar New Year. As in imperial times, the brightest students congregate for mass examinations to enter the civil service; and, as in the past, the number of jobs is a tiny fraction of those seeking them, adding to a growing problem of graduate unemployment. Cronyism and the age-old taste for gambling show through in runaway stock exchange speculation, and the tendency towards insider dealing. The former Portuguese colony of Macau, reunited with the PRC in 1999, outdoes Las Vegas as a gambling centre. At the end of 2008, betting on horse races was permitted for the first time since 1949.

Chinese medicine has enjoyed a revival, and the regime seeks to promote traditional culture in the face of imports from the US, Japan and Hong Kong. Despite repeated iconoclastic attacks, a Confucius renaissance began in 2005, with a lavish birthday party for the philosopher attended by 3,000 people. The doctrine of a 'harmonious society' proclaimed by President Hu to lessen national disparities has strong Confucian overtones. A book extolling the sage's teachings has sold more than 4 million copies, and his name has been taken as the brand for PRC cultural institutes round the world.[9]

The ancient creed of Daoism is also staging a comeback; in 2007, the government sponsored a six-day forum to examine and promote its main text, *The Book of the Way and Its Virtue*. The previous year, a world Buddhist forum was held in Zhejiang province (and the regime has shown how seriously it takes the potential threat of the Dalai Lama naming his successor by introducing a law to regulate reincarnation). A poll in 2007 found that 300 million people could be described as religious – treble the official total. Sixty per cent of believers were aged between sixteen and thirty-nine.[10] A century after the Boxer rising against the foreign religion, Christianity experienced a revival, both in officially sponsored churches (which involved conflict between Beijing and the Papacy) and in informal 'house churches'; by 2008, the estimate of the number of Christians in the PRC went as high as 40 million.

Destruction of old urban areas has been unrelenting, but it was somewhat checked in Shanghai when entrepreneurs realized that Art Deco buildings from the 1920s and 1930s could attract high-paying customers as clubs, restaurants, bars and hotels. Materialist Communism has not brought an end to ancient customs and beliefs. For 2008, three traditional festivals were reinstated as public holidays, including the Dragon Boat Festival believed to date back to the fourth century BC; the mythical beast lives on in the Dragon's Mouth region on the lower Yangzi round Shanghai, Dragon Seal wine and Dragon Head Enterprises in agro-industry. The geomancy of *feng shui* is widely followed. Graves are swept to honour the dead, who are comforted by offerings of paper and cardboard artefacts to use in the afterlife. In Hebei province south of Beijing, the corpses of single young women are buried alongside defunct male bachelors so that the souls of the men shall not lack partners; in 2007, a man was accused of killing six mentally disturbed young women to sell their bodies as 'ghost brides'.

A survey by the National School of Administration in 2007 showed that just over half of county-level civil servants did not reject physiognomy, astrology and divination. The lunar probe of 2007 was named for a goddess said to have flown to the moon. The number 8 is auspicious in some dialects because it sounds like the word for wealth – the opening ceremony of the Beijing Olympics began at 8 p.m. on the 8th day of the 8th month of the 8th year of the millennium. Births in the lucky Year of the Pig in 2007 rose by 20 per cent. And had it been an utter coincidence that the Communist Party chose as eight the number of its 'Immortals' in the 1980s and 1990s – as if they were the modern equivalent of the eight gods of Daoism?[11]

Though national unity is a prime concern of the regime, regional differences – cultural, linguistic and gastronomic – remain strong. A survey by the Education Ministry reported in 2007 that only 53 per cent of 50,000 people questioned across China could 'communicate effectively' in the official national tongue. Despite a huge investment in transport infrastructure, links are still insufficient – China handles about a quarter of world rail traffic on 6 per cent of global track. It is quicker and cheaper to import coal to Guangdong province in the south from Indonesia or Australia than to bring it from the mines of the north. Half the country's road haulage firms are reckoned to own a single truck. The era when villages had no contact with one another because of the topography and lack of tracks may be gone, but this is still a patchwork of a nation, on a continental scale.[12]

In another imperial inheritance, China is the last great colonial empire on earth, hanging on to ethnically separate Tibet and the vast Muslim lands of Xinjiang, despite unrest in both territories which spilled over into riots and a central government clampdown in the first in the spring of 2008 and into outbreaks of violence in the second during the 2008 Olympic Games. In Tibet, Beijing blasts the 'splittism' of the Dalai Lama and his followers and expresses surprise that the people are not more grateful for the assistance being given to the local economy, including the building of the world's highest altitude railway to Lhasa and the development of mineral fields in the Himalayas. In Xinjiang, China's main domestic source of oil and gas, separist movements linked to Muslim terrorist groups were blamed by Beijing for the violence, sometimes with vague evidence. In neither case was the PRC ready to face the fact that it was seen as an occupying power, resented by the locals as Han Chinese flooded in to change the population balance and take most of the best jobs.

Some 40 million people of Chinese descent live abroad. In countries such as Indonesia, Malaysia and Thailand, they play a leading role in business, and have been subject to persecution, in many ways like the Jews of Europe. Old and new emigrant families from the provinces of Guangzhou and neighbouring Fujian dominate Chinatowns from south-east Asia to Europe and the USA. If their wealth was put together, the Overseas Chinese would form a formidable unit in the global economy. Their 'patriotic' investments were a significant factor in helping the mainland's economic take-off in the 1980s. Chinese gangs have joined the exodus, undertaking robbery, protection rackets and drug trafficking. 'Snakeheads' smuggle compatriots to the West, sometimes with tragic results as the migrants are drowned at sea or suffocate in lorries. When they arrive, there may be further perils, as in the tragedy in Morecambe Bay, England, in 2004, when twenty-three Chinese cockle-pickers were swept away by the tide.

Rightly, the Chinese pride themselves on being the heirs of the world's oldest continuous civilization, stretching back at least to the bronze age of the Shang dynasty of 1600 BC. They can be regarded as belonging to a common culture rather than a naturally cohesive country, a factor which buttresses the feeling of being special and differing from the inhabitants of mere nation states. Today, there can be no doubt that a new version of China is being born. Yet it cannot exist apart from its history. As Confucius is said to have said, understanding what the future holds requires grasping the lessons of the past. In other words, to comprehend the most important new force in today's world, one has to see where China has come from and what has shaped it.

PART I

End of Empire

For more than 2,000 years, the emperors of China were like no other sovereigns on earth, claiming to be intermediaries between Heaven and Earth who ensured cosmic harmony and embodied a universe of meaning. In the mythology of their rule, their special nature and that of their country were as important as the vastness of their domains. China was a culture and a civilization with an unparalleled history, rather than a nation state in the Western sense. While Europe broke into separate units after the fall of the Roman Empire, China remained wedded to the preservation of its imperial system, despite two major periods of disunion. Its inhabitants saw it as a place of exception which had nothing to learn from elsewhere: 'Our China must be regarded as the root of all other countries,' as a character remarked in a classic nineteenth-century novel. Presented with a world map at the start of the twentieth century, a provincial governor said it must be wrong because it showed the Pacific. 'The United States borders upon China,' he explained. 'It must do so because China is the centre of all nations.'[1]

In 1644, Manchu warriors from the north-east had come through the Great Wall to take Beijing from rebels who had moved into a vacuum left by the decline of the Ming ruling house. Extending their authority across the country, they ruled as the Qing ('Pure') dynasty. Under three great emperors, who ruled from 1661 to 1795, China reached an apogee, its influence stretching over 3.7 million square miles, including Taiwan, Tibet, the northern steppes and the huge western desert land of Xinjiang. From the start, the Qing adopted Chinese methods of government and traditions. But there were limits to the multi-cultural, multi-ethnic nature of their rule. The Han people, who constituted the bulk of the population, were made to shave their foreheads and wear pigtails as a sign of submission. Inter-marriage was prohibited. Nor were Han allowed to emigrate to Manchuria. As a result, the rulers were always foreigners to most of their people.

The empire was so large and so apparently successful that the Qing felt no need of the rest of the world. At its height, their realm may have accounted for a third of total global wealth. In 1793, the emperor contemptuously brushed aside the gifts brought by a British mission, telling the envoy, Lord Macartney: 'We possess all things.' Macartney's view was rather different. 'The empire of China is an old, crazy, first-rate Man of War, which a fortunate succession of able and vigilant officers have contrived to keep afloat for these hundred and fifty years past, and to over-awe their neighbours merely by her bulk and appearance,' he wrote after getting back to Britain. 'But, whenever an insufficient man happens to have command on deck, adieu to the discipline and safety of the ship. She may, perhaps, not sink outright; she may drift some time as a wreck, and will then be dashed to pieces on the shore; but she can never be rebuilt on the old bottom.' China's history in the nineteenth century would show who was right.

I

Sons of Heaven

Sitting on the Dragon Throne in the Forbidden City in Beijing,* China's emperors personified a system based on Confucian teachings which exalted the harmony of society and the planet, and demanded awe from all. Expressing their majesty and power through elaborate ceremonials and art, the dynasties which ruled China claimed semi-divine status. The ruler was set apart, rarely appearing in public apart from such symbolic occasions as his procession to the great circular Temple of Heaven in the south of the capital to offer prayers to the gods. He usually ate alone, choosing from a lavish array of dishes brought by eunuchs. At night, his chosen concubine was brought into his chamber wrapped in a red silk gown and laid naked at the foot of his bed.

Imperial mythology and Confucian tradition gave social and administrative glue to a country which covered only 7 per cent of the surface of the globe but contained around a fifth of its population. Dynasties operated on the basis of filial piety, the cornerstone of old values. In return for unquestioning allegiance, the sovereigns promised to be benevolent, caring for the welfare of their people and invoking divine protection on their behalf. A master–servant relationship ran from the court down to rural villages. Every man, it was said, regarded those above him as tigers to be feared, and those below him as dogs to be kicked. The empire reached back to 221 BC, when the First Emperor established himself in Xi'an after his kingdom of Qin had won out over warring states. His dynasty was one of the shortest-lived, enduring only until its fall under his son in 207 BC. Ruling houses came and went in

* The city's name (meaning 'north capital') was transliterated at the time as Peking; but I have used the current Pinyin style of Beijing throughout for clarity, including the period when it was no longer the capital and was known as Peiping ('northern peace').

cycle of rise and fall that would become engraved on the national psyche as they won and lost the Mandate of Heaven granted by the gods. Chinese civilization reached apogees under the Tang and Ming dynasties and prospered under less-remembered sovereigns. But there were constant threats from the nomads of the steppes, and two major invasions from the north by the Mongols in the late thirteenth century, and the Manchus, in the mid sixteenth century. Yet the idea of unifying rule from the centre had been implanted by the First Emperor and remained the foundation for the country, while the Mandate of Heaven contained the idea – however imperfectly implemented – that the rulers had a duty to care for the people.

China was rarely as cut off from the world as subsequent history pretended. The Silk Road linked it with Central Asia, the Middle East and the Mediterranean. Sailors and traders went to south-east Asia, India and Africa. But China believed it was special, and the Qing expansion of the empire under the Three Great Emperors from 1661 to 1795 marked a high point. The realm reached westwards into Central Asia, and other neighbours were brought under control. This was a Manchu construction, in which the Middle Kingdom, for all its importance, stood alongside the other domains to the north, where the ruling house was most at home. Still, China was bound to predominate, so its customs became the public face of the Sons of Heaven from distant lands.

In a society arranged by strict and elaborate stratification, princes, mandarins and gentry figures of the Manchu Qing dynasty, which had seized the throne in 1644 to rule over the far more numerous Han Chinese, had specific ranks, denoted by robes and badges. Proper behaviour and sincerity were held to be all. As the classic text the *Daxue* ('Great Learning') put it: 'Thoughts being sincere, hearts are rectified. Hearts being rectified, persons are cultivated. Persons being cultivated, families are regulated. Families being regulated, states are rightly governed. States being rightly governed, the whole kingdom is made tranquil and happy.'[1]

In such a culture, it was only natural that the capital was laid out to exalt the regime and its ruler. The Forbidden City sat at the heart of the metropolis, which, after some false starts, became the centre of the empire. The Sons of Heaven resided behind a 52-metre-wide moat and 10-metre-high walls that ran for two and a quarter miles round what was known as 'the Great Within'. Halls and gates were set on marble platforms amid huge courtyards. Symbolism was everywhere – power expressed through carved dragons, longevity by phoenixes in the inner palace. Imperial edicts were carried on ornate trays under umbrellas of imperial yellow to the balcony over the Tiananmen Gate to be read out before being lowered and distributed round the country.

Emperors might be quasi-divine, but it was not assumed that dynasties were for ever. The cycle of rise and fall had run through China's history. The Mandate of Heaven was, itself, eternal; but who held it was a very different matter. When the gods showed their displeasure, for instance by permitting major revolts or visiting particularly severe natural disasters on the country, it was time for change. Ambitious military commanders or rebel leaders could claim that they were the ones now qualified to mount the throne. Thus, the eternal melded with the temporal in a system which preserved itself by being able to accommodate fresh blood at the top without bringing fundamental verities into question.

A backward-looking concept of existence predominated, along with the proclamation of imperial authority over the whole realm which did not always accord with reality; the early decades of Qing rule had seen recurrent revolts, including one that stretched over ten provinces. Preserving stability rather than considering change was the watchword. The regime's view of its mission 'seems to be to keep records of past occurrences, legalise faits accomplis, and strangle whatever comes before it in embryo,' wrote the acute Western observer of the later nineteenth century, the British Customs chief, Robert Hart. The Confucian *Great Learning* enjoined 'keeping the state in order' as the path to universal peace. 'Generation after generation has upheld Confucian teachings, stressing proper human relationships, between ruler and minister, father and son, superiors and subordinates, the high and the low,' wrote a leading scholar-general of the mid nineteenth century. 'All in the proper place, just as hats and shoes are not interchangeable.'

Among those who should know their place and keep to it were women, who were meant to be obedient wives and virtuous mothers, and little else, despite the occasional presence of 'literati women' who read, studied and wrote poetry in the 'inner chambers' of their homes. Put into arranged marriages at an early age, women were generally not allowed to socialize with men outside their family, and their husbands would not think of introducing them to acquaintances or mentioning them in conversation. Their status was symbolized by the bound feet Han men found alluring – a ban on the practice by the early Qing had no effect. Husbands were free to take additional wives and concubines and to visit prostitutes. An imperial official who met foreign traders recorded how embarrassed he was when they presented their wives to him.[2]

The male line was all that counted; only men could carry out the essential practice of ancestor worship. Infanticide of baby girls was common – a visitor to Fujian province in the 1880s was told that, in some districts, a third of female babies were drowned or strangled. The one thing women could draw on was the veneration by their children demanded by Confucianism, and the dominance that mothers-in-law exercised over their daughters-in-law, who could count the years till they achieved similar power.[3]

To govern their continent-sized country with a population of more than 410 million by 1850, the emperors depended on a bureaucratic system refined over the centuries but too small to be fully effective – there were only 40,000 civilian and military officials. The rulers held powers of taxation, military affairs, law-making and appointments. Below the emperors sat the Grand Council, the Grand Secretariat, six boards and nine ministries, provincial governors and magistrates. Communication with the ruler was through memorials to the throne, which then issued its edicts. Court censors were meant to keep emperors informed of matters affecting government and the people. In the corridors and shadows of the Forbidden City lived a couple of thousand eunuchs, known for their intrigues and despised by the whole men around them; many were miserable and vulnerable, though a few rose to exercise power behind the scenes and enrich themselves accordingly.[4]

China was split into eighteen provinces, 1,300 districts and 143 departments, grouped under administrative prefectures. The magistrate in each district was the key functionary, acting as mayor, sheriff, judge, coroner, tax collector, surveyor, prison governor, registrar, organizer of imperial examinations and bailiff. Since they could not do all this, and were too few in number to exercise effective grassroots control, a system of self-surveillance operated. Households were organized by the thousand, then sub-divided into groupings of a hundred and then ten. Headmen kept a register of everybody in each group, recorded comings and goings, and reported to magistrates on such offences as theft, gambling, kidnapping and money coining. Villagers were required to tell the headman of any illegal behaviour they encountered – failure to do so was a crime.

Magistrates were supposed to be 'the father and mother officer' of districts, applying Confucian principles to ensure harmony and stability, exercising benevolence and commanding reverence as a result. They were meant to have absorbed the Chinese tradition by having passed the rigorous three-stage imperial examination rooted in Confucian classicism. But, by 1850, only 60 per cent had done so. Another 20 per cent had bought their degrees and the rest been elevated by such channels as 'recommendation' or recognition of their 'meritorious record'. When they started out, at least, they lacked practical knowledge and depended on private secretaries. These men had studied administration and have been rated by a historian of local government under the Qing as 'respected as men of integrity'; but some were accused of taking bribes, forming factions and falsifying accounts.

Rather than acting as 'fathers' for their districts, magistrates easily became oppressors from their *yamen* headquarters. The administrative code laid down from Beijing was rigid and did not take account of regional differences and requirements. There were tough central government revenue targets to meet, and local expenditure had to be financed through fees and other duties. Magistrates were expected to make up for their low salaries by extracting 'squeeze' from the people they administered. They were appointed for a spell of only three years to any one district and so lacked local roots. Their enforcers, the *yamen* runners, were often corrupt bullies and thugs – the magistrate's 'claws and teeth'.[5]

Inside the *yamen*, clerks, estimated to number more than a million across the country, controlled the day-to-day flow of business. One reformer reckoned that they were the true holders of power in China. Many were locals who used their knowledge to maximum personal advantage. They took a cut of salaries that went through their hands and charged for work on legal cases. The fees they levied were, a magistrate remarked, 'as numerous as the hairs on an ox'. Peasants in Henan province complained that they were 'more ferocious than demons. You need money to lodge a complaint and, even then, the official may not approve it. If he does approve, there is no guarantee that his underlings will carry out his orders. And every step along the way requires money. One law suit can bankrupt an entire family.'[6]

Across the country, working with the magistrates and higher provincial officials, the rural gentry were key to the system, and to the maintenance of stability. While they can be seen as a class, there were many differentiations within their ranks; they might have wealth without position or position without wealth. Most were landowners; many held imperial degrees and had links with provincial and national government. As the century drew on, an urban gentry class became increasingly important, but its members had family connections in rural areas. Buying of land by merchants, and investment in urban enterprises by gentry members, created a network of interests.

By the mid-century, the gentry numbered 1.4 million, or 7.2 million with families. They arbitrated land disputes, organized relief during natural disasters, cared for the poor and ran public works, in return for which they received local power and privileges. Their sons made up most of the candidates in the imperial examinations, which began locally, progressed to provincial level and culminated in a test in front of the emperor in Beijing. The system was beautifully designed to capture the best and brightest for the regime, instilling in them the traditional values embodied in the texts on which the examinations were based. By offering material advancement to clever young people, the regime co-opted them, rather than letting them form a challenging intellectual class as happened in the West. Culture, society and politics thus melded with one another. When a gentryman invoked classical values, he was perpetuating tradition, stating the superiority of Confucianism, proclaiming the doctrine on which the empire rested, and asserting his own position.

However, by the middle of the nineteenth century, the fault lines of the Qing empire were becoming ever more critical. At the centre, since everything depended on the emperor, there were no effective organized checks and balances. Dissent was equated with disloyalty, making free discussion difficult. Memorials to the throne denounced bad behaviour by officials, but challenging news was not welcome. The pursuit of conformity made initiative dangerous. Though meant to be impartial, the censors often indulged in partisan point-scoring and factional court politics.[7]

The era of the Three Great Emperors stretching from late seventeenth century to the end of the eighteenth marked the heights of Qing rule, but, for all its glory and majesty, the reign of the last of the trio,

Qianlong, left a questionable inheritance. Though China may have accounted for a third of the world's wealth, high spending, expansion of the army, frequent wars and the cost of administering the empire strained the fabric. Taxes covered outlays, and China's merchant class was booming, but, the emperor reflected, if people did not become more frugal, the regime risked disaster.

His successor, Jiaqing, who mounted the throne in 1796, faced disorder and natural disasters. An attempt to strengthen imperial finances by cutting official salaries aroused resentment. The Han Chinese elite was, in any case, mainly a fair-weather friend, semi-detached from the foreign dynasty. Social cohesion was breaking down – a scholar, Zong Zizhen, warned that 'the wealthy vie with each other in splendour and display while the poor squeeze each other to death.' This, he added, would 'fill the space between heaven and earth with darkness'.[8]

In 1813, rebels marched on Beijing, and the Son of Heaven narrowly escaped assassination before they were driven away. Seven years later, he died of a stroke and was succeeded by the largely ineffectual Daoguang emperor. One thing his court did do, however, was to order an end to the export of opium by the British from India to the southern port of Canton,* the only place where foreigners were allowed to trade. But the traders took no notice and the government in London backed the commerce to compensate for the boom in imports of tea from China. By the late 1830s, 1,400 tons of opium were being landed annually. Though conventional history depicts the British as having introduced the drug to China, use of opium in the Middle Kingdom went back much further – an imperial edict sought to ban it in 1728. What concerned the court in 1840 was that China was getting opium in exchange for its exports to Britain rather than silver which it needed to back the currency. An energetic commissioner, Lin Zexu, was sent to Canton to enforce the ban. The merchants agreed at first, and saw their opium stocks thrown into the Pearl River. But, after an affray involving British sailors, the Royal Navy sailed in. The island of Hong Kong was seized – the Foreign Secretary, Lord Palmerston, said the rocky outcrop was far from what Britain sought.

The First Opium War, in June 1840, was a walkover for the British, who out-gunned the Chinese on land and at sea. They took charge of

---

* Now transliterated as Guangzhou.

Canton and moved up to the Yangzi, where they threatened imperial tax barges. The Treaty of Nanjing of 1842, the first of what came to be known in China as the 'unequal treaties', ceded Hong Kong to Britain and opened to foreign trade the ports of Amoy (now Xiamen), Foochow (now Fuzhou), Ningpo (now Ningbo) and Shanghai. As well as being compensated for the narcotics destroyed by the commissioner and being allowed to continue the opium trade, British citizens were granted immunity from Chinese law. Humiliating as the experience was, the emperor did not appear worried. He told a mandarin that the foreigners were 'not worth attending to'. Another official put them 'in the class of dogs and horses'. The dynasty's mindset was rooted in the great arc of territory from its homeland in Manchuria through Mongolia to Tibet and Xinjiang. Surrounded by tributary states the rulers did not grasp the threat from European maritime expansion. Since they had no aspirations to take the Mandate of Heaven, the foreigners did not present a fundamental menace, and would, it was assumed, leave in due course.[9]

So the court went along with what became known as the treaty port system, granting concessions to foreigners to establish settlements, with their own administrations and courts. After the British came the French, and, at the end of the century, the Germans, while the Russians expanded from Siberia into Manchuria where Japan also established itself after inflicting a crushing defeat on China in 1894–5. Americans arrived, but their government refrained from taking a slice of the melon. The result was 'an informal empire' of foreigners in a country that was too big to be colonized, but could be exploited economically.

A disproportionate role in China's troubles would subsequently be attributed to this intervention. Post-imperial Western guilt exaggerates the responsibility of foreigners for China's woes from the mid nineteenth century onwards. The effect of their arrival was certainly significant, but it was often indirect, certainly for the bulk of the population who never met them. The country's primary troubles stemmed from domestic sources, not from the British warships that routed the imperial junks on the Pearl River. Nor was it foreigners who held back economic and material modernization; on the contrary, their concessions in Shanghai were the most advanced part of the nation, while Chinese visitors to Hong Kong returned impressed by conditions in the colony.

Still, the foreign challenge came at a tricky time for the dynasty. The sheer size and diversity of the country made it very difficult to administer, demanding strong emperors, which the nineteenth-century Qing were not. The conquests of their predecessors meant that they ruled a vast land made up of two very different sections – 'Outer China' of the Far West and the northern steppes, and the smaller but much more heavily populated 'Inner China'. The first was divided, in turn, between Manchurians, Muslims, Mongols and Tibetans, while the second could be split into eight major regions, from the wheat-growing north to the rice paddies of the south, from the eastern coastal ports to the wild western mountains of Sichuan and Yunnan. Farm yields were higher in the south than the north, encouraged by the intensive use of labour and the warmer climate. The north had more migrant workers, natural disasters, crop failures, violence and banditry.

Though they would develop a racial consciousness in opposition to the Manchus, the Han of Inner China were hardly homogeneous. Physically, a tall, sturdy inhabitant of Shandong in the north-east was different from a smaller, slighter Cantonese in the south. A mandarin from Beijing or an old-school scholar from the ancient imperial capital of Xi'an had little in common with a merchant from Shanghai. Each province, each region, each city claimed some special virtue, be it for the excellence of its food, the bravery of its men, the beauty of its women, or the quality of its coffins. While people paid obeisance to the ruler, loyalties were, above all, local, circumscribed by the constraints of everyday life. As lines in the Confucian *Book of Odes* put it:

> We get up at sunrise.
> At sunset we rest.
> We dig wells and drink.
> We till the fields and eat.
> What is the might of the emperor to us?

Fragmentation was accentuated by mutually incomprehensible verbal linguistic groups, which meant that, despite the common written characters of Mandarin, people from one region could not understand what those from elsewhere said. Feuds over land divided communities. In cities, 'native place associations' catered for men from specific provinces or areas, keeping alive provincial roots and welcoming travellers from home; by the end of the nineteenth century, there were 800 such groupings across China.

The disparities of the nation were accentuated by variations of climate and topography, from the frozen winters of the north-east to the semi-tropical forests of the south-west, from mountain ranges to deserts. Northern China was subject to both droughts and floods, and generally went short of water. (The vagaries of the weather and demands of agriculture made irrigation a vital skill.)

The value of coins varied from one province to another. Different ones were required for different transactions. Mexican, French Indochinese and Spanish dollars circulated. Though Confucius, in the words of one historian, spread 'his ancestral mantle over China as a whole', each area had its own customs, cults and sects – foreigners were surprised by the way so many different beliefs were tolerated so long as they did not challenge the existing order; if they did, they went underground. Each city had its own god, who was thought to inhabit the walls and ditches surrounding it. The north-west was scattered with 'praying trees' believed to harbour beneficial spirits. The malicious dragon of the Han River was said to conjure up adverse winds and plant rocks in the path of boats. In the north, foxes were both worshipped and exorcised, conflated with enchanting female partners of celestial bureaucrats.[10]

Secret societies proliferated, some like the Triads of the south and the Green Gang of the Lower Yangzi beginning as self-help organizations, but then becoming involved in robbery, protection rackets, prostitution and gambling. Sects outlasted all attempts at suppression, going under such names as the Yellow Lotus, Red Eyebrows, Yellow Turbans, Red Beards, Big Sword, Long Spear – and, as the century ended, the Spirit Boxers.

Many provinces were cut off from one another by natural barriers, and poor transport routes. Most regions were self-sufficient. Peripheral communities existed in virtual isolation, perpetuating ways of life that stretched back centuries. Official restrictions on the movement of grain, which were meant to ensure that each region kept enough to feed itself, militated against the growth of a national supply chain.

For foreign visitors, China seemed an unchanging land, its cities, towns and villages as they had been for centuries, with their rabbit warrens of streets, temples, courtyard residences, teahouses and wine shops, brothels – and filth. Urban streets were open sewers; in the countryside, human waste was used for fertilizer, breeding parasitical worms. Lack of elementary hygiene nurtured plagues and pestilences, with polluted water a major contributor. Like education, health care was patchy at best in rural regions, where people depended on folk remedies and shamans.[11]

That is not to say that China was entirely the static, backward country that Westerners sometimes painted. The second half of the eighteenth century had seen the flowering of a rich merchant elite. At the junction of land and water routes, great cities prospered. In the north, Tianjin, the port gateway to Beijing, became famous for the wealth of its merchants, particularly the holders of the imperial salt monopoly, who built compounds that covered whole city blocks. They showed off their ease by breakfasting at two in the afternoon, and staged funeral processions stretching for a mile. The Middle Yangzi was dominated by three cities making up the conurbation of Wuhan – Wuchang for government and the military, Hankou for commerce and Hanyang for industry. Lying at the confluence of four big rivers, they handled a thriving traffic in tea, vegetables, cotton, leather, opium, coal and timber.[12]

Such cities housed a very small class of wealthy people, among them big landowners and holders of imperial monopolies. At the southern end of the Grand Canal, the commercial elite constructed palatial homes and commissioned artists to turn out repetitive paintings in the classical mode. The salt manufacturers of Zhidong in Sichuan pioneered highly capitalized and productive enterprises. Opium merchants thrived as the drug became an integral part of the economy, serving as a substitute for money, helping to finance military projects, alleviating pain and providing magistrates with tax revenue to meet their quotas in years when other crops did badly.[13]

A banking network stretched out from the north-west, establishing agencies in the main cities. Pawnshops were common. Market towns formed a vital link between villages and the surrounding region. But commerce ranked at the bottom of the Confucian scale of values. The pursuit of material gain was seen as the enemy of morality and harmony, while China lacked the external stimuli that Europe and North America received from global economic connections.

Agriculture dominated, and, through land reclamation, irrigation and introduction of new crops, provided general self-sufficiency. Machinery was rare. With coal mines located far from the main cities, there was none of the nearby energy supply for industry enjoyed by factories in Britain, the United States or Northern Europe. Handicrafts continued to dominate manufacturing, above all spinning and weaving, much of which was done at home. Most goods and crops were sold locally; wider distribution was discouraged by transport taxes as well as by poor communications.

All of which appeared to the Chinese and their rulers to be quite acceptable – the country was doing what it had always done and saw no need to evolve. With agriculture estimated to have accounted for almost 70 per cent of the gross national product, China was in what the historian Mark Elvin has termed a 'high-level equilibrium trap' which has also been described as 'involution' – growth without development in which output rose without basic change in operating methods. The system was not broken, so why fix it?[14]

But, beneath the seeming solid state of the nation, the structure was, in fact, weakening. The demand for silver to pay for imports raised the price of the metal, in which taxes were paid. The common copper cash currency depreciated, cutting the real value of wages. Dependent on traditional levies, many of which were pilfered on their way to the centre, and failing to develop new sources of revenue, the imperial court was growing short of money. Tax farming was inefficient. Gentry refused to pay, or kept the cash for themselves. Tax revolts flared up.

Infrastructure was decaying, epitomized by the deteriorating state of the once glorious Grand Canal that carried rice to the capital. Imperial highways formed an impressive network radiating out from Beijing, but most roads were tracks just wide enough to take a sedan chair or a wheelbarrow. Often, they simply consisted of land left vacant at the edge of fields. The defensive walls of towns were allowed to crumble as the money allocated to their repair went into the pockets of officials. Contractors made sure that the dykes along the Yellow River were badly maintained so that they would have regular work when the waters flooded over into the neighbouring countryside.[15]

Land represented a safe store of value, security, social status and family continuity, but was essentially static, and was not seen as something to be developed by greater productivity or new methods. Plots could be tiny; families, particularly in the north, would own several, but they were separated and could not guarantee a living.[16]

Though fresh crops were introduced, farming technology remained much as it had been for a thousand years. The price of metal meant that tools were mainly made of wood. The mass of peasants provided an endless flow of cheap labour. Small farmers unable to make a living from their fields were forced to offer their services to landlords, who could largely determine how much they were paid. Most peasants lived on the edge of subsistence in homes of earth and mud, bamboo and bricks, with paper over the windows. The diet was sparse and unvaried – rice, sorghum, beans or grain flour. Salt and meat were rare treats; the future Red Army leader Zhu De recalled that his peasant family had meat only at lunar New Year.[17]

Opium smoking spread steadily from towns to rural areas during the nineteenth century. Growing poppies became an increasingly attractive source of farm income as the domestic crop competed with the drugs imported by the British – they could be cultivated on poor soil during the winter months when nothing else would grow. The uncertainties of rural life made banditry a tempting proposition for young men who, in the north, could expect to be hired for agricultural work for only thirty or forty days of the year. Some gangs were linked to anti-Manchu societies which looked back to the last Han dynasty, the Ming. Some claimed to rob from the rich to help the poor. But the overwhelming motivation was to make a better living than could be got from the land, spiced with excitement and escape from the monotony of rural life.

The result was a deterioration of law and order. The self-policing system in villages and towns was abused by headmen who used it to do down rivals, or took bribes to turn a blind eye. Imperial forces were backward, with honours bestowed on Manchus for prowess at using bows and arrows on horseback. Many descendants of the soldiers who conquered China in 1644 had become parasitical and isolated from the population, congregating together in Beijing and garrison towns.

The regime's Chinese 'Green Standard' troops frequently lived on plunder, extortion and oppression – a group of 3,000 soldiers sent to the border area between Guangxi, Hunan and Guizhou provinces in 1850 demanded 60,000 labourers to move its baggage. Hearing complaints of pillage and rape by his men, an imperial prince was said to have replied that it would be best for the people to move their homes to avoid them. Generals pocketed the pay of their men, and inflated troop numbers to indent for as much money as possible; if an inspection was ordered, they could hire coolies for the day to impersonate the non-existent men. 'Our troops have not a tincture of discipline,' a provincial governor wrote to a colleague. 'Retreating is easy for them, advancing difficult ... all alike useless.' Desertion rates were high.

Though the emperor supposedly had a monopoly on maintaining armed forces, the gentry built up local militias as the dynasty proved incapable of assuring its citizens' protection.[18]

2

Upheavals

Those who thought that Heaven was removing its benediction from the Qing dynasty found plenty of evidence from nature as the second half of the nineteenth century dawned. The Yangzi and Yellow rivers both flooded, while drought scourged northern provinces. Lack of rain hit the grain crop. Famine swept through Guangxi in the south. There were earthquakes, plagues and swarms of locusts. Special prayers in the Forbidden City failed to produce an improvement. Moneylenders showed no pity to debtors, and bandits roamed. As a song put it after a string of calamities in eastern China:

> This year famine,
> Next year flood,
> Grass, roots, tree bark gone for food.
> Deep in debt,
> When the debt comes due – one picul* is repaid as two.[1]

One observer wrote:

Year after year the crops are a failure by what appears an act of God. Then the farm animals are eaten, then there is no seed for new crops, then the small farm is sold and the money soon expended, and the choice comes between begging and stealing, and often not even this choice, as there is but little to steal, and the strong take that.

In famine areas, parents sold their children for the price of a meal. Or they ate ground-up stones, which could lead to death. Or they resorted to cannibalism.[2]

The disasters fanned a string of large-scale uprisings, which arose

---

* A small unit of weight.

from poverty, oppressive taxes, a decline in famine relief operatons, anti-Manchu sentiment and resentment against imperial officials and troops. In the hard-hit central-eastern region, a major revolt brought together peasants, bandits and fast-riding horsemen under the leadership of a landowner who had branched out into salt smuggling. Known as the Nien,* the rebels rampaged across four provinces between the Yellow and Huai rivers. Establishing bases in walled towns and repulsing imperial forces, they took over local administration, promising less corrupt and fairer government as their leader nurtured dynastic ambitions.[3]

In the south, clans and secret-society members combined in the Red Turban revolt in Guangdong. Guangxi experienced fifty-four risings in a decade, during which most of its cities changed hands, sometimes several times. In both provinces, Triad members of the century-old Heaven and Earth Society staged anti-dynastic risings, as well as extending their money-making activities. Drawing membership from river pirates, including one gang whose female leader was a former prostitute, they forced farmers to join their ranks, ran gambling dens, and extorted money from merchants and opium traders.[4]

Followers of the White Lotus sect, who worshipped a sacred Buddhist Mother and had staged a ten-year uprising at the turn of the century, rose again in Henan and Shandong provinces. In isolated Yunnan, in the south-west, local people rebelled after a massacre by Han officials that was estimated to have killed tens of thousands of Muslims. They set up a 'Chinese Sultanate' in the Kingdom of Pacified Souls in the city of Dali, which they occupied after a battle costing further tens of thousands of lives. Other Muslims revolted in Gansu and Shaanxi provinces. Further west, an insurgent leader named Yakub Beg made himself ruler in Xinjiang, with his capital in the trading city of Kashgar.[5]

The Qing found it hard to assert themselves against challenges on such a scale. The Daoguang emperor died in 1850 and was succeeded by Xianfeng, a weak twenty-year-old who had good intentions but proved ineffective and soon withdrew to the Summer Palace to leave the job of running the empire to officials.

Rebel generals often proved better than imperial commanders. Their men were more motivated, drawing on local knowledge and sympathies.

---

* Some authors render the name as Nian.

Imperial forces and officials in their garrisons and *yamen* headquarters could not keep track of guerrillas who melded with local bandits. As a prefect in the wild Guizhou region lamented: 'As soon as the official sets forth, the rebels flee. As soon as he has gone, they congregate again.'

The largest of these challenges originated in 1850 among poor southerners of the Hakka minority in the Guangdong–Guangxi region. Lasting for thirteen years, the Taiping revolt took up to 20 million lives, devastated wide areas of China, created a flood of refugees, and brought a shift of power that further weakened the throne.

Its leader, Hong Xiuquan, was a village teacher who repeatedly failed the imperial civil service examination. He proclaimed himself the son of the Christian God after making a connection between a missionary tract and a delirious vision in which he ascended into the sky to meet a bearded, golden-haired man who told him to wipe out the demons on earth. He identified these devils as the Manchus, and declared that he had a mission to raise a divinely blessed army to eradicate them and Confucianism. His crusade was rooted strongly in the tribulations of the peasants, but was also explicitly linked to racial tension between the rulers and the Han. The Manchus wanted to 'reduce the number of us Chinese', a tract declared, and had 'unleashed grasping officials and corrupt subordinates to strip the people of their flesh until men and women weep by the roadside . . . the rich hold the power and the heroes despair.'

The Taiping Tianguo ('Heavenly Kingdom of Great Peace') preached a form of egalitarian Christianity with Chinese characteristics. Land and treasure would be shared out, the sexes separated and opium outlawed. As a Taiping song put it:

> Those with millions owe us their money,
> Those who are half-poor–half-rich can till their fields.
> Those with ambitions but no cash should go with us.
> Broke or hungry, Heaven will keep you well.[6]

Hong and his young confederates found their first supporters among the badly treated Hakka minority. In 1851, after careful preparations, they took the city of Yongan, with its rich storehouses, and their army swelled to 60,000. It was not all plain sailing; the Taiping failed to take the walled city of Guilin, and fell into a bloody ambush on the Xiang

River. Still, most managed to escape, and forged north into Hunan province and the rich Middle Yangzi region.[7]

By the time it reached the great river, the Taiping army numbered 100,000. It captured the three Wuhan cities, massacring thousands of inhabitants. Heading east, it achieved its main target of taking the imperial southern capital of Nanjing. The emperor wrote that his anger at the loss of the city was 'greater than I can bear'. Manchus there were systematically butchered. Hong, described as rather a tall man, with an oval face, large bright eyes and a sonorous voice, was carried into the centre of the capital of his Heavenly Kingdom in a golden palanquin borne by sixteen men. He wore a crown and a robe embroidered with a dragon. Four lieutenants, also styled 'kings', surrounded him. All were in their twenties or thirties.[8]

Buoyed up by money and valuables seized on their advance, the rebels appeared to threaten all China. Their armies rampaged through a dozen provinces. One got to within 100 miles of Beijing before being halted by bad winter weather and the mobilization of militia by the merchants of Tianjin; for once, imperial forces showed tactical intelligence in encircling the enemy, digging a canal to flood their camp, and then massacring them. Other armies ranged along the Yangzi – Wuhan changed hands several times – or forged back south.[9]

The dynasty was enfeebled not only by the generally poor performance of its troops but also by an abrupt decline in its revenue; the dislocation meant that Beijing received only one seventh of expected tax takings. Salvation came from gentry leaders who saw the rebels as a visceral threat to their position. Since the central government could not cope, they stepped in. Their primary motivation was self-defence, but their action would end up affecting the whole imperial system.

This had already begun with the formation of local forces to carry out police duties and ward off bandits – a British interpreter noted how these formations made people less awed by Beijing, which could not offer similar protection. So as not to break the imperial monopoly on the right to raise armed forces, landowners pretended that all they were doing was to step up local policing. But they abrogated taxation powers to pay for these outfits. Ties between gentry chiefs in different provinces enabled them to put together large armies which drew on local roots, in sharp contrast to Manchu troops isolated in garrisons far from their homes.

A dark-bearded scholar from a minor landlord family in Hunan, Zeng Guofan, emerged as the main leader of this gentry transformation that did not speak its name. Born in 1811, he entered the imperial bureaucracy after passing the superior examination at the age of twenty-seven. A memorial he wrote to the throne expressed his concern that officials were being appointed for their 'smart demeanour and smooth speech' instead of having their ability properly evaluated. He worried that functionaries were shirking their responsibilities, occupying themselves with trifles and keeping up appearances, and generally 'shilly-shallying'. The Taiping revolt, he warned, was 'not just a crisis for our Qing dynasty, but the most extraordinary crisis of all time for the Confucian teachings'. It was time for action. 'How,' Zeng asked, 'can anyone who can read and write remain quietly seated, hands in sleeves, without thinking of doing something about it?'[10]

A highly orthodox Confucian, he placed great emphasis on the virtue of 'sincerity' and collaborative effort in building up his army. 'If you win a battle, shift the praise to others,' he advised his lieutenants. 'If they lose a battle, go to their aid.' But he was also a strict authoritarian who placed no value on human life if its loss was necessary to achieve his ends. Turning from classical literary scholarship to army organization, he proved an excellent, clear-headed military manager, recruiting the best local leaders and ensuring that soldiers were disciplined and properly paid. His approach rested on the idealized Chinese family, the chief offering paternal care and demanding filial loyalty. It was rooted in the villages to which peasants owed their main allegiance. Eighty years on, Chiang Kai-shek would seek to follow Zeng's example against the outlaws threatening his regime – the Communists.

In recruiting subordinates, Zeng preferred *literati* scholars to military men; all the generals and members of his staff were imperial examination graduates. The army's local roots meant that it could draw on the clannish sentiments of the villagers and on rural Han groups which would not necessarily have rallied to the Manchu standard had the call come from Beijing. While the Taiping could stigmatize the dynasty as foreign devils, they could not use the same ethnic slur against the ultra-Chinese gentry. Still, for all his other skills, Zeng was not the best of field commanders – after a defeat in 1854, he tried to jump into a river three times to drown himself; his secretary pulled him out.[11]

His authority was expanded when Beijing was obliged by events to make him governor-general of Hunan. This opened major new opportunities for those round him. The web of contacts between them created a seedbed for men who would run China below court level in the next decades. No fewer than twenty-seven of Zeng's officers went on to become provincial governors, and 131 held other senior posts.[12]

They and the dynasty they served were fortunate that their foes never came together. Had the rebels formed an alliance, there can be little doubt that the Qing would have fallen. But all they had in common was their opposition to the Manchu rulers, and this was pursued mainly on an individual basis, despite some co-operation between the Taiping and Nien. Still, Zeng and his peers had to conduct an extremely long and bitter conflict. Allying terror and carefully plotted strategy, they methodically isolated rebel groups, depriving them of supplies, besieging their towns and starving them into submission. Their soldiers did not always live up to Zeng's Confucian ideals. Discipline deteriorated. Looting spread. At times, local militias fought to protect their home areas against the Hunan Army. Zeng, himself, noted that most of his officers 'cannot avoid fattening their private purses somewhat'.[13]

The campaigns were often confused, but one element ran through them all – the ruthlessness of all involved. Taking their relative lengths into account, China's strife exacted a much higher death toll than the partly contemporaneous American Civil War. The mandarin in charge of suppressing a revolt in Canton boasted of having beheaded the symbolic number of 100,000 people, regretting only that he had not been able to 'extirpate the whole class' – the overall death toll in Guangdong was put as high as a million. For his part, Zeng warned that, when pro-imperial forces swept down, 'every person will be crushed', while Hong said that 'all who resist us are . . . idolatrous demons, and we kill them without sparing.'[14]

Amid the fighting, the Europeans staged a fresh appearance with a British attack on Canton, in 1858, after a dispute arising from the arrest of Chinese sailors on a ship registered in Hong Kong, and the hauling down of its Union flag. The consul in Canton called for help from the colony as British houses were burned and a price was put on the heads of foreigners. A British-led force moved in, and the extremely fat governor was banished to India. In effect, Beijing accepted a dual system of government in the area, which led the local population to look to the foreigners to provide stability and act as a bulwark against the more oppressive imperial customs.[15]

The British and French then joined forces to seek the full opening of China to their goods, and showed their muscle by attacking Tianjin, east of Beijing. A Mongol general organized successful resistance, but the Europeans returned with more men. The city was taken after an assault on its forts from the rear, a tactic which a contemporary account said the defenders regarded as most unfair. Thirty foreign soldiers were captured, however, and were sent to Beijing, where they were tortured, and some died. The main force pressed on, routing the Chinese cavalry.[16]

The capital fell into chaos. There were riots and looting. The imperial army was in no mood to fight. Eighty thousand unpaid, undisciplined soldiers roamed the streets. Faced with imminent defeat, the emperor decided to move to his imperial hunting estate at Jehol, beyond the Great Wall. The Westerners arrived outside Beijing and set fire to the imperial Summer Palace in reprisal for the ill-treatment of prisoners taken on the earlier advance. 'You can scarcely imagine the beauty and the magnificence of the places we burnt,' one soldier, Charles Gordon, wrote to his mother. 'It made one's heart sore to burn them; in fact, these palaces were so large, and we were so pressed for time, that we could not plunder them carefully ... It was wretchedly demoralising work for an army.' But the capital itself was not occupied, and the Europeans stayed outside the city wall.[17]

The Xianfeng emperor left his brother, Prince Gong, to negotiate with the foreigners. Though only thirty, the ruler was seriously ill, brought low by debauchery and palsy, and dominated by reactionary figures who accompanied him on the 140-mile journey to Jehol. He had only one son, a five-year-old boy born to a concubine. By August 1861, he was too weak to write the edict naming his successor. A Manchu prince and a group of senior officials, headed by the senior censor, Sushun, had themselves appointed as a Regency Council. As the emperor lay close to death, the concubine made a dramatic appearance at his bedside, holding the boy and asking Xianfeng to confirm him as the next sovereign. Xianfeng replied that their son would ascend the throne, with the mother and the empress as regents. Then he died.[18]

The concubine knew that her life was in danger from the Sushun group, so she formed an alliance with the late emperor's wife, and with Prince Gong, an ambitious, arrogant and corrupt 27-year-old who had negotiated a settlement with the British and French in Beijing – the price was a large indemnity, the confirmation of concession rights and the ceding of 300,000 square miles of territory in the far north-west to Russia, which claimed to have played a peace-making role.[19]

The Sushun group had a major problem; the decree naming it as regent had not been stamped with the imperial seal, which a eunuch loyal to the concubine was said to have removed from the late ruler's bedchamber. But it was still intent on eliminating any opposition and set an ambush for the two imperial women as they made their way back to the capital. The concubine's former suitor and cousin, a Manchu general called Jung-lu, rode to their rescue. Meanwhile, Gong's troops captured the censor and his colleagues as they travelled south with Xianfeng's body. Taken to the capital, they were promptly executed – the original plan had been to skin Sushun alive, but he was despatched more mercifully by beheading. Two princes allied with him were allowed to hang themselves. Five others were disgraced.

On 11 November 1861, an edict announced that, in future, the former concubine would 'personally deliberate all government matters'. At the end of the month, this was approved by 197 senior figures. In keeping with the rules, the new emperor called himself her 'servant-son'.[20]

This marked the emergence of one of the most extraordinary figures in modern history, who came to be known as Cixi, the Empress of the West (from the location of her palace in Beijing), or, more simply, the Dowager Empress. Born into a noble but undistinguished Manchu family in Anhui province in 1835, she had been picked as a lowly graded imperial concubine at the age of seventeen. This meant abandoning a plan for her to marry Jung-lu, a slim man with a head the shape of a huge light bulb, who would, however, come to play an important part in her life and was rumoured to have carried on a liaison with her. Her enemies alleged that the boy emperor was actually their son.[21]

Five feet tall and illiterate when she came to court, Cixi was said to have had a 'sweet feminine voice'. After her death in 1908, she was painted in lurid colours as a sexually rapacious killer who poisoned rivals or had them thrown down wells, a deeply sinister and reactionary force using her wiles to pervert China. She was compared to the Tang dynasty ruler Wu, another concubine, who became China's only female emperor after murdering anybody who stood in her way in the late seventh century, or an equally bloody Han dynasty figure, the empress

Lü, from the end of the second century BC. In the 1970s, parallels would be drawn between them all and Mao Zedong's last wife, a latter-day concubine who pulled the strings of the Cultural Revolution.[22]

The lurid portrait was based largely on rumour and the imaginative writings of an English forger and pornographer living in Beijing, Edmund Backhouse, who claimed that he was unable to satisfy her 'unsatiated lust' and taste for unorthodox sex when they allegedly first coupled. The story spun by this homosexual native of Darlington was artfully pitched to fit Western preconceptions about the mysterious, Machiavellian court in the Forbidden City, with its eunuchs, rituals and decadence behind the screens that surrounded the throne. But it also owed much to the Chinese tradition of inventing scandal about dead rulers.[23]

That is not to say that Cixi was not ruthless with opponents, or had any compunction in plundering the imperial treasury – she was generally believed to have diverted funds from the navy to build herself a marble boat folly at the Summer Palace (no proof of this was forthcoming). Her clothes filled 3,000 camphor chests. Her jewels were ornate and extremely valuable. Though court regulations set a ceiling of a dozen on the number of maids anybody should have, she was surrounded by twenty. Like Wu and Lü, she was highly superstitious and, as she aged, began to present herself as a Buddhist goddess, with an acquired taste for Passing Cloud cigarettes.[24]

A highly accomplished politician, she used her position and the manipulation of dynastic power to stay on top of the imperial system, drawing on Manchu traditions to preserve solidarity among the ruling class around her. Aware of the nature of a female regency, which obliged her to give her decisions from behind a screen curtain by the throne, she was intent, above all, on establishing her own legitimacy as the central cog in a coalition made up of the occupant of the throne, the imperial widow, Gong, senior court officials and the leaders of Manchu clans, backed by the allegiance of the bureaucracy and gentry-scholars. Going to the extreme of the great-women-of-history approach, the correspondent of the London *Times*, John Bland, a collaborator of Backhouse, wrote that 'for fifty years hers was the brain, hers the strong hand, that held in check the rising forces of disintegration.'

The reality was more nuanced. As the British head of the Customs, Robert Hart, put it in a typically sagacious analysis, 'The policy of the central Government in China is not to guide, but to follow events.' Meeting her and the imperial widow in 1869, the gentry-general Zeng Guofan found their ability 'anything but exceptional'. They lacked training in administrative matters. Cixi's command of Chinese was poor, and she mixed up characters in her writing. As her long rule drew on, she was increasingly surrounded by old men who remembered the chaos of the mid-century rebellions and put stability above everything else. To maintain that and to preserve the Qing from the dangers lapping around the throne, she came to be seen as indispensable – 'without [her] attending to functions from behind the curtain, how could we have come this far?' asked a senior court official in 1887.[25]

While Cixi preserved her position for almost half a century and held the regime together, there was a central dichotomy for the Qing. Was the prime loyalty to China, or to the tribal clan? Did China or the Manchus come first? What would happen if the two diverged; for instance, if the court adopted policies which threatened the descendants of the conquerors of 1644 for the good of China, or, on the other hand, if it put the nation in jeopardy by backing Manchu priorities?[26]

Thirteen days after the death of the emperor, a gentry army took the river port of Anqing in Anhui province, which the Taiping had held for nine years. After the battle, the river was filled with the headless bodies of rebels. The next flashpoint was Shanghai, the target of a Taiping campaign in the autumn of 1861.

The city had grown hugely since being opened up as a trade port by the Treaty of Nanjing forced on the Qing by the British in 1842. Divided into a Chinese city, a French Concession and an International Settlement run by the British, it accounted for half the country's foreign trade. Linked to the interior by the Yangzi and close to the Grand Canal, Shanghai was conveniently sited as a channel for Chinese products the world wanted. Trade boomed – its exports of tea rose from a million pounds in weight in 1844 to 80 million in 1855, and of silk from 6,433 bales in 1845 to 84,970 just before the Taiping revolt. With the growth of commerce, Western banks moved in, led by the British, bringing modern financial practice to one small part of China.[27]

Trouble loomed when adherents of a secret society, the Big Swords, took control of the native city, and the Taiping advanced up the Yangzi. Imperial troops were a rabble who would have little chance against the rebels. So the city's elite inhabitants asked Zeng Guofan for an army. A 'surprise force' was sent in under the command of a Zeng protégé, Li Hongzhang, who despatched 6,500 men from his army in Anhui on chartered British steamboats escorted by Royal Navy ships. He also backed a 3,000-strong Chinese force raised by an American mercenary, Frederic Ward, a long-haired wanderer who rode on the battlefield in a frock coat smoking a cheroot and with only a riding crop as a weapon.

The battle for Shanghai was decided by a highly unusual event – snow fell for fifty-eight hours in January 1862. The Taiping froze; ice blocked their ships. Li's troops and Ward's army, which was equipped with mortars and artillery, triumphed, though rebels remained in outlying areas. The American took Chinese nationality, married the daughter of a local banker, and was awarded the imperial order of the peacock feather, third class. In the name of the infant emperor, his force was given the title of the Ever Victorious Army. In September 1862, he led it into a fresh battle south of Shanghai. Suddenly Ward put his hand to his abdomen, saying, 'I have been hit.' Dying at the age of thirty, he was given full Chinese funeral honours.

His American successor, Henry Burgevine, displeased Li Hongzhang, and switched sides three times before being caught by imperial troops and 'drowning' while being taken across a river. In his place, command of the Ever Victorious Army went to Charles Gordon, the British soldier who had lamented the lack of care taken in pillaging the Summer Palace two years earlier.

Gordon, who would become a Victorian imperial icon after his subsequent death at the siege of Khartoum, was a lonely martinet, a devout Christian typical of his age who fought to overcome his sexual desires. After the expedition against Beijing, he had decided to stay on in China. His first impression of the Ever Victorious Army was: 'you never did see such a rabble as it was,' but he gave it thorough training, banning the use of opium. In fighting along the waterways round Shanghai, he used artillery and pontoons to overwhelm the enemy. He went into battle carrying a rattan cane, though he kept a revolver under his tunic.

With Shanghai safe, gentry forces under Zeng launched a fourteen-pronged drive to eradicate the rebellion for good. It was an enormous undertaking, striking up the Yangzi at the heart of Taiping power. With the tide of war shifting, Zeng had huge resources at his disposal – funds, food, weapons and ammunition from half a dozen provinces plus the riches of Shanghai and help from French and British gunboats. Known as 'surrounding chess', his long-term strategy was to cut off the rebels in the countryside while tightening the noose round their capital. His brother led a force of 20,000 men westwards towards Nanjing, but was met by a far superior Taiping army, and did well to avoid annihilation. A lengthy stalemate ensued, during which the rebels launched counter-attacks. But gentry units prevented food getting to their Heavenly City.[28]

Li Hongzhang moved against the silk city of Suzhou, held by 40,000 Taiping. The attack failed. But rebel leaders quarrelled, and surrendered, expecting to be spared. Li, however, had them all executed, and half the defenders massacred, as the city was looted. Gordon was not allowed to send in his troops, to prevent his seeing what was going on; when one of Li's staff visited him, he pulled the head of a rebel, which he had somehow procured, from beneath his bed, and held it in the air in re-proach. At the start of 1864, after Li Hongzhang decided to disband the Ever Victorious Army, the Englishman went home.

The reverse at Shanghai, the loss of Suzhou and the tightening of Zeng's noose marked the beginning of the end for the Taiping. Their Heavenly State was already in trouble, poorly administered and abandoning the promised egalitarianism for lavish ceremonies and high living by the leaders. In some places, a reign of terror was instituted. Hong proved to be an ineffective chief as he dallied with sixty-eight wives and listened to the music of an organ taken to his palace from a Christian church.

The 'kings' around him fell into bloody power battles. The best commander, Shi Dakai, the 'King of the West', whose wife and mother had been killed by rival rebel chiefs, left Nanjing and wandered across China before being surrounded by superior imperial forces in the wilds of Sichuan. This gallant knight of the rebellion surrendered on a promise that the lives of his men would be spared. The imperial commander let 4,000 go, but massacred 2,000 while they slept in a temple. The King of the West was sliced to death.[29]

By the end of November 1863, Zeng's forces surrounded Nanjing. They encircled the rebel capital with a wide moat and got the foreigners in Shanghai to ensure that merchants there halted river traffic. Inside, the rebels were starving. Hong proclaimed that they would be sustained by manna from Heaven. But he himself died on 1 June 1864, probably from eating poisonous weeds. A month later, the troops under Zeng's brother blasted their way through the towering city wall, and subjected

Nanjing to another of the bloodbaths that marked the mid-century rebellions. A Taiping army escaped to the south, but was destroyed after being caught in a mountain pass. A remnant group continued to operate in the Guangxi–Guizhou region until 1871, but, thirteen years after it had begun, China's greatest rebellion of the century was over.

Despite their internal contradictions and blood fissures, the Taiping had put forward a root-and-branch response to the challenges facing China. They had also pushed anti-Manchu sentiment to the extreme, not in pursuing a nostalgic evocation of a Ming restoration but in wanting to replace the dynasty with something completely new. This was too strange and foreign to put down roots, however, particularly in the countryside, where the wholesale rejection of familiar ways by the rebels set up a wall between them and the local inhabitants, facilitating the mobilization of grassroots militias by the gentry. The reasons for their success and failure would guide another importer of a rebellious foreign doctrine in the following century, Mao Zedong.[30]

Though Zeng became governor-general at Nanjing and was raised to the rank of a Senior Guardian of the Throne and First Rank Marquis, with the double-eyed peacock feather, the court showed nervousness about the power of the men who had saved it. Zeng was ordered to disband his army. Other gentry generals were dismissed or pressed to resign. But the court had need of them once more when two Nien armies ranged across central and western China in 1866. One column of mounted rebels, said to stretch for fifty miles, scored a string of victories, broke through defences along the Grand Canal and swept into Shandong. Another army of 50,000 men got as far as Xi'an, which they besieged.

The court was forced to call in Zeng. His first response was that he could not help because the disbanding of his anti-Taiping army meant that he had only 3,000 troops, who were needed to garrison Nanjing. Having made his point, he changed his mind, on condition that he was allowed to raise an adequate force. He and Li Hongzhang went back to war. There was an initial success when the main Nien chief was betrayed by a subordinate, captured and executed. But Zeng made little headway in the rebel heartland of Shandong and Anhui. So he handed over to the younger, extremely energetic Li, who extended the 'surrounding chess' strategy of his mentor with an approach known as 'strengthening the walls and cleaning up the countryside'. Superior forces, with Western guns, encircled rebel units, depriving them of food, weapons or support. Starvation spread; in one rebel county, people ate the crushed bones of the dead and resorted to cannibalism.[31]

By 1868, Li, in alliance with the local anti-bandit Old Crow Society, had defeated the Nien in the east, but the other rebel unit still represented a big threat. Abandoning the siege of Xi'an, it headed towards Beijing, joined by a force of 3,000 mounted salt smugglers, and got to within eighty miles of the capital before a combination of an army sent by Li and a force under another gentry general, Zuo Zongtang, saved the day for the Qing. On 16 August 1868, the last Nien leader dashed on his mount into a river and drowned. The rebel heartland in the Shandong–Henan–Anhui triangle would remain volatile, but the main rising originating there had been crushed after seventeen years, and ritual sacrifices were offered in celebration in Beijing.

The other revolts crumbled one by one in the following years. At the end of 1872, surrounded by enemy forces, the leader of the Hui Muslims in Yunnan donned ceremonial robes, got into a yellow sedan chair and was carried to the south gate of his capital of Dali, where he swallowed a fatal dose of opium and ordered that he should be taken to the imperial camp. Though he was dead on arrival, the imperial commander had the body decapitated and then launched a ferocious attack on Dali; an official recalled that the roads were ankle-deep in blood and that no Muslim man, woman or child was spared. Hundreds drowned as they tried to escape across the lake below the city. The ears of the dead were cut off and more than 20,000 were put in baskets to be sent to Beijing. Women and children from the region were sold as concubines and slaves. Land, homes and other property were confiscated. A sign over Dali's main gate forbade 'traitorous' Hui to enter. Many Muslims moved into Burma and Thailand.[32]

Having helped to protect Beijing from the Nien, Zuo Zongtang, another native of Hunan, led the reconquest of territory in the northwest stretching over 220,000 square miles. A serious, practical man, with a round face, Zuo was a methodical expert at encircling and siege techniques, and utterly merciless. He took his time to ensure success. Though appointed governor of Shaanxi and Gansu in 1866, it was not until 1871 that he defeated his first main opponent, Ma Hualong, after besieging his fortress for sixteenth months. The defenders resorted to cannibalism before giving up – Ma was sliced to death, and thousands of his followers were ethnically cleansed from their home region on the border with Mongolia to other parts of China. Zuo then urged the court to adopt a 'Go West' policy to reassert Qing dominion in the great expanses of Xinjiang by defeating the rebels there under Yakub Beg. If China did not do so, he warned, Russia would spread its influence – it had already moved up on the frontier region on the Ili River. This dimension in China's foreign and security policy would flow through subsequent eras – the British, French and Germans were a constant irritant, but the Tsarist empire and its Communist successor represented a much greater territorial threat to China.

In April 1875, Zuo won the day and was appointed to head a campaign into Xinjiang, for which he raised loans from the Hongkong and Shanghai Bank, with customs revenue from Canton, Shanghai, Hankou and Fuzhou as surety. His opponent sent emissaries to London to try to get Britain to act as mediator. But, in 1876, a 60,000-man Chinese army surged towards his capital in Kashgar. Yakub Beg committed suicide at the end of May 1877, and his sons, who tried to continue the fight, fell out with one another. Russia agreed to withdraw from the Ili border area in return for a large indemnity. Xinjiang was declared a province of the empire.

For the Qing, the reconquest of the west meant the recovery of the fourth pillar of their empire – to go alongside Manchuria, Mongolia and China proper. Xinjiang was not left alone to pursue its traditional ways. In areas where ethnic and religious differences had contributed to the western revolt, campaigns were launched to sinicize the local people, a process that contrasted with the earlier, looser Qing rule. Han Chinese moved in to solidify the imperial presence, taking official posts, opening Confucian schools, establishing walled garrisons, and putting up Chinese names on the gates of their sections of racially segregated towns. To keep them apart from the locals they were prohibited from spending the night in the yurt homes of nomads, while Manchu troops were banned from visiting Muslim prostitutes. This pattern of colonial immigration and the tensions it aroused played out over the following decades, and continue to affect regional politics today, with Beijing, backed by Washington's 'war on terror', stamping down on any attempts by Muslims to claim real autonomy.[33]

*

The wars left an enormous legacy of death and devastation. In regions swept by the fighting, surviving peasant families huddled together in makeshift shelters, dressed in rags and starving. 'Smiling fields were turned into desolate wildernesses,' wrote an observer of the one-time Taiping heartland. Plains in central China, he added, 'were strewn with human skeletons; their rivers polluted with floating carcasses; wild beasts descending from their fastnesses in the mountains roamed at large over the land and made their dens in the ruins of deserted towns; the cry of the pheasants usurped the place of the hum of busy populations; no hands were left to till the soil, and noxious weeds covered the ground once tilled with patient industry.'[34]

The conflicts caught imperial finances in the double lock of increased military expenditure and falling revenue as warfare hampered tax collection. The currency was steadily devalued. Counterfeiting was widespread. Paper notes traded for only 3–4 per cent of their face value. In a bid to gain popular support, the dynasty stuck to a pledge not to raise land taxation, despite the crying need for funds. Greater austerity was preached at court. In areas where rebels had held sway, the gentry elite reclaimed its place in the social order, undertook welfare work, restored estates, and rebuilt ruined academies, libraries and *literati* clubs. Encouraging the rebirth of agriculture, as Zeng Guofan pointed out, reduced the danger that farmers would turn to banditry and create fresh widespread disorder.[35]

The recovery from the mid-century disasters was striking. Mass immigration boosted the population of the worst-hit regions. Land was sold cheaply, or given away. Easy loans were offered to purchasers of farms, equipment and seeds. Tenant producers were allowed to keep up to 70 per cent of their crops. Roads and bridges were repaired. Irrigation projects were undertaken. The silk industry expanded. Urban populations grew.

There was also an opening to the world with a mission sent to the West in 1866 under the command of a Manchu, who wrote that he was:

> Off to foreign countries, folk songs to collect
> Drawings to make, and history to learn.[36]

Foreign diplomats were received by the emperor, though all he did was express his good wishes to their countries. Language schools were established in Beijing and Shanghai. An appeal was sent to Queen Victoria offering 'anything that might be desired in the ways of concessions to British trade' in return for a halt to the export of opium to China – the British minister in Beijing said no reply should be expected. Under the 1878 Convention of Chefoo (now Yantai), Westerners were permitted to travel to the Upper Yangzi region. China's first permanent foreign envoy was despatched to London, where he was shocked by the immorality, but recognized the importance of the interplay of politics and economics, contrasting the 'real learning' of the West with the 'empty writing' practised at home. His report was not made public.

There were, naturally, blemishes in what became known as the Tongzhi Restoration, after the name of the young emperor. Carpet-baggers moved in to distressed areas; big landlords extended their holdings; there were disputes when farmers who had fled the fighting returned home to find themselves dispossessed. Yet, given the scale and length of the revolts, China was swift in getting back on its tracks.

However, a fundamental political shift was taking place. The gentry had always been a vital element in the system, but it now became more assertive, its leaders emerging as national figures. This boosted the position of the Han Chinese, who came to outnumber Manchus in senior provincial posts. The trend was towards greater provincialism, with significant implications for the central power. Gentry leaders punched a hole in the imperial tax system by levying duties on agriculture and controlling the *likin* tax on the movement of goods. Armies like those raised by Zeng and Li, which had been formed on a local basis, owed their prime loyalties to their commanders, not to Beijing, while the long civil wars and the perpetuation of sizeable militias installed violence and militarization as a characteristic of national life, closely linked to the provincial establishment. The pattern for much of the following decades was thus set in the dynasty's rescue from its greatest peril. Though there appears to have been little or no awareness at court, this would, in time, prove to be it's final challenge.

3

Strength and Weakness

Li Hongzhang, the victor of Shanghai who had presided over the massacre and looting at Suzhou, was a striking figure, over six feet tall and
with piercing eyes, a wispy beard and an impressive bearing. Born into
a cultivated scholar family in Anhui province on the Lower Yangzi in
1823, he passed third out of 4,000 candidates in the top grade of
imperial examination, his skill as a calligrapher being particularly noted.
Travelling to Beijing to sit the test in front of the emperor, he had written
a poem which began:

> A hero takes in hand a mighty sword.
> Ambition soaring o'er the Hundred Foot Tower
> In ten thousand years gone by
> Who else has shaped history?[1]

His subsequent career would mark him out as a key figure in China
during the second half of the nineteenth century, particularly after the
death of his mentor, Zeng Guofan, in 1872. Men like Li were modernizers in their fashion, but within the imperial context. They aimed to
strengthen the dynasty, not to change its foundations.[2]

Li reached his major civilian power base when appointed governor of
the key province of Zhili ('Direct Rule') round Beijing in 1870, a post
he held for a quarter of a century. His influence was extended when he
was also made commissioner for northern ports, giving him responsibility for negotiating trading agreements with foreigners, a role in which
he became more important for them than the Foreign Ministry in Beijing.

Using his official position to advance his business interests, Li
developed a big coal mining complex using modern equipment at Kaiping, south-east of the capital, founded the first cotton cloth mill in
Shanghai, and pioneered the establishment of a joint stock company,

with both state and private investment. He built a railway line to move the output of his mine to the port city of Tianjin, followed by other tracks that made Zhili the hub of China's belated railway system. His steamship line carried rice from Shanghai to Tianjin and Beijing, supplanting the much slower transport on the Grand Canal. He backed the creation of an experimental network of post offices, and the issue of the first Large Dragon stamps. Pointing out that foreigners with whom he negotiated in Tianjin could contact their capitals faster than he could get in touch with the palace in Beijing, he forced through the establishment of an Imperial Telegraph Administration.[3]

Li was notable for adopting a more realistic and subtle attitude to the foreigners than had been prevalent since the Qianlong emperor rebuffed the British Macartney mission in 1793. In a memorial to the throne, he wrote that the most important thing was not to arouse their contempt, which 'will thwart us at every turn . . . if they feel respect for China, all matters can be mutually arranged; and even difficult questions can be settled by compromise or agreement.'[4]

Quoting a Confucian analect, he noted that 'the requisites of Government are sufficiency of food, sufficiency of military equipment, and the confidence of the people in their ruler.' While the foreigners possessed these, China lacked them and so was weak. What was needed was to build up the country's material well-being. This should be done with 'extreme and continued caution' before confronting the Westerners. There should be no war, but, if it made the right preparations and was willing to wait, China would be victorious in the end. This strategy, akin to the policy Deng Xiaoping would adopt in pursuing material modernization a little over a century later, became known as Self-Strengthening – a term adapted from a classical text reputedly written by an early emperor: 'Heaven moves on strongly; the gentlemen, therefore, incessantly strengthen themselves.'[5]

Li's involvement in foreign affairs began when he settled a crisis with Paris after the killing of French nuns, priests and diplomats by a mob in Tianjin in 1870. Four years later, he negotiated a payment to Japan to get it to withdraw from Taiwan, which its forces had invaded. He then reached an agreement with London after a British diplomat was murdered in south-west China. In all this, Beijing exercised a useful ambiguity. Li was not a member of the Foreign Ministry which Prince Gong had set up, so his negotiations did not formally commit the empire.

If he succeeded, so much the better. If not, China retained its freedom of action. For Li, this provided room in which to manoeuvre and establish himself as the man with whom the Westerners could do business.[6]

Describing him as 'China's Bismarck', one contemporary British resident in China saw the likeness between the two men in Li's 'enjoyment of life, his brusque geniality, his impressive personality, his absolute freedom from scruples, and his astute wariness as to carrying his own ends'. He built up a secretariat of associates whom he placed in state-funded enterprises. He exemplified the 'statecraft' school of officials who believed in adopting a realistic approach to the challenges China faced rather than taking refuge in old formulae proclaiming the superiority of the imperial system.

Typical of his attitude, he told a British colonel that he could not understand the worship of Christ – 'Why, that man's life was a failure, and he was actually crucified at the end of it. Now, crucifixion is a very painful death, besides being a degrading form of punishment. How can you call yourselves followers of such a man?'

A British woman, Mrs Archibald Little, who wrote an early biography of Li, found him 'the most entertaining man I have ever talked with'. But an American former secretary of state, John W. Foster, who worked with him at the end of the century, described him as 'willing to be double-faced or even ten-faced', uniting 'the traits of cordial philanthropy and heartless cruelty, of truthfulness and mendacity'.[7]

With their recent experience of war, court figures saw the value of modern military equipment, and backed schemes by men like Li to build arsenals and shipyards. The empire bought iron-clad naval ships from Europe. A New Army was formed. Young officers were sent abroad to study. Foreign works were translated. The faith in the ability of foreigners to turn out weapons was such that some arsenals were entrusted to Westerners who were completely unqualified, including an English doctor.[8]

One of Li's secretariat, Xue Fucheng, drew up a wide blueprint for change, involving government backing for the modernization of transport and communication, the adoption of Western science, and the expansion of commerce and industry. Another practical scholar, Ma Jianzhong, who studied in Europe, saw government backing for the expansion of commerce as a means of improving the people's livelihood and expanding state revenues, emphasizing the importance of good laws, fair taxation, free expression of opinion through parliament and an end to corruption.

Other veterans of the wars against the mid-century rebels joined in the Self-Strengthening. The conqueror of Xinjiang, Zuo Zongtang, a man famed for his austerity, set up a shipyard, an arsenal and a woollen mill. Liu Kunyi, who had fought the rebels in central China, developed the city of Nanjing, where he became governor. Zhang Zhidong, who coined the saying 'Chinese learning for the fundamental principles; Western learning for practical application', took a more conservative approach, though this did not put a brake on his ceaseless activity; he was said never to go to bed because, if he lay down, he was haunted by the ghost of a wife he was alleged to have murdered. With one of the finest literary styles in the country, Zhang was as small as Li was large, and had an annoying habit of summoning people on the spur of the moment for supposedly urgent meetings, and then keeping them hanging around for weeks before he saw them; an American adviser suggested building a hotel where they could stay while they waited.[9]

Despairing of the military victories of the foreigners, Zhang wrote of how:

the barbarians swarmed in everywhere like moths or ants, and crept out here and there like so many frogs and insects. They suddenly forced their way past our stations and invaded our sacred demesnes; they burnt our pleasure gardens and spied out our cities and country places . . . Unless something is done at once, our country's vital strength will become more and more exhausted every day, while their power of mischief will increase in the same ratio.[10]

To achieve national revival by grafting Western technology on to Chinese roots, he began by setting up an academy and a printing works in Canton while he was governor there. Moved to run Hubei and Hunan provinces on the Middle Yangzi, he launched military and civilian schools, established a textile mill and a felt works, and promoted a scheme for a railway from Beijing to his new domain, as well as forming a local army corps. With Belgian help, he founded China's first iron-works in the city of Hanyang, which would become the home of some of the county's early trade unionists, who, in the next century, taught the Communists about labour organization. In case the Westerners tried to send troops to attack Beijing again, Zhang conjured up the idea of blocking their ships by sinking tiers of junks in the Gulf of Bohai leading to Tianjin and the capital, and then digging huge 'locust pits' on the shore to trap any soldiers who got through.[11]

Impressive as the action of Li, Zhang and their peers and protégés appeared, their enterprises were only a drop in the ocean for a country as large as China with so much ground to make up. Then, as now, there was a huge gap between the developing cities on the coast or in the Middle Yangzi, and the vast interior – a Western visitor to Guizhou in the 1880s reported that he did not see a single cart during his journey through the province; when his party finally came across one after reaching Yunnan, his bearers gazed in stupefaction at the broken-down contraption pulled by a buffalo. Though they might seem revolutionary – and, to reactionaries, deeply dangerous – the Self-Strengtheners were too few to enable China to catch up with other countries. Indeed, the pace of innovation in the West and Japan was far greater, so the gap actually widened.[12]

A listing of major new enterprises in 1885–95 by the historian Immanuel Hsü shows seven textile plants, three ironworks, two match factories, two mints, one paper mill and three mines, one each for gold, coal and iron. The Self-Strengtheners operated on the basis of loyalty to a system which was not designed to accommodate, let alone encourage, change. The necessary legal and administrative underpinnings were missing. Traditional remittance banks could not offer sufficient long-term capital, and attempts to set up a modern financial institution came to nothing. Though some young men were being sent abroad to study, especially to Japan, China had few experienced managers, and lacked the entrepreneurial spirit that powered the Industrial Revolution in the West. Companies such as those set up by Li had lax controls, particularly when the founders were diverted into another of their myriad activities. Li's steamship firm was looted by insiders and lost out in competition to British lines, while his coal mine got heavily into debt to foreigners.[13]

Apart from their membership of the Confucian elite, there was a strong practical reason why the Self-Strengtheners did not want to rock the political boat, and so never played the political role of Western Industrial Revolution entrepreneurs. Their business activities were intimately linked to their position as officials. They drew finance from the imperial treasury – three quarters of the initial backing for Li's shipping company came from official sources. By asserting their own management control, they were pioneering a form of back-door privatization, but they needed court favour, just as entrepreneurs today need at least tacit Communist Party approval.

What has been called 'defensive modernization' thus contained flaws at its very core. So long as they were seen to be pushing foreign innovations over traditional ways, the Self-Strengtheners would be suspect; to be fully accepted, the new technology would have had to have been viewed as Chinese. The reliance of the officially placed Self-Strengtheners on the provincial domains vested in them by Beijing meant that their enterprises operated on a local scale, rather than laying the foundations for national undertakings. Court favour could always be withdrawn, particularly when attacks from critical censors of the 'purist' school rose. Zhang and Li managed to maintain Cixi's support for most of their careers, enjoying regular preferment. Hongzhang and the Dowager regularly exchanged presents; he sent her valuable and foreign novelties while she reciprocated with scrolls, manuscript tablets, satin, sable and silk garments, and characters in the calligraphy she studied in pursuit of self-improvement. Still, both men fell from grace for a time. Official funding of Zhang's ironworks in the Middle Yangzi was halted, and he was ordered to sell it to private investors, which he did on disadvantageous terms. In the 1890s, Cixi's backing was not enough to protect Li when the court faction round the emperor turned against him. 'If the Dowager Empress has her way, he will be rehabilitated,' Robert Hart noted. 'If the emperor had his, the poor man's head would be off his shoulders before sunset.' Rather than anything so drastic, Li found himself stripped of the high ranks that had been bestowed on him, and retreated to await the moment to stage a return.[14]

Subsequently, Communist historians painted Li as the epitome of a 'surrenderist' scheming with the enemies of the people and giving away Chinese assets, while stashing his ill-gotten gains in foreign banks. As national economic policy shifted, this verdict was softened, but the towering Self-Strengthener is still a difficult figure ideologically for believers in 'socialism with Chinese characteristics' to approve of, even if he should have felt quite at home in the political economy of early twenty-first-century China.

In their own time, Li and his peers faced constant opposition from conservatives. Though he saw the need for modern arms and armies, their mentor, Zeng Guofan, feared that the telegraph and the railway would undermine China's values, and disliked the Western presence in

Shanghai. At an audience with Cixi during which she noticed that he had gone blind in his right eye, the two of them agreed that Christian missionaries were creating trouble, especially by promoting the interests of their converts. Putting the conservative case, a thinker, Yen Fu, argued that the difference between Chinese and Western knowledge was as great as that between the complexions of the two races. 'We cannot force the two cultures to be the same or similar,' he wrote after translating foreign works. 'Chinese knowledge has its foundation and function; Western knowledge has also its foundation and function. If the two are separated, each can be independent; if the two were combined, both would perish.'[15]

Railways were seen as a particular threat to the natural order, disrupting *feng shui* and disturbing the spirits of the ancestors. The first line, built by Westerners in Shanghai, was bought in 1877 by local authorities, which had the rails ripped up and the main station turned into a temple. Imperial censors warned that foreign countries were pulling up their rails because trains were so dangerous, and wanted to reduce their losses by selling the track to China, thereby menacing the employment of coolies and cart drivers. A governor of Shaanxi province at the end of the century explained to an American visitor why he had disapproved of railways: 'They bring in foreigners whom I do not like, and they throw men out of work.'[16]

There was also a financial–nationalist issue. The empire did not have the money with which to fund railways. So capital had to come from foreign syndicates, which saw the prospect of big profits in supplying China with infrastructure. The way the court and its officials looked abroad for funding, and committed tax revenue as collateral, underlined the country's weakness in the face of the modern world. Anti-Manchu nationalists could thus paint the rulers as being ready to work with Westerners to the detriment of the Chinese people. Urban gentry and merchants who wanted a slice of the pie bemoaned the failure of the Qing to stand up for China.

Zhang Zhidong accurately blamed the strictly limited success of modernization on a long list of failings – selfishness, lack of funds, the absence of a clear policy from the court, shortage of competent staff, interference, ignorance and the demand for quick results. 'When a mine had not yet been opened, a profit was expected,' he wrote. Enterprises were taken up by the state as urgent, and then allowed to go to waste.

'One digs a grave, the other fills it in,' he lamented. 'How could we expect any success?'[17]

Li Hongzhang answered the critics with the slogan 'Let us use the foreigner, but do not let him use us'. In a memorial to the emperor, he argued that 'if we can really and thoroughly understand their [the foreigners'] methods – the more we learn, the more we improve – and promote them further and further, can we not expect that after a century or so we can reject the barbarians and stand on our own feet?'[18]

It was a belief he stuck by all his life, but the results were, he admitted, disappointing. 'Affairs in my country have been so confined by tradition that I could not accomplish what I desired,' he replied when asked by a Japanese politician in 1884 why so little had changed in China, while Japan had modernized so rapidly. 'I am ashamed of having excessive wishes and lacking the power to fulfil them.' Li could see wider repercussions, too. 'In about ten years,' he predicted, 'the wealth and strength of Japan will be admirable – a future source of trouble for China'.[19]

As China rebuilt itself after the mid-century rebellions, Cixi steadily increased her power, with skilful divide-and-rule tactics, giving and withholding favours from behind the throne. The late emperor's low-profile widow was no rival, playing little part in decision-making before she died in 1881. Their co-conspirator in the coup of 1861, Prince Gong, had a chequered subsequent career. 'Extremely intelligent but lacks the steadfastness to be able to persevere in any view for any length of time,' Zeng Guofan judged. Gong and the Dowager had an uneasy relationship. He had her favourite eunuch killed, and she used her dynastic authority to have him censured for an alleged protocol insult to the Son of Heaven. On another occasion, however, she intervened to protect Gong from her son. As an accomplished politician, she knew the benefits of never letting others know exactly where she stood.

In 1874, Cixi demonstrated her steel after the death of the bisexual Tongzhi emperor. Her son had briefly assumed power on reaching maturity, but his health was in sharp decline, weakened by heavy drinking and syphilis he caught on clandestine visits to brothels. When out riding he sat hunched up on the saddle, looking very tired, his face sallow. His death opened up a fresh succession struggle, complicated by the pregnancy of his widow, who came from a powerful Manchu clan.

One course would have been to have waited for the child to be born.

But there was no certainty it would be a boy. In any case, Cixi wanted a fast succession that avoided the possibility of a new power centre at court forming round the widow. Elbowed aside, the pregnant woman killed herself. The scuttlebutt had it that Cixi had a hand in her death, and had even murdered her own son to prevent him falling under the influence of his bride and her clan – just as she would be alleged to have poisoned the other Dowager Empress. As so often when Cixi might be involved, the rumour mill worked at full speed, and nobody was the wiser.

With the unborn child out of the way, there were several possible candidates for the throne. One was the son of Prince Gong, but he was blamed for having abetted the late emperor in his debauchery. Instead, the Dowager decided on a four-year-old son of Gong's brother, Prince Chun. A remark which a senior official noted in his diary, and which was generally attributed to Cixi, had it that the new ruler should be 'amenable to proper training'. This was taken as proof that she wanted a puppet on the throne; it may, alternatively, have simply been a sensible observation that the dynasty should avoid a repetition of her son's bad behaviour.

Still, traditionalists were outraged at the choice of the new emperor, who was given the reign name of Guangxu. It broke the fundamental precept that each ruler must be from the next generation to his predecessor. Since this was not the case, the new Son of Heaven would not be able to pay filial obeisance to Tongzhi, as required by the code of rites. One censor was so scandalized that he committed public suicide during the enthronement. Reactionary Manchu princes instigated riots, and brought in wild Muslim horsemen to ride through the streets of Beijing to overawe the population. The *New York Times* reported talk of an impending civil war.[20]

To win out in her second succession crisis, Cixi could count on Gong, who approved what she was doing, on her own broadly based faction, on the court scholar, Weng Tonghe, who was the new ruler's tutor, and on powerful provincial figures. Li sent a 4,000-strong army on a forced march to the capital to back her. She also had the military protection of her one-time suitor, Jung-lu, who had risen to be one of the main Manchu commanders and controller of the imperial household. That was enough for her to win the day. But relations soon soured with Jung-lu, who was discovered having an affair with a lady in the palace, which led to Cixi having him exiled from Beijing.

In 1880, the Dowager fell so seriously ill with a liver ailment that there were reports she was dying. Recovering by the following year, she continued to accrete authority. In 1884, Gong, who had become expendable, fell from power, and the young emperor's father, Prince Chun, became the main male Manchu figure at court. He was married to Cixi's sister, and had assisted the 1861 coup. Respected as a scholar, he was less arrogant and more popular than his brother, Gong. His anti-foreign views gave him a patriotic sheen. A sad-looking figure with a drooping moustache and small goatee beard, he took pains not to be seen as a threat to the authority of the Dowager, who remained regent for two years after Guangxu came of age in 1887.

Outside the closed circle of the court, the country continued to be jarred by recurrent risings, on a smaller scale than the mid-century revolts, spurred by disasters, poverty, underground sects, bandits and anti-Manchu sentiment. When the dynasty acted resolutely, with the support of the gentry and merchants, these could be mastered. But they contributed to a drip-feed reduction in the authority of the central state, and the transfer of power to provincial power holders.

Events in the three cities of Wuhan in the early 1880s provide an example of the latent volatility. Drought and an awful harvest at the beginning of the decade raised local grain prices by 25 per cent, while the cost of cooking oil nearly doubled. Starving refugees crowded into the cities, lining up at street gruel kitchens. Even prosperous merchants in Hankou, which had become a treaty port in 1861, felt the pressure.[21]

There then appeared a poor man from Shandong, who had wandered round the country for years and was hailed by believers as the Great Teacher for his preaching of a transcendental unified faith and his calls for the overthrow of the Qing as he claimed the throne as the heir of the Ming. After a while, the Great Teacher departed on further travels, leaving his son and a lieutenant to organize a revolt from a Hankou shop-house belonging to a one-time martial arts instructor called Chang the Deaf. They drew on heterodox Buddhist sects and secret societies to raise a 4,000-strong force, the Flying Virtue Army. Thousands more men were said to be ready to join. Plans were laid for risings along the Yangzi and Han rivers, and in Shandong and Jiangsu on the east coast. At the end of April 1883, a group of wild-looking tea-chest makers who were part of the plot arrived in Hankou, spreading stories of impending violence to cause panic. Merchants closed their premises, and moved to the countryside or formed militia units. The authorities ordered the city gates to be shut.

Imperial troops were called in, and obtained information from a plotter who was arrested in a brothel, drunk. The gentry militias swung into action. Martial law was declared. Opium dens and brothels were closed. Nuns from Buddhist convents suspected of complicity with the rebels were sent home or sold as concubines. Arrests went on for months. Rebels were betrayed by members of their lineage clans and handed over to the authorities for a reward. Hundreds were executed, often after torture. The Great Teacher escaped; some reports said he was later captured and executed; others that he holed up on a holy mountain; and still others that he lived and died quietly in a village near Tianjin.

On 24 February 1889, a rainy, windy day in Beijing, a spectacular procession left the Forbidden City for the home of one of Cixi's nieces. At its head were nine white ponies followed by fine carriages, sedan chairs and a huge crowd of Manchu Bannermen troops* in red robes, holding aloft lanterns adorned with the character for fidelity. Sixteen bearers carried the young woman to the palace to be married to the Guangxu emperor, who was about to celebrate his seventeenth birthday. With her were two concubines, aged thirteen and fifteen. The bride's trousseau, carried by 4,000 men, consisted of 600 items, including golden chests, jewels, jade, furniture and mirrors ten feet high, all protected from the rain by oilcloth coloured in imperial yellow.[22]

It was no love match. The bride, slim, plain and three years older than her husband, disliked him and he her. Cixi had arranged the marriage to consolidate the power of her clan. She may also have hoped that an heir would avoid another succession crisis, but the marriage was childless. Indeed, it may never have been consummated – a report by a French doctor who examined Guangxu ten years later suggested that he was unable to sustain an erection.[23]

Cixi had also picked the two teenage concubines who accompanied the bride. They were sisters from Canton. One, known as the Lustrous Concubine, was dumpy and placid. The other, the Pearl Concubine, was

---

* So called because they had fought under a series of different banners in the 1644 invasion of China.

beautiful and lively. The emperor much preferred her company to that of his bride. But she soon abused her position to interfere with appointments and ensure that a cousin got particularly high grades in his imperial examinations. When the scandal exploded in 1894, Cixi ordered that the two young women should be degraded, and, it was rumoured, flogged, though they were later restored to their earlier status. Their cousin was temporarily banished from Beijing.[24]

A week after the wedding, as the emperor passed his seventeenth birthday, an edict announced that Cixi would retire. She should have done this two years earlier, but had stayed on, ostensibly to coach the young man. Now, at the age of fifty-four, it was time for her to move to take up residence in the great estate of the Summer Palace, outside Beijing, which had been rebuilt in luxurious fashion after the depredations of the Anglo-French expedition of 1860. With its lakes, covered walkways, trees, plants and classical arched bridges, it was a favourite spot for the 'Old Buddha', as she was becoming known. She resided in the Hall of Happiness in Longevity surrounding two courtyards planted with magnolias. A hundred dishes were cooked for each of the two main daily meals.[25]

Though she ordered the dismissal of a censor who suggested that imperial memorials should still be submitted to her, the true extent of Cixi's withdrawal may be questioned. Her nephew was emperor of China, but she was still chief of the extended Manchu clans, seen by many of the princes and senior officials as the de facto ruler, whoever sat on the throne. She maintained contact with the Forbidden City through nobles, officials and a fifty-year-old eunuch, Li Lianying, who had inspired her nickname when he reacted to the way rain fell after she offered prayers by exclaiming, 'it is almost as if she was Buddha herself.'[26]

Like Deng Xiaoping when he retreated from day-to-day administration a century later, Cixi was not the kind of person to fade out of the picture. Like him, she could only consider her own experience and sagacity as essential to keep the regime from hitting the rocks, particularly given the doubts among her long-time associates about the younger men who had assumed at least nominal power. In each case, this would lead to the use of force to suppress political reform and consign the protégés to house or palace arrest as the old stagers imposed orthodoxy at the centre and blocked political progress which could have changed China.

*

Guangxu was fragile both physically and mentally, subject to mood swings and temper fits. He had lung trouble and a speech impediment, and fell into depressions. His tutor, Weng Tonghe, recorded how the emperor would burst into tears or fall into silent sulks if he did not wish to continue his studies. His mother had mistreated him, and his father had been absorbed with state affairs. As a boy, he had been ill-treated by court eunuchs. When he granted an audience to foreign diplomats, he struck the American minister, Charles Denby, as 'a delicate youth . . . small and thin and gives no promise of possessing physical strength'. His eyes were large and black, his face smooth and hairless. His voice was 'light and thin like a mosquito'.

In keeping with custom, the new ruler began with a show of benevolence. Taxes were remitted for the year. Prison sentences were reduced; men about to be beheaded or strangled would be allowed to live. Bannermen troops received an extra month's ration. All Manchu women over seventy got presents. It was promised that the imperial examinations would produce 'a large number of successful candidates'. Guangxu disliked high spending, and told provincial officials they faced the 'direst penalties' if they imposed levies to help pay for his wedding – though Canton was also instructed to come up with pearls as big as acacia nuts.[27]

The emperor ordered a one-third cut in the budget submitted to him for the imperial household; this alienated members of the court, who had no desire to tighten their belts, and embarrassed officials on the Board of Revenue, who suffered the humiliation of seeing their proposals reduced. Guangxu also gave vent to his particular hatred of eunuchs derived from his bad boyhood experiences at their hands. He had a near-fatal clubbing inflicted on one for a minor offence and sentenced another to be given eighty strokes with a stick for showing a lack of respect.[28]

The attempt to reduce spending and clamp down on corruption raised an unmentionable issue – the Dowager. She enjoyed luxury, and did not stint on spending at the Summer Palace. If there were to be cuts in the Forbidden City, it was only logical that there should be on her estate as well. But that was a step much too far for the young man. He also reacted explosively to a censor who mentioned reports that she was interfering in state matters – the errant official was banished to the Far West.

The new ruler read books which alerted him to China's plight and the way things were done elsewhere. Taking lessons in English and French, he ordered extracts from foreign newspapers, and looked at pictures in British and American illustrated weeklies. One story had it that, as a child, he had been enraptured by mechanical toys from a store in Beijing kept by a Swiss man. He became fascinated by the telephone, installing one in the Forbidden City, and had a miniature railway track built beside the lakes of the Summer Palace on which he and his aunt would ride on a little open carriage pulled by a small engine. He set his heart on making a proper train journey from Beijing to Canton as soon as the projected line was completed, and issued what was described as a 'red hot edict' condemning the director of railways for 'doing nothing too vigorously', as the *North China Herald* put it.[29]

The key imperial official was the ruler's former tutor, Weng Tonghe, who had come first in the top level of imperial examination in 1856, and, after holding a series of posts, was appointed to school the young emperor and instruct the Dowager. In the late 1870s, he became director of the Censorate and president of the Board of Punishment. Named to the regime's top government body, the Grand Council, he was made president of the Board of Revenue. Though a perfect establishment man, he showed an interest in new ideas as a patron of 'celebrity-scholars' who provided intellectual ferment in Beijing.

Weng has sometimes been seen as the leading figure in an 'emperor's faction' after the Dowager left the Forbidden City, but his loyalty was to the throne, rather than to the person of its occupant. In addition, his strong attachment to filial devotion meant that he would find it hard to side with Guangxu against his aunt, to whom he owed a special debt of piety since she had helped his father.

Reports from censors showed growing concern about weaknesses in the system. An imperial reply admitted that official circles were 'over-crowded by men of mediocre ability and often of low standing to the detriment of the public services'. The Board of Revenue should stop selling senior positions, it added. Lower ranks should be thinned out by 'frequent denunciations of incompetent and avaricious prefects, sub-prefects, department and district magistrates'. There was not much evidence of action being taken. The Treasury needed the money from the sale of degrees, and local officials were well used to defending their interests through connections, bribery and simple refusal to follow instructions from the centre.[30]

Another censor noted how bureaux set up to levy taxes on the transport of goods to fund gentry armies were 'dotted like stars' across the country, outside Beijing's control. The throne's central problem was that, as now, the officials who were meant to take remedial action had a direct or indirect interest in perpetuating the existing state of affairs.

As for the intrusive foreigners, many in the gentry saw the imported ways as threatening their position in their home provinces. There was strong resistance to Westerners in Hunan, where one who penetrated the provincial capital of Changsha in 1886 was put into a closed sedan chair and carried from the city. European travellers in Yunnan and Guangxi were banned from contact with locals. A merchant in Guangxi who bought salt from Europeans was beaten to death. A medical missionary who settled in the old capital of Xi'an in the mid-1880s fled after a mob burned down his dispensary. A Manchu prince was reported to hold that the strangers all came from a single island which was now almost depopulated because so many of its inhabitants had gone to China; they pretended to be of different nationalities on different days of the week merely in order to mislead the Chinese. But, however annoying the Westerners were, they were not the main threat China faced under Guangxu's rule. That came from across the sea to the east.

In 1894, one of the great international conflict lines of modern times opened up between China and Japan. Their struggle for mastery in East Asia, detonated by Tokyo's ambitions as it adopted Western methods at the end of the nineteenth century under the modernizing oligarchs of the Meiji Restoration, would cost tens of millions of lives and fuel deep antagonisms, sharpened by the weight of history. The first outbreak of Japan's expansionist drive came in Korea, where Tokyo and Beijing jockeyed for influence.

China's weakness was an open invitation to the Meiji empire, which had undertaken root-and-branch reform after Commander Perry's expedition of 1852 brought it into contact with the outside world. Territorial expansion was viewed as the sacred imperial way to free the island nation from economic vulnerability, provide a living space on the Asian mainland and spread the message of Japanese superiority.

With rare exceptions, such as Li Hongzhang, the Chinese had no conception of what was going on. For them, Japan was an inferior country, its inhabitants known derogatively as *wojen* – 'dwarves' – who owed their culture to China. The hollowness of that view should have been apparent in the 1870s, when Japan invaded Taiwan and Beijing had to pay to get it to withdraw. The kingdom of Korea was the logical next step. The peninsula had long been under China's suzerainty, but Tokyo began to try to move across the Korean Strait in the early 1880s, backing a rebel faction at the court in Seoul. China and Japan sent in troops. Li Hongzhang negotiated an agreement in 1884 for both to withdraw their forces, and undertake not to return them without consultations. In 1894, a new crisis erupted as the Korean monarch faced a peasant rebellion and asked for Beijing's military help. When the imperial court agreed to this, Japan reacted by sending in a far larger detachment, which took Seoul, stormed the palace, disarmed garrisons in the city and captured the ruler. A prince they appointed in his place denounced Korea's treaties with Beijing. China's plenipotentiary fled. Deploying a line of propaganda it would use over the next fifty years, Tokyo claimed a duty to 'lead the little Kingdom along the path of civilization' and to make sure this was not impeded by another power – that is to say, China.[31]

Officials and scholar-advisers in Beijing advocated a tough response. Cixi was indignant. There were bad omens in China – plague, cholera and floods, followed by scorching weather. A strange double halo formed round the sun. Failure to meet the challenge from Tokyo would be a further sign of dynastic decline which the Qing could not risk.[32]

A declaration of war from the court said China had always 'followed the paths of philanthropy and perfect justice' in helping 'our small tributary' in its troubles; now, it was difficult to reason with the Japanese, who were referred to repeatedly in the text as *wojen*. They had shown themselves to be bellicose bullies, indulging in unforeseeable treacherous conduct, it went on. Li Hongzhang, who had just been awarded the highest imperial decoration, the three-eyed peacock feather, was told to gather all China's armies 'to root the *wojen* out of their lairs'.[33]

Li hoped that foreign powers would save China the trouble of fighting by checking the invaders. But the Qing enjoyed little sympathy from governments abroad, and the young emperor was anxious to stand up to Japan. '999 out of every 1000 Chinese are sure big China can thrash little Japan,' wrote Robert Hart.[34]

On paper, China had just over a million men at arms to throw into the war – 325,000 of them Banner troops, about the same number of

'Green Standard' Han soldiers, plus 400,000 other men said to have undergone training. The real numbers fell some way below these totals, however, and some elite Manchu forces still prided themselves in their expertise with bows and arrows rather than guns. Japan's 270,000 troops were well trained and had modern arms. Tokyo had also broken China's military cable codes.[35]

Qing armies were split between regional and princely chiefs; Japan's were unified. The Chinese command system managed to be both suffocatingly centralized and extremely chaotic, the generals milling around in a fog of uncertainty. On the other hand, Japanese commanders were given clear objectives and left to get on with the job in pincer attacks which flummoxed the Chinese.

The Qing forces set up a defensive position in early September 1894, behind walls and earthworks at the northern Korean city of Pyongyang. They thought they had plenty of time – the enemy was not expected to arrive for a week. So they indulged in an autumn festival feast, drinking and gambling late into the night of 14 September. But the Japanese marched through the surrounding mountains, and attacked before dawn the next day under cover of a heavy artillery barrage. After some delay, the Chinese came out to face them, but were promptly annihilated. 'Our comrades fell like mown grass,' a survivor recalled. The Chinese cavalry galloped off, only to be cut down by Japanese lining the road they took. The remaining defenders raised white flags on the walls, and then fled – again many were killed as they passed through an enemy gauntlet. Japanese records showed them suffering 189 dead and 516 wounded, while the Chinese death toll was 2,000, with 6,000 taken prisoner.[36]

The focus now switched to the sea, providing the first test for the navy of thirty warships which Li had built up with purchases from Europe, despite the depredations of members of his family, who had pocketed the money allocated for explosives and packed shell casings with sand. Two days after the Japanese took Pyongyang, they won a six-hour naval battle at the mouth of the Yalu river on the Korean border. China lost four ships. None of the Japanese vessels was sunk, though some were seriously damaged.[37]

The Chinese army now formed a defensive line on the Yalu, which was 200 feet wide and 11 feet deep. The Japanese built a bridge across it. Despite grand plans to assemble forces from across the empire, Chinese reinforcements were nowhere to be seen. The defenders fled. Japanese forces crossed into Manchuria, and drove on to the strategically placed, ice-free harbour city of Port Arthur,* which was taken after desultory fighting. Most of the Chinese soldiers ran away – according to an eyewitness, the chief civilian official changed into simple cotton clothes and escaped on a boat to Tianjin.[38]

When they entered Port Arthur on 21 November, the Japanese soldiers were outraged to see the heads of some captured comrades hanging from cords, noses and ears cut off. Two disembowelled bodies dangled from a tree, the eyes gouged out. In a pre-echo of future massacres, the victors killed indiscriminately. They drove a group of Chinese into a lake to drown. Civilians were tied together and shot en masse. Soldiers paraded in the streets with human heads held aloft on bayonets. In a bank, they stuck severed heads on the spikes running along the top of a partition.[39]

'The defenseless and unarmed inhabitants were butchered in their houses and their bodies unspeakably mutilated,' an American correspondent, James Creelman, reported in the *New York World*. 'There was an unrestrained reign of murder which continued for three days. The whole town was plundered with appalling atrocities.'[40] Creelman's dispatches, putting the civilian death toll at 2,000, drew a response from the foreign minister in Tokyo, who said that there had been 'no intention to harm or molest non-combatants', but that soldiers 'transported with rage at the mutilation of their comrades by the enemy broke through all restraints . . . to inflict vengeance without discrimination'.

Despite all the reverses, Beijing proclaimed great victories. Drawings of the war sold in the streets of Chinese cities showed the enemy being overwhelmed, and Japanese prisoners tied upside down to staves as they were carried to execution. But, as reality seeped home, a scapegoat had to be found, and the target was Li Hongzhang. Dismissed from his posts, he was stripped of his three-eyed peacock feather decoration and imperial yellow jacket. He had already come under attack in the summer, in a detailed report by a censor which inveighed against 'the immense wealth, the power and the influence of the scions of the Li clan'. Court memorialists denounced him as 'incompetent, arrogant, unprincipled',

---

* Named after a Royal Navy lieutenant, William Arthur, who had taken his damaged frigate into the harbour for repairs in 1860.

adding that 'his name stinks in the nostrils of his countrymen'. Li warned his much-criticized, profiteering brother, Hanzhang, the governor in Canton, that 'the mind of the emperor is inscrutable'. 'Take care and act.' The brother made an unsuccessful suicide bid that night.[41]

To show solidarity with the war effort, Cixi ordered 15,000 fur coats to be sent to soldiers fighting in freezing Manchuria, and donated 3 million tael for food for the troops. Court banquets for the winter solstice were cancelled. Orders were issued to cashier generals who failed in their duties. An imperial decree enjoined strict discipline, prohibiting looting or stealing from markets: still, observers noted that, when Chinese troops approached, villagers shut their doors and closed their stores.[42]

Prince Gong was recalled to take charge. 'Although not entirely recovered from his bodily ailments of former years,' an imperial edict declared, he 'still has the appearance of being unimpaired in vigour of intellect'. A request by the emperor to provincial governors to suggest what China should do produced a majority in favour of paying an indemnity to Japan. But no territory should be ceded. There was talk of buying the Chilean fleet to make up for China's weakness at sea, and of moving the capital to the west.[43]

On 12 February 1895, Japanese troops took the important port of Weihaiwei on the Gulf of Bohai, in Shandong, after a twenty-three-day battle in freezing temperatures amid raging winds and towering waves. This enabled them to destroy Chinese warships left at their moorings and seize 100,000 tons of coal on the docks. The imperial admiral committed suicide by drinking poison in his cabin. The invaders could now control maritime traffic to Tianjin and Beijing, as well as having their army poised north of the capital. If they so wished, they might move on the heart of the empire. A European from the Imperial Customs Service was sent to inquire about peace terms. The choice of a Westerner avoided the direct involvement of the court; his activities could be disowned as those of a man unfamiliar with Chinese protocol and procedure. The Japanese turned him away on the grounds that he did not carry proper credentials. Another mission was sent, under the American former secretary of state John Foster. It, too, was rejected. Japan had no interest in halting the fighting when it was on top.

In desperation, the court turned to the man it had disgraced, entrusting him with the peace mission. There was, as in the past, an ambiguity about this. If Li Hongzhang got a satisfactory agreement, that would be to the credit of those who had sent him. If he failed to do so, or returned with a shameful peace, blame could be heaped on his head. His critics did not let up. A memorial to the emperor said Li wanted the enemy to win since he had large investments in Japan. He was accused of having held up supplies to the Chinese army and diverted funds into his own pocket while 'rejoicing at our defeats and deploring our successes'. His execution, a censor added, would inspire imperial troops to annihilate the enemy. But Cixi knew she and the empire had nobody else who could deal with the foreigners. The critical censor was banished to the Far West to 'expiate his guilt and serve as a warning to others'.[44]

On 19 March 1895, as Japan took the Pescadores Islands off Taiwan, Li arrived by steamer in the southern Japanese port of Shimonoseki with a delegation of more than 100 people, including his son. Tokyo had turned down a Chinese request to hold negotiations in Tianjin or Port Arthur, which would have enabled the empire to pretend that the enemy was coming as a supplicant.

The negotiations with the former prime minister, Ito Hirobumi, were conducted in English. Ito spoke the language after travelling to America to study constitutional affairs. Li, who towered over the diminutive Japanese, used an interpreter. According to the Japanese record, the Chinese proposed that his country and Japan should unite against the white races; Ito did not take this up. Then Li proposed an immediate armistice.[45]

In keeping with the policy of 'getting the barbarians to fight the barbarians', he warned the Japanese that third powers might intervene if they felt their interests were threatened. Ito modified Japan's initial terms, but still demanded large swathes of territory and a big indemnity. He also noted that Japanese troopships were on their way to China, and more were ready to sail, leaving Li with a straight choice, between accepting Tokyo's terms or seeing the enemy advance resume.

The talks were suddenly thrown off balance when a Japanese youth fired a single revolver shot at Li as he was being driven back to his temporary residence. The bullet lodged under his nose. There was a huge reaction of shock from the Japanese – their emperor sent his personal physician; the empress rolled bandages and despatched two nurses. Li was reported to have received 10,000 letters of condolence. Given the victim's advanced age, the doctors did not dare to put him under an anaesthetic, and the Chinese statesman decided not to be operated on, but to resume the negotiations as soon as possible.

The shame at what one Japanese newspaper called 'the mad deed of a miscreant' put the invaders on the back foot. 'The scoundrel has undone the great achievement of the nation,' a field marshal exclaimed. Tokyo felt obliged to offer a three-week armistice. Plans to march on Beijing were put on one side, though Taiwan was retaken.

Standing in for his father, Li's son received Tokyo's new peace terms on 1 April. Japan demanded the whole of the Liaodong Peninsula in Manchuria, as well as keeping Taiwan. Other territory to be acquired in the north-east included the Qing's home region in Manchuria containing the tombs of the ancestors. The people of occupied areas were to be obliged to become Japanese citizens. China would keep out of Korea. An indemnity was demanded equal to the annual Chinese imperial budget. Japan would be admitted to the treaty port system of the Western powers, and seven Chinese cities opened to its firms, which were allowed to build factories there. Japanese goods were to be exempt from the *likin* transport tax. 'The battle of arms and men has reached its conclusion,' a Tokyo newspaper observed. 'Now the battle of commerce begins.'[46]

As Li travelled home with these terms, princes, ministers and provincial governors advised the emperor to reject them, but to increase the indemnity to buy off territorial concessions. Two hundred thousand troops were said to have been assembled to defend the capital. However, as Ito had remarked, Japan was sending in more than fifty troopships. The treaty was accepted.

Chinese military casualties in the war were estimated at 35,000. Though the official Japanese toll was 739, with 230 dying subsequently from wounds, the real figure was certainly considerably higher – some accounts put it at 17,000. Cholera spread on crowded troopships sailing back to Japan, where it claimed 40,000 lives. Still, the ease of the victories greatly boosted Japanese self-confidence – and military spending, while waking up the West to the new power in the East. 'Before, we did not know ourselves, and the world did not yet know us,' a leading journalist wrote. 'But now that we have tested our strength, we know ourselves and are known by the world.'[47]

Some Chinese units had fought bravely, but their overall performance and the court's handling of the crisis further reduced the empire's international standing. 'At no time in her history has China been so poor and so weak,' lamented a report drawn up by a scholar, Yu Tsan. For Robert Hart, 'China's collapse has been terrible, and the comical and tragical have dovetailed ... in the most heart-breaking, side-bursting fashion.' The shell of the imperial egg had been cracked, in Humpty Dumpty fashion, he went on. 'Everything that China should have yielded gracefully to others when asked for will now have to be yielded to Japan's hectoring. Japan will then pose and say to all creation – "That's the way to do it, and it's I that did it."' The voice of the Shanghai British establishment, the *North China News*, described China as 'one vast jellyfish'.

However, in defeat, Li's longstanding belief that China would be able to use the foreigners to cancel each other out finally came into play. When word of the proposed territorial arrangements leaked, European powers with interests in China were worried. 'The Mikado might become the Chinese Emperor and Russia would need hundreds of thousands of troops to defend her possessions,' the finance minister in St Petersburg, Count de Witte, remarked. So pressure was put on Tokyo to reduce its gains. Backing off, Japan renounced its claim to the Liaodong Peninsula in return for an additional indemnity, though hanging on to Taiwan. Russia and its European ally, France, could now present themselves as China's true friends in comparison to the British, who were closer to the Japanese.

After his services arranging the peace treaty, Li was not punished again for the defeat, but it was felt best for him to spend some time out of the country. So he went on a lengthy tour of Europe and the United States, his first destination being St Petersburg for the coronation of a new tsar, during which he pursued his policy of enlisting Russia against Japan. In Britain, he met Gladstone, expressing astonishment that the daughter of a man as important as the Liberal leader had not been able to find a husband. Asked by the Duke of Devonshire if he had ever shot grouse, he replied, 'No, but I have often shot rebels.'[48]

4

Reform and Reaction

Defeat by Japan was followed by a wave of natural disasters. The harvest failed in Sichuan; floods hit Anhui, Jiangxi and Jiangsu; the Yellow River broke its banks and spilled water six feet deep over land housing more than a million people. There was famine and plague in Jiangsu and Hunan. Tianjin and the surrounding region suffered a severe drought. Long stretches of the Grand Canal ran dry, and were used by farmers to house animals while locals took bricks from the dykes to build houses.[1]

Pirates sailed along the rivers of the Pearl Delta in the south; British warships were sent in to restore order on several occasions. Muslims revolted in Gansu and Shaanxi. There were risings in Anhui, Shandong, Sichuan and Guangxi. Wuhan suffered from outbreaks of arson, one of which was reported to have killed a thousand people. In Nanjing, mobs attacked rice stores as merchants held back supplies to push up prices. On the Huai plain in eastern China, 30,000 peasants took part in a violent protest against their distress. At Chinese New Year, at the end of January 1898, Beijing observed a total eclipse of the sun, a highly inauspicious sign. The following summer was exceptionally hot in the capital, the thermometer reaching 106 degrees Fahrenheit in the shade. The mood, wrote Robert Hart, was one of 'general gloom and depression'.

Public finances were in chaos, dragged down by indemnities to foreign powers. Inflation rose, aggravated by crop failures and a fall in the value of silver, on which the currency was based. The price of flour in Beijing and rice in Shanghai nearly doubled between 1892 and 1898. In Suzhou, rents jumped by 65 per cent in the 1890s. Increased land taxes sparked demonstrations.

Growing exports of food exposed farmers to international price fluctuations. The trade deficit rose as other nations competed with China's traditional sales abroad of tea and silk – the second had taken over from the first as the main export. Imported coal was sold for less than that mined domestically. Handicrafts were hit by imports, notably cotton goods from Britain, while Japan threatened to become the 'England of the Orient'. Some 700,000 plain grey cotton shirts made in Lancashire were sent up the Yangzi from Shanghai to Sichuan each year, undercutting local production despite the cost of shipping them across the globe. Not only were the foreigners profiting at the country's expense, but the Chinese themselves were unable to co-operate; they 'act like vultures over a dead body whenever there are profits to be realised', observed one writer.[2]

Such weakness set off a fresh scramble among foreign powers in a process known as 'splitting the melon'. The European powers worked both singly and in combinations that reflected the line-up on the other side of the world. A German member of the Imperial Customs suggested that Britain and his country were milkmen whose joint interest lay in keeping the China cow alive while France and Russia were butchers who wanted to carve it up.[3]

Despite the war of 1894–5, Japan managed to present itself to the Chinese authorities as less oppressive than the Europeans, and as a fellow Asian power. It established concessions in Hangzhou, Suzhou, Hankou, Tianjin, Xiamen and Fuzhou – but not in Shanghai, where the Japanese moved into a district of the International Settlement that became known as 'Little Tokyo'.

The agreement that the Japanese could set up factories in treaty ports was rapidly taken up by other powers; it was estimated that 136 foreign-owned manufacturing and mining enterprises were founded between 1895 and 1913, in addition to some 100 which had existed illegally before. Changes in the price of silver helped to make Japanese goods more competitive – exports jumped from 8 per cent of total Japanese trade in the first half of the 1890s to 25 per cent by 1914, while investment from Japan rose to 13.6 per cent of the total in China over the same period, far less than Britain's 37.7 per cent, but not far behind Germany and Russia and ahead of France.[4]

The court hoped to exercise 'barbarian management', turning the foreigners from 'outer barbarians' into 'inner barbarians' who would somehow become less aggressive as a result. But, alongside military defeat, the Qing became increasingly dependent on outside money –

between 1894 and 1896, the throne borrowed 350 million yuan from foreign banks. The pledging of tax revenue as collateral risked setting up a vicious downward spiral. While foreign military incursions provided the most dramatic sign of the power of imperialism, the more pervasive impact of indebtedness and reliance on foreign funding accentuated China's fragility.

The foreign presence was not all negative, however. Western mercenaries had helped the fight against the Taiping and the Nien. Foreigners made the Customs Service into one of the most effective arms of the administration, supplying a third of imperial revenue. Its inspector-general since 1863, the slight Ulsterman Robert Hart, became the best-known Westerner in China, a fixture in Beijing in his big, gas-lit suburban house, where he held tennis and dancing parties each Wednesday, played the violin, and maintained a private brass band. He had a Chinese concubine who bore them children, but they were sent out of the country when Hart married a woman from Northern Ireland. Often acting as adviser to the court in dealing with foreigners, he worked seven days a week, standing up at a lectern for fear that the Beijing air would lull him to sleep if he sat down. He was waited on at table by eight servants even when he dined alone. One of his subordinates put Hart's success down to his methodical ways; everything ran like clockwork under him, though, personally, he was 'a most entertaining companion, a teller of countless good stories, fond of fun and merry company'.[5]

In a judgement very different from the disdain expressed by many Westerners, Hart considered, after four decades in China, that its people were:

well-behaved, law-abiding, intelligent, economical, and industrious – they can learn anything and do anything – they are punctiliously polite, they worship talent, and they believe in right so firmly that they scorn to think it requires to be supported or enforced by might – they delight in literature ... they possess and practice an admirable system of ethics, and they are generous, charitable, and fond of good works – they never forget a favour, they make rich return for any kindness.

In Britain, he reflected, the rule was 'Break, but never bend', while in China it was 'Bend but never break.'[6]

Hart foresaw the day when an army of 20 million Chinese would 'make residence impossible for foreigners, will take back from foreigners everything foreigners have taken from China, will pay off old grudges with interest, and will carry the Chinese flag and Chinese arms into many places . . . thus preparing for the future upheavals and disasters never even dreamt of'. When he eventually left the country in 1908, he was awarded the highest imperial decorations. Military bands played 'Home, Sweet Home' as the train pulled out. After his death in Britain in 1911, he was given the rare title of Senior Guardian of the Heir Apparent.[7]

Other foreign influences were, however, increasingly unwelcome as European powers pressed for further concessions in the late nineteenth century. Germany, a latecomer, expanded aggressively in Shandong on the east coast, using the murder of two of its missionaries by a mob as a pretext to send in its fleet and land troops. 'Is it just to oppress us while we are struggling to emerge from the constraints of our ancient civilization, while improvements and progress steadily continue?' Li Hongzhang asked in an interview with the *New York Herald*. 'Should China be distressed by having her shores invaded and her territories occupied because of an occurrence which Western countries would deal with by law and not by war?'[8]

Arrogating to itself the right to land its forces, take action and demand territorial concessions, Germany established a settlement in the port of Qingdao, including a brewery and Bavarian-style houses on the city's hills, while prospectors travelled to isolated parts of the province seeking mineral deposits. An envoy from Berlin envisaged the sturdy inhabitants of Shandong becoming 'Chinese Germans' in what would be a German province of China. This aggressive attitude spurred others to lay down fresh demands. Britain got an undertaking that no other power would be allowed to assert itself along the Yangzi, and gained leases on territory north of Kowloon opposite Hong Kong Island, and on the port of Weihaiwei after Japan was persuaded to withdraw its forces from there. Pursuing the Great Game with Russia in Central Asia, Britain also concluded agreements with Beijing over Tibet, where Chinese influence had greatly declined. France established itself across the border from its possessions in Indochina. Japan was assured that no other power would be allowed to expand in Fujian province on the east coast. Though not for want of trying, only Italy failed to find its place, which was taken by conservative Manchu princes as a sign that the foreigners could be resisted. The United States kept above such territorial buccaneering, advocating an Open Door policy to prohibit discrimination by treaty port powers against other countries.

Russia presented a special dilemma for the court. Though the defeat of Muslim rebellions in the west had asserted Beijing's hold on 'outer China', the Tsarist regime still constituted a latent threat in the north. It was not primarily interested in trade, as the British were, but in territorial expansion. On the other hand, it had come to China's aid in putting pressure on Japan to withdraw from the Liaotung peninsula in Manchuria in 1895, and had loaned Beijing money to start paying off the indemnity incurred in the peace settlement. Its main motivation was to block Tokyo, but Li Hongzhang, Zhang Zhidong and other leading figures, who felt let down by Britain's refusal to stand up to Tokyo, saw China's interest as lying in an alliance with the Russians. Cixi agreed.

Visiting St Petersburg after concluding the treaty with Japan, Li was authorized to negotiate an agreement allowing Russia to extend its Far Eastern railway through Manchuria to the sea at Vladivostok, with the right to station guards beside the lines. A secret clause committed the two countries to defend each other against any attack by Japan. Li was reported to have received a very large bribe for his co-operation, and became even more of a target of patriotic reproach. As he passed through Singapore on his way home, Overseas Chinese pelted him with refuse. Hostile censors kept up their criticism. When Li went to the Forbidden City to report on his trip to the emperor in the early hours, a man in black surged out of the shadows and belaboured him before being overpowered.[9]

Still, a second agreement, greased by more graft, expanded the Russian zone in Manchuria. Tsarist officials acted at least as arrogantly as the other foreigners. The chargé d'affaires in Beijing adopted bullying tactics with the Foreign Ministry, treating China like a subject province. Moving in to Port Arthur and the other big Manchurian harbour of Dalian* after the Japanese left, the Russians landed heavy guns, and asserted sovereignty by refusing to recognize Chinese stamps on mail. They demanded, unsuccessfully, that all British staff on Chinese railways should be dismissed, and objected to the Hongkong and Shanghai Bank lending the Chinese £2 million for a railway in the north-east. They blocked the establishment of a government Bureau of Mining because it

---

* Transliterated then as Dairen.

would have been headed by a British official, and their diplomats joined with the French in lobbying to prevent a pay rise for the staff of the Customs Service because it was led by Hart. Not that St Petersburg was alone in such jousting. London sabotaged a project for a French–Russian railway line, while Germany blocked a plan by an American syndicate for a line in Shandong, which it considered its territory.[10]

'I have paced about from morning to night and cried bitter tears, I have vacillated back and forth and felt beset by calamity until suddenly awakening with a plan,' the Guangxu emperor had announced in an edict issued three days after the ratification of the pact with Japan in May 1895. He lamented that he could not follow calls to reject the treaty and continue the war. But the 24-year-old monarch insisted that the humiliation should mark a new start. The edict went on:

Hereafter, the sovereign and his officials, and persons high and low, must with firm resolve wipe out age-old abuses, exert every effort for the two great tasks of training soldiers and stockpiling provisions, and make detailed plans to promote the new and do away with the old. Allow no slacking, do not pursue empty forms, do not neglect long term planning, do not [blindly] follow old ways, and be realistic in everything in order to bring about real self-strengthening.[11]

Guangxu was in tune with his times. The scale of China's defeat brought a wave of national questioning and a growing desire to make a fresh start. The humiliation at the hands of Japan undermined the authority of the old system represented by Cixi and her associates. Young men taking the imperial examination in Beijing drew up petitions for reform, which were spread through the new printing technology. Outside the Censorate Office in the capital, they staged China's first student demonstration. As well as calling for repudiation of the peace treaty, they asserted that citizens had the right, or even the obligation, to hold their rulers accountable. They wanted China to build up a modern army, a state banking system, a railway network and a merchant fleet, as well as promoting agriculture and industry. Backward areas should be helped. Taxes should be raised. Modern education should be fostered. The skills of Overseas Chinese should be enlisted.

In similar vein, if with less sweeping goals, intellectuals and senior figures in the establishment plunged into political discussion which made the later 1890s a watershed in initiating the kind of public debate which was familiar in the West, but had been kept under wraps in China. Between 1895 and 1898, 103 study societies, 183 modern schools and 62 publishing houses were set up in a movement that became known as 'Young China' which sought to combine modernization and liberalization in a way the Self-Strengtheners had not done. Scholars were encouraged to revive the old pattern of engaging with officials in the hope that their ideas would be noted. Issues were debated more openly and more quickly than ever before, and developments in Europe and America were held up as examples for China to consider.

With its strong foreign influences and printing industry, Shanghai was the main centre for new newspapers and magazines spreading the idea of change. In Beijing, fifty scholars from the prestigious Hanlin Academy opened a forty-room Book Depot to publish original works and translations, as well as a forty-four-page journal. 'Natural Feet' associations were set up in major cities to agitate for an end to foot-binding. Lectures on foreign nations and their ways were held. Western books were translated, and libraries launched to make them available. The progressive governor of Hunan established the School of Current Affairs in Changsha, where schools teaching English did good business. Elite intellectuals known as celebrity-scholars acted as goads on officials.[12]

The old Self-Strengthener, Zhang Zhidong, gave cash to a modernizing 'National Strengthening Society' and sponsored newspapers, including one that employed Cantonese scholar-reformers. He sought to reconcile reform with tradition in a noted essay which posited 'five kinds of understanding' needed by the Chinese – that their country was not as good as others, that it could be colonized like India and Vietnam, that drastic change was needed in institutions and society as well as technology, that the essence of Chinese learning lay in its application to practical matters and that the Chinese should remain Chinese wherever they were.

Military matters were at the forefront of the reform movement. Army schools were opened, and foreign instructors recruited. New armies were set up. The commander of one, a Li Hongzhang protégé, Yuan Shikai, joined the National Strengthening Society. Unless China 'undertook some measures for her own preservation, nothing could save her falling to pieces', he told a British visitor. When Zhang Zhidong established a military academy in Hubei, it attracted 4,000 applicants for 120 places. Soldiering was no longer looked down on as it had been for centuries, and the new armies, much influenced by the Japanese example, became seedbeds for reformist and revolutionary movements.

The over-arching question was whether the regime could absorb change, or would have to shatter. 'There must be a dynastic cataclysm before wholesale reform can operate,' Robert Hart concluded. Knowledge from abroad challenged the foundations of the Chinese world; science and geography undermined the cosmological beliefs on which the status of the Sons of Heaven and their empire rested. Intellectuals reinterpreted classical texts to try to find an answer. Some stressed the place of self-cultivation and practical statecraft, using arguments that paralleled Western utilitarianism, but also sought a universal, moral context in which to place the pursuit of national wealth and power.[13]

The emperor gave enthusiastic leadership from the top. An edict in July 1895 listed steps to be taken to modernize China – railway building, currency reform, machine making, mining, creation of a postal administration, army training and stockpiling of military provisions, demobilizing of surplus troops, reorganization of the navy, establishment of modern schools, overhaul of taxes on the movement of goods, tightening up customs administration, surveying uncultivated land, and eliminating redundant bureaucracy. A question on current affairs was included in the imperial examination, and preparations were made to hold a special test in economics.[14]

At the end of 1895, a decree declared that railways were 'the most important factor in the maintenance of trade as well as an undertaking which will employ the masses. In view of this, therefore, we have decided to encourage railways in every way, in order to make them an accomplished fact of this empire.' Proposals were advanced for lines linking Shanghai, Ningbo, Wuhan and Canton.

An imperial message to Zhang Zhidong told him to encourage merchants in the Lower Yangzi to set up more cotton and silk works, and to commission boats to carry their goods. Big mills were duly established in Suzhou, Wuxi, Hangzhou, Shanghai and Ningbo. A decree said capital should be brought in from Overseas Chinese, which, it was held, would reduce corruption. 'Follow the Western model completely, with merchants in full charge and officials defending merchant interests,' the emperor ordered.[15]

Commercial bureaux were to be headed by 'affluent, experienced and prominent gentry and merchants', along with trade offices on major roads and water crossings. The governor of Zhejiang proposed that official funds should be granted to inventors of new machines. Urban gentry were attracted by the potential for profitable investment in modernizing projects. A top degree holder, Zhang Jian, gave up his official career to establish a cotton mill and plantation company in Jiangsu. Mining was developed in Hunan and Sichuan. Plants were built for matches, processed food, silk reeling and printing. In 1897, a National Post Office was based on the local operations which already existed in Shanghai. Postmen were issued with conical straw hats, white tunics and baggy trousers. Ornate post boxes had dragons curling round their legs. Severe punishment was threatened for anybody found mistreating the horses that pulled the postal wagons.[16]

An associate of Zhang Zhidong, Sheng Xuanhuai, epitomized the new bureaucratic-capitalist spirit. Put in charge of a General Railways Office, his ambit extended to shipping, the telegraph, iron and textiles. Another of the late Qing figures whose interests seem to have known no boundaries, he took over and integrated Zhang Zhidong's steelworks in Wuhan with iron ore and coal mines, while also founding the first Chinese academic institution that taught mechanical engineering and architecture. He held the governorship of the customs at Tianjin, and encouraged the development of Shanghai, where he lived in a large house with a two-storey colonnaded entrance – he was known as 'Shanghai's brain'.

In May 1897, Sheng became chairman of China's first modern bank, set up by imperial decree with the right to issue notes. He saw this as essential if foreigners were to be prevented from dominating his country. Still, he needed foreign expertise, and so hired a general manager from the Hongkong and Shanghai Banking Corporation, an institution whose practices he vowed to follow in every respect. Enjoying imperial protection, the bank was an immediate success, attracting foreign clients as well as Chinese enterprises. In its first eighteen months, it opened branches in a dozen cities, increasing deposits and loans by 50 per cent. To raise more capital, the regime launched Good Faith Bonds, paying 5 per cent interest – Prince Gong set an example by subscribing.[17]

There were, inevitably, problems in all this activity. 'We only want men who have practical knowledge and who keep posted with the times,' a decree declared. But such people were few and far between – when 300 telegraph stations were set up, there was great difficulty finding staff. At the Shanghai Post Office, the horses were described in an internal report by the European management as being 'of such miserable appearance that it is an act of cruelty to allow them to be driven to pull delivery vans'. A contract was concluded with the Dallas Horse Repository Company to provide better animals.[18]

Despite the imperial bonds, funding remained short, and financial management could be lax. Sheng had to turn to an American syndicate for a US$40 million loan for the railway link between Hankou and Canton, while the line from Beijing to the Middle Yangzi was allocated to a British syndicate. Some schemes were of doubtful commercial value, riding rather on a cloud of nationalist optimism. When it came to military training, the empire had trouble finding suitable teachers – the Germans were too aggressive and the Russians insisted that their officers should act independently of provincial officials; so finally the Chinese opted for the Japanese, sending 700 Chinese cadets to study across the sea, among them the future Nationalist leader, Chiang Kai-shek. In China itself, military schools were organized on Japanese lines. 'Let there be no doubt about it: the bulk of China's military affairs will be Japanized,' wrote Tokyo's minister in China. 'Japanese power, slowly but surely, will spread through the Asiatic continent.'[19]

In the oppressively hot summer of 1898, the emperor decided to give the reform programme a new lease of life. On 11 June, an edict told officials to commit themselves to propelling China towards 'wealth and power'. Guangxu showed the document, drafted by the senior mandarin, Weng Tonghe, to Cixi at the Summer Palace. She did not object.

There followed a flood of decrees – forty in all in what became known as the Hundred Days, during which the emperor celebrated his twenty-seventh birthday and kept to at least one tradition, offering prayers for rain, which were duly followed by showers. The programme of reform flowing from the imperial Vermilion Pencil was extraordinary in its scale and speed, creating big backlogs on the telegraph lines. The incoming traffic was heavy, too. Between mid-August and mid-September, court secretaries transcribed 660 memorials by hand. In theory, Guangxu had to read everything, drowning him in paperwork. To account for all the activity, a rumour circulated that reformers had administered him a magic red pill containing a potion from the Ming era which made whoever swallowed it subservient to whoever provided it.[20]

Education was to take pride of place in shaping the new China. The 'eight-legged' examination system would be overhauled, with more attention paid to practical subjects and less to poetry, which was dismissed in an edict as 'the hollow, useless and unpractical method' of an obsolete age. Nor would the 'empty accomplishment' of calligraphy earn recognition. A great university would be opened in the capital complete with a medical school; a 280-room palace was allocated as its premises and received a flood of applications. Youths were to be sent abroad to be trained in subjects for which there were no teachers at home. Each provincial capital was to be given a seat of advanced, Western-style learning; temples were to be turned into educational establishments, with each district town getting a primary school at which, it was stated, opium users would not be allowed to teach. (The emperor, himself, spent two hours a day taking English lessons from a Chinese who had lived in the United States – the ruler was said to have a sharp ear and a good accent.)[21]

Edicts ordered the bureaucracy and provincial governorships to be streamlined. Sinecures were to be abolished, among them the directorship of the Imperial Banqueting Hall. There would be monthly budget statements. Agriculture and industry were to be developed. A national cash currency would replace provincial coins. Foot-binding was to end.

In the army, spears and bows and arrows would be replaced by modern weapons. A fleet of thirty-four warships was to be built, and naval academies formed in maritime and river provinces. Volunteer forces and militias would be set up in every city, town and hamlet as the nucleus of a great national army to foster a military spirit. As these decrees were issued, the first consignment of 2,000 Mauser rifles and four quick-firing artillery guns made at the Hanyang ironworks was sent to an elite army unit in Beijing.

Recognizing how little the throne really knew about the country, the reformers proposed an information revolution. An edict told newspapers that they could write freely on political subjects 'to enlighten those in authority and tear off the veil which hides in obscurity the misgovernment of officials'. Editors and writers were 'not to hold back just criticism nor are they in future to avoid what has hitherto been considered forbidden subjects, for fear of giving offence to the persons criticized, as this will obstruct his Majesty's earnest desire of enlightening his Ministers and the masses'. Court officials and censors were warned not to place obstacles in the way of memorials to the throne, 'for only through such sources can the emperor learn the exact state of affairs in his Empire.' When senior members of the Board of Rites denounced a subordinate for having put forward ideas for reform, they were punished.[22]

The emperor showed his resolve to adopt the reality of the world around him when he was brought the draft of diplomatic credentials to be taken by the new Chinese minister to Korea. In keeping with tradition, his title was elevated three spaces above that of the king of the former tribute state. Guangxu took up his Vermilion Pencil and placed the two of them on the same level. 'Korea is independent and no longer a vassal to us,' he told officials. 'Well then, what's the use of affecting such hollow forms of arrogant pride and pretending an empty superiority over that country? . . . What is the use of fighting for such superiority which amounts to nothing more nor less than paper and ink superiority?'[23]

In all this, the emperor and those around him faced what one edict termed 'the bane of the deeply-rooted system of inertness and a clinging to obsolete customs'. Sweeping aside centuries of tradition was bound to arouse widespread opposition among the most affected, the very people on whom the dynasty depended to rule China. The Manchu nobles were outraged to learn that they were to lose their privileges. The end of the examination system would destroy the defining feature of the gentry-scholar class. Changes in the administrative structure would cost thousands of bureaucrats their jobs. Freedom of information and greater accountability would undermine the power of the civil service. Anti-foreign circles were alarmed to hear that the emperor had ordered a study of opening the whole of the coast and the Yangzi to international trade, while a dilapidated imperial palace in Beijing was to be fitted out as a hotel for foreign guests. Rumours spread that he was planning to make the court wear Western clothes.[24]

There were some official enthusiasts for the imperial programme, such as the progressive governor of Hunan. But most senior provincial functionaries dragged their feet, as shown by fresh edicts at the end of the summer berating them for slowness. The 'severest punishment' was threatened for those who showed themselves lukewarm. The excuse given in response was that it had been necessary to wait for the decrees to arrive by imperial messengers in case the cabled versions contained mistakes or omissions. The emperor ordered 'a stop to all such excuses'; telegraphed messages were to be taken as gospel.

For all his enthusiasm, Guangxu had trouble imposing himself at court. The Grand Council managed to block a proposal for a parliament and, with the Board of Civil Appointments and the Foreign Ministry, delay consideration of some other plans. The ruler lacked weighty allies. The death of Prince Gong in 1898 removed a veteran source of stability at court. Rather than trying to patch up his bad relations with Li Hongzhang and co-opt him into the reform process, Guangxu approved dropping the old Self-Strengthener from his post dealing with foreigners. Most seriously, the senior court official, Weng Tonghe, was dismissed four days after the promulgation of the edict of 11 June launching the Hundred Days, which he had drafted.[25]

The sudden decision to sack the most important civil servant at court, on which the Dowager appears not to have been consulted, was probably not a matter of policy – Weng had gone along with the reform programme – but simply a case of the young ruler's desire to be his own man, and his headstrong, short-tempered refusal to brook opposition. Robert Hart reported that the former tutor was said to be interfering too much and had tried to stop his master reading extracts from Western weeklies. The announcement of his dismissal accused him of mismanagement, grabbing excessive power and bad manners towards the ruler. Though not mentioned, there were also accusations that he had taken a bribe from Russia to back an extension of its concessions. Stripped of all his posts, Weng was banished to his home district in Jiangsu province.[26]

With Gong and Weng gone, the Grand Council consisted of four much less weighty figures. Its head was an ineffective Manchu prince. Of the two Han Chinese, one was seventy-four and had been appointed because of his familiarity with bureaucratic methods, while the other had only been on the council since March 1898 and was too junior to carry much influence.

The strongest personality was Kang-i, a Manchu who had built up a good record as governor of Guangdong, Guangxi and Shanxi over ten years, but was hardly in the class of Weng. Appointed to the council in 1894, he believed in repairing the system rather than altering it radically. Though he made practical proposals for change, he was in Cixi's camp, maintaining contact with the Dowager and her favourite eunuch.[27]

Subsequent accounts would attribute a substantial role in the reform process to a Confucian scholar from Canton, Kang Youwei, a square-headed young man who, like the Taiping leader, Hong Xiuquan, had failed the imperial examination but was still convinced of his special destiny. After retreating, like Hong, to live in the mountains and consider his future, Kang came to the conclusion that he was a sage. 'I became joyous and laughed,' he recalled. 'Then, thinking about the sufferings of the people of the world, I became sad and cried.'[28]

Highly active, Kang set up a school to teach his beliefs, helped to found the Do Not Bind Feet Society, and made a name for himself with works alleging that the Confucian texts then in vogue were forgeries. That this was probably not the case did not matter. Kang wanted to be free to interpret the teachings all Chinese respected to support the ideal of a utopian, classless, universalist society under a sage-king, in which all would have the right to self-determination and humanism would rule, ending discrimination such as that against women. In the early 1890s he submitted memorials to the throne on how to strengthen the nation but they evoked no interest. The court was more concerned with renewing the imperial gardens, Kang complained.

However, he found an articulate associate in another southerner, a sharp-faced, accomplished scholar and skilful writer called Liang Qichao, who believed that China needed a constitutional monarchy. He and Kang collaborated on books and pamphlets contrasting nations which had embraced progress and those which had resisted it. They pointed out how railways and roads fostered commerce, how agricultural and mining colleges improved production, and how patents encouraged inventions. The dynasty would be strengthened if politics was shared with the people, with a parliament acting as a bonding bridge between rulers and citizens, they argued. In this way, China would be revived, its people reinvigorated and made more patriotic.

In the reform maelstrom of 1898, Kang Youwei thought he had finally found his hour of power and influence. He attracted the attention of a senior official, Zhang Yinhuan, an English-speaking diplomat who was close to the emperor. Zhang, who had been China's minister in the United States and represented his country at Queen Victoria's Diamond Jubilee celebrations in 1897, wrote in his diary of Kang's 'ramblings', but added: 'this is a rare talent. Ought to look after him properly.'[29]

Presumably at Zhang's suggestion, Kang was invited to a meeting also attended by Li Hongzhang and the Manchu general Jung-lu, who had ended the seven-year banishment for his affair with a court lady and been appointed governor-general of Zhili and commissioner for North China. This was before Weng Tonghe's dismissal and he was also present – he had called Kang a 'wild fox'. The only account of the encounter was written by Kang, and has to be read with this in mind.

Jung-lu said the institutions of the ancestors could not be changed. But what use were they if China was incapable of preserving the realm of the ancestors, Kang asked. Were the six boards of government to be abolished and existing institutions and rules to be thrown away, Li inquired. Traditional laws and government had weakened the nation, and would ruin it, Kang responded. 'Undoubtedly they should be done away with,' he added. 'Even if we could not abolish them all at once, we should modify them as circumstances require.'[30]

When the emperor was given an account of the discussion, he was intrigued and asked to see Kang's memorials. Impressed, Guangxu decided to receive the Cantonese. According to the reformers, the meeting stretched over five hours, the longest audience the emperor ever gave; an official who was received afterwards said that it lasted for, at most, an hour.[31]

Contemporary press reports had the visitor evoking the example of Peter the Great of Russia, saying that, if the emperor took China on a similar route, 'succeeding generations will indeed glorify your Majesty's deeds and loudly proclaim the name of Guangxu for all time.' When Kang insisted on the need to reform the imperial examinations, the monarch replied that such changes 'were certainly necessary if China really desired to be strong and independent'.

According to an account written by Liang Qichao, which must be judged on the nature of the source, Kang warned that foreign incursions meant that China would soon perish.

'Today it is imperative that we reform,' the emperor replied.

Previous attempts had been only superficial, and had not changed the institutions, Kang went on, attacking the examination system for blocking understanding of foreign countries. 'It is so,' Guangxu responded, by Liang's version. 'Westerners are all pursuing useful studies while we Chinese pursue useless studies.'

The Cantonese paid tribute to the ruler's 'sagacity', and his reforms. At that, the emperor glanced outside the screen surrounding him, and asked, 'What can I do with so much hindrance?' Kang said he should use his authority to work with new men. Relying on conservatives would be 'like climbing a tree to seek fish'. As the meeting ended, by this account, Guangxu said that, if Kang had more ideas, he should send them straight to him, rather than going through the bureaucracy.[32]

Kang was joined in Beijing by one of his greatest admirers, a 33-year-old reformer from Hunan, Tan Sitong. Tan, who came from a family of officials, had developed an acute moral sense. After a series of family deaths, he took to writing poems obsessed with mortality. A high romantic, he attacked traditionalism as no better than hypocrisy and robbery. The foreigners who had invaded China were, he believed, 'forces of humanity and righteousness sent by Heaven to give China the punishment she deserves'. Tan was one of four reformers appointed at Guangxu's behest as secretaries to the Grand Council to 'assist in matters concerning the new policies'.[33]

Kang showered the throne with proposals. He prodded a censor to attack the president of the Board of Ceremony, and came up with the idea that the emperor should seek a wise 'recluse scholar' in whom he would entrust matters of state – there could be no doubt as to whom he had in mind. From all this grew the picture of the Cantonese and his associates as the men behind the drive for reform, a version they encouraged in their later writings. Though they were certainly very active propagators of new thinking, and were interesting as representatives of the reformist intellectual class, that story exaggerates their role. The reform edicts had started three years earlier, at a time when Kang was unknown at court. The summons for the Cantonese to see the emperor in 1898 came a week after the decree launching the Hundred Days and the day after Weng had been dismissed. The reform train was powering ahead under Guangxu's direction well before the southerners got on board. When they did, Kang's only post was as a junior official at the Foreign Ministry. According to the historian Luke Kwong, who has put the record straight, he only had one meeting with Guangxu.[34]

The real driver of the reform was the most obvious candidate – the ruler himself. After nearly four decades in which court politics had been conducted to preserve a coalition of interests and power, an emperor finally asserted himself. The trouble was that he had neither the strength nor the administrative apparatus to make reform stick, made some bad political mistakes, and had to cope with the lurking presence of Cixi at the Summer Palace. Still, this unique episode in Qing history marked the start of a long-term search for change that would be derailed time and again by reaction in a pattern that condemned China to political stagnation at the top.

One of Guangxu's worst errors was to seek counsel from the Japanese politician Ito Hirobumi, who had negotiated the peace treaty with Li and visited China in September 1898. The emperor thought he could offer useful advice on modernization based on his country's experience. At the same time, the reformer Tan Sitong had meetings with army officers from Tokyo, while two of Kang's associates produced proposals for an alliance between China, Britain and Japan.

The idea of any foreigner – let alone a Japanese – steering Chinese affairs was an anathema, and led critics to allege that the reformers were ready to sell out the nation. There was also a sub-plot at work, stemming from Li's links with Russia; when his faction played up the Ito issue, it was to weigh the scales against Tokyo and in favour of St Petersburg. Not, as it turned out, that the visitor was interested in becoming a consultant to the court. He told the London *Times* that, while many edicts were being issued, they were not acted on. There could be no change until the court was removed from the influence of reactionary, parasitic Manchu notables, he added.[35]

For the radicals, two notables were a particular obstacle – Kang-i in the Grand Council and Jung-lu, president of the War Board, vice-regent at Tianjin and commissioner in the north. Cixi's former suitor was well regarded by his officers for having forsaken civilian preferment to follow a military career. Said to be near-illiterate, he was known for his lavish lifestyle – his horses were even finer than those of the emperor. He had no inhibitions about profiting from his positions; after being appointed to Tianjin, he grabbed a local gold mine from its owners. Though conservative, he saw the need for army reform, adopting Western drills for his men and science lessons for officers. While loyal to the dynasty, his prime devotion was to Cixi, both as chief Manchu and as the woman whom, in another life, he might have married.[36]

The Dowager had cultivated ambiguity since the launch of the reform programme. She had not objected to the decree that started the Hundred Days. She accepted the sacking of Weng Tonghe, and the sidelining of her old supporter, Li Hongzhang. But, by temperament, she would not have favoured root-and-branch change, and could only watch with concern as the coalition over which she had presided since the 1860s broke up. The wilfulness of her nephew must have worried her, but, for the sake of the dynasty, it would be hard for her to move against him.

That, however, was just what Kang Youwei and those around him feared, setting off another dramatic, if muddy, episode in the late summer of 1898. Rumours flew that Cixi intended to use a visit by her and the emperor to Tianjin to get Jung-lu's troops to detain and depose the ruler. At the same time, tension was ratcheted up by news that other forces commanded by Manchus were moving towards the Beijing–Tianjin area.

Kang and his associates decided that the reform cause needed soldiers of its own to counter this threat. This force would kill Jung-lu, surround the Summer Palace and do away with Cixi. They fixed on the New Army general Yuan Shikai as the man who could help them. Born into a farming family in Henan, he had been adopted as a boy by the childless son of one of Li Hongzhang's commanders, and enjoyed the patronage of the Self-Strengthener as he rose through the military ranks. Having served as viceroy in Korea before the war with Japan, he now headed a unit based in Tianjin, which a British visitor found to be 'the only army in China complete in all detail, according to European ideas'. As a modernizer and member of the National Strengthening Society, the short, bullet-headed commander seemed a logical choice.

On 14 September the 39-year-old general was received by Guangxu. Yuan was suitably deferential, which the emperor took as a sign of support, and appointed him vice-president of the War Board. The following morning, when he went to the Forbidden City to express his appreciation, Guangxu told him there would be no pause in implementing the changes.

Yuan promptly called on Li to pass this on. The old man spread the news. Manchu princes met, and a delegation, including Li, went to see Cixi. Li's tame censor unleashed a memorial blasting the reformers and accusing them of being part of a Japanese conspiracy backed by Britain. The arrival at that moment of three telegrams announcing the sighting of British ships off Tianjin strengthened the charge, though it turned out to be a coincidence.[37]

Still counting on Yuan, the reformers sent their young zealot, Tan Sitong, to see him in the Beijing temple where he was staying. There are two versions of what transpired, a lengthy one in Yuan's own journal, a shorter one in Liang Qichao's biography of Tan, each written with an evident purpose in mind. What transpires from both was that Tan sought to engage Yuan in a plan he said had the emperor's backing to stage a mutiny against Jung-lu and besiege Cixi in the Summer Palace. In Yuan's account, Tan said he had recruited men from Hunan who would go inside and kill her while the general disposed of Jung-lu.

When Yuan played for time, the reformer said he would receive instructions from the throne written in the imperial Vermilion Pencil on 20 September. Meanwhile, Tan produced a mandate in black ink in calligraphy that looked like Guangxu's. 'We have resolved to reform, but old Ministers are reluctant to lend their support,' it read. 'We cannot force the pace, lest Her Gracious Majesty, the Dowager Empress, should be displeased. We hereby command Kang, Tan [and two other reformers] to find a better approach.'

Yuan pointed out that this document made no mention of killing Jung-lu or besieging the Summer Palace. Tan said the original was being held by another reformer and that what he had shown Yuan was a copy made by Kang. The general concluded it was a forgery, and said he would not turn traitor. At that, by Yuan's account, Tan saluted and left.

Returning to Tianjin, the general told Jung-lu everything. It appears that Cixi was informed. She had probably decided to act in any case after meeting with senior nobles, just as Deng Xiaoping and Communist elders would meet before suppressing the reform demonstrations in 1989. At dawn on 21 September, the Dowager left the Summer Palace for the Forbidden City to tell her nephew that the Manchu Clan Council was unanimously opposed to his reforms, and had asked her to resume the regency.

One dramatic account, attributed to Guangxu himself but which probably mixes some truth with a good deal of melodrama, has her confronting him in a huge audience hall lit by lanterns and flickering candles. She accused him of betraying her trust and falling into a plot laid by Cantonese, who wanted to drive out the Manchus. 'Punish me according to the law! I deserve it. I am not fit to rule,' the emperor is said to have replied.[38]

Jung-lu and Yuan Shikai were called in, the second pale, his gaze directed at the floor, unable to look the ruler in the eye. Eunuchs brought writing implements. Trembling, the emperor sat at a small table and

Cixi dictated an edict. Issued on 21 September, it said the ruler had asked her to return to advise him in the crisis through which China was passing. She had graciously consented, 'a blessing indeed for all our subjects'. Guangxu, the princes and ministers would perform obeisance before her the next day.

Guangxu then made his aunt's dawn journey in reverse, going to the Summer Palace, where he was held on the southern island in the lake for the rest of his life, just as Deng would keep the unseated reformist Communist Party chief, Zhao Ziyang, under house arrest after removing him from power ninety-one years later. A Manchu lady-in-waiting, Der Ling, recalled that when he was alone with young people like her, Guangxu would laugh and tease, but 'as soon as he was in the presence of Her Majesty he would look serious, and as if he were worried to death.'[39]

The Son of Heaven appears to have hoped to be allowed to return to power, studying English and reading books supplied by the Society for the Diffusion of Christian and General Knowledge in China. But there was nobody to stage a counter-coup on his behalf. The compilers of the Imperial Almanach were said to have been told to leave the entry for his name blank in case it was decided to depose him – sixteen robes for a new ruler were alleged to have been ordered from the silk works in Suzhou. Naturally, there were also rumours that his aunt was slowly poisoning him, or that he had already been murdered – when a French doctor examined him, reports spread that the man he saw was a stand-in.[40]

In fact, Guangxu was in genuinely poor health. The strain of the Hundred Days had undermined his already weak constitution and heightened his mental fragility. In the years to follow, he would be diagnosed as suffering from headaches, fever, back trouble, poor lungs, loss of appetite, weak pulse and heartbeat, and ejaculations provoked by sudden stimuli, stress or loud noises.[41]

As the Hundred Days ended in disaster, Kang Youwei escaped to Japan, evading a search of a steamer on which he travelled. Liang took the same course. Fearing collective punishment, Kang's family fled their homes. After reaching safety in Japan, the southerner sent an open letter to newspapers in China enclosing two 'secret decrees' he said were written by the emperor in mid-September. One stated that Cixi had become 'more and more enraged' and that Guangxu needed help; the other told Kang to go abroad and 'devise means to save us'. Their authenticity is uncertain, but, in exile, Kang inflated his role and added spice to the mill by serving up allegations that the Dowager's favourite eunuch had not really been emasculated, and that she had sex with him. Ironically, the regime played along by spotlighting him as the evil ringleader of a plot to undermine the nation, which enabled it to avoid fundamental questions raised by the Hundred Days – again as the Communist Party version of the events of 1989 would be used to mask the fault lines in modern China.[42]

Zhang Yinhuan, the diplomat close to Guangxu, faced probable execution before foreign pressure brought about his release, and he was banished to Xinjiang. Six other reformers were less fortunate, being arrested and beheaded. One was Tan Sitong, who died as a martyr upholding his principles in keeping with Confucian righteousness. He could have escaped but let himself be captured in keeping with his morbid, romantic psychology. The story went round that he had gone to his death declaring, 'Blood will have to be spilled for the revolution. Let mine be the first.'

Though reform had been brewing for three years, the Hundred Days of 1898 had been too sudden, too little thought out. As Tan Sitong noted before his execution, 'Desiring instant reform led to overstepping and consequently nothing was accomplished at all.' The historian Zhang Kaiyuan argues convincingly that this impatience was to become a recurrent source of weakness in attempts to change China, with a constant search for instant fixes and a belief in the effect of grand declarations. The 1898 reformers might speak of democracy, but their prime aim was to strengthen China by decree without bothering to seek popular support, following in the age-old pattern of top-down authority.[43]

The lack of the kind of middle class which was playing such a major role in Europe and the United States meant there was no natural constituency for change. The reform programme, and the headlong way it was promulgated, was bound to arouse the fearful opposition of officials and power holders. Yuan Shikai's decision to side with Cixi and Jung-lu condemned the movement to immediate failure, but it is doubtful that there was ever a real chance of him going along with Tan Sitong's proposal, if only because of his sense of ambition – his decision made him one of the Dowager's favourites and he was appointed governor of Shandong as his next step up the ladder.

Many reforms were dismantled, but some survived, including modernization in the army. Personnel changes were not entirely in the direction of reaction – the progressive governor of Hunan was sacked; but so was the hardline Manchu governor of Hubei. Nor was the post-1898 period anything like as intellectually stagnant as later reformers would make out. At the pinnacle of the new education system, the university in Beijing set up under the reforms was not only preserved but also further modernized under the influence of the ubiquitous Zhang Zhidong, with the traditional curriculum removed from its pedestal and classes taught in medicine, law, agriculture and science. At the heart of the new philosophical line was the *ti-yong* system, set out by Zhang, which embraced the study of Western ways but insisted that Chinese learning was essential. 'The old learning is the fundamental thing; the new learning is for practical use,' as he put it.[44]

This provided a distinctively Chinese form of modernity, a platform for the next generation that offered a means for China to adopt foreign ways without reneging on its special character. Still, the overall conservative current was clear. Jung-lu moved 10,000 loyal troops into Beijing, and held meetings with the Dowager from which others were excluded. On the Grand Council, Kang-i took an increasingly conservative line.

Once more, Cixi was the core of the imperial administration. When she and her nephew appeared together, she sat on a throne on the same level as him, rather than concealing herself behind a screen as she had done earlier. But her policy for her resumed regency remained opaque. Li Hongzhang recalled that, when he presumed to ask her about her plans, she became 'alive with wrath and angry words' – either because of his forwardness or because she was embarrassed at her lack of convincing answers.

The coalition approach she had practised since rising to power in the 1860s had diminished imperial authority. The era of the great emperors of the High Qing had given way to minority rule, regency and the search for equilibrium. The dramatic switchback pattern of the Hundred Days and its muddled end – with the emperor still on the throne but a prisoner in the Summer Palace – further undermined the majesty of the throne. It was becoming increasingly difficult for the Qing to command the support which the system assumed that the dynasty enjoyed. This became apparent at the beginning of 1900, when the son of a highly conservative Manchu, Prince Tuan, was named as heir apparent. The choice was unfortunate since he turned out to be a lecher, who soon acquired an unsavoury reputation. But what was most striking was the breadth of the criticism it aroused. This was not, as in Cixi's choice of Guangxu, a matter of breaching Confucian rules. The choice of the next ruler provoked protests from lower officials, urban gentry, merchants and Overseas Chinese. The politicization of such social groups and of Chinese living in treaty ports was now becoming an uncomfortable fact of life for the ageing Qing.

5

On the Ropes

Pull down the telegraph lines!
Quickly! Hurry up! Smash them . . .
When at last all the Foreign Devils
Are expelled to the very last man,
The Great Qing, united, together,
Will bring peace to this our land.[1]

So proclaimed a wall poster in eastern China. By the late 1890s, the foreigners were serving as scapegoats for China's ills. In the front line were the Christian missionaries who sortied out of the 'informal empire' of treaty ports and foreign concessions to work in towns and villages across the country. For Protestant and Catholic churches in Europe and America, the hundreds of millions of Chinese were an irresistible magnet. Like the businessmen of today who dream of cracking the China market and selling to hundreds of millions of consumers, missionary societies envisaged the day when they would 'plant the shining cross in every hill'.[2]

For the Western powers, faith and trade were to bring enlightenment to the Chinese. If force was needed to achieve this, so be it. Most missionaries favoured armed intervention because, as one wrote, 'their task will, by this means, be rendered less difficult, probably, than by the slow and laborious process of moral suasion.' The Chinese, argued an American, S. Wells Williams, would grant nothing unless stimulated by fear, 'because they are among the most craven of people, cruel and selfish as heathenism can make men, so we must be backed by force if we wish them to listen.' Other missionaries saw opportunities in China's natural disasters. One, reflecting on a drought which led to cannibalism, thought that it provided a chance to 'demonstrate the power of religion . . . to recognize all men as brethren'.[3]

The number of missionaries doubled during the 1890s to reach 3,000. Often accompanied by their wives, the men penetrated inland provinces where foreigners had hardly ever been. As well as their churches, they offered education, welfare and health care. Some also used their protected position to intervene in legal disputes on behalf of converts. This was much cheaper for the converts than bribing officials, but aroused popular hostility, and infuriated the bureaucrats.

Consciously or not, missionaries could be highly provocative. Their mixed services were contrary to the Chinese tradition of separation of the sexes in public. The presence of single women among them was seen as a sign of immorality. The mannish dress missionary women often wore raised suspicions that they were actually men who were pretending to be female to sneak into Chinese homes and seduce the women there. In Shanxi province, a group of twenty-five Swedish women proselytized, alone or in groups, playing the guitar and singing hymns; a British traveller reported that, when these ladies prepared for bed, local men pushed holes through the paper over the windows of their rooms and refused to go away, laughing and chanting insults.[4]

A widely disseminated pamphlet said that Christians worshipped a Chief Devil who had been so wicked that he had been executed. Missionaries were said to take a daughter from each converted family for their sexual pleasure and enjoy *droit de seigneur* before performing marriage ceremonies for Chinese women. In Canton, a tract in the name of the local commander-in-chief accused them of kidnapping Chinese children and scooping out their hearts and eyes; they also fed pregnant women converts a pill which led them to 'allow themselves to be defiled', after which the placenta was drawn out and chopped up to make magic potions. The first preachers to reach Hunan were forced to leave, and three were killed by a mob when they presumed to return. The governor-general of Shandong dismissed converts as 'weed people', and another official suggested that they should be obliged to wear Western dress so that, when retribution came, they could be singled out for punishment. In Manchuria, the use of cameras by missionaries was taken as proof that they were plucking out eyes to give the power of sight to their magic boxes.[5]

In 1870, an anti-Christian riot had taken the lives of fifteen Europeans in Tianjin in an episode that set a pattern for the future and showed just how far apart the Chinese and Christian cultures were. French nuns at the Notre-Dame des Victoires orphanage in the city had been offering payment for Chinese children put in their care. This led to 'child brokers' kidnapping infants and selling them to the orphanage. The nuns were particularly keen on giving ill and dying children a passport to paradise by baptizing them before they expired, so they harboured many infants who subsequently perished. This fed rumours that, behind the convent walls, the children were bewitched and mutilated, their hearts and eyes being used to make magic medicines.

A magistrate who went to investigate found nothing. As he left, the excitable French consul demanded an apology and, not getting one, fired a pistol shot. This killed the magistrate's servant. A mob attacked the convent and its church, burning it down, and slaughtering ten nuns, two priests, three Russian traders, and the consul and his assistant. Four British and American churches were also destroyed. Foreign warships sailed in. Li Hongzhang negotiated a settlement – eight people were to be beheaded and twenty exiled, while France was to receive compensation. An envoy went to Paris with the offer but was told the French were too busy with the war with Prussia to talk to him. He sailed for home via the USA, but, when he reached New York, he was summoned back to Paris, where the government simply accepted a letter of apology from the Chinese empire.

Over the following decades, the pattern persisted of European Christians behaving in ways that outraged Chinese, of wild rumours and occasional attacks on churches and missionaries. Western governments threatened force in response, and China agreed to executions and indemnities. In 1891, anti-Christian riots broke out along the Grand Canal and around the Yangzi river port of Wuhu, leading the British to send in gunboats to help imperial forces restore order. In Sichuan, a rumour that missionaries had kidnapped children and boiled them for their flesh set off severe rioting.

A deadly attack came in August 1895, when a hundred members of a Chinese vegetarian sect attacked houses in the hills of Fujian occupied by British missionaries. They grabbed two teenage girls as they were picking flowers at dawn, stabbing one but failing to hold the other – she burst into her parents' home crying, 'The vegetarians are coming!' The attackers pulled five missionary women from their beds and made them line up outside – they begged for parasols to protect them from the sun. According to the report in the *North China Herald*, a man carrying a red flag then ordered the women to be killed. The missionary houses were set on fire; the ashes of four Westerners were found inside. A baby was stabbed through the eye. Two children died later of their wounds. When assistance arrived, the villagers refused to help carry the coffins to the burial ground. One of the missionary women, who had feigned death, survived to tell the tale despite having a broken skull and gashed face.[6]

The court was well aware that such episodes could spark off fresh Western demands on it. Officials were ordered to stamp down on anti-missionary outbreaks. Twenty-five of the attackers of Fujian were executed, and twenty-one jailed or banished. After a British priest was hacked to death by secret-society members in a remote part of Shandong, an imperial decree stressed the treaty rights enjoyed by missionaries.

Nowhere was the populist anti-foreign feeling stronger than in the perennially unstable region of the Huai plain south of the Yellow River, which had bred the Nien revolt in mid-century, and where natural disasters continued unabated, and drought struck as the century drew to a close. For the country people of the region, the foreigners were akin to the demons and devils which populated their folk religions. A wall poster proclaimed:

> No rain comes from Heaven.
> The earth is parched and dry.
> And all because the churches
> Have bottled up the sky.[7]

The area was full of secret societies, young men living on the edge of the law, banditry, and salt and opium smuggling. A governor-general of Shandong noted that 'large numbers of unemployed people move about, form groups, and turn to plunder. In summer, when sorghum grows tall, bandits hide in the fields and stage surprise attacks on unsuspecting passers-by.' The province's large population of 37 million meant that there were always plenty of people ready to join any movement that promised to improve their lot or protest about living conditions – in 1898, 30,000 participated in a revolt against the price of salt.[8]

Resentment at the foreigners and their religious emissaries had been stoked by the German military intervention in Shandong in 1896, which had not only established the Europeans in Qingdao but led Beijing to agree to sack senior anti-foreign officials and build churches and homes for Germans. In the spring of 1899, the Germans caused further anger by launching a military expedition to protect their mine prospectors. The aggression of some German Catholic missionaries enraged locals. So did the aid they offered their Chinese followers; in one case, 4,000 secret-society members converted en masse to gain the help of the Europeans.

As a result, Shandong saw an estimated 1,000 anti-foreign incidents and protests. By the mid-1890s, the region experienced the first manifestations of what was to become the best-known Chinese grassroots upheaval – for the outside world, at least. Because of the way it was directed against foreigners, the Boxer Rising, and its subsequent siege of the legation quarter in Beijing, has been the subject of a shoal of books, and a Hollywood film starring Charlton Heston and Ava Gardner. But, dramatic as that fifty-five-day episode was, its deeper importance was in its effects on the dynasty and on the balance of power in China.

The discontent of the Boxers lay in traditional causes of peasant revolt – poverty and natural disasters – accentuated by the tribulations of their home region. But they were radically different from the Taiping and other mid-century risings in that they supported the dynasty and made violent hostility to the foreigners and their ways part of their battle cry of 'Support the Qing, destroy the Foreign'. Thus, though they certainly constituted a rising, the often-used description of the movement as the 'Boxer Rebellion' is wrong, unless one considers a Chinese attack on foreigners as the action of rebels.

The Boxers combined extremism and loyalty, drawing on old folk traditions and seeing themselves as a divine army marching to eradicate the demons threatening their country. In this, they resemble both the Taiping and the Red Guards of the Cultural Revolution of the 1960s. In each case, there were important differences – the Boxers were pro-dynasty unlike the rebel Taipings, and were a rural phenomenon unlike the mainly urban Red Guards. But the similarities are also striking, particularly between the Boxers and the youth unleashed by Mao Zedong. Just as Red Guards attacked what they saw as a corrupt Communist elite but venerated the Chairman, so the Boxers turned on oppressive officials, but dedicated themselves to the Qing. In each case, the senior bureaucracy on which the regime depended was appalled, and the outcome left the supreme power badly bruised, bequeathing a legacy to be held up as a terrible warning of the price of anarchy and heightening the fear of people power among members of China's elite, whether imperial officials or Communist cadres.

The Boxers United in Righteousness first appeared in the spring of 1898 during a dispute over the building of a Catholic church in the Shandong town of Liyuantun. Claiming invulnerability from their rituals, they drew on entrenched rural beliefs and traditions, on operatic dramas performed at county fairs, on ancient gods and heroes, and on boxing and martial arts skills. The simple nature of their rituals and roots in the countryside and market towns made them both familiar and accessible to ordinary people.[9]

Their righteousness was the *yi-qi* of the martial arts tradition, embodying loyalty, integrity and altruism. Some were remnant Nien; others came from secret societies, including one led by Big Belly Li, who was said to have a third eye hidden in the folds of his enormous stomach. As well as eradicating foreigners, they advocated killing corrupt officials, and laid down a code of behaviour:

> Do not covet wealth.
> Do not lust after women.
> Do not disobey your parents.
> Do not violate Imperial laws.[10]

One description of rituals had the person involved dropping to the ground as though falling asleep. 'After a while he rises and kowtows to the southeast. Then his eyes open wide and he pants from the mouth. His strength rises through his body. Picking up his weapons he dances wildly and his power is greatest. He practices three times a day. When the magic is exhausted, his strength is expended. This is called "shedding the magic".' Another account told of charms written on strips of cloth, such as 'Patriarch, Duke of Zhou; Immortals of the peach blossom; Golden Bell protect my body.' Incantations were burned and swallowed. Teachers beat initiates with bricks and staffs. 'After chanting a spell for three nights, one can withstand swords,' the account went on. 'It is said that after chanting for a long time, even firearms cannot harm one ... But if one loses concentration, then the blade will enter.'

Though the Boxers believed that women polluted their magical powers, a separate female branch of the movement appeared. Known as the Red Lantern Shining, its members were said to be able to fly, walk on water, attack foreign ships at sea and block their guns. In Tianjin, they were headed by a young prostitute who had been imprisoned for a transgression against foreigners. Elsewhere, as the historian Joseph Esherick, puts it, 'their very existence indicates that some young women also found an opportunity to escape the confines of Confucian patriarchy and join in mysterious and no doubt exciting activities with their peers, outside of the home.'[11]

Growing in numbers, the rural guerrillas adopted dress characteristic of past risings – red or yellow turbans adorned with charms, red leggings, red armbands and white charms on their wrists. The toughest fighters, known as the 'black corps', wore red robes and black bandanas. They called their group leaders 'Old Teacher'. Foreigners were 'Primary Hairy Men' and Christian converts 'Secondary Hairy Men' – people who used foreign goods were 'Tertiary Hairy Men'. All three were to be liquidated.[12]

Unsuccessful in their attempt to stop the churchbuilding, the Liyuantun group marched off through the Shandong countryside, proclaiming anti-foreign slogans. The authorities, who wanted no more trouble with the Europeans, suppressed them. But the following year, amid a drought and famine which they attributed to the Christians, the Boxers staged new outbreaks. Foreign pressure forced the court to dismiss the Shandong governor-general, who was blamed for the trouble. But his replacement took the same approach, subsidizing the Boxers and recruiting them into his militia. After eight months, he was moved to Shanxi.

Sweeping out of Shandong and joining other Boxers in Zhili province in the spring of 1900, the disorganized, illiterate peasants moved north and west towards Beijing. They had little formal organization and little idea of what they were going to do. Near the town of Baoding, eighty miles south of the capital, they burned a Christian church and killed twenty converts, who were subsequently buried by their co-religionists in a cabbage field. In April, there was another violent clash in a nearby town. A church was burned down and thirty converted families killed, their bodies thrown into wells. Boxers attacked railway and telegraph lines, gaining wide support from farmers and peasants. In the capital, sympathizers began to assault converts.[13]

The Boxers presented the court with a major problem. They were an obvious threat to authority and order. Their rituals linked them to subversive secret societies and cults. Initially, officials took a tough line.

The governor-general of Zhili ordered the execution of 100 'robbers and malcontents' after an early attack on a British missionary, and troops were sent to try to stop the advance on Beijing – in one clash an imperial colonel was killed. The court was well aware of the danger of the movement sparking off fresh foreign intervention, with attendant demands.

But an ambivalence was evident. The British consul at Tianjin noted how a magistrate called the Boxers 'good citizens on bad terms with the Christians'. A decree following the Shandong killings said 'societies' should not be condemned as a whole since some aimed at self-protection and preservation. Cixi's own views were moving against the foreigners. The court's firm line on the Italian demand for a concession had paid off. The missionary link with the reform group from the Hundred Days made foreign ideas suspect to the regime which installed itself in the autumn of 1898. The fact that the would-be sage, Kang, had escaped on British ships was an additional cause for resentment. So was the way in which foreign pressure had saved the diplomat official Zhang Yinhuan. Even worse was Western lobbying against replacing Guangxu with the son of the influential Manchu Prince Tuan – the father was well-known for his anti-foreign views. The Dowager called leading Boxers to Beijing and ordered court attendants to learn their arts. Manchus began to hire them as guards.

As so often, Cixi was showing an acute short-term political ear, at least as far as her key constituencies were concerned. Nor were the foreigners united. As the British wavered between diplomacy and naval action, Russia played its role of China's best friend, reportedly telling the court that it need not pay attention to calls to put down the Boxers. Japan's foreign minister alleged that Prince Tuan, who now headed the Foreign Ministry, was in the pay of the Russian minister in Beijing, and that St Petersburg wanted the Boxers to devastate North China before its forces moved in to restore order.[14]

In that context, ragged and unorganized as they were, the young men who were surging through Zhili were obvious candidates to become the dedicated foot soldiers the dynasty lacked. After decades of humiliation, they might represent a way for China to hold its head high again. In mid-June, they cut the railway line between Beijing and Tianjin. In the capital, Chinese troops shot a Japanese diplomat, and British marines had to intervene to rescue Chinese Christians under attack, killing forty people in the process. A large group of Boxers, which had been allowed through the gates, massacred converts and burned the cathedral in the south of the city. The Western legations opened their quarters to fleeing Chinese Christians. In Tianjin, the foreign quarters were shelled, and the Boxers, backed by Chinese troops, massed outside.

Russia now changed policy to back intervention, assembling a 4,000-strong force in Port Arthur, while a British-led force set out from Tianjin in answer to a call from Sir Claude MacDonald, the British minister in Beijing, to protect Westerners in the city. A decree from the Forbidden City told imperial forces in Zhili to resist the foreigners, but it was the Boxers who swung into action, flinging themselves against the column from Tianjin as it paused to repair a damaged railway. The attack was so violent that it overcame the superior arms of the British, killing sixty-two members of the expedition and cutting the survivors off.

On 16 June, the Dowager and emperor presided over a meeting of ministers and princes. An official dismissed the Boxers as rioters without magical powers. Cixi interrupted. 'Perhaps their magic is not to be relied on; but can not we rely on the hearts and minds of the people?' she said. 'Today China is extremely weak. We have only the people's hearts and minds to depend upon. If we cast them aside and lose the people's hearts, what can we use to sustain the country?'[15]

Before another meeting the following day, the anti-foreign Prince Tuan showed Cixi an ultimatum supposedly drawn up by the powers which was then read out to the full session. A forgery, it called for the emperor to be placed in a designated residence,* and for foreigners to collect all imperial revenue as well as taking command of all military matters. A fourth alleged clause, which was not made known, probably demanded the removal of the Dowager. She was outraged. 'Today they have opened hostilities, and the extinction of the nation is before us,' she declared. 'If we fold our arms and yield to them, I will have no face before my ancestors when I die. Rather than waiting for death, is it not better to die fighting?'

Matters were made worse when troops landed from Western ships occupied the forts commanding the approach to Beijing. Cixi sent emissaries to the legations, whose diplomats made it clear that they knew nothing of the four demands produced by Tuan.[16]

---

* Given his confinement in the Summer Palace, this was actually already the case.

The court told foreigners to quit the city. The diplomats, some of whom were fresh from African postings where muscular imperialism was the order of the day, refused and asked for a meeting at the Foreign Ministry. No reply was received. The combative German minister was stopped and killed by Chinese soldiers.

The foreigners refused to leave the legation quarter. MacDonald dug in his heels, relishing reversion to the role of a military man which he most enjoyed – he would describe events as 'very good fun'. As well as their own safety, there was the matter of the Chinese Christians who had been given shelter. When the court extended the evacuation deadline, it blamed the disorder in the city on the 'ill-feeling between the people and the converts'. Clearly, if the foreigners went, the latter would be massacred, sacrificed to the Boxers.[17]

On 20 June, China declared war. There was no communication with the enemy. An edict merely blamed the foreigners for starting the fighting. The Boxers, who were praised as 'righteous soldiers', were to be taken into the imperial militia. At 4 p.m., troops encircling the legation quarter opened fire, and the fifty-five-day siege began.

It was Cixi's greatest mistake. Her rise to power had taken place against the background of the previous foreign attack on Beijing. Now she had allowed herself, and the dynasty, to be led by an anarchic, peasant movement made up of young men who believed that reciting spells and swallowing magic incantations written on strips of paper gave them the protection of the gods. It was a sign of the bankruptcy of the regime that also believed in its invulnerability.

In the north-west, 32,000 converts were reported killed. Tens of thousands died in Zhili, Henan and Manchuria. Before the declaration of war, the death toll among foreigners totalled nine. But now many more perished – forty-nine in Manchuria and eleven in Zhejiang, slaughtered by a mob thought to be in league with a vegetarian sect.

The most notorious act involving foreigners occurred in Shanxi, where, after receiving a message from the court instructing that foreigners should be killed, the governor, who had formerly been in charge of Shandong, invited forty-five missionaries to visit him with their children in the capital, Taiyuan. When they arrived, he had them arrested and led down a narrow, crowded street to a wide-open space in front of the gate of his *yamen*, decorated with a huge screen of a dragon's face. Stripped to the waist, they were beheaded, first the Protestants and then the Catholics, first the men and then the women – and finally the children. An eyewitness recounted that the governor became impatient with the deliberate pace of the executioner, and ordered his bodyguards to join in with their broad swords – one of them removed the spectacles of a woman missionary before dispatching her.

When the white-bearded Catholic bishop asked why this was being done, the governor personally slashed him across the face before he was decapitated. The heads were hung in cages, and the bodies thrown outside the city walls to be eaten by wolves and wild dogs. Extreme violence against the Westerners and their converts spread to other towns in the province – in one case, sixteen were slaughtered after being found hiding in a shed in a Chinese temple; in another, fourteen were grabbed and murdered by soldiers, and buried in a deep pit when local people asked that the bodies should not be left lying on the ground.[18]

Senior officials in some provinces were of a different mind, abhorring both the Boxers and the popular revolt they epitomized. The governors along the Yangzi, including Zhang Zhidong, reached an implicit accommodation with the British, while Yuan Shikai protected mission stations in Shandong, though 300 converts were killed in the province. Li Hongzhang, who was so enfeebled by age that attendants had to carry him to his writing table, had been sent in semi-exile to the south. From there, he despatched a memorial to the throne warning that its fortunes were 'being staked on a single throw'. 'My blood runs cold at the thought of events to come,' he continued. 'Under any enlightened sovereign these Boxers, with their ridiculous claims of supernatural powers, would most assuredly have been condemned to death long since . . . your Majesties . . . are still in the hands of traitors, regarding these Boxers as your dutiful subjects, with the result that unrest is spreading and alarm universal.'[19]

In the central Yangzi region, revolutionaries tried to take advantage of the chaos by staging a revolt aimed at forming a new government for southern and central China under the Guangxu emperor, with a national assembly based in Shanghai. After a premature rising in Anhui alerted the authorities, the plotters' headquarters in Wuhan were raided on Zhang Zhidong's orders, and the leaders were executed.[20]

In the capital, the siege of the legation quarter would cost the foreigners some 250 lives. The empire's artillery bought from Germany fired from a range of only 150 yards. Mines exploded under the French legation. Water was short and food was rationed. The foreigners ate horsemeat and uncleaned rice – suet pudding made from mule fat was an occasional treat. An officer noted that the women 'looked very peaky'.[21]

At court, the militants held sway. Five officials who counselled peace were executed. In the Grand Council, Kang-i took a bellicose line. Still, there were subtle undercurrents from the start. Letters were sent to MacDonald, seeking a settlement which would spare the foreigners but leave the Chinese converts unprotected – he refused such a deal. Jung-lu had never been keen on the alliance with the Boxers, and his troops allowed flour, vegetables and water melon to be taken through their lines for a time. The gunners seemed to aim high. Storming assaults stopped just as they seemed about to break through the makeshift defences. As Robert Hart reflected, probably 'somebody intervened for our semi-protection'. An attack on the Catholic cathedral in the capital also failed, blamed by Boxers on women inside who exposed themselves and waved 'dirty things' to counter the magic.[22]

Li's memorial to the throne warned that there was no way to resist the foreign forces. He was proved right. When Boxers tried to invade the concessions in Tianjin, they were mown down by Japanese and Russian troops, who took the Chinese part of the city, shooting at random, looting and plundering. Arriving there soon afterwards, a young British lieutenant, Richard Steel, recorded in his diary a ruined city in which 'the whole river is polluted with dead Chinese'.

At the beginning of an oppressively hot August, the foreigners assembled a force totalling 54,000 soldiers and marines and fifty-one ships. Eight countries took part, with Japan contributing much the biggest national contingent of 20,800 men and eighteen ships. Having trounced China in their war five years earlier, Tokyo welcomed this as an occasion to assert its presence as a modern nation alongside the forces sent in by Britain, France, Russia, the United States, Germany, Italy and Austria. Faced with such a coalition of powers, the Chinese could only feel that the whole world was against them.

Twenty thousand of the foreign troops marched on Beijing, under British command, moving along roads surrounded by high crops, laying waste villages on their way. On 14 August, in the words of a Methodist missionary in the legation quarter, 'we listened joyfully, tearfully, hysterically to the welcome roll of artillery and the click, click, click of the sharp-spoken little machine guns.' The expeditionary force had arrived.

It stormed the capital, and had little difficulty in driving off the Boxers and Chinese troops.[23]

Richard Steel, the British lieutenant, noted in his diary:

The sight in the Legation beggars any description. Any amount of women, children, and men crowded round us, shaking hands and cheering till they were hoarse. The Chinese all around having recognised we were in, opened a tremendous musketry fire, and one couldn't hear oneself speak. However, no one minded at all. The shots were high, and only two men were hit . . . everyone plies us with drink and tea and bread etc.[24]

'The loot is fabulous but we are not allowed to touch anything,' Steel wrote to his uncle in India, lamenting that the French and Japanese – 'the brutes' – had got in first. He recorded that American troops shot 'every Chinese that showed his head'. Killing and pillaging was widespread under what missionaries sought to justify as 'the ethics of loot'. The Summer Palace and the great Hanlin Library that contained many of the country's historical manuscript treasures were among the targets for destruction. Then some of the foreign troops moved south to the town of Baoding, indulging in what were described as 'punitive picnics'. Far away to the north, the Russians took advantage of the situation by launching savage attacks along the Amur river on the frontier; Chinese sources said more than 15,000 local residents were killed. Less bloodily, Western financiers, including the future US president Herbert Hoover, took advantage of the unsettled times and foreign power to seize the big Kaiping coal mine founded by Li Hongzhang.[25]

By the time the expeditionary force arrived in Beijing, Cixi and the court had decamped as they had done in the face of the British–French expedition four decades earlier. Valuables they were unable to take with them were buried to await their return; the foreign troops did not find them. Cixi suffered the indignity of having to disguise herself as a peasant. Another of the stories attached to the Dowager has her ordering the Pearl Concubine, who had argued that the emperor should not flee, to be thrown down a well by two eunuchs before she left – it has also been argued that this was just one more of the lurid tales made up after Cixi's death.

Accompanied by Manchu guards and eunuchs, as well as the chief of the reactionaries, Prince Tuan, the imperial party headed first for the Manchu homeland to the north-east. But, once they had crossed the

Great Wall, the road ahead was deemed too dangerous because of bandits. Pausing to decide what to do next, the Dowager ate two eggs and noodles. She changed into the robes of the dead wife of a magistrate, boarded a sedan chair, and, accompanied by cavalry, headed west along the top of the wall towards Shanxi province, with its loyal governor. The journey was arduous, especially in contrast to the luxury the travellers had been used to all their lives. 'I cannot tell you how fatigued I was,' Cixi said later. 'So long as I live, I cannot forget it.'

At one point, a soldier shot at her. The bullet missed. A guard grabbed the man and beheaded him on the spot. 'Before I was just like a piece of pure jade,' Cixi reflected, 'but [now] the jade has a flaw in it . . . and it will remain there for the rest of my life.' The emperor, according to a prince who accompanied him, 'reviled everyone', his face dirty, his hair dishevelled, his clothes sweaty.[26]

In the Shanxi capital of Taiyuan, the governor laid out gold and silver plate, and recounted how he had killed the missionaries. Power in the region lay with a general who supported Prince Tuan. The chauvinistic prince argued for continuing war on the foreigners. However, as news spread of the massacre of the Westerners in Shanxi, the court feared yet another punitive expedition directed against it. So it moved on to the old imperial capital of Xi'an, and, turning on the Boxers, declared them outlaws, calling on Li Hongzhang to open negotiations with the foreigners in Beijing.

As the imperial party was carried through the rough, poor countryside, Cixi saw China as it really was for the first time, and could only have noted the contrast between the reality and the lies she had been fed for so many years about the condition of the nation. A famine which contemporary estimates said killed 2 million people was gripping the region. The plains were deserted; refugees huddled in caves outside Xi'an; consumption of cats and dogs, grass and weeds was followed by the appearance of what an American traveller, Francis Nichols, described as 'a horrible kind of meat ball made of the bodies of human beings'. Cholera and dysentery spread while men in carts toured the countryside buying children to be sold as household slaves in more prosperous areas.[27]

In Xi'an, the imperial party lodged in an old building in a park which had been abandoned after the story spread that it was haunted. To keep the business of government going, council meetings began at 4 a.m.

Guangxu was seen to stare at two large French clocks, brought from Beijing, which kept bad time but appeared to fascinate him. The heir apparent, meanwhile, lounged with his companions on a terrace, smoking water pipes and opium, or staged riotous nocturnal expeditions into the city which, on one occasion, led to them being thrown into jail – when they tried to pull rank, the local governor refused to bend, and Cixi backed him up.

Li concluded his negotiations in Beijing in early September 1901. The old man's last act for the throne – he died two months later in what a French visitor described as 'squalid quarters' in Gold Fish Lane – was extremely onerous. The post-Boxer agreement provided for the destruction of forts protecting Tianjin and Beijing. Foreign forces would be stationed on the approaches to the capital, and guards posted at the legations. China was not to import any arms for two years.[28]

The governor of Shanxi was ordered to kill himself. A prominent Manchu prince who had backed the Boxers committed suicide, while another was banished. More than 100 officials were punished. Prince Tuan was exiled to the Far West, and Cixi decided that his dissolute son should no longer be heir apparent.[29]

An indemnity equivalent to £67 million was to be paid over thirty-nine years at 4 per cent annual interest. Reflecting its growing position in China, Russia took 29 per cent, Germany got 20 per cent, and France 15.75 per cent. Britain, enjoying rich privileges in the Yangzi and Canton area, was content with 11.25 per cent. Since payments by Beijing would come out of imperial revenues, the foreign powers now had a direct financial interest in the continuation of a centralized unitary state. If a break-up of China halted payment, they would be affected. Rather than using their military power to split the Chinese melon completely, much better to continue the treaty port system, which provided a quasi-imperial position in major cities at minimal cost, under a government too weak to stand up to the foreigners.

The blossoming of the system meant that the empire was peppered by twenty-five concessions and leases stretching from Manchuria to Guangdong, and reaching inland to Hankou. The British, French, Germans and Russians were joined in this later stage of the penetration of China by the Japanese, the Belgians and, after an initial rebuff, the Italians, who secured a toehold in Tianjin after the Boxer debacle. Britain held Hong Kong and Portugal Macau. The French were acknowledged to have a zone of influence in the south-west; the same went for the Germans in Shandong and the British in the Lower and Middle Yangzi.

The heavy expense entailed by the Boxer agreement forced the court to raise fresh cash. Tax revenues were, however, not enough. To meet the financial requirements, China was obliged to get new foreign loans and commit more future revenue from customs, salt duties and other sources as collateral, further impoverishing the state.

The Boxer episode manifested the strength of grassroots anti-foreign sentiment, and buttressed the link in Chinese minds between foreign aggression and Christianity. The first secretary of the Chinese Communist Party, Chen Duxiu, would hail the rising as 'the great and tragic prologue to the history of the Chinese national revolution' and praise the Boxers for having acted to 'save part of the reputation of the Chinese people'.* But if the Boxers embraced a crude form of nationalism, what this amounted to was unclear. Was it no more than anti-foreignism at the service of a dynasty which, itself, came from beyond the Great Wall? Westerners bore some blame for China's plight, but the prime cause lay in the empire itself and its rulers. The Qing were losing a power game they had failed to fathom, and the country was coming to realize this. It was time to attempt reform.

* Interpretation of the Boxers remained a sensitive matter more than a century later. In 2006, a Chinese newspaper was temporarily closed down after publishing an article which took a harsher view of the rising.

6

Final Act

As was only fitting, Cixi herself symbolized the new direction the regime was to take by completing her return from her flight by travelling the last 100 miles to Beijing on a train in a sleeping compartment with a European-style bed, along with her opium-smoking paraphernalia. Moving to the Forbidden City, she was, according to Hart, most gracious, bowing and smiling at crowds of foreigners gathered to watch her return at the beginning of 1902. 'The Court is over-doing it in civility,' the Customs chief observed. 'Not only will Dowager Empress receive Ministers' wives, but also Legation children!' She even let herself be photographed in the rebuilt Summer Palace, protected from the elements by a ceremonial parasol, the air around her sweetened with incense.[1]

Leaning on the arm of a British woman as she showed the foreigners round her favourite residence, Cixi stopped from time to time to point out a beautiful flower or a view of the lake. Her living quarters at the palace had heavy wooden furniture, seating platforms and coloured glass chandeliers. The wife of a British official, Lady Susan Townley, noticed how the emperor trailed round after his aunt, his chin 'weak and undecided', only speaking when she addressed him. In her chamber, Cixi invited Lady Susan to climb on her brick *kang* bed, covered with cushions and bolsters. Cixi and the emperor joined the Englishwoman, and the three of them sat there cross-legged.[2]

While the 67-year-old Dowager settled back into the Summer Palace, a programme of change emerged which would equal what had been promulgated during the Hundred Days. The most reactionary officials were gone; the old Manchu princes were retired; Kang-i had been cashiered as part of the Boxer settlement. Reform-minded officials and nobles took the helm, among them the veteran Zhang Zhidong.

'Unless we cultivate talents, we cannot expect to exist,' an edict declared. 'Unless we promote education, we cannot cultivate talent. Unless we reform civil and military examinations, we cannot promote education. Unless we study abroad, we cannot make up deficiencies in education.' Accordingly, modern schools were set up – 35,787 in 1907, and 87,272 in the next five years as pupil numbers trebled to 2.9 million. The old imperial examination with its 'eight-legged essay' was replaced with ten questions on political and administrative history and foreign affairs and foreign learning – only three were on the classics. Then the government announced that the examination system would be done away with altogether in 1906.[3]

When it came to girls, the regime hesitated, regarding their education as incompatible with tradition. The first schools for them were, therefore, private, funded by gentry and merchants, and their wives. In 1906, however, there was a change after Cixi was reported to have told an American doctor of her wish that 'the girls of China might be taught'. In 1907, the government committed itself to female education. By 1911, there were 141,430 girl pupils in China.[4]

The administration was modernized. Army reform was pushed ahead. Industry and commerce were promoted. The long-awaited rail track from Beijing to Wuhan was completed; if it could be extended south to Canton and west to Sichuan, this would provide the framework for a national system. A five-man constitutional investigation mission was sent to the West to study governance there. Received by Cixi and the emperor on its return, its members warned that opposition to a constitution and anti-Han policies would 'lead to self-destruction and the fall of the state'. The ban on intermarriage between Manchus and Han was duly lifted; the decree also encouraged an end to foot-binding. As pressure for a parliament rose among gentry, intellectuals and students, Cixi agreed to reorganize central government by setting up eleven ministries, and to allow discussion of a constitutional regime.

Steam navigation, previously suspect like railways, was authorized in shallow waters throughout the empire. Lecture halls were opened for talks on foreign countries and science. In Tianjin, a model prison was established at which convicts learned printing, weaving, dyeing and shoe making, and were provided with fifty Singer sewing machines, though their leg shackles were not removed as they worked.[5]

A big drive was mounted against opium smoking, which had grown to such an extent that some big urban centres were reckoned to have more than a thousand narcotics shops and dens. Use of the drug by Chinese soldiers was seen as one reason for their poor performance. The memory of Commissioner Lin, who had tried to stamp out the trade in Canton, was invoked, and one of his descendants headed an anti-opium campaign in Fujian that lasted for fourteen years. The crusade melded neatly with the growing sense that the national fibre needed strengthening. But there were two problems – the reliance of many farmers on the crop and British insistence on the right to bring in the drug from India in the name of free trade.[6]

Yuan Shikai took over as governor-general of Zhili and military commissioner for North China from Jung-lu, who died in 1903 after several years of ill-health during which Cixi sent him presents of ginseng. The younger general reorganized the army, implemented bureaucratic reform and centralized his administration, while also treating with foreigners, weaving a network of associates in key northern posts, and solidifying his position with judiciously arranged marriages of offspring. In the Middle Yangzi, the evergreen Zhang Zhidong promoted agricultural innovations, engaging American specialists and experimenting with new seeds at a farm near Wuhan.[7]

Novels flourished, particularly in Shanghai. Most were sentimental, but there was also politically coloured fiction, encouraged by a belief that books could play an important part in modernization. One writer, Wu Woyao, devoted a 100-chapter work to describing social ills, official incompetence, cowardice and corruption. Another, Li Baojia, wrote satirically of officials, Chinese justice and ill-judged reforms.

Groups in Tianjin, Guangdong, Hunan and Yunnan campaigned to improve the condition of women. In Beijing, a Manchu princess organized a calisthenics display by schoolgirls. In Changsha, a young woman who had studied in Japan set up a Free Love Marriage Lecture Society, which was, however, banned by the governor. Shanghai had a Women's Chinese and Western Medical School, Women's Education Protection Association, Society for the Promotion of Hygiene, Girls' Patriotic School and the Women's Handicraft Training Centre. In Canton, women vowed not to use American flour to protest at the US legislation against Chinese immigration. An intellectual, Chen Xiefen, asked how, after thousands of years of slavery to men, Chinese women could still 'follow them, thereby becoming slaves of those enslaved by foreign races'.[8]

Women preferred to set up their own groups rather than join male-led reformist organizations. As the manifesto of one explained:

A great catastrophe hangs over us. We Chinese women are about to be sold, all will become the slaves of England ... Some ignorant males say that they do not want us to meddle in this political matter ... Such talk is nothing more than breaking wind. We women are people too! But because our locations and methods differ from those of men, we must establish our own organization, whose aim is nevertheless the same – to rescue the nation.[9]

The new atmosphere was manifest in an increased international presence. After the imperial ban on emigration abroad was lifted in 1893, enterprising families from the south and east coasts sailed to new homes round the Pacific Rim. In the early years of the twentieth century, 100,000 people a year left the port of Xiamen.[10]

The urban population leapt by up to 10 per cent a year, swollen by farmers and peasants seeking a more prosperous life. At the start of the century, Shanghai had forty-six enterprises with more than 500 staff each. By 1912, Jiangsu province, surrounding the growing metropolis, contained 386 plants, 263 of them with more than twenty-five workers. Factory conditions were primitive, with very long hours, draconian discipline, poor safety and no health care. Still, wages might amount to four or eight times as much as the men could have made if they had stayed on the land.[11]

The commercial world could be a jungle – Zhang Zhidong described it as a system in which 'each person selfishly plots private gains, everyone cheats everyone, con artists abscond with money, the slow and dim-witted get taken, with the result that people regard investing money as too dangerous, making us unable to compete with Western merchants.' To try to bring some order, a Ministry of Commerce was established in 1903, and work began on a commercial legal code.[12]

Businessmen increasingly saw economic development not only as a way of making money but as the key to enabling China to find its place in the modern world. This created a natural bridge between them and reformist gentry who wanted the country to be strengthened through reform and increasingly substituted the concept of the nation for that of the dynasty as their prime loyalty. Both groups were also anxious to free themselves from centralized control. In 1904, the business community got satisfaction with the authorization of chambers of commerce, which provided a forum to meet and lobby for modernization.

Some entrepreneurs followed the Self-Strengtheners' model of operating from an official base, such as the judicial commissioner of Zhili, who began with a mining company, and then branched out into textiles, banking, glass and a waterworks. Other holders of scholarly degrees preferred to take the risk of going private, even if they often drew on public investment funds. In Shanghai and Canton, a fledgling bourgeois business class emerged. In Tianjin, the rich holders of the salt monopoly invested in cigarettes and match factories, banks and insurance firms, glass, candle and cement plants, spinning mills and a 'Harmony Accordion Manufacturing Company'. In Nantong, south of Shanghai, an upper degree holder, Zhang Jin, established a model town with factories and a cotton mill, paved roads, a theatre and schools as a demonstration of modernization which he continued till his death in 1926.[13]

The Imperial Bank set up in 1897 had run into trouble after a wave of counterfeit notes from Japan started a run on the institution, and provincial officials switched back to the more familiar traditional remittance system. Still, the court was aware of the need for modern banking, and, in September 1905, authorized the establishment of the Bank of the Board of Households, with shares split between the board and the public. Three years later, the name was changed to the Great Qing Government Bank (Daqing). Acting as China's central bank, it took over the issuing of notes, handled the finances of the imperial treasury and customs revenues, and conducted official financial dealings with foreign governments. The Board of Revenues became its largest client, keeping large amounts of silver on deposit. With that kind of status and resources, the new institution succeeded in taking over the remittance business, and attracting the funds of provincial authorities. In seven years, Daqing increased its deposits and loans seven-fold, and paid shareholders dividends of up to 34 per cent. Another new state establishment, the Bank of Communications, was launched in 1908 to centralize funding for railways, steamship lines, and telegraph and postal services, administering the funds of the Ministry of Posts and Communications and with the right to issue notes.[14]

Private banks were established, starting in Shanghai, Ningbo and Hangzhou. Edicts gave them official protection, and stipulated that the accounts of customers could not be divulged without their consent. As a result, the number of modern banks rose to seventeen by 1911, with deposits and loans increasing 4,000 per cent. Apart from their regular business, they helped to stave off financial panics, and their shares became favoured investments.

Overseas Chinese, whom some still looked down on as despicable for having deserted the Middle Kingdom, were embraced in treaty ports as a source of ideas and capital. Shanghai, strategically located at the mouth of the Yangzi, and with its booming foreign concessions and Chinese businessmen, became one of the major cities in Asia, a symbol of the progress China was seeking. Internal migrants flocked there from all parts of the country. Foreigners introduced innovations in their settlements – electricity and gas, sewage and running water, along with their legal system and business practices. Though an argument has been made that the treaty ports drained economic activity away from the surrounding regions, the growth of enterprises in Jiangsu province round Shanghai or the development of the Middle Yangzi round Hankou point in the opposite direction.

The self-regulating foreign areas remained a living insult to China, but many locals moved into them rather than living within the walls of the native section. As one Chinese resident of Shanghai wrote:

In the international settlement, the roads reach everywhere. In the [native] city, the roads are narrow. The international settlement is exceptionally clean. Its cars do not leave a cloud of dust. People who live there think of it as paradise. In the [native] city, although there is a street-cleaning bureau, the stench from the river attacks the nose, and latrines lie adjacent to one another ... the difference between the city and the international settlement is that between heaven and earth.[15]

In the north-east, the economy grew fast after Japan followed its victory in the war against Russia of 1904–5 by concluding an entente with the enemy and, in effect, dividing Manchuria into two equal zones of influence. For the Japanese, the immediate attractions of the region were its mineral reserves, agriculture and huge forests. But, beyond that, military victories had bolstered their belief that they had a manifest destiny to pursue in Asia, and that security for their islands could best be achieved by expansion. The first step was to establish leadership over the far bigger nation across the sea, supposedly bringing China the benefits of modernization while actually making it a subservient state.

With strong support from Japanese investors, who received a regular 6 per cent dividend, a consortium built the South Manchurian Railway, with 700 miles of track, hundreds of locomotives, and thousands of wagons and carriages imported from America. Owning coal mines and land on either side of the lines, the SMR developed schools, parks, administrative buildings, public offices, libraries, hospitals, storage depots, a flour mill and a hotel, as well as tunnels and bridges. Its work-force staff rose to 13,621 in 1908. With its own guards posted along the tracks, it operated independently of the Chinese authorities, a self-regulating foreign enterprise answerable only to its bosses in Tokyo.

The Japanese modernized Port Arthur, and developed Dalian as a big port for the region's main export, soy beans. After the imperial ban on Chinese moving to Manchuria was lifted, between 300,000 and 400,000 people a year were estimated to have emigrated during the early years of the twentieth century, tripling the population to 15.4 million by 1911. For the time being, Japan had enough to satisfy it, but the urge to spread further, and more forcefully, would rise in tandem with national self-confidence over the following decades, leading to the most devastating results of any of the foreign interventions into China.[16]

Sweeping as the post-Boxer reform programme was, the changes were not always quite what they seemed; nor were their results what had been hoped for as the structures to replace the old system were lacking. The end of imperial examinations meant there was no set manner of choosing and appointing administrators. Key posts in new government bodies were still taken by Manchu princes and generals, and the proportion of Han in the top ranks of administration in Beijing actually declined.

The props that had underpinned Chinese rural life were steadily weakening. Land was bought as an investment, not held as an asset to be handed down from generation to generation. Among the gentry, the idea of public duty and community spirit frayed, while the lure of personal and material advancement rose, epitomized by the increase in the ranks of absentee landlords using local agents who became feared for their bullying behaviour. The decline in the tradition of city dwellers returning to their home villages when their parents died weakened the link between the urban elite and the countryside. As land prices dropped, small farmers found their main store of value falling while inflation, caused, in part, by the cost of the reforms, powered ahead – the price of wheat, barley, sesame oil, wine and pork doubled from the late 1890s to 1908.

New schools were short of trained teachers. The liberation of women lacked real official backing. The Education Ministry rules defined female education in terms of producing 'virtuous mothers'. The traditional virtues of Chinese women had to be upheld, it added, and 'all evil talk of allowing them to run wild, or of liberty (such as not heeding the distinction between male and female, selecting one's own spouse, holding meetings and giving speeches on political matters) must be strictly eliminated to maintain public morality.'[17] The anti-opium drive provoked protests from farmers who relied on the crop for their livelihoods. There were violent demonstrations against grain prices and taxes. One confrontation in Shandong involved 40,000 people, of whom 1,000 were killed in the subsequent repression. Protests which, in the past, had been on a single issue, such as taxes, now became part of a wider agitation that took on a strong political complexion.

Irrigation works which had been a hallmark of Chinese agriculture fell into disrepair through lack of care and money. Fresh natural disasters aggravated matters in Zhili, Jiangsu, Anhui and along the Yellow River. Sichuan counted hundreds of thousands of starving people after a drought in 1902. The distress boosted membership of secret societies, in which many gentry families also had at least one member.[18]

Rural revolts became more frequent. Secret societies maintained opposition to the dynasty – the Heaven and Earth Society, the Elder Brothers and the Benevolent Righteous Society, which staged an abortive rising in Henan in 1906 after its leader drank animal blood and recited magic spells to confer invulnerability. Rebels assassinated the governor of Anhui and tried unsuccessfully to kill the naval commander in Canton. There were risings in Yunnan and Guangdong.[19]

In 1906, after severe flooding on the Hunan–Jiangxi border, an anti-dynasty group called the Hong River Society planned a revolt, under the leadership of an illiterate firecracker maker, with two former army drill instructors as lieutenants. A Revolutionary Vanguard of the Southern Army of the Chinese National Army was formed. Students preached radical messages. In reaction, the gentry reinforced its militias, press-ganging one male from each family, and arresting secret-society members.

Despite counsels of caution from the firecracker maker, 20,000 men from the Revolutionary Vanguard went into action armed with swords, lances, farm implements and a few muskets and rifles, its men proclaiming: 'Rob the rich and aid the poor.' Imperial forces put them down easily, and savage repression was visited on the area. Radical students were arrested; very few escaped death. Though he had not joined the rising, the firecracker maker was executed. 'Killed and wounded rebels were cut into pieces and their livers removed by the troops, who ate them mixed with their grub,' a missionary wrote.

Four years later, riots in the Hunan capital of Changsha showed the volatile currents at work between the people, officials, the gentry and foreigners. Inflation, flooding and hoarding had doubled food prices. Arguments between local women and shopkeepers escalated into violent demonstrations. An official promise to open the city granaries was not kept. After fourteen people had been shot dead by guards trying to hold back the mob, the governor's *yamen* was burned down. Popular anger turned on the British since they had used their influence to prevent a halt to the export of grain from the province, which was popularly regarded as the best means of alleviating the shortage. Missionary posts were attacked.[20]

Local conservatives thought they could use the protests to undermine reformers, whom they identified with the British. They called for an end to railway construction, disbandment of the New Army, and closure of modern schools, as well as the opening of the granaries and the diversion of funds used for reform to pay for food for the people. There was a ready audience among workers who resented the foreigners not only for their strange ways, but also for their recruitment of masons from Hankou to build European-style houses. The violence spread across Hunan with attacks on churches and schools. Over the border in Hubei, rice riots and mob disturbances broke out. The regional New Army moved in to restore order. The governor-general of Hunan and Hubei had the leader of the original protest executed, along with several other craftsmen. Conservative gentry were reduced in rank.

The disturbances were dramatic evidence of the limited appeal of reform, which was blamed for tax increases and was identified with foreigners. Most people remained true to old ways. Given the huge disparity in numbers between those on top and those below, and the authoritarian nature of the imperial system, the prospects for reasoned progress commanding general adherence were slim, and violence remained the usual way of settling arguments.

In cities, bad conditions spurred workers to join secret societies. Strikes were usually accompanied by machine-breaking. Shanghai had fifteen stoppages in 1904–6 and twenty-four in 1909–11. In Hankou, 9,000 workers at a tea-brick factory went on strike for pay rises, and then attacked a rival Russian plant. In Wuchang, employees at a cotton mill stopped work to protest at the punishment of three colleagues, and there was a riot at a hide plant after a manager made off with the wages.[21]

Meanwhile, the constitutional debate polarized opinion. Pressure for a parliament rose steadily among reformist gentry, but the dynasty was intent on retaining control. Speaking for political tradition, the aged Zhang Zhidong decried talk of democracy, saying most Chinese were still too 'vulgar and rustic' to participate. 'Even supposing the confused and clamorous people are assembled in one house, for every one of them who is clear sighted, there will be a hundred others whose vision is beclouded; they will converse at random and talk as if in a dream – what use will it be?' Zhang asked. It could be a present-day official explaining why China is not ready for democracy, and needs continuing guidance from the top.[22]

For all the enthusiasm and initiative in establishing new businesses, the overall effect of the economic expansion was limited by the size of the nation and the backward starting point, as during the Self-Strengthening era. It has been estimated that, in 1911, China had only about 600 enterprises using machinery. Chinese capital in modern ventures was just 6–7 per cent of what was invested in agriculture. Some new enterprises collapsed. Too often, enthusiasm was substituted for planning.

Despite the metropolitan growth, urban dwellers were still in a definite minority. Though Shanghai saw its population treble to 345,000 over twenty years in 1900, its industrial workforce was only 76,000. Across China, traditional handicrafts remained a far bigger source of employment than factories. The new commercial legal code was impressive, on paper at least, setting up a system for corporate registration, standardizing weights and measures, and covering trademarks, bankruptcy, agriculture, shipping, mines and railways. But the regime's approach was strictly top-down. Beijing would decide what was best for business.

In 1907, the Shanghai General Chamber of Commerce said the weakness of commercial legislation was 'enough to make our entire circle of merchants cry'. A business newspaper complained that companies were subject to a policy of 'peel off the skin and suck the marrow'. 'Every day the government talks about protecting businessmen and promoting trade, but in the end it has failed the big test,' lamented the *China International Daily*.

There was undoubtedly a strong dash of special pleading in this. Yet the point was not whether the complaints of the merchants were fully justified, but that their negative feelings built up yet another source of alienation between progressive elements in society and the dynasty. Whatever the government might seek to do, its intentions – then as now – were subject to obstacles at local level, where entrenched interests ruled and officials used their positions to move in on enterprises. Plundering of business by state functionaries was reported in Guangdong, Jiangsu, Zhili and Guangxi. Reflecting on the opposition he faced from conservatives, an entrepreneur complained: 'We encourage new production – they oppose us by saying our regulations are oppressive; we develop new varieties of grain – they say it is tainted; we process tobacco by machine, harvest trees and open mines – they damage [our enterprises] on the grounds that we are interfering with geomancy or *feng shui*; we employ women as factory workers – they accuse us of harbouring women for lewd purposes; we make local products that imitate foreign goods – they hit us with interfering regulations.'[23]

The discord between the central administration and the business–urban gentry in the provinces became focused on the question of recovering rights which had been signed over to foreigners in return for loans. This rights recovery movement chimed in with growing resentment at foreigners, sharpened by American legislation against Chinese immigration that provoked a boycott of US goods. For the court and Cixi, now in her seventies, the rights issue presented a tricky problem. The cost of reforms had worsened government finances, on top of the strain of paying indemnities, particularly the Boxer levy. State expenditure was 25 per cent above revenue. Beijing's problems were replicated in many provinces. In Sichuan, the governor was forced to raise taxes on tobacco, wine, salt and opium, introduce a lottery and mint coins to pay for reforms – a process that was known as 'cutting out the flesh to cure the boil'; as always, the burden fell disproportionately on the poor.[24]

For the state, the easiest way of raising immediate cash was through more foreign loans. There was no shortage of offers from Western and Japanese consortia and banks. But the court had to put up collateral and, to do that, had to own the assets in question. This meant keeping them out of the hands of private Chinese investors, or reclaiming those which had been privatized. Gentry leaders and businessmen therefore had two causes of complaint – the state was preventing them from participating in infrastructure development while it was selling out China. A cartoon showed the Kaiser declaring: 'This government is like a dog following us. If we get the land, we will let him have some bones and then he will be satisfied.'[25]

Economic interests and nationalism melded for the gentry and businessmen, and, increasingly, for members of what was meant to be a major prop for the regime, the new armies formed after the defeat by Japan and relaunched by a decree of 1901 in eight provinces.

These forces constituted only 175,000 of the estimated 600,000 soldiers in China. But they were by far the best trained and equipped. As a cutting edge of national revival, they became seedbeds for reformist ideas, and attracted a better, more educated class of recruit than the old formations. Proper pay grades and promotion procedures were instituted. Thirty-five military schools opened, teaching modern methods of waging war, along with science and foreign languages. Political discussion inevitably followed, including the rights recovery issues. In addition, hundreds of Chinese cadets were being trained in Japan, where they came into contact with Chinese revolutionaries and exiled refugees from the Hundred Days, and could only be struck by the pace of change across the sea.[26]

The new armies thus became a potential danger to the Qing. They had not helped the court during the Boxer Rising. While not disloyal, their prime allegiance was to their commanders, like the anti-rebel armies of the mid nineteenth century – when a governor of Sichuan was posted to the south, the forces he had raised in the province went with him. As officers joined the rights recovery movement and barracks became the scene of debate on the future of the nation, it became increasingly probable that the new armies would play a political role, backed with force.[27]

The first flashpoint in the rights recovery movement came in the Middle Yangzi region in 1904, when it became evident that the construction of the track between Hankou and Canton by an American syndicate was disastrously behind schedule. It then emerged that, in contravention of their agreement with the court, the Americans had secretly sold the contract to a Belgian group, which was thought to be backed by the French. Since Russia was building railways in the north of China, and the Hankou–Canton line was to link up with connections north to Beijing and west to Sichuan, this raised the prospect of Paris and St Petersburg, which were allies in Europe, dominating China's rail system, undermining the court's policy of sharing out work among foreign powers to keep them divided.

The powerful gentry in Hunan, the first province on the line south of the Yangzi, agitated for the contract to be cancelled. This was done in the summer of 1905 under the auspices of Zhang Zhidong. The project was split between the provinces through which the track would pass, with each responsible for building its section. In Hunan, the local elite took over, going to Britain for a £1 million loan to buy out the contract. In Canton, gentry members formed the Guangdong Railway Company, whose share offering quickly sold out – only Chinese were allowed to buy them. But the gentry and merchants involved in the southern end of the project fell out over further financing, and enthusiasm waned. By mid-1907, only seventeen miles of track had been laid. Another short railway was constructed with Chinese capital in the centre of Guangdong, but it was the British who built the line from Canton to the New Territories of Hong Kong.[28]

In Sichuan, the contract for a link between the capital, Chengdu, and Hankou was awarded initially to a local consortium formed under state auspices, but this was then privatized. The local gentry welcomed the chance to improve their finances, after many of them had suffered large speculative investment losses when a bubble on the Shanghai rubber market burst. Purchases of shares were made easier for landowners by a provision that they could acquire them against a commitment of future grain harvests.

A line was also recovered from foreign ownership in Shandong, and strong opposition welled up against the concession to the British of a track between Shanghai and the port city of Ningbo. One feature of this latter agitation was that women attended the protest meetings, and pledged to buy shares in a Chinese company if it was given the contract. Rallies were held at the new schools for girls in the region – pupils at one were reported to have asked for military drilling so that they would be able to resist the foreigners. Prostitutes rallied to the cause. 'All our sisters must form a group, for we cannot abandon our rights,' their proclamation stated. 'Anyone who is not sincere about this matter of railroad protection is not a citizen ... We must each ... resolutely buy stock.' Caught between its agreement with the British and the outcry, the regime put the project on ice.[29]

So far so good, from the nationalist perspective. But railways were a tough business, requiring technical expertise, proper financing and application. The foreigners managed to get a high price for their contracts – the American consortium netted US$6.75 million for relinquishing the Hankou–Canton line. Before long, the first flush of enthusiasm gave way to practical problems. As a Japanese consul noted in a survey of Chinese business:

No detailed research into the general socio-economic situation or the relations of supply and demand is done. No comprehensive consideration is given to projected income and expenditure. No such preparations, generally necessary for establishing industries, are made. On dangerous foundations caused by these vague and immature practices, perhaps to satisfy the demands of higher officials, perhaps to answer the clamouring of the people, with no understanding of the nature of industry, [Rights Recovery] combines the gullibility of officials with the ignorant views of the half-understanding gentry.[30]

The recovery movement was part of a broader questioning of China's relationship with the foreigners, which both drew on and augmented anti-Qing sentiment. Military defeats and the granting of concessions had induced a deep feeling of despair about the plight of the nation. If trade boomed in treaty ports, so did fears that the foreigners would destroy Chinese handicrafts. Cheap imports of iron undercut domestic product. Tea growing was increasingly hit by competition from India and Japan. The junk traffic on rivers was threatened by steamships run by Western firms. Though their conversion rate was pitiful, missionary numbers rose, and provoked violence in some places – preachers accused of poisoning water in Hunan were clubbed to death, leading Britain to send in a gunboat.

Writers of popular 'courtesan handbooks' drew an implicit grief-tinged parallel between their country's condition and beautiful women for hire who might survive by cleverness but were, in the end, powerless.

Literature evoked the plight of Poland as a metaphor for a once great but now impotent state, divided between foreigners. Intellectuals continued to wrestle with the problems of reconciling Confucianism with change, seeking a specifically Chinese route to modernization which would not mean jettisoning everything that had made the nation great. The private secretary to a Yangzi governor published, in English, a 'Chinese plea for the cause of good government and true civilization in China', which advised the foreigners that their only policy should be 'Let the Chinaman alone.' More stridently, a young pamphleteer in Shanghai, Chen Tianhua, raised a cry of alarm:

Ayah! Ayah! They're coming! They're coming! What are coming? The foreigners! The foreigners are coming! It's no good. It's no good for anybody: old, young, men, women, high, low, rich, poor, officials, scholars, merchants, craftsmen, all types of people from now on will be the sheep and cattle in the foreigners' corral, the fish and meat in their pots. They will be able to kill us if they wish, boil us if they want.[31]

Such sentiment exacerbated the danger to the Qing of being seen to side with the foreigners against the Han, an impression heightened when the jittery court ordered an end to the boycott movement against US anti-Chinese legislation. In 1905, some nationalists took matters into their own hands by organizing an anti-Russian movement, including a revolutionary Resist Russia Volunteer Corps. The shearing of pigtails increased, and was generally tolerated by the authorities even if it defied the badge of submission imposed by the dynasty for two and a half centuries. An eighteen-year-old student from Sichuan, Tsou Jung, summed up the anti-dynastic feeling in the first passage of a book entitled *The Revolutionary Army*:

Sweep away thousands of years of despotism, cast off thousands of years of slavishness, exterminate the five million bestial Manchus, wash away the humiliation of 260 years of oppression and sorrow, cruelty and tyranny, turn the Chinese soil into a clean land and all the sons and grandsons of the Yellow Emperor into George Washingtons. Then we may rise from death and return to life, retrieve our souls; come out of the eighteenth layer of hell and ascend to the thirty-third level of heaven.[32]

The young author was detained for sedition in the International Settlement in Shanghai, but the authorities there refused to hand him over to the Chinese; he died in prison, setting off rumours that he had been poisoned by Qing agents, though the cause was probably tuberculosis.

Radical movements sought to draw on national feeling, couched in terms of Han interests linked to despair at the foreign dynasty. These groups were tiny compared to the gentry-merchant reformers, and were often factionalized. They had little or no contact with peasants or workers. The one thing they had in common with one another and with the gentry modernizers was anti-Manchu racial sentiment, which served as a useful glue but did not constitute a positive policy. The exhortation to 'expel the Manchus' was a simple rallying cry; as a contemporary writer put it, 'even the dull-witted can understand it, talk about it, and act upon it, so that it will become influential and widespread.'

The shortcomings of radical groups were well demonstrated by the experiences of the man who would become a national icon, Sun Yat-sen. A native of Guangdong who was taken to Hawaii by a relative as a boy and then trained as a doctor and converted to Christianity in Hong Kong, he operated from outside China. His main base was in Japan, where he founded the Tongmeng Hui (United League) in 1905, calling for democracy, the end of 'Tartar' rule, national revival, a republic and equalization of land rights. Though he raised funds and support among Overseas Chinese, the doctor's impact in his home country was minimal. Ten risings staged by groups he led between 1895 and 1911 all quickly collapsed.

Other revolutionaries who had studied in Japan but refused to bow to Sun's leadership formed the Restoration Society when they returned to China, planning independent local risings that would put a premium on the assassination of senior officials and heroic individual acts, probably leading to martyrdom. Based mainly in Zhejiang province on the east coast, they established contact with local secret societies but, despite famines and flooding, rice riots and mass movement of refugees, seem to have made no attempt to enlist the peasantry.[33]

Among them was Qiu Jin, a young woman from a scholarly family in the province, who had been put into an arranged marriage with an older man, rebelled and escaped to Japan. Returning to China in 1906, at the age of thirty, she campaigned for female rights, writing poetry and founding a magazine which encouraged women to seek financial independence and study for the professions. She caused a scandal by riding a horse while dressed in male clothes – a photograph shows her in a

Chaplinesque pose in a dark suit and cap, holding a cane; for another, she wielded a short sword.[34]

Back in Zhejiang, she became director of a modern girls' school in a country town in February 1907 – the curriculum encompassed physical education courses, which included gun drill with live ammunition. A stockpile of Mauser pistols and other weapons was collected on the premises. The date of 19 July 1907 was set for a rising. But Qiu's main associate, her cousin, Xu Xilin, jumped the gun when he and a confederate got a chance to shoot at the Manchu provincial governor during a ceremony in the city of Anqing two weeks earlier.

Though Xu had forgotten his spectacles and his companion shot wildly, the official was fatally wounded. Xu ran into the street, waving a sword and calling on people to join him in revolt. None of the passers-by did so, but thirty or forty students attacked the local armoury. The guards there fled, after several had been killed. Imperial troops marched in and won a four-hour battle, after which the leaders of the short-lived revolt were beheaded – at the request of the governor's family, Xu's heart was cut out as a sacrifice.[35]

Qiu Jin's brother was arrested and gave information that led the authorities to her school. Resistance was brief; there was little ammunition left after the physical education gun drills. Two students died in the fighting; Qiu and seventeen others were captured. On 15 July, she was beheaded, at the age of thirty-one. As leader of the revolt and a significant figure, she was made an example of – the others caught with her were either acquitted or given relatively short jail sentences. By the end of the year, the first edition of her poems had been published. Lines she was said to have composed on paper given to her to write a confession became famous as a cry from the edge of the grave for China's plight: 'Autumn rain, autumn wind, they make one die of sorrow.' The words were probably the work of another author and attributed to her posthumously. No matter. China had acquired its female revolutionary icon.[36]

The abortive risings were part of a much wider recourse to violence, continuing a pattern set by the mid-century revolts and their ruthless suppression. Despite the reforms proclaimed by Beijing, the imperial system remained a straitjacket for most of the population, in which confrontation appeared the only way for the mass of poor people to make an impact. Computations by the historian C. K. Yang show 653 insurrections of varying size between 1896 and 1911, with the highest incidence in the region round the capital. They were set off by the usual rural causes, from natural disasters to refusal to pay taxes. The protestors included farmers, coolies, vagabonds, secret-society members. In just over half the incidents, gentry or men associated with them acted as leaders.[37]

The authorities found themselves fighting bush fires of protest that broke out without warning in one place or another, and which had to be quelled one by one. Most sprang from the countryside, but could spill over into towns, which became increasingly volatile with the influx of rootless workers. Ominously for the imperial system, though such protests had no common ideology or continuity, they often involved an attack on the local authorities in one form or another, and, sometimes, outright condemnation of the Qing.

On 14 November 1908, the Guangxu emperor died at the age of thirty-eight. There were, once again, allegations that, knowing her own health was failing, Cixi and her favourite eunuch had arranged to have him poisoned. The motivation was said to be her determination that he should not outlive her, while her eunuch had been told of a plan by Guangxu to have him put to death. Chinese historians with access to the medical records wrote in 1982 that he had, in fact, died of natural causes but then, in 2008, forensic experts concluded that he was killed by arsenic after finding lethal levels of the poison in his hair, stomach and burial clothes.

Cixi had, herself, had a slight stroke and several bouts of ill-health – a foreign lady visitor gave her pills, but she threw them away, preferring Chinese medicines. As 1908 drew on, she could not sleep and lost her appetite. Then she suffered from complications after a bout of influenza.

Still, there was business to attend to. The day after Guangxu died, she discussed succession arrangements at a 6 a.m. meeting of the Grand Council. Her first choice as heir having fallen by the wayside, she fixed on a grandson of her former swain, Jung-lu, as the next ruler. Aged two years and ten months, he was the son of a prince, who had married the late Manchu commander's daughter. He was given the reign name of Puyi. During his minority, his father would act as regent, while Cixi would retain supreme authority as Empress Grand Dowager. That decided, she went to lunch, where she ate a lot of pears, and fainted.

Reviving, she dictated an edict setting the new regency in place immediately since she was 'seized of a mortal sickness and without hope of recovery'.

Cixi then set out a valedictory decree retracing her career, which she said had been marked by 'calamities from within and aggression from without [that] have come upon us in relentless succession'. She insisted that it had been her 'inevitable and bounden duty' to assume the regency again after the Hundred Days. Now, all officials must work together to strengthen the empire's foundations, while the infant emperor must devote himself to study and abstain from personal grief at her passing. Mourning was to be limited to twenty-seven days.[38]

Having completed her last decree, and asserted the legitimacy of her 1898 coup, Cixi uttered her last words, which in the light of her extraordinary career and her use of eunuchs were ironic, to say the least. 'Never again allow any woman to hold the supreme power in the state. It is against the house-law of our dynasty, and should be strictly forbidden. Be careful not to permit eunuchs to meddle in government matters.'

At 3 p.m., Cixi turned to face the west, and died. She was seventy-three. Her body was taken to a mausoleum in the Western Hills outside the city built by Jung-lu. There it lay for a year before her funeral, which was reported to have cost the equivalent of a million pounds. Her personal fortune was reckoned to be sixteen times that. She was buried surrounded by jewels and treasures, and a large supply of Passing Cloud cigarettes.

After forty-seven years in power, Cixi left a country in which the central state and the main motive forces in society were on a collision course. Her achievement was to have avoided the breakdown of the system for so long. But her conservative approach had not been enough. She had made a terrible miscalculation in siding with the Boxers, and the policy of appeasing the gentry while refusing them real power was bound to end in disaster, fuelled by the spread of anti-Manchu feeling. For all her guile, Cixi belonged to an earlier age. China was changing, but those she left behind thought they could continue to give ground in a gradualist fashion while retaining real authority at the centre in the old manner.[39]

Provincial assemblies were, indeed, set up in all provinces, and a national assembly of regional delegates was to convene in Beijing the following year. But both were designed to be no more than talking shops and echo chambers for the regime. When an 'Outline of Constitution' appeared in 1908, it put off the convocation of a parliament for nine years. Executive judicial powers remained with the throne.

The assemblies were elected on a tiny franchise estimated at 0.42 per cent of the population, and reflected upper-gentry power – 90 per cent of members had gained the old imperial degrees, and most were early forty-year-olds from affluent families. They found common cause with the businessmen in the chambers of commerce, with whom they were often involved in investment schemes. Their motivation was double-edged. They wanted political reform and progress – but on their terms. The resulting weakening of central power would not necessarily be to the benefit of the mass of the people. Critics painted the gentry as 'tigers' who would 'make the people their fish and meat'.[40]

Unhappy at the nine-year wait, a petitioning movement pressed for faster change. Provincial assemblies, chambers of commerce, educational groups and Overseas Chinese banded together to lobby for acceleration, with the support of some governors. When the court agreed to reduce the delay to six years, the constitutionalists rejected this as still too long. At the end of 1909, provincial assemblymen sent a delegation to Beijing with a petition calling for the immediate convocation of a legislature. This was refused, so degree holders throughout China were approached to put their names to a second petition – 300,000 did so, representing more than a fifth of total gentry male numbers, which, given the organizational difficulties, showed the alienation of the class that had been a prime prop of the regime. An assembly of provincial delegates in Beijing produced more acrimony towards the central administration.[41]

A meeting of assemblymen in the capital formed what was, in effect, a political party, the Friends of the Constitution. Bringing together political and economic strands, this linked national and provincial activity, and strongly backed rights recovery. Discontent was sharpened by rises in taxes, duties on land, shops and houses, and rice requisitioning by the central state. From Changsha, the British consul reported that levies were being slapped on the slaughter of pigs and oxen, iron, paper, hides, timber, coal, salt, tobacco, oil, steamer tickets, the movement of farm animals, pottery, wine, wheelbarrows and brothels.[42]

The enmity of the new regent, Puyi's father, Prince Chun, led to the ditching of one of the regime's most competent younger figures, the modernizing general Yuan Shikai. The official reason was that he was obliged to step down because of a leg ailment. Going to a Garden of Longevity he built for himself in Northern Henan, Yuan was free to receive visitors, watch the situation and plot his return.

The court then showed its hamfistedness by forming a government heavily dominated by Manchus, which became known as the 'Clan Cabinet'. This made a mockery of its declarations that it was committed to working with the Han. Localized but potent quarrels heightened the tension. In Tianjin, the finance authorities backed a demand by German, French and Russian banks to force wealthy merchants to repay loans. As the confrontation sharpened, the powerful chairman of the Chamber of Commerce, Wang Xianban, known as the 'single indispensable person' in the city, was imprisoned. A hundred leading citizens, clad in gowns and caps, marched on the governor-general's *yamen*, calling for Wang's release, which was eventually granted. Though the dispute was a complex affair, it was easy to depict the central government as the friend of foreigners against the Chinese.[43]

The most provocative blow to gentry ambitions came in May 1911, when an imperial decree announced that all permits for the construction of main railway lines would be taken over by the Boards of Communications and Finance. This major centralizing move was swiftly followed by an agreement to give work on these projects to a British–American–French–German consortium which was offering the loans the court needed so badly.

Anger was particularly fierce in Sichuan, where the provincial assembly was dominated by rights recoverists. The governor criticized the body for spending too much time trying to 'supervise' his administration rather than helping it. The assembly president responded that examination of the use of tax revenue was essential if people were to be ready to pay money to the state. A pro-assembly newspaper led a sustained campaign against the police superintendent in the provincial capital of Chengdu, who had tried to impose his will on the city, forcing him to leave.[44]

On 17 June 1911, shareholders in the Sichuan–Hankou Railway Company held a meeting at which policemen sent in to ensure order joined in, shouting, 'We are also men of Sichuan; we also love our country.' Protestors marched on government headquarters. A Railroad Protection Female Comrades Association was formed.[45]

The railway minister in Beijing made things worse when he branded the protestors as troublesome schoolboys. On the morning of 24 August, a general strike was called in Sichuan. Two weeks later, the governor imprisoned nine protest leaders. In a demonstration in Chengdu, soldiers fired on the crowd, killing several people. Militiamen from outlying areas marched into the city to support the railway movement. Though troops repulsed them, more 'comrade armies' formed. Led by local gentry, the movement took power in several parts of the province; some militias ran out of control, ransacking schools, tax offices and police stations. Chengdu closed its gates against the rebels, and became increasingly isolated. The governor felt obliged to release the imprisoned rights leaders and open talks, in which he handed over authority to the assembly while he stayed in his *yamen*.[46]

Though Sichuan looked the most threatening challenge, the spark of the revolution that overthrew the Qing occurred down the Yangzi in the triple cities of Wuhan in October 1911. It came by accident, but set off a movement waiting to happen across the country that would lead to the extinction of the empire. Having survived for 267 years, the Qing had grown too weak and too unpopular to retain power over such a complex nation. The dynasty seemed to have lost the will to govern. The system it surmounted could no longer claim to offer effective rule. But there was no imperial pretender waiting in the wings. So the empire as a whole forfeited the Mandate of Heaven in the second decade of an even more troubled century.

PART 2

Revolution and Republic

The revolution which overthrew the 2,100-year-old empire of the Middle Kingdom began by mistake. It was a ragged affair that caught fire province by province. That it unseated the system which had survived so many challenges over the millennia was a reflection of the fragility of the central power, the strength of regional interests and the depth of the feeling that China had to change its ways.

Even before Puyi, the last emperor, abdicated at the age of five, a republic was proclaimed and the leading revolutionary theorist, Sun Yat-sen – who would become known as the Father of the Republic – was elected president. Lacking authority, he soon handed over to a military strongman. An experiment with a quasi-democratic legislative election ended in the assassination of the leader of the victorious party. Within a year of the end of the empire, China was back on a path of autocratic rule, initially from Beijing but then fragmented among regional warlords, some ruling domains the size of several European countries.

After a decade of anarchy on a national scale, Sun's heirs in the Kuomintang movement (KMT) led an army to unify the country, in alliance with the nascent Communist Party. This united front ended in 'White Terror', as the Kuomintang Nationalists set out to establish one-party rule that never met expectations.

There was neither a social nor an economic revolution. The gentry, which had been steadily accreting power since the middle of the nineteenth century, overthrew the empire to buttress its own position. The warlords were seriously reactionary. Force became the ultimate arbiter of politics, setting a pattern that persisted through the century. For the mass of the people, particularly in the countryside, life went on much as before, even if recurrent civil wars – large and small – instilled a new level of violence. The empire was gone, but the system which emerged to replace it was weak and did not connect with most of the population. Revolution, as a leading writer, Lu Xun, remarked, 'is a bitter thing'. Nowhere more than in China as the decades after the fall of the empire would show.

7

A Very Young Baby

On 9 October 1911, a bomb went off in the office of a revolutionary group in the Russian concession of Hankou, in the Wuhan three-city complex in Hubei province on the Middle Yangzi. Russian police arrived, and discovered the group's membership list. Chinese police raided another radical meeting place, arresting thirty-two people; three were publicly executed in high wind and rain at dawn on 10 October. Two soldiers then shot an officer who questioned them about weapons they were carrying. Their battalion, based in another Wuhan city, Wuchang, mutinied, killing officers and occupying the armoury. Other units joined in, bringing the number of rebels to some 3,600, facing 3,000 Qing loyalists. Several hundred men died in a battle for the local government headquarters, before it surrendered and the governor fled.

The rebels needed a leader. The choice fell on a short, squat, dark-skinned brigade commander, Li Yuanhong. Though a military modernizer associated with the gentry, he was anything but a revolutionary. He took some persuading. One story had it that he had hidden under his bed, and was pulled out, pleading, 'Don't hurt me!' A student pointed a rifle at him saying, 'as a slave of the Manchus, you should have been shot.' When Li still hesitated to take up the offer, he was shut up in a room while the gentry-dominated local assembly put his name on a proclamation of a republican regime. But, after he staged a hunger strike and was allowed to go home, the 47-year-old soldier agreed to take on the leadership.

A senior officer, Li was well placed to rally support in the army and in other provinces. The imperial court would find it hard to dismiss him as a rebel bandit. For the gentry, he was reassuringly unradical, and would oppose social upheaval. He was also a Han, not a Manchu. Thus, from the start, the character of the revolution and the ensuing republic was set – a military–gentry coalition that drew on ideas set out by reformers, but had no connection with the vast majority of the Chinese people or any taste for radical change. The political system changed; the social pattern persisted.[1]

A counterattack by imperial loyalists in Wuhan flopped, and officials fled. Looting spread, but the gentry leaders made a point of reassuring foreign consuls that treaties would be respected. The police and militia were told to drive away 'disorderly people', and guard against 'cold and hungry refugees'. Across Hubei, local leaders took charge, joined by secret societies. Magistrates deserted the throne. In places, Manchus were killed; later, in Xi'an, the death toll was said to have reached 10,000.

Twelve days after the Wuchang revolt, the army rose in Hunan, to the south. The governor fled. A senior local scholar, Tan Yankai, declared that China needed 'a civilized revolution with the co-operation and dedication of the great families and ancient clans, and the military officers'. A populist revolutionary was stabbed to death in the back by an army commander when he tried to take power. Other radicals were murdered, and a former imperial official was appointed as 'pacifier' of secret societies. Tan Yankai emerged as the provincial strongman, launching a career that would stretch through provincial and national politics to his death in 1930.[2]

By the end of October 1911, the revolt affected seven provinces, where military governors worked with elite-led civil administrations, backed by assemblies of gentry and merchants. The radical Tongmeng Hui (United League) movement led by Sun Yat-sen played a significant role in only a couple of places. In Shanghai, a league member, Chen Qimei, who had strong links with businessmen and secret societies, became military governor after taking part in an attack on the arsenal; to maintain the initiative, he sent his associate, Chiang Kai-shek, whom he had called back from military studies in Japan, south to the historic city of Hangzhou with a 'Do or Die' unit that stormed the government *yamen*. In Guangdong, another Sun associate, Hu Hanmin, took over after the imperial governor fled when the merchants in Canton turned against the empire.[3]

Sun himself acknowledged that 'this time I did not expend an ounce of strength.' When the revolt broke out, he was fund-raising in Denver, Colorado. He did not have his codebook with him, and was unable to decipher an encrypted cable from an associate telling him what had happened. Instead, he learnt about the rising from the local newspaper. Rather than returning to China, he went to Britain and France to seek assurances that they would not aid the Qing.

The revolutionaries were united only by their rejection of the dynasty. There was no new claimant to national power. The Qing still held the throne, its hopes resting on support in the north, including its homeland of Manchuria, where the governor organized imperial forces, suppressed radicals and banned newspapers from reporting the revolution. But controlling China north of the Yellow River was not enough for a dynasty that still claimed the Mandate of Heaven. An attack had to be made on the rebels. To do the job, the throne called in China's leading soldier, Yuan Shikai.

Despite the hostility of the regent that had led to his being sent into internal exile in his home province of Henan, the 52-year-old general was the only man who could command sufficient army loyalty and organize an effective campaign. He laid down stiff conditions, including command of all imperial forces and political reforms, and solidified his own position by having a rival murdered. Under his command from Tianjin, Qing forces moved down the railway line to Wuhan, where resistance was ineffective. The imperial army burned the Chinese city of Hankou, while keeping clear of the foreign concessions. The revolutionaries suffered an estimated 28,000 dead. But Yuan was also in secret negotiations with Li Yuanhong, and the victory in Wuhan was irrelevant. A dozen more provinces declared independence of the Qing, including the home of the rights recovery movement, Sichuan, where the new governor had his predecessor decapitated, and rode through the streets displaying the head.

On 14 November, Yuan took the train to Beijing to be received at court. The next day, he formed a government of ten Han and a single Manchu. He blamed the country's condition on the lack of a strong, responsible administration. A constitutional monarchy was needed, he added. His foe, the regent, abdicated.[4]

The dynasty's position was further weakened when revolutionary forces took the old summer capital of Nanjing. After Yuan and Li decided they could work together, negotiations were held with the regional groups, and an agreement for a unified republic was signed in a Beijing bookshop on 20 December. A provisional assembly was called into session in Nanjing.[5]

As to who would head the republic, the document was vague, saying merely that the president would be 'he who overthrows the Manchu regime'. The revolutionaries of the United League wanted the job, but were divided. Sun Yat-sen was at sea on his way back to China. Huang Xing, his lieutenant, enjoyed considerable support. But a younger reformer from the Middle Yangzi, Song Jiaoren, was also well regarded, as was another party member, Wang Jingwei, who had narrowly escaped execution after trying to assassinate the regent in 1910.

Sun's arrival in Shanghai at Christmas 1911 was hardly auspicious. A gunboat sent out to greet him could not locate the ship in thick mist. Driven to a house in the French Concession, Sun discovered that his colleagues were in conference with a representative of Yuan Shikai. When they met their leader, the revolutionaries were taken aback to find that he had brought with him an American hunchback, Homer Lea, dressed in a uniform with big shining buttons and medals, who had become Sun's adviser after offering to train Chinese militia in the United States; he was soon sidelined.[6]

Born in a village in southern Guangdong in 1866, Sun was rare among the revolutionaries because of his extensive experience of the world outside China, and his ability to speak English. The wife of another revolutionary recalled that, unusually for a southern Chinese, he did not like rice, and preferred her to fry an egg or open a jar of beef bouillon when he came to visit. At the age of twelve, he had been sent to live with an elder brother who had emigrated to Hawaii. Later, he studied medicine in Hong Kong, where he converted to Christianity. Adopting the revolutionary anti-Manchu cause, he travelled frequently to canvass support from Overseas Chinese, and was good at cultivating Western media. Participating in only one of the risings by movements he led, he did most of his plotting in Japan.[7]

The dapper, womanizing doctor became a celebrity abroad after being detained for five days in the Chinese embassy in London in 1896, before the English housekeeper informed a British friend of his, who raised an outcry in the press and Parliament which got him freed. It was never clear if Sun had called at the embassy of his own free will, or had been kidnapped – probably the latter. The incident increased his profile in the Western press, to which he contributed articles, some ghost-written by British sympathizers.

In 1905, he founded the United League, with a sixteen-character charter calling for democracy, the end of 'Tartar' rule, national revival, a republic and equalization of land rights. Sun, himself, slimmed this down to his Three Principles of nationalism, democracy and the people's livelihood. The first would later be taken as applying to the Western and Japanese concessions, but the main message at the time was the anti-Manchu refrain, the glue that bound the gentry, revolutionaries and secret societies together. The national identity which Sun posited was that of the Han, with a subsidiary role for the Muslim, Mongol, Manchu and Tibetan inhabitants of China.[8]

The doctor's teachings could be imprecise to the point of impenetrability; he could also be highly impractical. But there were some things on which he insisted, including his devotion to the creation of a united republic that would preserve national integrity and whose interests ranked above those of the individual. He demanded dictatorial powers for himself in the organizations he founded, but took a less autocratic view of the regime he hoped to usher in. A republic, he wrote, was like an automobile – officials were the driver, but the people were the owner. Alternatively, the president was the factory manager and the people the shareholders.[9]

In Shanghai at the end of 1911, Sun considered that his long revolutionary record entitled him to the presidency. At a meeting with delegates from the Nanjing assembly, he surprised them by his direct way of speaking, unlike the circumlocutions habitual in China. There was some opposition from the young Song Jiaoren, who argued that, after legislative elections due at the end of 1912, China would best be governed by a parliament and prime minister, with only a figurehead chief of state. His face red, Sun countered that he would not 'stand apart like some holy excrescence while the great plans for the revolution are ruined'. The Nanjing assembly, representing seventeen provinces, stuck with the idea of a strong presidency.[10]

On 29 December, it voted overwhelmingly for Sun to take the job. Though he got no votes, Li Yuanhong was appointed vice-president. On the night of 1 January 1912, the doctor was inaugurated in a hall in Nanjing lit by bright electric lights. Handed the seals of office, he pledged to 'overthrow the despotic Manchu Government, consolidate the Republic of China and plan for the welfare of the people'. With peace restored, and the republic firmly established and recognized, he would, he said, step down. He noted tensions between the central state and the provinces, and promised a new era in their relations. Taxes would be reduced to lessen the burden on the poor. The neutrality of foreign powers was gratefully noted. To establish historical continuity, he visited the tomb of the first emperor of the Ming dynasty, which was revered for having been the last ethnic Chinese ruling house, and declared that the nation was free after 268 years of alien rule.[11]

There was an immediate wrangle about the new republican flag; in the end, a compromise was reached on a standard consisting of five horizontal stripes in red, yellow, blue, white and black. Sun moved into the quarters of the former governor-general, a charming set of classical buildings round a small lake. Visitors found him serious and thoughtful.[12]

His long-time associate, Huang Xing, took charge of daily business. Though his title was war minister, he was, in effect, prime minister. Continuing the line of Hunanese who would play a prominent role in China's evolution, the stout, mustachioed Huang had a first-class degree in the imperial examinations, and inspired confidence. Yuan Shikai called him 'candid and honest, a hero and a gentleman'.[13]

The administration's authority was highly circumscribed, however. The military governors and gentry leaders who ran much of China owed nothing to Nanjing. As Sun's secretary, Hu Hanmin, recalled, 'the ministries existed only in name.' Some ministers never took up their jobs. Expenditure, particularly on the army, raced ahead of revenue. There were persistent rumours that Yuan was providing large bribes to selected members of the administration. Sun showed scant practical respect for democratic processes or cabinet solidarity. He attended only three parliamentary sessions, and issued bonds worth $300,000 without any consultation.

The new regime had a particular problem in dealing with women, who had backed the revolutionary movement, joined some armed actions, formed medical brigades, raised funds, acted as spies and smuggled weapons (in Guangdong, posing as brides, they hid guns and explosives in their trousseaus). The Alliance for Female Participation in Politics agitated for just that, with branches in five cities. Women founded a bank and companies in Shanghai and Nanjing, some of which excluded male employees. But, despite soft words from Sun, the constitution made no mention of gender equality.

When parliament discussed the issue, women were not allowed to listen to the debate; sixty broke into the upper chamber, clashed with armed guards, smashed windows and boxed Song Jiaoren's ears. With Sun mediating, an agreement was reached that they could listen to debates. But then a law was promulgated that restricted membership of the legislature to men aged twenty-five or above. Only in progressive Guangdong were seats in the provincial assembly reserved for women, chosen by a female electorate.[14]

In the first month of 1912, China was in an extraordinary situation. A republican president sat in Nanjing. Yuan was prime minister and in command in Beijing. An infant emperor, Puyi, was in the Forbidden City, with no regent.

Sun lacked the armies or the authority to give the dynasty the final push. Only Yuan could deliver. Realizing this, and recognizing his own weakness, Sun sent the general a cable to say that he was ready to hand over the presidency. On 16 January 1912, Yuan Shikai was driven to the Forbidden City to present a petition from his cabinet calling for what amounted to abdication. As he left the palace, revolutionaries threw four bombs at his carriage. A dozen guards were killed. Ten of the attackers were caught; three were shot.

As a sign of imperial faith in him, Yuan was elevated to the status of first-class marquis. On 17 and 19 January, the leading Manchu and Mongol princes discussed his petition. The former regent favoured abdication, but four nobles called for war. A Tartar general proposed killing Yuan, and replacing him with the Manchu governor of Manchuria. There was talk of fomenting a new Boxer rising to defend the dynasty. Puyi's mother listened silently, weeping and hugging her son.[15]

Nine days later, the Manchu leader of a royalist party was seriously wounded by a bomb in a Beijing street, dying the next day. An assassination bid was made against the imperial general commanding Tianjin. Refugees from court sought shelter in foreign legations. Observers noted that Han soldiers in the capital outnumbered Manchu forces – if they followed the racial course of their colleagues elsewhere, the throne would be lost militarily. Believers in the power of *feng shui* geomancy traced the trouble to a decision by the dynasty to abandon the Summer Palace – power, they believed, had stemmed from the force passing from the Western Hills through its gates towards Beijing; now that the gates were closed, all was doomed.[16]

Yuan was suspected of having fomented the assassination attacks to raise tension. A message to the court from forty-two army commanders called for abdication. 'My own and the boy's lives are in your hands,' the dowager screamed at the prime minister's emissaries. 'Go and tell Yuan Shikai nicely that he must save us.'

On 12 February 1912, the abdication of the last emperor was announced. The country was in turmoil and its people suffering great tribulation, the edict from the throne said. 'It is clear that the minds of the majority of the people are in favour of the establishment of a republican form of government,' it went on. Sovereignty would be handed to the people as a whole under a republic. 'We the Empress Dowager and the Emperor will retire into a life of leisure, free from public duties, spending our time pleasantly and enjoying the courteous treatment accorded to us by the people and watching with satisfaction the glorious establishment and consummation of perfect government,' it added.[17]

The wording had been drafted in Nanjing, and sent to Beijing. There, a sentence was inserted giving Yuan responsibility for uniting the nation and installing the republic. In a message to provincial governors, he stressed the rapid deterioration of the situation and the government's lack of money. Dedicated to national unity, he rejected a proposal that Manchuria should become an imperial haven – the once vigorous governor there retired as 'a broken man living in fear'.[18]

Puyi was allowed to continue to live in the Forbidden City, but the empire was over, brought down in the end by a fatal combination of its own mistakes and the incompatibility of its system with the nation's evolution, as the gentry who had saved it in the mid nineteenth century demanded more power and resisted imperial centralization. Apart from the Manchus and traditionalists, nobody seems to have mourned its passing. The dynastic cycle of rise and fall had been played out as so often over the centuries. The difference this time was that there was no new claimant to the throne.

Three days after the abdication edict, Sun Yat-sen announced that he would resign as president by 1 April, making way for Yuan. Sun tried to get Nanjing retained as the capital. But when a team from the assembly went to Beijing to discuss the matter, the general's troops staged a nocturnal attack on the house where it was staying, forcing the delegates to flee in their night clothes. Other northern forces insisted that the new president must stay in the old capital. The delegation let itself be convinced.[19]

On 10 March, Sun was driven to the National Assembly in Nanjing with a military escort that included a general riding on horseback in tweeds. 'It will be my object to help my 400,000,000 countrymen, and to endeavour to make the blessings of the Republic a reality,' the doctor declared in his farewell speech. Only one member of the legislature rose to sing his praises and return his valedictory bow – the official explanation for this lack of enthusiasm was that the seated members wanted to show that equality ruled among all men.[20]

As Yuan was elected president by the legislative assembly, fireworks lit the sky. At a grand reception, Sun hailed his successor as 'the friend of the Republic, the devoted and valued servant of the cause'. As a national helmsman, the general was a more reassuring figure than the doctor for the gentry, armies and foreigners.

Sun thought it would take ten years for the republic to implant itself. Still, he claimed that the two principles of nationalism and democracy had been achieved, and 'only the principle of the people's livelihood has yet to be realised.' He was certainly right on the last point; as he spoke, famine in the northern plains put 800,000 people at risk, another 300,000–400,000 needed help in Anhui and the Yangzi was in danger of flooding.[21]

If nationalism meant simply replacing the Qing with Han rulers, then the doctor was correct on that score, too. But, beyond the simplistic racial platform, the nagging question remained of what Chinese nationalism meant. It was most easily defined in terms of what it was against – the Manchus and the foreigners. So was it anything more than Han patriotism and exclusivity? If not, that was not much of a base on which to build a modern state. As for democracy, a general with a dubious record was now president and the franchise for the national elections later in 1912 was based on a property qualification that excluded the vast majority of the population, including women.

Yuan kept Li Yuanhong on as vice-president, though the one-time rebel chief stayed safely out of Beijing in his Yangzi power base. The general installed an old friend as prime minister, and a military associate, Duan Qirui, as army minister. The Nanjing forces headed by Huang Xing were demobilized. 'Alas! Tremendous noble works have flowed away like water,' Huang wrote in a poem on his thirty-ninth birthday, in October 1912. The revolution was a very young baby, the new president told an American diplomat, and 'must be nursed and kept from taking strong meat'.[22]

Sun became Director for Construction of All Railways in China – 'transportation is the mother of industry, the railway is the mother of transportation,' he declared, embarking on a lengthy inspection tour of existing tracks, accompanied by several young women secretaries. One of them, Soong Ailing, eldest daughter of a leading Shanghai tycoon, Charlie Soong, particularly attracted his attention. An emancipated young lady who scandalized the neighbours by riding a bicycle, she did not reciprocate.

On his trip, the 'Father of the Republic' drew 70,000 miles of track on a six-foot-square map. The lines were all completely straight, regardless of the terrain. When reporters boarded his train, the doctor's Australian adviser, W. H. Donald, arranged for the map to be mislaid to avoid revealing another example of Sun's lack of realism.[23]

The victors bettered themselves with positions and perks. A Bureau for Examining Meritorious Service distributed cash among those who had served the revolutionary cause. The gentry further expanded its influence. The urban elite prospered. But peasants still could not afford salt. Rents and taxes rose. A single national highway linked the north with the Yangzi and the south. Urban growth was largely restricted to the treaty ports with their foreign concessions. The highest estimate for the number of modern factories was only 1,759.[24]

Yuan faced two main challenges – extending Beijing's control over the provinces, and restoring the ruined finances inherited from the Qing. He sent trusted associates to bring Manchuria to heel, and edged out Sun Yat-sen's ally, Chen Qimei, as military governor of Shanghai. Generals closely linked with him took charge of key northern provinces. But the attempt to extend central control was hampered by poor communications, and the unwillingness of provincial gentry to relinquish privileges and autonomy acquired in the last decades of the Qing and magnified by the revolution. The Sichuan gentry sought to limit official posts to men born in that province. In Hunan, Tan Yankai ran things much as he wished in collaboration with the local elite. Guangdong declared home rule under Hu Hanmin and a leading local figure from the 1911 revolt, Chen Jiongming. The southern province showed what the revolution might have become in different hands, but also the practical problems that confronted reformers.[25]

Ambitious programmes were drawn up in the province for education, health care, sanitation and the law. A start was made on land reform. Local industries were encouraged. Limestone was kept for local use, instead of being exported to Hong Kong. Campaigns were launched against gambling and opium; in Canton, a score of wealthy addicts were sentenced to clean up the riverside Bund, clad in their furs and silk coats but manacled with fetters and chains.[26]

Kowtowing ceased. A single form of address, the equivalent of 'Mister', was introduced instead of old expressions of deference. Modern buildings went up, including the Sincere department store, which was so popular that it charged an admission fee. Modern young urban men donned Western clothes, in the words of a newspaper, 'combining the hats, boots and trousers of New York with the coats of London and the waistcoats of Berlin'. Ten women members of the provincial assembly were picked by a female electorate, and women's associations bloomed. A weekly newspaper was launched 'to cultivate morality and protect the rights and privileges of womanhood'. Parents who bound their daughters' feet were threatened with loss of civic rights.

But all this came with a price tag, and growing financial problems forced Hu and Chen to slow down the pace of change. After negotiations for an American loan fell through, Guangdong had to turn to Beijing for help. Yuan's chief secretary undertook to provide funds, but in a scheme that put the province in thrall to the central authority while the president hatched a plan to set Hu and Chen against one another.

The independent attitude of provinces compounded Beijing's own financial woes. Inefficient collection and the siphoning off of funds at local level meant that revenues probably ran at only a third of what they should have been. Customs duties were mortgaged to foreigners to pay interest on loans or meet indemnities from the Boxer Rising. The empire had left big debts. The upkeep of armies, which bolstered the new ruler, was costly, and Yuan aggravated the situation by raising new forces to strengthen his hold.

In search of temporary relief, a £1 million loan agreement was negotiated with a supposedly Belgian bank – a railway project was put up as collateral. The bank turned out to be a Russian front, and pressure from other European powers scuppered the deal. Yuan denied any knowledge of it, and dropped the prime minister as the scapegoat. But the Senate rejected the new government he appointed. Legislators were subjected to a poster campaign of denunciation, bomb threats and demonstrations calling for their heads. Four generals warned that, if the Senate did not back down, 'we shall execute its members.' The legislators caved in. Yuan's men were approved. Military power ruled. So much for Sun Yat-sen's declaration that democracy had been achieved.[27]

The new government's immediate job was to complete talks for a £10 million loan from a six-nation consortium which demanded draconian terms, including control of collection of the salt tax and of how the loan would be spent. The government split on whether to accept. Yuan named a fresh administration that agreed to the proposal. The Senate gave approval. To avoid nationalist protests, the signing on 27 April 1913 was carried out secretly late at night – the Chinese representatives sneaked into the building through the back door.

The agreement was bad business for China. The interest terms meant that, if it was repaid in full at the end of its forty-seven-year term, its £10 million would have cost the country nearly £43 million. Two thirds of the first instalment was used to cover Puyi's allowance, running costs of the presidential office, ministries and the legislature, disbandment of troops in Hubei, and payments for the Beijing garrison and Manchu Bannermen troops. Europeans were appointed to oversee the salt administration, and head a new Audit Office, to which government departments had to apply for authorization of expenditure. If the revolution had been meant to assert China's national rights, the new regime had, within eighteen months, acceded to foreign control never suffered under the Qing.

The loan negotiations were held against a steadily fraying political situation in which Yuan showed his colours all too clearly. At the request of his vice-president, he organized the assassination of a Li rival who was visiting Beijing from Hankou. Despite Sun's accolade a little earlier, the ruler's behaviour alienated him and the more radical revolutionaries sufficiently for them to form the Kuomintang – or Nationalist Party – ahead of the national legislative elections at the turn of the year. The doctor took a back seat in the campaign, leaving the electioneering to the thirty-year-old revolutionary from the Middle Yangzi, Song Jiaoren, who had argued for a parliamentary system over a presidential regime.

Song believed that a cabinet backed by a strong party in the legislature was the best way of checking Yuan. An excellent organizer, he shuttled round the country building support among gentry leaders. Policies on land redistribution and women's rights were dropped as Song connected with the mainstream of the 1911 revolt and preached a message of re-creating 'the mighty accomplishments of our ancestors over the past five thousand years – in conquest, administration, expansion of our national territory, and the elevation of our national prestige'.[28]

Sensing the threat, Yuan banned 'secret organizations'; what constituted 'secret' was left undefined, but the measure could be used against the KMT if need be. Then, when Song visited him in Beijing, he proffered a book of blank cheques, which the young man handed back. The poll was a triumph for Song, showing that the elite electorate took a dim view of the president's ambitions. The Kuomintang won 269 of 596 seats in the lower house of the legislature, and 123 of 274 in the upper house. Alliances with smaller parties would enable it to form a majority. That would make Song prime minister, and help him to pursue his goal of parliamentary government.

Having failed with bribery, Yuan fell back on violence. His aides established contact with a disenchanted former revolutionary in Shanghai who headed an underworld gang. He recruited a young man in a tea house to shoot Song with a Browning revolver as he boarded the train to Beijing to claim his political prize. The politician was taken to hospital, but doctors were told not to operate until they received permission from the capital. By the time this arrived, peritonitis had set in, and Song died. A Western woman doctor said he could have been saved if she had been able to act immediately.

Yuan's administration tried to blame the deed on a secret society in Shanghai. Then it conjured up a 'Women's Assassination group'. But police located the man who had set up the killing, and arrested him in a brothel. The assassin was also caught. Their trials revealed Beijing's involvement. Pleading tooth trouble, the prime minister left the capital to become governor of Zhili, where he died in unexplained circumstances. The two men arrested in Shanghai also suffered mysterious deaths.

The murder of Song ended China's only experiment in contested national elections. Though the KMT initially pursued legal avenues, nobody put much faith in parliament being able to deal with Yuan. Sun Yat-sen called for his forcible overthrow, and three parties which catered for workers and peasants formed an Anti-Yuan Shikai National Citizens'

Coalition. Opposition rose further when the terms of the foreign loan became public. Yuan tried to organize a round robin message of support from provincial governors, but six of them, including Tan Yankai of Hunan and Hu Hanmin in Guangdong, refused to join in. The governor of Jiangxi province, who backed the Kuomintang, ordered 7,000 rifles from abroad.

The president used remaining cash from the loan to get KMT members of parliament to defect. Those who resisted were harassed. Li Yuanhong was named to take over in Jiangxi, which bordered his Middle Yangzi base. Hu Hanmin was told to quit Guangdong for faraway Tibet; Chen Jiongming was appointed to replace him. The governor of Anhui, whose loyalty was suspect, was transferred to remote Gansu in the north-west. Seven provinces declared independence from Beijing. That began what was known as the Second Revolution.

The provincial gentry was unenthusiastic, seeing no need for a fresh upheaval that might compromise their recent gains. Many of the new armies were on Yuan's side. The fighting was ragged. Soldiers looted at will. A one-time imperial general, Zhang Xun, who had begun his ascension when Cixi noticed him as a stable boy, led a force that sacked Nanjing; 'everywhere charred walls without roofs; the contents of houses broken and cast on the street; fragments of shrapnel on the walls – withal a depressing picture of misery,' wrote the American minister to China, Paul Reinsch.[29]

In Guangdong, Yuan's appointment of Chen Jiongming to succeed Hu Hanmin as governor did not split the revolutionaries as he had hoped. But the provincial administration had lost the support of the merchant class, which despaired of the worsening financial situation that led to bank notes being discounted by 50 per cent. A 4,000-strong force sent by Beijing took Canton. Suitably bribed, local army units mutinied. The victors invited the city's police chief to a feast, and killed him. Chen fled.

The province's home rule was annulled. The local assembly was dissolved. Devolutionary measures were reversed and newspapers were shut down while Confucianism was extolled and traditional dress encouraged. Restrictions on gambling and opium were lifted. British backing for Yuan was rewarded with a resumption of limestone exports to Hong Kong.[30]

In Shanghai, the former military governor, Chen Qimei, also failed to muster the support of businessmen for a fresh offensive. They had been alienated by his attempts to wring money out of them, and had no wish for fresh trouble. Pro-Yuan troops repulsed an assault on the arsenal. Chen fled to Japan with his sworn brother, Chiang Kai-shek, and his mentor, Sun Yat-sen. In exile once again, the doctor formed a new group, the Chinese Revolutionary Party. Small in numbers, it stood aside from other anti-Yuan movements. Its chief insisted on complete authority, and had members fingerprinted. This was too much for his long-time lieutenant, Huang Xing, who went off to the United States.[31]

The doctor's latest spell in Japan was notable for another, very different event. After failing to get anywhere, on his railway tour of 1912, with the eldest daughter of the Shanghai businessman and republican backer Charlie Soong, he had more success with her beautiful younger sister, Qingling. She fell for him, and he for her. The Methodist tycoon disapproved – if only because Sun already had a wife. Soong tried to keep his 23-year-old offspring away from the fifty-year-old revolutionary. But she climbed out of a window of the family house and sailed to join the doctor in Japan. In October 1915, they married, launching her on a career that would make her a patron saint of the left until her death in 1981 at the age of eighty-eight.

In Beijing, the rump of non-KMT legislators confirmed Yuan as president. He posed for a formal photograph in a uniform with large, braided epaulettes, a wide sash, a thick, embossed belt, sword, plumed helmet and a plethora of medals, his moustache reaching to his chin, his thick neck emerging from a tight collar. A new cabinet included the reformer from the Hundred Days movement of 1898, Liang Qichao, who wrote bitter, not unjustified, criticism of parliament as a bunch of lazy incompetents whose debates were 'like a squabble between fish-wives or naughty children'.

Northern generals moved into government. The gentry-scholar leader of 1911, Tan Yankai, was replaced as governor of Hunan. Yuan felt uncomfortable with his vice-president far away in charge of a key region, so he called Li Yuanhong to Beijing. In his place, he sent his lieutenant, Duan Qirui, to run Hubei, while also entrusting him with the Army Ministry.

In November 1913, the KMT was outlawed. Troops surrounded the party's Beijing office. Its remaining members of parliament were prevented from entering the legislature. This meant that the chamber lacked a quorum, so could not hold valid sessions. The KMT's legislative leader, C. T. Wang, telephoned the journalist and adviser W. H. Donald to say that Yuan's gunmen were outside his house. The Australian suggested that the politician disguise himself as an old woman and tell a servant to drive him to the Methodist Mission. Enlisting the co-operation of the American legation, Donald then got Wang to Beijing station, where, still in disguise, he boarded a train to the safety of the foreign concessions in Tianjin.[32]

By the end of 1914, Yuan could count a dozen provinces under his direct control, with central government troops sent in to back up his governors. A new constitution expanded the powers of the president, allowing him to declare war, sign treaties and appoint officials without legislative approval. Then Yuan decreed that his term of office would be limitless. To enforce and extend his authority, he used martial law, secret police and terror – the toll of executions in Henan in the year after the collapse of the Second Revolution was put at 21,000. The killing reached into the elite: twenty-one gentry were executed in one day in Zhengzhou.*[33]

Revolutionaries and anti-Yuan soldiers fled for their lives. Some joined outlaw bands, the most celebrated of which was led by Bai Lang ('White Wolf'), who has been seen by some writers as a 'social bandit', a politically aware figure who teetered on the brink of playing a truly revolutionary role. Born in 1873 into a family which owned thirty acres in the hills of western Henan, Bai joined a modern army in the last years of the Qing, but an unjust arrest in a local feud alienated him from the authorities. Married with five children, he turned to banditry in 1911, forming a group of peasants in his home district.[34]

Three years later, his 'Citizens' Punitive Army' was said to number 10,000. From its mountain hide-out in Sow Gorge, it stormed towns, burned down official buildings, and attacked officials and the well-off in hit-and-run raids across Henan, Hubei, Anhui, Shaanxi and Gansu. The bandits received regular pay, and appear to have been quite well-disciplined. Their chief, who wore a leather jacket and white fur hat, could show a social side, handing out food and coins to the poor. A government report noted that village women and children thought of

---

* Then rendered in English as Chengchow.

the bandits as their own family and regarded soldiers as enemies. A song about Bai as a Robin Hood had it that:

> He robs the rich, helps the poor and delivers Heaven's fate.
> Everyone agrees; Bai Lang is great!

KMT members made contact with him in 1912. During the Second Revolution, Huang Xing tried to get the outlaws to blow up train lines to hinder the movement of Yuan Shikai's troops. Proclamations written by KMT agents and posted by Bai's men denounced Yuan and called for justice. But the term 'revolution' meant nothing to the bulk of the bandits, and Bai over-reached himself with an epic march to the north-west. When government forces launched a campaign against their home ground in Henan, his soldiers returned to their farms; their first attachment was to their land and their second to banditry. Wounded and deserted by all except a few loyalists, Bai went home, too, to die in the summer of 1914. Government troops dug up the body, cut off his head and hung it, decomposing, from the wall of the provincial capital.

As he consolidated his power, Yuan looked back in time. He appointed as the new head of the cabinet a former Qing official who appeared at functions in his Manchu-era robes. Imperial forms of address were revived. Service under the dynasty became an aid to promotion. At a New Year reception in the Summer Palace, twenty generals in blue uniforms unrolled a carpet in front of the president.[35]

Egged on by an American adviser, Yuan prepared for the ultimate step. In 1915, petitions were organized from provincial leaders calling on him to become emperor. Coercion and fear appear to have played a considerable part in this, but the monarchical movement could also argue that a return to the past offered the best chance of stability and modernization on late Qing lines. To form a court for himself, the president appointed six dukes, eleven marquises, twelve earls, four viscounts and sixteen barons.[36]

On 23 December, he stepped into an armoured car at the Forbidden City to be driven to the Temple of Heaven. The road was covered with imperial yellow sand. On arrival, Yuan transferred to a vermilion coach and then to a sedan chair, on which he was carried up the steps to the altar. There, he shed his military uniform for a traditional robe of purple with circular dragons. Ninety minutes later, he was driven back to the

Forbidden City, having been declared emperor, taking the reign name of Hongxian ('Constitutional Abundance'). A National Congress of Representatives rubber-stamped the move. Yuan so overawed its carefully selected members that an official attempt to get a few negative votes for form's sake failed.

If the new emperor aimed to lead the Chinese equivalent of the Meiji restoration which had presided over Japan's modernization, he was in for a rude awakening. His position was much weaker than it might have appeared. Japan, Russia, Britain, France and Italy were all critical. Yuan lost the backing of constitutionalists from the imperial era such as Liang Qichao. Public opinion was not impressed, with the gentry resenting his pretensions to claim the Mandate of Heaven. Intellectuals, scholars and students were hostile. Nor could Yuan count on traditionalists – he was still the man who had betrayed the Qing. An officially spread story of a divine dragon appearing up the Yangzi, which would confirm the new dynasty, aroused chuckles. So did a tale of a vision of an imperial dragon hovering over the master's couch.[37]

Seeking to increase centralization, Yuan proposed to abolish the provincial system. That alienated not only the gentry but also military men he had appointed as governors. His decision to sack the ambitious Duan Qirui from his dual posts as governor of Hubei and army minister was a worrying portent for other lieutenants, as was the creation of a Central Command to concentrate military power.[38]

Yuan also faced difficulties from Japan, which in January 1915 presented China with twenty-one demands that went far beyond what the European powers had imposed. They provided for Tokyo to take virtual control of Shandong, Manchuria and Fujian. Its advisers would occupy key positions in the administration. Police departments would be run jointly, as would big coal and steel works. Japan would get a railway concession in central China, and become the sole arms supplier.

According to W. H. Donald's account, the Foreign Ministry in Beijing called him in for advice. Though deeply hostile to Tokyo's expansion, the Australian reflected the widespread defeatism bred by the great military reverse of 1894–5 and the humiliation at the hands of the foreigners in 1900. China, he thought, had no alternative but to submit to the territorial claims. Japan had allied with Britain and France against Germany in the World War, so would get their backing against China. Tokyo's proposal to run China's administration was rejected, but there was no overall refusal of the demands. When an edited version of them was published, omitting some of the more sensitive points, protests broke out in major cities. Nineteen generals declared their readiness to fight for China. Yuan did nothing. Japan got what it wanted in Shandong, extended its sway in Manchuria and gained other concessions. The ruler's unpopularity deepened.

The central government's financial situation, meanwhile, got worse and worse. Budgets were finalized up to a year late and bore little resemblance to reality, with a soaring gap between expenditure and revenue. The only refuge lay in foreign loans; more than £40 million of them were raised on railway projects; but the terms were onerous. The First World War dried up European finance, and domestic bonds had to be issued at a 73 per cent discount.[39]

Ironically, the regime's financial travails came at a time when the economy was enjoying something of a growth spurt. The World War lessened the pressure of imports from Europe, while Chinese raw materials were in demand by the belligerents. The currency doubled against the US dollar and sterling, increasing China's international purchasing power. The trade deficit fell sharply. New indigenous enterprises helped to push annual growth to as high as 13.8 per cent.

But most of the activity was centred in the treaty ports and Manchuria, beyond the state's orbit. Nor were the men leading the expansion beholden to the government. They were independent businessmen, often with international links, who stood outside the system Yuan was seeking to impose, and certainly had no desire for the restoration of strong imperial authority.

The radical revolutionaries had not given up completely. There were small-scale revolts in Shanghai. The first was put down by the military governor, a graduate of the Greenwich Naval College in London. Two revolutionaries then attacked his car with a bomb and pistol fire, killing him. Another assault, organized by the returning Chen Qimei and Chiang Kai-shek, hit the British-built local flagship, police stations, the telephone exchange and electricity station. But it soon fizzled out, and Chen was then shot dead by agents of Yuan. Chiang escaped, and went into hiding.[40]

A more significant threat to Yuan emerged on the other side of China when, on Christmas Day 1915, a self-styled National Protection Army, also known as the Anti-Monarchy Army, marched out of Yunnan in the far south-west. Other southern provinces joined it. Northern generals put up only token resistance, sensing that it might be time to desert the new emperor.

Visiting Yuan in his red and gold palace on 18 March 1916, W. H. Donald warned him that China might break up. His host said only seven provinces were unhappy. Seventeen, the Australian corrected him. The ruler looked washed out, as if dying. When the journalist insisted on the need to stop the fighting between north and south, the new emperor slouched forward, arms resting on a table.[41]

'You must abdicate,' the no-nonsense Donald said. 'You must stop this make-believe.'

'I am tired,' Yuan replied, getting up and shuffling out.

Three days later, he issued an edict ending his three-month-old monarchy, becoming president once more. This hardly helped. Yuan's imperial pretensions had destroyed his credibility, and he now seemed even more vulnerable. In the early summer of 1916, he talked of quitting, so long as the British would give him a safe conduct. But the British did not want him to step down, fearing the instability that might follow. It was the American minister, Paul Reinsch, who offered guards to accompany Yuan to Tianjin, while Washington agreed to lay on a destroyer to take him onwards.

Then, Yuan changed his mind. He did not want foreign protection, he decided, but an immunity from the advancing southern armies. He asked Donald to go to Shanghai to see opposition leaders there, including Sun, who had returned clandestinely from Japan. They gave the Australian an assurance of a safe conduct for the old soldier, which was relayed to Beijing. There was no word back from Yuan. He had died of blood poisoning.

8

Warlords

As vice-president, the portly, walrus-moustached, 52-year-old Li Yuan-hong automatically succeeded Yuan Shikai. He received visitors in a reception room of the Forbidden City, oil cloth on the floor, a gaudy Western chandelier hanging from the ceiling – an American described the vases as 'straight from a five-and-ten cent store'. The new president appeared unassuming. He was far from his base on the Middle Yangzi, and could not match the power of the northern generals of the Beiyang Army, the force originally commanded by Yuan, in particular Duan Qirui, the army minister who had been named as prime minister in the late ruler's will.[1]

At meetings in late 1916 and in January 1917, the generals threatened to act against anybody they judged to be disrupting national unity or making unreasonable demands. The soldiers thus imposed themselves while the gentry entrenched its local positions. Not that the Peiyang group was cohesive. Though they agreed on the need to sustain their collective, its members' internal rivalry was intense, and they relied on provincial commanders who, in turn, depended on the co-operation of grassroots militarists. Thus the pattern of devolved power was set, with effects that would be felt long thereafter.[2]

The inevitable showdown between Li and Duan came over the policy on the First World War. Duan had close links with Tokyo, from which China contracted major loans in 1917–18 in exchange for fresh economic concessions. He wanted to follow Japan's example in declaring war on Germany. Parliament was recalled to pass the necessary legislation, but, when loans he had approved with Japan came to light, the outcry forced Duan to resign. President Li sought support from the other northern generals, but they were not forthcoming. Isolated, Li called in the imperial general, Zhang Xun, who had taken Nanjing during the Second Revolution with his pigtailed soldiers.

Zhang, who was said to be paid by Germany to support its cause, was still devoted to the dynasty that had raised him from being a stable boy – hence his nickname of the 'Mafoo General', the first word denoting his original profession. A squat figure with a big head and protuberant ears, who wore a peaked skullcap, he compared the republic to 'a gardener who grows his cabbages with their roots up in the air' or a new porcelain shop selling bright, cheap ware. 'In time,' he went on, 'it is all broken, and the people go back to the old shop.'[3]

At the end of June 1917, Zhang rode through Beijing on a blanket of yellow imperial sand at the head of his troops, aiming to restore the infant Manchu ex-emperor, Puyi, to the throne. At the end of a lengthy banquet, the red-faced general, who had drunk heavily, sent men to get Li to sign a decree for the Qing restoration, which he did. With that in his pocket, Zhang went to the Forbidden City at 3 a.m., prostrated himself before the eleven-year-old Puyi, and announced the return of the empire.

Imperial flags were hoisted across the city. Kang Youwei, the ideologue of the Hundred Days of reform in 1898, reappeared, writing edicts to restore the Son of Heaven. But Duan Qirui marched on Beijing with an army from Tianjin. The old stable boy surrendered, seeking safety in the German legation. Puyi reverted to being a prisoner in the Forbidden City. Li resumed the presidency, but Duan, who regained the post of prime minister, was clearly the strongman at the head of what was known as the Anhui Clique. Before long, the president stepped down, moving to Tianjin to await the turn of events.

Another northern general, Feng Guozhang, became head of state and soon clashed with Duan. The main issue was the prime minister's adoption of Yuan Shikai's centralizing policies, which led him to send forces to assert control of the Middle Yangzi region, where two commanders had declared independence of Beijing. Feng took a softer line with provincial barons, and advocated peace. But Duan gained the support of six governors in north and east China, and Feng was forced to appoint a Duan ally, General Cao Kun, as pacification commissioner for Hunan and Hubei, in addition to his governorship of the key province of Zhili. To bolster his position, Duan turned to the warlord of Manchuria, Zhang Zuolin, who headed what was called the Fengtien Clique, from the name of his capital (also known at the time as Mukden and now as Shenyang). It was said that Duan won over the ex-bandit by telling him of an arms shipment for another militarist, which the Manchurian seized.[4]

Zhang and Duan triumphed over President Feng at the end of February 1918, when Manchurian troops surrounded Beijing. But other northern generals became alarmed by the prime minister's ambitions, an agreement he reached with Tokyo to train and equip a large army for himself, and the summary execution of a senior general who was lured to his fate in Tianjin. Wu Peifu, a general who had won victories for the northerners in Hunan and expected to be made governor of the province, was alienated when Duan awarded the job to a personal associate. Wu and southern provinces joined the call for peace, and the slippery Cao distanced himself from the prime minister.

Though Feng was forced from the presidency and replaced by a Duan-friendly general, the strength of opposition to his private ambition obliged the premier to step down, too. A reconciliation conference held in Shanghai in the spring of 1919 split into factions, which set the pattern for the years ahead.

Duan remained at the head of the Anhui group. But, having gained in supplies, weapons and influence, the Manchurians lined up against him alongside the governors in Zhili, Hubei, Jiangxi, Jiangsu and Henan. Wu Peifu marched north from the Middle Yangzi, while Zhang Zuolin's Fengtien army headed south towards the capital. The war which erupted in July 1920 lasted for five days. Pincer attacks forced Duan to flee to the concession of his Japanese friends in Tianjin. The Zhang–Wu victory launched the full warlord era that had been brewing since Yuan Shikai's death, and would mark China, in one form or another, for three decades to come.

Despite the crass materialism and lack of interest in ideas shown by the warlords, the start of their era saw an intellectual upsurge which would have an even longer heritage, through to the student demonstrations in 1989 and to reform movements of today.

Implementing a secret wartime agreement with Japan, the Western Allies granted Japan the former German concessions in China at the Versailles Peace Conference in 1919. This was particularly galling because Tokyo had actually done no fighting, while Beijing had also joined the anti-German coalition and sent 100,000 labourers to work on the Western Front. But Britain, in particular, favoured Japan as its prime East Asian ally, and Tokyo extracted a further series of concessions from Beijing in the name of protecting China from Bolshevism, enabling its soldiers to move about as they wished.

In Paris, Chinese blocked the route of their country's delegates to Versailles to sign the treaty. In Beijing, 3,000 students protested in the foreign legation quarter on 4 May. When police moved them on, they marched on the house of the pro-Japanese minister of communications. They beat on the gates, broke a window and climbed in, opening the door from the inside. The guards were overwhelmed.[5]

The minister escaped in the confusion, but the protestors caught a Japanese visitor to the house and a former Chinese envoy to Tokyo. The first was pelted with eggs from a nearby grocery shop; the second was badly beaten up with legs torn from an old iron bed. The house was trashed, and set on fire. Thirty-two of the demonstrators were arrested but released on bail. Demonstrations broke out in other cities. Japanese goods were boycotted or destroyed.[6]

Thus was born the May Fourth movement which encapsulated the frustrations and ambitions of young intellectuals who despaired of the state of the country. They traced China's woes to Confucian tradition. A new culture was proposed, with a simpler language capable of discussing modern issues without reference to ancient texts. The scholar Hu Shih promoted vernacular Chinese in literature, breaking the tyranny of the classics and encouraging pragmatism.

The movement's iconoclasm stretched far and wide. The importance of the individual was stressed against the mass conformity imposed by the traditional system. Among those who read and noted European exaltations of the importance of the individual was the young Mao Zedong.

Despite its nationalism, the movement embraced Western thought, raising, once again, the question of whether adopting foreign ways meant becoming less Chinese, or whether China could finally find a comfortable, confident place in a wider world. Connections were drawn between how people lived and the cultural and political context. Attention was paid to the status of women, the nature of modern marriage and family relations. The character of Nora in Ibsen's *A Doll's House* became an icon for women in the movement for having broken out of the conventional cocoon. Mao, whose articles at the time advocated independence for women and a free choice of partners, looked forward to an 'anti-feudal and anti-imperialist culture of the masses'. What China needed, declared Chen Duxiu, a prominent radical academic, was a 'Mr Science' and a 'Mr Democracy' – the first advancing positive, rational thought in place of the classics, the second offering a new system of morality along with political freedom. Only thus could China survive the contest of Social Darwinism with the West and Japan.[7]

The most celebrated Chinese work of fiction of the epoch, Lu Xun's *The True Story of Ah Q*, published in 1921, presented a national allegory in its tale of a cowardly, cunning dissembler and petty thief who ends up being shot when mistaken for a revolutionary. All that had happened since 1911 was that 'the Manchus have left the banquet', Lu wrote. The condition of China had not altered. 'Our vaunted Chinese civilization is only a feast of human flesh prepared for the rich and mighty,' he went on. 'And China is only the kitchen where these feasts are prepared.'

Lu's first major work, *The Diary of a Madman*, featured a man who found that, between the evocations of benevolence, righteousness, truth and virtue in his history book, there appeared the words 'Eat Men'. The nation's culture was one of serving masters who triumphed in the misery of the multitude, and the Chinese were marked by 'vileness and cowardice', Lu concluded. He thought the mass of the population too inert to offer a way forward through democracy. When faced with power, they dared not resist; when they gained authority, they became cruel, heartless and tyrannical; when defeated, they resigned themselves to fate.[8]

Some members of the movement embraced Marxism, seeing salvation in an emerging working class, 'casting my iron flower in the forge, flames around me', as one put it. For Marxists, China presented a problem. It had not gone through a bourgeois stage of development, so, in strict orthodoxy, it should not be ready for revolution. But the Bolsheviks could not ignore the potential of such a country.

Moscow sent several emissaries to try to organize a party, helping its cause by announcing the renunciation of Tsarist-era railway and concession rights in China. One of the agents worked with Chen Duxiu to draft a manifesto, and a preliminary session was held of the potential leadership of a Chinese Communist Party. In June 1921, Hans Sneevliet, an overbearing Dutch agent from the Communist International – the

Comintern – arrived in Shanghai, and arranged a meeting in a deserted girls' school in the French Concession to which thirteen of the fifty-seven declared Communists in the country were invited – among them, the young Mao from Hunan. Sneevliet, who offended some of the delegates with his aggression, brushed aside objections from the locals that China's working class was not ready for the proletarian revolution and had no grasp of Marxism.

The meeting was disrupted when a stranger looked into the school. Fearing that he was a police spy, the delegates decamped to complete their deliberations aboard a pleasure boat on a lake in the rain. There, they proclaimed the establishment of the Chinese Communist Party (CCP). The following month, the fiery-tempered Chen Duxiu became the fledgling party's secretary, giving it the imprimatur of a leading figure from the May Fourth movement.[9]

Though the CCP adopted the orthodox line on the dictatorship of the proletariat, it was more independent in other ways. It spoke of uniting with the Comintern in Moscow, rather than following its orders, and decided to cut links with other Chinese parties, going against Lenin's instructions for Communists in countries like China to co-operate with the 'revolutionary bourgeoisie'. While Marxist members of the May Fourth movement joined the CCP, others took a more reformist view, and found natural allies in progressive business circles, leading to a flowering of liberal thought that gained a wide audience through the press in Shanghai.

Beijing University continued to be the intellectual beacon it had become in the late imperial era. Political debate flourished, though parties were few and the KMT proved a disappointment; Sun Yat-sen stood aside from May Fourth – he generally disapproved of any movement he could not control. Foreign models were much sought after. The Shanghai columnist Zou Taofen presented readers with Ataturk, Gandhi, Marie Curie and Einstein as examples of progressive individuals who made a difference. Bertrand Russell came from Britain and Thomas Dewey from America to lecture. (In an aside which might apply to some of today's over-enthusiastic visitors, Lu Xun remarked acidly that Russell had 'praised the Chinese when some sedan chair bearers smiled at him'.) Chinese scholars explored new approaches to economics, geography, science and medicine while archaelogists discovered the remains of prehistoric Peking Man.[10]

The power behind the throne: the Dowager Empress Cixi with her favourite eunuch and two attendants.

Prince Gong: co-conspirator who was
bested by the Dowager.

Elder statesmen: Li Hongzhang and Gladstone.

British merchant: John Charles Oswald in his company's tea-tasting room in Fuzhou
around 1890.

The Last Emperor: Puyi (*standing*) and his father, Prince Chun.

The Dowager's defender: Manchu commander Jung-lu.

End of revolt: Boxer captives.

Early-twentieth-century Shanxi:
(*above*) coalminers, and (*right*)
three generations of women from
one family, with bound feet.

Strongman: Yuan Shikai (*centre*) and Chinese generals.

Revolutionaries: Nationalists meet in a Shanghai drawing room in late 1911 (*second left* Sun Yat-sen; *centre, seated*, Huang Xing).

Warlords: (*from top, clockwise*) Zhang Xueliang, the Young Marshal of Manchuria; Li Zongren, leader of the Guangxi Clique; Yan Xishan, the Model Governor of Shanxi; Feng Yuxiang, the Christian General.

The founder and the heir: (*left*) Sun Yat-sen and his wife, Soong Qingling; (*right*) Chiang Kai-shek and financier Soong Ziwen (T. V. Soong).

Top brass: Kuomintang leaders meet for the party's 2nd congress in Canton in 1926 (*third left*, Wang Jingwei; *fifth left*, Chiang Kai-shek; *then*, Borodin, Soong Ziwen, Eugene Chen; *far right*, Soong Qingling).

The Paris of the Orient:
Chinese young people
adopt Western dancing in
one of Shanghai's many
entertainment spots.

Spreading revolution: Kuomintang poster
of bringing an evil landlord to justice.

No quarter: street
executions as a
Communist-led rising
in Canton is suppressed
at the end of 1927.

However, Mao's claim that May Fourth marked the moment when the proletariat took command of the Chinese revolution was utter nonsense. Like its predecessors in imperial days, the movement was run by intellectuals and students, and had little or no link to industrial workers, let alone the peasants. It contained hope for the future, but also a streak of pessimism. In the face of the naked power of the warlords, what could a group of young intellectuals achieve? As a leading writer of the period, Ding Ling, asked, 'When will it be light?'

Civilian government was weak in the extreme, with governments appointed by whichever militarist controlled Beijing, which retained an importance since the customs revenue went to the administration there that was also recognized by the foreign powers as the government of China. Between 1916 and 1928, there were twenty-six prime ministers and nine changes of head of state. Parliament was feeble, devalued and corrupt. Regional potentates withheld tax revenue on a massive scale – in 1926, only a quarter of the salt levy reached Beijing. Central laws and regulations were ignored.

The one bright spot was in foreign relations, where efficient Chinese diplomats took part in international conferences and negotiated with Western powers and Japan. But, though they maintained the pretence of speaking for China, their country belonged to others, who had little or no interest in foreign nations except as a source of loans and arms. This extraordinary collection of self-made men pursued selfish ends to the extreme, based on force in a meritocracy of violence.[11]

As the historian Hsi-sheng Ch'i has suggested, China could be seen as a continent, split into rival states, with the warlords as the equivalent of kings in early medieval Europe, asserting their authority over their domains at the centre of a complex system of relationships and obligations with subordinates, family and friends, based on teacher–pupil links, patronage, clan membership, sworn brotherhoods, and shared local or educational backgrounds. In this analogy, the central government was like the papacy at its weakest, with whichever general controlled Beijing acting as pope-maker. No single militarist was strong enough to take charge of all China at the head of the national government. There was no Napoleon or Oliver Cromwell. Below the main players stretched an array of petty militarists, such as the fifty in Sichuan.[12]

Subordinates were taken by the leaders as adopted sons, like feudal baron-vassals. For the most part, self-imposed rules for mutual protection were observed, with defeated enemies allowed to escape in anticipation that they would return the favour one day if the fortunes of war changed. But the strains of constant conflict led Wu Peifu to complain by the middle of the decade that 'betraying one's leader has become as natural as eating one's breakfast.'[13]

As with displays of extravagance at medieval courts, conspicuous consumption was a sign of status. Zhang Zuolin was said to own the biggest pearl in the world and Wu Peifu one of the largest diamonds. In Shandong, the provincial baron ate off a forty-piece cut-glass Belgian dinner service; an American visitor recorded that, along with 'sinful quantities of costly foods', the illiterate ex-coolie served French champagne and 'sound brandy'. Some gambled to excess – Zhang Zuolin once lost $1 million in a night.[14]

Like European monarchs, the warlords needed strong territorial bases for tax revenue. Their self-protection and expansion led to a patchwork of alliances in which diplomacy was carried on to the brink of war. They contracted loans from foreign financiers and bought weapons from across the world, hiring mercenaries, in particular White Russians, some of whom, in dark-green uniforms and thigh-length yellow boots, drove armoured trains from which they machine-gunned civilians. The Manchurian warlord had 400 Japanese soldiers, a one-armed Old Etonian adviser called Sutton, a Russian inventor working on aircraft with movable wings supposed to be able to take off as soon as the motor started, and a German engineer, who was locked up in a vermin-infested jail after being convicted of killing a boy who called him a foreign devil.[15]

Their employer, Zhang Zuolin, had begun as a bandit in the north-east; when asked where he had been educated he replied that he was a graduate of the 'school of the forest'. Short and physically slight with delicate hands, a deceptively gentle face and gold-capped teeth, the warlord had initially put his men at the service of the empire, summarily executing revolutionaries. He switched to the republic in 1912. Known as the Old Marshal (his son was the Young Marshal), he held sway over a region of 300,000 square miles, as big as Germany and France put together, and with a fast-growing population. He was careful to get on with Japan, whose investments made the north-east the most industrially developed part of China outside the treaty ports, with thriving cities, including Harbin, which became a magnet for White Russians after the Bolshevik Revolution.[16]

The Manchurian's ally in Shandong, the 'Dogmeat General' Zhang Zongchang, stood over six feet tall and was known for his extreme violence. His wives and concubines were Chinese, Koreans, Japanese, French and White Russians, plus what a visiting journalist described as 'one bedraggled female who said she was an American'. With 'the physique of an elephant, the brain of a pig and the temperament of a tiger', Zhang called himself a 'big, round-faced, long-legged overfed ruffian', though he also affected the title of Great General of Justice and Might. Popular myth gave him a penis as long as a pile of eighty-six silver dollars.[17]

The square, dark-skinned Marshal Yan Xishan ruled Shanxi, west of Beijing. Taking power in the province in 1917, he became known as the Model Governor, seeking modernization on his own terms behind the wall of mountains surrounding his domain. He promoted the development of coal and iron ore mines and the growing of high-grade cotton, while propounding a philosophy which he said brought together militarism, nationalism, anarchism, democracy, capitalism, communism, individualism, imperialism, universalism, and paternalism. To dispel lethargy and improve behaviour, he promoted an Early Morning Rising Society and a Heart Cleansing Institute, encouraged water control and tree planting, and clamped down on foot-binding. He was described by another regional leader as 'an artful man [who] never showed his inner feelings'.

The son of poor farmers, the northern warlord Feng Yuxiang was a giant of a man. He worked as a bricklayer, labourer and servant before joining an imperial army, and then branching out on his own. He spouted progressive ideas and sought aid from the Soviet Union. Preaching frugality, he liked to present himself as a peasant – he received an American journalist for an interview squatting on the ground in his underwear, chewing water-melon seeds. But he also used a private train, and consumed enormous breakfasts to enable him to eat sparingly during the day. Unlike most warlords, Feng lacked a base and was constantly on the move.

Having been converted to Methodism and married the Chinese secretary of a YWCA branch, he was known as the Christian General; as they marched, his men sang songs on the need to conserve ammunition to the tune of 'Hark! the Herald Angels Sing'. Feng was said to baptize them with fire hoses, though he replied that the areas in which he operated were too poor to have such devices, and he preferred to do the job in Baptist fashion by having them wade through rivers. His decision to change sides in a contest for Beijing in 1924 earned him a second nickname – the Betraying General.[18]

Wu Peifu, the victor of Hunan who had then turned against the ungrateful Duan Qirui, was the dominant militarist in central China. The most cultivated of the warlords, having obtained an imperial degree, he prided himself on his calligraphic skills, though there were suggestions that he enlisted the help of his secretary. With receding, dark-reddish hair and brown eyes, he was dubbed the Philosopher General and hung George Washington's portrait on the wall of his study. A fierce patriot, he refused to enter the foreign concessions even for much-needed medical help, though he enjoyed British support in their common area of interest in the Middle Yangzi.

For a time, he impressed foreign observers as the man who might unite China, but he proved incapable of that role. He toyed with revolutionaries; his true colours were shown, however, when he had striking railway workers summarily beheaded beside the track, absorbed bandit gangs into his army, and felled trees that anchored the banks of the Yellow River to provide cash-generating timber. He drank heavily, both Chinese spirits and imported brandy. In an implied reproach, Feng Yuxiang sent him a large porcelain vase filled with liquid; Wu drank from it, and then spat out the mouthful on finding that it was water.[19]

The three-man 'Guangxi Clique', who had schemed their way to running their south-western province, enjoyed a solid local base, and were genuinely reformist, encouraging education and welfare, though the poverty and backwardness of their region limited them – their leader, Li Zongren, recalled his terror when he first saw a steam engine on a visit to Guangdong. They paid their bills from the tax on opium transported through Guangxi from Yunnan to Guangdong. A British intelligence report described Li as 'small, sturdy and ugly. Gives the impression of great mental and physical vigour, and of being possessed of moral and physical courage to an unusual degree.' The second member of the clique, Bai Chongxi, was a clever tactician, a Muslim who ate pork and drank wine and had eleven children; he was compared to an icon of early Chinese military skill, Zhuge Liang, famed for his clever tactics and use of subterfuge. The third Guangxi figure, Huang Xuchu, a small, apparently unassuming man, was an effective organizer and administrator. Between them, the clique members conjured up images of the classical heroes of the *Romance of the Three Kingdoms*, each playing his appointed role as they alternated between government and rebellion in pursuit of provincial autonomy.[20]

In the huge but sparsely populated territory of Xinjiang in the Far West, Yang Zengxin, an imperial official who had declared for the republic, dispatched two rivals by beheading them as they sat at table during a banquet. Adopting divide-and-rule tactics towards the majority Muslim communities, he gave his relatives and cronies key posts and ran a system in which corruption was rampant. Yunnanese by origin, the governor tried to isolate the territory from the rest of China, exploiting its resources to swell his bank accounts in the foreign concession of Tianjin. He imposed strict censorship, and was said to have kept the key of the telegraph office with him at night. He also did all he could to exclude Russian influence, particularly after the Bolshevik Revolution. Factories were banned since they might foster a working class that could organize against his regime.[21]

Another Yunnanese, the illiterate Ma Fushing, controlled the most westerly part of China, round the Silk Road city of Kashgar, claiming the region's mineral and oil rights as his personal possession. The British consul-general described him as 'a short, grizzled, monkey-like man with a long, wispy moustache and fierce eyes, resplendently arrayed in a saxe-blue Chinese Field Marshal's uniform several sizes too large for him, complete with plumed hat, several rows of stars and medals and gold lace epaulettes the size of hassocks flapping from his shoulders'. But Ma was very far from a comic opera figure. He had his victims fed into a large hay-making machine to amputate their limbs joint by joint – if this stopped short of death, they might be chained on a bench below a wall on which they were nailed. Eventually, even Yang Zengxin had enough. His troops marched on Kashgar, and captured Ma as he slept. He was shot the following day. His body was tied to a crucifix for people to revile and defile.[22]

The remorseless military build-up saw the combined warlord armies rise from 900,000 men to 1.5 million by the middle of the 1920s. To take the main events year by year in a chronology that illustrates how loyalties shifted:

In 1920, Wu Peifu and Zhang Zuolin drove the forces of the

Manchurian's former ally, Duan Qirui, from Beijing, while, in central China, Hunan declared self-rule.

In 1921, war broke out between Hunan and Wu, which the warlord won, while Sichuan troops tried unsuccessfully to invade Hubei.

In 1922, Wu won a war against his ally of 1920, Zhang Zuolin, for control of Beijing, where he installed a 'Cabinet of Able Men' with Li Yuanhong as president again. But internal rivalries undermined the government, the cabinet fell apart, the treasury was empty. Zhang declared Manchuria's autonomy.

In 1923, Li was ousted from the presidency and replaced by the veteran northern general Cao Kun, who won office with massive bribery. An army allied with Wu invaded Fujian.

In 1924, war broke out between Jiangsu and Zhejiang provinces. Wu and the Christian General engaged in another fight with the Manchurians, but Feng defected to the enemy to gain control of Beijing. Cao was forced to resign as president. Duan returned to head the government. Feng's troops forced Puyi to leave the Forbidden City; the last emperor went with his wife to live in Japan's concession in Tianjin.

In 1925, the Dogmeat General attacked Jiangsu, Anhui and Shanghai, but was beaten off by a local warlord. A Yangzi general staged an unsuccessful rising. Backed by the Christian General, Zhang Zuolin's principal subordinate tried a coup, which failed. Wu Peifu staged a comeback in the Middle Yangzi, and declared war on the Manchurians.

In 1926, after reaching a truce with the Old Marshal, Wu turned on the Christian General, who announced his 'retirement' and took a train to Moscow. Zhang Zuolin formed an alliance with warlords in Shandong and the eastern provinces of central China.

Despite the growing extent of warlord struggles, the size of China meant that substantial areas remained unaffected, with local elites asserting themselves and branching out into commerce and industry. As in Yuan Shikai's time, modern business did well in Manchuria and the foreign concessions. Across the Great Wall in the north-east, Japan reached a modus vivendi with the Old Marshal which benefited both sides as the foreigners pursued long-term strategic aims by pouring in investment, opening modern factories and making their railway a state of its own.

In Shanghai, where the population rose to 2.5 million, foreigners put up monumental banks and office buildings along the riverside Bund and pioneered Art Deco apartments. A growing number of Chinese moved into the two Western settlements, finding them more comfortable and safer than the native city. Leading Chinese figures were granted seats on the Municipal Council, which ran the International Settlement. The Chinese Ratepayers Association, merchant guilds, commercial associations and chambers of commerce acted as theatres for competition between new- and old-style local businesses. The General Chamber of Commerce declared its independence of Beijing, and negotiated directly with the local warlord.[23]

Canton also developed its waterfront, and had a plethora of factories making everything from matches to plastic shoes. Its labour movement provided a strong impetus for change, fuelled by a series of successful strikes and the holding of the First National Labour Conference in 1922, attended by delegates from twelve cities, most of them drawn from the immediate region. The southern city was a 'real-life laboratory for anarchists, missionaries, anti-imperialists, socialists, Western-educated reformers and unionists, all toying with schemes for societal regeneration and grass roots collective action', as a historian has written.[24]

Yet, in keeping with the weakness of central administration and despite attempts to paint the period in brighter colours, China's economy as a whole was in poor shape. The trade deficit rose with the passing of the opportunities offered by the First World War. For several years in the 1920s, the country had to import rice and wheat. Rural unemployment was put at 87 million. Infrastructure remained backward. Though railways were important to move warlord troops, construction of track was limited – little more than one third of that put down under the empire. By the mid-1920s, China had 5,237 miles of railways, mainly in the north, less than in Britain in 1850. Lines were damaged in fighting, hampering transport of civilians and goods. There were just 21,000 miles of highways across the whole country. In many areas, the traditional means of transport by waterways or on the backs of coolies persisted. A 1923 report from Sichuan noted men carrying loads of 160 pounds on their backs for fifteen miles a day.[25]

An international conference in Washington in 1922 intended to reorganize the nation's finances decided to wait until there was a cohesive central government to deal with. A consortium of banks from Britain, America, France and Japan was set up to issue fresh loans – but only when it could be sure they would be used properly.

Rather than interesting themselves in coherent economic development, the warlords grabbed what they could, using the force at their disposal. Villagers were made to hand over food, carts and pack animals. To escape looting, towns had to pay a 'departure levy' to get retreating troops to go quietly, and a 'welcome payment' to the arriving troops not to make trouble. In some cases, urban guilds stumped up money to prevent troops mutinying after their commanders stole their pay. During disasters, relief supplies were plundered.

Banks were obliged to extend loans that would never be repaid. Chambers of commerce were pressured into buying worthless bonds. Printing presses spewed out money with little or no backing; in one case notes were run off a duplicating machine. Extortion from railway companies was frequent. In Wuhan, Wu Peifu appropriated cotton, silk, cloth and hemp factories and the Hanyang ironworks. He looted the treasury of a railway line, before raising a mortgage on land along its track and a loan against its property. Turning to the Chinese River Steamship Administration, he arrested the company's boss and freed him only when he undertook to hand over the firm.[26]

Warlords slapped duties on everything from night soil to prostitutes in their quest for funds. A survey in the mid-1920s reported 673 different land taxes, some collected up to thirty-six years in advance, some applied retrospectively. Levies weighed heavily on the transport of goods; one militarist put a 100 per cent impost on railway freight, including food during a famine. In Sichuan, salt was subject to twenty-seven different duties. In Henan, there were taxes on sesame and melon seeds, wattle and persimmon cakes.[27]

Opium was a major source of funds. Drug monopolies were sold off, and taxes slapped on production, transport, sale and use. That did not stop warlords fining farmers for growing poppies, or establishing Suppression Bureaux that confiscated narcotics and then sold them. The proceeds of the traffic were reckoned to have reached 50 million yuan a year in Yunnan, 20 million in Fujian and Gansu, and 10–30 million in Sichuan. In places, opium became a form of currency, taken by soldiers as pay and by kidnappers for ransoms.

The exactions of 'resident' warlords who held on to settled territory could be onerous enough; 'itinerant' military units were often much worse, as they took what they wanted before moving on. Granaries were broken open, and men were press-ganged into service, when they did not volunteer to join armies that offered the promise of a new life away from the vagaries of rural existence. Worst hit of all were areas where undisciplined warlord forces and bandits overlapped, with little or no distinction between them. Such was the chaos that some warlords, rather than asking for interest on funds deposited with foreign banks, offered to pay for the security the Western institutions provided. 'Better to be a dog in peace than a man in troubled times', as a saying went.

A Japanese account from Shandong reported that:

Not only have arson, theft and rape occurred everywhere, as if wild beasts were on the prowl, but murders and kidnappings are performed in broad daylight. Peasants in the same locale are pillaged two or three times by outsiders. Bandits and warlord factions abscond with their chickens and dogs. The people are without houses, without food and their plight has become extremely miserable . . . no matter how much time elapses, the same conditions continue to persist.[28]

At the start of the warlord era, in 1920, bad harvests and drought caused famine in Zhili, Shandong, Shanxi, Shaanxi and Henan. Relief agencies estimated that 40 per cent of the population were destitute in some areas, and noted that many millions were living on sawdust, thistles, roots, tree bark and flour made of ground stones and leaves. One district in Hubei had no rainfall for the whole of 1920, a hailstorm in 1921 that damaged spring crops, a frost in 1923 that had the same effect, and then heavy flooding. Across the country, famines are thought to have taken 4–6 million lives in 1921–2. A third of farmers were believed to be in debt, paying interest that could reach 200 per cent a year.[29]

Banditry boomed. Some gangs were small, localized groups of drifters. Others were more permanent, sometimes led by sons of reasonably well-off farmers who found they had no means of advancement and were turned against society by real or perceived injustices meted out to them. One of the most famous bandits, known as Old Foreigner for his height and bushy hair, led 10,000 men to occupy Henan and Anhui cities. There were a few women bandit chiefs, such as Mama Chao with 600–700 female followers in southern Shandong, and, in Anhui, a woman known as Two-Gun Chang, who went into action with a pistol in each hand.[30]

Undisciplined warlord soldiers became bandits, and vice versa. The dividing line between protective and predatory force was often thin. If a gang leader was strong enough, he might parlay this into a position with a regional militarist, and absorption into his army. 'To become an official, carry a big stick,' went one saying.

The weakness of the central state and its inability to provide a modicum of law and order made local officials that much more ready to turn a blind eye to marauding bands or compromise with them. As a rule, armies did not pursue outlaws, but reached agreements. The bigger, more cohesive bands saw themselves as heirs to the tradition of upright outlaws opposing bad rulers enshrined in the popular tales of the *Water Margin* saga. As one song had it:

> Bandits make a stir,
> Impoverishing the wealthy, enriching the poor.
> They kidnap for ransom and eat all they can hold
> Then the leftover silver they give to the old.[31]

The reality was a lot less appealing. Kidnapping became a growth industry, the prey known as 'tickets' – 'lottery tickets' for the rich, 'pawn tickets' for the poor, 'quick tickets' for young women if their families wanted them back before night fell. When captives were killed, the ticket was 'torn up'. If payment was not immediately forthcoming, the victims' ears might be sent to their homes as encouragement. Or they could be subjected to punishments – 'Burning the God of Good Fortune', in which their bodies were burned with incense sticks, or the 'Carpet Bed', in which they were made to lie naked on thorns, or 'Housekeeping', in which their feet were nailed to the floor if the bandits left their base.[32]

One kidnapping in May 1925 was unusually well documented owing to the presence among foreigners grabbed from the Blue Train Express from Nanjing to Beijing of the editor of a Shanghai newspaper, John Powell. A gang of about a thousand bandits, under a petty warlord who called his force the Shandong People's Liberation Army, stopped the train in Shandong at night, and looted it down to the light bulbs. They led thirty foreigners away on a long, arduous journey through the mountains to their fort; as they passed through villages, the inhabitants crowded round to see their first Westerners. Some captives rode on mules, but most were on foot. A very fat Italian lawyer had to be carried for part of the way. Many of the victims wore the clothes in which they had been sleeping, though the Italian's young female personal assistant was in a shirt and tight black bloomers. Among the group was a sister-in-law of John D. Rockefeller Jnr, whose maid concealed her mistress's jewels under her nightdress.

In the fort, the captives were fed dog meat and scorpion flesh. A missionary, who contacted them, got a local man to take in ham and a collection of New Testament bibles, which did not go down well with a massively built Jewish car dealer from Shanghai among the prisoners. Then a Shanghai advertising agent, Carl Crow, got relief parcels sent in. Exploring the surrounding peaks after his guards passed out from drink, Powell stumbled across another fort with a room full of kidnapped children.[33]

Negotiations were held, with a Shanghai gangster and two Americans as go-betweens. The bandits wanted their region to be separated from Shandong, under international control. They did not get that, but the authorities agreed to pay them cash and integrate them into the army, as well as giving the foreigners compensation. However, they made the mistake of releasing their captives before getting the money, which was grabbed by the Shandong troops, who subsequently machine-gunned 600 of the bandits and beheaded their chief.

As well as outlaws, secret societies were particularly important in unsettled areas like Shandong, Henan and Hebei; some reached up into Manchuria. Members of the biggest anti-warlord group, the Red Spears, in central-northern China, assembled with weapons in the evening to worship spirits, burn incense, recite magic formulae and carry out military practice, swallowing ashes of amulets with mystic inscriptions to confer invulnerability. Before a military confrontation, the Grand Master appeared with one shoulder bared and a sword between his teeth, a magic flag in one hand, leading a goat. The goat's head was cut off, its blood scattered on the flag, the earth dug up and the animal's entrails wrapped round the waists of the troops. Then battle could be joined.[34]

The Spears resisted taxation, protected villagers from being press-ganged and repelled bandits, though some members went in for much the same line of work. With 3 million adherents, the movement could muster 100,000 men to attack a city. In 1925, it helped Wu Peifu to take Henan after he promised a three-year tax holiday, on which he reneged, driving the society into bitter rebellion. The Spears were said to have killed 50,000 of his soldiers, a measure of quantity rather than a precise number, but still a sign of their strength.[35]

Members of the Iron Gate Society for young unmarried women, which was descended from the Red Lantern wing of the Boxers, chanted magic formulae to divert enemy bullets into baskets held in their left hand. Other groups established rudimentary local administration, including the United Village Society of Shandong, which organized guard forces for villages, linking them together to resist big bandit bands. In the same province, the Limitless Society recruited soldiers known as 'labourers', who were forbidden sexual intercourse and the meat of wild animals. After massacring a local official and his family, they fought off an army attack, forcing its commander to reach a ceasefire.[36]

The Big Sword group carried on the anti-Christian ideology inherited from the Boxers. The Spirit Soldiers of Sichuan and Hubei, designated by their yellow turbans, attracted 100,000 members and controlled forty districts, refusing to pay taxes, resisting warlord advances and blaming foreigners for the evils of modernization as they awaited the restoration of the pre-Qing dynasty. Another Ming restoration movement, the Heavenly Gate Society of Henan and Hebei, beat off warlord troops and killed an emissary sent by the Christian General; an attack by his troops forced the sect's leader to flee, but he returned to defeat a division of the warlord's men and to reclaim his territory.[37]

For the young Mao Zedong, there was a certain dialectical logic in what was happening; order could only come out of disorder, chaos was part of the historical process, he argued. But, in real terms, there was no guarantee that the anarchy would ever end. The national fabric which had frayed in the last six decades of imperial rule was being ripped apart by a combination of political, military, economic and social factors. That made it all the more surprising that an answer should come from the obscure and irascible military lieutenant of a man whose resources paled beside those of the great warlords.

9

Ice and Ancient Charcoal

While the major conflicts of the warlord era were unfolding primarily in northern China, Sun Yat-sen never abandoned his idea of establishing a power base in his home region of the south. In 1917, after Yuan Shikai's death, he had set up a Nationalist Republic of his own in Canton. This flopped, but he returned in 1922 to try to mount an expedition from Guangdong to unify China.

The province was under the influence of the 1911 revolutionary Chen Jiongming, who was known as the 'Hakka General', because of his roots among the minority Hakka people in the area. He pursued serious reform, with a provincial constitution limiting military spending to one third of the budget. Chen Duxiu, who was later to head the infant Communist Party, was put in charge of education, which was to get 20 per cent of government expenditure. Students were sent to study at an anarchist college in France. Taking a federalist approach, Chen favoured the establishment of an association of southern states, leaving the rest of China to the warlords of the north and centre. Though he allowed Sun to use Guangdong as a springboard, he had no time for the doctor's expedition. The hagiography of Sun by both Nationalists and Communists has sullied Chen's reputation. But, at the time, he was described by the British consul in Canton as one of the ablest generals in China. Soviet agents called him a brilliant organizer, who had the sympathy of the masses.

Sun was joined in Guangdong by his main military aide, Chiang Kai-shek, the revolutionary who had plunged into what he called 'a life of debauchery' after the murder of his patron, Chen Qimei, by Yuan Shikai's agents in Shanghai. Chiang appears to have become a member of the powerful underworld Green Gang there, and tried, on one occasion, to seduce a thirteen-year-old girl in a hotel in the International

Settlement. She fled, but, two years later, he persuaded her to marry him, despite a nineteen-year age difference. (He had legally separated from his first wife, whom he had wed as a teenager in an arranged village marriage, and who bore them a son.) On the honeymoon, the groom infected his bride with gonorrhea; the doctor warned them that the German treatment he administered would make them both sterile. Still, she seems to have forgiven him, and went with him to Guangdong.[1]

In the spring of 1922, Sun and Chiang (accompanied by Chiang's wife) set out from Canton on a flotilla of boats along rivers leading north. Theirs was a hopeless quest, and the doctor was soon forced to give up. Egged on by Chiang, who hated Chen, Sun decided that the Hakka General was his adversary. Hurrying back to Canton, he warned that he had 'poisonous shells capable of finishing off sixty battalions in three hours'. That was enough to provoke Chen's principal lieutenant into a night-time attack on Sun's residence. The doctor escaped to a waterside fort, where loyal boats awaited him. His wife, Soong Qingling, fled through the countryside as shells fell around her, rejoining him on the river. Behind them, his manuscripts were destroyed as their house went up in flames.

Sun spent six weeks on a gunship on the Pearl River with Chiang and their wives. For safety's sake, they moored off the sandbank which housed the British concession in Canton. Eventually, they decided they had had enough and took advantage of a safe conduct from the British to go to Hong Kong. From there, they returned to Shanghai.

Sun remained convinced that he needed a power base in the south from which to launch his cherished expedition to the north to reunify China. Lacking an army of his own, he funded mercenaries from other southern provinces, who planned an attack on Guangdong. The cash appears to have come from his Overseas Chinese backers.

The Hakka General was encountering the classic problem of Chinese reformers. His administration was running out of money with which to pay for its changes. Merchants were alienated by tax rises. As the mercenaries advanced on Canton, Chen fled to his home area in the east of the province. At the end of February 1923, Sun travelled south to lead the new administration, accompanied by Chiang.

Apart from his southern roots, Canton had distinct attractions for the doctor. The distance from the north meant Guangdong was free from the influence of the major warlords. Though most of the city was still a jumble of traditional streets and small shops, it was relatively prosperous by the standards of China of the time, and, in the judgement of the historian Ming Chan, 'perhaps the most politically open and liberal city under Chinese rule'. With 800,000 inhabitants, it had new factories, a labour movement and strong overseas links. The streets were being improved, and the city wall was being torn down to make more room.[2]

Still, the regime was rackety. The mercenaries demanded heavy subsistence payments, which were often withheld from soldiers by officers. When his men complained about not being paid, a commander replied, 'Since you have guns, why should you be short of rations?' Troops indulged in robbery, piracy and kidnapping, and ran protection rackets, gambling, prostitution and drugs. Strapped for cash, Sun's administration forced merchants to lend it money, auctioned monopolies and official jobs, and slapped taxes on everything from pigs to dancing halls offering the services of Russian women. Bank notes fell to a fifth of their face value. Sun tried to grab customs duties earmarked for Beijing, but had to retreat in the face of threats from foreign powers, which were paid their indemnities and loan interest from the revenue. An American visitor described Canton as 'probably the most misgoverned city in China'.[3]

The doctor left much of the administration to others, while he expounded his principles of nationalism, democracy and the people's livelihood. The first of these did not stop him seeking help from abroad in his quest to unite China. The United States and Britain rebuffed him, but he found a friend in the Soviet Union and a junior ally in the infant Chinese Communist Party.[4]

The Comintern agent Hans Sneevliet, who had orchestrated the formation of the CCP, forced its unwilling members to collaborate with Sun's Nationalist KMT, which the Kremlin declared to be a revolutionary party. The Chinese Communists would have preferred to maintain their separate identity, but Moscow favoured united-front tactics. So the CCP buckled, and went along with an arrangement for its members to join the KMT.

The relationship had major ideological implications for the Communists. Given the heterodox nature of their much bigger ally, they had to moderate their policies. They were now in league with a movement that contained plenty of landlords and businessmen. That was fine by Stalin, but it dismayed Trotsky with his doctrine of permanent revolution. As a result, the united front became a function of the battle between the two men fighting thousands of miles away, neither of whom knew anything much about China.

Before going to Canton in 1923, Sun had deepened the KMT–CCP relationship in talks with another Soviet envoy, Adolf Joffe, that ended with a joint statement declaring the need for national unity and independence. At the doctor's insistence, it added that China was not ready for Communism. To a friend, he compared Soviet help to a straw held out to a man drowning in a river. 'England and America, on the bank, shout at me on no account to clutch at the Russian straw,' he went on. 'But do they help me? No. They jeer and at the same time tell me not to clutch the Russian straw. I know it is a straw, but better than nothing.'[5]

He sent Chiang to Moscow to try to enlist Soviet aid for the unifying expedition of which he still dreamed. His lieutenant met Trotsky, and was shown Red Army training exercises. But the Comintern refused to back the KMT campaign to the north. Such an expedition, it told Chiang, would be premature, adventurous and doomed to failure; the party's first task should be to develop an army and win over the masses.[6]

Condemned to carry the bad news home on the Trans-Siberian Express, Chiang railed in letters to his wife against the Soviets for their ignorance and narrow outlook. Only a third of what they said could be believed, he wrote. Their sole aim was to boost the CCP at the KMT's expense. Instead of returning to Canton to report in person to Sun, he stamped off to his home village in Zhejiang province to sulk.[7]

Unknown to Chiang, Moscow's answer to the KMT approach had already turned up in the south in the shape of Mikhail Markovich Gruzenberg, using the alias of Borodin. His job was to organize Sun's party on Leninist lines while other advisers helped it to set up an army. An experienced Comintern agent, the thick-set, 39-year-old Russian, with a heavy moustache, shaggy hair and deep bass voice, swiftly proved his worth by rallying an ad hoc force to repel an attack on Canton by Chen Jiongming. Then he went to work to solidify the united front, using not only his own skill and experience but also big subsidies from Moscow.[8]

For the USSR, the prospect of establishing a base of influence in the world's most heavily populated nation was irresistible. China, declared Lenin, was seething and it was Moscow's duty to keep the pot boiling. Canton was promising soil given its labour movement, its progressive experience under Chen Jiongming and its proximity to Hong Kong, which meant it could be presented as a launching pad against British imperialism. Sun rejected class struggle, and Borodin found Canton a 'veritable Babel', calling the doctor 'an enlightened little satrap', but each side needed the other, and the KMT leader told supporters in the United States, who asked if he knew the adviser's real name, that Borodin was 'China's Lafayette'.[9]

A KMT Congress in January 1924 adopted the Russian's organizational plan, which put the party above the government, duplicating ministerial organs in Leninist fashion. This, and the absence of electoral democracy, meant that whoever controlled the central party institutions could exercise autocratic power, whether from left, centre or right.[10]

Sun's Three Principles were the guiding ideology. The doctor was elected as the KMT's life president. Communists got ten seats on the forty-one-member Central Executive Committee, and headed the important Organization Department. They also took a leading role in revolutionary work among the peasants. A Communist son of a rich Cantonese landowner, Peng Pai, set up training institutes for small farmers and a union for rickshaw pullers. In 1926, Mao Zedong, who had been promoted with the backing of the KMT left to take charge of the Propaganda Department, was appointed to the Peasant Movement Committee. While other Communists still hankered after autonomy from Sun's party, their future leader was very happy to collaborate.[11]

Having adopted Borodin's organizational ideas, which accorded with his insistence on autocratic leadership, Sun was careful not to let himself be led along the Bolshevik ideological path. He had a reference to the leading role of workers and peasants expunged from the KMT manifesto. Two thirds of party officials were reckoned to be non-leftists.

At the end of 1923, the doctor also made a secret attempt to diversify his foreign backers by outlining a sweeping plan to the American minister in China, Jacob Schurman, who was visiting Canton. According to the *New York Times* correspondent Hallett Abend, who saw the record of the conversation, the KMT leader proposed that the US, Britain, France, Germany and Italy – but not Japan – should send in forces to take over China's provincial capitals from the warlords, assuming control of railways, rivers, ports and telegraph and dispatching experts to modernize them. After five years, elections would be held and authority would gradually revert to the Chinese. For a man who had made a fetish of nationalism and whose city was plastered with anti-foreign placards, it was a mad idea, and has, not surprisingly, been expunged from the Sun-ist canon. Having rejected the League of Nations, the US Congress would not agree in any circumstances to troops going to China in an ultimate imperialist undertaking. The other powers Sun had in mind were equally frosty. The doctor renewed his appeal, but got nowhere. He was left with his single 'straw'.*[12]

Having overhauled the KMT political organization, the Soviets set about giving it an army. The first senior military adviser Moscow sent in was drowned as he crossed a river on horseback. His successor, Vasilii Konstantinovich Blyukher, who adopted the pseudonym of Galen, would have a major impact on the evolution of China. From a poor peasant family, the 34-year-old general was a hero of the Russian civil war. Powerfully built, with the arms of a boxer, grey eyes, bushy eyebrows, a black moustache and shaven head, he was described by an American journalist as 'fiercely energetic, a tough taskmaster . . . forever stomping about, filled with ideas'. He got on well with the Chinese, enjoying their food, unconcerned about matters of status so long as affairs were dealt with efficiently. No ideologue, he warned that revolution was 'not so simple'. A visiting Soviet diplomat reported that the Chinese had such confidence in him that 'his every statement on questions pertaining to military operations was considered to be law.'[13]

Galen thought an army of only three or four well-trained divisions would sweep its way through the warlord forces. He insisted on the limits of what the Russians could do; holding up both hands, he pointed to one little finger – that was the USSR, the other nine were the Chinese. Still, Moscow's role was essential. Soviet freighters brought in rifles, artillery and ammunition. A military academy was established on Whampoa Island outside Canton in the Pearl River. The aim was to produce an elite force, operating on Red Army lines with political commissars; they included the cultivated, handsome son of a mandarin family, Zhou Enlai, who had joined the Communist Party while working in France in 1921 and had been sent back to China by Moscow.

Having sulked enough in his home village, Chiang Kai-shek came back to Canton to head the military school. Under him, Whampoa

---

* Sun engaged Western help of a different kind in the person of a British arms dealer, Morris 'Two-Gun' Cohen, who acted as his bodyguard.

became a key element in the KMT power structure, producing graduates whose influence would be felt for more than two decades. It combined Russian teaching, Japanese techniques Chiang had experienced as a cadet across the sea, and strands from Chinese tradition. The young men were paid and well looked after, with decent food. They were told to proselytize for the revolution and lead by example, to be austere, daring and brave, not to gamble or visit brothels. Chiang imposed a martinet regime, upbraiding pupils for leaving a button undone. Collective responsibility provided for the execution of units which retreated without orders, including officers.[14]

The numbers of students at the academy swelled from 645 in the first class in 1924 to 3,000 graduates by 1926. Some came from Mongolia, Tibet, Thailand, Korea and Vietnam, among them a revolutionary called Nguyen Ai Quoc, later known as Ho Chi Minh. At the opening of the academy, Sun acknowledged that, after thirteen years, the revolution was 'just an empty name and . . . a complete failure'. To change that, the new army would supply the necessary muscle.

From the start, the make-up of the academy was not as revolutionary as the Russians would have hoped. Educational requirements meant that three quarters of the initial intake was made up of sons of landlords, middle-income peasants or officials. Many party branches asked to recommend young men were run by non-leftists. Cadets were nationalistic, but this did not make them adherents of the left. A strong rightist group soon emerged as Chiang, given his distrust of the Soviets, imposed a traditional father-figure system with which students were familiar. As with Borodin's reorganization of the Kuomintang, there was no guarantee of the new model army following the political course the Russians envisaged. Once they got beyond the immediate control of the Soviet advisers, the military and the political movements could each use the efficiency bestowed by Moscow for their own purpose, and, if they combined in the person of a single leader, their authority could be irresistible.

The political climate in Canton was volatile. Three days after the inauguration of the Whampoa Military Academy, a Vietnamese threw a bomb into a dinner held for the visiting French governor of Indochina in a hotel in the foreign concession. Several guests were killed. The Western authorities slapped restrictions on access to the area for Chinese. Sun's government protested. A workers' picket cut off the concession. Though a compromise was reached, the radicalism of the workers rose, encouraged by the Russians and the KMT left.

Merchants, who had turned against 'Sun the Windbag', set up a self-defence militia, numbering anywhere from 6,000 to 12,000 men. Similar groups sprouted elsewhere in Guangdong. In response, the government founded an armed Labour Volunteer Corps. The merchants ordered nearly 10,000 rifles and pistols from Europe. When these arrived on a Norwegian cargo ship in August 1924, Sun ordered them to be seized and taken to Whampoa. The merchants protested with business strikes.[15]

Despite all this, the doctor decided to have another try at an expedition to the north. He thought the war between Wu Peifu and Zhang Zuolin might enable him to re-enter national politics; he intended to back the Manchurians, apparently untroubled by allying with a reactionary warlord. But his forces were pitifully small; Chiang refused to join in, arguing that control of Canton was more important. Most Whampoa cadets stayed behind.[16]

Fighting between the Nationalist KMT forces and the merchants broke out on 10 October 1924. Whampoa cadets participated in an assault on the fortified business district. Shells rained down as hand-to-hand combats raged along rooftops. Reports of the death toll varied wildly – from thirty to 284 for the government, 50–200 for the merchant forces, and 300 civilians. Up to 1,000 buildings were destroyed. The new army had been blooded. The British Communist Party sent a cable of congratulations for the 'gallant struggle against foreign Imperialism and native capitalism'.[17]

During the battle, Sun returned briefly to Canton for a lantern-lit parade of 20,000 people for his birthday. He called at Whampoa, where Chiang recorded him as saying, 'Even if I should die, my conscience will be at peace.' Then, he sailed down the Pearl River to Hong Kong on his way to Shanghai and Beijing to seek a wider role, calling Canton 'a city of death'. Visiting Japan before heading for the capital, he blamed his country's woes on the West and proclaimed 'the doctrine of greater Asia'. The war in the north opened the way to a 'great central revolution', he added. Unfortunately for him, the ally he sought had no interest in him, Zhang referring to the KMT as 'the cancer of China'. Reaching Beijing, Sun had abdominal pains and fainted. On New Year's Eve, he entered an American-funded hospital.[18]

In the south, the KMT army got a second chance to prove itself in action when Chen Jiongming advanced on Canton at the beginning of 1925. The performance of Chiang's forces was mixed. Communications and maps were poor; a leading commander collapsed under the strain and hid under a bush; the planned scaling of the wall of an enemy city turned into a fiasco when the storming party was not provided with ladders. Still, with the advice of Galen, the Nationalist forces triumphed in what was known as the Eastern Expedition, chasing their foes across the border into Fujian.

The campaign ended with the reported capture of 12–13,000 rifles, 110 machine guns, 8 million cartridges, 1,500 shells, 30 old cannons, 6 modern mountain guns and 3 wireless sets. Political commissars under Zhou Enlai promised peasants land reform. Disciplined Whampoa soldiers did not plunder, press men into service or loot towns. Their wounded got extra pay, and the dead were properly buried. Even the normally hostile *North China Daily News* acknowledged 'a really fine body of troops, well armed and sternly disciplined and, in every way, superior to any who might be expected to oppose them'.[19]

While the Whampoa troops fought his old foe, Sun underwent an operation in Beijing that found terminal liver cancer. In mid-February, he was moved to the home of a KMT member in the capital, where he was joined by Borodin. He dictated his last will and a political testament, calling for the masses to be roused to obtain international equality for China. Another document, drafted by the Russian, expressed the 'fervent hope' that China and the Soviet Union would advance together to 'victory in the great struggle for the liberation of the oppressed peoples of the world'.

On 12 March 1925, Sun died, aged fifty-nine. His second wife and son wanted a Protestant ceremony since he had been a Christian – just before he expired, he was reported to have murmured, 'As Christ was sent by God to the world, so God also sent me.' Others thought a foreign religion unsuitable for a nationalist revolutionary. So two services were held. Flags on the Soviet legation were flown at half-mast. A coffin was brought from Russia; it was said to be like Lenin's, but Reuters reported that it was 'not new', and was made of tin with a thin bronze covering. It was not used.[20]

Sun may have been an ineffective administrator and a continually frustrated dreamer, but he was the figurehead round which the regime in

Guangdong and Kuomintang supporters elsewhere in China gravitated. Funeral ceremonies were held across the country. In Wuhan, 8,000 people attended a tribute. In death, the doctor became a lay saint as he had never been in life, the basis of a new secular religion that rejected both warlords and imperialism. His heirs, on both the left and right, would make the most of that, their task facilitated by the imprecision of the doctor's thinking. Two years after his death, KMT soldiers put his portrait in the place of crucifixes in Christian churches; one of their posters declared: 'Jesus Christ is dead. Why not worship something alive such as Nationalism?' The Sun myth, epitomized by avuncular portraits and the reading of his will at KMT meetings, created a new political culture, buttressed by propaganda, slogans and speech-making that appeared to offer an escape from the warlord jungle.

Belonging to the extended Sun family was a passport to respect – his son, Sun Fo, remained a prominent figure for decades and his widow held a revered place as the bearer of her husband's legacy, described by a British visitor as 'the flame in the paper lantern carried at the head of the Nationalist procession'. More prosaically, Sun's name was used for a make of cigarettes which appealed to the patriotism of smokers, and for a brand of olives whose advertising said that their consumption would commemorate him.[21]

The reality was that the Nationalists faced a raft of problems in Canton. Prices were shooting up; unemployment increased; the city was hit by strikes. New taxes were imposed; still, teachers' pay fell eight months in arrears. Crime rose. Some banks stopped handling cash because of the number of robberies. Mercenaries kidnapped and levied summary fines at will.[22]

Matters were aggravated by the lack of a clearly designated heir to Sun. The two main contenders were Wang Jingwei and Hu Hanmin. Wang, the dashing revolutionary who had tried to assassinate the regent in 1910, was the more popular, a good orator and closest to Borodin. Aged forty-one, he had been at the doctor's bedside in his last days, taking down his will. 'An ambitious man, capable of resolute and energetic action, when he is certain of having behind him power and support,' a Russian report noted. A photograph shows him in a white suit, his hair wavy and pomaded, his face full, his eyes cheerful. A Soviet woman interpreter described him as 'a humbler of female hearts'.[23]

Four years Wang's senior, Hu was more in the traditional scholar-administrator mould. He had gained experience as governor of Guang-dong after the revolution, and had worked closely with Sun during the doctor's brief spell as president. Slim, with receding hair and large round spectacles, he lacked Wang's personal magnetism, and his indifference to the corruption of his brothers earned him unpopularity. The third major figure, Liao Zhongkai, was a manager, not a leadership contender, while Chiang Kai-shek was seen as a military man with no claim to a big role in civilian administration.

That was a serious misjudgement of the fiercely ambitious 38-year-old, showing a failure to appreciate the importance of military power. Chiang was easy to underestimate. Known for his bad temper, he appeared to KMT leaders as a rough, provincial type who spoke with a strong regional accent and lacked their ideological veneer. His wife overheard Wang's imperious spouse, Chen Bijun, and smart ladies from Shanghai deriding him as a peasant. But Chiang was perceptive as to where power lay. 'If I control the army, I will have the power to control the country,' he told his wife. 'It is my road to leadership.'[24]

To start with, Wang Jingwei came out on top. Backed by Borodin, he got the better of Hu Hanmin to become chairman of the National Government of the Chinese Republic proclaimed after Sun's death. Hu was sidelined as foreign minister: since nobody recognized Canton, there was little foreign relating to do. Liao Zhongkai handled finance, and caused alarm among corrupt elements in the regime, including Hu's brothers, by launching a campaign against graft.

The mercenaries were also criticized, their chiefs accused of collabor-ating with the government's enemies and of being in the pay of Wu Peifu. In response, they occupied the arsenal, and seized telephone, telegraph and lighting services, dug in east of Canton, and threw up barricades on the riverside Bund. KMT troops advanced against them, and full-scale fighting began in which government gunboats bombarded mercenary positions. A thousand Whampoa cadets crossed the river at night in a surprise assault. After six days, most mercenaries had surren-dered or fled. The government gained 16,600 rifles, 120 machine guns and 20 cannons.[25]

The victory came at a moment when a national anti-foreign move-ment was heightening the radicalization across China. In Shanghai, on 30 May, a junior British police officer ordered Sikhs under his command to fire into a crowd marching to support strikers at a Japanese-owned weaving mill. Eleven demonstrators died and dozens were wounded. A wave of boycotts revived the nationalist spirit of the May Fourth movement.

In Hong Kong, trade unions called a strike for improved working conditions, equality of treatment for Chinese, the end of child labour, reversal of rent rises, the right of Chinese to vote for members of the legislative council, and an end to racial discrimination. Tens of thousands of strikers left the colony for Canton, where they were given food and shelter – the Russians supplied them with funds in a bid to weaken the imperialists.

On 23 June, a large anti-foreign demonstration marched down the tree-lined Bund by the Pearl River. As it came abreast of the bridge to the Shameen sandbank that housed the Western concessions, firing broke out; the Chinese insisted that the British and French started it, but the British consul pointed the finger at Whampoa cadets among the protestors. At least fifty Chinese died, twenty from the academy. One foreigner was killed – a French merchant hit by a bullet in the head; four were injured.

The Shameen sandbank came under siege behind its network of concrete blockhouses, barbed wire, and sandbagged machine-gun nests. Indian reinforcements were dispatched from Hong Kong to strengthen the defence. Eight foreign warships anchored in the river. On the other side, more workers arrived from Hong Kong, swelling the numbers living in improvised camps to 100,000. British products were banned. Some of the strikers staged robberies, ran protection rackets and sprang colleagues from jail. Water, food and electricity were cut off from missionary hospitals; at a foreign asylum for the insane, strikers turned 300 inmates out on to the street.[26]

The atmosphere was made even more febrile by rumours of a right-wing coup. On 20 August, the small, slight KMT manager, Liao Zhong-kai, was assassinated by gunmen as he arrived at party headquarters. Martial law was declared, and a hundred arrests were made. Chiang shot a suspect dead at point-blank range. A list of names found in the pocket of one of the assassins, who had been killed by guards, led to a member of a secret society set up by a brother of Hu Hanmin. The foreign minister went into hiding in a derelict building, but was found and sent to Moscow to experience the benefits of Communism.[27]

The reconstituted National Revolutionary Army (NRA) then repulsed a fresh offensive by Chen Jiongming, who fled to Hong Kong, where he remained in exile until he died in 1933. Canton was now run by a politico-military triumvirate of Wang, Chiang and Borodin. It seemed to be solidly leftist, under the influence of the adviser and needing the steady flow of money and arms from the USSR. But Chiang retained his reservations about the Soviets. At a lecture, he drew a goose and a stove on a blackboard. The bird represented Russia; if it was not cooked very soon, he warned, it would get so big that it could catch the cook and do the cooking itself, putting the Chinese on the fire.[28]

In the middle of March 1926, a murky affair erupted which appears to have started with an attempt by left-wingers, who may have known of the general's sentiments, to kidnap him and ship him to Moscow. Chiang exploited the situation skilfully to launch a coup of his own. This was facilitated by Wang being confined to bed with diabetes, and by the absence of Borodin and Galen, who were visiting the Christian General in the north.

Communists were rounded up, among them Zhou Enlai. Soviet advisers were put under 'protective custody', and some were sent home. Chiang got the KMT Central Executive Committee to pass a resolution that 'comrades of the left . . . should retire for a while'. At the beginning of April, Wang left for Hong Kong on his way to exile in France. Returning from his trip to the north, Borodin had no alternative but to go along with the way in which the power structure he had established was being used against the left. He had to agree to the removal of Communists from official posts or their downgrading – Mao was among those sacked. CCP instructions were made subject to KMT approval. Chiang's victory heightened the militarization of the regime, and his next move was to send the Revolutionary Army on its biggest campaign to date, one which would change the face of China.

On 1 July 1926, the KMT government in Canton issued a proclamation: 'To protect the welfare of the people we must overthrow all warlords and wipe out reactionary power so that we may implement the Three People's Principles and complete the National Revolution.' Chiang Kai-shek was given overriding powers to lead the expedition to the north of which Sun Yat-sen had dreamed and which, though rarely remembered outside China today, would constitute one of the biggest campaigns between the two world wars and would show that, whatever his deficiencies as a battlefield commander, Chiang was a consummate military politician.

Watching the Cantonese leave on their expedition to the north in the high summer of 1926, Hallett Abend of the *New York Times* judged the undertaking to be 'hopeless folly'. The New Revolutionary Army (NRA) was heavily outnumbered by warlord troops. Its soldiers, Abend noted, were 'mostly little men . . . clad in ill-fitting cotton uniforms of dirty grey or dusty yellow'. Behind them, Canton was still unsettled by the strikers. Money was short and, though Chiang had asserted his supremacy, divisions between the right and left of the Kuomintang simmered just below the surface.[29]

Still, the Nationalists had advantages which the warlords could hardly grasp. For all its internal dissonances, the KMT was a real, organized political force, with a wide-ranging appeal that could win the support of nationalists, democrats, modernizers, technocrats, progressives, seekers after social justice, educational reformers, entrepreneurs, and all who wanted China to achieve internal peace, modernize and play its proper world role. Though Chiang had sidelined them from leadership politics, the Communists motivated the grassroots, and worked with peasants. As one of the army's marching songs proclaimed:

> The future belongs to the clean, fresh blood of youth.
> Between us and the ancient-minded men
> There is ice and ancient charcoal.[30]

The KMT had been able to attract young men who had come back to China after being trained in Western methods, such as the brother of Sun Yat-sen's wife, Harvard-educated Soong Tzu-wen – T. V. Soong. Having worked at the International Banking Corporation in New York, he brought order to the Canton financial system, building up a silver reserve to give the currency a rare solidity. In charge of the Finance Ministry, he doubled tax income in two years. Private savings held in banks rose sixfold. Smuggling and corruption were attacked. Government securities were successfully floated. All of which provided new funds for the forces to add to Moscow's gold.[31]

The NRA was well-structured, trained, decently led and amply supplied with Soviet arms, including a few planes. It had the services of Galen. Its soldiers had been blooded in the two Eastern Expeditions, as well as the battles with the merchants and the mercenaries. They were genuinely motivated, generally paying for food and abstaining from the wanton behaviour of warlord forces. They were backed by propaganda workers and the Blood Flower Troupe to perform revolutionary dramas. 'Soldiers and the people are like one family,' went an anthem. 'If we sing the song of love for the people every day, heaven, earth and man will be at peace.'

The KMT could attract support from regional figures who shared its antipathy towards the warlords of central and northern China. An alliance was formed with the trio of Guangxi generals. An opium-smoking local commander across the border in Hunan, Tang Shengzhi, turned to the Nationalists for help after being ousted by allies of Wu Peifu. The former Hunan governor, Tan Yankai, who had run the province after the revolution before being ejected, had gone to Canton, where he became head of the Political Council. Thus, despite its claim to want to eradicate warlordism, the KMT was, itself, part of a warlord coalition, led by a man whose power base was the military.

Chiang Kai-shek could also draw on contacts in the Shanghai business community from his days there, for advice, political backing and funding. An important figure in this respect was a financier called Zhang Jingjiang, who had made money in France and the United States before returning home to become a central player in the city's politico-financial-underworld nexus. Known as 'Curio Zhang' from his time in the antiques business in Paris, he suffered from creeping paralysis of the spine, which forced him to walk doubled over. An early sponsor of Sun Yat-sen, he had got to know Chiang as one of the doctor's aides – it had been at Zhang's house that the soldier first met his teenage bride.

The Northern Expedition's first target was Wu Peifu and his allies in Hunan, across a mountain range from Guangdong. Helped by Tang Shengzhi, the main NRA column made fast progress, and was joined by militarists from Guizhou and six other generals to whom Chiang offered benefits. Red Spear militias harassed warlord forces. Though he used high-flown rhetoric to declare that the campaign would determine 'whether the Chinese nation and race can restore their freedom and independence', the general also took a more down-to-earth view of his new partners. 'They are willing to ally with me or anyone else, just so they save their skins,' he told his wife. 'They are all stinking opportunists!' It was a problem that would stay with him to the end.

After capturing the Hunan capital of Changsha, the expedition continued north along the railway line to take a major base at the junction of the huge Dongting Lake and the Yangzi. The next objective was the three-city complex of Wuhan. Ahead of the army was a supposedly impregnable bridge called Tingsiqiao that spanned a steep gorge.

Waking up to the extent of the threat, the Philosopher General boarded his train to provide personal supervision of the defence of the bridge, with a force of 10,000 men. But the Nationalists were guided by peasants along hidden paths to attack, and, after twenty-four hours of bitter fighting, they emerged victorious, with a Communist-led 'independent regiment' playing a big role. Two thirds of the defenders were captured or killed. Many drowned as they fled; some were run over as Wu's train steamed out. It was a great victory, but, in a sign of discord to come, the Guangxi and Hunanese commanders kept their troops back from the fray.[32]

Wu tried to enlist the help of his one-time protégé, the eastern warlord Sun Chuanfang, whose influence extended over Zhejiang, Jiangsu, Anhui and Jiangxi, with Nanjing as his capital. But Sun showed how right Wu was to have reflected on the lack of loyalty among warlords. Chiang was already in secret negotiations with him, and the eastern militarist preferred to wait for the outcome of the struggle in the Middle Yangzi, calculating that he could only benefit if the contenders weakened one another.

At the beginning of September, the southerners reached the Wuhan city of Wuchang, which they besieged. Wu fled across the river to Hankou. Meeting the warlord over breakfast, the journalist John Powell found him depressed and drinking heavily. He carried a frayed copy of a classic military text from the third century. 'They didn't have any machine guns or airplanes then,' he remarked ruefully.[33]

Protected by its strong walls, Wuchang held out for five weeks; the Nationalists entered the city on the symbolic date of 10 October, the fifteenth anniversary of the 1911 rising there. Across the Yangzi, the general in charge of the defence of Hanyang took a large bribe and surrendered. The third city, Hankou, was now at the mercy of the southerners, and Wu decided it was time to flee to Henan. The soldiers he left behind, described by a journalist as 'shabby and dirty . . . ill and famished', contrasted with the 'civil and well-disciplined' Nationalists.[34]

It had been a breathtaking achievement, won by military skill, politics, populist appeal and graft. Though everything was, naturally, not perfect, the NRA soldiers fought with bravery, determination and speed unknown in all but the best warlord units. Among them was a female 'Dare to Die' unit led by 'Canton's Joan of Arc', who was photographed in jodhpurs, knee boots, a belted tunic and army cap. The combination of the NRA and the promise of modernization and land reform gave the Northern Expedition an appeal of a kind that proved irresistible.

'It is impossible to avoid the conclusion that the Cantonese have achieved amazing things,' wrote the correspondent of the *North China Daily News*. Their cause was further helped by a negotiated end to the long-running strike in Hong Kong and Canton, which removed instability in the home base. To continue the parallel with medieval Europe in the previous chapter, the expedition marked the eruption of a peripheral power on to the centre stage, on the model of England of the fourteenth and fifteenth centuries. The previous focus on northern China shifted as southern militarists asserted themselves nationally.[35]

Some later writers would portray the expedition's success as stemming primarily from the political revolutionaries, but this was to overstate their importance. Areas where cadres from the Communist-led Farmers' Institute were active certainly showed their radicalism. There were peasant risings as the NRA approached, and peasant associations sprouted in its wake. In Changsha, workers' organizations helped to chase out Wu Peifu's troops. But the core of the campaign was still military force. The victories that made the warlords retreat were won by arms and bribery, not evangelism or the masses. A contemporary poster reflected reality in showing a soldier with a fixed bayonet moving ahead of a peasant, worker, clerk and student.[36]

Having taken Wuhan, Chiang decided to strike out to the east, into Jiangxi on the route to his next objective, Nanjing and Shanghai. For unknown reasons, he did not consult Galen; perhaps success had gone to his head or he simply wanted to be his own man. After capturing the provincial capital of Nanchang, the Nationalists were forced back by an attack by the warlord Sun Chuanfang, who inflicted the worst casualties they had suffered. Galen was called in and engineered a counteroffensive, using air support. Nanchang was retaken. The Nationalists could now claim to have conquered half a million square miles with 170 million inhabitants. The NRA and allied armies totalled 260,000 men. It had lost 25,000 soldiers, 15,000 of them in Jiangxi.

Politicians from Canton, most of them on the left of the party, moved the government to Wuhan, where they were joined by Borodin. They wanted to press on up the middle of China to confront the Manchurians and capture Beijing. But Chiang remained fixed on advancing to Nanjing and Shanghai, the first symbolizing the short-lived republican government under Sun Yat-sen, the second a great potential treasure house. Pursuing his plans, the general received two visitors from Shanghai, who travelled up the Yangzi to meet him.

One, Pockmarked Huang, was the patriarch of the Shanghai underworld and its all-powerful Green Gang, whose help Chiang wanted to enlist to counter the Communist-led trade unions in the city, which were mobilizing to set up a Soviet. In return, Huang asked for freedom for the gang to expand its businesses in opium, prostitution, gambling and labour racketeering. There is no record of Chiang's response, but events would show him ready to clinch a deal.

The other visitor was Soong Ailing, the oldest and cleverest of the three daughters of the late Shanghai tycoon, Charlie Soong. Short and plump, Ailing was a commanding presence, keeping in the background but pulling many of the family strings. Educated in the United States, she had withstood the attention of Sun Yat-sen on his train expedition in 1912, and then married a scion of a Shaanxi banking family, Kong Xiangxi (H. H. Kong), who claimed to be a descendant of Confucius and had a lucrative connection with Standard Oil. Kong had been appointed industry minister in the Wuhan government, though he was no more left-wing than his brother-in-law, the finance minister T. V. Soong.[37]

Travelling on a private steamer to meet Chiang, Ailing carried with her a warning and a simple proposal, according to the memoirs of Chiang's wife, which may have been coloured by her husband's subsequent treatment of her. She records him as having told her immediately afterwards that the eldest Soong sister said the left would eliminate him unless he got the support of the Shanghai business world. Her family could arrange that. In return, Chiang should appoint T. V. Soong and H. H. Kong as finance and prime ministers and marry her youngest sister, Meiling. That, Ailing calculated, would enable her clan to control the army and the government.[38]

It was just what the general wanted to hear. The fact that Meiling had been overheard dismissing Chiang as 'a peasant' a few years earlier was of no import. He had long wished to enter the charmed Soong–Sun circle; according to Sun's widow, he had made advances to her through an intermediary after her husband's death. But there was a snag; he already had a wife.[38]

To get rid of her, according to her memoirs, he spun a plan for her to go to America for five years while he and Meiling wed. Then, he pledged, they would resume their life together. He told her he was sure she would agree since it was the way to unite China. 'After all,' he added in her account, 'true love is measured by the sacrifice one is willing to make.' Shocked, she went to her mother's home in Shanghai to weigh her options while Chiang resumed the move towards the Yangzi Delta.[39]

The advance brought the NRA face to face with a new foe in the shape of the Dogmeat General of Shandong, an ally of the Old Marshal in a northern warlord coalition known as the Anguojun, or National Peace Army. At the end of February 1927, Zhang Zongchang took his private train to join his troops in the Lower Yangzi, accompanied by his harem, sitting on a lacquered hardwood coffin as he drank and chain-smoked. Galen organized an offensive that drove the enemy back along the river towards Nanjing while the Muslim member of the Guangxi Clique, Bai Chongxi, led an army up from the south. Senior local officials defected. Towns paid the Shandong troops to leave peacefully.[40]

Though the advance was going well on the battlefield, political tension was rising sharply in the KMT. The civilian leadership in Wuhan tried to rein in Chiang, cancelling the special powers granted to him at the start of the expedition, and making him answerable to a commission which included a Communist and one of his fiercest critics, the justice minister, a man who struck the visiting *Manchester Guardian* journalist, Arthur Ransome, as 'a brilliant man but with something seriously wrong with his brain'. Learning of the steps taken against him, the general, who was in the Yangzi river port of Jiujiang,* banged his fists on his head and smashed a vase, weeping and cursing. When an emissary from Wuhan handed over handbills denouncing him as a putative dictator and letters urging him to fall in line, Chiang broke down, storming round his house, and refusing to eat or talk.[41]

Calming down the next morning, he summoned loyalists to plot a

---

* Transliterated at the time as Kiukiang.

counter-attack. His best defence was to go on the offensive to strengthen his position on the Nanjing–Shanghai front. He bought the support of regional political and military figures, and his forces moved steadily down the Yangzi. While Wuhan became increasingly radical, the general showed his true colours as his men executed Communists and closed down leftist organizations along their way.[42]

In Shanghai, the Communists and their allies in the labour movement called a general strike which was joined by 100,000 workers. Chiang and the equally anti-Communist Bai made no attempt to speed up their advance. As a result, the strikers were at the mercy of squads of warlord executioners, who put the heads of decapitated workers in wooden cages hung from lampposts. An armoured train, the *Great Wall*, operated by White Russians working for the Dogmeat General, steamed in, decorated in sky blue, primrose yellow and black – a journalist described it as 'a sinister thing of beautiful colour'. The foreigners in their settlements called in reinforcements to guard them against trouble. By mid-February, there were twenty-three warships in the river. Fresh troops arrived from Hong Kong, Vietnam and the Philippines – according to the *Lancet*, the British had so little to do that their main health problem was venereal disease.[43]

Though their strike had been suppressed, it was no secret that the unions and the Communists planned a repeat when the NRA got to the outskirts of the city. This could be portrayed either as fifth-column aid for the Nationalists, or as a bid to set up a Soviet, or both. It was a major threat to Chiang since the strikers would greatly outnumber his troops. Accordingly, he developed the plan he had discussed with Pockmarked Huang.

The gang boss, who was also chief of Chinese detectives in the French Concession, sat at the centre of a web of connections and sworn brotherhoods. The epitome of an old-style 'godfather', he held court in a teahouse in the morning and played cards in the afternoon before spending the evening with a concubine; his wife, a former brothel keeper, made her own fortune in the night soil business. But Huang was no longer the man he had been. Real power in the underworld Green Gang had passed to younger men, who were better organized and knew how to exploit the narcotics trade to the full.

Their leading figure was Du Yuesheng, known as 'Big Ears', for the obvious physical reason. Born in a fishing village, he had moved to

Shanghai, where Huang's wife took him under her wing. Finding his niche in running gambling dens, he rose steadily through the ranks of the Green Gang. By 1925, the physically slight, opium-addicted Du was eminent enough to throw a dinner for the Dogmeat General, for whom he provided a woman with each course.

With Huang and another associate, Zhang Xiaolin, who was in charge of relations with warlords, Du ran the Three Prosperities Company, which moved 40,000 chests of opium a year. Another of their outfits, the Black Stuff Company, extorted money from opium dens. Du, who sent pallbearers to deliver coffins to those who resisted him, cut deals with the police of the French Concession, where he established a home with his drug addict wife on one floor and two teenage mistresses on separate storeys; the mistresses bore him six sons, who were protected by White Russian bodyguards. With Huang acting as intermediary, he was just the man Chiang needed to beat off the threat from the Communists.

Big Ears set up a militia, the China Mutual Progress Association. The French consul-general, who was much concerned to 'struggle against the Soviet commune', arranged for concession police to protect its head-quarters, and supplied 450 guns. The co-operation of the administration of the International Settlement was also vital since it lay on the route to the main Communist stronghold in the working class area of Zhabei.* The French police chief, Captain Fiori, arranged a meeting for Du with Sterling Fessenden, the American chairman of the Municipal Council of the settlement. A short, plump man who had a taste for dancing with tall women, Fessenden was later described by a State Department official as a 'feeble creature who had gone to pieces in the Far East and was conspicuously unfit for his position'.[44]

When Fessenden arrived at Du's home, he noticed stacks of rifles and sub-machine guns in the hall. With Fiori present, he was easily persuaded to give permission for the armed militiamen to drive through the settlement. He later told the journalist John Powell he feared that the Communists would try to seize the concessions, resulting in 'widespread disorder and bloodshed, involving the lives of thousands of Americans, Britons, and other foreign residents as well as tens of thousands of Chinese who lived in the foreign-administered sections of the city'.

* Rendered then as Chapei.

Union members gave flesh to such fear as they took up fortified positions in major buildings, and raided police stations for weapons, roaming the streets and summarily executing 'running dog' employees of foreign firms. After fighting that took an estimated 300 lives and burned 3,000 buildings, the unions gained control of Zhabei. A general strike was declared as units of General Bai's army broke through the city's southern line on 18 March 1927. The garrison commander had been bribed to hand over the defence plans.

For all their fearsome reputation, the Dogmeat General's men hardly fired a shot, though the Russian train put up a brief show of resistance before its crew surrendered. 'It would be a mistake to say that the Northern resistance collapsed,' the *North China Daily News* noted. 'None was ever offered.' Warlord troops tried to join the refugees pressing to enter the foreign concessions. An American journalist, Henry Misselwitz, called them 'the most desolate, dispirited body of men I ever saw in my life. Their uniforms were ragged and torn, scores were wounded and poorly bandaged – disintegration seemed to possess the very souls of these men.'[45]

Faced with the show of strength by the unions, Bai advanced carefully – the NRA had only 3,000 men in the city. Chiang did not arrive until 26 March; his first rendezvous was with Pockmarked Huang. Evidently satisfied with planning for action against the left, the general sailed off up the Yangzi. As the strikers ignored an order from Bai to return to work, speculation grew that the left would declare a Soviet at a major rally being called to greet Chiang's old rival, Wang Jingwei, who was about to land at Shanghai on his return from exile in Europe. In the French Concession, a mob stormed the gates on the Boulevard des Deux Républiques. Foreign Communists flocked in; according to John Powell, some lived high on the hog, buying themselves Western cars, until the visiting leader of the American Communist Party, Earl Browder, called them to order after eating only bread and water at an elaborate banquet.[46]

The danger of anti-foreign sentiment spilling over into major violence was shown in Nanjing, which the Nationalists took the day after entering Shanghai. The Dogmeat General's men fled, looting, burning and raping as they went. The incoming Nationalist Sixth Army, which was not controlled by Chiang, attacked foreign houses and offices, shooting dead the British harbourmaster and the port doctor, and badly wounding the British consul. The American vice-president of the university was also killed, along with a French and an Italian Catholic priest. The Japanese consulate was ransacked. Two dozen American women and children had a perilous escape across fields under fire. After Western ships moored in the Yangzi shelled the city, the attacks stopped.

Chiang blamed the Nanjing Incident on the Communist head of the Sixth Army's political department, 'bad characters', northerners in southern uniforms, and 'what might be called an anti-missionary movement'. Several dozen soldiers were executed. But the Nationalists protested at the bombardment by foreign warships, and, in Shanghai, anti-imperialist placards covered walls. Foreign governments and the communities in the settlements were in uproar. The American Chamber of Commerce in Shanghai passed a resolution calling for armed US intervention. The *North China Daily News* ran an article entitled 'How to Spot Communists at Moving Picture Shows and Other Public Gatherings'.[47]

Fears of Communism were heightened at the beginning of April when, with the agreement of Western diplomats, the Old Marshal sent his men into the embassy quarter of Beijing to raid the Soviet legation and hustle away Chinese Communists sheltering there. Among those held was the country's leading Marxist theorist, Li Dazhao, who was swiftly tried and executed; his seventeen-year-old daughter was tortured for three days before being strangled. Documents seized from the legation were said to show plans for revolution in China.

To put the finishing touch to his preparations in Shanghai, Big Ears Du invited the most powerful Shanghai labour leader, Wang Shouhua,* to dinner. Wang had good reason to accept; if a Soviet was formed, it would want underworld neutrality. At 8 p.m. on 11 April, his chauffeur-driven car passed through the gates of Du's house in the French Concession. In the entrance hall, he was met by another of the Green Gang triumvirate, Zhang Xiaolin, who told him he should dissolve the pickets and change sides. Wang refused. At that, four gangsters set on the union leader. One, known as 'Old Crow', tried to throttle him. At this point, Du was said to have appeared at the top of the stairs, his gaze and voice disembodied by opium. 'Not here!' he cried. 'Not in my house!' The goons stuffed Wang into a sack, and, thinking him dead, drove to waste ground to bury him. As they finished digging the grave, Wang moaned. The gangsters interred him alive.[48]

---

* Also known as He Songling.

A few hours later, 2,000 armed members of Du's militia fanned across the city before dawn, wearing blue uniforms and white armbands with the character for 'labour'. At daybreak on 12 April, a bugle call rang out from army headquarters and a siren sounded on a gunboat in the river. That was the signal for the attack on the labour movement, which was joined by Nationalist soldiers. Leftist strongholds were stormed. Men were shot and beheaded in the streets. There was a report that captives were thrown alive into the furnaces of locomotives at the South railway station – though this may have owed more to the imagination of the French novelist André Malraux than to reality, it came to symbolize the ferocity of the repression, setting a pattern for what was to come.

As if the morning of 12 April had not brought sufficient evidence of what they faced, demonstrators, headed by women and children, marched to army headquarters in protest in the afternoon. They were met with machine-gun fire and bayonets. A Purification Committee was established. Green Gang men moved into the union headquarters to set up a new labour organization under their control. In all, between 5,000 and 10,000 people may have died. Many of the 300 prisoners taken to the military camp at Longhua, on the outskirts of the city, were executed there. 'It was a bloodthirsty war,' Chiang's secretary, Chen Lifu, wrote. 'I must admit that many innocent people were killed.'[49]

Among those who got away was Zhou Enlai; at one point, he was arrested, but escaped – this was said to have been arranged by Chiang to repay a debt for an occasion when the Communist saved him from violent leftists in Canton. Zhou and his wife hid in the Western Astor House hotel. To meld with the other guests, Zhou dressed in a three-piece suit and bought a pair of leather shoes, while his wife wore smart Chinese outfits with high heels. After two months in a room overlooking the river, they headed out of Shanghai. Their sojourn makes it all the more probable that Chiang let them go since it is virtually certain that the hotel's native staff included members of the Green Gang, who would have informed Du of the couple in room 311, and that he would have told the general.[*][50]

---

* The story came out in 1973, told by Zhou to the visiting President Georges Pompidou of France as they stood on top of the Broadway Mansion apartment block overlooking the Astor House, which has reopened as a hotel with 311 as one of its standard rooms.

The 'White Terror' spread out from Shanghai. In Huangzhou, girls and boys were reported to have been beheaded for speaking out, while men were broken on the rack or hung up in cages to die of hunger and thirst. In Canton, real or suspected Communists were roped together, taken to the parade ground and shot. Hunan was the scene of a particularly savage and prolonged confrontation as the right sought to eradicate the rural radicalism engendered there by the Communists, who hit back with a large-scale revolt known as the Autumn Harvest Uprising, setting off a provincial conflict that would stretch for a decade, at the cost of an estimated 300,000 lives.[51]

In Shanghai, sixty business groups sent a congratulatory telegram to Chiang after the 12 April purge. But it was their turn next as the capitalists were shaken down by the KMT and the Green Gang. A Financial Commission was set up to decide who was to pay how much. If cash was not forthcoming, the gangsters or the security forces went round. Assets reported to be worth $7 million were grabbed from a flour magnate. An arrest warrant was issued against a conservative business leader who refused to raise $10 million; when he fled, his shipping company was appropriated and Chiang took one of his houses. Cash was raised by kidnapping, thinly disguised as the detention of suspected subversives. 'Millionaires were arrested as "Communists",' noted a contemporary observer; victims included the three-year-old son of the owner of the Sincere department store.[52]

The Westerners welcomed the restoration of order, and the end of the Communist threat. For them, the events beyond the barbed-wire fences ringing the concessions was of little concern, though six Royal Air Force planes were parked at the race course just in case. On the day the purge began, ratepayers in the International Settlement met to discuss a motion to keep Chinese out of their parks and gardens.[53]

For their help, the rightist KMT regime that was set up in Nanjing by Chiang in competition with the leftist government in Wuhan rewarded Du and his colleagues by letting them develop their criminal empire even further. The French agreed that their naval boats would protect craft carrying drugs, and, in return for cash, let the gangsters open gambling houses in their concession. The authorities in the International Settlement reached a financial accord for the Green Gang to sell narcotics there. When a government opium monopoly bureau was set up with the declared aim of eradicating drug use over three years, it was headed by

Zhang Xiaolin, the Green Gang boss who had watched as the labour union leader was bludgeoned in Du Yuesheng's home.[54]

The attack on the united front by the KMT right was inevitable, given the competing ambitions on either side, transforming the 'awakening' of China into a bloody settling of scores in the latest upsurge of reaction and force. The repression in Shanghai on 12 April 1927 began a violent power struggle between left and right that would take millions of lives in twenty-two years of national dislocation. Sixteen years after the overthrow of the Qing, aspirations to build a nation that could evolve on rational lines, respecting individuals and seeking happiness for more than the elite power-holders, were thrown into jeopardy once more.

10

Divided We Stand

The Kuomintang's success could not leave China's biggest warlord indifferent. Zhang Zuolin was a man of the north and had quite enough to occupy him there – he was planning to make himself emperor; an imperial porcelain set was being designed, and, when the Old Marshal drove round Beijing in an armoured car, the streets were closed and strewn with imperial yellow sand. But the Nationalist advance demanded action.

The Marshal's 26-year-old son, Zhang Xueliang, the Young Marshal, led an army across the Yellow River north of Wuhan while the Dogmeat General regrouped his forces to advance on Nanjing. Though the Shandong soldiers got close enough to shell the city, they were turned back, allowing Chiang's troops to move northwards through eastern China 'like lemonade through a straw', as a newspaper put it. A 70,000-strong army fielded by the KMT government in Wuhan won a series of tough battles for railway towns against the Young Marshal, sustaining heavy losses but forcing him to retreat behind the Yellow River, where he set up a strong defensive line with artillery.

The younger Zhang was not a happy commander, and developed a serious drug habit as a result. 'I smoked opium out of anger and the pressure of leading an army,' he said in a television interview in 1992. 'An army doctor tried to help me by using a dose of medicine to get rid of the addiction. In the end I got rid of the opium but became addicted to the medicine.' This was morphine, which he took so often that his back was covered with needle pricks.[1]

Both wings of the Nationalists thus gained the breathing space they needed, but their internal split widened. Wuhan expelled Chiang Kai-shek from the KMT. A mass meeting in the leftist capital denounced him as the 'counter-revolutionary chief'. The general was untroubled, and won an ally in the veteran ideologue Hu Hanmin, who had returned from exile. The other returnee, Wang Jingwei, resumed his association with Borodin in Wuhan, where the government sought to keep the united front alive as mass organizations and trade unions sprouted – there was even one for Buddhist priests and nuns.

Demonstrators marched through the streets of Wuhan waving banners calling for world revolution. In the surrounding countryside, more than 2 million peasants and small farmers joined Communist-led associations, which confiscated big estates and shared out grain. Courts sentenced 'evil gentry' and their lackeys. Merchants were heavily taxed. Students demanded the power to sack teachers. Under the leadership of Sun Yat-sen's widow, women's institutes were established. A Russian aviator came in to fly daily displays.

The new spirit impressed even the *North China Daily News*, voice of the British establishment in Shanghai. 'No matter how one may dislike certain phases of the present Nationalist movement, there is one out-standing fact – the people, in general, seem to have entered into a realm of freedom and safety never before enjoyed,' its correspondent wrote. People worked together, he added. Shopkeepers were not afraid of being robbed. Women and girls could go out on their own safely – provoking a group calling itself Husbands of Emancipated Women to complain that their wives did not come home at night, and acted 'like alley cats'.[2]

Borodin, who drove round in Wu Peifu's former car, preached calm and 'the long view'. Though suffering from malaria, he was always cogent in analysing the problems of China. 'His slow, resolute way of talking, his refusal to be hurried or to get excited, his insistence upon the fundamental lines of action that determined detailed events, gave a spacious, deliberate character to his conversation,' an American correspondent, Vincent Sheean, wrote after several meetings.[3]

However, Wuhan's writ ran over only two provinces, which meant its tax base was low. So it had to impose heavy levies to pay for its army and to meet the cost of reform. Revenue was badly affected when pro-Chiang troops took a major Yangzi customs post. Steep taxes alienated merchants. Cholera killed thousands. Army officers, who had bought landed estates, were unhappy at land redistribution. Unemployment rose as strikes led big factories to close down. Inflation soared, and the finance minister, T. V. Soong, left for Shanghai, lamenting the way his 'beautiful bank notes' had been devalued.[4]

As the economic situation deteriorated, the government stepped up its attacks on the foreigners, scoring a notable success when Britain agreed to return its concession after it came under assault from a large crowd. British troops and any civilians who wanted to leave sailed down the Yangzi. As they were leaving, the garrison realized that it had forgotten to notify the Sikh guards; somebody was sent back to fetch them but found a Sikh delegation marching in a celebration of this victory over imperialism.[5]

The difference between the two rival wings of the party was summed up by the contrast between Wuhan and the city 450 miles downriver that supplied Chiang with his funding. 'Nothing more intensely living can be imagined,' wrote the British author Aldous Huxley of Shanghai. It contained half China's motor cars and its biggest shipyards. Its multi-storey department stores were the acme of retailing. Smart young Shanghai Chinese picked up Western fads in clothing and behaviour; the women marcelled their hair and wore flapper dresses. The spectacular Art Deco buildings in the foreign concessions made it a world architectural centre as well as the home of literature, art, film and political debate. Its night life was famed for its raciness, with many tens of thousands of prostitutes.

Shanghai had China's first stock exchange, centre of wild speculation and insider dealing. Entrepreneurs came from all over China and abroad, a few great tycoons and a mass of smaller operators. Foreigners cut a dash. H. E. Morris, owner of the *North China Daily News*, had a complex in the style of the British Home Counties covering a whole city block. The Iraqi Jew Victor Sassoon, a horserace-loving crippled First World War veteran, lived in a half-timbered hunting lodge and an apartment with a 360-degree view atop Sassoon House on the Bund. Noël Coward wrote *Private Lives* in forty-eight hours while laid up with influenza for a weekend in Sassoon's Cathay Hotel. Elly Kadoorie, another Iraqi Jew, danced the tango in a 400-square-foot ballroom lit by 3,600 bulbs at his white-painted Marble Hall mansion. Silas Hardoon, who started work as a warehouse watchman, lived with his Eurasian wife and ten adopted children in an estate with three houses, pavilions, artificial hills, lakes and bamboo groves, but still collected the rents from his property empire in person, working from an untidy office with no carpet, curtains or heating.[6]

Japanese ran a third of the city's cotton mills. Fifty thousand White Russians poured in, becoming shopkeepers, bodyguards and dance hall hostesses, some claiming to be princesses. The number of Chinese living in the concessions far outnumbered the foreigners. Though some were rich, most had grinding lives, labouring for very long hours in factories, pulling rickshaws or working as dockside coolies, doing any menial jobs they could find, sleeping on the pontoons by the river or in the streets, begging and selling daughters into prostitution. In silk mills, children worked for eleven hours a day, soaked to the skin by steam, their bodies swaying with exhaustion while overseers stood by with clubs. 'Yellow unions' run by the Green Gang and its associates, some from the KMT, took their cut, using strikes and strike-breaking to extort money from employers. The visiting Albert Einstein described the workers of Shanghai as 'cruelly abused and treated worse than cattle ... a working, groaning, yet stolid, people'. As a saying went, the city was a thin slice of heaven on a large slice of hell.[7]

For some, immorality and modernity seemed inextricably linked. Chen Duxiu, the May Fourth academic who had gone on to head the Communist Party, denounced the city's inhabitants as consisting of 'traitorous businessmen' who collaborated with foreigners, swindlers, prostitutes, gangster politicians, or peddlers of promiscuous romances and superstitions. Others blamed the pleasures the city offered for sapping the construction of the nation.[8]

As he climbed the stairway of the Great World entertainment centre, owned by Pockmarked Huang, the film director Josef von Sternberg saw:

gambling tables, singsong girls, magicians, pickpockets, slot machines, fireworks, birdcages, fans, stick incense, acrobats, and ginger ... restaurants, a dozen barbers, and earwax extractors ... jugglers, herb medicines, ice cream parlours, photographers, a new bevy of girls, their high-collared gowns slit to reveal their hips, exposed toilets ... shooting galleries, fan-tan tables, revolving wheels, massage benches, acupuncture, hot-towel counters, dried fish and intestines, and dance platforms serviced by a horde of music makers competing with each other to see who could drown out the others ... girls whose dresses were slit to their armpits, a stuffed whale, story-tellers, balloons, peep shows, masks, a mirror maze, two love-letter booths with scribes who guaranteed results, rubber goods, and a temple filled with ferocious gods and joss sticks.*[9]

*

* The Great World still stands, with distorting mirrors in the entrance, but features karaoke and gymnastics by schoolchildren in place of the entertainment Sternberg witnessed. Once impressive, it is now overshadowed by the surrounding modern tower blocks.

Though its army had repulsed the attack by the Young Marshal, the government in Wuhan felt in need of a powerful friend against the Manchurian troops, which were still a threat as they dug in along the Yellow River. Its choice was the Christian General, Feng Yuxiang, who was anxious to expand his influence into the Yangzi region after returning to China from an extended trip to Russia and raising a new army. His progressive statements and the backing he received from Moscow made him acceptable as a partner.

A delegation led by Wang Jingwei travelled to the rail junction of Zhengzhou* to meet him. Feng arrived on the back of a lorry, wearing a simple uniform and munching bread; only later did it emerge that he had travelled to the outskirts of the city in a private train. The KMT delegation laid out plans for a second phase of the Northern Expedition to Beijing, sidelining Chiang. To gain the warlord's backing, it agreed to his demands – command of the campaign against the Young Marshal, control of Henan and provinces conquered, plus a handsome payment. Feng encouraged the visitors by calling Chiang a 'wolf-hearted, dog-lunged, inhuman thing'.[10]

However, in separate talks, to which the Communist members of the delegation were not invited, he demanded the dismissal of Soviet advisers and the sacking of Communists from positions of authority. Ever pliant, Wang and his non-Communist colleagues said they were ready to go along. Naturally, they kept this secret. In Wuhan, Borodin could insist: 'Marshal Feng is our friend.'

But when the fighting against the Manchurians resumed, the warlord's soldiers held back until Wuhan's crack troops had done most of the work. Then Feng sent his cavalry to speed along the south bank of the Yellow River to take Zhengzhou with little opposition. Total casualties for his army were put at forty, compared to 14,000 for the Wuhan troops. The KMT politicians might have kept in mind their new ally's alternative nickname, the Betraying General.

Learning of the Zhengzhou conference, Chiang fixed a rendezvous with Feng at another key rail junction, Xuzhou.† The warlord put on a fresh display of humility for his arrival. The carriages on his train were empty. In a boxcar sat a husky man in a shabby uniform. When the

---

* Then rendered as Chengchow.
† Then rendered as Hsuchou.

fellow got out on to the platform, Chiang asked him where Feng was. 'I am Feng Yuxiang,' the peasant-like soldier replied with a smile. As a band played, he shook hands with the smartly uniformed greeting party, who later discovered that he had made most of the journey in his carriage, only moving to the boxcar as it approached its destination.[11]

As usual, Feng was out for what he could get, and Chiang was always a good payer. He promised the Christian General $2 million a month, and control of Henan. Getting Feng's agreement to back Nanjing against Wuhan, Chiang issued a warrant for the arrest of leading leftists, including Borodin. The warlord sent Wuhan a cable denouncing the way in which radical elements had wormed their way into the KMT there, reiterating his demand for the Russians to go home and advising that members of the administration should go abroad 'for a rest', while its troops joined him. 'I make these suggestions sincerely and expect you to accept them,' he concluded.[12]

Feng's volte-face could not have come at a worst time for Borodin, who was suffering from malaria and had broken an arm in a riding accident. His American wife, Fanya, had been arrested by northern troops on a Russian steamer on the Yangzi, and taken to Beijing to be tried. On top of all this, the policy he had implemented since arriving in Canton was suddenly reversed.

Ever since the first contacts with Sun Yat-sen, Stalin had insisted that the united front was the only valid policy to pursue in China. That meant tailoring rural reform to fit the KMT, and not seeking to establish a separate army. But the White Terror showed the danger of collaboration. After denouncing Chiang, and retrieving a photograph he had been about to send to the general, Stalin ordered a change of policy, and dispatched a new emissary to Wuhan, Mahendranath Roy, an Indian Brahmin with a face which looked as though it had been sculpted.

A telegram from Moscow on 1 June 1927 told the CCP to pursue agrarian revolution, form a 70,000-strong Red Army, and inject new blood into the KMT Central Committee in place of 'vacillating and compromising' veterans. After years of being browbeaten into collaboration, the Chinese Communist leadership did not know whether to laugh or cry at the new orders. Chen Duxiu said it was like taking a bath in shit. Borodin called the cable ludicrous. Roy made things worse by disclosing the message to Wang Jingwei, who termed it unacceptable. The envoy replied that it was an ultimatum. 'If the Kuomintang will not collaborate,' he told the Politburo, 'we must regard it as an enemy.'[13]

After six weeks of discussion, the Wuhan KMT decided on 15 July to expel the Communists from its administration and send the Russians home. Packing up to leave after learning that his wife had escaped from Beijing to Japan through a mixture of bribery, helpful friends and good luck, Borodin told the journalist Vincent Sheean that the Chinese revolution had suffered only a temporary setback. 'It will go underground,' he continued. 'It will become an illegal movement, suppressed by counter-revolution and beaten down by reaction and imperialism; but it has learned how to organize, how to struggle. Sooner or later, a year, two years, five years from now, it will rise to the surface again. It may be defeated a dozen times, but in the end it must conquer. What has happened here will not be forgotten.'[14]

After a farewell ceremony with tea and fizzy drinks, the Russian undertook an arduous road journey to reach the railway from Mongolia to Moscow. Ill and bad-tempered, he reflected that, like all bourgeois parties, the KMT was 'a toilet which, however often you flush it, still stinks'. Arriving in Moscow four years to the day from his first encounter with Sun Yat-sen, he became the director of an English-language newspaper. Arrested in a purge in 1949, he was sent to a Siberian prison camp, where he died in 1951.[15]

Four days after Borodin left Wuhan, Communist-led troops staged an armed rising in the Jiangxi capital of Nanchang at Moscow's urging. Zhou Enlai was in command, and several men who would become leading Red Army figures were involved, including the future overall commander, Zhu De.* The insurgency was soon weakened by desertions, the high summer heat, contaminated water and a lack of ammunition. After a week, it was crushed. The revolt would be celebrated later as the founding moment of the Red Army. At the time, it was just the latest in a string of major reverses for the CCP. The survivors marched off to take the port of Shantou,† hoping to receive Soviet supplies there. Delirious with fever, Zhou was put on a small boat that sailed to Hong Kong through seas so rough that the occupants had to be tied down to avoid being swept over the side. Those who remained

---

* The hotel which served as headquarters for the revolt has been turned into a museum where one can see the bedrooms occupied by the Communist leaders and what are said to be some of their weapons.
† Then rendered as Swatow.

behind in Shantou suffered another defeat from a Nationalist attack, and scattered into small bands seeking safety where they could find it.[16]

It was time for Galen to follow Borodin home. Unlike his compatriot, who had feared arrest if he travelled via Nanjing or Shanghai, the Soviet general went to see the commander who owed him so much. Chiang recorded that, finding the Russian greatly depressed, he told him not to feel too bad about leaving. 'I hope that this is not the last time we shall see each other,' Galen replied. 'So, till we meet again!' Chiang found it 'one of the most moving partings in my life'.[17]

Back in the Soviet Union, Galen was steadily promoted, reaching the rank of marshal and joining the Communist Party Central Committee. Eventually, he fell victim to Stalin's purges, and, after being tortured by the police chief Lavrenti Beria, was executed. Not knowing this, Chiang asked Stalin in 1939 to send him back to help the Nationalists. When the Chinese envoy mentioned the alias of 'Galen', the dictator did not recognize it. An aide murmured the Russian name to him. No, Stalin said, the general was unavailable because he had been shot for giving secrets to a Japanese woman spy.

The turn of events in Wuhan opened the way for a reconciliation within the KMT, which reunited in Nanjing. This was bad news for Chiang. The bloodiness of his purge had shocked many party members, and the Guangxi Clique began secret talks with Wang Jingwei about forming a new administration without him. The general's position was further weakened when the army of the eastern warlord Sun Chuanfang caught his troops in a trap while advancing towards Nanjing.[18]

Outmanoeuvred at the Military Council in August 1927, Chiang left Nanjing for his home village of Xikou in Zhejiang, where fireflies glistened amid the tall grass and bamboo by the river. In his absence, the Guangxi generals showed their military skills in repulsing a six-day attack by 30,000 of Sun's troops. They also mastered a revolt by the military commander in Wuhan, Tang Shengzhi, who fled to Japan. But their administration was weak. The Green Gang and the Shanghai businessmen cut funding. Chiang's agents staged a rally by his supporters in Nanjing which was dispersed by security forces – three people were killed and seventy-five wounded. Wang went to Canton, from where he showed his usual fluidity by opening negotiations with the general.[19]

Drinking green tea and munching nuts, Chiang told a journalist visiting Xikou that he was too much a part of the revolution, and it too much a part of him, for him to get out for good. From time to time, he travelled to Shanghai for meetings with associates. He also had personal business to attend to, pursuing his scheme to marry Soong Meiling, and presenting his wife with tickets to sail to the US on the liner the *President Jackson*. She agreed to go.[20]

With her out of the way, the general told questioning journalists that she was a concubine whom he had dropped. Learning of his remarks when she reached New York, his wife was distraught. By her own account, she ran round her room on Riverside Drive, tearing her hair, raving and shouting with such force that the janitor was called. Wandering the city, she added, she was about to throw herself into the river when an old man restrained her and walked her home.*

To get the blessing of the Soong matriarch, Chiang went to Japan, where she was undergoing medical treatment. Charlie Soong's widow had a low opinion of soldiers, and disapproved of her daughter's suitor for not being a Christian. He could do nothing about the first, but he undertook to read the Bible. As Qingling remarked, 'He would have agreed to be a Holy Roller to marry Meiling.'[21]

The wedding was held in Shanghai on 1 December 1927. After a Christian marriage ceremony at the Soong home, the 26-year-old bride and forty-year-old groom went to the Majestic Hotel, where white roses arranged in the shape of wedding bells hung on the walls and a Russian orchestra played Mendelssohn's 'Wedding March'. They bowed three times to Sun Yat-sen's portrait beside the KMT flag. A Western singer intoned the hymn, 'O Promise Me'. The general declared that the marriage union meant that 'I can henceforth bear the tremendous responsibility of the revolution with peace of heart.' But the couple insisted theirs was not a political union. It was made known that he had learned the English word 'Darling', and had written to his new wife telling her, 'Thinking about the people I admire in this life, you, my lady, are the only one ... My lady, your talent, beauty and virtue are not things I can ever forget.'[22]

---

* Returning to Shanghai in 1933, she lived on funds from Chiang and earnings from language teaching before moving to Hong Kong in the early 1960s to a house bought by her former husband and an associate. She died in 1971 after writing her memoirs for a New York publisher. The book was stopped by the US authorities on behalf of the Chiang regime in Taiwan, and then the manuscript was bought up and buried by Chiang's son. It finally saw the light of day after a copy was discovered by the scholar Lloyd Eastman.

Energetic and determined, Meiling had studied at a Wesleyan college in Macon, Georgia, where her English acquired a southern twang, and then at Wellesley College, outside Boston. Back in Shanghai after graduating in 1917, she undertook social work, notably to alleviate child labour and encourage the YWCA. Short and somewhat plump in the way of her family, she had moved in smart social circles that included the Young Marshal of Manchuria. She also met Borodin in Wuhan, where he had lectured her on world events; according to the Shanghai-based writer Emily Hahn, the Russian was so smitten that he wrote her name over and over on a sheet of paper with the addition of 'Darling'. As the years went by, she would become an increasingly prominent member of the Chiang regime, particularly for foreigners, whom she dazzled as the mysterious, sexy Dragon Lady, with the advantage of speaking perfect English. A saying had it that of the three Soong sisters, one (Ailing) loved money, one (Meiling) loved power, and one (Qingling) loved China.*

Ten days after the wedding, Stalin intervened in China once more, again with disastrous results. On his orders to the CCP, Communists in Canton staged a rising on 11 December. Officers and merchants were shot out of hand, police stations stormed, and major buildings looted. Rickshaw pullers from the Communist trade union acted as a revolutionary vanguard. A Soviet was set up promising food, clothing, housing and an eight-hour day. Ye Ting, the Communist regimental commander from the Northern Expedition, took military charge.

But the rising did not arouse popular support, and the counter-attack by the Canton army was swift. Armed members of the mechanics' union joined the troops. Executioners in fur caps and knee boots beheaded bound suspects in the streets. The *South China Morning Post* reported the indiscriminate shooting of women – 'mostly of the bob-haired type'. Children's bodies lay piled in the streets. An American educator, Earl Swisher, watched seven boatloads of prisoners being pushed into the river, and shot. The *North China Herald* wrote of a 'city of the dead'. The Russian consulate was stormed, and the bodies of five diplomats left on the lawn. The total death toll was put at 5,700. Ye fled to the Soviet Union.[23]

---

* Though it has come to typecast the sisters, the saying is unfair to Meiling. She certainly relished power, but her patriotism is hardly in doubt.

Along the southern coast, there were reports of the hearts of alleged subversives being eaten, and their severed heads pickled in brine. Communist suspects were shot in the streets of Wuhan. Nanjing broke off relations with Moscow. Soviet legations were closed, cutting off money and support for the CCP. Thus ended a terrible year for the Communists, who scattered to havens in mountain territory. One of their organizations put the number of dead in the repression of 1927 at a very precise 37,981.[24]

Events in Canton strengthened the call for a strong leader of the reunited KMT. Deluged by messages urging him to return to power, Chiang issued a circular telegram to major figures advocating party unity. The KMT formally asked him to come back. On 1 January 1928, his armoured train steamed to Nanjing from Shanghai. It was time for the Nationalists to turn back to the unification of China by launching a campaign against the biggest warlord, the Old Marshal, in his forward base in Beijing.[25]

The nature of war in China was changing. Battles which would have ended in the past with limited casualties were now fought to the death. Soviet advisers had introduced new tactics, particularly flanking movements. Weapons had grown more sophisticated. Though the Christian General told his men that bombs were no more dangerous than the droppings of birds, aircraft made their appearance. The piecemeal funding of the warlords was no longer sufficient.

Despite his weaknesses as a battlefield commander, Chiang was well suited to the changing conditions. He grasped the importance of finance and resources, of political control and coalitions which, however temporary, isolated opponents. In the spring of 1928, he teamed up with the Model Governor of Shanxi, Yan Xishan, and the Christian General, Feng Yuxiang, with his reconstituted Kuominchun (National Army).

Fielding 700,000 men against 400,000 for their northern foes, they elaborated a three-pronged strategy against Zhang Zuolin – the Nationalists would drive up eastern China from the Yangzi while Yan and Feng moved on Beijing from the west and south. Nanjing put a fresh squeeze on the Shanghai business community for funds, and hired a German First World War veteran, Colonel Max Bauer, as senior military aide – an extreme right-winger, he compared 'the strength, dignity, soundness and goodwill' of the Chinese with the degeneration of white races. Soviet advisers accompanied Feng's army, while White Russian émigrés fought for the marshal. Anti-warlord militias joined in once more, the Red Spears and Heavenly Gate Society staging guerrilla attacks on the northern troops and helping to capture the city of Luoyang* in Henan.

The KMT forces took the Shandong capital of Jinan without a fight. The provincial warlord, Zhang Zongchang, fled to Beijing through starving refugees from the countryside camped round the city walls. Among the Nationalist booty was an armoured train with a Russian crew who, by one report, were paraded through the streets with 'stout rope pierced through their noses'. Chiang came in to congratulate his men and instruct them to remain disciplined. After he returned to Nanjing, trouble broke out with a Japanese garrison guarding settlers in Jinan. It was not clear who fired first, but the Japanese soldiers took drastic action. They ransacked the provincial Foreign Affairs Commission, killing sixteen of the staff. According to Chiang's Japanese biographer, Keiji Furaya, they cut out the commissioner's tongue before shooting him in the head.[26]

Anxious to avoid trouble and get his troops back on the campaign, Chiang sent orders for them to leave Jinan. The Japanese issued a twenty-four-hour ultimatum. But some Chinese soldiers preferred to stay on rather than marching north. Japanese artillery and planes used this as a pretext to pound the mile-square old city. The next day, Chinese soldiers were allowed out through the walls, but were then ambushed. The official death toll was 3,000. Hallett Abend of the *New York Times*, who arrived by train at this point, put it at more than double that.

Anti-Japanese boycotts and demonstrations were staged in Shanghai, Canton and Wuhan. Against all the evidence, Chiang was depicted as a man who had defied the foreigners. In fact, he issued a proclamation calling for Chinese to disguise their feelings, storing up their thirst for revenge till they could fight back. First, he believed, victory had to be won over the marshal in the north.[27]

With KMT forces advancing from the east, the Model Governor's grey-uniformed army coming through the mountainous border with Shanxi, and Feng's cavalry speeding across the northern plains, Zhang Zuolin decided it was time to go home. Just before dawn on 3 June 1928, he was driven to the station in the centre of Beijing in a convoy of twenty cars. The warlord was reported to be smiling broadly as he

---

* Transliterated then as Loyang.

got into his cobalt blue private carriage, serenaded by a military band. The Dogmeat General accompanied him for the first leg of the journey.

Not trusting Feng, who had turned on his allies in his previous foray into Beijing in 1924, Chiang arranged for Shanxi troops to be the first inside the walls of Beijing, moonlight glinting on their bayonets. The Guangxi army settled in the north-west of the city. The handover was most civilized. Five thousand Manchurian soldiers stayed behind to ensure order until Yan's men arrived. The only serious fighting was round the Summer Palace, though some of the retreating Manchurians were later harried by Feng's forces.

Despite Tokyo's policy of working with Zhang, Japanese officers in the Kwantung Leased Territory in Manchuria thought it was time to get rid of him and to install a more pliant successor in the person of his morphine-addicted son. As the Old Marshal sat smoking in his compartment while his train pulled into the outskirts of his capital of Mukden in the early morning, Japanese soldiers set off a bomb on a bridge above the track. Blood pouring from his body, the warlord was taken to hospital, where he died. The Japanese officers had hoped the outrage would bring out Manchurian troops, providing them with an excuse to fight back and escalate a conflict. But local forces remained in their barracks, and the Japanese consul advised Tokyo there was no need for action to protect its nationals. The Kwantung Army blamed the blast on three Chinese opium addicts whom they rounded up and prepared for execution. One escaped, and told the story to Zhang's son.

Slim and broad-shouldered, the Young Marshal was described by an interviewer as looking more like 'a sensitive poet or scholar than the off-spring of a "bad man"', with deep-set eyes, prominent nose and long, graceful hands. He wore Western clothes and loud ties, played tennis and polo, gambled and drove cars at high speeds. Still, visiting him in Mukden, the Australian adviser W. H. Donald found that 'his face and his hands were thin and pale . . . and his body occasionally shook convulsively.' After fifteen minutes of the meeting, Zhang left the room for a fix.[28]

In Tokyo, Prime Minister Tanaka and the main adviser to the emperor wanted to sanction Kwantung officers for the assassination. But a powerful association of officers by the name of the Issekikai, whose members had known of the murder plot, closed ranks to protect them. The cabinet went along with its suggestion that the only punishment should be for having failed to guard the railway properly. Tanaka was humiliated, and resigned soon afterwards. Manchuria was clearly identified as a stamping ground for Japan's military hawks.

The victors in the second stage of the Northern Expedition gathered to celebrate in Beijing.* They paid homage to Sun Yat-sen's coffin at its resting place in the Western Hills outside the city, Chiang breaking down after reading a eulogy. Meeting local dignitaries, the KMT leader made it plain that the capital was to be moved to Nanjing. There was an unfortunate incident when one of Feng's generals broke into the tomb of Cixi, the Dowager Empress, and looted her valuables. The last emperor, Puyi, who was living in the Japanese concession in Tianjin, wrote that he was so affronted by this insult to the Qing that he vowed unending hatred of the Nationalists. A rumour spread that a particularly fine pair of pearls had been given to Madame Chiang, who had them attached to her slippers.

This was only a minor blemish on what seemed a time for real hope. The blue and red flag of the Nationalists, with its sun and twelve rays, was the symbol of a fresh start for China. In a new administration in Nanjing, the Model Governor became interior minister and the Christian General minister for war. The autonomist-minded Guangxi Clique stayed on board, ever-grouchy but part of the team. People really wanted the new order to succeed, as a contemporary journalist noted. A visiting British intellectual, Arnold Toynbee, remarked on Chiang's 'cool-headedness and restrained vitality'.[29]

A new political system provided the apparatus of a modern state, with Chiang as chairman of the State Council. Five government branches – the Yuan – were established. The Executive Yuan was in charge of ministries, economic affairs and relations with provinces, while the Legislative Yuan debated and approved legislation, voting on foreign policy and budgets. Two other bodies handled appointments and justice. The fifth, the Control Yuan, was to ensure ideological purity and discipline.[30]

T. V. Soong worked on a national budget and set up a Central Bank. Measures were promulgated to standardize provincial currencies, taxes,

---

* As the capital moved to Nanjing ('southern capital'), the northern city's name was changed to Peiping ('Northern Peace'). For simplicity's sake, I will continue to refer to it as Beijing.

and weights and measures, draw up a national land register and abolish both tax farming and the *likin* duties on the movement of goods. Projects proliferated. Under Chiang's Shanghai business patron, 'Curio Zhang' Jingjiang, a National Reconstruction Commission built power plants and radio stations. The Post Office network was expanded to total 12,000 bureaux by the early 1930s. An airline was launched. Plans were elaborated to build 5,000 miles of railway track, check river flooding, and encourage mining and agriculture. The working day was set at eight hours. Child labour would be banned. Workers would get notice periods and share in profits. Salt tax revenue was to pay for education. Civil service salaries were to rise to eliminate corruption. Campaigns were launched against foot-binding and cigarette smoking. Sport was encouraged to foster a new, healthier generation combining competition with team work.

Industrial output jumped by up to 10 per cent a year – from a low base indeed, but still a pointer to progress. A slump in the world price of silver, on which China's currency was based, boosted exports and helped manufacturers by increasing the cost of imports from countries on the gold standard. Foreign holders of silver found China a profitable home for their hoards, swelling bank reserves and enabling interest rates to be cut.

The government stepped up its efforts to gain a proper place in international affairs. The US led the way in restoring China's tariff autonomy. The Nanjing Incident of 1927 was formally closed with an agreement with London by which the Nationalists accepted Chinese responsibility, apologized, but also blamed the Communists. Recognition by foreign powers meant that Nanjing received the revenue from the customs service administered by the foreigners, though it had to pay indemnities such as that imposed after the Boxer Rising. Chinese diplomats were posted to Europe, Washington and Latin America, and sat in international bodies. Chiang learned more English from his wife – according to the writer Emily Hahn, this stopped after he greeted the British ambassador with the words, 'Kiss me, Lampson.'[31]

Nanjing saw a sprouting of new buildings in a style known as 'Chinese Renaissance', combining modern and classical features. A nine-storey headquarters was built for the leadership on the site of the old Taiping palace. A stadium for 30,000 spectators was erected, surrounded by tennis, baseball and basketball courts, a boxing ring and what one

British visitor described as 'the best open-air swimming bath that I have ever seen'. A drive was launched to get rid of prostitutes and beggars in the city, replace rickshaws with public transport and tear down slums. Foreign experts were appointed to the new regime – some, like Henry Ford, on condition that they would not have to go to China.[32]

Sun Yat-sen's body was brought from Beijing to a massive mausoleum in the foothills of the Purple Mountains outside Nanjing. A two-mile-long procession moved with it for six hours along the route from the city centre to his new resting place, at the top of 400 broad granite steps, with a blue-tiled roof, blue, red and gold cornices, stained-glass windows, wooden pillars and a mosaic of the KMT flag on the ceiling.

Despite the euphoria and enthusiasm in the new administration, critics were not hard to find. Sun's widow, who was living in Shanghai, was vituperative about Chiang. The doctor's former secretary, Hu Hanmin, thought that the party should exercise full control over the government and army, while the leftist Reorganization Society pressed for real democracy. But Chiang and his associates selected the bulk of delegates to a Party Congress in March 1929, which decreed that the KMT should practise 'political tutelage' on behalf of the people until the end of 1935. Not surprisingly, given the composition of delegates, the meeting did nothing to rein in the leader's power.[33]

In reality, the government was a lot weaker than it appeared. It controlled only five provinces in the Yangzi region. The tug-of-war between the centre and the provincial barons was too deeply embedded to be undone by a single military campaign, however successful. While Nanjing's army, bolstered by purchases of planes, rifles and field guns from Europe, could overpower any single province at a time, it could not impose itself on the nation as a whole. Nor could it be defeated. So a stalemate evolved in which most provincial leaders chose to follow or disregard central instructions as it suited them. For the warlords with whom he had allied to beat Zhang Zuolin in 1928, Chiang was one of their number, rather than the sole ruler of China. When he tried to get them to cut their armies, they resisted; when the administration sought to control them or to extend its reach, they rebelled.

The ever-volatile Guangxi group was the first to break ranks, seeking to put a protégé into the governorship in Wuhan in the spring of 1929. It mustered a force of 60,000, which Nanjing trumped by sending in an army of 100,000 men, who sang marching songs to the tune of 'Frère

Jacques' and sheltered under umbrellas from heavy rain as they advanced along the Yangzi. Deploying his usual second weapon of bribery, Chiang induced 5,000 of the Wuhan defenders to switch sides. The Guangxi generals fell back to Guangdong before fleeing to Hong Kong.[34]

More seriously, an anti-Nanjing coalition was set up in Beijing under the title of the Enlarged Conference of the Kuomintang, which brought together a varied crew of politicians ranging from Wang Jingwei and KMT leftists to right-wing traditionalists. The Model Governor and the Christian General, who disliked Chiang's attempts to build up authority and to cut their forces, joined in. On paper, the rebels had twice as many soldiers as the central army's 300,000 men. But Chiang got 100,000 of the enemy to switch sides by bribery. Fighting, largely along railway lines, was extremely bloody as it stretched through the bitter winter. Nanjing claimed that its forces inflicted 150,000 casualties, and suffered 30,000 deaths, with twice as many wounded. Other estimates spoke of overall casualties of 250,000, 100,000 of them for the central government. Towns were ravaged, and crops destroyed. Nationalist troops experimented with poison gas, only to have it blown back at them when the wind changed.[35]

Looking fit and confident, Chiang travelled to the front in an armoured train. His original German adviser, Max Bauer, had died of smallpox during the campaign against the Guangxi rebels, and he was now accompanied by another far-right German, Colonel Hermann Kriebel, who had shared a jail cell with Hitler after taking part in the Munich beer hall putsch attempt. The KMT leader recounted that, at one particularly dangerous moment when his troops risked being cut off, he had prayed to the Christian God, pledging to convert if he was victorious. A snowstorm blew up, preventing the enemy from advancing and allowing reinforcements to arrive to win the day. However, the key player was not divine, but the morphine-addicted young ruler of Manchuria.[36]

Zhang Xueliang had not turned out to be a patsy as Japan's Kwantung Army had hoped. His backbone was further strengthened when he took on the ubiquitous adviser W. H. Donald, who tried to wean him off his drug habit with a regime of long horse rides, physical exercise and golf. Zhang arranged the assassination of his father's pro-Japanese chief of staff. As mah-jong was being played after a dinner he gave for the general, the Marshal excused himself, saying he felt ill. That was understood as a pretext for him to go off for a morphine dose. After he left the room, his bodyguards ran in and shot the chief of staff dead.

Zhang wanted to defy both Japan and Russia, using railway politics as his weapon. He developed Manchurian lines to compete with the Japanese, and seized the Russian-controlled Chinese Eastern Railway (CER). This second initiative went badly wrong when it led Moscow to send in an army under Chiang's former adviser, Galen, which routed the Manchurians.[37]

However, Zhang was strong enough militarily to decide the outcome of the civil war in the north. If he sided with the Beijing rebels, Nanjing could not hope to win, and China might well revert into warlordism. If he allied with Chiang, the central government would have a good chance of putting down the rising, and establishing a proper state. The Marshal could thus use his position to strike a bargain that would confirm his control of Manchuria and leave him as the main figure in the north. Though a visitor reported that he regarded the Nationalist regime as 'rotten to the core', he saw the KMT's principles as China's only hope.[38]

The Beijing group made a serious mistake in including Zhang's name among members of its State Council without consulting him. At a post-midnight meeting with his commanders, the Marshal decided to go for the Nanjing option, and threatened to attack Beijing. The Enlarged Conference gave up. As usual, Chiang let his foes off with minor punishments, knowing that he might need to work with them another day. The 29-year-old Manchurian was appointed deputy commander of Nationalist armies and military governor of North China.

Chiang, who kept his bargain for his delivery outside Kaifeng by converting into the Methodist church at a ceremony in Shanghai, now turned to politics, having his old rival, Hu Hanmin, detained at 2 a.m. after a dinner at the general's home. Hu's supporters in the south promptly formed a movement to defend the politician and attack the man who had ousted him. Joined by Wang Jingwei and Sun Yat-sen's son, Sun Fo, the rebels sent an army into Hunan. But Chiang got a Party Congress in Nanjing to pass a constitution strengthening the power of the presidency, which he assumed; he also became prime minister by taking the chair of the Executive Yuan. Beset by its own divisions and lack of resources, the revolt fizzled out.[39]

Chiang's military and political victory did not bring China a lengthy period of calm to implement the reforms it needed. The divisions of the nation were too strong. In many ways, it was a federal state. But there was no formal federalist mechanism, no agreed means by which disputes could be settled without war.

The price of Zhang Xueliang's adherence to the regime was his retention of territorial autonomy in the north-east and the extension of his military authority across the Great Wall. In 1930, after having done penance for his part in the northern revolt with a spell abroad, the Model Governor of Shaanxi returned and picked up where he had left off, running his province independently of Nanjing. Though the Christian General remained in seclusion, painting and writing poetry, one of his former lieutenants took control of Shandong, executing KMT members and reaching pacts with the Japanese.

In Hunan, provincial authorities held back tax money to build up local forces. Further west, the largest province, Sichuan, was controlled by local militarists, while wild Guizhou was a law to itself under a particularly backward warlord. On the border with Burma and Indochina, a one-eyed militarist, Long Yun, who seized power in 1927 after having a rival beheaded as he sat at table at a banquet, ruled Yunnan as he wished, drawing revenue from opium and tin mines that used slave labour. In the Far West, Xinjiang was the scene of a series of warlord coups and Muslim revolts. The governor of Guangdong perpetuated the province's autonomist tendencies and the Guangxi Clique came back from its short exile to run the province on the basis of the 'three selfs' – self-determination, self-sufficiency and self-defence.

Though Nanjing emerged on top again and again, each confrontation demanded the application of resources, time and attention, which could have been better spent on state-building. The military nature of the regime was accentuated, as was the sense of living in permanent crisis. Programmes elaborated in the capital were far beyond the resources of the economy, and were often not well planned. Even in advanced areas, roads were still likely to be pitted with holes. Constant warfare had destroyed railway tracks in the north and, increasingly, Chiang made sure that new lines were laid mainly for military purposes.

Symbolically, the national stadium at Nanjing was inaccessible owing to lack of public transport, and there was not enough water to keep the swimming pool filled – photographs showed its sides cracking. Despite attempts to replace them with buses, the number of rickshaws in the new capital rose, and, while slum clearance was welcomed, prostitution was far from being eliminated. Meanwhile, Beijing was left to decay. As the great writer Lao She noted, its influence was taken to other cities as its people moved out – Beijing-style lamb was served in Qingdao, Beijing cakes were on sale in the streets of Tianjin, there were policemen and servants in Shanghai and Hankou who spoke the Beijing dialect and ate pancakes with sesame paste, while pallbearers took the train to Nanjing to carry the coffins of high officials. But, back home, the imperial capital's grand spaces were poorly maintained, its inhabitants deprived of the perks of being at the centre of power.[40]

Economically, the rural world had not shared in the good fortune of the manufacturing sector in the first year of the Nanjing era. Now, China suffered from growing competition which helped to double the trade deficit between 1928 and 1933. In 1902, the country had exported 34 per cent of the world's tea; by 1932 this was down to 9.8 per cent. Agricultural prices slumped; in 1933, rice was selling on the wholesale market in Shanghai for 55 per cent of the 1931 level. The silver advantage of the late 1920s disappeared when major Western countries left the gold standard. In 1935 the silver standard was replaced with a managed currency, but this did little good.[41]

While industry grew in some cities, the number of workers in modern factories was still only 1.5–2 million. Unemployment and destitution increased in Canton, Wuhan and Beijing. Labour conflicts in Shanghai became more frequent and larger. Though the modern sector developed in coal, iron and banking, traditional handicrafts and domestic enterprises were estimated to provide around 70 per cent of added value in manufacturing. Industrial safety standards were low – deaths of coalminers were far above the level in Japan, for instance, with recurrent disasters that took hundreds of lives.[42]

The overwhelming bulk of state revenue came from the customs, salt duty and excise levies – supplemented by the take from opium, which exceeded $100 million by 1934. Corporate and income tax made only a small contribution. The administration and provinces tried to augment their earnings with an array of 'special taxes' on everything from sedan chairs to each stage in the life of pigs – from birth through trough feeding and intercourse to butchery; a survey in Chiang's home province of Zhejiang showed that such levies increased the overall tax payment by 45 per cent.[43]

Nanjing was always short of funds. The main cause was the money demanded by the army, which took up half of total state expenditure. The Farmers' Bank turned into a front for channelling money from opium to the military. Loan servicing accounted for another 32 per cent of the budget. Government credit was so low that it had to offer up to 20 per cent annual interest on bonds. T. V. Soong resigned as finance minister in protest at military spending, and was replaced by another member of the family, H. H. Kong, who believed in simply printing a lot more notes, which boosted inflation and devalued the currency; that made China attractive for foreign investments, but they went mainly to foreign firms in treaty ports.[44]

Though there were laudable initiatives, plans for expanding health care and education never lived up to their targets. By the mid-1930s, a population of 450 million had just 30,000 hospital beds and 5,000 doctors. If the number of secondary schools trebled in ten years, the peak of pupil numbers did not exceed half a million. Private schools provided scattered pockets of primary and secondary learning, but the state education budget was only 15 per cent of what was needed to achieve the goal of free schooling for all. Farmers and rural labourers wanted their children to work – as a rural teacher reflected, school 'can't compare in practical importance with gathering firewood, reaping the rice, shepherding and so forth'.[45]

Corruption remained a constant and corrosive element, helping to win the loyalty of those who shared in it, but breeding widespread alienation among those who did not – or who thought it was simply wrong. Party officials in Nanjing bought fine homes, ordered lavish meals, sent their children to private schools in limousines, and spent long weekends at homes in the foreign concessions of Shanghai. Officials took shares in companies whose activities fell within their remit. Well-placed figures from the Soongs downwards used their status and connections to increase their wealth – Ailing speculated on the basis of information she overheard from her finance minister husband, sometimes in cahoots with Big Ears Du.[46]

Like the later empire, the regime depended on the rural gentry to act as a local government force. Chiang encouraged the *baojia* system of local militia which would be loyal to the regime, keep order and produce citizen-soldiers to fight both bandits and political opponents. Villages were reorganized into administrative units of 100 households under a headman. Above them were salaried officials with policemen under their command. In theory, they were subject to approval by the inhabitants and under a supervisory committee. In fact, they often acted as what one observer called 'petty tyrants with armed police to support them', working with magistrates, gentry and landlords. To make matters worse, they were often not local people and lacked roots or empathy with local problems.

Estates were increasingly run for absentee landlords who had moved to cities by agents who had no interest in local affairs beyond getting rents paid and skimming off their take. Where the old elite remained in place, it could find co-existence difficult with the new breed of land-owners, made up of army officers and party functionaries. This was part of a general fraying of rural society as tenancy increased at the expense of the traditional family-owned smallholdings. Moneylenders became even more grasping, and interest rates rose. Land distribution grew more unequal. Promised rent reductions either never saw the light of day, or were manipulated to the advantage of landlords, who had no motive to improve the land they let out.[47]

However, in some areas more-efficient farming methods were introduced. A study of Hubei and Shandong between 1890 and 1949 found that the peasant economy of northern China performed quite well. Other research suggests that agriculture grew more rapidly than the population in the 1930s. The National Agricultural Research Bureau reported that in 1933 average farm income, at $42, fell below average outgoings. But there was an improvement in 1936-7, with bumper harvests and the short-term effect of a new currency system which, by fuelling inflation, raised prices for agricultural products by 45 per cent over the 1933-5 average. Some rurally based textile works did well, as in Gaoyang county in Hebei, which counted 533 factories and commercial firms employing 120,000 people.[48]

On the debit side, co-operatives set up to help the smallholders were often looted by local officials; it was said that only half the funds reached the intended destination in some provinces. Rural taxes were as great a burden as ever, and spurred protests, as did rent rises. While most of the farmers, who made up 70 per cent of the population, remained productive, they worked within the limits of the technology available to them, consisting mainly of traditional tools and human waste as fertilizer. One estimate blamed up to a quarter of rural deaths on diseases spread through the use of excrement, but imported fertilizers paid 50 per cent duty.[49]

As always, the rural world was buffeted by natural disasters, and farmers were increasingly affected by growing integration into world markets, which made them subject to fluctuations far beyond their control or knowledge. International price movements of silver, in which taxes were paid, and copper, used for everyday transactions, could be devastating. An interruption of trade with the Soviet Union ruined tea merchants in Fujian, their decaying mansions standing as mute testimony to former prosperity. The sugar industry in the same province was devastated when Japanese colonists in Taiwan cut the price of their sugar. Alcoholic brewing in Jiangxi was hit by US prohibition. Japan became a major competitor in silk.[50]

In the mid-1930s, a collection of writings by Chinese authors about rural conditions provided illuminating snapshots of life in the country-side, the power of oligarchic buying cartels and big companies, official involvement, and the situation of peasants and farmers, to which I have added other on-the-ground evidence from the time.

In one community of 3,500 people in southern Hubei, which may stand for countless others, life had been getting progressively harder since the early 1920s under the impact of war, depression, famine and plagues. The gap between rich and poor families had widened; only eighteen of the 500 families in the village owned more than 100 *mou* (16.5 acres) while 75 per cent held 20 *mou* (three acres) or less. Implements were rudimentary. When the price of the main crops of sorghum, wheat and peanuts fell sharply in the 1930s, the local farmers could not make a living wage. Increasing banditry led to a twenty-four-hour guard system, and men took narcotics to stay awake. Most women aged over fifteen still had bound feet. Children worked on the land from the age of seven or did domestic chores and looked after younger kin. Half the boys and three quarters of the girls did not go to primary school – for those who did, a secondary education was beyond their parents' means.[51]

Further west in the centre of Shaanxi, average farm revenue covered only a little over half the cost of production and taxation. The gap was filled by loans, mortgages, sale of land and any valuables, and reduced standards of clothing and food. In the hardest times, vegetable husks were the only nourishment.[52]

In the east, silk worm farmers were at the mercy of monopoly owners of the filatures where the threads were extracted. These big families extended their influence over co-operatives, fixing prices virtually at will. As a result, a report in 1937 found that 'while the industrialists can enjoy huge profits ... the silk peasants cannot even make a living wage.'[53]

In Shandong and Henan, the British American Tobacco Company (BAT), which produced 60 per cent of China's cigarettes, encouraged peasants to grow tobacco by distributing seeds and promising immediate cash payment for crops. But the cultivation and curing of the leaves required an investment of capital that plunged many farmers into debt. When it was time to take their produce to the collection centres, lines of carts and wheelbarrows snaked across primitive paths, falling into deep mud in storms. Once at the depots, the crowd was such that it could take twenty-four hours to reach the front of the line. People were trampled to death in stampedes to get to the head of the queue. Farmers were so anxious not to see their crops spoiled that they took off their coats to cover the leaves when it rained, shivering through the night in the open while guards with whips kept order. When they presented their crop, the growers were at the mercy of agents, who might reject their sole source of livelihood or pronounce it of poor quality and worth only a low price.[54]

The hatred aroused by middlemen in the tobacco trade was such that, when the Christian General's troops arrived in the area in 1927, farmers burned down the imposing tobacco company building constructed by a comprador on the Beijing–Hankou rail line. BAT resumed operations there two years later, employing a new agent who was chairman of the tobacco industry association in Shanghai and an official at the Finance Ministry in Nanjing – and, according to a detailed report filed in 1936, a dab hand at dispensing 'squeeze' to obtain results. By the early 1930s, half a million farmers in the region depended on tobacco for their living. The new comprador had a monopoly on buying their crops, and his agents rarely offered anything but the lowest prices. From 1934, even these dropped sharply; by 1936, the average annual income was not enough to cover payment of debts incurred in buying coal for baking leaves.

Farmers who faced extreme difficulty in supporting themselves and their families from the land turned to alternative sources of income. In poverty-stricken Gansu, in the west, they earned a few coins by taking the place of men sentenced to a beating for misdemeanours; if they died, their families were not paid. More usually, peasants hired themselves out as coolie labourers, sometimes merely to get food in return for work. A highway between Hunan and Sichuan was built with what was, in effect, press-gang labour, working in arduous terrain in freezing weather, driven on by whip-wielding foremen, without enough food to survive. Officials pocketed payments destined for skilled stonecutters, who were reduced to destitution. Not surprisingly, there were riots, in one case led by a man who claimed to possess magic water that conferred invulnerability.[55]

A traditional alternative source of rural revenue was weaving on looms, either rented for use at home or in workshops where the peasants might find themselves spinning for fifteen hours a day. When crops were bad and farm income fell, the number of people desperate for work enabled employers to reduce wages. Falling prices caused by Japanese competition exacerbated the situation – in parts of southern China, the cost of labour dropped by 70 per cent between 1930 and 1934. In some southern areas, wages fell to only 6 per cent of the market price for finished goods. When retail prices got too low, the merchants who collected cloth from home weavers simply suspended operations, leaving the peasants with their produce, no buyers and rent to pay on their looms.[56]

Like so many others, they were obliged to borrow money to survive, risking a downward spiral of debt. In one district of Sichuan with 144,000 inhabitants, 73 per cent of adults were in debt in 1936. A survey of 1,898 pawnshops in 1933 showed three quarters charging monthly interest ranging from 3 to 8 per cent. In the silk zones of Jiangsu and Zhejiang, the rate went to 100 per cent for forty days. Half the moneylenders and pawnshops covered in a national study demanded repayment within a year. Most such outfits belonged to officials, landlords and merchants – a former Hunan governor possessed eighty pawnshops in Beijing. As terrible flooding in central China in 1931 forced many people to borrow money to buy food, the annual interest rate rose as high as 300 per cent. When foreign relief aid arrived, the lenders took 60 per cent of it as repayment.[57]

'Rural China,' concluded the economist Yao Hsin-ning, 'is now bankrupt.' The British social scientist R. H. Tawney compared farmers to 'a man standing permanently up to his neck in water so that even a ripple is sufficient to drown him'. Returning from a trip to the northern countryside, the poet Xu Zhimo wrote that his blood chilled at the sight of 'children that look no longer human [who] actually fight over lichen and mosses that their bony fingers scratch off from the crevices of rocks and stuff into their mouths, in their desperate effort to assuage excruciating hunger and cold! Lord, wherefore such were caused to be born!'[58]

One crop seemed to flourish in troubled times, though there could be catches here, too. Opium was subject to prohibition decrees and assurances of action to the League of Nations. The regime proclaimed that it was eradicating the drug; after pressure from the embassy in London, a display of an opium den was removed from the exhibit on China at Madame Tussaud's Waxworks. But, in the early 1930s, China still produced 12,000 tons of narcotics a year, and the drug remained a major source of income for farmers, traded by soldiers, officials, outlaws and the underworld gangs of big cities. It was a source of relaxation for workers, a diversion for the better-off, and a pain relief for millions. In some areas, it was the main cash crop. The regime drew funds from the traffic. Army officers sent to police poppy areas were paid off by growers, or imposed heavy taxes on them – in Anhui, 20,000 people took part in a protest at the fees.[59]

Farmers from Yunnan to Gansu to Anhui depended on poppies to lift them from the precariousness of rural life. Growers became users; a third of the adult population of Yunnan was thought to be addicted. Sichuan had twenty-eight morphine plants round Chongqing. When prices dropped steeply in 1934, growers were reduced to eating tree bark and pond weeds in some parts of the province.[60]

In Shanghai, Big Ears Du sought respectability by branching out into legitimate businesses and was described by the *China Yearbook* as 'a well known public welfare worker', but narcotics remained at the heart of his operations. He ran ten drug refineries, the two largest of which earned $40,000 a day and paid $5 million a year to the government. He himself was showing the effects of addiction; a Polish investigator from the League of Nations, Ilona Ralf Sues, who met him in his office, described him as:

a gaunt, shoulderless figure with long, aimlessly swinging arms, clad in a soiled, spotted blue cotton gown; flat feet shod in untidy old slippers; a long egg-shaped head, short-cropped hair, receding forehead, no chin, huge, bat-like ears, cold, cruel lips uncovering big, yellow decayed teeth, the sickly complexion of an addict ... He came shuffling along, listlessly turning his head right and left to look whether anyone was following him ... Eyes so dark that they seemed to have no pupils, blurred and dull – dead impenetrable eyes.

The fingers on his bony hands were 'brown, opium-stained claws', she added.[61]

Marxists paint the Nanjing Decade between 1928 and 1937 as a time when the bourgeoisie took control in league with the military. This fitted their need for a stage in the progress towards the Communist victory of 1949. But the true character of the regime was very different. The nascent bourgeoisie which had emerged in the Yuan Shikai and warlord period was treated ruthlessly, squeezed for money and excluded from real power. When Nanjing wanted to nationalize the big Shanghai banks, it used force, including Green Gang muscle. As a leading member of the Shanghai corporate elite, T. V. Soong provided a useful veneer calculated to appeal to foreigners, but his authority was always fragile. His youngest sister, Meiling, was equally popular abroad, particularly in America; but her husband always limited her access to the inner circle of his power – the army and the KMT.

What Chiang and the Kuomintang hankered for was a form of state capitalism harking back to the late imperial era. Well-connected businessmen would have a role to play, and might be useful in facilitating foreign loans. The bourgeoisie could enjoy a comfortable life so long as it did not challenge the regime, and kept its head down. But true power would be held by the central military-political group round the leader.[62]

As for the urban workers, the regime was keen to avoid the rise of leftist trade unions, and preferred 'yellow unions' run by co-operative underworld labour bosses among unskilled workers. Though Communist influence persisted in more advanced sectors of factory employees, the biggest organization, the General Labour Union of Shanghai, was relaunched after the 1927 purge under the control of allies of Du, whose command of the powerful Post Office union gave him access to correspondence. Labour reforms mooted at the start of the Nanjing Decade were shelved. Legislation to cut the working week, guarantee holidays and limit the slice of wages taken by labour contractors was ignored or turned into a dead letter. Children were employed from the age of nine rather than the statutory fourteen. The requirement to provide them with education was met in only a quarter of the plants. Instead of eight weeks' maternity leave with pay, women got an average of $18 with no time off. While there were strikes, notably at the BAT factories and silk mills in Shanghai, the regime's readiness to leave the regulation of labour to the underworld won it a large degree of industrial peace, at heavy cost to the workers.[63]

Chiang, the martinet, workaholic control freak, who had himself promoted to the rank of generalissimo, was aware of the fragility of the administration he headed. 'I have observed that many of the staff members do not seem to know what they are supposed to do while others do not know how to work at all,' he had told the State Council in 1929. 'That is why our organisation becomes worse and worse ... many staff members just sit at their desks and gaze into space, others read newspapers and still others sleep.' For all the good intentions, R. H. Tawney noted that 'nothing is being done, that no one is very hopeful that anything will be done, that there is little finance or administrative staff, that the last official concerned in the business was not wholly above suspicion in the matter of money, and that his successor cannot visit the areas which most need attention for fear of being kidnapped.'[64]

Inertia was the regime's most powerful enemy, Chiang declared: 'Everyone is sitting about and doing nothing.' There was no respect for laws, he added. Party workers spent too much time putting up posters, shouting slogans and issuing manifestos, rather than on real work. 'The revolution is in danger of failing, and the entire nation has gradually lost trust in the party,' he lamented. The new elite was seen as 'a special class; nowhere do the masses regard us with good will.'

In part, this was the result of the growing ideological straitjacket within which Nanjing operated. The gulf between the regime and intellectuals propelled progressive thinkers and writers into opposition. The poet Xu Zhimo wrote to a friend in England of a China marked by 'sordidness instead of nobility, hostility and mutual destructiveness, rather than fellowship and cooperation, dead and infectious dogmas, not living principles, run wild. Like stalking corpses to plunge the whole nation into yet greater disaster and suppress the creative fountain of the human spirit!'

Since the party epitomized the nation, no dissent could be allowed, in theory, at least – even if the weaknesses of the regime meant it had trouble imposing its will, and often had to compromise with non-KMT forces in civil society. Mass movements were an anathema. The Chen brothers, Lifu and Guofu – nephews of Chiang's Shanghai mentor, Chen Qimei – imposed conformity on the education system and clamped down on the press and the arts. As the regime moved to what the historian Frederic Wakeman has termed 'Confucian Fascism', a band of ultra-loyalists dedicated to the Generalissimo secretly founded a praetorian guard known as the Blue Shirts under the much-feared political police chief, Dai Li, a man with a crisp military manner, sharp eyes and tiny, delicate hands who was described as walking as if he had a ramrod for a spine, and was celebrated for the number of his mistresses, some of whom worked for the police and travelled with him on official missions. Enjoying Chiang's complete trust – he was the only man allowed to carry a pistol in the leader's presence – Dai Li's terror apparatus grew steadily, using torture, executions and arbitrary imprisonment against real or imagined enemies of the regime.[65]

Between 1929 and 1935, 458 literary works were banned for slandering the authorities, encouraging the class struggle or constituting 'proletarian literature'. A draconian press law was introduced in 1930. Film directors were told that their work should be 30 per cent entertaining and 70 per cent educational, to promote 'good morals and demonstrate the spirit of fortitude, endurance, peace and the uprightness of the people'.[66]

Though the regime was not strong enough or sufficiently centralized to exert repression on the scale of Nazi Germany or the Stalinist USSR, progressive writers and intellectuals were marginalized, harassed and, at worst, arrested and killed. The Shanghai journal *Life Weekly*, which reached a readership of half a million under the editorship of a May Fourth figure, Zou Taofen, was closed down. Dai Li's secret police shot dead the secretary of the League for the Protection of Civil Rights as he got into his car outside his home with his son. The editor of a leading Shanghai newspaper was ambushed and killed. In 1931, a prominent young writer, Hu Yepin, was among twenty-two people executed after being arrested at a Communist meeting in Shanghai – his wife, the writer Ding Ling, whose work pushed the boundaries of feminism and sexuality, was arrested two years later, and went to join the Communists after escaping in 1936.

A cutting allegory of China, *Cat Country* by the Beijing writer Lao She, carried the sense of despair to a pitch of high irony, telling of a Chinese who landed on Mars, where he found a population of cat people who were lazy, dirty, cruel, undisciplined, disorganized and addicted to drugs. Politics consisted of endless brawls. The cat emperor had been overthrown, and replaced by the Ruler of Ten Thousand Brawls. Then the 'small people' had invaded and slaughtered all the cat people except for ten who escaped to a mountain. There, they went on fighting among themselves until only two were left. Caught by the invaders, they were put in a wooden cage where they bit one another to death.*

Chiang blamed the May Fourth movement for having sapped the nation by dismissing the enduring strengths of China's culture. As a result, 'the educated classes and scholars generally lost their self-respect and self-confidence. Wherever the influence of these ideas prevailed, the people regarded everything foreign as right and everything Chinese as wrong.' What he proposed was a revival of classical values, including filial piety, with himself as the national father figure. The Chinese were to conduct themselves like dutiful children. He presented his gritty, disciplinarian mother as an icon, and saw his own Spartan lifestyle as a model. A massive change in behavioural patterns was, he declared, needed for national revival.[67]

The Generalissimo tried to bring the whole nation into line with his New Life Movement to encourage order, cleanliness, simplicity, diligence, promptness and precision, founded on Confucian principles of *Li* ('propriety'), *I* ('right conduct'), *Lien* ('honesty') and *Chih* ('integrity', 'honour'). There was nothing at all wrong with some of the campaign's precepts – for instance, to stop spitting in public or to kill flies and rats. But given the challenges China faced, particularly from Japan, it seemed glaringly beside the point to order skirts to be lengthened, to ban permanent waves and mixed bathing, or to forbid women to lead male dogs through the streets. People could only see instructions to eat in silence and go to bed early as either an intrusion into their private lives or laughable or sinister – in Wuhan, a New Life fanatic poured acid over a woman he thought was wearing too skimpy clothes and, in Chongqing, a magistrate ordered two fat pigs eating sugar cane pulp in a park to be shot as an offence to public decency.[68]

* The narrator gets back to China on a passing French spacecraft.

The hypocrisy was blatant. Streets were swept and buildings cleaned up in Potemkin Village fashion when the Chiangs passed by, but then the old dirty ways resumed. Officials went on enjoying the 'wine, women and gambling' forbidden by the growing list of prohibitions. Big Ears Du lorded it over the Shanghai drugs trade. Though careful to abstain in public, Madame Chiang paid no attention to the ban on smoking when in private. As the *North China Daily News* observed, 'the New Life Movement would have its best chance of success if, like charity, it could begin at home.'[69]

To go with its attempted moral revolution, the regime set out an economic reconstruction movement, which also contained elements of sense. Advised by eminent foreign experts, it did good work in helping the silk and cotton industries. But it had to operate through provincial authorities, which often had their own agendas. Its budget was far too small at $270 million over five years, and even that was not fully funded. Many projects were linked to Chiang's military plans.

The Generalissimo remained aware of the failings of the regime he headed. In 1936, when optimism was boosted by good harvests and an unusual degree of political stability, he warned that 'if we do not weed the present body of corruption, bribery, perfunctoriness and ignorance, and establish instead a clean and efficient administration, the day will soon come when the revolution will be started against us as we did against the Manchus.' But he lacked the tools with which to bring about the scale of change required, and knew that to do so would risk his own position. The country might be in trouble but he, as a man of destiny, had to distance himself from responsibility. 'I am the Generalissimo; I do not err,' he declared. 'China cannot do well without me.'[70]

Expert at operating on different planes which met only in his person, the Nationalist leader exploited all the contradictions in the country to his own ends, as Zhou Enlai observed. That was the mark of his skill as a political tactician, but left China bereft of a wider vision and without the kind of government able to implement the reforms it needed. This would have been grave enough in any circumstances, but took on a particularly menacing aspect as Nanjing faced two opponents with most definite visions of the future, which would prove very different from the perennial threat of the country's provincial barons. Chiang dubbed one a disease of the skin, the other a disease of the heart. The first was temporary and could, he hoped, be dealt with by patience and forbearance until

'Chinese virtues' triumphed. The other, being home-grown, was more serious and had to be eradicated before it grew into a tumour that would infect the nation. Between them, the two maladies would be the twin nemesis of the Nationalist republic, feeding off one another as they ushered in a much more radical change than the fall of the empire.[71]

PART 3

Wars Without End

The coming to power of the Communist regime which rules in China to this day is often seen as the inevitable result of the combination of popular discontent and the genius or monomaniacal power lust of Mao Zedong with the weaknesses of the Nationalists, their failure to evolve a modern state, their oppression and social dislocation heightened by raging inflation. There is, indeed, a retrospective logic to events in China from the early 1930s to the proclamation of the new order in 1949. But the two decades before the final regime change were filled with false starts, reversals and near-disasters which could have led to a very different outcome.

Having won power, the Nationalists faced a rolling, double-edged military conflict that engulfed China from 1931 to 1949. Tens of millions died. Vast areas were ravaged. At the end, the economy and society were brought close to ruin. On three occasions, the Communists appeared to be on the brink of annihilation while the Nationalists were constantly buffeted by enormous challenges which they were ill-equipped to meet.

For fourteen years, the country faced armed aggression by Japan that descended to the most savage depths. The United States embarked on a quixotic but arm's-length mission to save China from itself, and the Soviet Union played a thoroughly self-interested role. The civil war that followed Japan's defeat perpetuated the century-old tradition of resolving political disputes by mass violence, and pointed to a troubled future under a relentless autocrat that would take tens of millions more lives.

The Communist 'disease of the heart' and the Japanese 'disease of the skin' were intimately entwined in determining the future of hundreds of millions of people. As Mao Zedong subsequently told Japanese who apologized for their country's behaviour, he would not have ended up in power had it not been for their country's invasion. Beyond that, however, the Nationalist–Communist–Japanese triangle sat above, or below, a host of other currents running through

China in the 1930s and 1940s, which make 1949 far more than the victory of a new creed or a single man, whether he was an unmitigated monster or a great visionary – or both.

I I

Enemy of the Heart

The year of 1927 had been a terrible one for the Chinese Communist Party (CCP). Only six years old, it was brought to its knees by Chiang Kai-shek's White Terror purge and the end of the united front, which led to the ousting of the Party chief, Chen Duxiu, who turned to Trotskyism.*
Under his replacement, another intellectual, Qu Qiubai, the Party experienced fresh catastrophes with the failed military revolt in Nanchang, the bloody debacle of the attempted coup in Canton, and the collapse of the Autumn Rising in Hunan, Hubei and Jiangxi.

New Russian advisers arrived, controlling the Party's direction and funding. Through the Comintern, the Soviet Union tightened its grip on the CCP, which held its 1928 congress in Moscow. Qu was sacked for 'left adventurism' – he would be arrested and executed by the Nationalists eight years later. His successor was a Shanghai sailor and dockhand, Xiang Zhongfa, chosen for his proletarian background. He was a figurehead; real power lay with Li Lisan, a Hunanese in his late twenties, and with Zhou Enlai, who returned to Shanghai to work underground. Li imposed draconian discipline, and insisted that the Party concentrate on urban action. Zhou developed a support system of shops, property companies and clinics. He set about rebuilding the Red Army, and ran death squads, known as 'dog-killers'.[1]

Anybody who could be accused of being a Communist was in danger from the Nationalist police and troops as well as the regime's underworld allies. Summary executions were frequent, sometimes by live burial. Torture was routine. Jails were often lingering death traps, with little food and awful conditions. In one case, which led to an outcry from

---

* He was arrested by the KMT but an international campaign saved him from execution, and he was amnestied in 1937, dying in obscurity five years later.

left-wingers outside China, police in Shanghai's International Settlement arrested two dozen participants at a secret meeting, among them five writers, and handed them over to the Chinese authorities. Manacled hand and foot, they were held at the Longhua barracks on the edge of the city for a month before being led through a long, dark tunnel to the execution ground to die.

The bitterness bred by such repression and the premium put on self-preservation would contribute powerfully to the paranoia and purges that became a Communist Party hallmark. So would the uncertainties of a revolving leadership, and the dominant influence of Moscow. Though Li Lisan cleaved to an orthodox Marxist line in insisting that revolution would come in the cities, the industrial proletariat was small, and showed little interest in Communism, particularly after the 1927 purge closed down leftist unions.

On the other hand, though they might not grasp even the basics of the creed and remained wedded to traditional ways, oppressed peasants and poor farmers provided an obvious reservoir of support. If it could harness the rural masses, the Party might gain a new lease of life. The empathy that was really felt by the CCP for the peasants has to be questioned in the light of its conduct up to the end of the century. But rural bases still became the key element in the movement's survival. Between 1927 and 1934, more than a dozen were established. Most were in isolated regions, where Nationalist forces were not strong. Though the leadership in Shanghai assumed that it had Leninist control of the Party, the isolation of the bases and poor communications meant they enjoyed considerable autonomy; it took six months for instructions from Shanghai to reach a Soviet in Jiangxi in 1928, and nine months for the conclusions of a Party Congress to get to another. As a result, local bosses could rival or overshadow the official leadership, perpetuating the familiar Chinese tug-of-war between the centre and the provinces.[2]

Once more, force counted for more than ideological awareness: one CCP organizer recalled in Hubei that he asked a peasant, 'Are you a revolutionary?'

'I am,' came the reply.

'In what way are you a revolutionary?'

'I kill local bullies and evil gentry.'

'And then?'

There was no response.[3]

The survival struggles left the base leaders with few scruples, and little inclination to compromise. As the writer Simon Leys has put it, terror and paranoia were in the Party's DNA from the early days. Its chiefs harked back to the long tradition of the rural outlaw world, drawing on the classic saga *The Water Margin* to justify robbery, kidnapping, extortion and murder under the guise of 'smashing the landed tyrants'. Like the renegades of the past, they welcomed adherents from wandering gangs or former warlord troops, particularly if they were armed. All of which further fostered the climate of violence endemic to the CCP from 1927 onwards and fanned by the KMT's continuing White Terror.

A base originally set up by 200 partisans in the mountains of southern Hubei grew into the E-yu-wan* Border Region Special Committee in a strategically placed location by the province's frontiers with Henan and Anhui, north of Wuhan and west of Nanjing and Shanghai. Local people were ready for recruitment after bad harvests followed by heavy flooding. There was also a heritage of rural radicalism in the area bequeathed by farmers' associations of the first Northern Expedition and the Wuhan Republic period. Expanding their activities, the guerrillas staged attacks on the Beijing–Hankou rail line, and, in 1929, were strong enough to capture a county town.[4]

He Long, an uneducated former cowherd and bandit who had participated in the 1927 defeats, headed a Middle Yangzi base in his home area in West Hubei–Hunan. He arrived with twenty men and eight rifles, but his group had grown strong enough to take two county towns two years later. This base then grew to cover seven districts with a 20,000-strong army, productive enterprises, land reclamation, and campaigns against opium, gambling and superstition.[5]

In the south-east, a base in the mountains of Jiangxi developed the local economy with manufacturing outfits and appears to have taken a moderate line on land reform. On the Hunan–Jiangxi border, the young Mao led 1,500 men from the Changsha area to bandit country in the Jinggang highlands, where he was joined by survivors of the Nanchang rising under a former warlord soldier, Zhu De. At the end of 1928, a Northern Expedition veteran, Peng Dehuai, linked up with them with 1,000 men.

---

* Transliterated at the time as Oyüwan. The name is a contraction of the areas it covered.

Mao, who had warned that the revolution would 'not be like a dinner party', implemented his belief that 'it is necessary to create terror for a while in every rural area, or otherwise it would be impossible to suppress the activities of the counter-revolutionaries in the countryside or over-throw the authority of the gentry.' Public executions of class enemies began; in one captured town, the local chief was tied to a wooden frame and speared to death.[6]

Before he began his ascent at Jinggang, Mao had been a lesser figure in the CCP. His erratic early career had taken him through working in a library in Beijing, and at a school and a bookshop in Changsha. A voracious reader but still ideologically unfocused, he had been appointed to middle-rank posts during the united front in Canton. While other Communists preferred to keep their distance from the Kuomintang, Mao worked closely with the Nationalists. In the united front in Wuhan, he headed the Peasant Department for a time, though his growing radicalism led to his being replaced.

The failed risings in Hunan and observation of the intense repression there pushed him further to the left, and confirmed his belief in violence. Convinced of the complete correctness of his views, he was already driven by ferocious ambition, manipulative skill, tactical political genius melded with strategic vision – and a belief that he alone knew how the Chinese revolution would be won.[7]

During his time in Jinggang, Mao married for the third time – he had long left his first wife from an arranged marriage in his home village and had abandoned his second and their children in Changsha. His new bride, the daughter of a tea house owner, was a Communist who had fled to the bandit area to escape the White Terror of 1927. Since Mao could not understand the local dialect, she acted as his interpreter, and they were united in an informal manner at a banquet prepared by the wife of a bandit chief. Attractive and refined, she was described as having eyes like 'a pair of crystals'. At the time of their union, she was eighteen and her husband thirty-four. A song heard at the base had it that:[8]

Commander Zhu [De] is hard at work – carrying rice through the ditches
Commander Mao is hard at work – making love.

Nationalist attacks forced the base to transfer across the border into Jiangxi in cold winter weather in mid-January 1929. Four thousand men and a hundred women moved in single file along icy ridges, half of them armed only with spears. Mao looked ravaged, his hair straggling down to his shoulders. When the Communists paused in a town, enemy troops surprised them, killing hundreds. But, reaching Jiangxi, they took the town of Ruijin ('Rich Metal'), catching the defenders unawares at a Lunar New Year feast. Communist slogans were painted on the walls. Propaganda and discussion meetings were held. Red Army tunics, leggings and caps were run up from Nationalist uniforms on captured sewing machines.[9]

As newcomers arrived to join it, the base grew steadily to rival E-yu-wan in size. As well as agricultural resources, it had minerals, particularly tungsten. By the middle of 1931, it covered 10,000 square miles, mostly hilly or mountainous terrain. There was, however, friction with the leaders of an earlier Jiangxi base, while Mao's insistence on following his own policies got him into periodic trouble with the leadership in Shanghai. At one point, this led to temporary exclusion from the Party for insubordination. But, despite recurrent illnesses, he survived through his clever politics, strong personality and obfuscation – he kept his expulsion secret and sidelined an agent sent in by the centre to tame him.[10]

Mao's methods at the base set the pattern for the next four and a half decades. His treatment of colleagues was unyielding, and his pursuit of power relentless. Though this does not excuse him in the least, he was hardly alone in this – just stronger and better at vicious infighting. His theory of the 'mass line', which pretended that policy was determined by the wishes and interests of the masses as interpreted by the leadership, had an obvious appeal in contrast to the elitist top-down approach taken by Moscow-led CCP chiefs in Shanghai. While others debated detailed points of ideology, Mao presented a broad brush recipe based on peasant ferment (induced if it could not be spontaneous), armed force, guerrilla war and iconoclasm against any temple gods that stood in his way – all to produce, in the words of the historian of his thought, Stuart Schram, a man who was part emperor, part peasant rebel, part revolutionary leader. In Jiangxi, he honed the last two attributes; it would be a long climb to the first.

Despite its reverses, the CCP was always on the lookout for an opening. The leadership thought one had occurred when Nanjing became embroiled in the war with northern opponents in 1930. Following the line of the Comintern, Li Lisan imposed a co-ordinated campaign against urban centres, and rejected Mao's argument for a rural-based strategy. Between them, the base armies mustered 65,000 men, not many by the standards of the war in the north, but still enough to pose a challenge if they were properly targeted against vulnerable cities. Mao and Zhu De, who submitted to the Party line, were ordered to advance on Nanchang while forces from the two bases in the Middle Yangzi moved against Wuhan. A third group under Peng Dehuai, who enjoyed semi-autonomy from Mao, was given Changsha as its target. Workers in the cities were expected to rise in revolt as Communist troops approached.

Peng's army was the only one which achieved its target, taking the Hunanese capital and proclaiming a Communist government from its headquarters in the American Bible Institute. But a Nationalist counter-attack recaptured the city after eleven days. Having failed to get any-where against Nanchang, Mao and Zhu marched to join Peng's re-treating forces. Together, their armies numbered 20,000 men, much the biggest single force the CCP had ever fielded. Li ordered them to mount a second attack on Changsha, which they besieged. But the defenders stood firm and inflicted heavy losses with artillery, planes and help from Western gunboats moored in the river.

Mao's second wife and their children were in the city. Arrested, she refused to denounce or divorce the husband who had abandoned her and made no attempt to contact her or the children during the battle for Changsha. After being held for three weeks, she was shot outside the city wall, leaving behind highly moving poems, some dedicated to Mao, which were brought to light seven decades later by his biographer, Jung Chang. By then, Mao had led an unauthorized retreat to the base.[11]

Li Lisan carried the can for the failed campaign. He was replaced at the head of the CCP by a group known as the 28 Bolsheviks, who had returned to China after studying in the USSR.* The setback strengthened the position of the bases in the CCP. In a report to Moscow, Zhou Enlai named the E-yu-wan army and the Mao–Zhu De outfit as the Party's two main forces.

No sooner had its troops returned from Changsha than the Jiangxi base found itself under attack from an 'encirclement campaign' launched by Nanjing with 44,000 men, many from ragbag former warlord forces.

* Unlike his predecessors, Li was not caught by the police and lived on until he was tortured to death during the Cultural Revolution.

The Communists implemented the tactic of luring the enemy into the base and fighting on home territory, an approach laid out by the classic Chinese strategist Sun Tzu, and, like many of his other teachings, adopted by Mao. The trading of space for time worked militarily, but exposed the population to the attackers. Sacrificing peasants was not, however, something that ever troubled the future Great Helmsman.

The defenders scored victories with well-laid ambushes. In one town, they caught a division as it relaxed. Its commander, who was made to crawl round confessing his sins, had his tongue cut out, and his cheeks pierced. He was decapitated, and his head, wrapped in a red cloth, was nailed to a board by the ears to be floated down the river towards KMT forces. Deceiving the Nationalists by putting on the uniforms of the defeated unit, the Red Army routed another division. It was time for the government army to retreat.[12]

The Communist victory was all the more striking for having been won during the biggest internal purge the Party had seen. The target was the A-B (Anti-Bolshevik) League, a defunct KMT group which was conjured back into life to provide a pretext for Mao's group to grab control of the original Jiangxi base party, which predated his arrival. Its leaders were accused of allying with landlords and rich peasants, and of being 'mountaintopists', who put their local concerns above wider CCP interests. A meeting of the enlarged Party branch, with Mao's men in a majority, ordered the dissolution of the local organization and, by a secret vote, the execution of its four founders. It was the first case of Chinese Communists liquidating one another.

In the initial stage of the purge which developed against the non-existent A-B menace, some 1,000 people were killed. Then, Mao ordered the repression to be stepped up, with 'merciless torture' of suspects, who duly implicated others in an ever-widening ring of innocent victims. Killing spread to the army – in one week, 2,000 soldiers were shot and a whole company was slaughtered after its commander questioned the need for the purge. In the small market town of Futian, surviving Jiangxi leaders were arrested and savagely tortured; their wives had their breasts cut open and their genitalia burned. In a rare act of resistance, a battalion commander staged a mutiny, which freed the Jiangxi leaders.[13]

A stand-off ensued as two Communist forces faced one another across a river. But Mao's senior colleagues on the spot did not oppose him, while the leadership in Shanghai ended by backing him and ordering the execution of the remaining local leaders. Party solidarity ruled. The purge resumed. An army which had opposed Mao was disbanded, and all its officers arrested. As the Nationalists withdrew, the internal killing ebbed. Its scale and savagery are still kept under wraps in China. The death toll is impossible to establish, but ran into tens of thousands. Just as the White Terror of 1927 saw the bitter coming of age of the Kuomintang, so the Jiangxi purge marked what Mao biographer Philip Short calls the 'loss of innocence'.

Chiang Kai-shek next turned his attention to the other big base above the Yangzi, E-yu-wan, run by a leading CCP figure, Zhang Guotao, with its Fourth Red Army under the tactically accomplished Xu Xiangqian. The base had expanded steadily, setting up a textile factory and farm co-operative along with a post office and a mint – both Nationalist and Communist banknotes circulated in some areas. A Children's Corps was formed. Women's liberation was pursued.

Born into a rich family, the tall, confident Zhang would be damned by orthodox Communist history for his subsequent falling out with Mao, but, at the time, was the more powerful of the two. A participant in the May Fourth movement, he had been among the founders of the Party, going on to hold a string of senior posts as well as leading strikes of railway and factory workers. After the 1927 crackdown, he went to the Soviet Union, and was elected to the Politburo at the Party Congress held in Moscow the following year. Always outspoken, he opposed Comintern policies towards China, and was arrested by his hosts for a time. Allowed to return home, he became general secretary of E-yu-wan and chairman of its military committee. A believer in armed force, Zhang kept his faith in proletarian urban power as the motor of the revolution, and tended to see the rural soviets as a pretext for territorial occupation. The protection the Red Army could offer peasants was more likely to win them over than land redistribution, he believed. But terror also played its part, as in the liquidation of 3,000 members of elite households in a border area in 1929.[14]

At the beginning of 1931, the Nationalists launched an 'encirclement campaign', using planes and deploying three or four times as many men as the 50,000-strong Fourth Red Army. But the Communists showed greater mobility and employed superior tactics, moving swiftly from one side to the other of their circular territory. With peasant backing, they repeatedly caught the enemy by surprise and made the most of their knowledge of the terrain, while augmenting their strength by absorbing captured troops. A second campaign against the base in May used scorched-earth tactics, moving inhabitants out of border areas. But it, too, failed, for the same reasons.

Zhang followed Mao's example in announcing the discovery of a plot by the A-B League to free a captured Nationalist commander and other prisoners of war, blow up a hospital and kill Communist leaders. The plan was said to involve former KMT soldiers, landlords and gentry who wanted to stop the redistribution of land. At least 1,000 people alleged to have been part of the League were killed in a purge for which Zhang may have drawn inspiration from his time in Moscow. Like Mao, he wanted to wipe out the original local Communist leadership. When protests were held against the killings, Zhang had 600 people arrested; most were shot. The repression continued into 1932, engulfing the base security chief, who was among those executed. The total death toll has been put at anywhere from 2,500 to 10,000.[15]

The other Yangzi base, headed by He Long, was also swept by a purge estimated to have killed well over 10,000 people, including the execution of 90 per cent of the officers in one Red Army corps as KMT spies or anti-Bolshevik agents. Killing their own had become a habit for Communist leaders.[16]

Nanjing accompanied the campaigns on the Yangzi with a fresh drive against the Jiangxi base, led by Chiang's long-time associate from their days at the Whampoa Academy, General He Yingqin. A short, bespectacled figure, who was always smartly turned out, He had joined Sun Yat-sen's anti-Manchu alliance and undergone military training in Japan. After taking part in the first KMT campaigns in Guangdong, he played a prominent part in the Northern Expedition, but then failed to support Chiang against Wang Jingwei. The two generals were, however, reconciled, and, in 1930, He became minister for military administration as well as chief of staff, posts he held for most of the rest of the republican period. The senior lay Catholic figure in China, he built up a large landholding in his native Guizhou province, and was suspected of harbouring pro-Japanese sympathies.

Though he commanded more than 100,000 men, He did no better than the earlier attack in Jiangxi. In five battles during two weeks, 30,000 Nationalists were reported killed, wounded or captured. The

Red Army seized 20,000 rifles. Chiang decided to take charge himself, and, with a force of 130,000 men, forced the Communists to retreat across a 400-mile semicircular front – as Mao said, knowing how to run away was a prime requisite for a guerrilla.[17]

Advised by German officers, the Nationalists devastated huge areas. Some units collected the heads of victims, then, finding them too heavy, took only the ears instead – one division was said to have 700 pounds of them. Harried by peasant resistance and suffering from lack of food and the effects of foul water, the KMT soldiers massacred civilians and stole any food they could find. Zhu De recalled 'villages burned to ashes, and the corpses of civilians lying where they had been shot, cut down or beheaded; even children and the aged. Women lay sprawled on the ground where they had been raped before or after being killed.'[18]

Driven back to the foot of a mountain 3,000 feet high, the main Communist force escaped by climbing the heights at night, but it then made a bad mistake in staging a frontal assault, which cost 4,000 casualties. Still, enough survived to pull back to the core base and declare the Chinese Soviet Republic there, with Mao as its chairman. 'From now on,' he declared, 'there are two totally different states in the territory of China. One is the so-called Republic of China, which is a tool of imperialism. The other is the Chinese Soviet Republic, the state of the broad masses of exploited and oppressed workers, peasants, soldiers and toilers.'[19]

Mao's appointment had Moscow's approval. But his authority was, in fact, limited. Zhang Guotao, who was head of the other main base and with whom Mao's relationship was always uneasy, was made one of his deputies in the new republic. Though remaining as political commissar of the First Front army in Jiangxi, Mao lost his military command. The new set-up was meant to unite the Soviets spread across central and southern China, but had no means of doing so given the poor communications and the scattered nature of the enclaves.

Nationalist attacks and internal purges apart, the CCP had another serious cause for concern at this time, involving its leading assassin in Shanghai, a Green Gang member called Gu Shunzhang. Described as 'a master of disguise and deception', he had been trained by the Russians and was said to be able to strangle victims without leaving marks. His hobby was to appear as a magician at the roof garden of the Sincere department store, dressed as a foreigner with a large false nose and small moustache.[20]

In 1931, Gu set off as a member of an entertainment troupe performing in Yangzi cities. His secret mission was to infiltrate the Nationalists to discover their plans, and, possibly, to kill Chiang Kai-shek.
Magician he might be, but he was none too discreet, attracting police
attention by meeting known leftists in his hotels. Arrested and taken to
Nanjing, he was given two hours to choose between death and life. He
went for defection.[21]

Gu told his captors not to send news of his detention to the secret-
service headquarters in Nanjing. They took no notice. What he knew –
and they did not – was that the principal secretary of the intelligence
chief in the capital was a Communist mole. After reading news of Gu's
capture, he fled and tipped off Party leaders in Shanghai, including Zhou
Enlai, who escaped in the garb of a priest. Before he left, Zhou ordered
the beheading of Gu's family: only a boy escaped.

The magician turncoat became a member of the KMT Central Executive Committee, and was active in hunting down political foes. But he
subsequently fell foul of party factions, and was executed for supposedly
having 'reverted to Communist ideas' – though rumours said this was a
lie to enable him to engage in deep-cover work.[22]

On the basis of Gu's revelations, Nanjing was able to roll up the
CCP machine in Shanghai, capturing its wireless transmitter to cut
off communications with Moscow and the bases, thus enhancing their
independence. A few people bribed their way to liberty, but some 24,000
were killed or imprisoned, and 30,000 more were said to have bought
freedom by confessing and defecting to the KMT.

Among those picked up and killed was the former CCP secretary-
general, Xiang Zhongfa, who was detained in the French Concession,
and done away with at the killing ground at Longhua. A more obscure
figure, the future Madame Mao Zedong, Jiang Qing, was said by her
enemies to have bargained her way out of prison by agreeing to work
for the secret police. The main intellectual centre of opposition to the
regime, the Left Wing Writers' League, which had encouraged books
and films on real-life problems, was harassed. In response, the leadership
in the bases heightened the hunt for counter-revolutionaries and sent
killer squads to eliminate KMT agents.

Other opponents of the regime – real or imagined – were at risk as
the purge widened from Communists. A potential Nationalist rival from
Chiang's province of Zhejiang was shot on a bus. Deng Yanda, the

one-time dean of the Whampoa Academy, who headed the small 'Third Party' that sought to navigate between the KMT and the Communists, was arrested in the International Settlement in Shanghai. Taken to Nanjing, he was executed with the greatest discretion outside the city walls. There was a murky element to the affair; Deng's arrest came soon after he had defeated a pro-Communist faction at a congress of his party. Rumours swirled that he had been betrayed by internal opponents egged on by the CCP.[23]

As well as the effects of the Gu defection and of the purges, the CCP bases faced renewed KMT campaigns as Chiang consolidated his political position in Nanjing. Scenting victory at last, he geared up for new offensives in Jiangxi and against the E-yu-wan base. But, as would be the case on several key occasions, external events came to the aid of the CCP as, once again, military and political developments intermeshed to complicate matters for the central government.

First, Nanjing had to confront the rebellion launched by southerners using the ousting of Hu Hanmin as a pretext to try to unseat Chiang. Though the revolt fell apart, it diverted central regime troops from the anti-Communist campaign. Then nature took a hand as heavy rain brought widespread flooding to central China; a downpour in Hubei fell for twenty-three days in temperatures that exceeded 100 degrees Fahrenheit. Though 2 million people were inoculated, cholera spread. A quarter of a million refugees crowded into Wuhan, where human and animal corpses floated in huge cesspools. White slavers bought girls from their starving parents.

Other events also provided causes for concern – Chiang was the target of an assassination attempt in Nanchang and T. V. Soong was shot at in a Shanghai railway station. Chiang also had a personal decision to make involving his son, Ching-kuo,* born of his first village marriage, who had gone to the USSR in 1925 at the age of fifteen. Showing leftist sympathies, and treated badly by his father, he had made the trip voluntarily. But now Moscow tried to barter his return for the liberation of a Polish Communist agent being held in Shanghai.

Whether Ching-kuo actually wanted to go home was unclear. He seemed quite happy in the Soviet Union, taking up with a Russian girl and getting a taste for vodka as he worked in engineering plants.

---

* This Wade-Giles transliteration is still in use. In Pinyin, the name is Jiang Jingguo.

Softening, Chiang wrote in his diary: 'I miss Ching-kuo very much.' But he decided that, as he put it, he should not 'sacrifice the interests of the country for the sake of my son'. The theory that he was ready to make concessions to the Communists to regain his son flies in the face of the evidence.[24]

Still, the Nationalist chief did not let disasters, family problems or assassination attempts distract him from his new campaign against the Jiangxi base. But, in September 1931, events in the north-east forced him to head back to Nanjing and call off the offensive. Japan's Kwantung Army had attacked in Manchuria. The triangle of the next fourteen years had taken shape, with the deep irony of the CCP benefiting from the aggression of the fiercely anti-Communist foreigners against the Nationalists.

12

Enemy of the Skin

While Chiang was preparing his latest assault on the Jiangxi Communists in September 1931, the Young Marshal of Manchuria, Zhang Xueliang, was undergoing medical treatment at the Rockefeller Hospital in Beijing. Though a cover story was spread about a minor ailment, the doctors were trying to wean him off his morphine habit. He was in poor shape to exercise the northern command of 250,000 troops with which Nanjing had entrusted him after he allied with the Nationalists to defeat the big rebellion of 1930. Meeting him earlier in the year, Hallett Abend of the *New York Times* was shocked to see a 'sickly, emaciated, drug-blurred individual . . . a physical and mental wreck'.[1]

On the night of 18 September 1931, Zhang left the hospital to dine at the British Legation, going on to attend a performance by China's most famous Beijing Opera performer, Mei Lanfang. As he did so, a detachment from the Japanese army in the Kwantung Leased Territory in his home city of Mukden strapped forty-two packs of gun cotton on the railway line by a barracks on the way to the main station. The explosion caused little damage – the next train to pass jumped the break in the track and steamed on. But the Kwantung Army used it as a pretext to take over the city on the night of 18–19 September. When Japan's consul-general raised objections, an officer with a drawn sword told him to shut up. Reinforcements moved in from Korea.[2]

Returning to his residence in Beijing from the opera after midnight, the Young Marshal received the news. He telephoned Chiang Kai-shek, and they agreed to do nothing, hoping that the Japanese action would be limited and that foreign powers would intervene to reverse the situation. Zhang Xueliang was described as 'pale and anxious', and may have sought relief in morphine. When he tried to contact officers in Mukden, the switchboard operator there told him, 'I can talk no more. The

Japanese have entered my office.' The Marshal was said to have fainted. Coming round, he wept.[3]

What was known as the Mukden Incident followed a period of rising tension in the north-east. Manchuria had a somewhat ambivalent status. It had provided the last imperial dynasty of China, which had largely adopted Chinese traditions. The separate Manchu identity persisted, but Han immigration after the ban on movement was lifted at the end of the nineteenth century meant that the majority of the population came from south of the Great Wall.

In Japan, Manchuria was portrayed as a 'lifeline', and made the subject of romanticized writing about its 'red setting sun'. The war with China of 1894–5 had led to the unsuccessful attempt to grab the Liaodong Peninsula in the south of the territory. After defeating Russia in their conflict in 1905, Tokyo had gained control of the Kwantung Leased Territory in eastern Manchuria, which was run as a separate state from its headquarters in Dalian, complete with its own army. With a fifth of China's land area but only 5 per cent of its population, the region seemed a natural colony and destination for emigrants from the overcrowded home islands as America clamped down on entry into California.

The Social Darwinism in vogue in Japan justified saving Manchuria from the 'insincere' Chinese, and as an element in manifest national destiny. A leading politician, Prince Konoe, thought it 'only natural for China to sacrifice itself for the sake of Japan's social and industrial needs'. Rising unemployment under the impact of the Great Depression, growing hardships at home and food problems made expansion across the sea all the more attractive. For those who envisaged an anti-Communist crusade, the north-east was an ideal springboard for an attack on the Soviet Union.[4]

Pressure for action was sharpened by the contempt many Japanese felt for the Chinese after the crushing victory of 1894–5. One military specialist believed that three or four divisions and a few gunboats 'would be quite enough to handle the Chinese'. Hawks found an ideological leader in Ishiwara Kanji, a lieutenant-colonel in his early forties who combined Buddhism with knowledge of modern warfare. His real target was the USSR. Japan could sustain an anti-Communist war for twenty or thirty years if it had footholds all over China, he thought. To begin with, 'the only path left open to us is the development of Manchuria and Mongolia', neither of which, he argued, was really Chinese. The Japanese would exercise political leadership and run big industry, Chinese provide labour and operate small industry, Koreans grow rice, and Manchurians tend animals.

Ishiwara's ideas were shared by his superior, Colonel Itagaki Seishiro, a tough, hard-drinking officer in his mid-forties known for his determination and ruthlessness. Skilled at kendo fencing, the colonel belonged to a secret society dedicated to Japan's expansion in Asia. In touch with radical rightists at home, the two officers prepared a pretext which would enable them to take over Mukden.

Time seemed to them to be pressing. Zhang Xueliang had not proved to be a Kwantung Army puppet. He had launched reforms and built railway tracks to compete with Japan's powerful South Manchurian Railway (SMR). He saw the future of Manchuria as lying in ever-closer identification with China, which was planning to end extra-territorial rights in 1932, threatening the end of the Kwantung Territory. 'I am Chinese,' Zhang told a Japanese representative who urged him to follow Tokyo's wishes. Japan would object to further integration, he told the American journalist Edgar Snow, but 'we are prepared to defend ourselves.'[5]

Afraid of matters getting out of control, the government in Tokyo tried to rein in the army. The chief of the Intelligence Section of the General Staff was sent to Mukden with a letter warning against provoking an incident. A less suitable envoy could hardly have been found. Before leaving Tokyo, he tipped off Colonel Itagaki that his plans for a coup were known. Taking his time, he travelled to Mukden by boat and train, rather than flying. On arrival, he went to a restaurant with Itagaki. He was then taken to a geisha house to sleep, still without having delivered the government's message. In any case, there was no way that the military plotters were going to listen to the civilian ministers.

Following up its seizure of strategic positions in Mukden, the Kwantung Army grabbed government offices, the four major banks, the main agricultural company, cotton mills and coal mines, power plants and railways, the post office and the telephones. The residences of Manchurian generals and senior officials were ransacked for treasures, down to a collection of six dozen ancient eggs owned by the head of the Finance Bureau.[6]

Carpetbaggers moved in from Japan and Korea, opening opium dens, gambling houses and brothels, and trailing along behind the soldiers as they fanned out across southern Manchuria. The American comedian Will Rogers, who was visiting Mukden at the time, remarked: 'It wasn't Horace Greeley who told young men to go West – it must have been the Japanese.' An intriguing figure, Dohihara Kenji, head of the Kwantung Special Service Division, who had travelled over much of China in repeated undercover operations during the warlord and republican periods, was put in charge of running Mukden. He spoke several Chinese dialects like a native, dressed in a scholar's gown and had excellent contacts among militarists, including the Model Governor of Shanxi. He had been an adviser to the Old Marshal, and was suspected of having played a role in his murder.

To head a nominal 'peace maintenance' government, Dohihara fished out a Qing-era official in his seventies with a straggling white beard, who wore silver guards over his three-inch fingernails, grown in the traditional fashion to indicate his abstinence from manual labour. His administration declared Manchuria's independence from China. He told Edgar Snow he only took the job under threat of imprisonment or execution, and was acting under duress.

Having consolidated their position in Mukden, Japanese forces assaulted other towns in southern Manchuria, their planes attacking defenceless civilian targets. Emperor Hirohito, it was noted, regarded this as 'only natural in view of conditions at the time'. Zhang Xueliang's effects were sent to him in 417 packing cases, with a note lamenting his 'forced absence' and regretting that it would be impossible for him to return home because the Mukden climate was unhealthy for him. The Marshal did not, however, receive his $100 million treasury.[7]

Guerrilla actions were mounted against the Japanese in the north of Manchuria. An opium-smoking, illiterate warlord, Ma Zhanshan, defeated a Tartar force operating for the foreigners, and then, in the winter, held the main enemy up for a few days at a river in the most northerly province of Heilongjiang. But he retreated in the face of the Kwantung Army's strength. After taking the northern city of Qiqihar,* a Japanese general, a professorial figure barely five feet tall, replied to questions from journalists about criticism from the League of Nations. 'What do those talkative gentlemen in Europe know about conditions

---

* Transliterated then as Tsitsihar.

here?' he asked. 'We are establishing peace and order in Manchuria. Their activities are very tiresome.'

Western powers put pressure on Tokyo not to attack the big southern industrial centre of Jinzhou,* 150 miles south of Mukden. But, meeting at the home of the army spokesman, Major Watari, a group of young officers decided to go ahead. Planes bombed the city's railway yards, and preparations were made to send soldiers from Mukden by rail to 'restore order'. Remonstrations from Washington halted the troop movement for the time being, but it was too late to reverse the tide, and proposals by Moscow for a common anti-Japanese front with the US and China got nowhere.[8]

The Manchurian troops withdrew from their territory on New Year's Day. Jinzhou was occupied. Apart from the Soviet-held Chinese Eastern Railway, Japan now controlled all Manchuria's lines, minerals and ports, and fertile agricultural areas, which were the world's biggest producer of soya beans.[9]

The officers in Manchuria had, in effect, declared themselves independent of the government. The command in Korea had flouted Japan's constitution in not seeking approval before moving men to join the Kwantung Army. At the end of the year, the cabinet in Tokyo fell, and was replaced by a government that approved the taking of Manchuria. The Kwantung officers had staged the biggest land grab since the First World War. China was set to become its devil's playground for fourteen years.[10]

The loss of Manchuria was of a different nature from the earlier foreign interventions. Japan could not be bought off with concessions. The amount of territory relinquished could not be shrugged off as peripheral. Nanjing was faced with the choice between accepting a fait accompli or trying to organize resistance, a choice that would continue to face it for the next six years.

The initial popular response was a wave of nationalist anger. In Shanghai, 50,000 demonstrators demanded death for anybody who traded with the enemy. There were riots in Tianjin. The Communists called for resistance. The *China Times* published a song urging 'Kill the enemy! Kill the enemy! Hurry up and kill the enemy!' Another newspaper

---

* Transliterated then as Chinchow.

added to the flames by printing the full text of a memorial alleged to have been written in 1927 by the then Japanese prime minister, General Tanaka Giichi, setting out a plan for world domination starting with the occupation of Manchuria and Mongolia, followed by the conquest of China. It was a fake, perhaps of Russian origin. But it chimed very neatly with what many Chinese expected from the nation whose rise they had watched with concern since its victory over them thirty-six years earlier.[11]

In Nanjing, 6,000 young people, including 300 women dressed as nurses, marched to demand to be sent north to fight. Anti-Japanese students attacked KMT headquarters. Demonstrators waved banners proclaiming 'Death before Surrender' and 'Supreme Sacrifice' as they called for 'the Entire Nation to come to the Rescue'. Some invaded the Foreign Ministry, breaking windows and assaulting the minister, who was carried out by guards, his clothes torn off and his face covered with blood.[12]

Japanese goods were boycotted – imports fell by 40 per cent in the last four months of 1931 and by 90 per cent in 1932. Chinese banks in Shanghai stopped offering facilities to Japanese firms. Chinese businesses refused to work with Japanese spinning mills. In December, the Shanghai Japanese Industrialists Association begged Tokyo for large loans to avoid bankruptcy.[13]

Chiang Kai-shek declared that an hour of unprecedented gravity had struck the nation. A huge map of Manchuria was put up in the centre of Nanjing, replacing a poster advertising toothpaste. To foster national unity, Chiang had his KMT rival, Hu Hanmin, released from house arrest, and held a meeting with him, Wang Jingwei and Sun Yat-sen's son, Sun Fo, which agreed to call a 'Reunification Conference'.

However, the Nationalist chief had decided not to resist, which has been widely seen as the first episode in the appeasement of the revisionist Axis powers that would stretch up to 1939. That verdict takes little account of the conditions and realities of the time. Chinese troops were no match for the enemy. If Nanjing threw in its best soldiers, its control of China as a whole would be weakened. For the KMT leadership, a great patriotic crusade to recover Manchuria might all too easily get out of hand, creating the kind of mass movement it distrusted and coming under the influence of the left and regional barons. With their roots in southern and central China, the men running the regime had little natural affinity for Manchuria. A Japanese report had Chiang remarking: 'If

Japan will be satisfied with Manchuria, well, we aren't happy about it but we can pretend they aren't there.'[14]

The professed opponents of aggression, the League of Nations, offered only words and the dispatch of an inquiry mission that condemned Japan but also criticized the Manchurians. The Western powers and the USSR did nothing, while Chiang asserted his authority with a typically sinuous manoeuvre, submitting his resignation to the KMT Central Committee on 15 December 1931 and saying he wanted to open the way for 'more competent men'. As the Nationalist chief withdrew to his home village in traditional fashion, the Young Marshal resigned his military positions and flew to Shanghai.

'More competent men' were notably absent when the 'Reunification Conference' met in Nanjing. The rotund Sun Fo took over as head of government, but it barely functioned as the Shanghai money tap was turned off. Provincial leaders flexed their autonomy. In mid-January, Chiang returned as military commander, flying to Nanjing with his wife in their new Sikorski seaplane, equipped with a couch and armchairs. Wang Jingwei, ill with diabetes, became head of the government. The Christian General and the Model Governor rallied in the name of national solidarity.

Chiang's first act was to launch a fresh offensive against the Communist E-yu-wan base, but it was poorly co-ordinated, falling into ambushes and losing 20,000 men killed or taken prisoner. A campaign against the other Middle Yangzi base also failed. But Nanjing's attention was soon diverted back to the 'enemy of the skin'.

Japan's military attaché in Shanghai was a specialist in dirty tricks and, at the beginning of 1932, fomented a series of incidents in the city to heighten the already high state of tension. Hawks in Tokyo and Manchuria wanted him to distract attention from the expansion in the northeast, while the Imperial Navy, which had ships moored off the city, was keen to show that it could do as well as the Kwantung Army.

The attaché paid Chinese thugs to attack five visiting Japanese Buddhist monks, two of whom subsequently died. Across the sea, newspapers ran graphic reports and calls for vengeance. A mob from the 'Little Tokyo' district of Hongkou* attacked a towel factory, setting off a fire

---

* Transliterated then as Hongkew.

that killed two Chinese. A rally by Japanese inhabitants degenerated into street fighting, in which shop windows were smashed and vehicles trashed.[15]

Five hundred Japanese marines landed from ships in the river. The Chinese authorities declared martial law. Tokyo responded by sending in a cruiser and twelve destroyers. The naval commander, Admiral Shiozawa, told the *New York Times* correspondent, Hallett Abend, over cocktails and caviare on his flagship on 28 January that the full attack would start that night.

At 11.05 p.m., his vessels began to bombard the heavily populated workers' district of Zhabei. Japanese marines drove through the streets on motorcycles mounted with guns, firing at random. Westerners took taxis from restaurants, night clubs and ballrooms to see what was going on, some still wearing evening dress. They generally thought the Japanese were right to teach the uppity Chinese a lesson. The Defence Committee of the International Settlement entrusted the protection of Hongkou to Japanese elements in the concession's Volunteer Corps.[16]

In the morning, *ronin* hoodlums brought in from Japan killed hundreds of civilians. Twenty thousand Japanese reinforcements began to pour in, advancing across fields outside the city and assaulting a line of forts on the coast. Planes staged low-level bombing raids, including an attack on a clearly marked Red Cross refugee camp and another on the huge Wing On Cotton Mill, where women workers died at the reels. By early February, shells were landing in Zhabei at an average of one a minute, igniting huge fires.

The big North Station was set alight, great holes gaping in its roof, blood along the tracks. A train was reduced to a mass of charred steel, the bodies of some of those inside thrown thirty feet by the impact of the bombs. The headquarters of China's largest publisher, the Commercial Press, was devastated. At the National Oriental Library, flames destroyed priceless ancient manuscripts. Chinese crowded into the foreign settlements. Air attacks cut the railway line to Nanjing, which was also shelled by Japanese ships on the Yangzi. The government moved to the safety of the Henan city of Luoyang.

In contrast to the lack of army resistance in Manchuria, the Chinese fought back in Shanghai. The main force involved was the Cantonese Nineteenth Route Army, which Sun Fo had moved to the city to act as his military shield on the Yangzi. It owed no loyalty to Chiang Kai-shek, containing officers who had trained under the Soviet advisers at Whampoa and retained left-wing sympathies. It was, in effect, a free agent, but it refused to go home until it was paid off. Receiving journalists at receptions where pâté de foie gras and Martel cognac were served, the army's forty-year-old commander, Cai Tingkai, a tall, dark-skinned man with chestnut eyes, vowed not to cede a foot of ground.[17]

Joined by Green Gang members, his soldiers fought from house to house, sniping at the Japanese from rooftops as the enemy's armoured vehicles were blocked in the narrow streets below. Outside the city, moats, deep trenches and barbed wire defences slowed down the advance of the invaders. Tycoons, local people and Overseas Chinese contributed money. Big Ears Du offered his support. A 1,000-bed field hospital was set up, and the Shanghai press radiated defiance.

Subsequent accounts would depict Chiang Kai-shek as taking no part in the battle, leaving the politically unreliable Nineteenth Army to be destroyed by the Japanese. This fits in with the conventional picture of him as devoting the years from 1931 to 1937 to appeasement, and being ready to let the enemy chew up forces he felt he could not count on. But it is misleading. Chiang did, indeed, hold back for three weeks as Nanjing hoped that the West would put pressure on Tokyo to stop its aggression – or that the fighting would hit the foreign concessions and bring in the powers to halt the battle. But, once more, foreign help was not forthcoming, the League of Nations issuing a verbal reprimand to Japan, and telling off the Chinese for the assault on the monks. The Japanese were allowed to use the International Settlement to unload tanks, armoured cars and lorries, horses, artillery, guns and munitions.[18]

The central government then sent in its German-trained troops in their Western uniforms and steel helmets. They fought well. Cai paid tribute to them for their 'courage and fortitude'. A hospital visitor who saw their wounded attested to their 'excessive bravery'. In the fields outside the city, one brigade staged five charges in an hour. Others held out in trenches protected by four metres of barbed wire. But Japan poured in more men and its 200 planes widened their bombing range. In all, the Chinese are estimated to have committed 63,000 men to the battle, though this may be an overstatement given the depleted condition of some divisions. Japan said it sent in 47,000 men; the Chinese put their numbers at 77,000.[19]

On 18 February 1932, Cai rejected an ultimatum from the invaders.

'My only answer is gunfire and bombardment,' he said. But he was then fooled by the Manchu mistress of the Japanese attaché, who inveigled her way to a meeting with him at which she said she had secret information about the invaders' strategy. This led the general to concentrate his forces on one sector of the front and to leave the coast south of Shanghai unguarded. That was where the Imperial Army landed its fresh reinforcements, which advanced to turn the Chinese line.[20]

On 3 March, a ceasefire was reached. The Route Army headed south to join anti-Communist operations; central-government forces moved west along the Yangzi; the government returned to Nanjing. As the Chinese withdrew, the Japanese went on a murderous rampage. Civilians were killed at random, some taken to a racecourse to be bayoneted. Property and goods were destroyed or dismantled and loaded on to ships for Japan. A puppet administration was set up in Zhabei, and was to encourage opium dens and brothels.[21]

Estimates of Chinese military dead ran from 4,600 to 6,080, with up to 10,000 more missing. Japan's consulate put deaths for its country at 385, with more than 2,000 wounded. The death toll was probably higher, but by how much cannot be known. Though not precisely established, the civilian toll was much greater. More than 200,000 people sheltered in seventy makeshift camps. Half a million may have fled. More than 300,000 of those who stayed were without work. The city government reckoned damage of $1.5 billion, involving 12,000 dwellings, 4,000 shops, 600 factories, 200 schools and five colleges. The municipal economy was badly hit, affecting tax and customs revenue. Food supplies were hit by the devastation of farm land round the city.[22]

With British and American mediation, a settlement was worked out under which China accepted the demilitarization of its biggest metropolis. Japan withdrew forces from Chinese areas; Nanjing was allowed to post only police in the city. Demonstrators showed what they thought of that by pelting the main Chinese negotiator in the face with coins. He signed the settlement while being treated for his injuries in hospital. The Nationalists called a National Emergency Conference to discuss the situation, inviting figures from outside the KMT; but it achieved nothing and Chiang and his colleagues refused to cede any authority. In Japan, the settlement contributed to the assassination of Prime Minister Inukai Tsuyoshi by a naval officer who considered him too moderate, but, for the army and the expansionists, Shanghai was, essentially, a sideshow. Having distracted attention while the Kwantung Army completed its campaign in the north-east, they were ready to switch back to their main purpose.

On 9 March, six days after the ceasefire in Shanghai, the independent state of Manchukuo was formally inaugurated to rule Manchuria. Its creation was, in part, a precautionary move by Tokyo, which was trying to rein in the Kwantung Army: better to have a structured state than an army running wild. The last emperor of China, Puyi, was fetched from the Japanese Concession in Tianjin, where he had been living since being expelled from the Forbidden City in 1924. He was installed with the title of chief executive of the 'paradise of benevolent government' in Changchun, renamed Xinjing* ('New Capital').[23]

Again, the international community was not prepared to do anything. Washington said that, once the new state was established, it expected Japan to withdraw and so saw no need for action. Moscow sent a senior general to the Far East to review the situation, but was not ready to act. Tokyo walked out of the League of Nations after finding itself in a minority of one in the voting on the report by the mission sent by Geneva to investigate events in the north-east. It could paint the international body as racially biased; had it objected to French possession of Indochina or Britain's advance in Tibet? Nanjing was, Reuters reported, 'depressed' by the turn of events.[24]

Puyi could count on the backing of a handful of old imperial loyalists. A former official from the late Qing era, Zheng Xiaoxu, who denounced the Republicans as a bunch of thieves, became the first prime minister. His doctrine of the 'Kingly Way' sought to promote autocratic, benevolent government and co-operation with Tokyo. But there was never any doubt where power lay. An American living in Harbin suggested that the new state might better be called 'Japanchukuo'. Authority was concentrated in an official from Japan who combined the posts of garrison commander, governor of the Kwantung Territory and 'ambassador extraordinary and plenipotentiary'. Japanese forces expanded to 100,000 men, the soldiers operated as they wished – in a reprisal for the killing of several of them by Red Spears guerrillas, 3,000 people were reported to have been massacred in nine villages near the industrial city

---

* Transliterated at the time as Hsinking.

of Fushan. Elsewhere, peasants were herded into 'protected hamlets', which were often rudimentary and poorly supplied. The official *Manchuria Daily News* listed the enterprises the Kwantung Army controlled as banks, post, railways, telegraphs and telephones, the wireless, aviation, slaughter-houses, lotteries, horse-racing, livestock markets, forests, gold, navigation, iron, coal and petroleum deposits.[25]

In Japan, the Manchu dream was extolled as a paradise, and a million people moved to Manchukuo in its first decade of existence. The puppet state was seen as an essential ingredient in recovery from the Great Depression, a valuable source of raw materials and an ideal theatre for heavy industrial growth in the cause of economic imperialism. Manchukuo became part of a yen bloc, and trade and Japan's investments soared.[26]

Japanese headed boards to administer the territory, and enjoyed preferential terms in acquiring land. A building boom got under way. Roads were laid, and an airline was inaugurated. Plans were set in motion to expand the railway network from 5,000 to 15,000 miles in five years. Mining was developed – by 1936 Manchurian railways carried 45 per cent of the combined coal output of China and Manchuria. Department stores from Japan opened branches in cities such as Harbin, where women in kimonos and wooden sandals walked respectfully behind their menfolk and the imperial flag fluttered above.

Not that the occupiers were united on the form their economic imperialism should take. Businessmen from Japan wished to operate independently, but faced strong pressure for state capitalism, particularly from Kwantung officers who wanted to organize a homogeneous military-industrial complex. The army aimed to dismantle the South Manchurian Railway conglomerate to get control over its dozens of constituent companies and direct them to military production. Though the well-organized staff and management protected the SMR, the command economy proponents got the upper hand elsewhere with the adoption of a policy known as 'one enterprise for one industry'. This made Manchukuo radically different from the economic imperialism seen in the treaty ports, and could serve as a model for future Japanese colonies.

The new state took over the customs duties that had previously gone to Nanjing and drew income from vice. Gambling houses and brothels proliferated – there were said to be 70,000 Japanese prostitutes, as well as a similar number of Koreans. The military police and the army special services operated opium dens.

White Russian gangs proliferated. There was a scandal when one kidnapped the Jewish son of the Russian émigré owner of the main hotel in the city. An accomplished pianist with French citizenship, Simeon Kaspe was held for a $300,000 ransom before being killed after his father countered with a lower offer. Under French pressure, the authorities arrested six of the kidnappers, who were tried in a Chinese court which was still sitting in Harbin. Four were sentenced to death, and two to life imprisonment. But the Japanese intervened to have the judge arrested, and a new panel of Japanese judges ordered the six to be released on the grounds that they had 'acted from patriotic motives'. The large Jewish community in Harbin began to pack up and move down to Shanghai.[27]

Despite the strong Japanese military presence, Manchukuo was so big, covering 300,000 square miles, that outlaw activity continued in the vast empty spaces, membership of gangs swollen by disbanded Chinese soldiers. Contemporary estimates put the number of 'resistance bandits' at anywhere from 100,000 to 150,000. The Manchurian Communist Party linked up with some of the bandit groups, but was badly hit when a police raid on Party headquarters in Harbin led to the arrest of 155 members, forty-two of whom were executed.[28]

Ma Zhanshan, the warlord who had resisted the Japanese in northern Manchuria, became the leading symbol of resistance, though his main interest was in survival on his own terms. He established a base in virtually inaccessible mountains by the Amur River in a building equipped with six German-made grandfather clocks synchronized to strike loudly one after another. He then switched tack and agreed to join Manchukuo, provided he became war minister and got a large supply of gold bullion. After the Japanese agreed, Ma promptly used his position to move arms to his base. Then he broke with the regime, and made off with 1.5 million silver dollars in addition to his bullion, sending a statement to the League of Nations denouncing Manchukuo's self-determination as a myth and warning that Japan would move into north China.[29]

Back in the north of the territory, Ma fought battles which, according to Hallett Abend, showed 'considerable strategic brilliance'. Still, attacks by superior forces forced him to flee to Outer Mongolia, a Russian preserve where the Japanese could not pursue him. On the way, he dressed a corpse in his uniform and sword; falling for this, the Japanese took the uniform and sword to Tokyo to be presented to the emperor as evidence that Ma had been killed. The following day, he reappeared at the head of a band of ragged followers on his way to Russia, eventually getting back from there to China. Japanese newspapers were forbidden to mention him. From shame at having misled the emperor, some Japanese officers committed hara-kiri.[30]

With the Shanghai battle over and the establishment of Manchukuo tacitly accepted, Nanjing launched campaigns against the two Yangzi Communist bases involving 400,000 men – roughly double the total number of Red Army troops they faced. The offensives were much the best prepared, drawing on the advice of the chief German adviser, the former army chief of staff Hans von Seeckt, and on lessons learned from the history of Zeng Guofan's fight against the Taiping.

The Nationalists imposed a tight blockade, using scorched-earth tactics and reducing people in border areas to near-starvation by destroying crops. Applying the anti-rebel policy of the 1850s, 'volunteer' village units were established. New roads linked Nationalist forces. Communists were summarily shot. As Chiang put it, 'a thorough house-cleaning is being carried out.'[31]

The Fourth Red Army in the E-yu-wan base had grown to around 70,000 men, but its quality had deteriorated and peasants switched sides in search of survival. Allowing themselves to be drawn into positional battles, the Communist forces were pushed back towards the middle of the base, where they would be a sitting target for a major assault using planes and artillery. The only course was a break-out, which began on 20 August 1932, leaving behind a residual guerrilla force that would hold on in the mountains for a decade. The withdrawal went against orders from the Party leadership. Mao, who saw Zhang Guotao as his main long-term rival for control of the Party, denounced him for 'warlordism and flightism'. The march through Hubei, Hunan, Henan and Shaanxi reduced the Fourth Army to 10,000 men. But, at the end, it reached a safe area of Sichuan to set up a new Soviet. Back in the former stronghold, the Nationalists massacred anybody thought to have Communist sympathies, in one case burning 300 patients alive in a hospital and digging huge pits in which victims were buried alive – in one instance 3,500 people, according to a Communist account.[32]

Chiang turned his attention to Jiangxi, where the base had undergone a leadership change after the arrival of the Moscow-aligned group of 28 Returned Bolsheviks from Shanghai, further undermining Mao's position. At a meeting to discuss the situation in Manchuria, one partici-pant branded him a 'right opportunist'. The Chairman stalked out, asked for sick leave and went with his wife to live in a temple on a volcanic hill, where he brooded in a depressed frame of mind, writing poetry and trying to keep in touch through newspapers and documents sent to him. Though still nominally head of the Soviet, Mao was replaced as political commissar of the First Army. 'The only thing for me to do was to wait,' as he reflected later.[33]

Before marching into Jiangxi again, Chiang had to deal with a sensitive top-level political matter which, once more, he turned to his advantage. Wang Jingwei launched a withering attack on the Young Marshal. Despite the months that had elapsed since the Mukden Incident, he said, 'there has been absolutely no achievement to your credit.' In a typical gambit, Wang offered his own resignation – on condition that the Marshal did the same, which, the politician added, would be 'an ines-timable blessing to China south of the Great Wall'.

Zhang did step down as commander in the north, but this changed little. Though Chiang took over, his focus on the anti-Communist drive in central China left the Manchurian still effectively in command. Wang was isolated. When the whole government resigned, he departed for treatment for diabetes in Germany. T. V. Soong succeeded him. The cabinet withdrew its resignation. The net result, wrote the *North China Daily News*, was that Chiang 'became the Government of China'.[34]

For the Jiangxi campaign, Nanjing deployed nearly 150,000 troops in a ring, along with 100,000 men sent in to drive the Red Army enemy into this trap. Aircraft staged bombing runs and provided surveillance. The tide of war shifted from week to week, but the Communists escaped annihilation. Though the Germans had trained its elite forces, most of the KMT army was still of poor quality. Some units concentrated on stealing food, and turned to banditry. Commanders thought in terms of defence, not offence.

Yet again, the worst sufferers were the ordinary people caught up in the fighting. Locals were press-ganged into service and made to pay special taxes. 'Weeds are growing rank in the rice fields, homes lie in ruins, bleak and forlorn, village upon village is totally depopulated, here and there a family huddles together in a shack, facing the winter's cold and gradual starvation,' a League of Nations expert reported. 'If anything is calculated to make the Chinese peasant turn spontaneously to Communism,' concluded the British writer Peter Fleming, after visiting the front, 'it is having troops permanently billeted on him.'[35]

Success in withstanding another offensive led the CCP to adopt what was known as the 'front forward line' of sending an army northwards to attack the Nationalists. Mao opposed this, but was overruled, and branded again as a 'right opportunist'. At the beginning of 1933, the new Party boss arrived from the Shanghai headquarters. Bo Gu, still only in his mid-twenties, was a graduate of the University of the Toilers of the East in Moscow, and had been sent in on Soviet instructions to impose the orthodox, urban line. With bulging eyes and black-rimmed spectacles, he looked like a teenage schoolboy, but he was decisive. He undermined much of Mao's power base, backed by a new Comintern adviser, the German Otto Braun, whose hectoring style went down badly. In the face of Bo and Braun, who enjoyed Zhou Enlai's support, Mao risked eclipse; but the focus of national attention was, once again, far away to the north.[36]

At the beginning of 1933, the Japanese announced that they had found two bombs hidden in the garrison which the Boxer Treaty entitled them to maintain in the coastal town of Shanhaiguan in Jehol province. To 'clear evil elements', they shelled and bombed the town. Then they began to advance southwards.[37]

Lying between the Great Wall and Manchuria, Jehol was run by Tang Yulin, a short, thick-set former bandit in his early sixties known for his cruelty, corruption and encouragement of the drugs trade – when the Young Marshal and the Australian W. H. Donald drove into the capital of Chengde through a blizzard in early 1932, the only soldiers they saw were guarding an opium factory in the grounds of Tang's palace. He was a master at wringing money out of the population, forcing them to use notes from his bank, which depreciated to 5 per cent of their face value. He raised land levies, and collected them years in advance under a 'crop anticipation' tax. On the proceeds, he gave banquets complete with shark's fin, swallow nest soup, lotus buds, pork with crisp crackling, fish and chicken washed down with fine cognac while his military band played outside.

The steep mountains of the province should have provided excellent defensive terrain, but there was no co-ordination, no attempt to fortify passes. When Japanese planes flew in, soldiers on the ground waited till they had gone a safe distance before opening fire, not wishing to incur attacks. Zhang was responsible for the overall defence of the north, but he appeared detached, more concerned with receiving the writer Bernard Shaw and directors of the London *Daily Mail* at his headquarters in Beijing than with conducting a war.

After being pummelled by Japanese bombs and shells in narrow valleys, Tang's army broke and ran. In the morning of 4 March, the day of Franklin Roosevelt's inauguration in Washington, Japanese planes staged a heavy attack on Chengde. Then 112 soldiers from a Kwantung brigade drove in on trucks, followed by lorries carrying Korean 'comfort women'. Chinese soldiers and refugees streamed south, among them a military band with a punctured drum. The steep pass south of Chengde was jammed with rickshaws, wheelbarrows, carts, camels, motor cars and people on foot. Japan had added 67,000 square miles and 3.8 million people to its domain in China, along with a lot of poppy fields to feed the narcotics business.

Finally, somebody had to pay the price for the losses in the north-east. On 8 March 1933, Chiang Kai-shek went by train to the town of Baoding, south of Beijing, to meet the Young Marshal. In a five-minute session, he told Zhang that China was like an unstable ship which could only be righted by dropping one of those on board. The old Whampoa hand, He Yingqin, would take over in the north. 'We came into China to effect national unification,' Zhang told his troops. 'But the result is that we are now homeless.'[38]

The Manchurian flew to Shanghai in his Ford aircraft. Though a brass band played on his arrival, his reception was cool. 'Do you remember that you have lost Manchuria? And now, through you, Jehol is lost to China,' read a scroll put up when he went to meet officials and journalists, who boycotted a press conference when guards frisked them for weapons. At the urging of the adviser W. H. Donald, the Marshal underwent successful treatment for his drug addiction, and then set out on a lengthy trip to Europe, flirting on the sea voyage with Mussolini's daughter, whose husband, Count Ciano, was returning from a diplomatic posting in China.[39]

Just as Manchuria had led to Jehol, so Jehol led the Japanese to the Great Wall. The Chinese put up some spirited resistance, in one case fighting with broadswords. But General He Yingqin proved no more able than the Young Marshal to stop the enemy. The defences were not co-ordinated. Sitting on the Great Wall, Gerald Yorke of Reuters watched as 'cars, lorries, wagons and camels struggled by in a confused mass. Transport which had not heard the news was still moving up from the south. The two streams met in the gateway below. A pony fell. All was confusion and shouting.'

For all their prowess, the Japanese did not want an urban battle for Beijing. The experience of Shanghai served as a warning, and they were much more impressive on the open spaces, where planes, armoured vehicles and artillery could be used to full effect. So they issued demands instead, following the lines of the demilitarization of Shanghai, on a far bigger scale. As the price for not attacking Beijing, where martial law had been declared, Japan called for the removal of Chinese troops from an area of 115,800 square miles, containing 6 million people.

Chiang Kai-shek agreed to this, though keeping it secret for fear of the outcry that would result. A signing conference was arranged for 31 May at the Japanese consulate in the walled costal town of Tanggu. Two Japanese destroyers sailed in with their guns loaded for action. At the consulate, the Chinese were kept waiting in the hot sun at the gate for nearly ten minutes. Inside the building, they were greeted by low-ranking Japanese officials. When the Chinese said the agreement was purely military and without political significance, they were told to shut up and sign, which they did. The accord contained a pledge to clamp down on anti-Japanese activities in China.[40]

For the expansionists, the Tanggu Truce was not simply an extension of Japanese power in China, but also a further step on the path towards replacing the Westerners in Asia; a map in a textbook for Japanese primary schools showed Japan, Manchukuo, China, Indochina, Thailand, the Philippines, the Dutch East Indies, and Malaya and Singapore with three flags flying over them – those of Japan, Manchukuo and China, a China which, it went without saying, would observe Tokyo's desires. Between the Mukden Incident on 18 September 1931 and the Tanggu agreement of 31 May 1933, the Japanese claimed to have inflicted twenty times as many casualties as they had suffered, with 200,000 Chinese killed or wounded – including civilians. Foreign observers thought the figure for the invaders was likely to be more than 30,000, but the ratio was still overwhelmingly in their favour.

On top of its recurrent authority problems elsewhere in the country, Nanjing had virtually lost control of northern China. As well as the four provinces of Manchukuo, the Japanese dominated nearly all Hebei province north of Beijing, and the city of Tianjin, their position further strengthened when Moscow sold them its stake in the Chinese Eastern Railway in 1935. Chinese commanders made deals with the occupiers. A Military Council in Beijing played along. The dominant general in the north, Song Zheyuan, did not keep Nanjing fully informed of dealings with the Japanese, while passing on to the invaders what Nanjing was telling him.[41]

With their eyes on the territory's gold, iron ore and coal deposits, and its strategic position on the Soviet border, the Japanese encouraged an autonomist movement in Mongolia to rebel against Chinese rule. Launching economic warfare, in north China they smuggled in mountains of goods, cutting Chinese customs revenues. In Manchukuo, policies were further toughened, including land seizures and forcible large-scale resettlements. Near Harbin, a large bacteriological laboratory, Unit 731, was set up to carry out experiments on thousands of live prisoners.[42]

As if this was not enough, Nanjing faced a fresh wave of criticism and revolt after the contents of the Tanggu Truce were leaked. Returning from Europe, Wang Jingwei compared China to a man whose life was in grave danger. The National Salvation Society set up after the loss of Manchuria inveighed against the failure to fight, and gained the support of Hu Hanmin from Hong Kong. In Shanghai, Sun Yat-sen's widow organized a conference to denounce 'the base betrayal by the Chinese ruling classes and the Kuomintang'.

In the east-coast province of Fujian, the Nineteenth Route Army of Shanghai fame, which was unhappy over pay and a subsidiary role in the fight against the Communists, joined a revolt of Social Democrats, Third Party members, Trotskyites and former members of the Wuhan regime. A 'government of the producing people' was set up in the port city of Fuzhou, but it failed to gain wide support and alienated the local gentry with radical proposals. Its hopes that Guangdong would join the cause were dashed as Chiang paid off the warlord there. The Nationalists built airfields across the border in Zhejiang, and launched bombing raids on Fuzhou and other undefended targets. After two months the rising collapsed. General Cai went on a world tour as the hero of resistance to the Japanese.

Meanwhile, a political crisis blew up between Chiang and T. V. Soong, who had taken a stronger public line on Japan and had negotiated a $50 million American loan which he wanted to use to stabilize the economy and cut the budget deficit; Chiang, predictably, preferred to channel it to military purposes. Soong resigned. According to Hu Hanmin, he said that 'being minister of finance is no different from being Chiang Kai-shek's dog. From now on, I am going to be a man, not a dog.' He was replaced by his brother-in-law, H. H. Kung, who fell in with Chiang's wishes, and set the printing presses rolling to produce more inflation-fuelling banknotes.[43]

The Christian General put in a fresh appearance at the head of an army which defeated Manchukuo troops, but was then cornered between the Kwantung Army and Nationalist forces moved up by Chiang, who had no desire to see Feng reassert himself. Faced with this double threat, his army melted away, and the warlord retreated to a mountain temple, where he devoted himself to writing poems on the national disgrace.

In the north-east, the Japanese had Puyi declared emperor of Manchu-kuo on 1 March 1934, to rule in a 'Reign of Tranquillity and Virtue'. Wearing a blue-and-gold gown with red sleeves and a fur coat, he was driven through Changchun in a bullet- and bomb-proof Lincoln limousine to the Altar of Heaven, where imperial-yellow silk draperies flapped in the cold wind. As scrolls were read, wine drunk and a calf sacrificed, Puyi, who had just celebrated his twenty-eighth birthday, took his place on an ebony throne with box springs supplied by Tokyo.[44]

A Kwantung Army officer, Yoshioka Yasunori, was appointed as attaché to the Imperial Household. A short man with a small moustache and high cheekbones, he had been Puyi's Japanese minder since his exile in Tianjin in 1928. When he reported Japanese victories, he insisted that the nominal emperor bow in the direction of the battlefield. Yoshioka installed green-uniformed Japanese police in the palace to keep watch on everything that happened there. The occupiers orchestrated all government appointments. Nor was Puyi's personal life immune. After his wife had developed a strong opium habit and given birth to a daughter by another man (the child was killed on Puyi's orders), the emperor took a concubine, but she fell ill and died – he suspected that the Japanese killed her because of her opposition to them. Yoshioka offered him photographs of successors, and personally vetted the fifteen-year-old Puyi chose.

*

Though a large swathe of territory had been lost, one benefit of the Tanggu Truce for Chiang Kai-shek was that it freed his hands to turn back to the war against the Communists in Jiangxi. From his summer home in the ancient shrine town of Lushan in mountains above the Yangzi, he prepared his 1934 drive against the base. This was to be bigger and better prepared than anything that had gone before.

To pen the enemy in, 3,000 'turtle shell' blockhouses were built round the edge of the base, linked by roads and bridges. Scorched-earth tactics cleared border areas. An economic blockade cut off food supplies. A big new airfield was built in the rear, with smaller landing strips at the front to accommodate 150 planes. Nationalist propaganda was pumped out in parades, stage shows, lectures, posters, cartoons and films – the first the country people had seen. Leaflets dropped from the air offered rewards to Communist soldiers to defect with their rifles. The capture of Mao and Zhu De would attract large sums, but less if only their heads were brought in.

Military trucks, mules, coolies, ambulances and marching soldiers jammed 700 miles of new roads. Just in case things went wrong and it came under attack, the provincial capital of Nanchang was surrounded by moats, trenches, barbed-wire emplacements, walls and square, tur-reted watchtowers which a Polish journalist found reminiscent of the Middle Ages.

Inside the base, Mao was on the sidelines, under virtual house arrest after being marginalized by Bo Gu, his ally Zhou Enlai and the German adviser, Otto Braun, who insisted that the best way of countering the blockhouse strategy was to make 'fast and close strikes' against them. Rather than luring the enemy into ambushes on favourable territory, the Red Army took the offensive. That proved very costly, and opened the Soviet to counter-attacks. The Chairman was powerless to alter this. When he attended the Second National Soviet Congress at the beginning of 1934, he found that everything had been prepared by a Central Committee meeting to which he had not been invited. Mao went back to his house in the country, received a few faithful followers, taught his bodyguard to read, and fell badly ill with malaria, his temperature shooting up to 105 degrees.[45]

As the Nationalists advanced slowly but surely, Communist desertions soared, and their execution squads beheaded laggards on the battle-fields. A fresh campaign was launched against 'counter-revolutionaries'.

Though he had an axe to grind, Mao was not wrong when he wrote that 'we milled around between the enemy's main forces and his block houses and were reduced to complete passivity.' By the end of September 1934, Nanjing's troops threatened to overrun the base. A diversionary break-out into Fujian by 9,000 men turned into a disaster: most of the force was destroyed and its leader executed, his head paraded in a bamboo cage.[46]

As usual, Chiang and his colleagues in Nanjing had other concerns to attend to. One of the Christian General's associates staged a revolt in the far north which was put down. Drought and then fresh flooding on the Yangzi affected tens of millions. Flare-ups with the Japanese threatened the settlement in Shanghai. The Kwantung Army issued protests at alleged infringements of the agreement in the demilitarized zone round Beijing.[47]

Still, at the suggestion of his wife and W. H. Donald, Chiang made an extended trip through regions of northern and western China never visited before by a republican leader. It was strange that Chiang should absent himself in the north when the campaign in Jiangxi was reaching its climax, but he appears to have enjoyed the journey, and even relaxed in public. Asked about rumours that he and Meiling were discussing divorce, he riposted that another tale had it that an office-seeker had offered him a dozen beautiful women. Both were false. He and Meiling 'acted like newly-weds', Reuters noted.[48]

On the other side of China, the leadership of the Jiangxi Soviet had come to the conclusion that staying in the base would mean its eradication. The bulk of the Red Army would leave for a safer enclave. As at E-yu-wan, a guerrilla force was to be left to continue the local struggle as best it could. The leadership might have preferred that Mao stay with it, but he made sure he was not left behind, moving to quarters on the exit route and joining the long column making its way over the Gan River; he noted that the huge baggage train made it more like moving a house than a military exercise. The official account has the Chairman wearing a grey cloth uniform and military cap, carrying two blankets, a cotton sheet, an oilcloth, a coat, a broken umbrella and a bundle of books, abandoning his two-year-old son, whom he would never see again as he set out on a decisive lap of his ascent to power.[49]

13
Mao's March

The Long March which took the First Red Army from Jiangxi to its eventual home in Shaanxi in the north lasted for a year. By most accounts, it stretched for 5,000 miles, though two British writers who walked the route in 2003 reckoned that it was 'only' 3,700. Still, the way the columns split up, wandered over the countryside and then rejoined one another meant that the total distance covered by the marchers as a whole is virtually impossible to establish.[1]

The terrain was often forbidding, and the political infighting bitter as Mao clawed his way back to the top. Suffering was extreme, particularly for women who marched on during their periods or when pregnant. As well as battle casualties and death from weather, disease or starvation, desertions were frequent. Losses were extremely high – only a few thousand of the 80,000 to 100,000 who set out from Jiangxi reached the new base at Yenan. In contrast to the glowing portrait enshrined in Maoist history and delivered to the West by the American writer Edgar Snow, the soldiers sometimes acted like bandits, robbing and kidnapping as they went. Peasants were press-ganged. Few of the marchers knew much, or indeed anything, about Communist theory. Half of those who set out from the south-east were under twenty-five and had no experience outside the base. Some were in their early teens. The Chairman was among the 4 per cent who were over forty.[2]

Soon after it ended, the march acquired a mythical status and became the central element in the Chinese Communist story, proof that the movement contained a special strength and an unquestionable visionary leader in Mao, its veterans forged through the experience to lead the revolution and the nation. As the French writer and politician Alain Peyrefitte has put it, the expedition was an 'epic poem' to Communism, in which defeat was spun into triumph. It has been described in countless books and articles, celebrated in Chinese songs and in films, its very name going down as a common phrase in English. In the autumn of 2006, a writer for the Chinese news agency Xinhua noted that 'even at a time of rapid economic development, the Long March spirit is still relevant to the Party's well-being and nation's development.'[3]

As with all such events, it became embroidered by exaggeration and, according to some writers, outright invention. But, as shown by evidence gathered by the writer Sun Shuyun, from forty survivors in 2004, it was still a triumph of survival, made all the more impressive by the confusion, fear and uncertainty that engulfed it from the start. The fact that it was led by a man who would turn out to be as monstrous a killer as Mao does not in any way invalidate that achievement by the marchers. So it retains a legitimate position in the iconography of China, and as a testament to human endurance, whatever the motives of those in charge. If the Chairman elided the event with himself, that does not mean we should follow suit. Nor does the idea that Chiang Kai-shek allowed the marchers to escape make sense; according to this thesis, his motive is said to have been to get his son back from Moscow, but he had turned down an earlier offer and repeated Nationalist attacks on the marchers hardly speak of a secret 'Reds for son' swap with Moscow.[4]

From the start, the marchers benefited from the help of southern warlords anxious to see them leave their territory, and from the work of decoders able to read Nationalist wireless messages. Zhou Enlai reached an agreement with the Guangdong governor which enabled the Red Army to move through the first ring of blockhouses. Other provincial barons later allowed the Communists to escape because they did not want to give Nanjing a reason to send in central government troops to exert control.

Having got through the Jiangxi–Guangdong blockhouses, the Communists headed west into Guangxi. Far away in Mongolia, Chiang attended a horse race and visited a Buddhist temple. Flying to Shaanxi, he denounced opium at a meeting of a thousand officials. Returning to Nanjing after visiting ten provinces on his protracted tour, he turned his attention back to the Communists, ordering an encircling move in front of the Xiang River in Guangxi.

But battle was not joined. This was not because Chiang wanted the Red Army to escape. Rather, the always stroppy Guangxi forces preferred to hang back to defend their city of Guilin from possible Communist attack. While the Generalissimo badgered the independent-minded south-westerners to advance, half the Communist force was able to cross the wide, shallow river. Then the Muslim Guangxi commander, General Bai, caved in, and a devastating attack was launched in early December, with the marchers split on either side of the waterway. Nationalists with fixed bayonets swarmed up hillsides to assault the defences the Communists had erected. Planes swooped on bombing and strafing runs. As one Communist veteran recalled, 'We were too slow and the enemy too quick.'

Zhu De sent a message to the forward units that the battle was decisive for the whole future of the Red Army. The fighting lasted for a week, and produced the biggest single setback the Communists suffered during the whole of the Long March. Some accounts reported that their strength was halved, with only 30,000 men escaping. Much equipment was lost as the rearguard baggage train struggled across the river. Peng Dehuai remembered hard fighting, while Otto Braun reported huge losses, saying Chiang wanted 'to destroy our main force while crossing the river'.[5]

After this disaster, the remnants of the Red Army turned north to head for a Soviet base the guerrilla commander He Long had established in northern Hunan. But Chiang prepared a killing field on its path, clearing the ground and marshalling troops, planes and artillery. Learning of this, the Communist leadership followed Mao's advice to turn west into the wild mountain terrain of Guizhou. The priority, he said, was to find a new secure base and to avoid further big losses in set-piece battles. It was the first sign he was returning to power, buoyed by the defeats suffered under the Returned Bolsheviks and Braun. His revival was underscored by a rejection of advice from the Comintern agent to stand and fight three local divisions in Guizhou. The German was suspended as military adviser, and the Politburo, in effect, adopted the Chairman's strategic approach as it declared that 'no opportunity should be missed to use mobile warfare to break up and destroy the enemy one by one.'[6]

In mid-January, the Red Army reached its next objective, the town of Zunyi lying amid mountains, waterfalls and great bamboo forests in rural Guizhou. At the end of January, a crucial meeting was held in the colonnaded, wood and brick former home of a minor militarist surrounded by flower gardens. A brazier in the middle of the small conference room did little to ward off the winter cold. More heat came from the crowd of participants.

Bo Gu and Zhou Enlai, who was in overall political charge of the army, led for the defence, blaming the abandonment of the base on Nationalist strength. Their own policies, they insisted, were not at fault. Mao then opened the prosecution, unusually for him reading from a prepared text. He attacked the leadership line in general, and Bo and Otto Braun in particular, but did not go for Zhou Enlai.

The loss of the Jiangxi Soviet had been due to the abandonment of the strategy advocated by himself and Zhu De, he charged. The main fault lay with Braun, while Bo Gu had failed to control the German, whose bullying had produced 'extremely abnormal phenomena' in the Military Council. Braun sat in a corner, chain-smoking as his interpreter translated the onslaught, which was followed by other attacks, including one by Peng Dehuai on the European as 'a prodigal son who squandered his father's goods'.[7]

The adviser pleaded that responsibility for the policies that had been followed lay with the leadership, not him. This turned the spotlight to Zhou Enlai as the senior military figure. He did not speak until the second day of the meeting. Then, reading the way the wind was blowing and aware that Mao had offered a tacit olive branch by not naming him, he abandoned the leadership group. In one of the survival self-criticisms that would pepper his career, he acknowledged that the strategy had been 'fundamentally incorrect'.

The resolution issued at the end of the discussions, which had a highly restricted circulation, attacked Bo for making 'serious political mistakes' and Braun for 'treating war as a game'. Both had shown 'extremely bad leadership'. Zhou's kowtow had been enough to save him. The resolution said merely that he had delivered a 'supplementary report' to the meeting and, even then, the characters for his name were omitted from all copies except those handed to the highest-ranking Party members.[8]

This was a sign of Mao's mastery of political tactics. Zhou could have been his main rival. By protecting him, the Chairman established a debt and earned an ally of experience and administrative ability. It set a pattern that would continue to the 1970s.

Mao contented himself with joining the Standing Committee of the Politburo and becoming Zhou's main military adviser. In February, one of his allies, Zhang Wentian, replaced Bo. Then a Front Headquarters was set up for the military which, in effect, sidelined Zhou. Zhu De, whose relations with Mao in Jiangxi had not always been smooth but who could always be dominated politically, was named commander. The Chairman became the army's political commissar. A new overall leadership troika was formed in which Zhou was outnumbered by Mao and Zhang. The Communists had finally and irrevocably acquired the leader who would rule them for the next four decades.

Mao's political victory marked a return to guerrilla warfare for the marchers, who followed an extremely confused path during the following months, heading into Sichuan, retreating back to Zunyi, and striking south towards the Guizhou capital of Guiyang. Chiang set up a headquarters to the north in the Sichuan city of Chongqing, and the campaign at the front was waged by a former Whampoa instructor, General Xue Yue, a short, hot-tempered man who had taken part in the Jiangxi encirclement campaigns before chasing the Red Army through Hunan, Guizhou and Sichuan.

Playing his usual political role, Chiang tried to assert his authority over the myriad warlords in Sichuan, with little success, but did manage to oust the local baron in Guizhou, where, despite denouncing the opium trade, he raised funds by having a state narcotics monopoly created in the province. The Nationalists won a battle north of Guiyang, though suffering substantial casualties. Blockhouses were constructed, but they were of little use as the Red Army dodged and weaved across the wild countryside, partly as a matter of tactics and partly simply to escape the enemy. Rain and cloud prevented the Nationalists deploying the air force much, but one strafing attack wounded Mao's wife in fourteen places, sending her into a coma from a head wound. She survived.[9]

The way ahead for the Red Army lay through neighbouring Yunnan, and then north to Sichuan. The Generalissimo flew into the far south-westerly province with his wife to pay their first visit to a region that was well out of the national mainstream, its principal links being with Burma, Vietnam and, to the north-west, Tibet.* The delicate but ruthless governor, Long Yun, greeted the visitors with champagne toasts at the airport outside the capital, Kunming. Cheering students in white and blue uniforms lined the road into the city. Nationalist flags flew every-

---

* An article in the *National Geographic Magazine* by an Austrian botanist, Joseph Rock, about his expeditions in the Yunnan–Tibet border region had just inspired the novelist James Hilton to invent Shangri-La in his 1933 novel, *Lost Horizon*. Several towns in the area have competed to be named the true source of this fictional place.

where. An open-air reception was held, at which a French banker got a 'furtive view' of Meiling's white silk bloomers when the wind blew up her skirt.[10]

Long Yun's main wish was to get the Communists out of his province, and remove the pretext for Chiang to send in central-government forces to chase them. As it moved towards the first bend of the Yangzi known as the Golden Sands, the Red Army found an abandoned vehicle with detailed maps of the country they would be crossing. There was no opposition when 18,000 of its soldiers reached the river, taking up to a week to move into Sichuan.

Stopping thirty-five miles on at the town of Huili, nearly 6,000 feet above sea level, they decided to head for the base Zhang Guotao had established in the north of the province. That involved traversing some of the most difficult terrain on the whole march, including repeated scaling of mountains. They had to cope with the local Yi people, who had spent centuries fighting incursions by lowlanders. A pact was sealed with them in chicken's blood by the chief of staff, Liu Bocheng, who had lost one eye in battle. But there were ambushes along the way as the army moved towards its next obstacle, the torrential Dadu River running down from the Himalayas.

The Nationalists resumed bombing the columns and ordered boats to be destroyed or moved to the far bank to trap the Red Army with its back to the waterway. There was a comforting historical echo for the government forces – a Taiping general had been caught on the Dadu seventy years earlier as he paused to celebrate the birth of his son, and his army had been wiped out. But one column got across the waterway after finding the boat of a local commander who had come to the near bank for a family dinner. The water was turbulent, and it took three days to get a division across. When planes started bombing, another crossing was needed. The choice fell on the chain bridge at Luding, 100 miles upstream, which would give rise to one of the most celebrated episodes on the march, and recent controversy about what happened there.

The official story, propagated by Communist propaganda, tells of a regiment arriving to find that the Nationalist defenders had removed the planks from the bridge and set a fire. This forced twenty-two Red Army soldiers to cross hand-over-hand along red-hot chains under intense machine-gun fire above the foaming torrent. A slightly different version by a Red Army soldier says that the first wave crept along the chains on each side of the bridge while their comrades laid planks and branches behind them.

The reality of what happened at the Dadu was considerably less dramatic. The Mao biographers Chang and Halliday have concluded that the whole story was fiction, and that 'there was no battle at the Dadu Bridge.' What appears most likely is that there was some fighting, but it was no more than a skirmish, with no hand-over-hand crossing of the river by soldiers grasping red-hot chains. The Nationalist command wanted to check the Communists at the Dadu while its main force caught up with them. A battalion sent to guard the bridge began to remove the planks in the evening, but stopped work because the soldiers were tired and slowed down by opium. In the morning, the Communist vanguard appeared on the far side of the bridge, preventing the removal of the rest of the planks. Fighting broke out, killing fifty government soldiers. When the main Red Army force turned up, the commander at the bridge telephoned for instructions, saying it would be difficult to hold out. After the line went dead, he panicked, ordering a retreat.[11]

While he ran the campaign from Chongqing, Chiang had equally grave causes for concern as his other enemy stepped up pressure to expand its influence further in the north. The commander of Japan's garrison in Tianjin put forward fresh demands, to which General He agreed on instructions from Nanjing. The Yellow River became the dividing line between Chinese rule and the invaders' sphere of influence. Later in the year, a Political Council was set up in Beijing, including the former warlord of Jehol, which publicly toed the Japanese line though it resisted more concessions.

Such successes encouraged the campaign by the invaders to establish puppet regimes in the name of 'autonomy'. This made limited head-way, in part because of rivalries between potential puppets – one candidate, the former eastern warlord Sun Zhuanfeng, was shot dead as he prayed in a temple, by the daughter of a man he had executed eleven years earlier. Still, a puppet administration took over a 30,000 square mile stretch of eastern Hebei. Receiving the American journalist John Powell, the nominal head of the zone explained how this operated. Japanese army advisers were sent to work with district magistrates; the gentry was instructed to raise 'peace preservation' forces trained and led by Japanese officers; farmers were compelled to join co-operatives controlled by the invaders; school textbooks came from the 'Sino-Japanese Cultural Society' and Japanese teachers moved into secondary schools.[12]

The region became a vast channel for Japanese goods to enter China, either smuggled or paying very low import duty and undercutting domestic products. *Ronin* gangsters and Korean criminals moved in to help run the trade, which was estimated to cost Nanjing $8 million a month in lost duties. Japanese ships chased away Chinese customs craft.[13]

As in Manchukuo, drugs were encouraged across northern China to raise money and sap the health and morale of the population. As well as domestic production, 30 tons of high-grade Iranian opium was being imported into Tianjin a year. Beijing had 100 drug shops and 300 opiate dens. Operators of the traffic claimed extra-territorial status. At pawn shops in one big town, a social worker reported, people were encouraged to take narcotics rather than money for their goods – a syringe could be rented on the spot.

Other outlets consisted of box-like structures erected outside houses with a sliding panel in one wall through which addicts would put their bare arms, with the requisite amount of money in their hand. John Powell visited a Japanese-run den of around seventy rooms in a six-floor house, each containing divans for ten to fifteen smokers. The brightly lit house was open round the clock and, he reported, the smell of opium was evident a full block away. Police in the Japanese concession of Tianjin did regular rounds of the dens to pick up the bodies of addicts who had expired and throw them into the river – through holes in the ice in winter – sweeping up some who were still alive in the process.[14]

From China, the Japanese drug traffickers spread their activities to the United States and Europe. By 1937, the League of Nations would estimate that 90 per cent of the world's 'white drugs' such as morphine were being made by the occupiers or their puppets. The British efforts of a century earlier were put in the shade by the new Asian imperialists.[15]

Shandong, where a comeback bid by the Dogmeat General ended when he was shot dead in a train station by the nephew of a general he had killed years earlier, came under the sway of a warlord who made accommodations with the Japanese. In Nanjing, rumours flew that some leading government figures were ready to conclude a pact to give Japan a completely free hand, leading to an economic union of the two countries.

Chiang Kai-shek was, more than ever, playing on several fronts at the same time.[16]

Having got across the Dadu river, the First Front Army headed to the Great Snowy Mountain range, rising to 14,000 feet. The journey was an ordeal of precipitous climbs, typhus, dysentery, air attacks and ambushes by fanatically anti-Chinese Tibetans – the queen of one tribe threatened to boil alive anybody who helped the Red Army. On 12 June 1935, the advance guard emerged from the mountains, and saw what it thought were enemy troops. Shots were exchanged before it realized that the others were men from the Sichuan Soviet headed by Zhang Guotao, the veteran Communist who had been forced to flee from the E-yu-wan base three years earlier. The two main Red Armies had finally met.

Zhang rode in through the rain with thirty bodyguards, their fine horses reflecting the contrast between them and the ragged First Front Army. The atmosphere was, at best, cool. Mao said later that the link-up produced his 'darkest moment' as he feared the loss of the supremacy he had established on the way from Jiangxi. At the first dinner of the two leaders, there was no serious conversation. Zhang complained later that Mao had shown no interest in hearing about his Fourth Army. Instead, the Hunanese extolled the virtues of chillies as a sign of revolutionary ardour. However much the union of their two armies might be celebrated in public, the two, who had not met for eight years, were bound to be deadly rivals for the ultimate Communist leadership.[17]

Zhang had four times as many troops as the First Front Army. Mao's men were exhausted and in poor condition, while Zhang's army had been able to rebuild its strength after its own long march from the E-yu-wan base on the Yangzi. Having chaired the inaugural meeting of the Communist Party, its leader could claim a much greater pedigree. He rejected 'guerrillaism' and advocated a review of the decisions reached in the conference at Zunyi, which had consecrated Mao's return to power. For his part, the Chairman considered Zhang guilty of elitism and insufficiently Communist.

Everything he had going for him bred a complacency in the ponderous Zhang. Mao, on the other hand, was never more determined or skilful than when the odds seemed to be stacked against him. Vitally, he had a majority in the Politburo because of the influence he had asserted during his march. At a three-day meeting in a Buddhist monastery lit by yak butter lamps, he showed his political mastery. Zhu De was appointed chairman of the Military Commission. Zhang accepted the post of his deputy, apparently thinking he could overawe the simple soldier. Zhang got a big job as general political commissar, and joint head of the combined Red Armies with Zhu. But Mao was in the ascendant as the debate turned to the next military move.

Zhang advocated heading west to set up a base among minority peoples on the fringe areas of China. Mao, who had experienced the hostility of the Tibetans and the Yis, thought this a thoroughly bad idea, and pressed, instead, for a march to a new enclave on the northern border of Sichuan. Taking advantage of Zhang's absence from a Central Committee session, Mao got the other man's proposal branded as 'flightist' and 'right opportunism', charges levelled against him when he left his original base on the Yangzi.

Split into two columns, the armies duly moved north through cold rain towards a huge swamp 11,000 feet up on the border of China and Tibet. Ahead lay a treacherous sea of icy black muck, with water many feet deep. Zhang's larger force included the headquarters unit and Zhu De. On the way, he tried to get Zhu to abandon Mao and wanted to change the line of march, refusing to enter the swamps. He had good reason for this. When Mao's column pressed on, it went through one of the most horrific experiences of the whole expedition. Marchers were sucked down to their deaths. The troops ate rats or unmilled grain – famished men took the undigested kernels from the bloody faeces of the dead, washed them and tried to eat them. Foul water provoked typhus and dysentery. There were ambushes from local inhabitants. By the time it emerged, the First Front Army was down to 10,000 men and women.[18]

Chiang sent troops to attack them, but they escaped to Gansu province in late September, though harried along the way by a local warlord's Muslim cavalry. Learning of a Soviet base area 600 miles away, Mao decided this should be the place where he and his army would stop running. In October 1935, a year after leaving Jiangxi, the remnants of the First Front Army straggled across the Liu Pan ('Six Twists') mountains into the loess country of northern Shaanxi. Coming out of the highlands, it encountered a column of armed men, led by Xu Haidong, a veteran of E-yu-wan. Together they rode to the base in Yenan (Yan'an) in

Shaanxi, where the Chairman slept in one of the caves that characterized the area, which would be his home for a dozen years.

But Mao and his depleted army were not Chiang's main concern in the autumn of 1935. Zhang's force was bigger and more threatening. It had held back from crossing the swamps after reaching a flooded river, and headed towards the Sichuan capital of Chengdu. Zhang kept Zhu De with him, as a virtual hostage, though the soldier may have become somewhat exasperated with the way Mao had bossed him around.

Large areas of countryside were devastated as the Nationalist defenders lost one battle but then won two more, obliging the Fourth Army to retreat to the west. There, Zhang joined with two other Communist units, but suffered a defeat on the Upper Yellow River, forcing him to move further west into barren country. Mao ordered this 21,000-strong Western Legion to head to the Soviet border to get supplies. Caught in strange territory, the legion was overwhelmed by Muslim warlord troops. Only 400 of its members managed to flee to safety. Captured women in the legion were sold as concubines.[19]

Zhang's forces were still wandering around when the First Front Army declared its march at an end on 22 October 1935, 369 days after setting out. A charade of unity was organized after the remains of his army got to Shaanxi the following year. Zhang was named one of Mao's deputies, but he was without power, and, after being purged, defected to the KMT in 1938 – he eventually moved to Canada, converted to Christianity and died in 1979.

The survivors of the Long March were less than 10 per cent of the original force, but they had maintained the existence of the First Army along with the political machine developed under their chief. This made it even more certain that the new revolution would come from the mouth of a gun under the control of a tight Party apparatus headed by a despot intent on acquiring the power that had belonged to the emperors. That, too, was the ambition of Chiang Kai-shek and the increasingly autocratic, militarized Kuomintang regime. From 1935 onwards, even more than during the campaigns in Jiangxi, the two major figures of twentieth century China were pitted against one another.

Mao and Chiang had a surprising number of traits in common. Both were born into non-poor rural families, Chiang in 1887, Mao in 1893. Both venerated their fervently Buddhist mothers, and had a poor opinion of their fathers. As teenagers, both were put into arranged marriages to older girls, whom they left as soon as possible. Later, they abandoned subsequent spouses, and married politically ambitious younger women. Each retained his provincial accent – Chiang that of Zhejiang province, Mao that of Hunan – and his taste for the local food. Both suffered from constipation – Mao told a bodyguard that he had his best ideas when straining to defecate.[20]

They were great political gamblers, never losing confidence in themselves as they manoeuvred to rule supreme. Each espoused the tactics of trading space for time. While they both headed movements proclaiming revolution, they also drew on Chinese tradition, and looked back to the struggle between the Taiping and the gentry. Each saw himself as the sole guide for the nation, believing in the power of the will and of armed force. Neither valued intellectuals. Both were heedless of the lives of others, including those of their own soldiers.

Yet their differences were more striking, not only politically but also personally. Mao was famed for his lack of grooming and peasant ways – throughout his life he rinsed his teeth with green tea rather than brushing them, with the result that they grew black, decayed and fell out. He did not bathe. Chiang always looked smooth, with an 'air of fastidious distinction', as a visitor remarked. The Chairman wore peasant clothes or a baggy grey outfit, the Generalissimo donned uniforms hung with medals, silk robes and a velvet trilby. Chiang was slim, erect, precise, his lips thin, his head shaven; Mao was described in 1936 by the admiring Edgar Snow as a 'gaunt, rather Lincolnesque figure, above average height for a Chinese, somewhat stooped, with a head of thick, black hair grown very long, and with large, searching eyes, a high-bridged nose and prominent cheek-bones'.[21]

The Communist shuffled and rolled as he walked, worked late at night and slept till the end of the morning. The Nationalist strode briskly around, rose before dawn, and went to bed at 11 p.m. Chiang stressed the need for respect, order and traditional hierarchies. Mao prized disorder, so long as he was on top, going through an endless reshaping of thinking to fit changing priorities. From the end of the Long March in 1935, Mao was in control of the CCP, its army and its organization, whereas Chiang had to work on a wider stage at the head of a more fragmented regime.

During the exodus from Jiangxi, the Chairman had fastened on the idea of presenting the CCP as the truly patriotic movement devoted to fighting the Japanese. He could safely proclaim this mission from Yenan, knowing that its geographical location meant the Party was in no position to do any such thing. Instead, it was Chiang and Nanjing that faced the invader. The Communists would never do anything like as much fighting against the joint enemy as the Nationalists, but the War of Resistance provided them with a second great iconic theme to put with the Long March as China imploded under the strain of conflict and national dislocation, opening the way to the ultimate resolution of the struggle between the two rivals.[22]

14

Total War

While accepting the loss of northern China and Manchuria, Chiang had not been as supine as post-1949 orthodoxy has maintained. Laying the groundwork for full-scale war with Japan, a secret National Defence Planning Council was charged with proposing how to deal with foreign aggression. This included building fortifications and strengthening troops in central China, constructing arsenals, development of the air force and preparations for chemical warfare. Nanjing told Tokyo it wanted to abrogate the Tanggu Truce, though it had no way of getting Japan to agree. It decided to adopt a forward policy in the north-west.

Missions were sent abroad to buy weapons, including a contract for German submarines. A $100 million dollar agreement was concluded with Berlin for arms in return for strategic minerals, such as tungsten in the former Soviet in Jiangxi. The air force was expanded; there was a nasty experience when a consignment of planes bought from Italy was found to consist of antiquated models, and their spare parts to be scrap metal. But a forceful American exponent of air power, Claire Chennault, was taken on, while Madame Chiang became Director of the National Aeronautics Board. Mercenary pilots were hired, and aircraft were put together from parts imported covertly from the United States so as not to alert the Japanese.

More German military advisers arrived, and some Chinese went abroad to gain experience – Chiang's adopted son attended an army academy in the United States and then joined the Wehrmacht as an observer.* As chief adviser, von Seeckt was succeeded by Alexander von

* Chiang had adopted the boy who had been born to a liaison between his sworn brother in Shanghai and a Japanese woman. The sworn brother had subsequently married and did not want to keep his son. Chiang seemed fonder of the boy, called Wei-kuo, than of his own offspring, Ching-kuo.

Falkenhausen, a tall First World War veteran with a vulture-like head who wore a pince-nez. He drew up a comprehensive strategy memorandum that proposed to locate the main troop concentrations in the Middle and Lower Yangzi, where a network of fortifications was being built. Upriver, Sichuan would be the 'last base of defence'.[1]

The problem was time and resources. The strengthening of defences would stretch over six years; broader proposals for national reconstruction would not be completed for ten. In August 1935, the newly appointed president of the South Manchurian Railway warned that the menace from the USSR meant that Japan had to pursue operations in northern China. 'The arrow has already left the bow,' he added. Tokyo increased the size of its standing garrison in the north from 2,000 to 5,000 men. A mechanized brigade was stationed south of the Great Wall, where it practised artillery bombardments. Japanese soldiers controlled the railway from Beijing to the sea, and a telegraph exclusively for their use was set up along the track from Mukden to the former capital. Marshalling yards and sidings were built to facilitate movement of troops.[2]

On the Chinese side, the backward condition of industry and the loss of Manchuria meant that the Nationalists did not have a heavy-manufacturing base on which to build a modern military machine. Most soldiers were illiterate and unacquainted with even primitive technology; a significant number were opium addicts. The porous tax system deprived the government of revenue to fund military spending. Chiang's adroit playing of army politics to advance loyalists and hold off potential rivals brought promotion of incompetent generals. His use of German advisers made him vulnerable if Hitler decided to give Japan a helping hand by ordering them home.

In an over-arching sense, China lacked the cohesion needed to underpin a major war effort, because of the weakness of civil society and of state organs, and the absence of either a meaningful political dialogue or an efficient autocracy, combined with the gulf between civilians and the all-powerful military. On top of which, the Nationalists had to fight the Communists and guard against regional revolts, as well as handling the threat from Japan.

However, Japanese attempts to set up puppet entities in northern China met with only limited success, and Nanjing could hope that, if it was able to demonstrate greater military strength when the showdown with Tokyo came, the adversary might back off and prefer to concentrate on the Soviet Union. Colonel Ishiwara, the architect of the Mukden Incident who had joined the High Command in Tokyo, wanted to limit expansion in China to focus on the Siberian frontier in pursuit of total war. At the same time, a power shift among the military in Japan strengthened central discipline, making freelance episodes less likely.

The Generalissimo also looked for a possible alliance with the USSR, calculating, correctly, that his bid to wipe out the Chinese Communists would not be a deterrent to Stalin's realpolitik. Diplomatic relations had been resumed in 1932, and, in 1934, Chiang sent a personal envoy to Moscow, without telling his colleagues in Nanjing. Talks followed in Nanjing between the Chinese leader's close associate, Chen Lifu, and the Soviet ambassador, Dimitri Bogomolov. Chen paid a secret visit to Moscow in 1935. That summer, the Comintern called for the creation of broad anti-Fascist fronts. A statement published in October in Paris by Chinese Comintern delegates advocated a united anti-Japanese accord including both the KMT and the CCP.[3]

Chiang calculated that, if Japan and the USSR went to war, China would occupy a pivotal position on the flank. If, on the other hand, Tokyo's navy took the initiative from the army and pursued policies that led to a maritime conflict with America, Nanjing could expect Japan's focus on China to diminish, and Washington to look to China as an ally. However, such geo-strategic calculations were of little help to the regime in facing criticism of its apparent passivity in the face of Japanese aggression. The Generalissimo, whose reputation would never recover from the circumstances surrounding him in the mid-1930s, could not explain what he was doing. As a result, in the face of grave national peril, the Kuomintang seemed inert; an eminent academic, Hu Shih, described it as 'dead, but not buried, and all unburied dead things cause trouble for the living.'[4]

In the early summer of 1936, the ever-rebellious Guangxi Clique seized on patriotic demonstrations after the death of the KMT ideologue Hu Hanmin to mount a new challenge to the central government in the name of opposing the invaders. It allied with the corrupt, super-stitious warlord of Guangdong, who encouraged his officers to tilt at a leather figure labelled 'Chiang Kai-shek'. Joined by General Cai, formerly of the Nineteenth Route Army and the short-lived Fujian

Republic, the Anti-Japanese National Salvation Army advanced into Hunan on 1 June 1936.

Chiang was well prepared. He had been bribing key military figures in Guangdong for some time. They defected or fled to Hong Kong. His secret police chief, Dai Li, sent a former dance hall girl to seduce the Canton air force commander, and pass on a promise of a substantial payment for every plane he handed over. Faced with this kind of counter-play, the Guangdong warlord decided that the game was up, and went to the British colony, where he had stashed away a fortune. Flying to Canton, the Generalissimo slapped an economic blockade on Guangxi. The remaining rebels gave up, in return for a monthly payment and a post on the National Defence Council for the main Guangxi strategist, the Muslim General Bai.[5]

Having dealt with the southerners, Chiang could turn back to the Communists, whose base, though poor, was growing and which received a propaganda boost with the highly favourable book *Red Star over China*, written after a visit to Yenan by the American journalist Edgar Snow. The Generalissimo was determined to end the internal threat before he confronted the Japanese. To achieve this, he had always counted on armed force, and he now prepared a campaign against the Shaanxi base. But he also put out secret peace feelers through Chinese in Moscow and through the underground in Shanghai. How serious he was must be open to question, but the talks, conducted by his close associates, the brothers Chen Lifu and Chen Guofu, got far enough for two Communist negotiators to travel to Yenan to report to Mao in February 1936.

Edgy exchanges followed, with each side setting conditions the other could not meet, in a pattern that would stretch through the ensuing decade. Nanjing's bottom line was that the Red Army should come under its control, which Mao refused to entertain. The Chairman was in an awkward position. He had identified the anti-Japanese cause as one the CCP should embrace, but if this meant a new united front which strengthened the Nationalists, that was not at all his goal. Nor did Mao want to help his old internal Party foes, the Moscow-trained comrades who backed co-operation with the KMT against the invaders and had the support of the Comintern.[6]

Mao had another problem when a Red Army offensive into neighbouring Shanxi in early 1936, which was presented as an attack on the

Japanese, failed in its real purpose of opening a supply route to Soviet-controlled Mongolia. After this, the Kremlin put its foot down. An envoy from Moscow arrived at Yenan with instructions for the Chinese Communists to agree terms with Nanjing. A Draft Agreement on Resistance to Japan and National Salvation was duly drawn up. The slogan of 'Resist Japan and Oppose Chiang' was replaced by 'Compel Chiang to Resist Japan'. The Nationalists were then emboldened to up their terms by a victory over Mongolian autonomists backed by Tokyo. The Generalissimo called for the Red Army to be limited to 3,000 men and for all senior cadres and officers to be exiled for six months, after which they would have to integrate into the Nationalist ranks. Negotiations died out.

Instead, Mao and his colleagues tried to get militarists in the north-west to line up with them against Nanjing. Though his troops had fought the Red Army in early 1936, the Model Governor of Shanxi had fallen out with Chiang over the continuing presence of Nationalist soldiers sent to help him, which he saw as a prelude to a bid by the central government to extend its influence to his province. So he reached a pact with the Communists, couched in the name of the struggle for national salvation against Japan. Mao also put out feelers to the generals who had scored the victory over the Mongolians, and sounded out the Guangxi Clique down south. Most important, the Communists established contacts with the man meant to be leading the fight against them.

After being cured of his morphine habit in Shanghai, Zhang Xueliang had gone to Europe, where he saw Benito Mussolini and the British prime minister, Ramsay Macdonald. The Young Marshal put on weight and took a house in Brighton, to host all-night poker parties. Returning to China, he had been reinstated by Chiang to take part in the anti-Communist campaigns being planned in Shaanxi. He hoped that he could build a new power base there at the head of an army of 80,000 men. But Nanjing began to exert its influence over the north-west, using a new railway line as one of its main tools. Funding for Zhang's army was cut, and a plan was announced to incorporate his best troops into the central forces.[7]

This prompted the Marshal to consider joining the anti-Nanjing alliance in the hope that it might be strong enough to drive the Japanese from Manchuria and enable him to return to his homeland. Mao, Zhou

Enlai and twenty-one Red Army generals wrote a letter to tell Zhang his real enemies were the Japanese and the Generalissimo. The Marshal had an all-night meeting with Zhou Enlai in a Catholic church. Further talks led to the signing of a secret Agreement to Resist Japan and Save the Nation in September 1936. According to Zhou, Zhang opened trading posts for the Soviet base, handed over arms, ammunition, radio equipment and medicine, and exchanged liaison officers, as well as telling the Communists some of his plans.

In a television interview fifty years later, Zhang gave this explanation of his attitude towards the Communists: 'It wasn't that I was sympathetic with them. But they were Chinese so why fight each other? We could talk with them ... Mr Chiang became very unhappy with me in this matter.'

A local military chief, General Yang Hucheng, who had an army of 36,000 men and was worried that Chiang was going to force him out, also reached a non-aggression pact with the Communists. As well as exchanging liaison staff, he and the Red Army agreed to stage fake battles to keep up appearances. Yang suggested to the Young Marshal that they go a step further by kidnapping Chiang when he visited Shaanxi at the end of the year, to force him to do what they wanted.

The Generalissimo arrived in the provincial capital of Xi'an on 7 December 1936. Meeting him, Zhang announced that he was no longer prepared to fight the Communists, and urged a political settlement. Chiang said the campaign would go on. He had brought a strong staff of senior officers with him, including one of his favourite commanders, Chen Cheng, and was ready to replace Zhang with more trustworthy men to liquidate the Communists. The Marshal decided to go along with Yang's proposal. At dawn on 12 December, 150 of his crack troops stormed across the terraces of the imperial hot springs outside Xi'an where Chiang was staying. The Generalissimo was doing his early-morning exercises, and escaped through the back window of his room clad in his nightshirt. He left his false teeth on a bedside table.[8]

Chiang made his way through the undergrowth behind the resort, fell down a gulley, injuring his back, and then climbed up a slope to hide in a cave. In the middle of the day, he gave himself up. Members of his party staying in Xi'an were rounded up. Zhang sent off a circular telegram to national leaders calling for the reorganization of the government, and the end of the war against the Communists. Political prisoners, including the 'Six Gentlemen' of Shanghai who had been detained for their anti-Japanese attitude, should be released, free speech allowed, and a National Salvation Conference held to implement nationalism, democracy and the people's livelihood.

In the capital, the chief of staff, General He, prepared to attack Xi'an from the air and by land. The possibility that this might kill the Generalissimo or provoke the rebels to assassinate him did not deter him. He brushed aside pleas from Madame Chiang not to attack as the emotional response of a woman. Her Australian adviser, W. H. Donald, now stepped in. He had the advantage of having counselled Zhang in Manchuria, and of having arranged his drug cure, so he might have some influence on the younger man. Donald was described by the British writer Christopher Isherwood as 'a red-faced, serious man with a large, sensible nose'. A teetotal bachelor, he did not speak Chinese and abhorred Chinese food. He could speak more frankly than the Soongs, and could always be disavowed if things did not work out.

When Donald arrived in Xi'an, he found the Marshal in a worried frame of mind. His non-Communist allies had not rallied to him. The KMT propaganda machine had revved up, and even anti-Chiang newspapers deplored the kidnapping. His captive was proving impossible to handle, refusing to speak as he lay on a camp bed in a cold, bare room, the blanket pulled up over his face, telling his guards either to obey him or to shoot him. The Australian got the Generalissimo moved to a house with steam heating, warned Chiang about pro-Japanese circles around him and flew back to Nanjing to confer with the Generalissimo's wife.

When news of the kidnapping arrived in Yenan, Mao had exulted. The Politburo Standing Committee called for the 'elimination' of Chiang, who should be tried by a People's Tribunal. But Moscow did not agree. Still seeing the Generalissimo as the best hope of maintaining unity in the face of Tokyo's aggression, the Comintern denounced the kidnapping as 'objectively detrimental' to the anti-Japanese cause. Zhou Enlai was dispatched to Xi'an to work for the liberation of the Nationalist chief – he travelled by mule and then in a plane sent by the Marshal for him; the anti-Communist American pilot said that he flew through rough patches on purpose, and enjoyed watching his passengers vomiting.[9]

A flurry of KMT dignitaries arrived in Xi'an, including T. V. Soong and the secret police chief, Dai Li, who, taken to see his master, fell to his knees and berated himself for having failed to protect him. Meiling flew in from Nanjing with Donald; she carried with her a pistol and a spare set of her husband's false teeth. The Australian recalled that, as they landed, she gave him the gun and said, 'Please shoot me if any soldiers touch me.'[10]

When he met her, Zhou faithfully followed the Moscow line, saying that her husband was the only man able to lead the country. That opened the way for the two men to meet on Christmas Eve. They had not been face to face since their time together as commander and political commissar at the Whampoa Academy in Canton in the mid-1920s. By all accounts, their meeting was extremely polite, with the Communist repeating that the CCP backed Chiang as the national leader against the Japanese. The Generalissimo said there should be no more civil war. 'All the time we have been fighting, I have often thought of you,' he added. 'I hope we can work together again.'[11]

Zhou then had a second meeting with Meiling. 'Internal problems should be solved by political means, and not by military force,' she said, blithely disregarding the weapons her husband relied on to win and maintain power. Zhou persuaded the local militarist, Yang, to be satisfied with a verbal assurance of unity. On Christmas Day, Chiang was freed, and flew back to Nanjing. Zhang, who had said he was ready to accept any punishment that might be meted out, made the same journey. Madame Chiang noted that it was the first time 'any high officer responsible for mutinous conduct has shown eagerness . . . to be tried for his misdeeds'.[12]

In the capital, cheering crowds greeted the Generalissimo, who wrote of 'living a second life'. Newspapers expressed relief that the crisis was over. The Nationalist leader headed for his home village of Xikou to recuperate. Zhang was tried, and sentenced to ten years' imprisonment, later changed to detention at Chiang's pleasure. The location of the comfortable prison chosen for him was intriguing – a hostel and then a temple just outside the Generalissimo's village. He would be held for half a century, moving between houses and caves all over China and then to Taiwan. Finally released in 1988, he converted to Christianity, married the companion who had shared his imprisonment and went to live with her in Hawaii, where he died in 2001 at the age of 100. In an oral history released after his death, he said that he and Chiang had a 'flesh and blood' personal friendship, but 'our political dispute was like the relationship between two sworn enemies.'[13]

Back in Xi'an, leftists tried to rally resistance, but, after six weeks, they collapsed in the face of a Nationalist column advancing on the city. Their leaders sacked the treasury and fled to Yenan. General Yang went off to Europe; when he returned in 1938, he was arrested.

The incident had repercussions within the leadership as Chiang named General Chen Cheng, who had shown his loyalty in Xi'an, as his eventual successor. But the most important result was to force Nanjing to give up the anti-Communist campaign. The relief at the peaceful outcome reflected a widespread feeling that unity was needed against the invaders. Chiang had to acknowledge national sentiment. When an aide suggested going through with the offensive against Yenan, he bent his head and did not reply. Thus, though he would remain a prisoner, the Young Marshal achieved his aim.

After its escapes from the 1927 purges and on the various long marches, the CCP once more avoided probable destruction, or, at best, marginalization in an even more isolated haven. Discussions on forming a united front resumed between Zhou Enlai and Chen Lifu. The Yenan base expanded across the provincial border into Gansu and Ningxia to form the area known from abbreviations of provincial names as the Shaan–Gan–Ning base, with its capital still at Yenan. Its borders were closely watched by the Nationalists, and the Communists ran into local resistance, particularly from the Ma brothers, three Muslim warlords who had ruled in the region since the 1910s and whose very fat leader liked to be fed ice cream by female nurses. But they were safe from the final offensive Chiang had planned from Xi'an.

The Red Army grew in size, Nanjing agreeing to fund 'reintegrated' territories and armies. Communist forces in Shaanxi became the Eighth Army of the United Front under Zhu De, while a second Communist unit, the New Fourth Army, was set up in the Lower Yangzi, including guerrillas who had been left behind at the start of the Long March. The two armies reached a combined strength of some 92,000 soldiers during 1937, and then doubled the following year.

Mao faced a challenge on another front, however, when the Chinese Comintern leader, Wang Ming, arrived in Yenan as the Kremlin's apostle of joint action against Japan. Stalin might have identified Mao as a man to carry the banner of revolution in China, but he made sure he had a solid Bolshevik bureaucrat on the scene as well. Nor was there any cause for complacency on the Nationalist side. China was suffering from a fresh outbreak of natural disasters, including bubonic plague, smallpox and famine that hit 30 million in Sichuan, Shaanxi and Henan. Politically, there was no hiding the weaknesses of the regime; a veteran figure, Lin Sen, who had been appointed as a figurehead president to undertake ceremonial duties for the Generalissimo, remarked that things were 'far behind what we had hoped for'. Above all, there was the growing certainty of a major confrontation with Japan for which the Nationalist regime had not had the time or resources to prepare itself properly.[14]

Privately, the adviser, Alexander von Falkenhausen, admitted that the Chinese army 'in its present state is not fit to face a modern war'. On paper, Nanjing had 2 million troops, but many units were understaffed. Half the officers promoted from the ranks were reckoned to be illiterate. In his study of the Chinese army, Michael Gibson calculates that only seventy-nine of the 165 divisions actually reported to Nanjing; the rest were under regional command, and only seventeen were of good quality. Another historian of the Sino-Japanese war, Hsi-Sheng Ch'i, counts far fewer divisions answering to Nanjing – thirty-one. For all the contracts for arms imports, there was still a serious shortage of heavy weapons, and air power.*[15]

On 7 July 1937, shooting broke out between a 100-man Japanese unit and Chinese troops beside a stone span over the Yungting River outside Beijing, known to the Chinese as the Lugou bridge† and to Westerners as the Marco Polo Bridge since the Venetian traveller was said to have visited it. The Japanese were conducting night exercises, and one of their messengers went missing – eventually he returned, and was variously reported to have got lost in the moonless night after stopping to urinate, having been taken prisoner by the Chinese, having visited a brothel, or having fallen in a gravel pit and passed out.

The Japanese used his temporary absence as a sign of alleged aggression against their troops, and protested at the 'unlawful firing' of rifles by the Chinese. When fresh shooting broke out from the Chinese before

* For this chapter and the next, I am particularly indebted to Hans Van de Ven, both in conversations and in his authoritative account, *War and Nationalism in China*.
† Transliterated at the time as Lukouchiao.

dawn, the Japanese advanced, but then a ceasefire was agreed. Despite this, tension rose in the area; on 26 July, Japan issued an ultimatum for two Chinese divisions to withdraw by noon the next day. Not waiting for this, they began an attack near the Summer Palace the following morning. Armoured vehicles moved in as planes strafed. Hundreds of Chinese soldiers were killed.

The town of Wanping near the Marco Polo Bridge came under heavy assault, its gates blown away. In another walled town, Chinese militiamen who had worked with the Japanese changed sides once the foreign troops had gone off to join the fighting. They killed hundreds of Japanese and Korean civilians, provoking a generalized slaughter by returning imperial soldiers. Hirohito authorized the dispatch of reinforcements to China.[16]

Japanese units bombarded a barracks south of Beijing and laid an ambush that killed 1,000 men who fled. A mechanized force, including fifty tanks, shut off all the roads into the former capital. On 8 August, Imperial Army troops occupied the city. Tianjin was subjugated by bombing. The psychological change since the Xi'an Incident meant that there could be no drawing back by Nanjing this time. Appearing in field uniform on the balcony of military headquarters in the summer capital of Lushan, his chest stuck out, his face stern, Chiang declared that 'the limits of endurance had been reached'. An Admonition to All Officers and Soldiers in the War of Resistance said that, since all hope of peace had vanished, 'all we can do now is to resist to the bitter end.' On 7 August, the final decision to pursue war was taken by the National Defence Council in Nanjing, attended by Chiang, the Model Governor, the Christian General, General Bai of the Guangxi Clique, Wang Jingwei, T. V. Soong, Sun Fo and thirty-four other high-ranking figures. Zhou Enlai and Zhu De went to Nanjing for discussions, which decided to keep the Communist Eighth Army in Shaanxi while the Fourth Army would operate in Jiangsu, above Shanghai.

In Tokyo, the emperor called for a 'war-ending' battle. His brother, Prince Takamatsu, forecast: 'We're really going to smash China so that it will be ten years before it can stand straight again.' In a message to the Communist Military Commission, Mao said a moment of truth had been reached at which it was imperative to enforce 'the policy of total resistance by the whole nation.' Von Falkenhausen told Berlin 'total war' had broken out.

Chinese resistance crumbled swiftly in the north. But Chiang had a fall-back position. He had built up the country's strongest defences in the Lower Yangzi area round Shanghai and Nanjing, which had always been at the core of the regime. In August 1937, he threw this into the battle, opening a second front which he hoped would swing the tide of war.

15

The Great Retreat

Shanghai had been demilitarized by the agreement that ended the fighting there in 1932, but now the central government moved in troops while Tokyo's navy, which was anxious to emulate the army's successes in the north, massed a fleet of thirty-two ships, carrying thousands of marines. Japanese naval planes raided the railway line to Nanjing. The Nationalist government declared martial law in the region.

In mid-August, after a typhoon had blown through the city, the 87th and 88th central army divisions, Nanjing's best, German-trained troops, wearing metal helmets and well armed and disciplined, began to attack Japanese positions in and around Shanghai. The invaders hit back with an artillery bombardment of the workers' district of Zhabei and the university area. China deployed 80,000 soldiers while Japanese forces on ships and in the International Settlement numbered 12,000.[1]

In the afternoon of 14 August, five planes from the Chinese air force flew in a tight V-shaped formation to attack a Japanese cruiser moored in the Huangpu River. By mistake, they dropped their bombs on crowded areas of the International Settlement and French Concession; more than 3,000 people were killed or badly injured. The next day, Nanjing issued a Declaration of War of Self-Defence. A General War Directive issued on 20 August opted for a war of attrition, to be waged by five war zones to deny Tokyo swift victory and exhaust it by fighting across huge expanses of territory, trading space for time. A non-aggression pact was announced with the USSR, and Soviet arms began to flood in, paid for in raw materials. At the same time, Nanjing also managed to maintain the German connection, von Falkenhausen helping to direct operations in Shanghai, eating hard-boiled eggs and drinking cognac at the front.[2]

*

The death toll of soldiers and civilians in the war which was now bound to engulf China will never be known. Estimates range from 10 million to twice as many, with most in the 15 to 20 million range – the very size of the discrepancies attests to the scale of human loss.* There was enormous material and moral damage. The official Nationalist history counts twenty-three campaigns fought by its troops against the Imperial Army, involving 1,117 major battles and 38,931 lesser engagements. This does not take into account the fighting between the Communists and the Japanese.

The scale of major campaigns was huge. At least 350,000 troops were involved at the peak of the battle for Shanghai. At the beginning of 1938, the Chinese massed 600,000 men over a front stretching from Jiangsu province to southern Shanxi. An offensive they staged the following year involved around a million troops. As late as 1944, the Japanese mounted a multi-pronged offensive that struck from the Yellow River to Guangxi province in the south-west, a distance of 900 miles as the crow flies. If China was a country on the scale of a continent, this was continental conflict, but one little noticed by the rest of the world until Japan's aggression stretched across the Pacific ten years after its first move in Manchuria.

In the north, some Nationalist troops fought well, but the old factor of regional interests raised its head once more. The Model Governor refused to co-operate with central-government forces, and held back his best soldiers. The warlord of Shandong avoided battle, while the Kwantung Army took over Inner Mongolia. Chiang posted some commanders far from their home regions to play politics and lessen the prospects of local insubordination.[3]

However, in Shanghai, where fighting stretched along a forty-mile front, the united Chinese troops included armies from Guangdong, Henan, Hunan, Sichuan and Fujian, as well as Nanjing's own units. Tokyo threw in reinforcements to bring its strength to 200,000 men, who found progress difficult in the rain-sodden terrain of fields, irrigation canals and swamps spotted with pillboxes and deep trenches.

---

* An official Nationalist account put military and civilian casualties at 11.65 million – 3.3 million military and more than 8.4 million civilians. Other estimates run between 15 and 20 million (see Eastman et al., *Nationalist Era*, p. 115). Chiang Kai-shek's adopted son put military and civilians deaths at 23 million. The Generalissimo spoke in 1947 of 10 million 'sacrifices', but it was not clear what this included.

Civilians constructed defence works and aided medical and relief work. Big Ears Du gave his bullet-proof limousine to the army. Sing-song girls comforted wounded soldiers in night clubs turned into hospices.[4]

The carnage in the city grew as civilian areas were bombed and bombarded amid vicious house-to-house fighting. As in 1932, the area round the North Station saw some of the fiercest combat. The streets of the Hongkou were littered with bodies of people shot by the Japanese. Across Suzhou Creek, Westerners watched the battles from the rooftops along the Bund. Another Chinese aerial attack on Japanese ships in the river ended in a fresh disaster – to evade enemy fighters, the pilot lightened his load by dropping a bomb; it hit the Sincere department store, killing 170 and injuring 470.[5]

From his headquarters north-west of the city, Chiang set a pattern which was to dog the Nationalist effort throughout the war. Often poorly informed, he issued badly formulated, unrealistic orders that took little account of the evolution on the battlefield. His refusal to allow any retreat as a matter of principle meant that good troops fell in protracted but unwinnable battles. The heavy guns on Japanese ships played an important role, untroubled by poor Chinese naval defences. Japanese air attacks were indiscriminate. Despite a Union Jack marking on the roof, one hit the car of the British ambassador, Sir Hughe Knatchbull-Hugessen, wounding him in the spine. Madame Chiang broke a rib when her open car hit a shell crater and she was sent flying through the air. Recovering, she was photographed tending to wounded in hospital, wearing a nurse's uniform.[6]

The Chinese were eventually worn down by the power brought to bear by the attackers. In one two-day period, 2,526 bombs fell on Shanghai. Thirty thousand Japanese troops landed on Hangzhou Bay to the south and moved up to attack the Chinese from the rear, slogging through cold mud like treacle, sliding down hills, tumbling into ditches and creeks, and drinking filthy water. Towns on their route were devastated – dogs grew fat on the corpses. There were too many bodies to count, a Japanese officer wrote in letters to his family.[7]

Finally, Chiang had to order a retreat in early November. To hinder the enemy, the Nationalist troops set off more fires on top of those caused by bombing and shelling. Despite the rain, the blaze stretched for more than five miles. Estimates of Nationalist losses in the ninety-day battle range from 180,000 to 300,000. Japanese casualties were reckoned to be in excess of 40,000, possibly as high as 70,000 men. More than 100,000 refugees crowded into camps in the foreign areas. Another 350,000 fled the city. The foreign concessions remained intact, and a Shanghai Municipal Commission was established to run Japanese-occupied districts.[8]

The Chinese retreat turned into a rout as the invaders outflanked defensive lines up the Yangzi, killing, raping and looting as they advanced. 'The farming area between Shanghai and Nanjing, once the most populous area on earth, was the graveyard of almost a million Chinese soldiers and civilians,' the journalist Rhodes Farmer reported. In the silk city of Suzhou, as an eye-witness put it, air raids sent 'tons of explosives hurtling down from the skies, exploding in a cascade of bits of human flesh, dirt, stone and mortar . . . The most dreadful nightmare could not compare with it.'[9]

Next, the invaders headed for Nanjing. Fortresses on the river were unable to stop their ships – the Chinese guns had obsolete shells, no rangefinders and sights dating from the end of the previous century. Japan also ruled the air. The Nationalists decided to abandon their capital and move to the tri-cities of Wuhan. But Chiang could not be seen to abandon the city without a fight, given its status as the Nationalist capital and the link with Sun Yat-sen. So a force was left to resist as best it could under Tang Shengzhi, the Kuomintang's early Hunanese ally on the Northern Expedition who had subsequently led a revolt and fled to Japan before returning to rally to the cause once more. He had 90,000 troops, who set up machine guns, dug trenches, and erected barbed wire, sandbag and concrete defences, as well as clearing a mile-wide belt of land round the city with fire. At a press conference at the end of November, the opium-addicted Tang pledged to live or die with Nanjing.[10]

But he was soon seeking an agreement with the Japanese to surrender, provided his men were allowed to leave peacefully. The enemy was not interested. Its planes bombed; an artillery barrage opened up; the huge city wall was breached. Aiming to save as many men as he could, Chiang ordered Tang to retreat over the Yangzi. It was too late.

Thousands died trying to cross the river. Fires and exploding ammunition dumps killed many more. Three thousand wounded soldiers lay on the concrete platform of the main station, their moaning sounding 'like the wind in a pine forest', according to an American who fed them gruel. Buildings erected during the past decade as symbols of China's modernization were set on fire. Amid the confusion, Japanese planes sank an American gunboat, the *Panay*, machine-gunning survivors in the river. British gunboats were also attacked. Washington and London were content with apologies from Tokyo.

After General Tang escaped on a small launch, the city's people became the victims of a rape that would mark its perpetrators in history, with hugely emotive political fall-out that persists to this day. The number of people killed by the Japanese troops remains open to question, though the precise number does not diminish the horror of what happened, or support Japanese revisionists who claim that there was no atrocity. The figure of 300,000 has been generally accepted in China, and has often been repeated in Western accounts. But recent examination of contemporary records reduces this to 100,000 or less. The historian David Askew has found that the flight of much of the population meant that there were only about 250,000 people left in Nanjing when the city fell. He puts the maximum number of people buried at 32,000. A key eye-witness, John Rabe of the German Siemens company, wrote of a death toll of 50,000–60,000 civilians and soldiers.

Rabe, the 'Good Nazi of Nanjing', set up a Safety Zone to shelter civilians. But the Japanese began to raid the enclave, first to seize Chinese soldiers sheltering there and then to grab anybody. Food inside the zone grew scarce. Japanese diplomats gave Rabe polite assurances, but the army called the tune, and it was bent on mass killing, including inside Rabe's zone.

Unlike the Nazis, the Japanese leaders issued no order to the troops to conduct the rape. The commanding general gave senior officers a scathing rebuke for the behaviour of their men after a victory parade on 17 December. But he left Nanjing two days later, and his words had no discernible effect. Chinese were roped together and machine-gunned, doused with kerosene and burned. Atrocity accounts told of thousands buried alive – or put in holes up to their necks and savaged by dogs. Others were used for bayonet practice, nailed to boards and run over by vehicles, mutilated and disembowelled, sprayed with acid, or hung up by their tongues. Martial arts swordplay was practised on defenceless civilians.

If the Japanese despised the Chinese in general, they had an even lower opinion of Chinese women, who were raped in enormous numbers, and then killed. Soldiers believed that raping a virgin would bring them prowess in battle. One trooper recorded that, while engaged in rape, his colleagues might consider the victim as a woman, but, when they killed her, 'we just thought of her as something like a pig.' Some women died with sticks rammed into their vaginas. Fetuses were ripped from the bodies of expectant mothers. Other women were taken to so-called 'comfort houses' set up for the soldiers, who called the inmates 'public toilets'.

The killers felt no shame at their savagery. Some photographed the killings, and sent the negatives to Shanghai to be developed. Staff in photographic shops there showed them to foreign journalists, who alerted the outside world to the horror. Seventy years on, some Japanese teachers and writers still deny that anything terrible had occurred, blaming such accounts on Nationalist propaganda and lying American journalists, saying that photographic records had been faked and indulging in extremes of obscene nit-picking. But the case against the massacre is singularly unconvincing and can only fuel nationalist hatred between the two major nations of East Asia to nobody's benefit – if this book argues for a more honest Chinese grasp of its history, the same is equally true for Japan, which cannot wallow in the notion that Nanjing saw only scattered executions and incidents.

Can the sustained mass bestiality of the Rape of Nanjing be explained? Perhaps not. But one element sprang from the tensions in the Japanese army since the Shanghai battle erupted. Many soldiers were backward country boys who let their passions run viciously free once they were released from discipline by victory. They had won; they would take their price. The victims were mainly civilians or soldiers who had shed their uniforms. That was in keeping with the way in which the Japanese soldiers regarded the people whose country they had invaded. One wrote in his diary of Chinese as 'ants crawling on the ground'.

It seems certain that the emperor knew the broad lines of the massacre. He still hoped that China could be defeated with one big blow, which Nanjing might provide. Japan followed the latest victory with tough peace proposals through the German ambassador, which the Nationalists rejected. Though still termed an 'incident' so as not to fall foul of American embargoes on supplies to war combatants, the fight in China was elevated to the status of a sacred struggle to extend the emperor's 'benevolent rule'. The Japanese commander said the Chinese should realize his troops were their real friends, ready to sacrifice themselves to rescue them from backwardness.

Having retreated to Wuhan, the Nationalists found themselves threatened by a two-pronged attack, along the Yangzi from Nanjing and down the railway from the Yellow River to the north. To check the first, booms were laid across the river and forts strengthened. To stop the second, Chiang had a huge force of 600,000 men, spread from Shanxi to Jiangsu. But the Japanese still advanced, and to the east took Shandong while, politically, they supervised the establishment of a collaborationist administration in Nanjing which absorbed some of the figures who had worked with the invaders in northern China.

Seeking to halt the enemy, Chiang ordered the dykes on the Yellow River to be blown, near the city of Zhengzhou, unleashing a flood that affected 6 million people as the waterway returned to the original course from which it had been diverted under the Qing dynasty. It was swollen by water from the melting snows of Mongolia and its bed was high because of the accumulation of loess silt. The banks of part of the Grand Canal were also opened to increase the effect. When the Japanese tried to get Chinese labourers to carry out repairs, watching Nationalist troops machine-gunned them. Some reports tell of half-a-million people perishing; others say the tally was much lower because peasants knew what was about to happen and fled in advance. The enemy was stopped, for the moment.

The Nationalists decided to make the major rail junction of Xuzhou,* close to the Shandong–Jiangsu border, into the next major testing point. Two hundred thousand troops were moved in to this region on the traditional route from northern China to the Yangzi. This zone was under the Guangxi commander, Li Zongren, described by the visiting Christopher Isherwood as 'a very polite, nut-brown man, with an enormous mouth and deeply intelligent eyes'. Troops from other parts of China were drafted in, including a northern army under General Tang Enbo. Chiang badly needed a victory to convince doubters that it was worth continuing to fight.[11]

A successful defensive operation in southern Shandong gave the campaign a good start. The Generalissimo flew in to confer with the Guangxi generals. Staying at Li's headquarters in a small temple, he took his host's bed, leaving him to sleep on a door taken off its hinges. Chiang placed a female spy in the general's staff in case of fresh plotting against

---

* Transliterated then as Hsüchou.

him. But, this time, the Guangxi Clique showed its military worth on behalf of the nation, and the regime it had so often opposed.

A trap was set up by which Chinese troops retreated into the walled town of Taierzhuang, north of Xuzhou on the Grand Canal, at the end of March 1938, drawing the enemy after them into the narrow streets between the fortress-like stone houses, while other units moved against the Japanese rear. General Bai, with his high-domed forehead, darting amber eyes, high-bridged nose and prominent chin, plotted the battle from a two-storey building standing by the railway station booking office.[12]

The Japanese fell into the snare, and were caught in fierce hand-to-hand fighting. As defenders sprayed them with kerosene, the town was described as a 'burning hell'. A Chinese 'Dare to Die' corps stormed in, some carrying long swords. Nationalist planes supplied by the Soviet Union appear to have enjoyed aerial supremacy for once. Tanks wheeled across the fields outside as Chinese snipers picked off enemy soldiers from foxholes.

'Battle cries shook the skies,' Li, who directed operations on horseback, wrote in his memoirs.

After grimly fighting for some ten days, the enemy troops had spent their energy and were running out of munitions and gasoline. Many of their motor vehicles had been destroyed, and those that remained had no fuel. The whole army broke and fled in disorder. Faced with this sudden victory, the morale of our men soared and they rushed after the enemy like a storm sweeping fallen leaves. There was no stopping them. Enemy corpses lay all over the plain, and vehicles, arms, and horses were strewn about.[13]

Li's account depicts him and his troops winning the battle virtually single-handedly. In fact, other Chinese units also performed well, including Tang Enbo's northern units. Li's claim of 20,000 Japanese casualties compared to 12,000 Chinese dead may well be an exaggeration – other sources put the Japanese losses at 8,000. But there was no doubt that this was an occasion for celebration for the Nationalists and their allies. Li called it the first happy occasion since the start of the war. Chiang hailed the 'concrete manifestation' of China's spirit, and pressed for a major offensive to take advantage of the enemy's disarray, involving 450,000 men.

Spirits rose in Wuhan, where the united front between the KMT and the Communists, which had been formally proclaimed during the Battle of Shanghai, took real shape. The leading returnee from Moscow, Wang Ming, arrived to promote the new Comintern line. 'Everything through the united front,' he declared, adding that this was 'no time to engage in a power struggle'. Red Army commanders came in for discussions. The Christian General and the Guangxi Clique joined the effort. Soviet aid grew, and Chiang hoped that Moscow's forces would attack Manchukuo. The dividing line was no longer between Nationalists and Communists, but between those who fought for China and those who betrayed the nation.

At the beginning of 1938, a high-level example was made of two warlords, one from Sichuan and the other from Shandong, who had been conspiring together. The Shandong militarist, a one-time subordinate of the Christian General, had retreated to allow the Japanese through the south of his province. Arrested after being lured to a conference and separated from his bodyguard by a phoney air raid alarm, he was taken to Wuhan, where he was court-martialled and killed with a shot in the back of the head. The Sichuanese was lying ill in hospital in Wuhan at the time. A plane sent by his staff to fly him home exploded in mid-air. General He Yingqin went to his bedside to tell him what had happened to his Shandong crony, and showed him copies of intercepted cables between them. Soon after He left, the Sichuanese had a violent spasm, and died two days later.

Reaching back to the days of the Wuhan leftist government of 1927, progressives and intellectuals sighted a new dawn as they moved upriver from occupied Shanghai. Secret-police activities were restricted. Factories which had been dismantled in the Lower Yangzi were re-erected. Foreign writers such as Isherwood and Auden, film-makers and the photographer Robert Capa came in to record the defence of the city, which was to be China's equivalent of the struggle of Madrid against Franco's fascist forces. The press was free. Bookshops flourished along Communications Road. The streets were brightly lit, neon tubes flashing out the colours of the national flag; a young army political officer, I Feng, compared the illuminations to beacons on a battlefield, though he was shocked to see that 'some of our heroic veterans who had fought a hundred battles were here, tipsy or drunk and lying in the embrace of prostitutes'; but he excused them since 'a fighting man will naturally try to feast on pleasure to the utmost while there is still time.'[14]

Following a policy of no surrender, the Generalissimo refused to receive the German ambassador when he sought to present a Japanese peace feeler. The diplomat was allowed to read the proposal to Madame Chiang, H. H. Kong, who had become prime minister, and Donald, saying he had been instructed to convey it to them without comment. 'I should think so,' Meiling replied.[15]

As was his habit, the Generalissimo accompanied his calls for national resurrection with biting criticism of KMT members for lax living, lack of enthusiasm, lackadaisical work, and pursuit of power and pleasure. They had 'almost become a special class', he added. 'The masses . . . are not only cool towards the party but have even become antagonistic toward it.' The former journalist Rhodes Farmer, who had gone to work for the Nationalists, recalled Chiang as acting like 'a man with a hundred pairs of hands and eyes, his eyes boring into visitors like gimlets'. 'Wherever I go is the Government and the centre of resistance,' he declared. 'I am the State.'[16]

His wife was also highly active – and emancipated for her country and time, though her husband liked her to walk behind him on formal occasions. She pushed for the development of the air force, launched a scheme to get Chinese women to sew 2 million winter uniforms for the troops, visited wounded soldiers and toured villages to tell peasants of their role in the war. Pursuing her welfare work, she drove an ambulance donated by American Friends of the Chinese People – at least for the cameras. A visiting writer, Edgar Mowrer, was bowled over by her sex appeal. Christopher Isherwood remarked that 'she could be terrible, she could be gracious, she could be businesslike, she could be ruthless', but also noted that, behind her public mask, she looked 'tired and far from well'.[17]

Through newspaper articles, interviews and radio broadcasts to the US, she hammered home the theme that other nations did not seem to care about Tokyo's expansionism. 'All treaties and structures to outlaw war and to regularize the conduct of war appear to have crumbled, and we have a reversion to the day of savages,' she noted. Did foreign silence denote 'the death-knell of the supposed moral superiority of the Occident', she wondered.

The fact was that the big powers had no desire to get into a fight over China, as had been the case since the Mukden Incident. Japan's modernization and its presence in the foreign settlement made it an honorary Western nation. Britain and the US did call a conference in Brussels to discuss what Tokyo called 'the special undeclared war' in China, but, when Japan boycotted the meeting, this initiative fell apart. Facing the rise of fascism in Europe, Britain had no desire to get embroiled in Far Eastern complications. For anti-Communists, Tokyo was a bar to the Soviet expansion on the other side of the globe. The United States was not ready for hostilities across the Pacific. The USSR was caught up in Stalin's purges.

Chiang looked beyond the immediate battlefields to national redemption, and permitted some political relaxation. An Organic Law provided for a National Political Consultative Council to 'unite all the forces in the country and bring together all ideas and views to benefit the formulation of national policies'. The government would be required to submit important domestic and foreign policies to the council before implementation. When the body met in July 1938, 120 of its 200 seats were allocated to the CCP, independents and smaller non-KMT groups, including the anti-Japanese standard-bearer, the National Salvation Association.

Economic plans included a crusade against speculation and corruption. Officials were to be held to a strict code of conduct while soldiers received political training, and associations of peasants, workers, students and other groups would help the war effort.

However, as so often, there were substantial clouds over the sunny intervals in Wuhan. The council's powers were limited; it could propose and criticize but not enforce decisions. Its membership was subject to vetting. It might be useful to Chiang and his colleagues as a way of forging a wider sense of national unity, but the KMT establishment was to remain at the core of the regime, epitomized by the granting of sweeping emergency powers to the Generalissimo. As for Mao, he saw the united front as a potential barrier to his personal and philosophical supremacy, and Wang Ming as a most unwelcome rival.

On the aid front, Chiang had seemed to have scored a signal success by retaining the services of both the Germans and the Russians, who occupied compounds near to one another in Wuhan, but avoided meeting. However, the Soviet army did not advance into Manchukuo since Stalin wanted to avoid war with Japan, and, in Berlin, the new foreign minister, Joachim von Ribbentrop, pursued an increasingly pro-Japanese policy. The Nazis recognized Manchukuo, and then cancelled military exports to China, after which the ambassador and the military advisers were ordered home.

As for the battlefield, the old regional fault lines reasserted themselves after the victory at Taierzhuang. In response to Chiang's proposal for a major attack, Li Zongren objected that full victory would be hard to achieve and made clear he would not risk more of the troops he had moved from Guangxi to his war zone. His refusal deprived other armies of the support they needed to advance. This gave the Japanese time to regroup and pour in reinforcements. They won a second battle at Taierzhuang, and took Xuzhou after their planes flattened the railway station, the airfield and the army barracks. An observer flying over the area estimated that half the villages were destroyed, many on fire.

On the day the Nationalists abandoned the city, two Chinese planes flew over Japan, dropping leaflets urging the population to stop their militarists – Chiang claimed that the flight would bring home their vulnerability. Closer at hand, the Anhui capital of Anqing fell. After heavy bombing, the city of Kaifeng was also lost. Air attacks spread to Wuhan.[18]

In the north, a puppet government was installed in Beijing as Japanese planes attacked cities and railway lines, and their troops took the Shanxi capital of Taiyuan after a siege. China alleged that the invaders were using poison gas. Lin Biao, the Long March veteran and commander of the Communist Eighth Army, led a rare fightback with an ambush of a supply column. But, though played up in Communist accounts, it was tiny compared with the reverses elsewhere.

After watching railway wagons filled with wounded soldiers on the Henan–Shandong border, Rhodes Farmer wrote that 'gangrene was everywhere: maggots writhed in the wounds. They suffered silently and died silently.' Hangzhou, a foreign resident reported, became 'a filthy, battered, obscene place . . . a city of dread'. In mountains by the Yellow River, Theodore (Teddy) White of *Time* found villages where every woman had been raped by the Japanese. Survival became a local matter, undermining loyalty to the Nationalists, just as the Qing's inability to defend people from the mid-nineteenth-century revolts had undermined faith in the dynasty. It was the key factor in China from 1937 to 1945, involving both self-defence and variable loyalties, as people were much more swayed by pragmatism than by nationalism.[19]

In some areas on the 2,000-mile border between Chinese and Japanese influence, both sides tried to collect taxes, each killing petty officials working for the other. Guerrilla-bandits kidnapped for ransom, accusing the victims of being traitors. Trade and smuggling flourished. Not that anywhere in eastern and central China was safe from Japanese planes: Chiang Kai-shek's first wife was killed in a raid on their home village – their son went to the house and erected a memorial stone pledging vengeance.

The fighting generated huge crowds of refugees. The Nationalist political officer I Feng saw crowds 'pouring headlong like a whirling flood down the main road on the southern bank of the Grand Canal. Some were tugging their oxen and donkeys with them, and others drove furiously in wagons. Those with no means of transport carried the whole of their property on their shoulders. Shouting for their fathers and crying for their mothers, supporting the aged and carrying their children in their arms, they poured along the road. Enemy planes gave no respite, but bombed and machine-gunned them continuously.'[20]

Still, for all their military success, the invaders were badly over-extended. Their expansion had been in a broad belt of territory in the eastern half of the country running from the far north to the Yangzi. Later, they would take Canton and stage punitive expeditions that reached into the south-west. But western provinces such as Sichuan, Guizhou, Yunnan, Shaanxi and Gansu were beyond them. While they won battle after battle against Chinese troops, they could not hope to achieve complete control, particularly when they came up against traditions of banditry and local autonomy. Big areas of provinces like Fujian, Jiangxi, Zhejiang and Hunan remained unoccupied, though anywhere might be the target of air attacks or sudden raids to grab food and resources.[21]

The occupation was compared to a net with the strings and knots representing Japanese positions around the much larger Chinese holes. Though China could not beat the enemy, the fact that the enemy could not beat it meant that up to a million imperial troops and a large air force were tied down for eight years, with the associated cost in material resources and planning skills. The strain on Japan of the China Front thus made it an important piece in the jigsaw of the Second World War, as Roosevelt always appreciated, even if Churchill complained about the attention paid by the Americans to a country he dismissed as 'four hundred million pigtails'. Parallels between the Japanese in China and the American experience in Vietnam, or more recently in Iraq, are evident. The Red Army commander, Zhu De, told a journalist that Japanese reliance on mechanized units meant that 'they cannot take advantage of the hill country, but must follow the easiest and most level route . . . so we always fight in the hills, not in open country.'[22]

Saving a big city such as Wuhan was a different matter. General Chen Cheng, Chiang's diminutive companion in the kidnapping at Xi'an, was in charge of the defence. On paper, he had 450,000 men under his direct command, though, as always, the number of men in the field was less than the official count. The Japanese advanced from north, south and east. Some armies held out successfully, such as a force in Jiangxi under the determined Cantonese general Xue Yue, who was helped by a big outbreak of dysentery among the enemy. But to the north of Wuhan, as the Yellow River floods receded, the invaders took Xuzhou and Kaifeng to control the railway line to the Yangzi. To the south, they captured Canton, opening the Pearl River for Japanese shipping and cutting supply routes from the South China Sea. On the east coast, they mastered Fuzhou and Shantou.*

Heavy air raids hit Wuhan. The river port of Jiujiang fell despite a four-to-one numerical superiority of the defenders – the Japanese followed their victory with a smaller-scale repeat of the Rape of Nanjing. Enemy ships rode over booms in the river on waters brought down tributaries that had been swollen by the Yellow River floods. With the enemy only twenty miles away, Chiang Kai-shek flew with his wife and W. H. Donald to Hunan. Behind them, there was no great battle for Wuhan. The Chinese melted away. The last line of defence reported by Japanese newspapers did not materialize – 5,000 orang-utans said to have been trained to throw grenades, seize machine guns and attack company commanders whom they had been schooled to identify. Chinese casualties in the war so far were put at up to a million. The Japanese admitted to 62,000 killed.[23]

Chiang established his new headquarters in a temple on the sacred mountain of Nanyue, 2,000 feet up amid seventy-two peaks in central Hunan. Chinese losses represented only a broken piece of jade, not the whole national tile, he said. The enemy was 'deep in the mire' having won only scorched earth and dead cities. He likened the situation to the fight against the Taiping, which had seemed lost in its early stages.

* Transliterated then as Foochow and Swatow.

As the military situation turned sour, he needed to lay out a case that victory could still be achieved to ward off a growing political threat from Japanese plans to set up a fully fledged collaborationist government, a logical step given Chiang's refusal to surrender and the problem of running occupied areas. Tokyo's policy was music to Wang Jingwei, the senior civilian member of the Nationalist administration, who favoured accommodation with Tokyo, and was anxious to get the better of the Generalissimo after more than a decade of rivalry.

Japan's initial efforts to 'pacify' the Lower Yangzi with agents brought in from the South Manchurian Railway had flopped. Now it wanted to set up a Chinese government which would be able to put up a front while Tokyo retained control, as in Manchukuo. Wang secretly sent an emissary to Shanghai to talk to the enemy, who was receptive to an approach from such a prominent figure. A draft agreement was reached by which Japan undertook to withdraw north of the Great Wall except in areas where there was a Communist threat. It would abandon its extra-territorial privileges and hand back leased territories to China. In return, the Chinese would co-operate in the anti-Communist fight, recognize Manchukuo, undertake economic co-operation and grant preferential mineral rights in the north.

Since he could not cross directly to Japanese-held territory, Wang slipped out of China to French Indochina. Arriving in Hanoi, he called for talks with Tokyo. The police chief, Dai Li, sent an assassination squad, but, entering the politician's villa at night, it killed Wang's secretary instead of him. The pomaded politician used the killing to denounce Chiang, going to Nanjing to establish collaboration with the invaders in the name of sparing China from war and pursuing what he said had been Sun Yat-sen's aim of forging collaboration between the two main East Asia nations.[24]

Chiang, meanwhile, did not stay long on the sacred mountain. The Nationalist leadership had moved on from Hunan to its new capital, the Sichuan city of Chongqing, on cliffs above the Yangzi. Safely beyond the natural barrier of the Yangzi Gorges, the Generalissimo radiated confidence. 'I dare say that, even if we lost fifteen provinces out of the eighteen, if only we could keep our Sichuan, Yunnan and Guizhou,' he declared, 'we could defeat any enemy, recover the lost land, restore our country, and accomplish our revolution.'[25]

*

It was from the first of those three provinces that Chiang led the Nationalist regime. For seven years, Chongqing would be China's capital, a remote inland city shrouded in such mist and cloud that the dogs were said to bark in fear when the sun broke through. The American scholar John King Fairbank described it as looking like 'a junk heap of old boxes piled together . . . There is no color. Nothing grows out of the rock, the stone is all gray and slightly mossed; people, houses, pathways all blend into gray, with the gray river swirling between.' The rats were famed for their size, the people for their surliness and suspicion of outsiders. Sewage ran through open drains, and rubbish dumps littered the steep steps down the cliffs to the river where human excrement was poured into 'honey barges' and stirred by naked men to be sold as fertilizer.[26]

Chongqing became an extraordinary melting pot as refugees moved in from other parts of China. Zhou Enlai headed a Communist mission. The Christian General took up residence on a hillside. Qingling Soong held court for leftists in her home, watched by the police of Dai Li's innocuously named Military Statistics Bureau – *Juntong*.

Dai commanded more than half a million men, including assassination squads, one of which killed the collaborationist mayor of Shanghai with a meat chopper as he slept, while another shot the puppet foreign minister dead in his home. A train carrying Chinese officials to the signing of a treaty between Japan and the regime being established by Wang Jingwei was blown up, killing seventy-four of those on board. Poisoning attempts were made on leading collaborators.[27]

A handsome man with delicate hands, a flat nose, dark hair, gold teeth and sharp, deep-set eyes, Dai described himself as Chiang's 'claws and teeth'. A Whampoa Academy graduate, he had organized the ultra-loyalist 'Blue Shirts' in Nanjing. He had arbitrary power of life or death, and was known for his constant love affairs. His most famous liaison was with the film star 'Butterfly' Hu Die, whose husband he paid off with a large sum of money and for whom he built a mansion outside Chongqing surrounded by tropical plants and exotic trees.

Dai ran a huge operation to bring goods into Nationalist areas to pierce the Japanese blockade, working with Big Ears Du. His Loyal and Patriotic Army carried the supplies and sold them at a large profit. His police organization ran training schools, camps and prisons, spied on the army, tortured suspects and engaged in the drugs trade. The chief peppered it with secret agents of his own to keep a watch on his subordinates. Very keen on codes and codebreaking, he hired an accomplished staff, including a wizard interceptor of enemy radio traffic and an American called Herbert Yardley, who had run the US interceptions service in the First World War and who, despite his heavy drinking and womanizing, proved adept at reading Japanese messages.[28]

A motley crew of foreigners like Yardley arrived in the new capital, but the long-time China hand W. H. Donald departed after daring to attack her elder sister's corruption to Madame Chiang. 'You may criticize the government or anything in China, but there are some persons even you cannot criticize,' she shot back. The Australian walked away as the blood leapt to his cheeks, and subsequently left for Hong Kong, from where he sailed to the South Seas on his yacht, called after Meiling. He later hid in the Philippines during the Japanese occupation, and, after the war, was taken to hospital in Hawaii, where he dictated his recollections to a local journalist before returning to die of lung disease in Shanghai in 1946 – Meiling attended his funeral, and had a cross of yellow and white chrysanthemums placed on the coffin.[29]

Nearly 2,000 factories and smaller plants brought from the Lower Yangzi region were reassembled in the KMT's western bastion in Sichuan. In the city were a Nanjing Hat Shop, a Hankou Dry Cleaners and a Shanghai Garage and Motor Repair Works. Cooks brought dishes from all regions. While most of the inhabitants were illiterate, universities shifted to the interior, and the Chongqing post office found itself handling 200,000 messages a month. Drinking water for most inhabitants came from the filthy river, but French wine and American liquor were served in smart restaurants. Six cinemas opened; chorus girls from Shanghai strutted their stuff; and a theatre played Eugene O'Neill's *Mourning Becomes Electra*. American-trained dentists advertised their services as traditional tooth-pullers operated in the streets. Thoroughfares were renamed the Road of the National Republic or the Street of the People's Livelihood, but rickshaw pullers still called them the Slope of the Seven Stars or White Elephant Street.[30]

The huge territorial losses suffered since July 1937 left the Nationalists extremely stretched. The provinces they still controlled were the least advanced. Output from the factories reassembled round Chongqing was far from enough to sustain a war economy. Chemicals that were essential for munitions were lacking. So was iron ore. For all Dai Li's blockade-running, Japanese control of the coasts made it hard to import equipment or materials, while enemy air raids cut off land and water routes. Many Shanghai businessmen preferred to stay put and chance their luck with the Japanese, or send their money abroad.

The disruption drastically affected government revenue; customs takings provided only 6.3 per cent of state income in 1939, compared to 67 per cent before the war. New taxes were introduced on consumption, incomes and profits. But the demands of military spending, which trebled between 1937 and 1940, made H. H. Kong's policy of printing money even more attractive to Chiang, despite its severe inflationary effects.

The money supply in government regions was further boosted when the collaborationist regime in Nanjing banned Nationalist banknotes, which flooded back into areas controlled by Chongqing. The Japanese used their military scrip to undermine the currency, restricting their opium trade to their own notes. By 1941, the salaries of Nationalist civil servants were worth 16 per cent of the 1937 level in real terms, while those of soldiers were 78 per cent down.

Chongqing might be beyond the reach of the Imperial Army, but Japanese planes began to bomb the city on 3 May 1939. The ensuing raids would make it the target of terror attacks which presaged the German blitzkrieg from the air in Poland that autumn. The protective clouds and fog of winter and spring gone, Chongqing was ravaged in months of attacks that set off huge fire storms through the packed wooden buildings. The main streets were filled with craters, wrecked buildings and crowds seeking safety. Hospitals, relief services and the fire brigade were overwhelmed. 'Chungking has become one vast cemetery,' a French missionary wrote.

A Japanese General Staff document of December 1938 set out a new overall strategy reflecting its belief that the war could not be won as quickly as had originally been envisaged. The focus was to be on mopping up in the rear and conducting anti-guerrilla operations. The invaders could only be encouraged by the conditions of the armies facing them. More than a million men were recruited or press-ganged into the KMT forces each year, but many of the best officers had been lost in the fighting along the Yangzi, and ordinary troops were of poor quality, sometimes marched to camps tied together with ropes round their necks, and stripped naked at night to prevent their running away. At the very top, Chiang was well aware of the deficiencies of his generals and their men. 'I have to lie awake at night, thinking what fool things they may do,' he said.[31]

Not that the Generalissimo was an impressive strategist or tactician. He interfered with commanders in the field, issuing contradictory orders and second-guessing them. Having risen in a climate of betrayal and double-dealing, and surrounded by potential rivals, he prized loyalty above ability. When his wife mentioned the particular incompetence of one general, he replied, 'But where do you find a man who is so obedient?' He allocated supplies with a political motivation, holding back arms and food from generals he distrusted, setting subordinates against one another to ensure his supremacy, and keeping hundreds of thousands of men on the edge of the Communist base.

Whatever their General Staff proclaimed as the new strategy, Imperial Army commanders on the spot do not appear to have taken much notice of the new, cautious approach. Successful advances were staged to take the Jiangxi capital of Nanchang and the Generalissimo's summer retreat at Lushan above the Middle Yangzi. The invaders captured the large island of Hainan in the South China Sea. But, in a month-long battle for the Hunan capital of Changsha in the autumn, the southern general, Xue Yue, showed his ability in forcing the enemy to retreat after drawing it into a series of traps – though the victory was accompanied by tragedy when the commanders in the city set alight a stock of inflammable material that had been collected to be put on fire if the Japanese got inside. Changsha burned for five days. Thousands died, and many of the homes of the 800,000 inhabitants were destroyed. Chiang flew in to preside at a court martial that punished the officers involved.[32]

The successful defence of Changsha followed another setback for the Imperial Army, at the battle of Nomonhan on the border between Mongolia and Manchuria. Japanese and Manchukuo troops had begun to attack a disputed border area in May. In August, Soviet forces under Marshal Zhukov mounted a major armoured counter-attack, using 500 tanks, mobile artillery, aircraft, paratroops and innovative mobile-warfare tactics to pulverize the enemy. Though little remembered now, the battle had a key effect on the evolution of the Second World War since defeat convinced the high command in Tokyo to abandon any idea of attacking in Siberia, and to focus on south-east Asia. Despite

Zhukov's victory, it also brought home to Stalin the danger of a two-front offensive – he concluded the pact with Berlin soon afterwards and then reached a non-aggression treaty with Japan.

Emboldened by Xue Yue's success, and hoping that Soviet forces might follow up Nomonhan by moving into Manchuria, Chiang Kai-shek issued a mobilization order for a winter offensive on 19 November 1939. Planned on a national scale, it was to involve eighty divisions – half the Nationalist armies. Guerrilla tactics were discarded as armies went into full positional battles.[33]

The campaign had an important political element. Wang Jingwei had just signed an outline accord with the Japanese and was denouncing Chiang as 'an aspirant dictator' lacking 'even the minimum moral and ethical qualifications of the normal human being' – the following March, he would be installed as head of a Reorganization Government of the Republic of China, which claimed to represent the true KMT heritage. The dangerous appeal of collaboration was evident when the Model Governor of Shanxi also reached an agreement with the invaders. For Chongqing, it was more important than ever to keep the flames of war alight, dividing China between patriots and traitors, and attacking in as many places as possible.[34]

The Japanese spoiled Chiang's big show with a landing in Guangxi which took the provincial capital of Nanning. Two months of fighting there tied down troops, tanks and 100 planes on which Chiang had been counting. But his campaign flopped for broader reasons. Though the KMT forces made brief incursions into Kaifeng and the Wuhan area, their weaknesses after the losses of 1937–8 were all too apparent. Equipment and co-ordination were poor. Armies gave up after a few days and retreated against orders. Commanders offered to resign rather than fight. By the spring of 1940, the offensive petered out. Nor did the Soviet army move into Manchuria.

Next, it was the turn of the Communists to try to assert their patriotic credentials with a campaign by their Eighth Army in the late summer of 1940, known as the Hundred Regiments Offensive, though many of the units were smaller formations. As well as wishing to provide backing for the anti-Japanese propaganda line, Mao and the Communists in Yenan wanted to hit at the blockhouse strategy the Imperial Army was using to pen them in. They also needed a success to strengthen their hands in discussions in which the Nationalists pressed for a reorganization of zones to bring their armies under greater control and move them north of the Yellow River.

The Communist attack, which got through the Nationalist forces surrounding the base, managed to cut some railway lines. But its frontal assaults were easily repulsed by the Japanese. Though propaganda heralded a great success, the campaign did no better than Chiang's Winter Offensive. The Eighth Army lost 22,000 men, while inflicting only 3,000–4,000 casualties. All Mao could say was that the Party had gained a useful propaganda weapon to use against the KMT.[35]

Now it was the turn of the Japanese, who launched a major offensive in central China to take the fertile plain of northern Hubei and the Yangzi port of Yichang,* where goods were transferred from big boats to smaller craft to make the final journey to Chongqing. The invaders also stepped up attacks on cities held by the Nationalists, dropping more than 27,000 bombs between May and September 1940.

At the end of this distinctly unpromising year, what the CCP called 'frictions' with the Nationalists erupted into a conflict which went down in the history of both parties as a moment of double-dealing that further envenomed their longstanding hostility. This concerned the 100,000-strong Communist New Fourth Army on the Lower Yangzi which the Nationalists wanted to move northwards. The Maoist concentration on Yenan and the war in the north has led to the Fourth Army's role being underplayed, but it was a formidable force and, through its links with Shanghai, was in many ways more advanced than the isolated northerners. It had grown out of the guerrillas left in Jiangxi by the Long March, and gathered strength from peasants, workers, students and intellectuals, showing ideological flexibility towards local leaders who felt threatened by the Nationalists.[36]

Its political boss was the man who had run the Jiangxi base from 1934, Xiang Ying. The military commander, approved by the Generalissimo, was the highly regarded Communist regimental commander from the Northern Expedition, Ye Ting. Its location was particularly sensitive since Chiang had made the Lower Yangzi his power base before the war. In the autumn of 1940, as the Nationalists sought to enforce their control, a substantial battle broke out in the area between their forces and the Fourth Army which the Communists won decisively. This posed

---

* Then transliterated as Ichang.

a double threat – of the Fourth Army establishing itself permanently in the area and, for Chiang, of a united-front army defying him. Chongqing set a deadline of 31 December for the Communists to move north across the river.

The deadline was not met but, at midnight on 4 January 1941, the Fourth Army headquarters units began to move from their base. Snow and rain bucketed down through icy winds. The lighting the Communists carried in the night made it easy for the Nationalists to track their progress. Instead of going north as expected, they moved south, raising suspicions that they were heading for their old guerrilla strongholds in Jiangxi.

Nationalist patrols opened fire. By 9 January, the Communists were under heavy attack. In Chongqing, Zhou Enlai went to see the Generalissimo. Chiang said reports of fighting must be wrong – he had agreed to a safe passage for the Fourth Army, had he not? As the tired, hungry Communists concentrated in a village called Shijing, Ye drafted a message to Chiang asking him to stop the attack. He sent the message to Yenan, but it was not immediately forwarded to Chongqing. Given its importance, this was unlikely to have been a slip-up. Mao and his colleagues had no interest in seeing Xiang and Ye establish an alternative Communist centre in the rich Lower Yangzi region. That may have led them to leave the Fourth Army to its fate.

The Nationalists unleashed an intense artillery and bombing attack. By the time Yenan finally passed the message on to Chongqing, it was too late. The vastly larger Nationalist forces overwhelmed the Communists. Estimates of the dead among the Fourth Army headquarters ranged from 2,000 to 10,000. Survivors told of women being raped, and captives being marched 400 miles to a camp – 'when they sickened, they were beaten; some were shot, and others were buried alive.' Ye was taken prisoner and held for five years; he died in a plane crash on his way to Yenan in 1946. His fellow commander, Xiang Ying, escaped, only to be killed by a companion, who made off with the gold he kept in a pouch.

Zhou Enlai told the journalist Teddy White that he was sure Chiang had not ordered the attack, but had let the local generals believe he would not mind if they did so. Was Chiang lying, White asked. 'No,' said Zhou. 'Someone was lying to the Generalissimo but the G'issimo lies to a certain extent, too.'

Despite its losses at the start of 1941, the Fourth Army would remain a potent force throughout the war, drawing on support from the growing Communist underground in Shanghai. But Zhou considered that the incident meant co-operation with the Nationalists to be finished, while Mao warned that 'those who play with fire ought to be very careful'. However, Moscow made its influence felt against a break, and the Chairman started to speak of the time that had to elapse until a full split with the KMT.

Feeling the wind in his sails, Chiang blockaded Yenan in a sign of the continuance of the civil war within the struggle against Japan. Nationalist cavalry attacked Communist forces in northern Henan, inflicting 4,000 casualties. CCP activities were banned in KMT-held areas, Dai Li's police stepped up arrests. The Communists reacted to the changing circumstances by merging their organizations in central China into a single bureau under the Party manager, Liu Shaoqi, with the Long March veteran Chen Yi in charge of the seven divisions of the New Fourth Army, each of which was given a specific area of responsibility.

There was good news for the Nationalists when Washington signed up for loans, a currency stabilization agreement and credits bringing its aid to US$245 million. But, as a whole, 1940 had been an annus horribilis for the KMT. Abroad, the Generalissimo's hopes of a Soviet–British–French alliance against Japan were confounded by the Nazi–Soviet Pact and the German sweep across Western Europe. The Vichy regime cut the rail link from Hanoi and allowed the Japanese to move into Indochina. Stalin recalled his pilots to serve Soviet interests closer to home and to avoid antagonizing Tokyo. Under pressure from Japan, Britain closed down the overland supply route from Burma, which was vital to bring supplies in to China from the south.

In China itself, the Wang Jingwei collaborationist administration in Nanjing presented an alternative government that might recruit Chiang's varied enemies, and hoped to draw on Japanese material support. Unlike collaborationist regimes in Europe, the Reorganized Government of the Republic of China did not differ ideologically from the national administration; rather, it claimed simply to be a better heir to Sun Yat-sen's thoughts. Wang launched a New Citizens' Movement to proclaim Sun's Three Principles, and advocated moral behaviour, science, economic development, frugality and a crusade against corruption. It made no more impact than Chiang's New Life campaign. The Nanjing collaborationists had less authority than the KMT in Chongqing, and Wang had a basic problem: he claimed to espouse Sun's Three Principles, but the first – nationalism – was vitiated by the fact that he depended on a foreign invader.[37]

The collaborationist leader made much of the symbolism of having his capital in Nanjing, and, if puppet troops in the north were included, could claim an army of half a million men. But the Japanese never trusted him entirely, holding back arms and keeping the collaborationist army carefully in check. Wang liked to proclaim that the anti-Communist sweeps which his men and the Imperial Army carried out jointly were winning the hearts and minds of the people, but they were primarily military exercises that cordoned off designated areas behind barbed wire and fences. The Japanese saw China as a land they could exploit, not as a potential partner.

Wang's regime was split into the familiar set of factions, and held together only by his personal aura. It drew on the acquiescence of businessmen, notably in Shanghai, who had no alternative if they wanted to hang on to at least some of their assets. It managed to get some Nationalist units to defect, though there were rumours that Chiang had approved of this since he was sure Tokyo would lose and wanted to preserve them for the later battle with the Communists. In reality, Wang could count on only a tenth of the collaborationist forces. Other armies answered to local commanders; one, in Suzhou, grew so threatening that the Japanese poisoned him at a dinner in 1943. Collaboration aroused little enthusiasm, and was primarily motivated by a desire to survive. Above all, Japan had never had any interest in anything but a master–servant relationship; Wang might fool himself that Sun Yat-sen nationalism would reach fulfilment in co-operation with Tokyo, but his masters saw the Joint Prosperity Scheme as operating strictly for their advantage.

However, the situation in 1940–41 was one which could give weight to a collaborationist policy. Britain was isolated in Europe; then Germany launched its devastating offensive against the Soviet Union. Neither of the main Western powers appeared ready to confront Tokyo, which had joined in the Tripartite Pact with Germany and Italy in September. In China, the united front had all but broken down. Chongqing was more isolated than ever territorially, and open to aerial attack whenever the enemy chose. A review of its army pointed to lack of initiative, co-ordination and equipment, and poor staff work, intelligence, logistics and discipline. The Japanese estimated that Chinese combat effectiveness had fallen by up to a third.[38]

Chiang launched a New Life-style campaign for the army and government. There was to be no smoking or drinking or gambling. Officers and civil servants were to go to bed and to rise early, with absolute obedience to superiors. Office stationery was not to be used for private correspondence, nor should badges of office be worn in places of amusement. Public banquets should be held only when absolutely necessary. None of this had a discernible effect.

In the north, the invaders turned on the CCP base with an assault under the motto of the 'Three Alls' – kill all, burn all, destroy all. By the time it ended in the autumn, the population of the Soviets had fallen from 40 million to 25 million. People living in areas taken by the invaders were herded into settlements guarded by blockhouses and used as forced labour. Railway defences were strengthened. Villages were encouraged to collaborate by being offered higher food allocations if they identified local Communists. Japanese troops burned what crops they did not seize. Young men were shipped off to work in Manchukuo.

In reaction, the Communists toughened up their demands from the farmers and peasants to support the diminished base. Harsh manual labour was imposed, and campaigns launched against anybody suspected of less than complete loyalty. After the failure of the Hundred Regiments campaign and the devastation of the Three Alls, the Eighth Route Army was not going to risk a full-scale fight with the Japanese. While nurturing the propaganda line that it alone was fighting the invaders, the CCP restricted itself to scattered guerrilla operations and was, in fact, considerably less active than the Nationalists as Mao concentrated on building up a power base from which he would be able to challenge for supreme power in China once somebody else had defeated Japan.

There was some relief for the Nationalists when, deciding that there was no point in seeking to placate Tokyo, Britain reopened the Burma Road and extended a £10 million loan. But 1941 saw more big Japanese offensives, though they did not always bring the victories to which the invaders had grown accustomed. In January, the invaders threw 150,000 men, 300 tanks and 100 planes against southern Henan. The Chinese fell back, cut off the Japanese rear and hit the enemy supply lines. They were so successful that they inflicted more casualties than they suffered, and forced a retreat in mid-February. Similar tactics again repulsed an assault in Jiangxi, where the Nationalists scored a signal triumph at the town of Shangguo that matched the battle of Taierzhuang, destroying around half the attacking force. However, the invaders scored a swift victory in Shaanxi, cutting off Chinese units there and establishing firm supply lines.

In September, 120,000 Japanese troops advanced in a second bid to take Changsha, supported by 100 planes, 20 naval ships and 200 motorboats that sailed down the Xiang River from the Yangzi. As in the previous battle for the Hunan provincial capital, the Nationalists under General Xue Yue lured the enemy into traps, cut their supplies and attacked from the flank, forcing them to retreat with heavy losses. The KMT position was also helped by the resumption of Soviet air aid and the growth of the Flying Tiger fliers organized by the American Claire Chennault. After the disastrous 1940, the following year represented a distinct improvement – or, rather, a sign that, when the Chinese held fast and executed a thought-out tactical plan, the Imperial Army could be less than invincible. The guerrilla war was also taking its toll in areas where the invaders could not exercise their superiority in planes, armoured vehicles and artillery. By the end of 1941, they had lost 185,000 dead since starting the war four years earlier. The conflict in China risked becoming unwinnable. Japan had already begun to expand into Indochina. Now, it was time to move elsewhere. On 7 December, Pearl Harbor was attacked.

To celebrate the news, Chiang Kai-shek put on a gramophone recording of 'Ave Maria'. In Shanghai, the Japanese took over the International Settlement (the French Concession had come under the control of the invaders after the fall of France the previous year). Settlement inhabitants were marched to camps, and those the Japanese had marked down as enemies, Chinese and foreign, were taken to prisons where conditions were primitive in the extreme, and torture or death was always just round the corner.*

On 9 December, China declared war on Germany, Italy and Japan.

* John Powell, editor of the *China Weekly Review*, who was one of those taken to the notorious Bridge House Prison, gives a harrowing account of conditions in *My Twenty-Five Years in China*.

The Generalissimo proposed to Washington that he should assume command of the whole war effort in Asia. Roosevelt did not take this up, but pledged 'immediate steps . . . to prepare the way for common action against our common enemy'. In a broadcast to the American people, he spoke of China's 'magnificent defense and her inevitable counter-offensive – for that is one important element in the ultimate defeat of Japan'. After four years of conflict, China was no longer alone.[39]

16

Tangled Alliance

The alliance between China and the United States was marked by much wishful thinking and frustration on the American side and by stubbornness and artful power plays from the Nationalists, with occasional bit-part appearances by the Communists. Though he hymned the Nationalist struggle, Franklin Roosevelt was set against any commitment of US ground troops to fight the Japanese in China. His 'Europe First' policy meant that there were not enough GIs to spare. Instead of men, China got aid to ensure that it continued to tie down up to a million enemy troops, and the help of the US Flying Tiger air force. Starting with a $500 million loan. T. V. Soong, who was now foreign minister, spent much of the war lobbying in Washington for assistance offered at a wildly unrealistic exchange rate which enabled insiders like him to profit mightily.

Looking further ahead, the president saw the Nationalists and Communists coming together as China emerged from the war as one of the Four Policemen of the post-war order, alongside the US, the USSR and Britain. Japan's defeat would produce a vacuum in the Far East which only China could fill, Roosevelt believed. In an acute analysis of the situation that followed Pearl Harbor, a KMT diplomat and minister, Fu Bingchang, noted: 'This should be a good year. Our enemy has been foolish enough to kill the hope of America and Gr. Britain to compromise by joining the Axis Powers, thus forcing the Democratic powers to regard us as one of them and give us better support. We have every hope of success and our future is extremely bright.' For both military and political reasons, Roosevelt was obliged to pretend that the Nationalists were more powerful and more democratic than they really were. A third successful defence of Changsha between December 1941 and January 1942 gave cause for rejoicing. The Nationalists staged eleven attacks in fierce fighting that saw one burial mound on which the Japanese had tried to set up an artillery position changing hands five times.[1]

But a dash of cold water came from the American mission in Chongqing which reported that the KMT forces were generally in such poor condition and the economy was so weak that proponents of reaching a settlement with Wang Jingwei's collaborationist regime and with the Japanese might gain the upper hand. That, it went on, could give 'the Japs free access to the resources of China and the manpower of China, thus fully developing the long predicted "Yellow Peril" '.[2]

Washington dispatched 'Vinegar' Joseph Stilwell, one of its toughest infantry commanders, to Chongqing with the mission of strengthening the Nationalist army into a force that would drive back the enemy and provide a launching pad in China for an invasion of Japan – the atom bomb that would end the war in the Far East was still a fledgling project whose military applications were only dimly grasped. Chiang could hardly refuse the advice if he wanted US aid, and Stilwell, who had previously served as military attaché in China and spoke the language, would be welcome for the material help he brought. But, despite the American's title of chief of staff, his authority would be strictly limited. General He would remain the Nationalist chief of staff, and generals would continue to report to Chiang. As well as the command confusion, there was a wider issue. For the Generalissimo, the army had always been an acutely political organization to be used and manipulated for his purposes. On no account would he let the foreigner upset the politico-military apparatus he had constructed over the years.

Nor did Stilwell's taste for offensive action and his abrasive personality help; he and the feline Chiang were about as different as two men could be, as the American showed when he told the *Time* journalist Teddy White, before he even got to his new job: 'The trouble in China is simple. We are allied to an ignorant, illiterate, superstitious, peasant son of a bitch.' Soon he was referring to Chiang in his diary as 'Peanut' – later it became 'the rattlesnake'.[3]

The general had the strong backing of the powerful US chief of staff, George Marshall. His mind-set, manner, offensive spirit and refusal to play politics would make him an authentic American hero for some, such as White and his Pulitzer Prize-winning biographer Barbara Tuchman. A dispassionate view suggests that he was the wrong man in the wrong place at the wrong time doing the wrong thing for the right reasons. His character did not make things any easier, but he had been sent on an impossible mission.

This was further complicated by his virtually impossible array of responsibilities – as well as his Chinese job, he was commander of all US forces in the China–Burma–India sector (CBI), and in control of supplies sent in under the Lend-Lease agreements extended to the Nationalists. He represented his country on war committees, and acted as liaison with the British – dislike for them was one of the few things he shared with the Generalissimo, who hated their imperialism and went out of his way to encourage Indian nationalists on a visit to the British Raj.

In addition, there was the running sore of a feud between Stilwell and Claire Chennault, the American champion of air power in China who argued that the war could be won from above, and enjoyed the support of the nominal head of the Nationalist air force, Madame Chiang. The tight-buttoned, rigorous Yankee Stilwell was bound to fall out with the expansive Texan leader of the Flying Tigers, who tolerated a brothel for his fliers and their black market activities. Speaking to Roosevelt in 1943, the general described Chiang as 'a vacillating, tricky, undependable old scoundrel who never keeps his word', while the airman said he thought the Generalissimo was one of the two or three greatest military and political leaders in the world, who had 'never broken a commitment or promise made to me'. A special element was added to their fight by their physical ailments – Chennault was very hard of hearing while Vinegar Joe had hardly any sight in his left eye and required a thick lens on his right eye. Meeting them, Britain's chief of staff, Alan Brooke, called Stilwell 'a hopeless crank with no vision' and Chennault 'a very gallant airman with limited brain'.[4]

Stilwell's mission began badly as he approached his fifty-ninth birthday in early 1942. The Chinese and British were routed by a Japanese offensive in Burma which cut off the supply link to China and posed a threat to the Raj. Nominally under command of the American, the Nationalist troops still took their orders from Chiang. When things got tough, they headed for home with as much equipment as they could take. Stilwell decided to go the other way, staging an epic trek through the jungle to India. It would make his name as a heroic figure. But, impressive as the walk was, it can be seen as an example of a general abandoning his command and his soldiers. Perhaps he felt some sublimated guilt, or just resentment at being defeated in his first field operation, for the reconquest of Burma would become a personal mission that significantly distorted his strategic priorities.

As the United States checked the Imperial Navy at the Battle of Midway in June 1942 followed by landings on Guadalcanal in the Solomon Islands, the Japanese concentrated on building up static defensive positions in China, including some 7,000 miles of blockades along railway lines and 7,700 fortified posts. 'Model peace zones' were established in the Yangzi Delta using harsh coercion methods. But the invaders were still ready to stage offensives. In April, American pilots returning from the first air attack on Japan – known as the Doolittle Raid after its commander – landed in Zhejiang. Seeing the danger of eastern China becoming a vast airfield for US attacks, Japanese troops swept over the area, employing biological weapons which had been tested on prisoners in Manchuria.[5]

Directed by Chiang personally from the other side of the country, Chinese resistance was chaotic. Heavy casualties resulted. An American colonel who visited the battlefield reported that most of the Chinese troops arrived tied to one another to prevent their running away. Their equipment was poor, and medical facilities non-existent. The regional commander remained at a villa fifty miles behind the front.[6]

In response to such performances, Stilwell produced his first memorandum to Chiang on army reform. This advocated a smaller, more efficient army, and a new command system, weeding out inefficient commanders. Chiang hit back with a complaint that China was being treated as an inferior ally by not being included in Allied military planning; on security grounds, George Marshall refused to allow Nationalist representatives to join meetings of Anglo-American chiefs of staff – his caution was justified since the Japanese were breaking Chinese codes and could read everything transmitted to and from Chongqing.[7]

The Generalissimo put forward what were known as the 'Three Demands', calling for US divisions to join in an attack on Burma, for 500 new planes, and for an increase in Lend-Lease supplies to 5,000 tons a month. All three were unrealistic; the US did not have men to send to a Burma–China campaign while Washington was despatching all the planes and supplies it could spare to Britain and the USSR. At the end of June, Chiang threatened to halt participation in the war unless he got his way. Madame Chiang berated Stilwell for not doing enough for the regime, and spoke darkly of the strength of those seeking peace.[8]

The Chinese were not wrong in their complaints. They never received parity with Britain and the USSR in US aid. That was the nature of the grand strategy of the anti-fascist alliance. So long as Roosevelt stuck to a 'Europe First' policy, China would always come second.

For the Communists at the beginning of 1942, the American involvement in the war meant little. They had more immediate matters to deal with. Japan's Three Alls campaign following the failure of the Hundred Regiments had seriously weakened the base in northern China. 'Things got steadily worse until we were in great difficulty, running short of grain, short of cooking oil and salt, short of bedding and clothing, short of funds,' Mao wrote.[9]

Like H. H. Kong, the CCP leadership stepped up the printing of banknotes to pay its bills. As in the Nationalist areas, this further fuelled inflation. With food prices rising steeply, programmes were instituted to raise production, bearing down on peasants and farmers. Frugality was preached for the masses. A new Party myth, the productivity miracle of Yenan, was born. In fact, the Politburo had found a new income stream.[10]

From 1942, as the historian Chen Yung-fa established in his ground-breaking study, opium became the biggest single source of revenue of the base, handled by the Local Product Company and referred to in the records as 'foreign trade', 'special product' and 'soap'. Though its use was banned in the Communist area itself, it was taken out by merchants and the Red Army. A senior figure told the Soviet adviser Petr Parfenovich Vladimirov that, though recognizing narcotics as morally reprehensible, the Politburo had decided to give them a vanguard financial role. By 1943, the Communists were producing nearly a million boxes of opium a year; the following year, drug profits contributed up to 40 per cent of total revenue of the base administration.

The trade has, naturally, been kept well hidden in post-1949 histories. Nor have they mentioned the contacts between the Communist spymaster, Pan Hannian, and Wang Jingwei and the collaborationist regime in Nanjing as both sought to strengthen themselves against their mutual enemy, the Nationalists. Vladimirov also reported a Communist liaison officer at Japanese military headquarters who moved freely between the enemy and the Fourth Route Army in the Lower Yangzi. A third element which has been well concealed is the Red Army's policy of evading military confrontation with the Japanese as far as possible after its reverses in 1940–41. Vladimirov observed in 1942 that the Communists had 'long been abstaining from both active and passive action against the aggressors'. The following January, he noted that their armies were 'strictly ordered not to undertake any vigorous operations or actions against the Japanese down to retreating under an attack and seeking, if possible, a truce'.[11]

Some fighting was inevitable as the invaders launched successive campaigns against the base areas – between the summer of 1941 and the end of 1943, there were four separate Japanese offensives on the Red Army's 11th division under Lin Biao. These involved 230,000 men and lasted for more than twelve months. Still, all the external evidence from Russian and American observers shows the Communists doing much less fighting than they claimed, then and subsequently, and certainly less than the Nationalists. But the myth that it was the CCP which constituted the prime source of armed resistance persists as one of the key claims to legitimacy of the regime since 1949.*[12]

Inside the base during these years, Mao developed his philosophy in a series of writings on politics and the arts which would become sacred templates, and bolstered his power with purges against 'factions which formerly existed and played an unwholesome role in the history of our Party'. The most prominent target was the Moscow-aligned champion of the united front, Wang Ming, who was fed debilitating but not fatal poison while he and his associates were marginalized politically.

A 'rectification campaign' attacked 'subjectivism, sectarianism, and party formalism'. The first meant book knowledge of Marxist Leninism and neglect of its practical application. The second referred to anybody who did not respect absolutely the authority of the Central Committee. The third applied to those who spoke in formal terms that ordinary people would not understand – Mao compared this to 'the lazy old woman's long, foul-smelling foot bindings which should be thrown in the privy right away'.[13]

As Mao's 'mass line' was imposed, new CCP intellectuals who had

---

* Though published in 1974, Vladimirov's account was ignored by writers who retailed the CCP's tale of its heroic performance against the Japanese and made no mention of the drug trade. Equally, though detailed by Chen Yung-fa in 1995, the extent of CCP involvement in narcotics was scarcely noticed before being suddenly presented as a revelation a decade later.

flocked to Yenan without having gone through the mill of the Long March were denounced at rallies and pursued by terror. This appealed to the tough veterans who had little time for the educated recruits from Shanghai and bourgeois circles. A writer, Wang Shiwei, who had criticized the Mao line in an essay entitled 'Wild Lilies' was taken as a scapegoat. He was arrested, but the Chairman ordered that he should not be executed – rather, he was held as a warning to others. Described as 'a young man with a grey, deathly look on his face', he was finally beheaded in 1947.[14]

In the autumn of 1942, a 'cadre screening movement' began under Mao's political police chief, Kang Sheng, the counterpart of the Nationalist Dai Li and every bit as fearsome and blood-stained. The Party had suffered a significant setback in southern China where Dai's men had eliminated many of its local organizations and guerrilla units after capturing the Jiangxi Provincial Committee. But the purge which Kang Sheng master-minded was concentrated on the Yenan base, which was alleged to have been infiltrated by Nationalist agents. Spies were 'as thick as fur', the Chairman warned. The definition extended to anybody thought ready to step out of line. At the end of the year, the 'screening movement' turned into a 'rescue movement', which would enable suspects to save themselves by confessing under torture. By July 1943, 1,000 'enemy agents' were reported to have been arrested, half of whom were said to have admitted to their crimes. Newcomers to the base were found to be 70 per cent politically unreliable. Forty thousand Party members were expelled amid a wave of suicides induced by the witch hunt. Eventually, the leader realized this had gone too far. Calling an end to the 'rescue movement', he admitted to a meeting that it had involved excesses; he had to bow three times to his audience before it applauded.[15]

Still, the main purpose had been achieved, and the pattern for the future was established. The CCP had to be purged of any groups that might challenge Mao, whose personality cult was being developed by leaps and bounds. The leading Party manager Liu Shaoqi gushed that 'Mao Zedong's leadership penetrates everywhere.' The song 'The East is Red' proclaimed him to be 'the people's Great Saviour' and pupils at schools in the base were taught to recite 'We are all Chairman Mao's good little children.'[16]

In this process, innocence or guilt was meaningless; if the leadership demanded evidence of sins, the suspect must provide it. The rationale was that a smaller, thoroughly loyal movement was better than a broader church; better a movement ruled by fear on the basis of an ideology that Mao could define – and redefine at will – than a party with room for debate and divergent ideas. Best of all, a closed, small-group leadership dominated by one man.

The Chairman's freedom of action was widened by the dissolution of the Comintern by Stalin in 1943 as a wartime gesture to buttress the idea that national Communist parties would henceforth run themselves. His status and that of the CCP were enhanced when Chiang agreed to allow a group of eight American soldiers and a diplomat, John Service, to set up in Yenan in 1944 – they were known as the 'Dixie Mission' because they were in rebel territory. The base controllers made sure that the visitors learned nothing of the rectification campaign, and opium poppies were destroyed along roads they travelled.

The Dixie Mission occupied a compound about half a mile from Yenan. There was no running water, and the latrines were some way off. The Americans lived in tunnels dug fifteen feet back into the hillside, sleeping on beds made of planks laid between trestles. The windows were covered with paper in place of glass. Heat came from charcoal braziers, but the smoke made the men ill, and threatened to choke them if the doors were closed. The hosts threw frequent dinner parties, and a projector was brought in, playing films to packed houses. There were evening dances – first to an old gramophone and then to a band the Chinese formed with a harmonica, violins, flutes and banjo-like instruments. The Americans showed off the conga. Mao and Zhu De were regular attendees, the Chairman appearing in white shirt and dark trousers and dancing with the girls.

The Communists, Service reported, were democrats who wanted to work with KMT liberals to reform China. A party of American reporters who followed gained an equally favourable impression, though Teddy White and Annalee Jacoby of *Time* noted how Mao was the object of 'panegyrics of . . . almost nauseating slavish eloquence'. In Washington, Roosevelt nurtured the idea that the Chinese Communists were 'agrarian socialists'; Chiang's warnings about their true nature could be dismissed as the pleading of a dictator who had to be supported for the time being but who would be cajoled by Washington into forming a coalition with the progressives one of these days.[17]

The formal consecration of Mao was reserved until late in the war, at the Seventh Congress of the CCP held from April to June 1945. Liu Shaoqi hailed him as 'not only the greatest revolutionary and statesman in Chinese history, but also the great theoretician in Chinese history'. A new constitution centralized authority, and elevated rural regions above urban areas. Mao stressed the importance of 'regeneration through our own efforts'. 'Relying on the forces we ourselves organize, we can defeat all Chinese and reactionaries,' he added. 'China has a vast territory and it is up to us to sweep it clean inch by inch.'

Having achieved so much, the Chairman could reach out for a façade of unity. Wang Ming was prevailed on to write a letter of self-criticism. Then, he and the Returned Bolshevik leader, Bo Gu, were elected to the Central Committee, though only to the two last places.

The mythologized deeds of the CCP on the Long March and in Yenan were valuable for propaganda purposes, but it was during these wartime years that Mao made sure he had a party which would manage the grassroots revolution to accompany the military victory he always saw as fundamental to gaining control of China. While the less ruthless, less focused Chiang was engaged in the constant business of running an administration and an army ill-equipped to handle the challenges they faced, Mao was building up a twin-headed machine which would take advantage of domestic foes' weaknesses to the full and be in good shape to impose itself on China as nobody had since the heights of the Qing empire.

The Nationalists, meanwhile, got a symbolic boost when the United States and Britain agreed in 1943 to waive all territorial rights in China. The immediate practical effect of this move, which coincided with the dissolution of the Comintern, was nil since the Japanese had taken over the foreign concessions after Pearl Harbor and put Westerners into detention camps. Nor had America any settlements of its own in China. But it did clear up one item on the Chinese agenda for the post-war era, and Chiang congratulated the British on having won a moral victory over themselves.

After the death of the venerable Lin Sen, the Generalissimo took his title of President of the Chinese Republic and the Chongqing regime went in for some political window-dressing. The People's Political Council was revived, with the Communists and six other non-KMT parties of the Democratic Federation allowed to join. In what appeared to be a liberalizing move, seats were no longer allocated to each group and three quarters of the members were to be elected. This was a clever device by the KMT, which controlled the polls. The smaller parties lost their guaranteed places. The Communists and the Democratic Federation decided on a boycott. Chiang could respond that he had tried, and that it was not his fault if the others rejected elections.

Such democratic sentiments were certainly not apparent in his ghost-written foray into the literary world, *China's Destiny*, which became an automatic best-seller as required reading for all who aspired to rise in the Nationalist ranks. Highly conservative, it insisted on the supremacy of traditional Chinese ways, and the need for order and discipline. All the country's ills were laid at the door of outsiders. Given the reaction this might provoke in America, a plan for an English version was shelved, supposedly at Meiling's suggestion. The State Department classified its copy of the Chinese original as 'top secret' to avoid embarrassing leaks. Still, its author was awarded the Legion of Merit, the highest US award for a foreigner.[18]

More immediately, China faced a fresh rash of natural disasters in 1942–3. There were floods and crop failures. Locusts swarmed over the centre of the country. Famine gripped Henan, where no rain fell in 1942 and the army of the Nationalist general Tang Enbo took from 30 to 50 per cent of farm output. An American information officer, Graham Peck, saw endless streams of refugees moving along the railway tracks, falling and dying where they lay, clinging to wagons 'like ants on a dead worm . . . For hundreds of miles the railroad was littered with the corpses of those who had been too weak to hang on.' People were packed into rail cars so close together that they could not move. Families sold their children. Tree bark was a frequent food. Cannibalism spread; mothers were said to exchange babies, saying, 'You eat mine; I'll eat yours.'

Visiting Henan, Teddy White of *Time* estimated the death toll from famine at 2 million. As many had fled the province, and as many again faced death. In one county, two thirds of the 150,000 people had nothing to eat; 700 were dying each day. Learning of the disaster, Chongqing ordered taxes to be remitted, but the local army said they had already been collected and could not be returned. Getting back to the wartime capital, White obtained an audience with Chiang, who said he had ordered tax remission, so the peasants must be all right. When the journalist produced photographs showing dogs eating corpses, the Generalissimo grew annoyed that his instructions were not being followed. He noted details on a small writing pad. Sanctions were taken, and grain was rushed in. The army even gave back some food.[19]

Militarily, there were fewer large-scale Nationalist confrontations with the Japanese, but less-intensive fighting continued. Stilwell pressed on with his planning to reclaim Burma with Chinese troops who, like him, had escaped from the campaign there to India, where they were being trained by the Americans – they received their wages directly instead of getting what was left after their officers skimmed off cash; they had health care and were properly fed, gaining an average of twenty pounds. At the same time, Vinegar Joe supervised the build-up of a force in south-west China which was to attack Burma from the east while the troops in India came in from the west. Having played tough with his Three Demands, Chiang got a commitment of 5,000 tons of monthly Lend-Lease supplies, but how they were to be allocated was still Stilwell's call.

Chinese criticisms of the American were now getting a hearing in Washington. Chiang sent T. V. Soong a message for transmission to his US contacts complaining that 'this man does not place much value on organization, concrete planning, and overall implementation.' A presidential aide, Lauchlin Currie, who was a secret Soviet agent of influence, recommended recalling Stilwell. Marshall resisted this. Undeterred, Vinegar Joe wrote that 'The Chinese government is a structure based on fear and favor, in the hands of an ignorant, arbitrary, stubborn man.'

In 1943, 'Madame Empress', as Stilwell dubbed Madame Chiang, enlivened Sino-American relations when she flew to New York in a leased TWA Stratoliner, initially for medical treatment for multiple ailments, including trouble with her back, teeth and sinuses, skin rashes, insomnia, exhaustion and pain as a result of the damage to her ribs in her accident in Shanghai in 1937. After a month in hospital, Meiling staged a barnstorming tour of America backed by the resources of Henry Luce's pro-Chiang *Time-Life* press empire. She became the first woman, and the first Chinese, to address a joint session of Congress, setting out her husband's strategy as 'not to accept failure ignominiously but to risk it gloriously'. She got an ovation. Staying at the White House, she brought her own silk sheets, and went on to address big rallies across the country as well as being guest of honour at a gala evening attended by the stars at the Hollywood Bowl.

Her aims were to raise popular support for China, get donations for her country and persuade Roosevelt to send in more planes. When she had talks with him, the president did not seat her on the sofa beside him, as he often did with guests, but put her in a chair opposite, with a card table between them, so as not to be 'vamped' by her. Her behaviour grew increasingly imperious, and Roosevelt soon had enough of her at the White House. There was a hiccup when Teddy White's epic story on the famine in Henan got through an inattentive censor and landed at Luce's news magazine. Hearing about it, Madame Chiang lobbied the publisher not to run it, and to fire the correspondent. Luce declined to get rid of White, but only 750 words of one of the outstanding dispatches of the war in China appeared in *Time*, with all mention of failures by officials, corruption and peasant anger excised.

A sub-plot to the visit was Meiling's relationship with the Republican whom Roosevelt had beaten in 1940, Wendell Willkie. In a piece of wartime bipartisanship, FDR had sent the ebullient businessman turned politician to Chongqing in the autumn of 1942, where the acidic Stilwell noted in his diary, he was 'immersed in soft soap, and adulation'. One evening, Willkie slipped away from a reception, as did Meiling. According to the sole source for what follows, the US publisher Gardner Cowles, who was accompanying the Republican, Chiang arrived some time later at the house where the two Americans were staying. 'Visibly furious', Cowles wrote, he stormed through the house, searching rooms, peering under beds and opening cupboards. At 4 a.m., long after the Generalissimo had left, 'a very buoyant Willkie appeared, cocky as a young college student after a successful night with a girl. After giving me a play by play account of what had happened between him and Madame, he concluded that he had invited Madame to return to Washington with us.'[20]

Cowles pointed out that Willkie could relinquish any hope of getting a second presidential nomination if he stepped off the plane with the Chinese leader's wife. Meiling was, he acknowledged, 'one of the most beautiful, intelligent, and sexy women either of us had ever met', but there was already gossip among journalists in Chongqing about the way the two of them had flirted in public. At breakfast, the politician told his friend that he was right, and sent him to withdraw the invitation, instructing him how to get to her private apartment on the top floor of a hospital, where they had evidently gone the previous night. When Cowles delivered the message, China's First Lady scratched her long fingernails down both his cheeks so deeply that he had the marks for a week.

During her US tour the following year, Meiling invited Cowles to dinner on the forty-second floor of the Waldorf-Astoria Towers, which she had taken over. She told him that, on their wedding night, Chiang had told her he believed in intercourse only for procreation and, since he already had a son, they would not sleep together. This highly unlikely tale was presumably meant as some kind of message to Willkie. Then she said Cowles was to get whatever was needed spent to clinch the nomination and the election; China would reimburse any amount. 'If Wendell could be elected, then he and I would rule the world,' she told Cowles. 'I would rule the Orient and Wendell would rule the Western world.' It was, as the publisher noted, totally mad, 'but I was so mesmerized by clearly one of the most formidable women of the time that this evening I would not have dismissed anything she said.' Unfortunately for her plans, Willkie's liberalism helped to deprive him of the nomination, and he died of a heart attack shortly before the 1944 election.

That was not Madame Chiang's only setback. Her husband, who was rumoured to be having an affair with his nurse, resented her high profile in the United States. They were reported to have regular rows, but her ambition was unquenched. Back in China, she enrolled the unwitting Stilwell in a plot by herself and her eldest sister to get rid of General He, and perhaps take over as war minister herself. At the end of 1943, she was ready to strut the world stage once more, this time in her husband's company. The scene was a summit in Cairo with Roosevelt and Churchill – Stalin stayed away and waited for the two Westerners to join him at their subsequent conference in Teheran. (One of his motives was a desire not to meet Chiang, since this might be taken by Tokyo as a reason to attack the Soviet Far East.)[21]

Held from 23 to 26 November in a complex of villas and hotels outside the Egyptian capital, the summit saw Roosevelt spending more time with the Chiangs than with Churchill, who griped at all the 'Chinese business'. The president feared that seeing too much of the British might be taken badly by the Kremlin, but he also wanted to get the measure of the Nationalist leader. Whether Madame Chiang was formally invited to attend or not, she made a big impression, sitting at the conference table with the three leaders, wearing a black satin dress slit up the side. She used her linguistic skills to control the discussion when China was involved, interrupting the interpreter with her version of what her husband was saying, and relaying comments from the others to him.

At one point, she shifted position, showing what the British chief of staff, Alan Brooke, called 'one of the most shapely of legs'. 'This caused a rustle among those attending the conference and I even thought I heard a suppressed neigh coming from a group of some of the younger members,' he added in his diary. Ignoring, as usual, the New Life provision against cigarettes, Meiling chain-smoked, using a long holder. She had eye trouble; when she consulted Churchill's doctor, he told her she would only get better when she was under less strain.

Her husband drove the others to distraction by constantly changing his mind over committing troops to an offensive to retake Burma. When the chiefs of staff met, the Chinese refused to put forward any proposals, causing George Marshall to lose his temper. The main Nationalist aim was to establish China's position in the alliance, and to get Roosevelt to pledge more support. The Chiangs made considerable progress at a dinner with the president, who promised a substantial amphibious operation across the Bay of Bengal against Burma to support a Nationalist land invasion. He said China should be an equal member of the Big Four, and recover Manchuria, Formosa (Taiwan) and the Pescadores Islands, with the Ryukyu Islands in the far north split with the Soviet Union. The US and China were to agree to come to one another's aid in the future, but the Generalissimo got nowhere with a request for a US–Chinese chiefs of staff organization or for China to join the existing Anglo-American body of their chiefs of staff. Roosevelt knew that Marshall would turn both down.

Chiang asked for Lend-Lease aid for ninety divisions, a $1 billion loan and payment of $100 million in gold for the use of labour to build a big US air base in Sichuan. He also made clear that China would hold on to Tibet. When Roosevelt said he favoured the return of Hong Kong to China, the Chinese leader responded that he would make it a free port. He and his wife listened politely as the president argued for a coalition government between Nationalists and Communists, but gave no ground.

The Americans also agreed to send an undercover mission to work with Dai Li's police; the aid and expertise given to the Sino-American Cooperation Organization, or SACO, as it was known, was meant to be against the Japanese but was actually used mainly to harass the regime's domestic enemies. Its headquarters at 'Happy Valley', outside Chongqing, became notorious as a place of arbitrary imprisonment, torture and death – a forerunner of other instances of US collaboration with political police forces of authoritarian governments.

Roosevelt professed to have been impressed by Chiang. In a broadcast 'fireside chat' after getting home, he praised the Generalissimo as an 'unconquerable man . . . of great vision [and] great courage'. As he left Cairo, the Generalissimo got news of a plot by young officers to kidnap him on his return, and force him to drop his more reactionary and corrupt subordinates. The conspirators approached the Americans, but got no sympathy. Dai Li had them arrested. Chiang ordered the execution of the ringleaders.

The summit might have gone well, but there was soon bad news from the president. Under strong pressure from Stalin at Teheran, the Western allies agreed on an invasion of France in 1944 to open a second front against Hitler. This would use all available landing craft, so Roosevelt decided to abort the amphibious operation in Burma. This, Chiang replied, gave rise to 'serious misgivings' – as a result, he would not go ahead with the planned land offensive into northern Burma from south-west China. Stilwell was equally disconcerted by the way things had gone and, in particular, the difficulty of pinning down Roosevelt. 'A brief experience with international politics confirms me in my preference for driving a garbage truck,' he reflected.

Despite his tart rejoinder to Roosevelt's cancellation of the landing in Burma, Chiang decided to proceed after all, to show what China could do. On 21 December 1943, Stilwell led the 50,000 Chinese troops who had been trained in India over the border while the other force in Yunnan – Y Force – moved towards the malarial Salween Gorge on the eastern frontier. The fighting was enormously harsh as the troops from India – X Force – crossed 200 miles of jungle, swamps and 6,000-foot mountains to attack strategic towns and open the route for supplies to reach China by land. At the head of his men, the 61-year-old Stilwell lived rough like them, and wrote after one climb: 'All out of shape. No wind, no legs . . . Felt like an old man when I staggered in.'[22]

To begin with, Chiang held back the Yunnan force on the border, not wanting to lose it in Burma and valuing it as a way of keeping the lid on the autonomist tendencies of the provincial governor. But US pressure, including a message from Roosevelt and a threat to halt Lend-Lease supplies, induced him to authorize Y Force to move through precipitous river country in the lower Himalayas where stiff Japanese resistance meant it was able to advance only twenty miles in a month. 'Generalship was atrocious, manpower was squandered. Ammunition wasted, and weapons misused and neglected,' the American diplomat John Paton Davies wrote.[23]

On 7 March 1944, X Force took its first objective, the town of Maingkwan. Labour gangs began work on a road and pipeline to China. As the soldiers advanced towards the next target, Myitkyina, on the narrow-gauge railway north from Mandalay, Frank Merrill, the commander of an American commando force taking part in the campaign, had a heart attack, and his men suffered badly from disease and casualties.

The battle for Myitkyina was won after two more very tough months. 'Rain, rain, rain, mud, mud, mud, typhus, malaria, dysentery, exhaustion, rotting feet, body sores,' Stilwell noted in his diary. 'A knockdown and drag-out affair.' But eventual victory opened the land route to China. Stilwell had his revenge on the Japanese, and had shown what could be done by well-trained and properly equipped Chinese troops, though the training had been conducted well away from the debilitating effects of the Nationalist military machine. Vinegar Joe was given his fourth star, a rank he shared with only four other American officers. The road from Burma to Yunnan would be named after him.

The focus on Burma may have contributed to the lack of preparation by Chinese forces to face an offensive launched by the Japanese in April 1944. At this late stage in the war, as the Americans drove forward to take the Marshall and Mariana Islands, the Imperial Army could still field more than 350,000 troops with 800 tanks and up to 15,000 vehicles to carve down through China. They had several objectives – to stake out a belt of territory stretching from their northern domains to the border with Indochina, where they had grabbed power from the French, to seize food and supplies, and to destroy US air bases in the south. Soldiers were instructed not to ill-treat the population; leaflets identified the real foe as 'the white-faced demons'.

By any standards, the early stages of Operation Ichigo ('Number One') were a stunning success. The kill ratio was put at forty Chinese for one Japanese. Sweeping across the Yellow River into Henan, the invaders devastated Tang Enbo's army. Chiang played politics, refusing to move troops blockading the Communist base in the north, and holding back supplies and reinforcements from the able Cantonese General Xue who was defending Changsha but whose loyalty he suspected. After forty-seven days of fighting, the Hunan capital fell. The Japanese pushed on, heading for the town of Hengyang, on the southward railway. Chiang ordered Xue to withdraw to Sichuan.[24]

As he had done in the past, Xue disobeyed, sending his crack Tenth Army to defend Hengyang. Claire Chennault argued that, if his planes received more fuel, they could cut the extended enemy supply lines by bombing. Stilwell refused to divert the fuel. The airman, not the most unbiased of witnesses, wrote later that Stilwell's aides told him the general was deliberately aiming to see the Chinese lose the battle in Hunan so that he could press his case to take over their army. That this may not have been simply the result of Chennault's animosity is indicated by an entry in Stilwell's diary noting that, if the Ichigo crisis was 'just sufficient to get rid of the Peanut without entirely wrecking the ship, it would be worth it'.

Ten thousand men of the Tenth Army dug in round Hengyang, outnumbering the enemy four to one. A US intelligence officer found that malaria was rife, arms were lacking and food was down to two bowls of rice a day. Yet the spirit of the defenders was 'absolutely amazing'. Teddy White reported that only a third of the soldiers had a rifle. A unit he joined had no vehicles, and only two antique French First World War artillery pieces. 'All that flesh and blood could do, the Chinese soldiers were doing,' he wrote. 'They were walking up hills and dying in the sun but they had no support, no guns, no direction. They were doomed.'

Chennault's planes parachuted down limited supplies of rice, medicine and ammunition as the town went up in flames. But Stilwell refused to authorize bigger drops on the grounds that this would 'set a precedent for further demands that could not be met'. His headquarters turned down a request channelled through Chennault for 500 tons of weapons for Chinese troops planning a flanking attack as a 'waste of effort'.

After seven weeks of fighting, the Japanese entered the town on 7 August. 'We are now in the midst of street fighting,' a Chinese commander radioed. 'Our men are all but wiped out. This is my last message.' Hengyang fell the following day. After a month's rest, the invaders resumed the offensive, entering Guangxi, with its big American air base and military training centre at Guilin. Chiang wanted this to be held at all costs, but Stilwell organized a withdrawal – as the Americans left, prostitutes hung out banners reading 'So long, buddies, and good luck'.

The great Japanese sweep had serious economic effects, destroying some of the limited Nationalist industrial base and further reducing its tax revenue. Refugees flooded out of south-western cities; Chinese soldiers charged them to board trains which steamed a few miles, and then stopped; the troops forced the passengers out at gunpoint, and went back to collect another load. In early November, the American air crews burned the last US installations in the south, and flew to safety in Sichuan.[25]

The Guangxi army of General Bai brought the Japanese to a halt after they had covered almost 1,000 miles. The invaders set the provincial capital of Nanning on fire before leaving. Some headed north towards Sichuan, but stopped at a mountain base, where Americans blew up a stockpile of 50,000 tons of military supplies. The sudden halt led to rumours of a secret agreement with Chiang under which the Japanese would not threaten Chongqing in exchange for a winding down of resistance elsewhere. When an American mentioned this to him, the Generalissimo responded with a dry cackle. There may have been a more prosaic reason – Tokyo had no interest in getting caught in winter fighting in the wilds of Sichuan, and would need all the forces at its disposal to confront the US advance across the Pacific bolstered by a big naval victory in the Gulf of Leyte.

Despite Ichigo, the withdrawal of the Imperial Army from China thus seemed imminent. Dai Li was believed to be working on agreements to ensure that occupation forces handed over their territory to the Nationalists, rather than leaving it prey to Communist advances. At Marshall's urging, meanwhile, Roosevelt stepped up pressure on Chiang to put Stilwell in full charge of the armies. 'I feel that the case of China is so desperate that, if radical and properly applied remedies are not immediately effected, our common cause will suffer a serious set back,' the president wrote. 'The future of all Asia is at stake along with the tremendous effort which America has expended in that region.'[26]

A new presidential envoy was sent to Chongqing. Patrick Hurley, a tall, mustachioed and eccentric former secretary of war who liked to emit American Indian whoops, was to try to get the Generalissimo to agree to expand Stilwell's authority. This would be extended to the Red Army, with Lend-Lease supplies going to Yenan. Two Communist emissaries told Stilwell they would fight under him, if not under Chiang. In his diary, Vinegar Joe became more and more irate with the Generalissimo, calling him 'the crazy little bastard [with] that hickory nut he uses for a head. He is impossible.' The Nationalist system, he added, must be 'torn to bits'. Another entry contrasted the KMT 'cesspool' with 'Communist program. Reduce taxes, rents, interest. Raise production, and standard of living. Participate in government. Practice what they preach.' The mass of Chinese people, he added, 'welcome the Reds as being the only visible hope of relief from crushing taxation, the abuses of the Army and Dai Li's Gestapo.'[27]

Stilwell got Marshall to draft a particularly blunt letter to Chiang, which Roosevelt signed, stating: 'I have urged time and again in recent months that you take drastic action to resist the disaster which has been moving closer to China and to you. Now, we are faced with the loss of a critical area . . . with possible catastrophic consequences.' There must be 'drastic and immediate action' with the American given unrestricted command. Otherwise US aid would be called into question.

Fearing its effects on his own more diplomatic efforts, Hurley urged Stilwell not to deliver a Chinese translation of the letter. But this was too sweet and savage a moment for the general to pass up. Calling on Chiang, he 'handed this bundle of paprika to the Peanut and then sank back with a sigh. The harpoon hit the little bugger right in the solar plexus, and went right through him. It was a clean hit, but beyond turning green and losing the power of speech, he did not bat an eye.' When he had finished reading, Chiang said simply, 'I understand' and sat in silence, jiggling one foot. Then he put the lid on his tea cup. 'That gesture still means, I presume, that the party is over,' Stilwell remarked. In a doggerel verse he sent his wife, he exulted that he had 'wrecked the Peanut's face'. But Stilwell, Marshall and Roosevelt had gone too far. They had no alternative to the Generalissimo and, if he would not give way, they had committed the grave tactical sin of leaving themselves without an escape hatch.

To win the last round, Chiang played the sovereignty card. It was, he noted, 'all too obvious that the United States intends to intervene in

China's internal affairs'. Agreeing to Roosevelt's demand would be to accept a new form of imperialism, making his administration no better than the Wang Jingwei collaborator regime in Nanjing, he told the KMT Central Executive Committee. His speech was leaked to the US embassy to be forwarded to Washington.[28]

The Generalissimo provided a way out by focusing his criticisms on Stilwell, personally. Replying to Roosevelt, he said he would accept another American, but that Stilwell was unfit for the job. During a sleepless night on 12–13 October 1944, Hurley drafted a message to the White House saying that, while he was a fine man, the general was 'incapable of understanding or co-operating with Chiang Kai-shek'. Retaining him might mean the loss of China. Before sending it, the envoy showed his cable to its subject. It was, Stilwell wrote, like 'cutting my throat with a dull knife'.

On 19 October, Stilwell wrote in his diary 'THE AXE FELL' as a more emollient general, Albert Wedemeyer, was named to take his place. After a final meeting with Chiang, he left Chongqing without briefing his successor, but took time to give his side of the story to the *New York Times*. To his wife, he wrote of 'hanging up my shovel and bidding farewell to as merry a nest of gangsters as you'll meet in a long day's march'. Stilwell was appointed to command the US Tenth Army in Okinawa, but the war ended before he could see action. Chiang refused to allow him to return to China. A visitor to his home in Washington heard him say that he would be proud to serve in the Red Army. He died in his sleep in October 1946. With his opponent safely expired, the Generalissimo attended a memorial service in Nanjing, and extended posthumous honours.

Wedemeyer, a soldier with Hollywood good looks, was also keen to reform and improve Chinese forces, but he went about it in a far more constructive fashion, achieving some useful results. The Nationalists put up a particularly stiff fight against an attack on a US air base in Hunan by enemy troops pulling back from Ichigo. Wedemeyer worked on plans for a grand offensive across the south, and authorized a fire-bomb raid on Wuhan by seventy-seven Stratofortress bombers on 18 December 1944, followed by attacks by locally based planes. Fires burned for three days, gutting the docks and warehouses and Japanese air force facilities.

On the political front, T. V. Soong was appointed as the equivalent of prime minister. Though suffering from stomach trouble and insomnia, the Generalissimo's rotund brother-in-law improved government, and brought in a former mayor of Shanghai reputed to be efficient and honest as finance minister. Though General He proved the eternal survivor as chief of staff, the more effective General Chen Cheng became war minister. If not sold on the need for wholesale change, Chiang appeared to recognize the need to strengthen the regime.

Patrick Hurley replaced the career diplomat Clarence Gauss as US ambassador and launched a bid to bring the Nationalists and Communists together, flying to the Yenan base on the weekly Dixie Mission supply plane on 7 November 1944. A tall, dapper figure with a handsome Roman face, Oklahoma-born Hurley had worked in coal mines and as a cowboy before prospering as a lawyer, going into politics and ending up as secretary of war under President Hoover – this entitled him to style himself 'General', which he liked to do, together with wearing a uniform decked with medals. He may have known the Washington ropes, but, in China, he was a stranger in a strange land. He called the Generalissimo 'Mr Shek' and pronounced the CCP Chairman's name as 'Moose Dung'.[29]

There was also some doubt about his mental abilities – an American adviser, Arthur Young, depicted him as 'a senile old man who couldn't keep his mind on any subject'. At a dinner in Chongqing, he toasted the short, brunette *Time* journalist Annalee Jacoby as 'the most important person in the world, my tall, blond goddess of a bride'. Alcohol may have played its part – a journalist recalled that the envoy kept him drinking for three hours before they sat down to lunch.

On a trip to Moscow earlier in the year, Hurley had been much impressed when the foreign minister, Molotov, told him the Chinese Communists were 'margarine Communists' – that is, not the real thing. This chimed in with the president's view of them as agrarian socialists and the positive view of the Yenan base propagated by the Dixie Mission. Mao had told the diplomat John Paton Davies that the Communists would collaborate fully if US forces landed in eastern China, provided the force was big enough and brought them supplies. In an interview in the summer of 1944, he had added that, if a satisfactory agreement was reached, Chiang would 'naturally' continue as president, and that the Communists would not overthrow the KMT or confiscate land.

Hurley had not told the Communists he was coming, and Mao had to be hurriedly summoned to the Yenan airfield. As the Chairman walked towards him, the ambassador issued his favourite form of greeting, the war cry of 'Yahoo!' Getting into the Communist leader's vehicle, a Chevrolet ambulance donated by the New York Chinese Laundrymen's National Salvation Association, the ambassador and Mao engaged in one of the more unlikely of conversations, with the Dixie Mission chief, Colonel David Barrett, interpreting. It was, the colonel recalled, not too easy because of 'the saltiness of the General's remarks, and the unusual language in which he expressed himself. His discourse, in addition, was by no means connected by any readily discernable pattern of thought'. That night, at a banquet for the anniversary of the Russian revolution, Hurley disrupted proceedings with yells of 'Yahoo!'

The Communists wanted a coalition government, a joint military council, American supplies and the freeing of political prisoners. Hurley thought this fair enough, and produced a paper that added democracy and liberty, which he and the Chairman signed, the ambassador styling himself as 'Personal Representative of the President of the United States'.

Returning to Chongqing accompanied by Zhou Enlai, Hurley was told that the Generalissimo was too ill to see him. But T. V. Soong warned him that he had been 'sold a bill of goods by the Communists'. Ten days later, Chiang shot down the pact by insisting that his armies should take over the Communist forces. Naturally enough, Mao rejected this completely, and threatened to put Hurley on the spot by publishing the document they had signed. Told of this, the envoy looked as if he was about to burst a blood vessel. 'The motherfucker, he tricked meh,' John Paton Davies records him as having said. Falling back on an old Oklahoma saying, Hurley added, 'Why do leaves turn red in the fall? Because they were so green in the spring.' After a message from the ambassador, the Communists agreed not to publish the document – for the time being, at least.

Worse was to follow for the envoy. Unknown to him, the US secret service, the OSS, had proposed to the Communists that 5,000 US airborne troops should use the Yenan base to attack the Japanese, while a division moved from Europe to work with the Red Army. American training teams would be installed. Equipment for 25,000 guerrillas would be brought in, including 100,000 Woolworth one-shot pistols. In return, the Communists would agree to make troops and militia available to the US.[30]

The OSS emissaries told the war minister, Chen Cheng, and T. V. Soong of the plan, asking them not to inform Chiang. No Chinese official was going to keep such news from the Generalissimo, who had Dai Li set up a briefing for Hurley. Enraged and embarrassed, the ambassador fired off a message to Roosevelt condemning those involved. The president sided with him. The initiative died a swift death. Still, sensing American friendship, the Communists suggested that Mao and Zhou Enlai should go to Washington on an unofficial basis to explain the situation in China. They hoped to see Roosevelt. There was no reply. Nor does there appear to have been any response to a request from the Red Army chief, Zhu De, to Wedemeyer for a $20 million loan to be used to buy over 10 per cent of the puppet forces in China.

On the ground, the last stage of the war with Japan saw the Communists advancing in east China, consolidating their hold in Shaanxi and the border with Henan, moving into Hunan and setting up positions round Shanghai. The central government, meanwhile, faced sporadic attempts by opponents to organize, notably in the south-west. But the dissidents were divided – the US consul in the Yunnan capital of Kunming described them as consisting of 'feudal barons and radicals, idealists and practical politicians'. Meiling and T. V. Soong flew to Yunnan to rally the governor by allocating him enough aid to fund three divisions.

The Generalissimo's position was further eased when Wang Jingwei died in November 1944 from natural causes in a hospital in Japan. His body was brought back to be buried near the Sun Yat-sen mausoleum in Nanjing – it was blown up with Chiang's approval after the war. There was no comparable successor to Wang, and the men left in charge of the dying embers of the collaborationist regime were in contact with Dai Li to smooth out their futures, while the commanders of puppet forces were working out deals to rally to the Nationalists after the war.

But there was unwelcome news that, at the Yalta Conference in January 1945, Roosevelt had agreed to the restoration of Tsarist-era Russian privileges in Manchuria as the price for getting Stalin's definite commitment to enter the war against Japan two or three months after the defeat of Germany. China was not consulted, though the president insisted that Moscow must sign a treaty with it to confirm the concessions. 'I feel more than simply hurt and sad,' Chiang wrote when he heard of the agreement.[31]

The Generalissimo's concern for the future increased when Roosevelt died in April 1945, though for a somewhat unexpected reason. He noted that the late president 'had at times shown a tendency to appease the Communists. But he set a limit to that ... After his death, I am afraid that the British will exert a greater influence on American policy.' The dropping of the atom bombs in August 1945 made the Yalta concessions to Stalin unnecessary, but Soviet troops had already overrun Manchuria, bringing the collapse of Manchukuo. Moscow put the death toll of soldiers and civilians in the north-east at 83,737 with 594,000 Japanese troops taken prisoner. There were also wide-scale atrocities against White Russians. Other sources say 180,000 Japanese were killed by the Soviets and angry Chinese, or starved to death. As booty, the Russians seized goods and equipment worth an estimated $2 billion. They also took prisoner the Last Emperor, Puyi, who was initially moved to the USSR, and then returned to China, where he underwent 'thought-education', and ended his life as a gardener in the Forbidden City in 1967.

Five days after the Soviets invaded the north-east, China and the USSR signed the treaty provided for at Yalta. Moscow recognized the Nationalists as the government of the Republic. The concessions agreed by Roosevelt were confirmed. But Manchuria was stated to be part of China and the USSR pledged non-interference in Xinjiang. However, the independence of Outer Mongolia was acknowledged, meaning that it fell under Moscow's sway.

When Japan surrendered on 18 August, the China run by the KMT was devastated by war, plagued by inflation, social ills, and the loss of manpower and industry. It was subject to the old regional divisions and, despite T. V. Soong's attempts to make government more effective, by weak administration and lack of vision. The absorption of former puppet troops did nothing to increase the quality or cohesion of central-government armies. Carpetbaggers fanned out into areas freed from the invaders and alienated the population. China regained Taiwan from Japan, but there was sharp tension on the island between native inhabitants and incoming Nationalists, who grabbed the best assets and imposed harsh military rule.

As so often, the Nationalists desperately needed a period of peace and quiet in which to try to construct a modern state, and a period of serious reflection as to what that state should be. As usual, they got neither. Two days before Hirohito surrendered, the Communists rejected an instruction from Chiang for their forces not to advance into territory formerly held by the invaders. Instead, they sent in troops to link up with the Soviets, and brought back units that had been sheltering in Siberia. The new invaders handed them 100,000 guns from Japanese stores, and 200,000 Manchukuo troops were recruited.

Desperate to check the Communists, General He organized joint operations with Japanese who had surrendered to retake twenty towns and cities in seven provinces from the CCP – until the end of 1946, some 80,000 Japanese troops were operating under KMT command. American air transport moved half a million Nationalist soldiers to the north, Manchuria and Taiwan. US troops landed in Beijing, Tianjin and other northern strongpoints. In theory, the American policy was to keep out of the conflict between the two Chinese sides. In fact, there was no doubt which party Washington was helping as Harry Truman toughened the US attitude to the Soviet Union and China became caught up in the Cold War.

So, no sooner was the fourteen-year conflict with Japan over than the Nationalists found themselves diving straight into a fresh conflict as the final act of the long struggle for control of China opened. In his diary, Chiang called the crisis the most serious since the Mukden Incident of 1931.

17

The Last Battle

On 28 August 1945, Patrick Hurley made his second trip to Yenan, to bring back to Chongqing the man the Nationalists had been fighting for nearly two decades. Under strong American pressure, Chiang Kai-shek had agreed to issue an invitation to Mao. At first, the Chairman demurred, offering to send Zhou Enlai instead. But Stalin was beginning to have doubts about giving the Chinese Communists too much backing. His aim was a weak China with which he could meddle as he sought to extend Soviet influence in East Asia. While he waited to see how that would work out, he was ready to back talks on a coalition government, and to urge Mao not to take an attitude that would cement the relationship between the Nationalists and the Americans.

The CCP chairman would later express resentment at the way he had been strong-armed by Moscow into leaving his base to meet the Generalissimo. But he probably realized that turning down the invitation would lose him potential support from America, and alienate Chinese who wanted the two sides to reach an agreement. Still, he said he would only make the trip if Hurley flew with him to prevent any attempt to bring down the plane. The ambassador agreed. 'How comical this is!' Chiang noted in his diary. 'Never imagined that the Communists could be so chicken-hearted and shameless.'[1]

Smiling broadly and waving his fedora hat in triumph, Hurley was first out on to the tarmac when the aircraft landed in Chongqing. Behind him, Mao wore a rumpled blue cotton uniform, and a solar topee. His hair was long, his face pudgy and soft. In a statement, he said political and military problems should be 'resolved in accordance with justice and reason, as well as on the basis of peace, democracy and unity. We must build a unified, independent, prosperous and strong new China.' Asked how he had found his first flight, Mao replied, 'Very efficient.'

The visit was all a novel experience for him in other, more important ways. He had been in soviets in Jiangxi and Shaanxi for almost two decades, interspersed with the Long March. He had grown accustomed to living an enclosed existence dominated by CCP politics, surrounded by people who subscribed to the cause. The only foreigners he had met were Comintern advisers, admirers like Edgar Snow and, most recently, the Dixie Mission and Hurley. His knowledge and judgement of the wider international dimensions affecting the situation were, as the historian Odd Arne Westad puts it, 'schematic and shallow, his analyses [built] on guesswork and castle-building'.

Now, he was entering the lair of an enemy which fundamentally disagreed with him and which, though it had performed badly and suffered greatly in the war with Japan, was still stronger than the CCP and enjoyed the backing of the most powerful country on earth. Even more than Chiang, Mao was a solo performer. Like the greatest emperors, he stood apart and assumed the Mandate of Heaven (Marxist-style). In Yenan, he was master; in Chongqing, he was, at best, an equal, forced to compromise in a way foreign to his nature and to his existence since he gained the upper hand in the Party ten years earlier.

Chiang was self-confident. According to Doon Campbell, the Reuters correspondent in Chongqing, he showed off the visitor as if to say, 'Look – isn't he a prize exhibit?' In a dinner toast, the Generalissimo even expressed the hope that 'we can now go back to the days of 1924'.[2]

The talks were conducted by negotiating teams, with Mao and Chiang holding the strings behind the scenes. The Generalissimo's tactics were characteristic. He would appear to give ground, but surrender nothing which he could not reclaim. Thus he agreed that a National Assembly might meet and even that there might be a coalition government; but he immediately added that all China must come under the Nationalist umbrella, even if, as during the war, the CCP was allowed its zones. The Red Army should be severely reduced, he added. To which Mao riposted with a demand for Communist governors in five northern provinces and the chairmanship of the Beijing military council, plus a substantial army.

At a dinner and during a tea party, Mao shouted, 'Long live President Chiang Kai-shek!' But, in his diary, the Nationalist leader complained that the Chairman seemed insatiable, adding, 'he does not hesitate to take advantage of my friendliness to make exorbitant demands.' Still, after three weeks of talks, a pact was announced to avoid fighting and form an all-party government. Each side wanted to appear in a positive light, if only to win favour with the Americans with their treasure chest of supplies. For the Communists, relations with Washington had been soured by the detention of a US intelligence mission in their territory in Henan, and the bayoneting to death by their troops in Shandong of an OSS captain, John Birch, whose name would subsequently be adopted by a far-right American group.*

As Mao left the next day, an agreement was unveiled to call a political consultation conference, guarantee civil liberties, recognize all political parties and release political prisoners. Zhou stayed behind to continue negotiations. The accord did not address the key issue of military strength or Mao's call for CCP control of five provinces. 'Neither side trusts the other and will make the first concession,' Campbell wrote in a letter home. 'Each wants territorial, military, civil, political control. Yet each side claps hands for democracy, unity, freedom, nationalization of the armies.' The emptiness of the accord was shown when Chiang put off the political conference until 1946. Nationalist troops were, meanwhile, leapfrogging into north and north-east China thanks to the American airlift.[3]

Mao had kept up appearances while in Chongqing, but, once he got back to Yenan, the strain broke through. He collapsed, lying prostrate on his bed, his body trembling and bathed in cold sweat, his hands and legs twitching convulsively. 'He asked us for cold towels to put on his forehead, but it didn't help,' an aide recalled. 'The doctors could do nothing.'

Recovering, he ordered operations to be stepped up in Manchuria. But the Red Army did badly – used to guerrilla warfare, its troops were no match for the Nationalists in set-piece battles. Attacks on cities played into the government's hands. Desertions soared.

The Soviet commander, Marshal Malinovsky, declared that his mission was 'to assist the Chinese government to establish its political power in the north-east'. The head of Moscow's occupation force in the former Manchukuo capital of Changchun declared that it was 'not permissible to oppose the Nationalist government', and sacked the Communist

---

* Birch's death followed an argument with a Communist military unit which had taken him prisoner. The US intelligence group was freed.

mayor. In an evident attempt to restrain the Communists further, Moscow agreed to a request from Chiang to delay the withdrawal of Soviet forces until the Nationalists felt ready to stand on their own in Manchuria.

However, when the time came to leave, in May 1946, Stalin switched again. He did not want to see the KMT troops that were pouring into the north-east to be too successful, so he ordered a huge quantity of weapons and equipment taken from the Japanese to be given to the Chinese Red Army, while the USSR dismantled Manchurian factories and shipped them across the border. As always, his aim in China was to produce maximum weakness, which the Kremlin could exploit for its own best interests.

The north-east would turn out to be a snare for the Nationalists, drawing their best troops into a region where they had never held sway. Communications lines were stretched. The local population was alienated by carpetbaggers and officials imported from other parts of the country. Urban Manchuria became what the historian Edward Dreyer has described as a 'kleptocracy'. Central-government forces depended on American transport. Commanders from southern and central China stuck to towns and cities, leaving the countryside open to the CCP as Mao heeded advice to focus on a base area along the Soviet border, and responded to an instruction from Stalin to seek a modus vivendi with the KMT by asking, 'Does this mean that we are going to hand over our guns to the Kuomintang?' To which the CCP Chairman replied: 'No, the arms of the people, every gun and every bullet must all be kept, must not be handed over.'[4]

Though civil war had begun in earnest by the end of 1945, one party did not give up pursuing peace – the Americans. Harry Truman upped the stakes by sending the most respected American public servant to try to bring order and agreement to China. Grey-haired and with piercing blue eyes, a country boy from Pennsylvania who drove himself to the Pentagon in a small black saloon, General George Marshall had organized the US war effort. He was known to be deeply honest and straightforward, a stickler for clear lines of authority and agreements that meant what they said. He had backed Stilwell almost to the end, and had exploded in anger at Nationalist prevarication at the Cairo summit of 1943. In other words, just about the least fitting man to send to China.

However, the mission appeared to get off to a flying start with talks that produced an agreement between Communists and Nationalists to set up a joint committee to arrange a ceasefire in northern China, announced on 10 January 1946. The next day, a Political Consultative Council of thirty-eight delegates met – the Nationalists had eight seats, the Communists seven and others came from smaller parties or were non-partisan figures. There was broad agreement on reorganizing the government and moving towards constitutional government with a national assembly. Marshall was treated as a hero when he made a short trip home.

He was guided by the continuing American belief that the Chinese Communists were merely rural reformers and the conviction that China could be led to democracy American-style. Like others before him, Marshall was impressed by a visit to Yenan while he became disenchanted with the Nationalists. Having agreed to what the mediator wanted in January, the KMT Central Executive Committee moved in March to limit the scope of the accord by reserving powers for the central government, seeking to perpetuate presidential rule, and insisting on a veto power in the national assembly. In reaction, the Communists and the small parties refused to go any further in implementing the January agreement. So the KMT simply went ahead on its own, calling a national assembly in November to promulgate a new constitution on its own terms.

An agreement reached in January to set a ceiling of 700,000 men for government forces and 140,000 for the Red Army fared no better. As spring arrived, fighting flared up in Manchuria, which was not covered by the ceasefire. The Nationalists drove the CCP out of Mukden and Changchun, and took their strongholds built up during the war with Japan in eastern China and along the Yangzi, including the reconstituted E-yu-wan base. The Communists, meanwhile, staged offensives in Shandong, on the rail track from Tianjin, and in Jiangsu.

Marshall decided it was time to wave his big stick. He forced the central government to agree to a fifteen-day ceasefire by threatening to end aid. The effect of this was to halt the Nationalist advance in Manchuria, and save the main remaining Communist city, Harbin, from attack. Thus, in pursuit of his mission, the American provided the latest of the lifelines that outsiders had dangled for the CCP over the decades.

The Red Army faced some trouble in the far north-east with a rising by members of the Yellow Rifles secret society, who, despite their name, fought with spears and bows and arrows. But they were suppressed and the Communists made the most of their hinterland with the Soviet Union, Mongolia and Communist North Korea – as Mao remarked, it was like sitting in an armchair. They gained time to regroup, and the Kremlin, anxious not to see Chiang triumph, provided aid and training that turned the Red Army from guerrillas into a modern, organized force. For the Nationalists, the Marshall truce thus became what Chiang would call 'a most grievous mistake' – but one he felt he had to go along with because of the evolving Cold War politics from which he could not escape.[5]

On paper, the Nationalists had a numerical advantage of more than three to one over the Communists. But their army remained plagued by inefficiency, regionalism and corruption. Most soldiers were illiterate peasants, often press-ganged, miserably treated, ill-disciplined and without any real allegiance to the regime. Many died on forced marches to the front; up to half of all new recruits were reckoned to have perished or deserted. Like warlord troops before them, they looted, pillaged and raped, forfeiting any pull the regime might have had on hearts and minds. Nor, with a few exceptions, were the Nationalist commanders up to the job. Their tactical skills were frequently fairly primitive and, from the days of the Whampoa Academy onwards, they had lacked training in the efficient disposition of large bodies of troops, supply and organization. The Nationalists were also harmed by the activity of highly placed Communist agents, including the assistant chief of staff, the head of the War Planning Board and the confidential secretary to General Hu Zongnan, the commander in the north-west.

On the civilian front, the failure of the regime to offer anything new once the war with Japan was over lost it support among its core urban constituency. In the countryside, landlords used private militias or government troops to punish peasants who tried to resist their exactions – in one village, an American journalist, Jack Belden, reported seeing two dozen bodies being dug out of a pit where they had been buried alive. Peasant bands hit back, sometimes organized by remnant Communists, sometimes perpetuating old outlaw traditions.[6]

Hyper-inflation undermined everyday life and ruined tens of millions. The government deficit for 1946 was four times that of 1945; it sextupled in 1947, and increased thirty times the following year. In Shanghai, the cost of living index at the beginning of 1946 was 900 times the level at the outbreak of the war with Japan. An economic reform programme was introduced in 1947 but made things even worse. An attempt to impose price controls failed through non-compliance, hoarding and the black market. When the controls were lifted, the index in Shanghai was more than a thousand times above the level of two years earlier. As the historian Michael Lynch has aptly put it, 'in 1940, 100 yuan bought a pig; in 1943, a chicken; in 1945, a fish; in 1946, an egg; and in 1947 one-third of a box of matches.'[7]

Corruption was endemic, at every level of society. Anybody with influence was likely to use it to extract 'squeeze' or make money. Chiang's family-in-law and associates such as Big Ears Du were implicated in major scandals involving the distribution of US assistance, currency manipulation, government bonds and an American gold loan.

The black market thrived. Aid supplies were hijacked and sold – blood plasma donated by the American Red Cross was on sale in shops in Shanghai for $25 a pint. During a fresh famine in Henan, Jack Belden reported seeing soldiers grabbing relief intended for an orphanage and selling it while the children died of hunger. Reconstruction of industry was halting. Unemployment rose as did labour unrest – there were 4,200 strikes in Shanghai in 1946–7.

Repression tightened. The Democratic League was harassed. A police colonel explained: 'If we think that a man is a Communist agent we grab him and it's up to him to prove that he is not. The Chinese masses are used to what you might call cruelty, they understand it, they have always understood it.' In Beijing, troops fired on a protest by 3,000 students, killing several. In Yunnan, Nationalist troops overthrew the autonomy-minded warlord. Police shot five dissidents in a demonstration there and arrested more than a thousand. Some reports told of thirty being buried alive.[8]

Chiang also suffered the loss of one of his key lieutenants, the police chief, Dai Li, who died in a plane crash flying through bad weather to an assignation with his film star mistress, Butterfly Wu. Abroad, the Generalissimo had to deal with Harry Truman, who did not share Roosevelt's romantic, nostalgic vision of China. When Madame Chiang made a fresh trip to Washington to try to rally support, the president refused to let her stay at the White House. Later, he would reflect that 'grafters and crooks' in the Chinese government had stolen a billion dollars from US loans. 'They're all thieves, every damn one of them,' he added. The Republican 'China Lobby' grew steadily in strength but only fuelled Truman's disdain.[9]

Though Marshall continued his efforts, neither the Nationalists nor the Communists had any more time for the envoy. Indeed, Chiang had become personally hostile, writing in his diary of the American's 'harsh' voice and face. Nationalist troops moved against the Red Army in Shaanxi, Jiangsu, Shandong, Henan and Shanxi. The CCP headquarters at Yenan was bombed. Overriding the mediator's objections, the Generalissimo launched an attack against the northern city of Zhangjiakou,* the last major Communist urban centre in China proper, which was located between two KMT strongholds.

Infuriated, the Americans put a short-lived embargo on the shipment of military aid in July 1946. 'Selfish interest of extremist elements, equally in the Kuomintang as in the Communist Party, are hindering the aspirations of the Chinese people,' Truman noted. The Generalissimo, who accused Marshall of doing 'irreparable damage', ceded to the extent of calling a short truce in Zhangjiakou – which the Communists rejected. The embargo was lifted, and Washington agreed to a huge bargain-basement sale of war surplus equipment to the Nationalists. The attack on Zhangjiakou resumed, and the city was taken on National Day, 10 October 1946, after a Red Army counter-offensive had been beaten back. At the end of the year, a new constitution was unveiled in the National Assembly in Nanjing, which had become the capital once more. It cemented presidential power but also, for the first time, recognized that provinces and counties might enact self-government legislation. As with so many other fine-sounding provisions laid down by the Nationalists, this meant little in practice.[10]

On 7 January 1947, Marshall went home. At their last meeting, he warned Chiang that the People's Liberation Army (PLA), as the CCP's forces now became known, was too strong to be defeated. In response, the Generalissimo forecast final victory within ten months. At the airport, the American attributed the failure of his mission to 'almost overwhelming suspicion' between the Nationalists and the Communists, aggravated by KMT reactionaries and 'dyed-in-the-wool Communists'. In truth, it had been doomed from the start since neither side wanted peace and harmony.

* Then known as Kalgan.

'Chiang is a murderer,' proclaimed a Communist song. 'Butchering countless Chinese. His face is covered with the people's blood.' In Communist-controlled areas, peasants were mobilized, willingly or not, providing both a base in the countryside and millions of support workers for the military. As in the Jiangxi base, they were encouraged to take retribution against class enemies into their own hands so that they would have a blood link with the revolution. They maintained defence lines, dug trenches, tended to the wounded and formed militias.[11]

Mao believed that the sheer mass of the peasantry meant that, if it stood together, it could dig up the twin mountains of imperialism and feudalism, provided strict political control stretched down to the grassroots, regimented by a mixture of force and the promise of land reform, and allied with the army. Framed by the personality cult and the ideology of revolution as defined by the Chairman, the political–military–peasant triangle fused into a blunt but finely calibrated instrument to which the Nationalists had no reply. The Communist victory was no spontaneous affair. It had been carefully honed over the years, and could now draw on all the elements put in place by the supreme leader during the long quest for ultimate power, including the weapons of terror and repression sharpened in Yenan.[12]

Greatly helped by the Soviet handover of between 700,000 and 900,000 rifles, 14,000 heavy and light machine guns, artillery, mortars, anti-aircraft weapons, boats and 700 vehicles, including tanks, the PLA was no peasant guerrilla army. Japanese prisoners of war were put to work, training soldiers and forming an air force. Russian advisers set up military schools in the area between Harbin and the Siberian frontier to teach the Chinese the use of modern weapons and the tactics of large-scale warfare.[13]

As for Mao, he was on the move in the early spring of 1947 after Nationalist forces under General Hu Zongnan, a Whampoa veteran who had acquired the nickname of the 'Eagle of the North-West', took Yenan.* This was, naturally, hailed as a triumph by the Nationalists,

---

* Jung Chang and Jon Halliday state in their biography of Mao that their investigations convinced them Hu was a Communist 'sleeper' who engineered repeated disasters that cost the lives of hundreds of thousands of Nationalist soldiers (pp. 312–18). They give no details of the evidence for this and Hu's son threatened legal action in Taiwan. As with other disputed elements in their book, the authors did not reply to inquiries sent through their British publisher on this point.

but Hu's confidential secretary had tipped off the Communists after being shown the secret attack plan, and the leadership escaped in plenty of time.[14]

An American, Sidney Rittenberg, who was with Mao, recalled the Chairman playing 'a sardonic cat and mouse game' with the Nationalist troops, keeping just ahead of them, but not so far that they would give up the chase. Then, when the KMT soldiers were exhausted, they would be led into an ambush where the PLA would bring superior force to bear to wipe them out. Mao described this as wear-and-tear tactics: 'Chiang thinks that when he seizes the devil's lair, he will win,' the Chairman told PLA commanders. 'In fact, he will lose everything. We will give Chiang Yenan. He will give us China.'[15]

The Nationalists had a host of other problems in Manchuria. The population was increasingly alienated, and offered no moral support for their armies. The north-east was garrisoned by units from other parts of China which were resented by the local population. Chiang distrusted Manchurians, and kept their former ruler, the Young Marshal, as his personal prisoner. Supply lines were becoming impossibly extended. Chiang continued to issue orders after his 9 p.m. conference in Nanjing that might take no account of the position on the ground and be outdated by the time they arrived.

KMT troops managed to contain an offensive launched from northern Manchuria in early 1947 under a Long Marcher, Lin Biao, after it had progressed for 150 miles. But, from its new positions, the PLA attacked rail and road links, and isolated major cities, which became dependent on supplies brought in by air – Claire Chennault ran an airline which could never meet the demand. Nationalist commanders kept their troops in their garrisons, leaving the countryside in enemy hands and facilitating the implantation of the CCP apparatus there.

There was also heavy fighting in Shandong, the traditionally turbulent province where the Communists had built up both their armed forces and their local authority. In two big battles, the Nationalists were estimated to have suffered nearly 100,000 casualties. The provincial capital of Jinan, containing 80,000 troops and 575,000 civilians, was taken by the PLA after an eight-day battle in September 1947. The American consul-general reported that the troops and population 'no longer consider [the] Nationalist Government merits continued support'.[16]

Communist forces crossed the Yellow River, and also advanced the following spring to the area of the old E-yu-wan Soviet above the Yangzi where some guerrillas had held on for fourteen years. That meant the civil war was being fought on two major fronts – the huge Manchuria-north region and the strategic triangle of Shandong, Anhui and Henan in east-central China. On 23 March 1948, Mao moved to a new base, south-west of Beijing. A month later, General Hu abandoned Yenan; his army was reckoned to have lost 100,000 men in the fighting in Shaanxi. The Communists claimed that 640,000 Nationalist soldiers had been killed and wounded in the civil war to date, and that more than a million had surrendered. As well as footsoldiers who changed sides, a pattern developed of defections by government commanders who found themselves surrounded and pummelled by the PLA's artillery.[17]

Chiang repeated a tactic he used against the Japanese, ordering the path of the Yellow River to be changed to split enemy forces on either side of the waterway. Dykes were built to return it to the course from which it had been diverted in 1938 to try to stop the advance on Wuhan. But the water in the heavily silted river rose above them, flooding 500 villages and displacing 400,000 people, heightening the regime's unpopularity in the region.[18]

In the north-east, the Generalissimo shuffled commanders, but to no avail, as Mao decided it was time to 'try for complete annihilation'. In the summer of 1948, Lin Biao launched an offensive in Manchuria with 700,000 men – twice the size of the Nationalist army. Changchun, the most northerly city held by the Nationalists, was starved into submission by a five-month siege that started in September. The death toll was put at anywhere from 120,000 to 300,000, mainly civilians who perished from disease, the cold and hunger. Human flesh went on sale for the equivalent of US$1.20 a pound. After a Yunnanese unit in the garrison defected, the city fell.[19]

Chiang flew to Mukden to direct operations. He sent half the garrison of 230,000 men there to relieve another big city, Jinzhou,* on the corridor up from the Great Wall. Then he left for Beijing without informing the war minister or the general staff. The PLA took Jinzhou on 15 October, and inflicted heavy losses on the relief column as it

---

* Then transliterated as Chinchow.

moved slowly south. That left Mukden short of troops and isolated, depending on supplies flown in by Claire Chennault's airline on a hundred shuttles a day. Food ran out. Corpses lay in the gutters as people fought and bribed their way onto trains and planes whose American crews stamped their cowboy boots on the fingers of those trying to clamber aboard so that they could close the hatches and fly off, in a pre-echo of the fall of Saigon in 1975. The garrison commander defected, and, on 2 November, the PLA marched up the empty avenues of the one-time capital of the Old and Young Marshals. The Nationalists suffered 400,000 casualties in all in Manchuria. Only 140,000 of their men escaped south of the Great Wall. The PLA acquired huge supplies of captured American guns, vehicles, tanks and equipment, along with more recruits from the KMT forces.[20]

Chiang saw the loss of Manchuria as 'the virtual beginning of another world catastrophe'. But the second front in the Shandong–Anhui–Henan–Jiangsu region was even more threatening, striking as it did towards the regime's heartland. One army, under a Long March veteran, Chen Yi, moved south from Shandong while the Central Plains Army advanced from the west under Liu Bocheng, yet another Long Marcher, known as the 'One-Eyed Dragon' from his disfigurement in a grenade explosion. Underlining the importance of the confrontation – known as the Huai-Hai battle because it was fought between the Huai River and the Lunghai railway line – Mao moved into a farmhouse behind the lines.[21]

The railway city of Xuzhou, centre of the big campaign in the Japanese war in 1938, held the key to central China. Fighting in the surrounding flat countryside began in freezing weather late in the year. Well over a million front-line troops were involved, plus as many bearers for the Communists, organized by the political commissar, Deng Xiaoping. Far from the popular image of a peasant army rising in revolution, the PLA, like the Nationalists, deployed heavy tanks and artillery – but to better effect than their foes. Though the government controlled the skies, its air force had been allowed to run down seriously; to avoid anti-aircraft fire, pilots tended to keep too high for accurate bombing. Communist intelligence drew on the local knowledge of peasant cadres. Nationalist commanders feuded. Chiang meddled with battlefield decisions.

As well as learning modern warfare techniques from the Russians, the

PLA retained the speed and mobility of the guerrilla days, surrounding enemy units while it pummelled them with artillery – the PLA radio taunted the 100,000-strong garrison in Xuzhou with being 'encircled as tightly as in an iron barrel'. Villages blazed for thirty miles as the Communists formed a twenty-mile arc north of the city. Nationalist units ran short of food. Defections rose. A KMT general shot himself after one defeat. Officers and officials stormed planes to fly out before the Xuzhou airfield closed. Burning fuel dumps sent up 8,000-foot plumes of smoke. After a counter-attack in early December flopped in the face of heavy artillery fire, KMT forces fell back to set up a defensive line thirty miles closer to Nanjing.[22]

In the north, meanwhile, 2 million refugees poured into Tianjin, where the defenders dug a fifteen-mile moat from behind which they hoped to negotiate with the Communists. Outside Beijing, Lin Biao's forces took the airport and the Summer Palace; they also captured the city's power plant, enabling them to control the electricity supply. The Nationalist commander, General Fu Zuoyi, fell into what appeared like a depression. Some of his staff were Communist agents; others favoured surrender. His daughter, who had joined the CCP, urged her father to give in. Fu began secret negotiations with Lin to avoid a battle for the former capital, and to assure his own future.

In this deteriorating context, the Nanjing government made a last attempt to introduce economic reform. The losses on the battlefield had seriously cut its tax revenue as inflation soared. Shanghai was the focus. The aim was to get rich people to exchange their gold, silver and valuables for new banknotes. Chiang's son, Ching-kuo, was sent in as the chief enforcer, and applied hard-edged methods he had witnessed in the Soviet Union against 'big tiger' targets. A leading speculator was executed. A son of Big Ears Du was arrested for stock manipulation; his father was so shamed by photographs of the young man in handcuffs that he stayed in his house for weeks before decamping to Hong Kong. Members of Ching-kuo's Bandit Suppression National Reconstruction Corps raided warehouses and set maximum prices at markets. Loudspeaker trucks parked outside the houses of rich suspects booming out orders for them to hand over their gold – a story was spread that the vehicles contained devices capable of detecting hidden precious metals.[23]

The campaign flopped, however, when the new notes plunged in value. Cynics might have wondered if the prime aim was to amass valuable bullion to be taken to the new haven the Nationalists were building on Taiwan in case of defeat on the mainland. The crusade to hold down prices created shortages as Shanghai shopkeepers sent their stocks out of the city to be sold in places where Ching-kuo's writ did not run, and farmers stopped bringing in food. When the price campaign was extended to Nanjing, Zhejiang, Jiangsu and Anhui, stores closed and goods became unavailable. Then Ching-kuo ran into family trouble by moving against H. H. Kong's son, David, a notorious profiteer. Meiling flew in to upbraid her stepson – one account said she slapped him in the face. His father told him he had to stop chasing the 'big tigers'. Ching-kuo resigned. Inflation roared ahead once more. People mobbed banks to withdraw their cash. The black market boomed even more. 'Business is better than working' went one saying. 'Hoarding is better than business. Speculation is better than hoarding.'[24]

The Communists upped the pressure on the Nationalist leadership by issuing a list of forty war criminals, headed by Chiang, followed by T. V. Soong, H. H. Kong, Meiling and a line of Nationalist generals, including the Beijing defender, Fu. The Generalissimo sought to increase support for the regime by naming a relatively liberal figure, Wang Wenhao, as prime minister. When the national assembly met, discontent was evident, even though opposition groups had been excluded. Still, it granted Chiang 'extraordinary powers' for the war against the Communists. In the poll for the presidency, he got 2,430 of the 2,699 votes. But, against his wishes, the troublesome Guangxi leader, Li Zongren, was elected vice-president.

In the United States, Truman's re-election dashed hopes of a more KMT-friendly Republican administration influenced by the China lobby. The State Department produced a White Paper saying the US had done all it could for China, and, in effect, would do no more. The new Secretary of State, George Marshall, had no love for Nanjing after his experience in China. The second Truman administration suspended aid. With Japan safe for the West, Korea divided and European colonial rule re-established for the time being in South-East Asia, the early Cold War was to be conducted in Europe, not in the Far East to save the Nationalists.

In early January 1949, the PLA began to breach the defences of Xuzhou. The defending commander fled disguised as an ordinary

trooper, but was captured.* Another general got away by being taken
out in a wheelbarrow. Planes flying shuttle runs to Shanghai were filled
with soldiers 'dying in their blood and excrement', as one pilot put it.
After another week's fighting, the last Nationalist units withdrew across
the River Huai. As they went, they blew up the main bridge, killing
thirty civilians on it. The Communists hailed the victory as their Gettysburg. The Nationalist Central News Agency reported: 'No longer of
strategic importance, Xuzhou has been evacuated.' Nobody was
fooled.[25]

With the PLA moving in on the capital, those who could fled Nanjing,
by air or on what were termed 'dispersal trains' heading south. So many
of its members left the city that the legislature lacked a quorum. The
strain was said to have driven the Generalissimo to drink a big glass of
whisky to get to sleep. The normally supportive *Time* magazine noted
that his prestige 'has sunk lower than the Yangzi'.[26]

In the north, the PLA captured Tianjin, whose inhabitants decided to
surrender rather than count on their moat. The newcomers fired in the
air as they marched past the great buildings in the former American and
British concessions. Six days later, after writing to Fu to urge him not
to give up Beijing, the Generalissimo told the KMT Central Committee
that he was stepping down as president 'in the hope that the fighting
will come to an end and that the suffering of the people can be lessened'.
Some committee members wept. His decision was, however, ambiguous
– he merely said that the vice-president, Li Zongren, 'will act for me'.

After making his announcement, Chiang was taken in his black
Cadillac to visit the Sun Yat-sen memorial on the edge of the city. In
the great hall, he bowed three times before the marble statue. From the
terrace in front of the monument, he looked out for a time over the
capital, then was driven to the airport to fly to Hangzhou with his son;
his wife was in Washington on an unsuccessful trip to raise support –
'looking for more handouts', as Truman put it. That night, before going
to bed, the Generalissimo told Ching-kuo, 'I feel most relieved after
unburdening myself of such a heavy load.'[27]

Returning to his home village of Xikou, as he usually did at such

---

* He was held in prison by the Communists until being pardoned in 1959, and appointed to
the People's Consultative Council. His rehabilitation was linked to a bid by Beijing to get
his son-in-law, a Nobel Prize-winning physicist living abroad, to return home.

junctures, he declared that the KMT had only itself to blame because of its failure to reform society or improve the people's welfare. 'The old system,' he noted, 'had collapsed before the new one could be established.'[28]

At the end of January, General Fu surrendered Beijing – under the deal, his name was removed from the list of war criminals. The PLA advance guard marched into the city six abreast in icy weather. They were followed by students carrying portraits of Mao and Zhu De, and soldiers riding in captured American trucks. Cheering crowds greeted them. The large portrait of Chiang outside the Forbidden City was replaced by an even bigger image of the Chairman. The 200,000 Nationalist troops in the region were integrated into the Communist forces.[29]

Mao entered the city in a procession of eleven cars and ten lorries. 'Today,' he told Zhou Enlai, 'we are going to sit the imperial examination.'

'We should be able to pass it,' Zhou replied. 'We cannot step back.'

From Xikou, Chiang continued to meddle with military affairs. Between walks in the hills and playing with his grandson, he telephoned instructions to army commanders, and received visitors, including Yan Xishan, the Model Governor, whose forces were holding out against PLA troops led by Mao's companion from the Jiangxi days, Peng Dehuai. Receiving two journalists from *Life* in his capital of Taiyuan, Yan had spoken of raising an army of Japanese mercenaries and using American planes to drop napalm on the enemy. Pointing to an array of white cyanide capsules on his desk, he said there was one for each of his 499 officers if the city was overrun; a single black pill was for him. He opened a cupboard to show the journalists cans of petrol which he said he would pour round his office and set alight before swallowing the pill to ensure that his body was not taken. But, when the city did fall, Yan was away seeking aid from Nanjing and meeting Chiang. Several hundred of his officers were reported to have swallowed their poison pills; Yan, who had taken the province's gold reserves with him, did not follow suit – surviving for another day was always a warlord trait, and he ended up as prime minister in Taiwan.[30]

From Shanghai, a Chiang loyalist, Tang Enbo, whose men imposed a reign of terror in the city, supervised the transfer of assets across the ninety-mile strait to Taiwan. Green Gang members loaded ships with gold, silver and bank notes worth hundreds of millions of US dollars from banks. The national collection of art treasures was also taken, as were four of the Generalissimo's bullet-proof limousines, and his special prisoner, the Young Marshal. The Nationalist leader spent his birthday there in October 1946, passing a week on the island with his wife and being presented with the former mansion of the Japanese governor-general as a gift for the occasion – damage done by American bombing was repaired and the avenue in front of the building was renamed Boulevard in Celebration of Chiang Kai-shek's Birthday. The likelihood of the island being needed as a refuge was rising by the week. It was attractive because its coast would be easy to defend since the Nationalists still had naval and air superiority. It also had no native Communists. Chiang intended to bide his time there until the outbreak of the war he believed must be coming between the Soviet Union and the United States, in which Washington would need him as an ally and thus help him to return to power on the mainland.

The arrival of the Nationalists was bad news for the islanders. As a Japanese colony since 1895, Taiwan had been run efficiently, if repressively. The standard of living had risen, literacy was high and health care decent. Now, under the Nationalists, native companies were discriminated against and the population found itself excluded from government jobs. Public service declined; a black market flourished; and the Nationalists declared monopolies for their own benefit. There was cholera and plague. In early 1947, a revolt was sparked by police shooting an old woman selling cigarettes in Taipei, in contravention of a monopoly. A 2,000-strong crowd gathered to protest, and beat two monopoly agents to death. Troops drove through the streets of the city, firing indiscriminately. Chiang appears to have thought it was the work of Communists, and that the Nationalists were facing a rebellion on the island. Reinforcements were brought in. As the repression widened, anywhere from 5,000 to 20,000 people were killed. Suspected opponents of the KMT were picked up and disappeared. The American embassy in Nanjing reported to Washington that co-operation between the Nationalists and the Taiwanese would be 'difficult for an indefinite time in the future'.[31]

On the mainland, Li Zongren's already fragile position was further weakened when, on Chiang's instructions, Tang Enbo refused to move troops from Shanghai to defend Nanjing. The Generalissimo wanted this army to go to Taiwan when the time came, not to be lost fighting for the Nationalist capital. When other senior officers urged Tang to change his mind at a meeting, he slammed the table, swept papers to the floor and threatened to shoot the head of the Operations Staff.[32]

Desperate, Li floated the idea of a US force to patrol the Yangzi, and stop the Communist advance. Truman and Marshall had no intention of becoming involved. The head of the US Military Advisory Group in China, Major-General Barr, blamed the Nationalist reverses on 'the world's worst leadership and other morale-destroying factors which led to a complete loss of the will to fight'. Truman thought Chiang had nobody but himself to blame. 'Only an American army of two million men could have saved the Generalissimo, and that would have been World War III,' he wrote later to a friend.[33]

Stalin showed more interest when the Nationalists approached him to act as an honest broker with the CCP. Preferring a weak China to a revived, nationalistic nation, he advised Mao to order the PLA to halt on the Yangzi. The Chairman took no notice; fourteen years later, he would note that the Chinese revolution had succeeded against Stalin's will, and trace the roots of the subsequent split with Moscow to the Kremlin's attempt to check him and force co-operation with the KMT.

On 23 April 1949, steel-helmeted troops of Chen Yi's Third Field Army in mustard-brown uniforms marched into Nanjing accompanied by a tank force. Mobs looted ministries as the defenders blew up the railway station and stripped off their uniforms. Li Zongren flew to Canton, which became the new Nationalist capital; most foreign diplomats stayed put. Nanjing's mayor drove off with 300 million yuan, but was beaten up by his chauffeur and bodyguards, who stole the cash. A dozen Communist soldiers burst into the bedroom of the American ambassador, pointed to the furniture and said, 'These will soon belong to the people.' Deng Xiaoping and Chen Yi went to the presidential palace and amused themselves sitting in Chiang's chair. A Nationalist newspaper advised that 'a strategic withdrawal must not be confused with a military defeat.'[34]

In an incident which threatened to bring foreign intervention, the PLA shelled a Royal Navy ship, the *Amethyst*, which was taking supplies to the British embassy, killing forty-four sailors. The captain refused to sign a confession of 'criminally invading Chinese territorial waters', and his vessel was trapped for 100 days before escaping under fire. Mao saw the incident as a sign of a new China which would 'brook no foreign interference'.

Upriver, Wuhan was taken by Lin Biao's troops moving down the railway line from Beijing. Bai Chongxi tried to put up resistance, but the ever-suspicious Chiang refused to allow the Guangxi general to receive supplies. Bai was forced to retreat to the south. The PLA took Henan and isolated Shaanxi, obliging the 'Eagle of the North-West', Hu Zongnan, to abandon his base at Xi'an and cross into Sichuan. In the east, the loss of Nanchang and Hangzhou, following the fall of Nanjing, isolated Shanghai.

Staying in the Moral Endeavour club in the city, Chiang wrote in his diary that:

Seeing the Republic of China on the verge of death, I am moving ahead with tears in my eyes. There is only one road ahead, but it is tortuous. Don't fear. The road has been blazed with blood by our revolutionary forefathers. We must move forward today – forward, never retreat. Around us is darkness; ahead of us are dangers. With a ray of hope and my allegiance to Dr Sun Yat-sen, I will continue my struggle without fail.

One of his secretaries committed suicide in despair at the situation, leaving a note reading 'the light is dying.'[35]

In Shanghai, Tang Enbo ordered a large moat to be dug and a ten-foot-high bamboo barrier to be erected – it was said that one of his relatives in the timber business had a lot of stock to get rid of. Civilians poured out of the city on to ships or clinging to the sides of locomotives and roofs of trains. But fighting in the countryside sent others fleeing in the opposite direction. The mayor resigned – bizarrely, his replacement proclaimed a Health Week and ordered the cultivation of 'victory gardens' to grow vegetables.[36]

As food ran short and inflation spiralled even higher, prisoners were put to work digging zig-zag defensive trenches. Martial law and a curfew were declared, though the Park Hotel continued to advertise 'dinner dancing under the moon'. Soldiers built sandbag emplacements at crossroads, and cleared fields of fire for their artillery, using grave headstones to build fortified positions. Anti-Communist parades were organized along the Bund, complete with drawings of Mao as an ogre. Foreigners boarded a big evacuation ship, the USS *President Wilson*. Afraid of being caught by the Communists, White Russians besieged refugee organizations seeking a new home – many were accepted by the Philippines.[37]

Black marketeers and alleged Communists were driven through the streets standing on the backs of lorries tied to strips of wood on which their crimes were listed. Then they were shot in Zhabei Park. Other suspects were taken to an interrogation and torture centre in an abandoned house in the old French Concession. Among those pulled in were Reuters correspondent Graham Jenkins and the editor of the *North China News*, George Vine, after the paper published the agency's account of the Communists crossing the Yangzi; they were sentenced to death, but freed after an American journalist, Clyde Farnsworth, pointed out to the police what bad publicity the executions would arouse in the West.

Paid off by the business community to leave quietly, Tang's men crossed to Taiwan or melted into the countryside. The general himself flew to Canton. On 24 May 1949, the vanguard of Chen Yi's army marched into the old French Concession area; the city's businessmen had provided them, too, with money and medical supplies to buy off trouble. There were scattered skirmishes, with sniping along Suzhou Creek by Nationalist soldiers on the roof balcony of the Broadway Mansion apartment block. In the Hongkou district, the streets were littered with uniforms discarded by Nationalist soldiers seeking safety in civilian garb.

Across the river from the Bund, men from an infantry division tried to resist but were cut off when soldiers further down the Huangpu defected. Pickets of workers took over factories. A huge portrait of Mao was hoisted outside the Great World entertainment centre. The opera star Yan Huizhu, a former Miss Shanghai, whose beauty was such that people said it made geese fall from the sky, put on a blue denim jacket and a pair of canvas shoes to go out to greet the conquerors. Welcomed by the Post Office band, the newcomers gawped at the buildings, and, dog-tired, slumped on to the pavement when they broke ranks. Observers noted their excellent discipline – they even refused offers of cigarettes.[38]

Li Zongren made another bid to enlist American support. But the ambassador, Leighton Stuart, told Washington that he could not envisage any US statement which 'would be effective in changing the course of military events'. Chiang interfered more and more, altering military plans, laying out his own projects and forming an Extraordinary Committee of the Central Executive Committee of the Kuomintang, with himself as chairman. He named the Model Governor as prime minister and Tang Enbo as governor of Fujian, across the strait from Taiwan. He negotiated with the Soviet Union about rights in Xinjiang. According to Li Zongren, some southern generals were so infuriated that they proposed a rerun of the Xi'an Incident by arresting Chiang, but this got nowhere.[39]

At this eleventh hour, the Nationalists promised a 'typhoon' of reform, including rent reductions for 52 million people. The Generalissimo flew to the Philippines and South Korea for talks with their anti-Communist governments. But the battlefield position was worsening by the week as the fall of Shaanxi opened the way for the PLA to enter Sichuan and link up with armies in Hubei and along the Yangzi. The commander in Xinjiang declared his loyalty to the Communists. Leaders of a revolt in the Ili region on the Soviet border died in a mysterious plane crash, leaving a more pliant figure to side with the Communists.[40]

Politically, as well as militarily, the CCP was laying the foundations for the future. In September, a Political Consultative Conference met in Beijing to draft a constitution for a new state. On 1 October 1949, Mao stepped out on to the platform at the top of the Gate of Heavenly Peace of the Forbidden City to proclaim the People's Republic in his high-pitched Hunanese accent. The PLA paraded with its captured American vehicles and tanks; fireworks lit the sky. 'A long, long life to Chairman Mao,' the crowds chanted. The next day, Moscow recognized the new regime. As in the last months of the empire, China had two governments, but the final outcome was as inevitable and even more swift than it had been for the Qing.[41]

'The past year has been the darkest and bleakest in my life,' Chiang noted in his diary. Outside Canton, KMT forces blew up the bridge over the Pearl River as the PLA approached, but it still took the city in mid-October. By then, Chiang and the Nationalist government, such as it was, had moved back to the wartime capital of Chongqing. The city was, Chiang's son recorded, 'in the grip of panic, terror, and an atmosphere of deadly silence'. Li Zongren declined to join the last stand – suffering from bleeding bowels, he went for hospital treatment in Hong Kong, and then flew to the Presbyterian Hospital in New York.[42]

But Chongqing was not safe, either. PLA forces led by the Sichuan native Deng Xiaoping closed in, forcing the Generalissimo to fly to the provincial capital of Chengdu. A police agent recalled that he left orders 'to kill all the people he hated'. Political prisoners held in a coal mine or in the 'Happy Valley' camp run with the Americans during the war against Japan were executed. So was General Yang, the man who had suggested the kidnapping in Xi'an and had been held in a house outside the city. Secret police shot him, his son, his daughter and six members of his staff and their families. Doused in acid, the bodies were buried, the general in a brick flower box.[43]

Chengdu was as chaotic as Chongqing had been. Soldiers looted at will; vehicles jammed the streets; crowds of refugees headed out of town. On 10 December 1949, Chiang flew to Taiwan from the country he had lost. There were still some pockets of resistance to the Communists: General Hu fought a final rearguard action in the far south-west. Hainan Island in the South China Sea held out until 1950. The Nationalists repulsed Communist attacks on isles they held between Taiwan and the mainland. Survivors from the battle for Xuzhou made their way to Burma, where they divided their time between growing opium and staging hit-and-run attacks across the border into Yunnan.

But, by the end of 1949, the Nationalist era was over. A new epoch had opened with a new emperor to bring an end to three decades of disunion. 'We should be capable not only of destroying the old world,' Mao declared. 'We must also be capable of creating the new.' That creation would involve heights and depths greater than what had been seen before as one man sought to impose himself as completely and as ruthlessly as any Son of Heaven.[44]

PART 4

The Rule of Mao

Victorious revolutionaries have a problem. After winning power as outsiders, they become the new establishment. They have to construct and manage society, building bridges rather than blowing them up. Few handle the transformation well, and things usually end up badly for the people on whose behalf they claim to have acted. Never was this more true than for Mao Zedong, who remained rooted in conflict and violence after the victory of 1949.

Thirty-eight years on from the 1911 risings against the Qing, China was once again ruled by an imperial force. But this did not bring peace or stability. Logical, scientific methods were displaced by utopianism of an increasingly extreme variety. Professionalism was subordinated to politics – 'Better red than expert', as a saying went. The exercise of the will and enthusiasm in implementing the dictates from the master was all. For Mao, the country and its 600 million people were, as he observed, a blank sheet of paper on which he could sketch the future.

Two strands from the past came to bear. There was the reassertion of central control, but also a continuing pattern of conflict that would prevent China from evolving as a state in which citizens could hope to be free of errant autocracy. The struggles decreed by the Great Helmsman would target not only class enemies, the Kuomintang, the United States, the Soviet Union, South Korea and India, but, above all, his own people and his own party. Their individuality was challenged by a regime that forced them to mobilize in the name of revolution, class warfare and national identity, and repeatedly turned itself against them. The despotic machine was, itself, prey to recurrent internal purges.

Mao's responsibility for the extinction of anywhere from 40 to 70 million lives brands him as a mass killer greater than Hitler or Stalin, his indifference to the suffering and the loss of humans breathtaking. People were fodder for his increasingly irrational dreams. So what if nuclear war killed half the earth's inhabitants, he once remarked; it would bring the destruction of imperialism, and the world would become socialist. But terror was not all. The Chairman represented something more, then and even now. One needs to go beyond his well-established culpability to understand the evolution of China from 1949 to his death in 1976, and its continuing influence on the nation of today.

18

The Winner

For most Chinese, the end of the civil war was an almighty relief after more than thirty years of conflict stretching back to the warlord era. Tens of millions had been killed. Industry, agriculture and the infrastructure had been hard-hit – in 1949, factory output was 44 per cent below its level of 1937. Overall, food production was at subsistence level, meaning that there were pockets of starvation. Half the railway network was destroyed. Inflation had ruined the economy. Important assets had crossed to Taiwan or gone to Hong Kong and South-East Asia, along with the skills of fleeing officials and businessmen. National morale was in tatters. Society had lost its moorings.

If the doctrines of the new rulers were not understood by the bulk of the population, the Communists still appeared to offer peace and stability as the People's Republic of China (PRC) rolled out across the country. But they faced enormous problems, above and beyond the shattered state of the nation. To begin with, there was their own history. For all its military prowess, organizational strength and ideological language, the Chinese Communist Party had been an outsider since the breakdown of the united front in 1927, often fighting for its life. Its essence had been shaped by struggle, with an ideology constructed in the isolated cocoons of Jiangxi and Yenan and subjected to recurrent internal strife. Its chief was a man not much interested in the business of government.

The new regime could shape its own mandate – the better days of the Nationalist republic were long forgotten. A state had to be built from the ruins of invasion and civil war. Yet the endless talk of the need to root out class enemies, overcome reactionaries and drive back counter-revolutionaries was a means of asserting and consolidating power, not a recipe for establishing a stable socialist society. Mao identified the industrial proletariat as the hard core of the new order, but only 5 per cent of the population of 600 million worked in industry – many of these were illiterate and so unable to read Party literature. While the CCP had acquired the habit of speaking in the name of the proletariat, its long isolation from the cities meant that it approached its core constituency on a theoretical base.[1]

On the other hand, the world it did know – that of the peasant – was given only a subsidiary role in building socialism. Grain, Mao believed, was the key link in the economy; the Chinese, he said later, should 'store grain everywhere'. But this did not mean a privileged place for the men and women who grew it. On the contrary, the role of farmers was to feed the workers who would construct the new paradise, but they were not, themselves, to play the vanguard role. The myth that Mao led a revolution whose prime aim was to improve the lot of the peasants has had a long life, but was always based on a misconception, which the Chairman never shared.

Had 1949 seen an uprising which united the bulk of the nation behind a common positive programme, the way ahead might have been clearer. But China had been conquered by an army backed by a political machine as the old order imploded. Despite all the words Mao had written over the decades about the future of the nation, the practical course for the People's Republic was poorly traced. Nor was it clear how the new regime would legitimize its rule. Those two fundamental weaknesses still face the CCP in the twenty-first century.

The leadership came from varied geographical and class backgrounds – the Chairman and Liu Shaoqi from Hunan, Zhou Enlai from the more sophisticated eastern province of Fujian, the PLA chief, Zhu De, and Deng Xiaoping from the deep interior of Sichuan. Some, like Zhu and Marshal Peng Dehuai, had grown up in dirt-poor peasant villages; Mao and Deng's families had been better off; Zhou came from an elite background.[2]

The long battle for power made the relationship between the CCP and the PLA central to the regime. Mao, who headed the Military Affairs Commission (MAC), insisted that the army must be subservient to the Party. But, as under the Nationalists, militarization reached deep into the soul of the civilian administration, giving the PLA political weight and a role that went far beyond simply fighting wars. The Ten

Marshals of the civil war had special status. Long Marchers formed an elite.

The military heritage was evident in campaigns executed like enormous guerrilla offensives to encircle, isolate and destroy targets, to raise production or reduce the amount of food people consumed. The mass line perfected in Yenan was applied, as Mao explained, to refine the 'scattered and unsystematic ideas' of the people, and then propagate them back until they 'embrace them as their own, hold fast to them and translate them into action'. The top-down approach of this pantomime of popular democracy might well have been understood by emperors who claimed similar omniscience. For Mao, it provided a means of obfuscating the basic contradiction between the people's will and autocracy.

Though everything was supposed to have changed in 1949, dictates still came from a far-off ruler to be applied through his local agents, backed by force, if necessary. For the Chairman, the poverty and blankness of the masses made them ideal subjects. 'Poor people want change, want to do things, want revolution,' he reflected. 'A clean sheet of paper has no blotches, so the newest and most beautiful pictures can be painted upon it.'*[3]

Still, in the context of 1949, the new leaders were ready to start out by being pragmatic. The Nationalist collapse had been much faster and more thorough than they had anticipated – Mao had estimated that southern China would not be conquered until the mid-1950s. Some of the cities won in 1949 were in chaos, forcing the new masters to act much more quickly and on a much wider scale than they had expected. They had to raise spirits and restore the sense of national identity, establishing themselves in a way the KMT had largely failed to do. They had to win over cities, which the Party had long seen as hotbeds of reaction. That pointed to flexibility at the top, and a readiness on the ground to adapt to local conditions, taking an opportunistic, improvisational approach when necessary.

The rulers also had to cope with the threat from across the Taiwan Strait as the Cold War saw Washington stepping up its support for Chiang Kai-shek, who insisted that there was still only one China – his KMT Republic. The island was under martial law and the Chinese

---

* Wittingly or not, the second part of the formulation echoed a comparison made by Sun Yat-sen between the Chinese people and a tray of sand that could be shaken into new shapes.

minority governed with no regard for the interests of the native population. In a theatre of the surreal, legislators elected in Nanjing before
1949 spoke as representatives of mainland provinces. Enjoying naval
and air superiority, the Nationalists blockaded the mouth of the Yangzi.
Shanghai and Nanjing were bombed, as was Guangzhou, where a raid
was reported to have killed 259 people.

KMT agents and other anti-Communist forces were active below the
Yangzi and in the north-west. Nationalist forces which had crossed to
Burma in 1949, and moved into the drugs trade there, staged hit-and-run
raids, with help from the CIA. Tibet remained outside Beijing's control.
America offered the anti-Communists there aid, including some CIA
involvement. In Taiwan, itself, the US intelligence agency backed a secret
group of pilots, known as the 'Black Bats', who flew more than 800
missions over the mainland up to 1967, dropping agents, testing China's
radar and collecting air samples.

A great problem for the PRC was the shortage of reliable and experienced officials. The 4.5 million CCP members represented less than
one per cent of the population – a recruitment drive was launched which
would swell the ranks by 3 million between 1949 and 1952. Party
cadres, who had gained experience in the north, had to be dispatched
to apply their expertise elsewhere, instead of building on their initial
endeavours. While trusted to follow instructions more faithfully than
locals, the newcomers lacked the roots that had been developed in
Communist areas of strength before 1949. Local guerrilla leaders
resented the outsiders, who were rather like imperial magistrates arriving
in their *yamen* from far afield. Such postings could also run into trouble
when, as in Guangdong, the newcomers could not understand the local
tongue.[4]

In the countryside, land redistribution was the main change offered
by the new regime to win support. It drew on deep and long-standing
grievances, and, to that extent, tilled genuinely revolutionary soil. But,
as shown by the eyewitness account from Shanxi by an American aid
worker, William Hinton, the broader precepts of the CCP meant little
to peasants, though dinned into them at Orwellian struggle meetings.[5]

Despite encouragement from the regime for poor peasants to 'speak
bitterness' for their oppression, the victory had not brought the full
eradication of old social patterns. In Guangxi, 13 per cent of cadres
trained to administer land reform came from the very landlord families

they were meant to be dispossessing. In Henan, property owners who had links with officials were protected. In other places, landlords divided property among clan members to minimize redistribution. In Guangdong, a senior CCP figure was reported to have done favours for a big landlord who was a relative. A murder case in the same province, in which a landlord killed the husband of his mistress, revealed the continuing influence of KMT veterans, and corruption by CCP investigators, including a local magistrate, who was distributing favours to his clan.[6]

In March 1949, Mao had declared that the time had come for the CCP's centre of gravity to switch to the cities, which were to focus on production rather than consumption. For nearly all the faithful, they were strange places. Apart from his trip to Chongqing in 1945, the Chairman himself had not been in one for more than two decades before he entered Beijing in 1949. Places such as Shanghai were viewed as lairs of reactionaries firing 'sugar-coated bullets' against the revolution. For their part, urban dwellers accorded the PLA a steadily less rapturous reception as the armies moved south. While soldiers gawped at buildings, urban inhabitants spread stories of country bumpkins who washed their rice in Western toilets, and were aghast at how it flushed away when they pulled the chain.

Even if it moved relatively softly against all except major class enemies in 1949–50, the Party was clearly out to permeate national existence. It intruded on civilian organs and everyday life at will. Intermediary communal bodies were brought under its sway. Local power holders were swept away. No sector was off-limits.

Propaganda deployed the icons of struggle – flags, heroic images, weapons and the use of the term 'comrade'. Troupes spread the message that 'Without the CCP there is no new China.' To rally support, jobs were given to some of the Nationalist turncoats of 1949. General Fu, who had handed over Beijing, went on to become minister for hydraulics. The Yunnan warlord Long Yun, who had gone into exile in Hong Kong after being ousted by Chiang Kai-shek and who had then ordered his troops to ally with the PLA, returned to join the upper house of the legislature. Madame Sun Yat-sen, who moved into a villa by the 'Rear Sea' lake in Beijing, was named as one of six vice-chairs of the regime. Her husband continued to be consecrated as the Father of the Republic, and the CCP came up with a 'Revolutionary Committee of the Chinese Kuomintang' to claim his legacy.

The past was drawn on in such gestures as Mao proclaiming the People's Republic from the terrace of the Forbidden City. In 1950, the leadership moved into houses amid the lawns and lakes of Zhongnanhai Park, a one-time hunting ground behind the old imperial compound. Mao went to live in the grey-tiled Hall of Beneficent Abundance built by the Manchu emperor Qianlong. Around the leader's dwelling were the Spring Lotus Chamber, the Chrysanthemum Fragrance Study and Harmony Hall. Indoor and outdoor swimming pools were built by the Hall of Purple Light for the Chairman to undertake his only form of exercise. When the emblem of the new regime was put up on the Tiananmen Gate, the workmen who moved the Republican insignia into a space at the back found similar detritus from the empire there.[7]

Scholars were recruited to serve the new order, Zhou Enlai stressing how the Chairman valued patriotic intellectuals. Chinese arts were extolled over American 'cosmopolitanism'. Mao's long-time CCP foe, Wang Ming, was hauled out of oblivion to become director of the Central Legal Committee – given his links with the Kremlin, this could be presented in favourable terms to Moscow, though he enjoyed no authority. There was an echo of the old united front in invitations to non-Communist parties to send delegates to a Political Consultative Conference held in September 1949, to establish the new state. The ever-hopeful Democratic League, which had been persecuted by the Nationalists, was seduced by having a leading member, the intellectual Wu Han, appointed a vice-mayor of Beijing.[8]

This was window dressing; the non-Communist politicians were known as 'flower vases' – there for decoration. Mao and his colleagues had not gone through the struggle of the previous decades to share power with anybody. The New Democracy proclaimed by the Party was, Mao declared, 'a joint dictatorship of all the revolutionary classes', with Leninist centralism ensuring CCP control. Though the administration included one minister from the Democratic League and one from the Communist-sponsored KMT, the minor parties were only allowed in on condition that they did not diverge from the CCP. A non-Communist vice-premier recalled that he was refused a list of the directors of provincial departments because he was not a Party member.[9]

There was thus a strange two-tone character to the opening year of the People's Republic. On the one hand, the CCP was enforcing its dictatorship and identifying obvious enemies to pursue. A general who helped to arrange the capture of Beijing recalled that, afterwards, hundreds of thousands of KMT members and soldiers were detained, and some executed. Reports in 1950–51 told of more than 2.6 million 'bandits' being wiped out. The PLA deployed a total of 1.5 million troops for a national campaign in response to Mao's call to 'resolutely eliminate bandits, spies, bullies and despots . . . Kuomintang agents and saboteurs'.[10]

At the same time, it was considered quite possible to modulate land reform according to local conditions, and to work with the patriotic 'national bourgeoisie', who had decided to stay in China. The Chairman admitted the need to learn economic techniques from those who were acquainted with them in order to ratchet up production and modernize everything from railways to sanitation.[11]

The regime's number two figure, Liu Shaoqi, spoke of tolerating some 'capitalist exploitation' if it achieved the right results, calling for discipline, managerial authority, firing of excess staff and 'reasonable' settlement of disputes. 'If we were to go as far as to eliminate the bourgeoisie in the struggle, it would result in the closing of factories, decline of production, and unemployment among workers,' he argued in a major speech in Tianjin – there was already considerable joblessness in cities. 'Today China does not have too much capitalism. China is not over-developed; Chinese capitalism is too weak and China is too underdeveloped . . . [We] should let the bourgeoisie exist and develop for several decades.' In the countryside, Liu called for a mild approach to land reform. At the People's Consultative Conference in June 1950, he said violent methods were no longer needed since landlords would have to knuckle under in any case. They might lose most or all of their land, but they should still contribute to the development process. The chairman of the CCP Bureau for Central and South China ruled that land reform must be conducted 'in accordance with law and reason'.[12]

In Xi'an, most businesses stayed in private hands. In Hangzhou, local leaders decided that the city's Consultative Committee should include 'a couple of bad elements who have influence in industrial and commercial circles so that these can be controlled'. The memoirs of Lucian Taire, a Western businessman in Shanghai at the time, record one rich Chinese manufacturer thinking he would be able to deal with the new state of affairs as he had with the old, and the head of a small-scale import–export firm expecting his patriotism to stand him in good stead. Zhou

Youguang, a Chinese banker who had prospered in the United States, recalled in his memoirs how excited he was to have come home after the Communist victory. Joining the People's Bank, he soon shed his Western suits for blue workers' clothes while extending loans to private firms. In 1950, more than 75 per cent of Shanghai's industrial workers were still in private enterprises. The new mayor, Chen Yi, encouraged traditional culture, and the local opera star, Yan Huizhu, who had gone out in a denim jacket to greet the PLA in 1949, found her career blossoming again.[13]

Identifying himself with the regime and it with him, Mao tapped into the old imperial psyche. He was everywhere, his head on the postage stamps and banknotes, his name invoked in a hymn schoolchildren sang each day. Terror played its part, but, to begin with at least, the Chairman commanded obedience as a paternal figure who would restore the order the people sought after the long years of disunion – in distant history, the First Emperor and then the Tang and the Sui dynasties had ended periods of war and discord; now the victor of 1949 would follow in their path as the bearer of the Marxist–Maoist Mandate of Heaven.

For all the murderous excesses of the ascent to power, and the even greater horrors to come, there was a time in the 1950s when the Chairman represented China in a way that had eluded Chiang Kai-shek. He was able to combine a quasi-supernatural aura with blunt peasant aphorisms, and to be presented by the propaganda machine as a caring patriarch with the people's welfare at heart. It is too facile to dismiss this as simply a vast, murderous confidence trick on the people of China (and foreigners). After all they had gone through, the Chinese were ready to believe – and first among the believers was Mao himself. The tragedy was that this belief laid the foundation for the disasters and vast inhumane excesses which were to follow at the behest of the new emperor.

The impression of returning normality was helped when inflation was brought down by reducing the volume of notes in circulation and setting up a national savings scheme. Well-off people who wanted to prove their loyalty followed instructions to put their savings in state banks so that they could be pumped into the public sector. A drive was launched to reduce population pressure in cities by persuading refugees to return to their rural homes, in some cases with payment.[14]

Minorities were promised a degree of autonomy, and were asked to identify themselves so that they could be properly recognized by the state. Social reforms were promulgated, including a 'patriotic public health campaign' in which rubbish was cleared up, latrines built and peasants taught how to remove parasites from human waste fertilizer. Epidemic control stations were established. Workers were organized into *danwei* units which promised accommodation, shops, schools and other facilities in self-contained communities. Women were declared to be equal to their husbands. Polygamy, the sale of girls and female infanticide were banned. More than a million women took advantage of a new divorce law. The All-China Women's Federation had 40,000 staff in eighty three cities.[15]

The Party set out to isolate and undermine secret societies, particularly those involved in vice, gambling, extortion and corruption. Action was announced against traditional sects and religions, which were pursued, as under the empire, for their heterodox beliefs and, as under the Republic, for embodying superstition. In large cities, beggars were sent to training colleges to learn an occupation, or dispatched to their home villages; recalcitrants were warned that 'those who do not work do not eat.' In Beijing, a campaign was launched to close brothels, and send the women to 'productive labour' at enterprises such as the People's Button Factory. A big drive was mounted against opium use – on the anniversary of the original imperial attempt to stamp out the trade in Guangzhou,* drugs and pipes were burned in a huge bonfire there.[16]

In practice, these campaigns had their limits and drawbacks. The *danwei* units, with their system of compulsory registration and personal files on members, constituted a coercive control apparatus that both fragmented and regimented the population. Despite success in combating typhus, plague and syphilis, health spending – starting from the very low level bequeathed by the Nationalists – never rose above 2.6 per cent of the state budget up to 1956; the cheapness of the mass inoculation campaign and the improvement in hygiene facilitated low expenditure. Attention was focused on cities, while most of those affected by major illnesses lived in the countryside, where health care remained rudimentary. Practitioners of traditional medicine and acupuncture were estimated to number almost half a million in the

* From now on, this name will be used instead of Canton.

mid-1950s. Old magical cures kept their pull, and large crowds sought relief at holy water holes.[17]

For all the promises of equality, women went on getting the less well-paid jobs, and were still expected to look after the household, queuing for food and necessities. The Shanghai Party secretary excluded female homemakers from the ranks of 'productive people'. Divorcees could well find themselves cut off from any family support system. Modern contraceptive methods were rare, in keeping with the Chairman's belief that a rising population was a source of national strength. In a series of reports in 1951, the *People's Daily* highlighted continuing family violence and abuse against women, some of whom did away with themselves in individual or group suicides. In 1952, a quarter of all criminal cases involved rape.[18]

In the countryside, a gender revolution might have provoked disaffection with the new order among men. In any case, since the victory of 1949 was held to have done away with social differences, there was no need for action specifically aimed at improving the lot of women. In Beijing, brothels reopened, designated by black gates. Some veteran revolutionaries shed their peasant wives for city women – they compared their original spouses to the dry bread of the poor and their new partners to round, smooth steamed buns. At the top of the tree, the Chairman, increasingly estranged from his wife, dallied on his wide bed with young ladies picked for him from Party and army ranks. As in the Yenan base, opium cultivation was pursued – again for export; output is estimated to have quintupled in five years, with a flourishing trade from Shandong to Japan.[19]

When 400 ethnic minorities answered the invitation to identify themselves, the authorities decided that this was too many, and set up a social science project to classify them. This boiled the number down to fifty, lumping together people who spoke different languages and, in some cases, lived in different parts of the country. These groups were then put under military supervision. Far from opposing the chauvinism of the majority population, the Propaganda Office stressed the revolutionary supremacy of the Han.[20]

Secret societies and superstitions proved difficult to eradicate. There were periodic risings. Daoists in Zhejiang staged three attacks on government offices, killing forty cadres as they called for the return of the empire. In Hubei, the Army of the God of War designated an eight-year-old boy as its emperor, and was active in sixteen townships, killing a Party secretary and attacking government offices before being routed. A cult in Hunan made swords, ships, and bows and arrows from paper to equip an 'army of the other world' which would come to fight for them. In Shanxi, a sect warned that the government was gouging out people's eyes and hearts to use in an attack on Taiwan.[21]

In the first year and a half of Communist rule, Mao was content to delegate domestic administration to Liu Shaoqi and his colleagues, letting others get on with daily business while he dealt with grander visions. The first of these was to establish himself and his country on the world scene. That meant going to see the other great Communist leader.

The Chairman had been angling to visit Moscow since 1947. Two years later, he had declared that Communist China would 'lean' towards the Soviet Union, and so away from the USA. The verb was important – though Mao would repeatedly seek favours from the Kremlin, he would not adopt the subservience manifested by Communist leaders in Eastern Europe.[22]

Stalin waited till the civil war was resolved before issuing an invitation to Mao to attend a gathering of Communist bigwigs in the Soviet capital. It was the first time the Chairman had left China. On the long train journey, he showed the nervousness which could affect him physically at times. As in Chongqing in 1945, he was not in control, and was about to face a man whose power exceeded his. Walking along the platform in Sverdlovsk, he staggered, his face white, pouring with sweat.[23]

What he wanted from the visit was the abrogation of the treaty signed by the USSR with the Nationalists in 1945 as a result of Yalta, and a new agreement with his government. But the past three decades gave him every reason to tread carefully. The prime factor in the Kremlin's China policy was always the preservation and advancement of Soviet interests. Preferring a weak nation in which he could meddle, Stalin had even urged the PLA to halt on the Yangzi in the spring of 1949, rather than conquer the whole country. Now, he feared that the PRC might follow the route taken by the independent-minded Tito in Yugoslavia, setting up its revolutionary stall in competition with Moscow.

Still, a splendid welcome was staged at the Kremlin on 16 December 1949, the Soviet Politburo lining up to greet the visitor. Five days later, Mao was an honoured guest at celebrations of Stalin's seventieth birthday, during which he paid glowing tributes to his host. Then the wind turned chill.[24]

The Chairman was left alone in a dacha outside the city. The Kremlin cancelled meetings. Stalin declined to take telephone calls. Permission was withheld for Zhou Enlai to come to Moscow to help negotiate a new agreement. The Kremlin maintained that it was still bound by the Yalta accords, disingenuously expressing concern that tampering with them could cause problems with Washington. Mao would recall his belief that Stalin thought 'our revolution was a fake'.

The Chairman lost his patience. 'I have only three tasks here,' he cried out: 'The first is to eat; the second is to sleep; the third is to shit.' Taken to Leningrad, he made a point of being unimpressed. Still, he refused to go home, and, on 2 January 1950, Stalin decided to take a softer line. Mao was told a new agreement could be concluded. Zhou was allowed in.

The accord took six weeks to negotiate. On 14 February, the Treaty of Friendship, Alliance and Mutual Assistance was signed, with the Soviet and Chinese leaders watching. When Mao alluded to Yalta, Stalin replied, 'To Hell with that.' On another occasion, he remarked, 'You're a winner now, and winners are always right.' He even made the unusual gesture of leaving the Kremlin for a Chinese reception in the ballroom of the Metropol Hotel.[25]

Under the treaty, Moscow agreed to go to China's aid if Beijing found itself at war. It extended a $300 million loan, half of it for military purposes. But this was spread over five years, and much of the first instalment was retained by the USSR to pay off debts China was said to owe.[26]

The industrial aid Mao obtained was less than he had hoped for, amounting to fifty large-scale projects. In return, in secret annexes, Manchuria and Xinjiang were recognized as being in the Soviet spheres of influence. The USSR was to get 'surplus' stocks of Chinese tin, tungsten and antimony for fourteen years, depriving Beijing of the chance to earn foreign currency by selling them elsewhere. Staff drafted in to provide technical expertise were guaranteed high salaries, while China compensated their employers for the loss of their services. In a condition which was kept secret because of its echo of the concessions of the Qing to foreigners, the Soviet advisers were not subject to Chinese law.

Yet the trip was not such a cave-in as it has recently been painted. It has to be seen in the context of the evolving Cold War. The PRC was still very weak. Facing the huge task of national reconstruction and the threat from US-backed Taiwan, Beijing needed a strong friend at a time when it felt hemmed in. Fifty big plants may have been less than Mao wanted, but they were valuable none the less at a time when there was no prospect of aid from the West. Moscow would find it hard to exploit Manchuria and Xinjiang, while Beijing was able to define what constituted 'surplus' minerals.

All in all, Mao could return to Beijing reasonably satisfied. His visit marked his country's re-emergence on the world stage, albeit only the Communist half of it. He had forced Stalin to take the People's Republic seriously and not treat it as a vassal state. Four months later, the Chairman made his next move, gaining an advantage over the Big Brother in Moscow at the cost of hundreds of thousands of Chinese lives.

Defeat in 1945 had ended Japan's colonialization of Korea, and divided the peninsula along the 38th parallel between the Communist North, under Kim Il-sung, and the South, which came to be run by the right-wing Syngman Rhee. Soviet and American occupation troops withdrew in 1949. Kim was anxious to unify the country by force, building up his army with Soviet equipment and returned soldiers who had fought in the PLA. Knowing that he enjoyed military superiority over the South, whose army was little more than a police outfit, he lobbied Stalin for backing, one motive being to emulate, on a smaller scale, the Communist achievement in China.

The Kremlin said no, fearing that the North might not win, and concerned about the effect on the Far East balance of power were America to come to the aid of Seoul. 'If you should get kicked in the teeth, I shall not lift a finger,' Stalin warned Kim. 'You have to ask Mao for all the help.' Then, as border incidents multiplied, the US secretary of state, Dean Acheson, issued a definition of the US defence perimeter in Asia which did not mention Korea. That could only further encourage Kim, and be taken by Moscow as a signal. In the spring of 1950, it gave the green light. On 25 June 1950, the North invaded the South, setting off a three-year war which, technically, continues to this day since the truce reached in 1953 was not followed by a peace treaty.[27]

Using Soviet tanks and planes, the 135,000-strong North Korean army routed its opponent. After only three days, Seoul fell. Harry

Truman ordered the US navy and air force in Japan to halt the advance. The United Nations decided to intervene; the vote was made possible by a Soviet boycott at the world body to protest at the refusal to pass China's seat from the Nationalists to Beijing. American units poured in, along with troops from Nato allies. Air supremacy devastated the northern supply chains. Up to half Kim's men were lost. Implementing a high-risk plan drawn up by General Douglas MacArthur, the American supremo in East Asia, US troops landed at the port of Inchon, near Seoul; Kim had ignored a warning from China and had failed to lay mines. This put them behind the North Korean front line, and cut the enemy off from its home base. The question was whether Washington merely wanted to roll back the enemy, or would strike north to inflict punishment for the initial attack.

Beijing could only be mightily concerned. Though Mao's policy in the Korean War has been portrayed simply as a cynical drive to get Soviet aid for his country's military machine, wider and perfectly genuine factors were at work. If the Americans destroyed Kim's state, China would lose a large buffer zone, and a hostile, better-equipped power would sit on the Manchurian frontier. In 1894, China had faced the Japanese across the Yalu River; now it might be the USA. The growing US–Japan relationship threatened a hostile nexus in north-east Asia, joined by Chiang Kai-shek. The *People's Daily* depicted a coiled American snake seeking to wrap itself round China.

But, if it was to go to Kim's aid, the PLA would need Soviet air cover, and Mao was cagey about Stalin's plan to pit Beijing against the United States. Others in the PRC leadership had serious doubts about intervention. As Marshal Nie Rongzhen, who was, in effect, PLA chief of staff, recalled it, the dissenters 'argued that, having fought wars for so many years, we had an urgent need to recuperate and rebuild, it would be better not to fight this war as long as it was not absolutely necessary.'[28]

Subsequent accounts, which may have been affected by the politics of history, have it that Marshal Lin Biao was unwilling to assume command of an offensive. On 4 October 1950, Marshal Peng Dehuai, Mao's old companion-in-arms and now the commander in north-west China, agreed to take on the job after spending a night sleeping on the floor of his hotel in Beijing – the bed was too soft for him. America and its allies surrounded China, he reasoned to himself when he awoke. 'The tiger always eats people, and the time when it wants to eat depends on its appetite.' US imperialism, he felt, had to be opposed, preferably in a long conflict to wear it down.*[29]

Zhou Enlai went to Moscow to see Stalin. A warning was sent to Washington through the Indian government that the PLA would move if the Americans continued their advance. 'We must enter the war,' Mao told Zhou. The Kremlin promised the air cover the Chinese needed by December. That was enough. Chinese units surreptitiously crossed the Yalu to set up preliminary defence positions. One surrounded 2,400 men from the 8th Cavalry Regiment, killing or wounding 800 of them in fighting in temperatures 20 degrees below freezing. MacArthur took no heed of Beijing; indeed, he may have relished the prospect of confronting the Communist power in the east. His staff put the number of troops the PLA would deploy at only a quarter of the 300,000 men who joined the full advance.

Using force of numbers, surprise and battle skills from the civil war, the highly disciplined Chinese army drove through the thinly stretched 400-mile American front, and surged down to the 38th parallel. Peng wanted to halt there, but the Chairman aimed for total victory. Seoul changed hands for the third time, falling to Peng's troops in January. But the advance ran out of steam. Its supply lines were extremely extended, and the Americans hit back. Out-gunned, the Communists retreated from the southern capital, which, by now, was in ruins, its population reduced from 1.5 million to 200,000. The Chinese suffered appalling losses, including men frozen to death in the extreme winter conditions. Peng flew to Beijing to remonstrate with Mao, but was told he was fighting a long war. The Chairman cabled Stalin that he expected 300,000 Chinese casualties on top of the 100,000 already suffered. Such a price, he added, would be worth while to inflict hundreds of thousands of deaths on the Americans and force them to back down.[30]

Truman declared a state of national emergency. Chinese caricatures showed him holding his head in despair, a swastika in the centre of the seal of the United States. MacArthur challenged the president repeatedly, wanting to expand the war to attack China, envisaging use of nuclear weapons and talking to Chiang Kai-shek about how he might invade the mainland. Truman sacked him. The prospect of American forces

---

* The account by Peng came from the time after he had been purged by Mao, when he had no reason to show obeisance to the Chairman.

threatening the PRC evaporated. The chief of staff, Omar Bradley, told a Senate committee that this would be 'the wrong war in the wrong place at the wrong time and with the wrong enemy'.

The military confrontation in Korea became a stalemate on the 38th parallel. When Kim proposed ending the fighting, Mao rejected the idea. Beijing moved factories and workers to the rear area in Harbin. It was not until July 1953 that a ceasefire was reached. In all, China sent in some 3 million men, of whom around 400,000 probably died – Mao's forecast.* Despite the loss of life, Beijing benefited in receiving up-to-date Soviet weapons, aircraft factories and an air force that amounted to 3,000 planes by the end of the fighting.

Both parts of China gained from the war. Taiwan was now a core element in US Cold War strategy in East Asia. The Nationalists could be sure that Washington would veto any bid to switch China's seat on the UN Security Council to the PRC. If Beijing attacked the island, it would find itself at war with the USA. The KMT dictatorship was part of the bamboo curtain surrounding mainland China, reinforced after the San Francisco Treaty of 1951 formally ended the Second World War in the Pacific.† Though the KMT was an oppressive minority on the island, it drew on administrators, economists, teachers and scientists who had crossed the Strait in 1949. Only 4 per cent as big as the People's Republic, at 13,900 square miles, and with a population of around 8 million, Taiwan was small enough to be run efficiently by the Generalissimo's dictatorship in a way that had been impossible on the mainland, with the solid backing of the United States.

For the PRC, the ability of its army to stand up to the technologically superior Americans was seen as proof of enhanced status, taken by Mao as vindication of his belief in the power of the will and the force of the revolution. It was also important that the Communist soldiers who fought and died were Asian, not Soviet. Liberation movements still drew funding from Moscow, but Beijing became the beacon of the anti-imperialist cause, particularly after the death of Stalin in March 1953.

---

* The military casualties of other major combatants were: North Korea, 215,000 dead, 303,000 wounded and 100,000 missing or captured; South Korea 46,000 dead and more than 100,000 wounded; the US 36,000 dead and 103,000 wounded; Britain, 1,078 killed, 2,674 wounded and 1,060 missing or captured.
† It was signed by forty-nine nations but, for diplomacy's sake, by neither the PRC nor the ROC in Taiwan.

Among those who perished in Korea was Mao's eldest son, Anying, killed in an air raid on PLA headquarters, where he was an interpreter. Zhou Enlai and Mao's staff decided not to tell his father for fear of the effect of the news. So the Chairman only learned of it three months later, when Peng apologized for not having better protected the 28-year-old. Mao had a troubled relationship with his son, who had been abandoned by his parents at the age of nine and grew up in poverty in Shanghai before being reunited with his father and sent to study in the USSR. Thereafter, the Chairman took a greater interest in Anying than in his other offspring, and prompted him to volunteer for Korea.[31]

When Peng let slip the news of Anying's death, Mao blinked slowly and trembled. Twice, he reached for a cigarette but could not manage to take one from the pack on the tea table in front of him. His bodyguard helped him. The only sound in the room was the hissing of the smoke he exhaled through his teeth. His eyes were red and moist, whether from emotion or the smoke the bodyguard could not tell. 'In revolutionary war, you always pay a price,' the Chairman said eventually. 'Anying was one of thousands . . . you shouldn't take it as something special just because he was my son.'

China extended its territorial reach in 1950–51 by invading Tibet in the name of old claims of sovereignty. The PLA had little difficulty in clinching victory, helped by the defection of people in eastern Tibet who disliked rule from Lhasa. In May 1951, an Agreement on the Peaceful Liberation of Tibet was signed, promising autonomy and the retention of its traditional forms of government, religion and society for its population of around a million. The sixteen-year-old Dalai Lama visited Beijing and applied to join the Communist Party – unsuccessfully.

Though outward forms were maintained, the accord was administered by a Chinese-dominated military committee. Traditional ways were soon under assault from modernization in the shape of roads, electricity and construction projects. Large tracts of Tibetan land were ceded to neighbouring Chinese provinces. In the border areas, resentment led to revolts, some backed by the CIA. But the accord held in the remaining Tibetan territory of 470,000 square miles of mountainous terrain as the Chinese ruled through a mixture of force and the help of local agents, while the Dalai Lama did not throw his weight behind outright opposition.

To the north, Xinjiang also became an autonomous region stretching over 635,000 square miles. According to a census in 1953, 75 per cent of its population of 4 million were native Uyghurs. One was appointed to chair the regional People's Council, but a Han Long March veteran ran the Party and military apparatus. Beijing soon stepped up migration measures to increase the Han presence. Men were moved in to work on construction projects. A railway was laid from Gansu to the Xinjiang capital, Urumqi. A KMT army which had defected in Nanjing moved to the Far West where it was disarmed and made into a 'production brigade', which was also joined by demobbed PLA troops. The head of the Xinjiang Production and Construction Corps (Bingtuan), Wang Zeng, who has been described as perhaps the closest any CCP military man came to being a warlord, presided over a vast conglomerate that ran businesses, farms and prisons, while offering Beijing border security and keeping the Uyghurs down.[32]

With Tibet and Xinjiang, Beijing had a 1.1 million square mile security buffer in the north-west, containing mineral resources and potential for emigration from crowded parts of the Han core. In Inner Mongolia, to the east, the local leader, Ulanfu, trod a tightrope between retaining the confidence of the people and satisfying Beijing, above all by resisting Soviet overtures to the 455,000 square mile territory. The People's Republic had thus shown that it could match the colonial scope of the last dynasty, forgetting talk of independence for Inner Mongolia or better treatment for Tibetans in the interests of the new Chinese empire, while stepping up the Sinicization of Xinjiang.

Spurred on by the militancy bred by the war in Korea and the feeling that it no longer needed to compromise with domestic foes, the CCP replaced its relatively pragmatic early approach with a renewed drive for revolution across China. In 1950–51, a 'rectification' campaign was launched against people identified as class enemies, counter-revolutionaries and spies – 28,000 were estimated to have been killed in Guangdong, alone. This was followed by two other offensives – the Three Antis (against corruption, waste and bureaucracy) and the Five Antis (which added in bribery and tax evasion). The targets were irreproachable; the snag was that they were often chosen on political grounds. A Thought Reform Campaign was mounted to bring intellectuals into line, and turn them from bourgeois imperialists into proletarians. Millions were caught up in the first of the rolling mass campaigns that would mark Maoist China. 'Take care to strike with sureness, precision and energy,' the leader instructed.

Neighbours were encouraged to inform on one another, children to denounce parents, workers to spy on colleagues. Party officials compiled dossiers on anybody who came to their attention; the contents determined whether the subjects got jobs, housing, welfare and a pension. To maintain the drive, enemies had to be found everywhere, all the time. Nobody knew when he or she might be classed as an imperialist lackey, a landlord, a bourgeois backslider, or a counter-revolutionary capitalist-roader. Accusations were enough; proof would be obtained through confessions. Self-criticism became an essential element in the system. The CCP held a monopoly on the truth, which its master could alter at will.[33]

In April 1951, the Ministry of Public Security distributed a manual advising 'How to Hold an Accusation Meeting'. Led by Party officials, the people would deliver their verdicts; the role of the courts was simply to implement them. Any notion of judicial independence or the rule of law was foreign to the New Democracy of the People's Republic.

In Xi'an, a crowd of businessmen was forced to attend meetings at which they confessed to 25,000 economic crimes – eight men who declined to take part were punished separately. In Shanghai, 99 per cent of businessmen were held to be guilty of at least one of the 'five poisons' – bribery, tax evasion, theft of state property, cheating on government contracts and stealing information for speculation. More than 3,000 people were arrested in the city in April 1951 and herded into the one-time dog racing stadium, the Canidrome, where American jazz bands had played in the 1930s. On 1 May, 500 executions were announced. Among those caught were Green Gang leaders, including the one-time godfather, Pockmarked Huang, who confessed his crimes under questioning and was shot. A few former KMT officials who could be useful to the new regime, such as a former deputy to police chief Dai Li, saved themselves by recanting and writing memoirs denouncing Nationalist rule.[34]

In Hangzhou, suspects were taken to a sanitorium on a hillside, where a slogan hung at the entrance reading 'Without a confession, no tiger can leave.' Those who submitted were issued with blue tunics and trousers as they lined up to admit their sins at the Department of Industry and Commerce. Each confession was met with a demand for more during morning-to-night interrogations. Residents' Committees denounced 'dirty rich people'. 'Smash the fierce onslaught of the bourgeoisie' became a slogan – as if the middle class had the means to stage an assault. The targets saw this simply as yet another attempt to wring money from them, and those who could decamped to Hong Kong or South-East Asia or further afield.[35]

The old spectre of provincial power holders going their own way revived as the Party and government worried about the emergence of 'independent kingdoms'. Reports told of local bureaucrats, from village chiefs upwards, treating their units as personal fiefdoms. Mao recognized the danger. 'In all our institutions, be they Party, government or military, as long as there is a lot of money and property involved, there will be a large number of big "tigers",' he wrote.[36]

At the grassroots level, the campaigns to instil discipline were expanded to political sessions through which the CCP's messages were spread to workers. In Tianjin, half the city's employees attended them. To step up its influence over people's lives, the regime began to tighten its grip on where Chinese lived and worked. In July 1951, Regulations Governing the Urban Population required that all city dwellers register with branches of the Public Security Bureau, starting a process that would lead to the removal of any right to free movement. In August 1952, another decree restricted peasant emigration to cities. In Shanghai, more than 300,000 people were sent back to Anhui, and the Party newspaper called for the population to be halved to 3 million.[37]

The *danwei* work unit system affected all areas of life, starting with housing and welfare and eventually leading to power over the right of couples to have children. Horizontal society was to be eliminated. Everything was to be regulated on a pattern laid down from the top, through the CCP's representatives, who might interpret the dictates from above with draconian orthodoxy – or as best fitted their own purposes. Nothing was to escape the Party's control.

Land reform, which had been launched in 1949, became more rigorous in a newly radicalized initiative. More than 100 million acres were redistributed. The crop area held by poor peasants doubled to 47 per cent. As with the moves against private businessmen, the campaign was more than economic, aiming to wipe out the remnants of the past that had survived the revolution and to achieve maximum social change. The landlord class, which had been a KMT bastion, was to be isolated and exposed to the people's justice.[38]

The main instrument was the class struggle. Village dwellers were put into more than a dozen classifications ranging from landlords through rich, middle and poor peasants to labourers, peddlers and vagabonds. 'Black' class enemies became non-people, excluded from the bonds of kinship that still ruled in villages. Rankings could be arbitrary – a teacher who rented out the little land he happened to own could be put down as a 'landlord' or 'feudal tail' rather than in the safer group of 'professionals'. The pressure of getting a politically correct ranking was heightened by the way in which children inherited their status from their fathers, perpetuating class membership through succeeding generations – if the son of a dispossessed landowner married the daughter of a peddler, their offspring would be landlords, however poor they might be. Some people were so anxious to avoid any danger of being put down into that category that they gave away their smallholdings.[39]

Again, tension was evident between the top and the base. A young southerner, who had organized the overthrow of landlords but then found himself marginalized by 'work teams' from outside, recalled: 'They told us that they could not trust us. They declared that we were not to participate in any of the activities of land reform and that we should stay at home and keep out of things. They even required us to ask permission if we wished to leave our homes. In some other villages, the local officials were actually locked in their houses.'[40]

Those targeted for attack were paraded on improvised stages, their heads bowed while peasants crowded around, and were encouraged by CCP work teams to deliver denunciations. Members of the crowd might mount the platform and beat the accused. Given the oppression they had suffered, there was no absence of charges – in a case cited by the historians of rural Guangdong, Sulamith and Jack Potter, five landlords hauled up in front of a village meeting were accused of murder, extortion, loan sharking, rape, property seizure and swindling. Two were shot right away, the others imprisoned.[41]

After the struggle meetings, the property of those found guilty, along with their animals and farm implements, was confiscated and distributed to the poor. Their homes might be ransacked. Temples and ancestral homes were taken over as housing. In this reordering of the rural world, peasants whose families had lived on, or below, the margin for generations got their revenge on those who had oppressed them, or had simply been better off. No quarter could be expected as the thirst for social justice running back to the Taiping and Nien revolts was given full rein by the new masters. There was no need to grasp Marxism–Leninism–Mao Zedong Thought to join in the settling of scores. 'All the appropriate emotions – envy, hatred, resentment and greed – were already present', as the Potters noted.

The exact number of people who died in the countryside and the cities during this period will never be known; estimates run from 800,000 to 5 million. The minister of finance, Bo Yibo, wrote of more than 2 million being eliminated. Mao and the public security minister, Luo Ruiqing, each mentioned a figure of around 800,000.

The toughening up heightened the position of Luo's ministry. Mao's original security and terror aide, Kang Sheng, had been sidelined in 1949 as a scapegoat for excesses in Yenan, and was sent off to be governor of Shandong – Mao let him know that he needed to watch himself. In his place, Luo directed an increasingly fearsome machine, which remains a key pillar of the regime to this day.[42]

As well as those killed on the spot, millions were deported to prison camps set up under the name of *Laogai* – 'Reform through Labour'. These drew on Soviet experience and Luo explained that 'forcing offenders to work and be productive can only prevent them from indulging in their counter-revolutionary activities.' Before long the system contained perhaps 15 million people; the fruits of prisoners' work made it self-financing.

As the mass campaigns forged ahead and the war in Korea was accompanied by increasingly strident attacks on America, the regime inevitably turned its attention to foreigners. Companies were taken over, starting with Shell Oil in April 1951. Chinese associations which had links with foreigners were investigated. Westerners were called in for interviews by the police at which they were asked about their friends, their books, their radio sets and what they thought of Marxism. An Italian and a Japanese were put on trial accused of plotting to assassinate Mao with a mortar bomb as he spoke on National Day on 1 October 1950. They were said to be working for the head of the wartime Dixie Mission to Yenan, Colonel David Barrett. The two men were executed after being driven through the capital standing up in jeeps. Zhou Enlai later apologized to Barrett.

In Shanghai, a 58-year-old American lawyer, Robert Bryan, was hustled from his home and taken to the old Ward Road Jail, where he was locked up in a sixth-floor cell lined with cork so that prisoners could not kill themselves by smashing their heads against the walls. Accused of spying, he was kept in solitary confinement for five months with minimal food; when he finally was given a court hearing, he was made to appear clad only in his underwear, which had not been washed since his arrest. After that, he was held as an ordinary prisoner, and put under mounting pressure to confess to spying. When he refused to do this, he was held down and given an injection after which, he said, he passed out. The next day, he was shown a confession with his signature at the bottom. After two more months in solitary, he was taken to the border with Hong Kong and released.[43]

In due course, nearly all the foreigners were told to leave China, or went of their own accord. Some were detained on charges of being US agents before being deported. As they left, they were subject to intensive checks; police probed into the sandwiches of a group of missionaries to make sure nothing was hidden there. By 1952, the new regime had virtually cleared China of the barbarians. Exactly 110 years after the initial concessions by the Qing, only a few true believers and a scattering of diplomats and representatives of other Communist powers were left.[44]

19
Plots and Plans

In this changing context, the first power struggle since 1949 broke out in the leadership as the ambitious Communist boss in Manchuria, Gao Gang, launched a power bid and became the first of a string of the Chairman's protégés to find just how uncertain his support could be.

Born at the start of the century, Gao had first come into contact with Mao in 1935, when the Long Marchers reached a small base he was running in Shaanxi. He established himself in the CCP's north-eastern bastion during the civil war and went on to run it after victory. Manchuria was a key economic region for the new regime; it contributed half the nation's industrial output, while its proximity to the USSR, plus the Soviet presence in its ports and railways, meant it absorbed the techniques of the Communist Big Brother. Gao's enemies thought him too close to Moscow, and speculated that he was trying to enlist its help to carve out an independent barony in the former stamping ground of the Old and Young Marshals. But the general view was expressed by Sun Yat-sen's widow after a visit to the area – 'Our north-east is leading the way.'[1]

Appointed chairman of the Central Planning Commission in 1952 as well as chairman of the Executive Committee for the north-east, Gao was promoted to the Politburo in 1953 as its sixth-ranking member. According to the Chairman's doctor, apart from his admiration for the younger man's efficiency, the leader marvelled at Gao's virility – he was said to have had 100 mistresses.[2]

Gao's ascent coincided with the application to China of planning, USSR-style. 'The Soviet road is the road all humanity will eventually take,' declared Liu Shaoqi. 'To bypass this road is impossible.' In September 1953, a Five-Year Plan was drawn up, though it was not formally endorsed until 1955. A state statistical bureau was established. A drawing in the *People's Daily* showed Mao examining maps, pencil in hand;

the wall behind him was covered with pictures of steel mills and hydro-electric plants.[3]

Almost 700 major plants were to be built, 156 of them supplied by the Soviet Union, including twenty-four electric power stations, iron and steel mills, petrochemical plants and oil refineries. The railways were to be greatly expanded, and the military machine modernized. Since the coastal cities were suspect for their Nationalist-era past and could be vulnerable to attack from Taiwan, three quarters of the projects were located in the interior in cities such as Chongqing, Wuhan, Lanzhou and Xi'an. Twenty-eight thousand Chinese went for training in the Soviet Union. Eleven thousand Soviet experts travelled to China, most involved in industry, but some advising on education and urban planning. The aid was paid for from peasant savings and requisitioned food.[4]

In this context, Gao flourished, and Mao took him under his wing, grumbling to the newcomer that Liu Shaoqi and Zhou Enlai were not moving far or fast enough. When their ally, the finance minister, Bo Yibo, proposed a new tax system, Gao and Mao attacked him as a 'right opportunist' for giving private firms equality of treatment with state enterprises. Bo offered self-criticism, which was deemed insufficient.[5]

The Chairman then moderated his attack, following his habitual tactic of keeping those around him uncertain as to his true wishes. Deng Xiaoping, secretary-general of the Central Committee, was called in to attack Bo's policies but cleared him of representing an opposition line. Criticism of Zhou was also softened to avoid impeding government work. The Chairman declared Liu selfless and honest. Mao's divide-and-rule tactics were nothing new, but they had a particular dimension at this point. Stalin's death had just come as a reminder of the mortality of even the most eminent Communist chieftains. Mao was in poor health. Gao needed to move fast.[6]

First, he gained the backing of the head of the CCP Organization Department, Rao Shushi, who had run the Party in eastern China before being promoted to Beijing. Then he sought to enlist military commanders from the civil war, suggesting to them that they did not enjoy sufficient authority in the new regime compared with Liu's associates. He also made contact with the powerful Party boss in Guangdong, and offered the economist Chen Yun the post of vice-chairman. But his scheme went awry after he talked to Deng Xiaoping, who told Mao of the extent of the plotting.

Since this threatened a Party split, Mao dressed him down, before leaving the capital at the end of December 1953 for a rest in Hangzhou, where he settled into a luxurious mansion beside the famous West Lake. With his tacit approval, Liu and Zhou launched a counter-attack. At one meeting, Gao was said to have threatened to shoot himself on the spot if he was condemned. He asked to see the Chairman, who refused to receive him. Gao and Rao were purged. Sent to prison, Gao committed suicide by taking an overdose of sleeping pills – according to Mao's doctor, the Chairman recounted that his one-time protégé had had sex twice on the night he killed himself, adding, 'Can you imagine such lust?' Rao was imprisoned and lived on till 1975.[*7]

Two civil war commanders Gao had unsuccessfully approached, Peng Dehuai and Lin Biao, were promoted, the first becoming defence minister in 1954 while the second joined the Politburo the next year. Deng took over the Organization Department, and, in 1955, advanced to the Politburo. The political influence of the north-east was reduced.

The outcome of the Gao Gang affair strengthened Mao's authority. Liu and Zhou could only be reminded that their positions depended on his favour. Bo Yibo was kept on, but after feeling the heat of recrimination. From time to time, Mao might choose to take a back seat and let others handle Party and state business. But when he wanted to assert himself, nobody could resist him. For the last three decades of his life, each directive he issued was regarded as gospel, to be picked up, and often exaggerated, by officials down the line – except for a time after the flop of his economic policy and the huge famine at the start of the 1960s, when even he had to beat a retreat. The idea that Mao was ever seriously constrained once he had made up his mind holds little water. The ultimate proof of his dominance was how many things he got extremely and tragically wrong on a massive scale observable to all – and how he survived with the mantle of the great leader unchallenged by the tough figures around him, standing squarely in the line of all-powerful first emperors. There was debate in the Politburo, but unanimity was required once a decision had been reached, and what has been called the 'bandwagon' tendency generally meant that leading figures preferred to fall in with the Chairman.[8]

The leader's status was buttressed by secrecy, isolation and control.

* In 2008, Gao's widow petitioned for his rehabilitation: there was no response.

His trips out of Beijing were surrounded by extreme security; railway lines were cleared of other trains and the air of other planes. Apart from stage-managed encounters with carefully selected members of the public, he met only CCP leaders and the chiefs of national and provincial governments, his staff and bodyguards – and the young women brought to his bed.

Below him, the contours of the new state were being filled out. In Leninist form, the Communist Party was more powerful than the government. Though the Central Committee was enshrined as the Party's leading body, the real power centre was the Politburo and its Standing Committee, which made the decisions on major issues; its members might also hold posts in the government. The Military Affairs Commission (MAC) controlled the armed forces, ensuring their loyalty and subservience to political decisions. Party congresses, plenums and work sessions set and confirmed policy; but long periods might elapse between their meetings, during which Mao could act unilaterally or in consort with a few associates.

Liu Shaoqi was number two in the regime as deputy chairman of the CCP and number two in the Politburo. Born in 1898 into a well-off farming family in Hunan, he was an early member of the Communist Party and was trained in the USSR, getting the theoretical grounding in Marxism–Leninism which Mao lacked. He made his mark as a labour organizer in the 1920s, masterminding a successful wage strike at a big coal mine in Jiangxi that ranked as one of the big union successes of the warlord era. Political commissar of the New Fourth Army when it was relaunched after the Nationalist attack, Liu organized Communist operations in Kuomintang 'white arcas', gaining a strong reputation as an administrator. Patient and painstaking, frugal and reserved, Liu was ballast for the mercurial Mao, described by the historian Roderick McFarquhar as 'truly grey in his eminence'.[9]

Even if he disagreed with the leader's more wilful policies, Liu's supreme loyalty to the CCP always kept him in line. He had taken a prime role in developing the Mao cult in the 1940s, proclaiming the Chairman to be 'the people's Great Saviour' who 'penetrates everywhere'. But he also told a conference in 1947: 'There is no perfect leader in the world ... If there is one, he only pretends to be such, just like inserting onions in a pig's nose to make it look like an elephant.' Five years younger than Mao, Liu was the obvious dauphin. His boss might allow criticism of him, as during the Gao Gang saga, and Madame Mao might resent the better-connected Mrs Liu; but the Chairman knew he needed his lieutenant to keep the show on the road.[10]

Prime minister, foreign minister and number three in the Politburo, Zhou Enlai was well liked at home and was the man of whom the world saw most. He combined an enormous capacity for work and mastery of the administrative machine with an ability to absorb criticism from his master and, on occasion, to hold two contradictory ideas in his head, balancing his essentially governmental role with the supremacy of the Maoist party. His suave manner led foreigners to imagine that he represented a more moderate strain of Chinese Communism. But Zhou would always follow Mao's orders.

His subservience to the Chairman may have been, in part, because he knew he was vulnerable to attack for his membership of the anti-Mao leadership group in the Jiangxi base, but it may also have been a case of a gifted but natural follower finding his lodestar. Though often seen as the more humane face of Chinese communism, he had a long history of condoning, or organizing, violence from his time in charge of the assassination squads in the 1920s to his chairing of the Central Core Examination Group, which questioned and tortured high-ranking cadres. In 1955, Beijing learned that a KMT ring in Hong Kong was plotting to put a bomb on a plane in which he was due to fly from the colony to Indonesia. Zhou took another route, but let the plane take off with a dozen minor Chinese officials and journalists on board. It blew up in flight, killing them all. That served two purposes – discrediting the KMT and enabling Beijing to put pressure on the British to expel Taipei's agents. The lives did not count.

The one-time warlord soldier Zhu De, who ranked fourth in the Politburo, commanded the PLA as well as being vice-chairman of the CCP. As defence minister, Peng Dehuai, a straightforward man who cherished his peasant roots, aimed to make the army more professional. His fellow marshal, Lin Biao, was more complex, an extreme neurotic who was frequently ill. Another Long March commander, the thick-set Chen Yi, became mayor of Shanghai and then a vice-premier.

The main economic figure, Chen Yun, who ranked immediately below Zhu De in the Party, was unusual among the leadership in coming from a proletarian background – he had been a typesetter in Shanghai. Having followed a quiet route to the top, he advocated a more organized approach than that favoured by the Chairman. The boss of the Beijing Party and municipality, Peng Zhen was a tough operator whose control of the capital was such that Mao would remark that no needle could penetrate his machine, no drop of water find its way through. The diminutive, bullet-headed Deng Xiaoping would become the second most important figure in China's post-1949 history after Mao, but, in the 1950s, he was still on the rise through the senior CCP apparatus. In 1955, Mao was sixty-two, Liu, Zhou and Peng Dehuai fifty-seven, Zhu De sixty-nine, Peng Zhen fifty-three, Chen and Deng fifty and fifty-one respectively, and Lin Biao forty-eight.

Under this leadership, the contours of the new state were established. A fresh constitution was rubber-stamped by the first session of the new legislature, the National People's Congress. It provided for a single candidate for each seat in elections, which, as one historian puts it, thus became 'a rite of adhesion to the regime'.[11]

A new currency was issued. The written language was simplified by the dropping of 1,055 characters – 515 were accepted as standard forms and 196 were added. Reading was to be from left to right. The Committee for the Reform of the Spoken Language made the Beijing dialect compulsory for official verbal communications (though the head of the committee, Chen Yi, had a broad Sichuan accent, which meant that people from the capital had great trouble understanding him).[12]

Despite being deprived of representation at the United Nations, China stepped out on to the global scene. Not wanting to see another Korean War on its southern border, the PRC encouraged North Vietnam to agree to a division of the country at the end of the French Indochina war. Beijing forged links with non-Communist governments such as India's, which turned a blind eye to the annexation of Tibet. It threw its weight behind the movement of non-aligned countries; Zhou Enlai starred at summits such as that in Bandung in 1955. The sharp hostility of the Eisenhower administration only helped – when Dulles refused to shake Zhou's hand at the Geneva conference on Indochina, China's stock could only rise among those who resented Washington's power. Having established its credentials in Korea by going to war with the Americans, China could claim to offer a non-Soviet path to revolution, incarnated by Mao. One of his great achievements, claimed Liu Shaoqi, had been to 'change Marxism from a European to an Asiatic form'.[13]

Taiwan remained a sore, Zhou saying that the American presence off the Fujian coast constituted a threat to international stability. Beijing launched periodic attacks from the mainland on tiny Nationalist-held islands close to the Chinese coast, but this did not stop the KMT constructing a new society in exile. In contrast to their failure to reform agriculture in China, the Nationalists organized the distribution of plots to owner-occupiers. American aid boosted the economy. Savings rates were high, and cheap labour fuelled growing exports.

Though the protection of the Seventh Fleet meant that the PRC could not envisage an invasion of the 'renegade province', Mao turned Taiwan to his advantage in a different way. He had failed initially to get the new Soviet leader, Nikita Khrushchev, to agree to provide China with atomic technology. But this changed when a protracted flare-up across the Taiwan Strait led Eisenhower to tell reporters that the US would not rule out using the bomb 'like a bullet or anything else'. If hostilities broke out in which America threatened to use its atomic arsenal against China, Moscow would have to throw its nuclear force into the balance on Beijing's side, or be discredited. Much safer, in the logic of deterrence, to let China have its own force with which it could stand up to Washington.

In a series of escalating agreements, Moscow undertook to provide the PRC with the equipment and knowledge to go nuclear, though the programme was a long-term project from which it could withdraw when it wished. Mao had dismissed the nuclear powers as paper tigers and would express insouciance about a new war that might kill half the world's people, but would eliminate imperialism and turn the globe socialist. Still, possession of the ultimate weapon would be a sign of how far the People's Republic had advanced. 'We must control the earth!' the Chairman declared.[14]

The results of the Five-Year Plan were trumpeted as proof of national revival. Official statistics showed gross domestic product rising strongly, along with industrial output. Monopolies were declared for agricultural products, and the government increased its stakes in private companies, which became increasingly difficult for the owners to run. Often entrepreneurs were only too ready to sell out after their recent experiences. In Shanghai, proprietors of textile mills paraded to beg to be taken over.

Soviet help enabled China to leap-frog the preparatory stage of development, but it was building on a very backward base, meaning that break-neck industrial growth took place without any real measures to ensure its sustainability. At the same time, the leader's purist vision of revolution was under threat as economic bureaucracy swelled and a managerial class emerged. Indeed, growth, in itself, contained an inevitable menace. As Mao would tell a student delegation in 1957:

Our China has two things, one, poverty, the other ignorance . . . the Chinese are illiterate. The standard of living is very low; the educational level is very low. Our revolution relies on these two things. If China becomes prosperous, just like the standard of living in the Western world, then [people] will not want revolution.

There were other, more immediate, difficulties. The inflexible application of central planning took no account of regional differences. Production priorities were dictated by national demands that did not help local needs. Between big state plants and small handicraft enterprises, there was little or nothing. Though the countryside housed 84 per cent of the population, 88 per cent of state capital investment was allocated to heavy industry in urban areas. The question arose as to whether the countryside could feed the industrial cities if their population went on expanding at 7 per cent a year. As the state grain monopoly diverted supplies, procurement quotas rose, rural reserves fell and, in places, hunger spread among the farmers.[15]

'The situation in the countryside is highly tense,' the Central Committee and State Council noted in March 1955, as mass riots broke out. In a typical fertile county in Jiangsu province, the farmers were left with only 35 per cent of their output. They reacted by under-reporting the harvest, trying to bribe officials, getting their womenfolk to sleep with village leaders to gain favoured treatment – and then began to attack cadres physically. In response, procurement was cut by a third.[16]

Mao worried that the distribution of land was creating a new ownership class, which would show what he called 'spontaneous tendencies towards capitalism'. So cadres were sent in to break the traditions of clan, lineage and local markets. Farmers were encouraged to pool labour. Agricultural Producers' Co-operatives (APCs) were introduced, to which they were obliged to contribute land, labour, tools and animals. The Chairman argued that larger units would automatically lead to greater mechanization and higher output (in line with conventional Communist orthodoxy), while Liu Shaoqi said machines should be introduced first to make the new units more attractive. As usual, the Chairman prevailed.

The co-operatives did not tempt the better-off, including those who had gained property from land reform and were loath to give it away. When farmers who had joined co-operatives were offered a chance to leave them in 1955, Beijing was unpleasantly surprised by the number who took the opportunity. Typically, Mao saw the answer in a more radical approach, hailing the advent of 'the high tide of Socialism'. 'Some of our comrades are tottering along like women with bound feet, always complaining "You're going too fast",' he declared in a speech in July 1955. As a result, China embarked on a headlong drive to bring farmers together in huge collective state-run units, cadres outdoing one another to shine by implementing the Chairman's wishes. New agricultural methods being introduced elsewhere in Asia were ignored; the concentration of numbers under the direction of the CCP was thought to be enough. The people's will, as epitomized by the leader, would overcome.[17]

By the spring of 1956, 92 per cent of peasant households had been collectivized, compared to 14 per cent the previous spring. Another change followed, by which farmers were paid only for the work they did, not for the assets which had been taken over. Land and equipment distributed in the earlier reform programmes thus became government property. In reaction, tens of millions left the countryside, boosting the urban population, and further increasing the strain on rural areas to feed it.

But there was no let-up in the ideologically led policies, which removed incentives, and disrupted marketing and distribution of food. Ignorant cadres set impossibly high targets with orders which they expected to be blindly followed whatever the outcome. In Henan, they decreed that cotton should be planted in wheatfields and vice versa. In one collective in Guangdong, farmers were told to reduce the pattern of plots in which they had always sowed rice; output halved.[18]

For the CCP, the countryside was still a reservoir to be pumped dry to feed the industrial workers, and provide government revenue. In 1952, the state directed 4 per cent of its expenditure to agriculture while drawing 23 per cent of tax revenue from it. Capital investment in farming accounted for only 8 per cent of the total.[19]

Hostility to collectivization led to physical attacks on officials. In

The leader and the lieutenant: Mao Zedong (*right*) and Zhou Enlai (*left*) in the Yenan base in Shanxi province in 1937 after the Long March.

Rape of Nanjing: Japanese soldiers compete to behead the most Chinese.

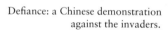

Defiance: a Chinese demonstration against the invaders.

New capital: the steps up from the Yangzi in Chongqing were renowned for their filth and slipperiness.

Allies at war: Chiang Kai-shek, Madame Chiang and US adviser Joseph 'Vinegar Joe' Stilwell.

Chongqing in flames: the defenceless wartime capital was subjected to intense
Japanese bombing.

Summitry: the Chiangs meet Franklin Roosevelt and Winston Churchill in Cairo at the end of 1943.

The three sisters: Ailing, Meiling and Qingling Soong (*in black*) meet Nationalist women soldiers.

Civil War – victims and survivors: (*top left*) Communist women prisoners; (*top right*) the Model Governor shows off his poison pills; (*bottom*) head of decapitated Communist stuck on a wall after his capture outside Shanghai.

Fighting and fleeing: (*top*) Nationalist troops prepare for battle in the civil war in Manchuria; (*bottom*) refugees crowd on to a train leaving Shanghai.

Loser and winner: (*top*) Chiang Kai-shek as the end approached for the Nationalist regime; (*bottom*) Mao Zedong proclaims the People's Republic in October 1949.

Life goes on: despite the scale of the fighting, many parts of China went on with their traditional existence as regime change unfolded.

some places, CCP leaders recognized that the peasants were being driven too hard. The CCP secretary for Henan compared them to beasts of burden. 'Human beings are harnessed in the field,' he wrote. 'Girls and women pull ploughs and harrows, with their wombs hanging down. Co-operation is transformed into exploitation of human strength.' There was also criticism from officials in Guangdong, Guangxi and Yunnan. But the centre remained unyielding.[20]

The stress on increasing farm production led to a fall in rural light industries as workers were kept on the fields. One slogan ran: 'What you plant, you eat. If you plant grain, you eat grain. If you bake bricks, you eat bricks.' So brick production dropped, and construction suffered. Unrealistic pricing policies were adopted as old market systems were disrupted. Peasant incomes fell. Some members of collectives had to borrow money to pay for anything other than the essentials provided for them.[21]

None of this caused Mao second thoughts. Though in a rare moment of reality he admitted that there had been 'black clouds all over the sky' in the first half of 1955, he said he thought that, overall, the hundreds of millions in the countryside had no cause for complaint. Soon, he went on, there would be no more poor peasants. The state and the collective farm system would solve the age-old problems of the rural world.

At the start of 1956, the Chairman forecast that the revolution could be completed within three years under the new slogan of 'more, faster, better and more economically'. Work began on an ambitious Twelve-Year Agricultural Programme while 'socialist transformation' was speeded up in industry. The city of Beijing led the way in what became known as the first 'Small Leap Forward' with a sudden spurt in the programme to turn private firms into joint state–private enterprises – that is, nationalization. The Chairman, Liu and Zhou appeared at a celebratory rally in Tiananmen Square with the capital's CCP boss, Peng Zhen.

The Small Leap failed. Food shortages grew, exacerbated by poor distribution and resistance to the collectives, plus the need to send food to the USSR to pay for imported machinery. Factories found it impossible to meet targets. Construction work slowed down. Labour tension rose. Wage reform brought some relief, but the cost of collectivization and the imbalance between the urban and rural worlds were arousing concerns among senior members of the Politburo. Liu and Zhou made their worries known, to which the Chairman reacted by wondering if the problem was that the revolution was not being pursued fast enough.[22]

There was also cause for concern from abroad. February 1956 brought the bombshell from Moscow of Khrushchev's speech denouncing Stalin for his crimes and the cult of personality. This contained obvious implications for Mao. Then came the rising of Poles and Hungarians in the summer and autumn. Communism faced a crisis. Putting great store by national independence, Beijing initially sympathized with the Poles. But events in Hungary, with the prospect that it might quit the Warsaw Pact and ally with the West, convinced Mao of the dangers of what was going on. So the PRC backed the suppression of the revolt, blaming the unrest on weak control from the Kremlin. But Mao also saw the need to give a fresh impetus to his own revolution. In search of this, he launched an extraordinary response to the challenges the CCP was facing, showing his own naiveté – and then his utter ruthlessness.

'Let a hundred flowers bloom,' the Chairman declared in May 1956. 'Let a hundred schools of thought contend.' Allowing disparate voices to make themselves heard could, he reasoned, resolve the contradictions in China, remove the roadblocks of his enemies of 'bureaucratism' and 'sectarianism', and get the CCP back on track. Later, this would be seen as a trap to get dissidents and critics to put their heads above the parapets so that they could be scythed down. Mao's post-facto rationalization would buttress that interpretation. Such reasoning, accompanied by falsification of a key speech, was necessary to maintain the myth of his infallibility. At the time, it is quite probable that the Chairman believed what he was saying. The iconoclasm behind what became known as the Hundred Flowers campaign was very much in line with the May Fourth movement and the philosophical tradition from which it stemmed. But how things turned out once he was forced to face reality would bring tragedy for hundreds of thousands.

The new line was quickly picked up in some places – in Henan, the editors of the provincial daily newspaper said they would no longer simply parrot the Party. Liu Shaoqi told journalists to make their products more interesting to readers. The Party journal, the *People's Daily*, doubled its size to eight pages, and announced that it would cover both the socialist and capitalist worlds, running items 'whether they make pleasant reading or not'. The head of the official Xinhua news agency went to London and Paris to study the operations of wire services there. His organization launched a newspaper, *Reference Information*, to reprint material from foreign sources. A young writer called Wang Meng published a short story which satirized the cynicism, bureaucratism and demoralization of middle-ranking officials. Moves were launched to strengthen respect for legal forms; Liu told a senior member of the Prosecutor's Office that it was 'necessary to protect the lawful rights of counter-revolutionaries'.[23]

Still, for the Party machine as a whole, Mao's speech came as a big shock. Only recently, the Chairman had launched a vicious campaign against a writer, Hu Feng, who had dared to step out of line, tell the truth about conditions in the country and call for freedom of debate; now Mao seemed to be encouraging the likes of Hu. The dislocation was such that, for once, the leader's word did not command immediate obedience. Confusion grew after the Chairman reacted to an attack on Wang Meng from four PLA writers in the *People's Daily* by defending the author. Mao estimated that 90 per cent of CCP members opposed his 'open-door rectification', and went as far as to tell a meeting of the Shanghai CCP bureau, 'I have no base.' Far from being deterred by this, he saw it as a sign of the need to step up the attack.

He had other reasons for concern. The economic growth campaign was running into major trouble. Spending increased too fast. In industry, the concentration on boosting output brought a decline in the quality of goods and a rise in industrial accidents. In the countryside, officials were pushing collectivization too rapidly, and imposing unsuitable equipment – heavy, double-wheeled ploughs were deployed in paddy fields, where they sank into the ground. There were bad floods in Manchuria and central China, where 14 million people were affected in Hunan and production of grain and cotton fell by 40 per cent.[24]

Led by Zhou Enlai and Chen Yun, senior economists insisted on the need to apply the brakes. A *People's Daily* editorial vetted by Liu Shaoqi put the problems down to officials having 'attempted to do all things overnight'. This was not to the taste of the leader, who wrote on the draft 'I won't read this'. But the editorial was still published, and 700,000 double-wheeled ploughs were scrapped as the Twelve-Year Agricultural Programme was abandoned.

There was a further setback for the Chairman at the Eighth CCP Congress, held in September 1956. The first such gathering for eleven years, it reaffirmed that China was ruled by a collective leadership, and adopted a proposal from Marshal Peng Dehuai, approved by Liu Shaoqi, to omit the reference to Mao Zedong Thought as the totem for the Party and nation which had been carried over from the wartime years and included in the 1945 constitution. The Great Helmsman went along; indeed, he had suggested it himself. But when the time came to put it into practice, he may not have been so pleased.

In addition, a resolution to develop industries in coastal regions 'positively and fully' ran counter to his stress on inland areas. There was also fresh talk about developing a two-line structure at the top of the leadership which would see Mao stepping back to the second tier in a largely honorary role. While he had mooted this in the first place in the early 1950s, it was the kind of idea that was unlikely to be attractive to him when it threatened to become a reality.[25]

Still, there were positive aspects for the leader. A bid led by Peng Dehuai to reverse the Chairman's insistence that industrial spending should take precedence over military expenditure failed. In the new ranking in the enlarged Politburo, Peng was demoted from eleventh to fourteenth place while Deng Xiaoping soared from fifteenth to sixth place and Lin Biao rose from twelfth to seventh. Peng was probably blamed for mistakes during his command in Korea and, possibly, by the Chairman, for the death of his son there. There was a lingering suspicion that he had listened rather too attentively to Gao Gang. The old soldier clearly sensed that his day was fading. 'I am old, out of favour and of no importance to the Chairman,' he wrote. 'I can return home to till the land. If I am disliked, let it be.'[26]

Overall, however, the congress could only be depressing for Mao, who withdrew from public life for three months. Then, at the beginning of February 1957, he was briefed by Zhou Enlai, who had visited Poland and Hungary, and advised that the CCP could only benefit by confronting its mistakes, as he said the Europeans were doing. In two speeches, Mao reiterated 'a policy of letting a hundred schools contend in literature and the arts and in academic thought and so on, and how to treat shortcomings in literature and art'. Distinguishing 'contradictions among the people from contradictions between ourselves and the enemy', he stressed the need to increase cohesion through a process he defined as 'unity–criticism–unity' – in other words, the launching of open debate would end up in greater unity. He also insisted on 'a new battle – the battle against nature – to develop our economy and culture, enable all our people to go through this transition period in a fairly smooth way, make our new system secure, and build up our new state'.[27]

The country's difficulties could not be blamed simply on counter-revolutionaries wanting to emulate what had happened in Hungary, he told a student delegation. To resolve its contradictions, he added, China required what became known as 'blooming and contending'. That would sweep away the institutional barriers to revolution in a new and softer way than the campaigns of the past. Mao's stance was enough to produce a steady swelling of criticism of the Party and government. Non-CCP voices were encouraged to join in. The chief Communist official for literary matters, Chen Yang, spelled out that even 'those who say counter-revolutionary things are not necessarily counter-revolutionaries'.[28]

With many newspapers remaining cautious, wall posters and meetings played key roles in spreading the word. They attacked repression and promotions made on the basis of Party and personal loyalty rather than ability. 'Local Party emperors' were criticized for extravagance and oppression of peasants. A reporter for the official Xinhua news agency, who travelled widely in China at the time, recalled how shocked he had been to discover that village leaders built fine houses for themselves while living standards for peasants were little better than before 1949.*[29]

The main thrust of the protests was that the Communist Party should pull back, and let the government get on with running the country while other parties should be permitted to emerge along with a free press. Though he estimated that 70 per cent of university students had landlord or bourgeois parents, Mao saw young people as the 'new-born forces' which would move the country forward. They reacted enthusiastically. The first of the 'big character' posters, which would become a defining element of agitation in China, appeared on 17 May on the Beijing campus.† It queried the way in which delegates to the National Congress of the Youth League had been selected. A second poster called for a 'democratic garden' where views could be expressed.

---

* An economist, Fei Xiaotang, who returned from the London School of Economics (LSE) to his home village in Jiangsu, about which he had written in the 1930s, concluded that conditions for farmers had deteriorated since then.

† A big-character poster consisted of one or several sheets of paper measuring at least 70 × 100 centimetres. Each character was seven to ten centimetres high, written in ink by brush (Leijonhufvud, p. 17).

A 'Democracy Plaza' was duly established on the campus, with a 'Democracy Wall', some of whose posters defended the CCP. The May Fourth example of open discussion about the icons of China's regimented life was being resurrected four decades on. Following the lead of the capital, students elsewhere joined in. Picking up the ball, intellectuals raised questions about society. Religious groups came out into the open in some places; in Hubei, police reported that Buddhists were 'chanting banned scriptures'.[30]

Mao called in the editor of the *People's Daily*, Deng Tuo, to upbraid him for the article against the author Wang Meng by the four PLA writers and for not having run the Chairman's February speech. Receiving him in his bedroom, the leader cried, 'You're not worth what you used to be. Shit or get off the pot!'[31]

The Chairman then went off on a long tour of China by train to talk to provincial barons. He attended carefully stage-managed meetings with the people, and made a much-publicized swim in the Yangzi at Wuhan. It might all be set up, but he could take the warmth and cheers he encountered as a sign that the people were with him, and that debate held no perils.

The early hesitations within the Party machine appeared to lessen as spring came and Mao assured CCP members they had no need to fear that the campaign would unleash 'ghosts and monsters'. Rectification, they were told, would not use harsh methods, but consist merely of 'gentle breeze and mild rain'. Still, Mao did not have a strong majority in the Politburo while, in some provinces such as Henan, officials made plain that they were carrying out the campaign against their better judgement. Liu Shaoqi was ambivalent, and used his command of the propaganda machine to get the *People's Daily* to run an editorial which pinned the prime blame for China's troubles on the bourgeoisie and intellectuals. The Chairman's reaction to this was to suggest that all provinces should have non-Party newspapers since they did a better job in spreading his word.[32]

As the debate swelled, the very nature of CCP rule came into question. As the editor of the non-Party *Guangming Daily* put it, 'In my opinion, the key lies in the idea that "the world belongs to the Party". I think a party leading a nation is not the same thing as a party owning a nation. I think this idea that "the world belongs to the Party" is at the bottom of all the sectarianism and the root of all contradictions between Party and non-Party people.' His view was echoed by a wall poster at Beijing University stating, 'We want Party leadership, but we are resolutely opposed to the Party alone making decisions and implementing them.'[33]

There was a major problem in all this. Mao was the incarnation of the Party. If it came under attack, he could not expect to be exempt. His 'Yenan talks', which had laid down the line on art and literature, were criticized, one writer calling them 'conservative, far beyond the situation now developing'. Then things got rougher. A poster warned that 'dissatisfied peasants could throw Chairman Mao's portrait into the toilet.' A university professor wrote of his 'arbitrary and reckless character'. Denunciations of the CCP talked of its 'malevolent tyranny' and 'Auschwitz fascist methods'. A Party deputy secretary in Beijing pasted up posters with the slogan 'Oppose the Soviet Union sending troops into Hungary.' Students' associations with names such as Bitter Medicine and Voices from the Lowest Level set up information exchanges with people living outside the main cities to circulate reports of the real condition of China. There were occasional outbreaks of violence.[34]

Having pushed the boat out so far, Mao had to cope with the doubts of those who kept his regime afloat. After the publication of the rectification directive in the *People's Daily* on 1 May, he was obliged to agree that the critics would be allowed free rein for only five weeks. In a memorandum to the Central Committee, he did not pull back from his campaign, but homed in on 'rightists', who had a simple choice – to mend their ways or 'go on making trouble and court ruin'. Once more, he retreated to his bedroom to consider his next move as his assumption that the revolution was popular enough to withstand debate was shown up as naive.[35]

As well as the intellectuals and students, there were protests from the proletariat in whose name the CCP claimed to rule. The number of strikes grew – Shanghai saw eighty-six in 1956. In Guangzhou, as many as half the dockers stopped work to protest at a new shift system that reduced their pay. In various cities, workers established 'Grievance Redress Societies' at their enterprises. The biggest movement, as usual, was in Shanghai where protests in the spring of 1957 involved nearly 30,000 workers at 587 enterprises, with more than 200 walkouts and 100 production go-slows. The influence of what had happened in Eastern Europe was evident – 'Let's create another Hungarian incident,' ran a slogan. In one district of the city, more than 10,000 workers joined a 'Democratic Party'. Anger rose against cadres who were seen as representatives of oppression. At an industrial plant, a union official was frogmarched to the Huangpu River, where his head was dunked in the filthy water at two or three minute intervals for an hour.*[36]

Some union leaders took note of what was happening at the grassroots and sympathized with the protests, seeing this as a chance to forge new links with the workers and shed their reputation as enforcers of the official line. The Director of the All-China Federation of Trade Unions, Lai Ruoyu, sought greater autonomy for his organization, and blamed the labour strife on bureaucratism among union officials and divisions between better-educated young workers and older staff.

In the early summer of 1957, Mao decided to lower the boom on the Hundred Flowers. He could not sustain his belief that differences were just a 'contradiction' that could be cleared up by debate. The rock of the regime – the Party – had to be preserved and, with it, his own supremacy. The *People's Daily* ran six editorials in as many days to denounce the 'rightist' attack on the CCP and socialism. After it had been leaked to the *New York Times* by a Polish source, Mao's original speech was finally printed, but with appropriate corrections by the author to make it appear that it had all been a trap laid for opponents of the regime, designed to lure out the snakes and 'poisonous weeds' of reaction so that they could be destroyed. Since his original encouragement for debate could not be wiped from the slate, the whole thing had to be turned on its head to provide fresh proof of the leader's wisdom and dedication to the revolution. Critics were accused of trying to overthrow the CCP, restore bourgeois dictatorship and 'resubjugate the Chinese people to the rule of imperialism and its running dogs'. By the autumn, Mao was able to dismiss the Hundred Flowers as a set of 'queer arguments' – as if they had nothing to do with him.[37]

Hardliners, such as the Beijing boss, Peng Zhen, pressed for harsh action. Deng Xiaoping was given the job of launching an anti-rightist campaign to 'squeeze the pus out of the abscess'. The attack spread well beyond those who had offered criticism, and served as an umbrella for settling of scores. In 1958, 43 per cent of criminal cases heard by courts

---

* Elizabeth Perry described the Shanghai strikes in a key article in the *China Quarterly* in March 1994 (from which these details are drawn), but they have received surprisingly little attention since.

involved alleged counter-revolutionary activities. The Chairman initially put the number of 'rightists' uncovered at between 50,000 and 60,000. Then, he raised this to 300,000 and finally, in a remark in 1961, to 400,000. A third of them were 'ordinary intellectuals' such as primary school teachers, he added.[38]

The Democratic League and the Beijing-approved Kuomintang came under sustained attack, with up to 40 per cent of their senior members exposed as having followed an 'anti-Communist, anti-people, anti-Socialist bourgeois line'. As a result, their already marginal influence declined even further. Journalists who had written critical articles were sacked, like the editor of the *Guangming Daily*, expelled from the Party and subjected to intense criticism. On the other hand, the editor of the *People's Daily*, who had so annoyed Mao by his initial lack of enthusiasm for the Hundred Flowers, was treated leniently, losing his job, but being given another in which he continued to influence the paper.

'Re-education through labour' was invoked to enable police to send people to camps without trial. Dai Huang, the Xinhua reporter who had been shocked by the lavish lifestyles of rural cadres, was denounced in big-character wall posters at the agency, one written by his wife. He was dismissed, thrown out of the CCP and sentenced to 'labour under supervision'. His wife divorced him. Among the other prisoners at the camp to which he was sent in Manchuria was a seventeen-year-old girl who had been overheard saying that 'American-made shoe polish is really good.'[39]

'At the beginning we were not treated too badly,' Dai recalled of the camp. Prisoners rose at 4 a.m. and worked till 7 or 8 p.m. After eighteen months, things got tougher, with frequent bullying by team leaders and repentant 'rightists' who thought that the viciousness increased their chances of pardon. Food rations were reduced to a small bread roll for breakfast and lunch, and a supper of porridge so thin that you could see your own face in it. Prisoners ate rats. Many died of starvation or in the extreme winter cold.

In 1960, a decision was taken that prisoners who had worked for central government departments would be allowed to return to their units. As he was about to leave, Dai found that biscuits he had been given for the four-day trip to Beijing had been stolen. He went to ask for a new supply at camp headquarters. There, he saw Party leaders eating meat and fish and white-flour rolls. Munching on a mouthful of pork, the Party secretary told him there was a big grain problem so 'everybody should take his own responsibility for his food ration.' Dai's request was rejected. When he weighed himself back in Beijing he found that his two years in prison had reduced him from 98 kilos to 41.

Judicial reform was halted, and senior legal officials severely criticized for encouraging such Western concepts as 'innocent until proven guilty' and 'benefit of the doubt'. Mao inveighed against one of his favourite targets, intellectuals. The principal student leader at Beijing University, Lin Xiling, was sent for severe 're-education through labour'. The leading woman writer Ding Ling, who had joined the Communists in Yenan after being arrested by the KMT in Shanghai in the 1930s, was dispatched to a camp in the north-east. The young author Wang Meng, whose story had been attacked in the People's Daily, was exiled to Xinjiang. University professors were ordered to clean the lavatories at the establishments where they had previously taught.[40]

The purge did not mean an end to the attack on bureaucratism and sectarianism. But Party unity was held to be sacrosanct – Liu told an Indian delegation that 'no matter whether the Party's line is correct or mistaken, the Party must safeguard its unity ... A Party split is more damaging than a defeat to the revolution.' Any remaining prospect of rational, reasoned advance towards socialism with open debate vanished. Class warfare was stepped up.[41]

In confident form once more, the Chairman forecast in the spring of 1958 that there were probably only a few more rounds to be fought before socialism triumphed. To achieve victory, individualism had to be slapped down while an 'all-people rectification movement' was launched against backsliding Party officials, with a 'mass struggle against bourgeois rightists'. At the same time, Mao reasserted his grip on rural policy; even though this produced disappointing results in 1957 as it had the previous year, collective farms were expanded along with increased state control and the closure of the remaining free markets. The Twelve-Year Programme for farming was brought out of hibernation, suitably changed but still based on the old principles.[42]

It was time for a vast national campaign to propel China to the front rank of world powers, the Great Helmsman decided. As was often the case, the international situation had an influence on internal Chinese policies; when external pressures grew, Mao usually adopted more radical policies to strengthen fortress China.

In this case, Cold War tension in Asia had been increased by an agreement between the US and Taiwan for the Americans to station missiles capable of carrying nuclear warheads on the island, making it, for Beijing, even more of an advanced base for counter-revolution within range of the Fujian coast. Dulles insisted on no recognition of the PRC, no trade and no seat at the UN – the secretary of state added that he thought Communism was only a passing phase on the mainland. The defeat of the domestic 'counter-revolutionaries' was held by Mao and his colleagues to be the political foundation for a fundamental economic breakthrough. Zhou Enlai, Chen Yun and the technocrats around them were forced on to the back foot. Dogma reigned. After all, the Chairman declared, imperialists were 'like the sun at five o'clock in the afternoon while we are like the sun at six o'clock in the morning. The East wind is bound to prevail over the West wind because we are powerful and strong.'[43]

He made that claim during his second visit to the USSR, for a conference of Communist parties in November 1957. (The flight from Beijing was only the second time in his life he had travelled by air, after his trip from Yenan to Chongqing in 1945.) There was no open disagreement with the Kremlin, but Mao returned home intent on following his own path of permanent revolution rather than submitting to Moscow. Nearly ten years after winning power, it was time for the People's Republic to strike out on its own, with a leap into the unknown that would end up taking tens of millions of lives as the revolution went off the rails.

20

Leaping to Disaster

'I have witnessed the tremendous energy of the masses. On this foundation, it is possible to accomplish any task whatsoever . . . there are still
a few comrades who are unwilling to undertake a large-scale mass movement in the industrial sphere. They call mass movement on the industrial
front "irregular" and disparage it as "a rural style of work" and "a
guerrilla habit". This is obviously incorrect.'[1]

So spoke Mao in the summer of 1958 after launching his biggest and,
to date, most disastrous initiative, the Great Leap Forward. In the
following three years, it would cause deaths estimated at up to 46 million
from coercion, forced labour and, finally, the worst manmade famine
ever seen on earth. Politically and socially, the Leap marked the start of
nearly two decades in which, under the Chairman's baton, China's
Communist orchestra departed from the generally logical score it
had pursued since 1949 to indulge in wild dissonances that would
threaten to bring the whole revolution to a juddering close. To begin
with, the Leap was not without sense, but, as political considerations
took command, it became more of a vision than a rational economic
programme, and unravelled into catastrophe.

The poor results of the first attempt at an economic bound ahead in
1956 had enabled the planners to implement an 'anti-rash advance'
campaign to rein things in. Their chief, Chen Yun, the fifth-ranking
member of the Politburo and an ally of Zhou Enlai, preached the need
for balanced growth, with a more measured farming plan. This, he
admitted, would take time. Mao did not want to wait.

The leader returned from his trip to Moscow at the end of November
1957 convinced that something new and different was needed to build
up the economy and revitalize the revolution. The experience of the

Hundred Flowers had closed the door on liberalization. Though CCP officials had shown their loyalty in rooting out 'rightists', the Chairman still saw them as an obstacle – 'a bunch of zombies with a slave mentality'. The planners lacked zeal, he decided, and adhered to the Soviet model at a time when Mao thought China should be finding its own path. (In any case Moscow was not going to be able to supply what China needed given the resources it was now directing at Eastern Europe.)

The Chairman declared that what he wanted was rashness; only those who were 'blazing red' could be counted on as China set itself the target of surpassing Britain economically within fifteen years. Experts were to be disregarded – or positively discriminated against. As a sign of the way the wind was blowing, the state statistical bureau was virtually dismantled. Economic decision-making was decentralized to enable provinces to operate more independently. A vast irrigation programme was launched, using conscripted labour, as Mao called for big increases in grain output, and promoted campaigns on everything from forestation to the eradication of pests.[2]

Industry, notably steel, was the core concern. Ministers and provincial bosses vied to outbid one another in their forecasts; those who were more realistic were purged. At a session in Hangzhou in January 1958, the Ministry of Metallurgy advanced a plan to more than double steel production to 20 million tonnes by 1962 and then to reach 100 million by 1977. Not to be outdone, the chemicals minister proposed constructing thousands of chemical fertilizer factories. Other officials offered 60,000 miles of roads by 1972.[3]

Liu Shaoqi contributed the notion that all rules and regulations considered to hinder the enthusiasm of the masses and of 'productive forces' should be revised or abolished. China would 'walk on two legs' with capital-intensive heavy industry in the cities and state-run rural communities combining agriculture and small-scale industrial production. Huge communes – the term was first brought into use by Mao's secretary and ideological helper, Chen Boda – were set up on a trial basis in Henan and Manchuria to pool resources in agriculture and local industry. Absorbing all private plots of land, they created a completely collective existence for members, with very long working hours and the virtual abolition of private life.[4]

To spur growth, a mad procedure was adopted by which the central government produced two plans. Meeting the targets of the first was mandatory. The second set, pitched higher, was to be achieved by extra effort. Provincial plans also came in two tiers – the first was aligned with the second set of central plans; the second was higher. This multiplication continued down the administrative ladder until, by the time a plan reached the local implementation point, the figures had gone up five or six times. Though some senior planning officials showed distinct signs of nervousness, the prospect of the vast initiative put Mao in the best of spirits. Unusually, he joined in the final banquet after a conference in the Guangxi capital of Nanning, wolfing down a fatty dish of snake and tiger, and swimming in the river the next day – the water was cold and he caught a chill.

Events moved ahead fast. Despite having offered self-criticism for backing the 'anti-rash advance' programme, Zhou Enlai was replaced as foreign minister by Chen Yi, though he continued to meet high-level visitors. In March 1958, Mao told a conference in Chengdu that China was at a stage where 'one day equals twenty years'. The meeting heard that farm production for the year would rise by 17–20 per cent.

As the Chairman redoubled his attack on the 'superstitions' of rules, regulations, and academic and expert views, the cult of his personality soared even further. When he remarked at a Party session that 'all of us here are students of a sort', the ideologue Chen Boda chipped in: 'Except the Chairman.' When he proposed that teaching materials in schools should be cut back, another follower suggested that the leader's sayings should be studied instead. 'We have to trust the Chairman to the degree of blind faith,' declared a Mao favourite, the Shanghai boss, Ke Qingshi. 'We should obey the Chairman to the extent of total abandon.' At Chengdu, Liu Shaoqi instructed delegates: 'In every respect – thinking, perspective, foresight and method – we are way behind [Mao].' It was an opinion that the Chairman could only share, elevating him to the superhuman status he had cherished for himself – as well as providing an extremely useful tool of mastery over those around him.[5]

In May 1958, the second part of the Eighth Party Congress approved the Great Leap Forward. Mao made five speeches during the meeting – a sharp contrast with his single intervention at the previous session twenty months earlier, when he had felt himself on the back foot. He spoke of the need to lift the lid and 'let the people explode'. Shanghai's Ke Qingshi was rewarded for his enthusiasm by being elevated to the Politburo, along with two other Mao devotees.[6]

In August 1958, the leadership took stock at its favourite seaside resort of Beidaihe. The harvest was excellent; the *People's Daily* had just declared that China's wheat output exceeded that of the United States and that the country could produce as much rice as it wished. When wild figures from a provincial chief raised the question of what would be done with all the surplus grain, Mao suggested that everybody should eat five meals a day.[7]

Official reports from the experimental communes were glowing. Mao, who was having Engels's *Socialism, Scientific and Utopian* read to him by his doctor, put his personal stamp on the increase in steel production. Reviewing the initial suggestion to raise the target from 6 million to 9 million tonnes, he told the minister concerned, 'Make it snappy! Let's just double it! Why dilly-dally? Let's make it 11 million tonnes.' By another account, Mao raised the prospects for steel output while in the water with his favourite swimming companion, the economist Bo Yibo. Unable to recall the figures, Bo suggested that they do another lap. Later that day, the Chairman announced that production would 'double next year'. Whatever its origins, the outcome was a ridiculously high target of 11.5 million tonnes. Hebei was to build seven iron and steel mills; Hunan planned more than a thousand small furnaces; backward Guizhou began building a plant to produce 40,000 tonnes of rolled steel a year.[8]

If there was a moment when Chinese Communism lost touch with reality, this was it. A fatal and self-contradictory mix of authoritarianism, self-delusion and anarchic devolution set in, which was to be reproduced in the following decade in the Cultural Revolution. Realists in the upper echelons would be on the defensive so long as Mao lived.[9]

By the end of 1958, 25,000 communes had been established, each averaging 5,000 households. Like every campaign the CCP undertook, this was to be a mass affair organized on army lines. Vast gangs of labourers were deployed on roads and great buildings. Huge establishments were encouraged because they made it easier to control large numbers of people – Xiuwu in Henan had 130,000 members, Shilong in Guangdong more than 100,000. Mao envisaged that some communes would become as big as cities, with roads wide enough to double as runways for aircraft, and each would have its own university, scientific research institute and hospital. In place of home cooking, mass canteens served food to all members, who were urged to eat as much as they wanted. As production had been collectivised, so was consumption. Those who did not eat enough were stigmatised as class enemies with white flags and drawing of turtles pinned to their back in a traditional badge of shame. Instead of cash payments, work points were allocated, which were exchanged for food. 'The notion of utopia mentioned by our predecessors will be realized and surpassed,' forecast Mao and Liu. Or, as a maker of farm equipment on a commune recalled:

It was real communism. The mess hall was great. We got to eat things made from wheat flour every day, and they were always slaughtering pigs for us. For a while it seemed that they were telling the truth and we were going to enter heaven. [We] said that 'Communism is heaven, and the communes are the bridge that will take us there.' We felt like we were crossing that bridge, could heaven really be far away?[10]

Visiting Anhui, Mao was shown a simple furnace said to be able to produce high-quality steel; the metal presented to him had, in fact, been made elsewhere, but the Chairman saw the process as the means of mobilizing mass labour on a local level to meet the targets he had identified as the essential 'link' in China's industrialization. Three quarters of a million backyard furnaces were set up to smelt iron and steel from pots and pans, bicycles and door knobs, scrap metal, scissors, jewels and children's pendants – the melting down of cooking utensils served the subsidiary purpose of forcing the owners to eat in the commune canteens. 'The more metal you collected, the more revolutionary you were,' as one commune member recalled.

Ministries in Beijing formed furnace teams. Their chiefs made well-publicized visits to help shovel scrap metal into the flames. Sun Yat-sen's widow, Qingling Soong, had a small smelter in her back yard. By the end of 1958, 100 million people laboured at the furnaces and associated enterprises. Mao looked out from his roof at the glow cast over Beijing through the night. Foreign visitors were mightily impressed, seeing a whole country on the move.[11]

In the communes, the military approach was evident once more. Members were organized into regiments, companies and brigades. Provincial leaders spoke of unleashing them in 'surprise attacks' on the fields. Hubei had an 'iron and steel army' of up to a million people, backed by motor vehicles and horse transport divisions. Guangdong counties were told to prepare as if 'going to war'.[12]

Peasants were mobilized in a drive to kill off grain-eating sparrows, defined as one of four pests to be eradicated, along with rats, flies and mosquitoes. The Chairman said children as young as five should participate in the anti-sparrow offensives, climbing trees to knock down nests and making as much noise as possible in the evening to scare the birds from alighting for the night. The idea was that they would die of exhaustion in flight. Such was the status of sparrows as public enemies that a Sichuan artist who specialized in depicting them did not dare show his paintings.[13]

This was a terrifying metaphor for the way in which mass campaigns – against humans – would subsequently be whipped to a frenzy. In Beijing, as he recalled half a century later, a young schoolboy joined a crowd going after an exhausted bird early one Saturday morning.[14]

'Get the little thief!' some shouted.

'Don't let the little bastard get away!' others cried.

'Kill it! Kill it!'

'Our workers are strong, our workers are strong,' a voice intoned over a loudspeaker.

The crowd surged forward screaming, 'Kill! Kill! Kill!' It then suddenly parted and the boy saw a large man holding a bird, its head covered with blood. The loudspeakers switched to a verse:

> You can fly, but stop you can't.
> The field is wide open.
> But you find no place to hide.
> You're hungry and tired.

As well as seeking to boost production, the Great Leap Forward was designed, once more, to ram home a new form of organization to replace old social structures. The new emperor's men were ever-present, stamping on tradition, leading indoctrination sessions, setting work teams to emulate one another and encouraging villagers to inform on their neighbours. In the Far West, communes were designed to replace the nomadic way of life amid campaigns against Islam, regionalism and Soviet influence. On the other side of the nation, in a commune in Zhejiang on the east coast, a shopkeeper was arrested for having offered presents of rice to people who had given him advice; he died in prison.[15]

*

The Soviets took a critical view of the Great Leap. Increasingly, Moscow was viewed by Beijing as an obstacle which had to be stood up to – and bested if possible. Anything the USSR could do, the PRC could do bigger. In Beijing, Tiananmen Square was expanded to be even grander than Red Square in Moscow. More than a million people worked on it in round-the-clock shifts for ten months, and 10,000 houses (and two imperial-era gates) were demolished to make way for the 136 acre (55 hectare) site. In unwitting anticipation of what was to happen there three decades later, the Beijing city boss, Peng Zhen, ordered that the boulevard at the top of the square should be strong enough to hold the heaviest tanks passing. The Great Hall of the People on one side of the square was to accommodate 10,000 people for meetings and 5,000 in its main banqueting hall. Zhou Enlai told the architects and engineers that it should be built to last for longer than the Forbidden City. The bridge planned over the Yangzi at Nanjing was designed to show that China could do as well as the Soviet experts who had put up the crossing upriver at Wuhan.

When Nikita Khrushchev visited China just before the Beidaihe conference on the Great Leap in the summer of 1958, Mao told his doctor he was 'sticking a needle up his arse'. He received the Soviet leader sitting by his swimming pool, and suggested that the visitor might fancy a dip. Khrushchev agreed, changing into one of the pairs of swimming trunks kept by the pool. However, he did not know how to swim, and had to bob about in a rubber ring while the interpreters dealt with the conversation between the men in the water.[16]

Though they appeared comradely in public, the Chairman resented Moscow's effort to dominate the world Communist movement. He also regarded a proposal by the USSR for a joint submarine fleet in the Pacific and Indian Oceans as a bid to assert military control (whereas it was, in fact, aimed against the US naval presence). Mao's attribution of imperialist motives to Moscow shocked Khrushchev, and the Kremlin had to ask what kind of allied co-operation it could expect as the PRC's military strength increased.[17]

Nor was Moscow's policy of peaceful co-existence with the West at all to China's taste, particularly when the visitor proposed to Mao that Beijing should pledge not to attack Taiwan. 'I told him that whether or not we attack Taiwan is our own domestic affair,' the Chairman confided to his doctor. 'As for the people's communes, what is so wrong about trying them out? . . . We will do something on the Taiwan front. We will definitely give the people's commune a try.'

On the way to Beidaihe after the meetings with Khrushchev, Mao fumed that the Soviet leader did not know what he was talking about. 'Maybe we can get the United States to drop an atomic bomb on Fujian. Maybe ten or twenty million people will be killed . . . Let's see what Khrushchev says then.' Three weeks later, the PLA began a heavy bombardment of the Nationalist-held island of Quemoy, off the Fujian coast.

Eisenhower reacted by saying that the United States would fight rather than let the PRC take the tiny island, but also stated his readiness to seek a negotiated solution 'acceptable to all parties concerned'. Mao did not want Quemoy. His aim was to stir up nationalist sentiment, show that he could give Chiang a hard time, and put Khrushchev in his place. America might remain the great enemy, but the USSR was fast joining it in the Chairman's mind.[18]

There may have been some inner logic to the notion that China could draw on the size of its population to produce a mass labour force in grassroots industrialization. But the approach was impossibly broad and horribly rushed. There was no prioritization, no serious planning, just the exhortation to produce. 'Stir up all energy, aim high, build socialism: more, faster, better, cheaper' went the slogan. In keeping with Mao's impatience, the first five aims were paramount; the last two were forgotten.

Despite a good harvest in 1958, targets were far too high to be met; in some provinces, requisitioning – in part to pay the Soviet Union in food for its aid or sell grain abroad – meant a significant fall in food reserves. The gross demands made on the farmers were relentless: 44 per cent of the harvest was taken in Jilin, 35 per cent in Inner Mongolia and 30 per cent in Jiangxi, though some was returned.[19]

The movement from the countryside to man industry deprived the rural labour force of many millions of working days a year. New and unsuitable agricultural methods reduced output below its maximal level. Huge transport backlogs built up. Despite all the efforts on the water front, floods and droughts continued.

Policies contradicted one another. The melting down of pots and pans for iron meant they were not available to bang to frighten off the sparrows. Killing the birds meant a proliferation of insects they would have eaten, thus destroying grain in their place; bedbugs were substituted among the 'four pests'. Exhortations to peasants to 'fill your bellies' in the canteens meant that food was gobbled up. In a Guangdong commune, the six-month rice supply went in twenty days, after which there were only sweet potatoes and cassava; when that was exhausted, the diet was reduced to thin gruel and grasses, and stomachs swelled from malnutrition.[20]

Metal objects fed into backyard furnaces were often of low quality; so the iron was unusable. But, such was the reluctance to admit any shortcomings that it was shipped off to secret depots. The extremely long work hours led to exhaustion and accidents. The emphasis on industrial production in communes meant that shortages of agricultural labour grew, aggravated by farmers moving to cities and towns. With the furnaces eating up fuel, coal supplies fell short. So trees were chopped down in enormous numbers, bringing an ecological disaster.[21]

Still a very poor country, with a backward infrastructure, China simply did not have the resources needed to achieve its goals, particularly given the big military budget. The rise in state spending, caused in part by expensive methods to try to turn pig iron from the new furnaces into steel, brought budget deficits, which were covered by printing money. So inflation rose. Real national income and wages declined, as did living standards.

The Chairman was unabashed, and the reality of the Leap was disguised by two fortunate coincidences. One was the good harvest of 1958 after less abundance in 1956 and 1957, for which not even the CCP and its leader could claim credit, though the Central Committee enlarged output well beyond the actual figures. The other, somewhat ironically in view of the deterioration in Sino-Soviet relations, was the way in which big plants set up by the USSR under the Five-Year Plan came on-stream, boosting industrial production. There was also massive lying, facilitated by the collapse of the central statistics bureau.[22]

'Imbalance and headache are good things,' Mao proclaimed. 'When everybody adds firewood, the flames rise higher,' declared Liu Shaoqi. By the middle of 1958, the media were trumpeting victories in every sector simultaneously.[23]

The time to overtake Britain economically was cut from fifteen years to seven, five and, eventually, to two. At one meeting, the normally restrained Liu stuck up his thumb and said, 'Right, it's going to be like this; this year a leap forward, next year once again a great leap forward, and the year after still another great leap forward.' The euphoria produced claims that wheat was planted so closely in Henan that rats could not penetrate the fields. A doctored photograph showed a field in Hunan where the corn was so thick that children stood on top of it.[24]

Though he relished the huge numbers rolling in from the provinces, even the Chairman could raise an eyebrow – he warned basic-level cadres, 'What is the use of exaggerating?' But the messianic, political nature of the Leap meant that it had a big built-in exaggeration factor.[25]

A novel about the period, *Pobiji*, told of a commune official receiving a telephone call from a superior who asked for poultry figures. The commune man immediately replied with invented numbers. When a colleague expressed surprise, he explained, 'Day in and day out, they telephone for figures of pigs, sheep and chickens . . . Who cares if they are true or false? Everyone is just going through the motions! Sometimes, you need to add a zero, or a few decimal points, only then will they believe you.'

For Mao, the Leap offered the exhilaration of romantic revolution he loved, vindicating him after the disappointment of the Hundred Flowers. He could see a revival of the spirit of guerrilla action and the Yenan era, with the CCP attacking industrial and agricultural targets instead of Nationalist ones. The rhetoric became ever more strident and expansive.

Undertaking an unprecedented number of provincial tours, the Chairman appeared like a hero-emperor amid carefully regimented adoring throngs. In Henan, he looked overjoyed as he stood in a cotton field, his sunburned face turned upwards as he proclaimed, 'The people's communes are good!' When he repeated the words on a visit to Shandong, they became a national slogan. On the train back to Beidaihe, his doctor noted that he had never seen his eminent patient so excited. He even spent a well-photographed half-hour working on the Ming Tombs Reservoir north of Beijing; Zhou Enlai was pictured pushing a wheelbarrow at the same site. Dr Li commented that it was the only moment in his twenty-two years with Mao that he saw him undertaking physical labour.[26]

By the autumn of 1958, the leadership could no longer ignore the problems the Leap faced. The harvest was good, but there were not enough peasants to bring it in, so industrial workers who had come from the countryside were sent home and 'shock battalions' were formed of school pupils, clerks, shop assistants and anybody else who could be found; the *People's Daily* laid down that their work periods should not be more than forty-eight hours, with six hours for sleep during that time. Still, the inexperienced shock troops worked less well than the absent peasants, and harvesting was unsatisfactory. Distribution problems compounded the shortfall, with some local Party leaders holding back supplies for the use of their communes, and the shock farmers diverted from work in the fields to attend political meetings.

Nor was the key component of industrial growth doing anything like as well as forecast. At a work session in Wuchang in November, an attendee noted that China's total iron output would reach only 7 million tonnes that year; just 40 per cent of that would be good quality. In addition, rain and cold winter weather in northern China was bound to affect the operations of small furnaces, while fuel was growing scarce in some places. Mao seemed to recognize reality when he said he would count it a success if 10 per cent of communes were run well, referring to a report from Hubei that put the proportion at 7–8 per cent. He acknowledged that he and his colleagues had pushed too hard, and that the work burden should be lightened. He also became aware of the fabrications being employed to make it seem that targets were being met – for instance, communes borrowing pigs from other places to present to inspectors as their own, or the practice of collecting grain from a big area and pretending it came from a single small plot, and then multiplying the figures on that basis.[27]

The Chairman noted that the six-month irrigation works target involved moving nearly four times as much earth and stone as in the winter and spring of the previous year. He foresaw that, along with simultaneous plans for steel, copper, aluminium, coal, transport, processing industries and chemicals, the overwork could cause the deaths of 50 million or more – showing his usual cavalier disregard for figures, he had begun by saying that half the population might perish, before scaling back the figure. 'If with a death toll of 50 million, you didn't lose your jobs,' he told the officials around him, 'I at least would lose mine.' Whether he would also lose his own head, he went on, 'would also be open to question'.

The planner Chen Yun was recalled. He advocated looking at the country as a whole, like a chessboard, rather than counting on a myriad of local efforts. Zhou Enlai and Deng Xiaoping were set to work to evaluate the situation. But the practical spirit which started to set in at the end of 1958 was strictly relative. At Wuchang, Mao accepted that the year's grain output was not the claimed 450 million tonnes; but he settled on 370 million, compared to a true total of a bit over 200 million. Though the leader admitted that he had been guilty of a lack of realism in the summer, targets for 1959 were still built on phoney 1958 figures, and so were hugely unachievable – grain, for instance, was to increase to 592 million tonnes.[28]

In October 1958, the defence minister, Marshal Peng Dehuai, made two provincial tours to see how the Leap was working. A tough, thick-set man, who genuinely cared for the peasants from whose ranks he had risen, his relationship with the Chairman had grown rocky over policy issues and as Peng sniped at the Mao personality cult. The marshal's high standing in the PLA raised the danger that the army might move outside the tight political control which had always been exerted over the power of the gun. As a pre-emptive move, Mao was advancing the more dependable Lin Biao. If Peng had to be disposed of, his successor was in the wings.

Peng's first provincial tour made clear to him what a disaster the Leap had become. A second trip, to his home province of Hunan, reinforced his concern. But to criticize the Leap was to criticize the leader. So, rather than 'agitating', Peng made only muted complaints after his tours.

He may have thought that he had no need to speak up because of the way Mao conducted one of his periodic violent switches of direction at a conference in Zhengzhou at the end of February 1959, where he rounded on excessive leftism, saying targets should be relaxed, communes should be reorganized, and grain requisitioning reduced. Strict egalitarianism was wrong, he added. Differences should be acknowledged; the more people worked, the more they should earn. 'I say – firmly implement right opportunism, thoroughly and to the end,' he added. 'If you don't follow me, then I'll do it on my own – even to the lengths of abandoning my party membership, and even to the extent of bringing a suit against Marx.'

It was another of the wild, fundamentally irresponsible shifts that could only bemuse and demoralize his followers, a fresh sign of basic immaturity and unfitness to rule as Mao threw his personal position into the equation, like a petulant child threatening to walk off with his toys if he didn't get his way. Perhaps, though, he was also intimidated by the scale of the disasters around him. By April, fifteen provinces were suffering drought, and 25 million people in five provinces needed urgent relief supplies of food. After Politburo members went to inspect their home districts, their findings forced Mao to acknowledge the need to reduce targets. There was also a challenge from a revolt in Tibet which was put down by troops rushed in by Beijing. The Dalai Lama fled to India, leaving the Pachen Lama as the most senior figure in Tibet – he was initially seen as a collaborator but was purged in 1962 after petitioning Beijing to moderate its policies.

At a Party Plenum in April 1959, Mao took the symbolic step of relinquishing the state chairmanship – Liu Shaoqi was to replace him. This made no difference to the Great Helmsman's real exercise of power as head of the CCP and supreme leader, but could be seen as a sign that he was acknowledging that the Leap had not worked out as planned. He also made another switch, as if harking back to the Hundred Flowers and blotting out the vast repression of the subsequent anti-rightist campaign.

The Chairman issued a paean of praise to constructive criticism. 'Speaking out should involve no penalty,' he declared. 'According to party regulations, people are entitled to their own opinions.' He lauded the example of two officials under the Ming and Tang dynasties who had been fearless in their criticism of their emperors, and a play about one of them was performed in Shanghai on the tenth anniversary of the revolution. China seemed to be on a roller-coaster ride in which consistency had no place, as its helmsman lurched from one position to another. The moment of truth would come in the summer of 1959, when the leadership gathered at a resort high above the Middle Yangzi for a session that would do much to define the top-level power relationships of the following decade and a half.[29]

Lushan, an ancient holy site much prized as a haven from the summer heat and humidity of the river valley below, had been the Nationalist government's summer capital under Chiang Kai-shek. A settlement of stone houses was built there in the early twentieth century, initially for foreigners and then increasingly occupied by prominent Chinese, including the Soongs and the Young Marshal of Manchuria.

The Communist leadership arrived by boat up the Yangzi. A newsreel film taken during the journey showed them in relaxed form, joking among themselves on deck; Deng Xiaoping was absent because he had broken his leg in a fall while playing billiards – Mao's doctor was told that Deng's nurse became pregnant while she was looking after him and was sent home to Shanghai to have an abortion. The foreign minister, Chen Yi, was kept in Beijing by pressure of work. Lin Biao also stayed away from the opening sessions; he had an aversion to wind, rain and water – all of which were prevalent at Lushan. When he did turn up, he stayed at the foot of the mountain, where the weather was less changeable.

Peng Dehuai asked to be excused, saying he was exhausted after a two-month trip to Moscow and Eastern Europe. He had also been occupied with the repression in Tibet and the strengthening of the PLA there. But a telephone call from Mao persuaded him to attend, and he settled into a bungalow amid tall trees.

In the next house to Peng was a remarkable survivor, the scholarly Zhang Wentian, who had been a member of the Moscow-trained leadership which elbowed Mao aside in Jiangxi. On the Long March, he was among those who switched camps to back the Chairman, becoming CCP general secretary from 1935 to 1945. After serving as ambassador to Moscow, he acted as Zhou Enlai's deputy for foreign affairs and a Politburo member. But he then came under a cloud, and was demoted to alternate membership of the Politburo. Two years later, Zhang failed to get the Foreign Ministry when Zhou was relieved of his post. So, apart from doubts he harboured about the Leap, he had plenty of reasons for resentment. During the conference, the forthright Peng and the canny politician-diplomat formed an unlikely alliance in which the second may have manipulated the first.[30]

The main sessions were held in an auditorium used by Chiang Kai-shek to plan the campaign which forced the Communists on to the Long March. There were side meetings between Politburo members and regional CCP chiefs to discuss the progress of the Leap. Speaking to delegates from the north-west, Peng told of what he had seen on his tours. He was still restrained, merely asking, 'Was the call for the whole people to make steel correct or not?' His hope must have been that Mao's onslaught on leftism at Zhengzhou marked a watershed. He could be comforted by news that, working in his villa at Lushan, the Chairman had decided to draw up lists of Party officials guilty of fabricating figures. But his expectations suffered a blow when the leader insisted that successes in the Leap far outweighed failures. As the days went by, Peng noticed that his remarks were not appearing in the conference bulletin like those of other prominent figures.[31]

So, on 14 July, he sent Mao a handwritten letter setting out his findings from his provincial tour and retailing the 'winds of exaggeration' he had encountered. He charged that the Leap had been a haphazard affair without 'plans for achieving the balances that were necessary'. His letter invoked the leader's favourite slogans so there could be no doubt that this was a personal charge. All the more so when, in an echo of a phrase used by Lenin, Peng attributed failures to 'petty-bourgeois fanaticism'. Whether the old soldier would have come up with such wording can be doubted; the hand of the more educated Zhang Wentian may have been present.

Instead of treating this as a personal message between comrades, Mao took it as a challenge that had to be faced down. Wearing a white robe and slippers without socks, he called four senior Politburo members and handed them copies, asking for comments. The letter was then circulated to other senior officials. That annoyed the marshal, who angrily asked the Chairman why he had circulated a private missive; Mao replied that Peng had not asked him not to show it to others.

Zhang Wentian then upped the stakes with a speech criticizing economic policy, saying reality had been ignored and the interests of the masses neglected. The fact that such a canny operator was ready to stick his neck out indicated that he thought there would be significant support for a campaign against the Leap. Chen Yi telephoned Peng from Beijing to offer congratulations. The finance minister, Li Xiannian, was impressed. Zhu De made a sharp intervention to say that it would not necessarily be bad if the mess halls, which Mao greatly prized, were shut down. As the Chairman noted, 'some comrades are wavering.' Complaints were being heard from PLA officers that the Leap was harming troops. Reports from provinces showed growing recalcitrance, with suggestions that the leader did not know what was going on. It was no longer just a matter of whether the Leap was working or not, but a question of Mao's unquestioned leadership.[32]

So there had to be a counter-attack. On 23 July, as Peng listened from the back row of seats in the auditorium, Mao made one of his most important speeches, starting on a light note – 'Now let me say something will you? I have taken sleeping-pills three times, but I can't get to sleep.'

Then he moved on to the offensive. 'Bourgeois rightists' were at work, he warned. 'We are under combined attack from within and outside the Party. The majority of comrades need to strengthen their backbones. Why are they not all strong? Just because for a time there were too few vegetables, too few hair-grips, no soap, a lack of balance in the economy and tension in the market, everyone became tense. People became psychologically tense . . . in the first part of the night you might be tense, but once you take your sleeping-pills the tension will go away for the rest of the night . . .'

There was 'a bit of petit-bourgeois fanaticism, but not all that much', he said. Turning to Peng, he observed that the defence minister had described himself as a 'coarse fellow'. 'Some people will waver in times of crisis and show a lack of resolution in the great storms of history,' the Chairman charged. 'They are different from rightists in that they are all engaged in building socialism. It is just that they lack experience. As soon as the wind starts blowing and the grass waves, they become unsteady on their pins and turn anti-adventurist . . . Some of what I say may hurt people. But if I remained silent now, this would not be in these comrades' interest.'

Mao was ready to shoulder responsibility, using typically robust phraseology: 'The chaos caused was on a grand scale and I take responsibility,' he said. 'Comrades, if you have to shit, shit!' he added. 'If you have to fart, fart! You'll feel much better for it.'[33]

But he made clear that others in the leadership had to acknowledge their parts. As for the military leaders, if they came out against him, he would go off to fight a guerrilla war of his own. It was, as at Zhengzhou, the ultimate threat, and underlined the leader's indispensability.

The revolt was quashed. Mao could shrug off attacks by Peng's supporters on him for being vain and despotic and for sticking to his policies for as long as possible before executing a 180 degree turn. He could count, as always since the Long March, on Zhou Enlai. Liu's rank as the heir apparent and his elevation to the post of state chairman gave him major positions to defend. Other leading Party figures, such as Deng Xiaoping and the Beijing boss, Peng Zhen, were compromised by their involvement in the Leap. The climate was such that, when a technocrat arranged for crates of substandard pig iron to be brought to Lushan to demonstrate the shortcomings of the programme, Zhou stopped him. The chairman of the State Economic Commission decided not to deliver a speech he had written pulling together critical analyses of the Leap by economists.

Such collective failure to stand up to the Chairman and to defend the change of course which had been recognized as necessary a few months earlier was a portent of what was to come in the 1960s. In the past, dissent had been allowed so long as discipline was maintained once a decision had been taken; now, merely questioning the Chairman was outlawed. At the same time, Mao abrogated to himself the right to shift policies at will, making him an elusive leader who might change tack at any moment, bringing potential disaster to those who had put their faith in his previous line. If the Leap was the start of a madness that would last till Mao's death in 1976, Lushan was the moment at which any brakes that had been applied to the Chairman in the past were lifted.[34]

Leaving the hall after his speech, the Great Helmsman bumped into Peng.

'Let's have another talk,' Mao suggested, according to his doctor, who was with him.[35]

'There's nothing more to talk about,' the marshal replied, his face red, chopping the air with his right arm. 'No more talk.'

'We have our differences, but we still exchange opinions,' the leader persisted.

'Talk is useless,' the defence minister replied, walking off.

Withdrawing to his quarters at Lushan, Peng lost his appetite, grew pale and lay on his bed with his head in his hands. He and his associates were accused of being 'bourgeois democrats' and of heading an anti-Party plot. Comparisons with the Gao Gang episode of the early 1950s were invoked. Given the deteriorating state of relations with Moscow, Peng's visit there earlier in the year was another black mark against him. Only his military comrade, Zhu De, had a good word to say for him, which was probably allowed as a way of placating the PLA.[36]

At a Party Plenum in August, Mao conjured up a subversive 'military club', and sent Zhang a letter to tell him his only course was to 'rectify, painfully'. He was sacked as deputy foreign minister. Two other alleged conspirators, the PLA chief of staff and the Party secretary of Hunan also lost their state jobs but, for the sake of CCP unity, they, Peng and Zhang all retained their Party rankings. Peng resigned as defence minister, telling colleagues he had made three promises to Mao – 'I will never become a counter-revolutionary. I won't commit suicide. I will support myself by the sweat of my brow.' Lin Biao became defence minister and reshuffled senior ranks in the PLA to assert Party authority. He also began to compile the *Little Red Book of Mao Zedong Thought*.

Though still formally a member of the Politburo, Peng was barred from its meetings and those of the Central Committee. Losing his home in the Zhongnanhai leadership compound, he moved to a house in a run-down part of southern Beijing, where he set up an experimental farm and devoted himself to study. Despite making a self-criticism, he persisted in talking of the social chaos caused by the Leap, and of destruction and loss 'beyond calculation'.

Mao was not going to take any notice of such remarks. The Leap was to continue, with targets that were lower, but still unrealistic. A new anti-rightist campaign was launched which affected 3.5 million CCP members and cadres, and as many people outside the Party. The Communist secretary of Anhui, who had tried to reduce peasant distress and had closed down mess halls, was purged.[37]

Though the biggest communes were reduced in size, loyalists like the Party secretary in Sichuan dismissed any criticism of them as 'completely counter to the principles of Marxism–Leninism and to the facts'. Mess halls were promoted. Once more, Mao lapped up phoney reports of triumphant harvests and insisted that only 15 per cent of peasants opposed the Leap. In the autumn, a figure of 270 million tonnes was promulgated for the grain harvest – 100 million above the true figure. Based on such false statistics, the state requisition took nearly 28 per cent of the crop, eleven points above the 1957 level. To raise more state funds, peasants were encouraged to increase savings from their tiny resources; Mao lauded a Shaanxi commune where the savings rate was said to be 45 per cent. He also latched on to the idea of a network of pig farms with 10,000 animals each; a pig, he once said, was valuable not only for its meat but as 'a walking fertiliser factory'.[38]

Urban communes were set up to parallel those in the countryside. Leftism, the target of Mao's attack at Zhengzhou, was now encouraged in factories. The head of the State Economic Commission, who had almost shot himself in the foot at Lushan, proclaimed a new slogan: 'Let the gates open to redness.' Orders went down from the top to maximize production and discard inherited Soviet management methods, an approach that was seen as being justified when Moscow reacted to the wave of criticism from Beijing by withdrawing its experts and advisers.[39]

Lin Biao extolled political work as 'the atom bomb of the spirit, much more powerful and more useful than the material atom bomb'. The Shanghai boss, Ke Qingshi, insisted that 'right opportunists' had failed to recognize the enthusiasm of the people, and the CCP chief in Guangdong denounced those who followed 'a safe and steady line'; the proletarian revolution, he said, was a rock which would withstand all storms and tides. The results were no better than before – output of steel, cement, machine tools and cloth all fell sharply; the one sector that did well was that of wrist watches, output of which went from 16,500 in 1958 to 622,000 in 1961. Grain supplies in Beijing, Shanghai and Tianjin ran very low. Mills in Shanghai had to close for lack of cotton. An enormous human disaster was brewing, stemming directly from one man's refusal to admit reality or criticism and from the reluctance of those around him to risk sharing the fate of Peng Dehuai.[40]

Grain output (million metric tons)[41]

	Total grain	Rice	Wheat
1957	185	86.8	23.6
1958	200	80.8	22.6
1959	170	69.3	22.2
1960	143.3	59.7	22.2
1961	147.5	53.6	14.25

Other crops (million metric tons)

	1958	1961
Sugar cane	12.50	4.27
Beets	3.00	0.80
Oil-bearing plants	4.77	1.80
Cotton	1.97	0.80

Livestock (millions)

	1958	1961
Pigs	138.29	75.50
Draught animals	53.60	38.10

Industrial output, billions yuan

1958	1959	1960	1961	1962
121	163	183	113	94

Steel, coal and cement, million metric tons

	1958	1959	1960	1961	1962
Steel	8.8	13.87	18.66	8.70	6.67
Coal	270.0	369.00	397.00	278.00	220.00
Cement	9.3	12.27	15.65	6.21	6.0

21

Famine and Retreat

In terms of lives lost, the famine provoked by the Great Leap Forward was the worst disaster of the twentieth century. The generally accepted estimate is that at least 30 million died.* The rural rate of 11.07 deaths per 1,000 inhabitants before the famine rose to 28.68 by 1960. The overall figure concealed far greater mortality in some provinces such as Anhui, where it reached 68.6.[1]

People ate tree bark and ground stones, and, in places, resorted to cannibalism, gnawing on flesh from corpses, and killing children to boil them for food. Men sold their wives to raise cash. Gangs of starving peasants attacked grain reserves and trains. The population effect was aggravated by millions of children not born to adults, who could not contemplate raising families or were physically unable to procreate. In Fujian, the birth rate fell from 37 per 1,000 in 1957 to 17 in 1961; in Beijing, from 42 to 25; and in Shanghai from 45 to 22.[2]

Farm output was hit hard by the new official system known as the 'three three', under which one third of farmland was harvested, one third planted, and one third left fallow – not only to enable the earth to replenish itself but also on the tragically ironic grounds that, since so much surplus grain would be produced if all fields were fully farmed, insufficient storage would be available. In 1958–61, the amount of crop-producing land dropped by 9 per cent. Average available grain per head of the rural population fell from 311 kilograms in 1958–9 to 223 in 1959–60 and 191 in 1960–61.[3]

The famine was aggravated by the excessive grain output figures which continued to be reported, producing high levels of state requisitioning

---

* A secret report to the Communist Party general secretary, Hu Yaobang, two decades later told of more than 40 million deaths.

from what was actually an insufficient reserve. The PRC went on exporting grain in the midst of its own disaster, some to pay the Soviet Union for plant contracted under earlier contracts, some sent to Communist Eastern Europe to show China's munificence. Mao welcomed exports as evidence of the success of the Leap.

The CCP and the government still insisted that feeding industrial workers must take priority. Net procurement of grain per head of the urban population rose by nearly 70 per cent between 1958 and 1960. Still, many city dwellers and factory staff went short. In Beijing, Mao's doctor, Li Zhisui, recalled, 'there were almost no people on the streets, and those who were, were thin and listless.' At the New Year dinner in 1961, his family ate only a thin porridge of rice and vegetables. There was far greater privation in the countryside, where villages were turned into ghost communities which took many years to recover. Provinces such as Sichuan and Henan, which were run by Party secretaries most loyal to Mao, suffered disproportionately, with widespread famine even if grain production remained good. Five other provinces each registered more than a million dead. Though hunger was widespread, famine was a rural phenomenon.

The chaos and experimentation of the late 1950s had undermined production methods. Distribution and transport were inefficient. Farm equipment had been neglected. On top of this, the weather turned against the PRC. In 1959 and 1960 there were droughts and floods; and the Yellow River burst its banks, killing an estimated 2 million people through either drowning or loss of crops. In 1960, lack of rain affected half the country's cultivated land. Eight of the twelve main rivers in Shandong ran dry. A dozen unusually strong typhoons battered coastal regions.

As people were reduced to utter desperation by hunger, the Great Leap thus ended with the Chinese being dehumanized in the most basic way. The mass killings of kulaks in the Soviet Union and the campaigns in the early years of the People's Republic were aimed at real or imagined categories of enemies. Now, there was no such discrimination. One simply died for being a peasant. People were 'not only dumb but also numb', a woman who survived in a famine-racked area recalled. Nobody cried when a family member died. 'You just carried on as usual,' she said. 'No fear of death, no emotion for the living.'[4]

*

Henan had been a testing ground for the Leap; one of its communes was given the name of 'Let Us Overtake England'. By the spring of 1959, the model province had become an object lesson in disaster. Much-vaunted measures of 'hydrological control' failed to stop large floods. A plague of locusts destroyed half a million hectares. Poor rainfall in 1959 brought severe drought, affecting 6.5 million hectares.[5]

Well before the Lushan meeting of 1959, only a fifth of Henan's counties had adequate grain stocks. In a special development region of the province, nearly all the cattle perished. Three and a half times as many people died in Henan in 1960 as in 1957, and the birth rate more than halved. Still, the Party boss built seven luxurious villas in the capital of Zhengzhou for visiting Politburo members.

In Sichuan, whose CCP chief was also an ultra-loyalist of the Leap, the population fell by 6 million between 1957 and 1961. In one district, a million people were estimated to have perished. China was a big country, the provincial Party secretary observed, asking, 'Which dynasty has not witnessed death by starvation?'

In Shandong, the death rate rose by 650,000, and 4 million people were hit by diseases caused by hunger. Though Anhui produced enough food in 1957–9 to satisfy its own needs, so much was taken away from the countryside that terrible famine resulted. In one county, up to a quarter of the people died of starvation. In all, according to a former senior official, 8 million died in Anhui during the Leap. Even in a city like Xi'an, which escaped relatively lightly, people got into the habit of testing for oedema by pressing their fingers on their forehead or legs in the morning to see if the indentation remained.

Bian Shaofeng, an Anhui woman whose teacher husband had been disgraced as a rightist in the repression of 1957, had gone back with him to live in their native village, where they became members of a commune. As early as the spring of 1958, food became scarce. The flour disappeared from their vegetable and wild grass porridge; then soup was made only of grass, or powdered sweet potatoes and yellow beans. As famine took hold, the commune members ate leaves, roots, worms, baby frogs and toads. They tried to catch rats, but were often too weak to do so. When they found an animal bone, they smashed it and boiled the fragments.

Of the thirteen family members in Bian's house, eight died of lack of food. Survivors did not report the passing of relatives so that they could receive the rations of the deceased. Bian kept the corpse of her five-year-old nephew hidden, and made excuses to get his supplies until the smell grew too strong. Returning from work, she saw the trunk of a man without legs or arms. A woman tending a cow nearby said his limbs had been chopped off for food – she had a chunk in her basket.

Amid all the suffering, cadres continued to impose draconian rules – members of Bian's commune were forbidden to pick up loose ears of corn in the fields. Some central leaders, such as Liu Shaoqi, tried to show solidarity with the suffering by refusing presents from the provinces and growing vegetables in plots by their homes in Beijing. As for Mao, when reality broke in, according to the compilers of his papers, 'the serious extent of the problem frightened him . . . his frame of mind was extremely grave. He couldn't sleep. He stopped eating meat.'

However, for many Party officials, the law of the jungle applied. A saying had it that the only people with 'big faces and strong legs' were cadres or cooks. There were cases of officials who buried adults and children alive for daring to beg for nourishment, or insisted on being supplied with large amounts of food, and watched indifferently as the peasants who provided them died of hunger. One rationale was that the CCP had suffered for the people, now the people should suffer for it; another line portrayed present suffering as the prelude for future abundance.[6]

Though Mao instructed that it should not be an extravagant affair, his sixty-sixth birthday party in Hangzhou, which he did not attend, on the grounds that he had a cold and preferred to miss such personal anniversaries, included bird's nest soup with baby doves, shark's fin soup and the finest of wine. The provincial security bureau boss fell down drunk.[7]

By 1960, there was no escaping both the catastrophic failure of the whole programme and the way in which Mao had accentuated the original disaster after Lushan. That year, the Leap was officially abandoned. Mao had another shock in store when it emerged by accident that his conversation on his private train, and perhaps elsewhere, had been bugged – by whom was not clear.

That was a minor incident compared to the heritage of the Leap. He could only retreat in the face of reality. The planner and economist Chen Yun re-emerged once more to the front line as a major policy switch was implemented to try to pull China out of its slump. The Chairman authorized measures to rebuild agriculture, reversing his past stress on industry ahead of farming. Zhou Enlai reasserted the role of the central government. Liu Shaoqi focused on putting the CCP back on track, bringing wayward provincial chiefs into line.

After the decentralization and anarchy of the Leap, conformity was to rule. So the administration promulgated Seventy Articles for industry, Sixty Articles for commerce, Sixty Articles for higher education, Thirty-Five Articles for handicrafts, Eighteen Articles for forestry, and Fourteen Articles for science. Literature and the arts got only Eight Articles. Thousands of construction projects were cancelled. Infrastructure investment was reduced to rationalize development. Work units were told to ensure that their members got cradle to grave protection. As 20 million peasants went back to the countryside, the residence system there was tightened up to prevent their returning to the cities; one effect was to widen further the urban–rural divide.[8]

Though he had to give his approval to the new policies, Mao was a smouldering fuse. This was not what he had led the revolution for. When the leadership met once more at Lushan in the summer of 1961, the leader maintained his distance, attending few of the meetings as he left others to shape policy. He diverted himself with nightly dance parties at an ugly concrete and glass villa built for him by the provincial committee, hidden from view behind trees and shrubs. Despite the presence of his wife, he had a liaison with a pretty local nurse, and went off to the river port of Jiujiang to bathe in the Yangzi and enjoy himself with young women at the town guesthouse.

When Mao loyalists spoke up at the conference, they were slapped down. Inspections of the countryside had shown just how bad things still were; some peasants were even making uncomplimentary comparisons with the Nationalist era. Provincial Party secretaries, who had backed the Leap most enthusiastically, were dismissed. Households began to regain responsibility from communes. The canteens were dismantled. The Guangdong Party chief, who had just been put in charge of south-central China, said that, if returning collectively held land to individuals so that they would not starve was capitalism, then 'I prefer capitalism.'[9]

A mass meeting of 7,000 cadres in Beijing in January 1962 saw an intricate dance. Lin Biao was gushing about the leader. Deng Xiaoping weighed in to stress the importance of results, which, he argued, should decide which agricultural policy was adopted. There should be no shibboleths, he added, producing a saying from his native province of Sichuan: 'It doesn't matter if the cat is yellow or black as long as it catches the mouse.'*

Though praising the Chairman, Liu Shaoqi admitted that the 'primary responsibility for the shortcomings and errors in our work in these past few years lies with the Party Centre'. Only 30 per cent of the disaster of the previous years could be blamed on natural causes, he added. The number two did not name names, but nobody present would have been unaware that Mao had declared himself to personify the Centre. The Beijing boss, Peng Zhen, dotted the i's by saying it would be bad if Mao was above criticism.

The Chairman was unmoved. He told Liu, Zhou and Deng that a tour he had made of Hunan convinced him the existing farm system was what peasants wanted. Deng promptly telephoned an aide to tell him to delete his reference to cats from the published text of his speech, and to insert a paragraph calling for consolidation of the communes.[10]

Addressing the conference, Mao said he did not want to avoid responsibility but spread blame widely. 'Any mistakes that the Centre has made ought to be my direct responsibility, and I also have an indirect share of the blame because I am Chairman of the Central Committee,' he said. 'I don't want other people to shirk their responsibility. There are some other comrades who also bear responsibility, but the person primarily responsible should be me.'

While his statement was qualified by its opening phrase, the meeting was electrified, and provincial bosses lined up to admit faults. His comrades at the top felt obliged to follow with far more searing self-criticism. Mao came away from the session even more hostile towards the Party bureaucrats. 'They complain all day long and watch plays at night; they eat three full meals a day – and fart,' he said. 'That's what Marxism–Leninism means to them.'[11]

By the 1962 summer work conference held at the resort of Beidaihe on the Bohai Sea, he was back on positive message. 'The future is bright,' he said. That did not mean he approved of what was being done to put

---

* When his remark became known later, the first colour was, for some reason, changed to white, and it has been repeated as that ever since (Ruan, pp. 4–5). Deng had taken the saying from another Sichuan native, Marshal Liu Bocheng.

right the damage of the Leap – far from it. He accused economic and finance officials of not reporting what they were doing, and setting up 'independent kingdoms'. While exonerating the PLA and Foreign Ministry, his criticism took in Zhou, Deng and Chen Yun.[12]

A particular target was Deng Zihui, the man in charge of agricultural reforms designed to put right the errors of the previous years and end the famine. One third of rural households had been granted responsibility for their affairs from the communes by then, and Mao was not happy at this vote of no-confidence in his vision. He asked his terror lieutenant from the Yenan era, Kang Sheng, to do a study of how private ownership of land had not worked in the USSR to use against Deng Zihui. He undermined a small group set up to press agricultural reforms by expanding it through the inclusion of trusted figures. As in the Peng Dehuai case, nobody stood up to the leader to defend Deng Zihui, who was sidelined.[13]

'Comrade, never forget the class struggle!' Mao declared. 'In the final analysis, are we going to take the socialist road or the capitalist road?' But, for the moment, class warfare could not be allowed to impede the work of recovery. So changes continued. Industrial working hours were cut. Millions condemned in rectification and anti-rightist campaigns were pardoned. Fifty thousand people were allowed to go to settle in Hong Kong. There was liberalization in the arts. The Chairman knew the moment was not ripe for another leap into the unknown. In any case, he had a different target to attack, the 'counter-revolutionary' Soviet Union.

Despite their differences, Mao had held Stalin in some awe. This did not apply to Khrushchev, whom the Chairman saw as not being a true Communist, lacking respect for China and short in the quality the Chinese always called for from others – 'sincerity'.[14]

Though Moscow was helping the PRC's atomic programme and agreed at the beginning of 1959 to provide technology for nuclear submarines, the Kremlin had not hidden its distaste for the Great Leap Forward. It acted towards China in a generally boorish, overbearing manner that was bound to get Mao's back up. Its search for a thaw in relations with Washington became even more suspect when Khrushchev went as far as to describe Eisenhower as a man of peace. Mao ordered up a collection of tales entitled *Stories about Not Being Afraid of*

Ghosts, designed to mock the Soviets for fearing confrontation with the capitalists.[15]

Clashes between Moscow and Beijing came out into the open at a series of international Communist meetings at which delegates exchanged insults. Khrushchev called Mao an adventurist deviationist, while the Chinese replied that the Soviet leader was guilty of 'patriarchal, arbitrary and tyrannical' behaviour, and was jettisoning Leninism. Next, Moscow withdrew its offer to supply China with an atomic weapon, and withheld research assistance. In July 1960, the USSR decided to halt aid and to pull out its 1,300 experts and advisers. At the same time, there were frontier clashes between Chinese and Soviet forces in Central Asia.

In December 1961, Beijing's proxy in Europe, Albania, which stood apart from Khrushchev's revisionism and received strong financial incentives from the PRC, severed relations with the USSR. The following year, though approving the construction of the Berlin Wall, Mao considered that Khrushchev behaved in a 'capitulationist' manner in the Cuban missile crisis. However, relations between the two Communist powers were still strong enough for Moscow to tell Beijing of the installation of missiles in Cuba before the crisis broke, while the PRC informed the Soviets of its plan to launch an offensive in the Himalayas against India at the same time. Whether this amounted simply to an exchange of information or to collusion remains an open question.

Moving across the border in October 1962 and helped by confusion in the Indian government, the PLA scored successes on a front stretching for 600 miles. Having established positions south of the border, it declared a ceasefire, and withdrew. It had got what it wanted, including a protective zone for the road to Tibet. The Chinese never gave any figure for their casualties; the Indians reported 1,383 dead and 5,500 missing or captured. Frontier disputes would still rumble on for more than four decades.[16]

The war reflected a realignment in Asia. The days of Sino-Indian co-operation in the non-aligned movement were well past. New Delhi could count on Soviet political backing against Beijing. By tilting India against the PRC, the war paved the way for strong relations between China and Pakistan.

Mao resumed the ideological struggles with nine polemics, starting in the autumn of 1963, which attacked the Soviet leadership for its denunciation of Stalin, revisionism and pursuit of peaceful coexistence. On 14 July 1964, relations were broken off.

Khrushchev's fall in October of that year led to Zhou Enlai travelling to Moscow to meet the successors, Leonid Brezhnev and Alexei Kosygin, but there was no improvement. Indeed, the Soviets made matters worse with a clumsy attempt to probe the prime minister on whether he would be ready to move against the Chairman. That was a non-starter, and Zhou immediately informed Mao. It could only fan suspicions that Moscow was plotting a coup in Beijing.

More than ever alone in the Communist world except for Albania and the parties of Indonesia and Cambodia, China went its own way. Maoism became a glamorous creed for revolutionaries in what was then known as the Third World, encouraging national liberation movements and forging links with some countries which had achieved independence though, as an article by a Chinese deputy foreign minister warned, 'the capitalist classes that control the political power of certain Afro-Asian states prefer to develop their economies along the road of capitalism or state capitalism.' In a twenty-year period starting in 1963, China provided Africa nations with loans amounting to $2 billion on very favourable terms, and sent some 150,000 workers to help on development projects, among them the 1,150-mile railway between Lusaka and Dar es Salaam, which involved 25,000 Chinese engineers and was finished in five years, two years ahead of schedule. With the Chairman's long-term associate Kang Sheng playing a major directing role, the PRC spent large sums on backing its favoured revolutionaries, and opposing what it saw as the increasingly revisionist stance of the USSR. Maoism presented itself as the authentic voice of the masses, in contrast to Moscow's bureaucratic approach, seducing guerrilla movements and Western leftists alike.[17]

The breach with the Soviet Union meant that the PRC had both the superpowers lined up against it. In Washington, successive secretaries of state from both parties followed the anti-China line from conviction backed by an awareness of the domestic political firestorm that would be provoked by any apparent softness towards the nation which many Americans thought had been 'lost' by US weakness in 1949. America was solidly behind Taiwan, and its retention of the Chinese seat on the UN Security Council, though it discouraged Chiang Kai-shek's schemes to attack the mainland in the aftermath of the Great Leap and famine.

The Treasury Department maintained an embargo on the PRC; the Department of Commerce blocked the export of anything from pens to condoms; Americans in Hong Kong were told not to buy fresh food because it might come from the mainland; the CIA mounted operations in China's frontier areas; and the United States' Information Agency spent millions of dollars on both open and covert propaganda. 'Peking's behaviour is violent, irascible, unyielding and hostile,' the secretary of state, Dean Rusk, summed up in 1966, while President Lyndon Johnson denounced the PRC for 'helping the forces of violence in almost every continent' and casting a 'deepening shadow' over Asia.[18]

As American influence increased in Laos and the US began its build-up in Vietnam, the Western enemy came to within a few hundred miles of Yunnan. Though North Vietnam was unwilling to throw its lot in entirely with Beijing given the aid it was getting from the USSR, Johnson claimed that the Chinese were urging on the government in Hanoi, and Beijing was certainly committed to a North Vietnamese victory. But there was not going to be another Korean War in Indochina. Plentiful aid was offered; 100,000 Chinese were sent over the border as labourers to free North Vietnamese to fight; Hanoi's air force was helped with joint exercises from a specially built airfield in southern China. If the North was invaded and China threatened, Beijing would send in troops and fight to the end. Otherwise, it would stay on the sidelines. While Maoist revolutionaries were encouraged in Africa and Latin America, the regime recognized its limitations closer to home when confronted with the far stronger superpower.[19]

The image of Mao defying the world establishment, in both Washington and Moscow, was a seductive one, but it took little account of China's weakness. Cash which flowed out to help fund friendly regimes in the Third World or finance guerrilla movements could, for instance, have been much better used for development at home. But, for the Chairman and his acolytes, that was not the point. They had declared their regime to be the standard bearer of world revolution, and would act accordingly. As with the Great Leap, the grand political vision was what counted, regardless of reality.

Not that the true state of the country was evident to outsiders at the time. Foreigners were given Potemkin Village tours of happy villages and pounding factories. Gaullist France recognized the PRC. The image of a strong nation was reinforced on 16 October 1964, when the PRC conducted its first nuclear test at the remote test site in the north-western oasis of Lop Nor. Mao celebrated with a little poem:

> Atom bomb goes off when it is told.
> Ah what boundless joy.[20]

Beijing denounced the test ban treaty between the US, USSR and Britain as an attempt to set up a monopoly club. Mao again attacked Brezhnev and Kosygin for practising counter-revolution and 'Khrushchevism without Khrushchev'. Speaking to a Japanese delegation, he outlined territorial claims on 1.5 million square kilometres of Soviet territory.

At home, however, it was time for consolidation. While communes were retained as geographical units, they were greatly reduced in individual size. Incentives were introduced, and rural markets permitted to operate again. Work units were reduced to teams of thirty or so people, which resembled old village groupings rather than the Leap armies. Small plots of land were handed back to private ownership. A mixed system thus began to emerge in the countryside, in some ways moving back towards the old meld of individual property and land held by lineage clans.

Grain output rose, and Zhou authorized imports to fill the granaries. Rationalized after the Leap, industrial production grew by 17–27 per cent in 1963–5. In the middle of the decade, output of steel, electricity, cement and heavy trucks was more than double the 1957 figure. China began to develop its own petroleum and petrochemicals sectors. Inflation was brought down as agriculture revived and the state cut retail prices. Urban overcrowding was reduced by sending more than 26 million migrants back to the countryside. By 1965, state enterprises paid 31 billion yuan to the government from their profits.[21]

A serious attempt at population control was launched, reversing Mao's earlier encouragement of a high birth rate. A conference held in September 1963 set a target of reducing the annual rate of urban growth from 33 to 20 per thousand inhabitants by 1965, followed by more gradual falls in the ensuing ten years. A Birth Control Office was set up. Campaigns were run to promote late marriage and the two-child family. After the second baby, according to the childless Zhou Enlai, the best thing for an urban husband to do was to be sterilized; he ordered the propagandists to 'create the right atmosphere' for this. Medical teams sent to rural areas were told to include birth control among their services; but the impact was blunted by opposition among health workers, who were not convinced about the new policy, by peasant resistance, by the political fear of being branded a 'Malthusian' if one encouraged contraception – and by the sheer scale of the problem.[22]

In some places, old practices re-emerged: in a Fujian county, brides were sold while idols were worshipped in sixty-seven temples, thirty-one of them newly built. At the grave-sweeping season in April 1964, official newspapers warned against lineage groups making pilgrimages to tombs. 'If we go with landlords and rich peasants to visit ancestral tombs, what class standpoint are we taking?' asked one paper.[23]

At the same time, a stricter work ethic was encouraged, with a soldier, Lei Feng, singled out as a model for the nation – an orphan, his hard work, devotion and selfless work for others made him a paragon of Communist virtue until he died at the age of twenty-two after being hit on the head in a freak accident.* In the new climate, expertise was no longer suspect; nor was 'red' politicization regarded as the key to success. The foreign minister, Marshal Chen Yi, argued in a speech in Beijing that students in technical schools should work on their specializations, rather than study Marxism–Leninism. At a conference, he reached back to 1957 to tell the audience, 'We still want a hundred flowers to bloom, so cast aside your inhibitions, and speak up with your opinions.'[24]

That could only be regarded with suspicion by those who had seen what had happened in the blooming of 1957. Mao might be lying low, but he had not changed his basic ideas. He launched an attack on the planner Chen Yun as a 'bourgeois character' (he was, in fact, a rare proletarian figure among the leadership) who 'leans consistently to the right'. Chen retreated to Suzhou on grounds of ill-health, remaining out of front-line affairs for more than a decade.[25]

With Mao's agreement, Liu Shaoqi launched the Socialist Education Movement (SEM) to clean out abuses in the CCP and make cadres responsive to the people. More than 2 million trusted Party agents were sent out to implement the SEM in the Four Clean-Ups and the Five Antis. Liu's book, *How to be a Good Communist*, became a bible. The reform teams, some as big as 130,000 people, included forty-five deputy

---

* Four decades later, an entrepreneur marketed condoms bearing his photograph to denote performance. The authorities told him to stop.

ministers. They combed through 2,530 state enterprises and communes. What they found was shocking for a regime which still believed in the purity of its cause.

More than 100,000 cases of speculation and profiteering were reported by the public. Waste amounting to 103 million yuan by officials was uncovered in just four cities. In parts of Hunan, things were so bad that local authority had been transferred to peasant associations because the CCP branches had collapsed or were controlled by renegade officials. In Fujian, local functionaries forced peasants to build them houses, using communal materials, held endless parties and expected gifts from guests at weddings and birthday celebrations. In one commune in Qinghai, in the north-west, 47 per cent of cadres were listed as meriting dismissal or disciplinary action. In Sichuan, more people were arrested in the last two months of 1964 than in the whole of the rest of the year. In a district outside Beijing, detained officials made seventy suicide attempts, fifty of them successful.[26]

Mao backed the SEM but saw that it could simply result in an efficient, cleaner bureaucracy which would be an obstacle to his desire for more revolution. Success would also buttress the authority of Liu, Deng and Zhou, and risk turning the Chairman into a mere figurehead. In the background lurked the spectre of China following the Soviet path, with the CCP becoming a bourgeoisified machine headed by grey men. So, for the Chairman, the struggle had to be relaunched, with the accent on class war and mass movement. If Liu Shaoqi's Party stood in his way, it would be time to replace it.[27]

Mao was not mistaken. Nearly two decades after it had taken power, the CCP had lost its initial appeal. To regain that, and to enable the leader to reassert his own position, a new populist link was needed, illuminated by a new dream, however fanciful. For that, the Chairman required a new cast of actors to play under his direction and to aim at not so new targets, first among them the man generally seen as his successor.

Though Liu Shaoqi was reconfirmed as head of state by the legislature in 1965, the distance between Mao and his number two widened. The president became the epitome of all that the Chairman disliked and feared in the evolution of the regime: a cautious man set on bolstering bureaucracy rather than pursuing revolution pell-mell. The signs of a looming divorce had become increasingly apparent. When Liu contracted tuberculosis in the spring of 1964, the Chairman ordered the Central Bureau of Health to stop giving special treatment to the leadership. He, of course, kept his own personal doctor; others were to go to the Beijing Hospital, along with members of the public. While cloaked in the language of democratization, the timing meant the decision was clearly aimed at Liu.[28]

At a Politburo work conference, the Helmsman took issue with the harshness of the SEM purge. He then noted ominously: 'There are at least two factions in our Party. One is the socialist faction, the other is the capitalist faction.' Without naming names, Mao accused Liu of wanting to stop him intervening in debates, and Deng of wishing to exclude him from meetings (the latter had suggested that he might prefer to rest because he was in poor health). Waving copies of the national and Party constitutions, Mao said that as a citizen and CCP member he had every right to speak at meetings. It may have seemed a ridiculous piece of grandstanding, but it was never safe to disregard such outbursts since their author could turn his paranoia into reality.[29]

At the end of 1964, the Chairman took the unusual step of inviting Liu Shaoqi to his seventy-first birthday dinner, but then subjected him to a diatribe against revisionism and the building of independent kingdoms. On the day Liu was re-elected to the presidency, 3 January 1965, Mao summoned him to his suite at the Great Hall of the People. Without telling him, the Chairman also called in Liu's wife so that she could witness his verbal attack on her husband. The couple looked at one another in silence. Fifteen years later, he would tell Edgar Snow that he had decided at that time that Liu had to go because he had disputed the assertion that there was a capitalist faction in the CCP which had to be rooted out.[30]

In place of Liu, Zhou and the bureaucratic pragmatisms, Mao assembled a spectacularly odd group of acolytes who existed in the reflection of his image. This first gang of four* consisted of Lin Biao, the defence minister, Chen Boda, the ideologue who drafted many of Mao's pronouncements, Kang Sheng, the ruthless police chief from the Yenan era,

---

* Only Jiang Qing would belong to what became known as the Gang of Four in the ensuing years, but the appellation seems as justified for the original quartet as for the later one.

and Jiang Qing, the Chairman's ferociously ambitious wife with more than a few chips on her shoulder.[31]

Lin was busy turning the PLA into Mao's ideological arm, with soldiers playing the role of model citizens. Politics must dominate everything, the army newspaper explained. Senior officers who wanted the PLA to concentrate on its professional role were put under pressure, as Lin raised the Mao cult to new heights by organizing the mass publication of the *Little Red Book* (the Chairman drew royalties from the hundreds of millions of copies).[32]

Born in 1907, Lin had trained at the Whampoa military academy and joined the Long March before his emergence as a leading commander in the civil war, heading the campaign in Manchuria and northern China. A vice-chairman of the CCP and member of the Standing Committee of the Politburo, he had a long record of poor physical and mental health, stemming in part from a war wound inflicted on him by a Communist sniper who shot him when he was disguised in Japanese uniform. He had become addicted to opium and morphine, a habit cured in the Soviet Union in 1949, but which may have left traces. Several sources diagnosed him as a manic depressive. A bodyguard said the marshal did not feel comfortable in a peaceful context, and needed a warlike environment to revive his energy. His uniform was cut so tightly that it seemed to be a second skin. Slight and short, with deep black eyes, he habitually wore his military cap, even indoors, to hide his spotty bald head.

Lin suffered from phobias, in particular of water and moving air; he could not bear to look at the sea. Mao's doctor recalled that the sound of running water could give him diarrhoea. He never bathed, but, like his leader, was rubbed down with hot towels. Nor did he use a toilet, squatting instead on a bedpan under an improvised tent made of a quilt. His wife fed him steamed buns dipped in water to give him liquids. The first time Dr Li was taken to meet the marshal, he was curled up in bed in his wife's arms, his head on her breast, crying like a baby as she patted and comforted him. He was suffering from a kidney stone, a painful ailment to be sure but not one which the Chairman's doctor felt should have reduced a leading soldier to tears.[33]

Lin's second wife, Ye Qun, had met him at the Yenan base, where she had a reputation as a woman of easy virtue. Despite her known lack of concentration, she headed his private office – their children referred to her between themselves as 'the Director' while calling their father

'Commander'. Ye aspired to play a political role to add to her rank of colonel in the PLA, and showed great determination in pursuing her goal. Given her husband's constant need for moral and physical support, she became a power player in her own right, the second powerful wife of the new turn of the revolution. Her literature teacher recounted an episode when a member of the marshal's staff approached Ye with a question from his boss as she watched a film. Lin had phlegm in his mouth and wanted to know if he should swallow it or spit it out. 'Tell him to spit it out,' she replied impatiently.[34]

Ye enjoyed Mao's favour. In 1967, he began to invite her to attend Politburo meetings. She did all she could to advance the career of her ambitious son in the military, but had tempestuous relations with both of Lin's daughters – one, Xiaolin, had been born to the marshal's first wife. The other daughter, Lin Liheng, known as 'Doudou', was the only person who dared to stand up to her mother. In 1966, Ye discovered a diary in which her daughter had written negatively about Mao; she burned it but, inexplicably, photographed the incriminating pages first and sent them to the Security Bureau. After one row with her mother, Doudou tried to kill herself; this matter was kept secret from her father. Mao and Zhou were both aware of the tension in the family, the Chairman remarking that there were 'two camps' in the house.[35]

Chen Boda, Mao's stout, moon-faced political secretary, was a bookish figure, prone to nervous fits, weeping and talk of suicide. Born in 1904, he had taken part in the Northern Expedition of 1926–7 before going to study in Moscow. Short and with a thick Fujianese accent and stammer that made his speeches virtually incomprehensible, he stood firmly on the left of the Party. The famine deaths, he said, were 'an unavoidable phenomenon of our onward march'.[36]

Chen was a key figure in developing each version of Mao Zedong Thought that would shape the 1960s. After the birthday dinner at which Mao ranted to Liu Shaoqi about revisionism and those seeking to run independent kingdoms, Chen was the only one who spoke up in the Helmsman's support; in the early hours, the Chairman summoned him to explain how he planned to get at his number two.[37]

Kang Sheng, the police and terror chief of the Yenan era, was, like Chen Boda, an alternate member of the Politburo. He had returned to Beijing in 1955 after semi-exile in charge of Shandong – he also suffered from ill-health. After carrying out the investigation into Gao Gang's activities for Mao, he steadily worked his way back to the centre, overseeing the simplification of the language, though, as a scholar, he probably detested the change. Joining the Central Committee Secretariat, he was active in promoting leftist causes, as well as informing the Chairman about what his own boss, Deng Xiaoping, was up to. He became a moving force in pushing revolution in Africa, the Middle East and Latin America, and got back in training as a terror expert by establishing a 'Special Case Group' to probe an alleged attempt to rehabilitate Gao Gang – the only evidence was an unpublished novel with a central character said to resemble the north-eastern boss; thousands were questioned, and a vice-premier was among those purged.[38]

Born in 1898, Kang had joined the CCP in Shanghai in 1925, and subsequently gone for training to Moscow, where he observed Stalin's show trials. In the Yenan base, he oversaw the purges with particular ruthlessness, perfecting the terror machine, riding round in leathers on a black horse followed by a dog. Described as a man 'with a heart of stone, who did not know how to cry', the thin-faced, short-sighted killer with a sparse moustache was a chain-smoker and drank heavily. He was also genuinely cultured, a skilled calligrapher, combining deep knowledge of Chinese classics and Marxism – the latter made him valuable in ideological assaults on Moscow.[39]

The fourth member of the new inner circle, Mao's wife, had a long power relationship with Kang. Born in 1914, Jiang Qing had been an actress in Shanghai under the name of Lan Ping – Nora in Ibsen's *Doll's House* was her favourite role. Her marriage to a noted writer in Shanghai ended in divorce. Involved in progressive politics during the dangerous 1930s, she was arrested by the KMT political police, and there were allegations that she had slept with her captors to win their favours or given them information in return for her freedom. As Japan attacked the city in 1937, she left for Yenan. Beautiful, pale-skinned and sophisticated, she did not fit easily into the dour, male-dominated base, or into the company of the tough female veterans of the Long March. She had an affair with a member of the Propaganda Office who came from Shanghai. Then, she attended a talk given by Mao, to whom she put some questions. Soon afterwards, seeking the Chairman one night to discuss a message from Chiang Kai-shek, Zhou Enlai found him lying on a grassy bank with Lan. She was twenty-four; he was forty-five.[40]

Mao was already estranged from his third wife, who had accompanied him on the Long March and been badly wounded in a Nationalist air attack. He had begun an affair with another young woman, but Lan replaced her. Taking the former actress under his wing, Kang Sheng encouraged her liaison with the Chairman. One evening, the police chief was seen playing the drums as she performed an aria from a traditional opera. For Kang, she was a protégée who could be useful in the deadly game of internal politics. For her, he was her stepping stone to the top.

But, though Mao's sexual appetite was well known by then, Yenan was a puritanical place. Revolution did not encompass free love. The new union was deeply disapproved of by many leading figures in the base. The Chairman's third wife had gone through hell on earth for the cause; now she was being ditched for an actress floozy. An investigation produced a report that Lan was suspected of having been a Nationalist agent. But she became pregnant with a daughter by Mao, and he was unshakeable. Without her, he told senior colleagues, 'I can't go on with the revolution.' The impasse was such that he asked for advice from that well-known agony uncle, Josef Stalin.[41]

In the summer of 1938, a deal was worked out, perhaps with a helpful word from the Kremlin, more probably by the combined efforts of Zhou Enlai, Zhu De and Liu Shaoqi. A divorce was decreed between Mao and his wife, who went to the Soviet Union for medical treatment. The Chairman married his mistress. But she had to agree to keep out of politics for thirty years, and to devote herself to looking after him. That gave her a smouldering resentment – 'You know in Yenan, I got into trouble for wearing a military cap,' she would recall indignantly in the 1960s. 'I was ordered not to wear it!' She was Ibsen's Nora kicking against the pricks of the CCP, further burdened in due course by her swain's philandering ways with other women.[42]

By the 1950s, the couple were distant from one another. In the leadership compound in Beijing, Jiang Qing, as she was now known, moved into a different courtyard from her husband, citing the varied hours they kept. While Mao took up with his procession of young ladies, his wife grew increasingly neurotic, paranoid, domineering – and ill. She went to the USSR for medical treatment. She suffered from ringing in the ears and hypochondria, complained about noises, draughts and bright lights. She thought her nurses were trying to poison her or scald her in her bath.[43]

Still, Mao came to see her as a useful ally, a potential piece on the chessboard ready to strike for his benefit. Though the thirty-year purdah had not expired, he began to send her documents for comment, and called her in to help him at the Lushan conference in 1959, where he also summoned his previous wife and caused her to have a fresh breakdown. Having proved herself, Jiang began to work on the cultural front, which had always been one of her husband's prime interests and in which she could claim some expertise. Appointed to head the CCP Propaganda Department's film branch, she worked little, never turning up at the office. The growing strength of her mentor, Kang Sheng, further buttressed her position. One of their fields of co-operation was the revival of traditional dramas, which both of them loved. But, as Mao developed an anti-classical agenda, they realized that this would not be the best way to proceed and dropped the traditional for modern leftism.

By the mid-1960s, Jiang was ready for a major political role. Though she did not command much respect from those running China, she had one great advantage. As Mao became increasingly isolated, she could claim to speak in his name. Portraying herself as the voice of the Chairman, she was irresistible, though nobody was to know how accurately she was conveying her husband's views.[44]

The choice of culture as her domain was fortunate for her, once she had shed her traditional baggage. Having picked up a remark by Kang Sheng about how novels provided a good cover for anti-Party thoughts, Mao decided it was time for a rectification drive aimed at writers and artists, who were told that their 'ideological remoulding' was weak. It was, the Chairman said, 'absurd that many Communists are enthusiastic about promoting feudal and capitalist art, but not socialist art'. A special group was set up to deal with cultural issues under the Beijing city boss, Peng Zhen.

This was in keeping with the Chairman's idea that culture was defining society. His wife ardently encouraged the campaign. It was her way of moving towards the authority which the elders of Yenan had denied her; a revenge element would run through her conduct in the next dozen years, though she insisted later that she was simply doing as her husband instructed. 'I was Chairman Mao's dog,' she would say. 'Whoever he told me to bite, I bit.'[45]

In the autumn of 1965, she accompanied Mao on a long stay in Shanghai – a projection room was fitted to their apartment in the old French Concession area so that she could vet films. She used the visit to

433

establish close links with the city's leftist intellectuals, ready to move when her husband gave the signal. Wiggling a finger, he described her as 'a scorpion'.[46]

The autumn of 1965 brought significant reverses for the PRC abroad. The Beijing-friendly Communist Party in Indonesia, which counted 3 million members, botched an attempted coup and brought about a bloody military counter-attack leading to the installation of the Suharto dictatorship. China's ally, Pakistan, meanwhile, failed to pursue a war with India which Beijing had hoped would weaken New Delhi. At home, Mao lost some of his most loyal supporters among provincial chiefs, either through the fall-out after the Great Leap or, in the case of the Shanghai boss, Ke, through a fatally mistaken medical diagnosis. But, by the end of the year, he was ready to launch his new offensive against those he had decided were enemies of the revolution.

First, Yang Shangkun, the director of the Party Centre's General Office, who controlled the flow of documents to the Central Committee, was fired. Though no reason was officially given for the disgrace of the Long March veteran, the bugging of the Chairman's train four years earlier was apparently advanced as one cause. To replace him, the Chairman appointed Wang Dongxing, the head of the Central Bureau of Guards, whom he had come to trust over the years. Wang vetted all visitors, including Mao's wife. He also supervised the 'Cultural Work Troupe' which provided the leader's women.[47]

Mao then embarked on a lengthy visit to the Lower and Middle Yangzi, travelling in an air-conditioned East German train. The trip did not interrupt the stable cleaning. The next victim was a seemingly unlikely target, the PLA chief of staff, Luo Ruiqing, the former security chief, who had presided over repression and the labour camp system. His treatment was an early example of just how determined the new group round Mao was in destroying its targets, and how it rolled over the old guard.

In 1959, 'Luo the Tall' had been appointed to the army job after the incumbent went down in the purge of Peng Dehuai. He seemed just the man Mao needed to ensure control over the forces. But he went native, backing training and modernization over Lin Biao's stress on politicization and guerrilla warfare. He tried to get his boss to tone down his extreme praise of the Chairman, disapproving of Lin's exaltation of the leader's thoughts since this devalued other Marxists. Mao's sympathy evaporated; 'Luo isn't worth the clothes on his back,' the Chairman told his doctor.[48]

In mid-November 1965, Luo further blotted his copybook by successfully defending the head of the General Office of the Military Commission, Xiao Xiangrong, who also took a dim view of Lin's instruction to 'give prominence to politics'. Hearing that Xiao had been cleared of the accusation that he was anti-Mao and belonged to a Peng Dehuai clique, Lin ordered the tribunal to reconvene to expose and criticize Xiao. 'A chicken should be used to scare the monkey,' the defence minister added – the monkey being Luo.

Lin's wife, Ye Qun, went to see Mao in Hangzhou with a dossier compiled against the chief of staff. Staying for seven hours, she accused Luo of bypassing her husband and wanting to take his place. In the following days, Mao insisted that those who did not put politics first were guilty of revisionism and 'opportunism'. He accused Luo of treating Lin as an enemy, of being a careerist dictator, and of being constantly 'in contact with people who engage in conspiracies'.

An enlarged Politburo meeting was arranged in Shanghai to try Luo in his absence – he was on a tour of south-west China. The dossier of allegations did not impress either Liu Shaoqi or Deng Xiaoping. The General Office chief, Xiao, was called in from Beijing and pressured to accuse his boss. When he refused to do so, he was sent into internal exile in the north-west, deprived of his freedom and subjected to investigation for 'serious errors'.

Unable to make the case stick, Mao and Lin had Luo summoned to Shanghai. Zhou and Deng showed him the dossier. When Luo started to deny the charges, the prime minister cut him off. But the tribunal would still not convict him, and broke up inconclusively. Feeling the strain, Mao took ten times his normal dose of pills to get to sleep.

Luo was flown back to Beijing while Mao celebrated his seventy-second birthday in the Jiangxi capital of Nanchang by drinking a little wine and taking a walk along the river. Though it was a windy day, the Chairman unbuttoned his shirt, catching a bad cold that turned into bronchitis. Despite coughing heavily and running a fever, he refused local medical care. Dr Li, who had been off working in the countryside, was summoned, and cured his patient with antibiotics. In a sign of his rising paranoia, Mao told him that the guesthouse was poisoned.

Finally, Luo cracked under the pressure, offering to resign and submitting the required self-criticism, though he denied ever having wanted to replace Lin. He was subjected to 'struggle sessions' with up to ninety-five people haranguing him. These were organized by a 'small group' set up to handle the case, which – despite the latter's earlier doubts – included Zhou and Deng. To escape, Luo jumped out of a third-floor window; he broke his legs, but survived. His suicide bid was taken as proof of guilt. Deng made light of the episode, describing Luo as having 'jumped like a female athlete diver, resembling an ice lolly.' 'How pathetic,' Mao commented.

After Luo, the next target was the Beijing boss, Peng Zhen, a formidable figure, both politically and personally, with his tall, burly frame, domed forehead and highly coloured complexion. Born in 1902, he joined the Party at the age of twenty-one, rising eventually to be a member of the Central Committee and Politburo, CCP secretary and mayor of the capital. As head of the top-level small group just set up, he was also, in effect, culture minister. This and his tight control of the capital were obstacles to Mao's plans which had to be removed.

The issue on which this battle was fought was, at first sight, both minor and ironic. But it was adroitly chosen and stands as a case study in the way the Helmsman operated, relentlessly pursuing his aim behind a cloud of subterfuge and apparent concessions, using others to advance his cause so that he could claim to be falling in with the majority and deny responsibility if things went wrong.

In 1959, Mao had praised the Ming-era official Hai Jui, who had stood up to the emperor and been dismissed for his pains. Wu Han, a historian who was also a leader of the China Democratic League and deputy mayor of Beijing, was encouraged to undertake a play on the subject. Then came the Peng Dehuai affair, and the Chairman decided that the work was a subversive attack on his own conduct. Now, Jiang Qing was determined to make it the spearhead of her first major assault; this suited Mao since Wu Han's position in the capital meant that his play could be connected with his boss, Peng.

Jiang turned to Shanghai leftists, led by an intense, bespectacled 48-year-old propaganda official, Zhang Chunqiao. A stout, 34-year-old writer, Yao Wenyuan, with a big, bald head like a melon, was called in to draft the attack. After being sharpened by the Chairman and his wife, the article was published in two Shanghai newspapers in mid-November

1965. It charged that the play had spread poison by dealing with rural matters in such a way as to encourage private enterprise and capitalism, so 'if we do not clean it up, it will harm the people's cause.'

The article was picked up by six east-coast CCP journals, but Peng told the *People's Daily* and other papers in the capital not to run it. He relented when Zhou telephoned to tell him of Mao's role, but he refused to abandon Wu – the *People's Daily* ran an editorial in favour of 'the freedom to criticize as well as the freedom to counter-criticize'. Any mistakes were attributed to historical faults, not political motives. In a bid to sideline the whole issue, Peng's men insisted that it was a purely academic matter.

Peng and members of his small group on culture then flew to see Mao in Wuhan with a report that backed up their contention that the issues involved in the play were not political, and stressed the importance of 'seeking truth from facts, and holding everybody equal before the truth'. Mao riposted that the article attacking the play was good; what he wanted to know was whether the dramatist was 'really anti-Party, anti-Socialist'. Kang Sheng, who was a member of Peng's small group, broke in to call the play 'a poisonous weed'.[49]

Mao appeared to give ground by observing, in his best Hundred Flowers style, 'Of course, if there are different opinions, they should be aired. You should all feel free to speak. Let different opinions be aired here.' He did not need to see the report by the Beijing group – 'You people work it out,' he added.

Peng took this as the green light. He and his group went off to browse antiquarian bookshops. Stopping in Shanghai on the way home, he told colleagues he had Mao's approval. But the leader was only biding his time. 'Reactionaries don't fall down unless you hit them hard,' he told Dr Li.

A trip Peng made to Sichuan, where he met the other Peng, Dehuai, can only have aroused further suspicions in the Chairman's mind – though the idea that they discussed a military coup seems highly unlikely since neither commanded any troops and Peng Zhen thought he had won the day over the play.

But Jiang Qing now geared up for fresh action, going to see Lin Biao, who had put her in charge of the PLA's varied artistic and cultural activities. Dr Li noticed that she was acting with a new assurance, freed from her hypochondria, walking briskly, no longer suffering from headaches or bothered by bright lights, noises, draughts or ringing in her ears. Her husband, however, showed the strain as during the crisis over Luo Ruiqing; he had even greater trouble than usual sleeping, sometimes staying awake for twenty-four hours at a stretch, and lost his appetite.[50]

This did not stop him launching into fresh denunciations of 'bourgeois intellectuals' and calling Peng Zhen the 'number one questionable person'. At a Politburo session, attended by the Beijing boss, in Hangzhou, Mao attacked the playwright Wu Han as no better than a member of the Kuomintang and the *People's Daily* as being only 30 per cent Marxist. Young leftist intellectuals must be given their heads, he said. Beijing, he charged, was being run as an independent kingdom. The atmosphere, as Dr Li recalled, was 'extraordinarily tense'.[51]

Lectures which Jiang Qing had given in her PLA role were published to warn of 'the dictatorship of a sinister anti-Party and anti-Socialist line which is diametrically opposed to Chairman Mao's Thought'. 'The literary field and most professors have stood as a black force trying to dominate our politics,' she charged. As a result, there was a desperate need for a 'Socialist Cultural Revolution'. The *Liberation Army Daily*, which ran extracts from Jiang Qing's lectures to military commanders, proclaimed that 'a Socialist cultural revolution demands that there be destruction as well as creativity. Without thorough destruction, there can be no real construction.'[52]

Kang Sheng told Peng and Zhou that Mao had accused the Beijing authorities of protecting bad people. That was enough for the prime minister to fall in line. A Party Secretariat session, under the chairmanship of Deng Xiaoping, convicted Peng of opposing the Chairman and contravening Mao Zedong Thought. At the suggestion of Zhou and Deng, Peng's small group on culture was dissolved, and a new body was established to draft a 'culture revolution document'.

The attack was pressed home by Mao in person at another Politburo meeting in Hangzhou, attended by Peng – the Chairman refused his request for a private twenty-minute prior meeting. Liu Shaoqi had been away on a tour of Asian capitals, but, on his return, the Chairman told him he had been chosen to deliver the verdict on his long-time colleague and the alleged co-conspirators. They were sentenced to imprisonment or house arrest but, once again, Mao held back from the death sentences passed on similar victims of Stalin's show trials – he had done well by getting away with such a travesty and knew better than to push things any further.

Next, the spotlight turned to the Propaganda Department chief, Lu Dingyi, who was required to offer self-criticism. As they arrived for a meeting to consider his case, Politburo members found a bizarre missive on their seats.

It arose from anonymous letters which Lin Biao's wife had been receiving, accusing her of sleeping around in Yenan, including an affair with the writer Wang Shiwei, who was subsequently executed. The marshal, the letters charged, had been cuckolded; the children might not be his. Ye found out that the author of the letters was Lu Dingyi's wife, Yan Weibing. Yan was arrested as a counter-revolutionary – her husband was sent away. Recalled to Beijing, he was accused of having mounted a campaign with his wife against Ye Qin and Lin Biao.

As they took their seats on 20 May, Politburo members found a note on their chairs in the marshal's handwriting, signed by him. It read: 'I certify that (1) when she and I got married, Ye Qun was a pure virgin, and she has remained faithful ever since; (2) Ye Qun and Wang Shiwei had never been lovers; (3) Laohu and Doudou [the Lin children] are my own flesh and blood; and (4) Yan Weibing's counter-revolutionary letters contain nothing but rumours.'

Lu denied that he had known anything of his wife's letter. But he hardly helped himself when, questioned by Lin as to how this could be true, he replied, 'Aren't there quite a few husbands who don't really know what their wives are up to?' Lin threatened to kill him on the spot. Years later, a drunk member of the security services told a Western author that the note from Lin ended with the words 'The Chairman can testify to Ye Qun's virginity [in Yenan].'[53]

22

Demons and Monsters

Mao saw the Cultural Revolution which began in the early summer of 1966 as 'the greatest revolutionary transformation of society, unprecedented in the history of mankind'. 'My countrymen are yearning for another spring,' he wrote in a poem. For the Chairman, Old China had existed within an old cultural framework, so New China had to forge its new culture, ways of thought, and behaviour patterns. The 'four olds' – old thoughts, old culture, old customs, old habits – were to be swept away. Like the foot soldiers of such earlier mass movements as the Taiping, the 'little devils' of youth, as Mao called them, were recruited to 'disrupt the palace'. A psychological biography of the Chairman has suggested that, like so many emperors of the past, he was seeking immortality by identifying himself with symbols that would live on after him. Fifteen years later, a Central Committee resolution described what ensued as 'the most severe setback and the heaviest losses suffered by the Party, the state and the people since the founding of the People's Republic'.[1]

The cult of Mao was at the core of the movement – more than 2 billion badges bearing the leader's face were made. The *Little Red Book* of his thoughts became the national bible, carried, in particular, by students, who quoted from it to upbraid suspected opponents and urge people to follow the Chairman's teachings. Like those of Confucius, the sayings of the Great Helmsman were held to provide an all-encompassing belief system covering everything from Correcting Mistaken Ideas ('Even if we achieve gigantic successes in our work, there is no reason whatsoever to feel conceited and arrogant') to War and Peace ('War is the continuation of politics') and Serving the People ('We should be modest and prudent, guard against arrogance and rashness, and serve the Chinese people heart and soul').

Huge portraits of the Helmsman went up everywhere. The leader had, in his own mind and to many of his people, become a superman who stood with the great figures of Chinese mythology and legend, well beyond any normal human bounds. He was both the emperor whose edicts had divine force, and the Monkey King of the classic *Journey to the West*, a free-spirited genius, who 'makes trouble in Heaven' as he saves his master – in this case, China. The country, he once wrote, needed people who were 'savage and rude' – they would replace the institutional organs of the Party and state.

The new movement harked back directly to Mao's celebrated observation in Hunan in the 1920s that a revolution was 'not the same as inviting people to dinner or writing an essay or painting a picture or embroidering a flower . . . a revolution is an uprising, an act of violence whereby one class overthrows the authority of another . . . to right a wrong, it is necessary to exceed the proper limit.' Less than twenty years after leading the CCP to power, the Monkey King wanted to open the gates to the biggest outburst of fervour he could muster, with no respect for the status of its targets.[2]

From the start, the rhetoric of the young shock troops was even more vengeful and extreme than in previous campaigns in the PRC. 'Beat to pulp any and all persons who go against Mao Zedong Thought,' advised an early wall poster. Nobody was to be safe. Since Mao was the 'red sun in our hearts', 'whoever dares to oppose him shall be hunted down and obliterated,' proclaimed the *People's Daily*. 'No matter who they are, what banner they fly, or how exalted their positions may be.'[3]

Under Mao, a Central Cultural Revolution Group (CCRG) took charge, headed by Chen Boda and containing Kang Sheng and Jiang Qing and their radical associates. Occupying seven villas in the Diaoyutai complex in the capital, the group was poorly organized. Kang, who used agents to egg on and direct militants, feuded constantly with Chen while, for all her authoritarian ways, Mao's wife often showed herself uncertain. The one thing that bound them together was their ambition, their hatred for the Party establishment and their adulation of the Chairman.[4]

Though most senior Party figures were excluded, Zhou Enlai came to play an important role in the CCRG, introducing some order. Once again, he was showing a flexibility calculated to ensure survival. His involvement was in sharp contrast to the urbane image he enjoyed abroad. At one point, it is true, he drew up a list of people who were not to be attacked under the Cultural Revolution, but, as with all such lists, the point was that those who were not on it were fair game. Neither Liu Shaoqi nor Deng Xiaoping seems to have grasped the nature of the challenge that was building up.

To get the ball rolling in the universities, Kang Sheng sent his wife, who was head of his private office, to see the Party secretary in the Philosophy Department at Beijing University (Beida). Nie Yuanzi was a 45-year-old Yenan veteran, married to a cadre in the Central Discipline Inspection Commission. As she recalled forty years later, 'we believed the Party was great and graceful and correct. You went wherever it pointed you.'[5]

Nie was highly critical of the head of the university, Lu Ping, for his alleged conservatism. Ideology apart, she had reasons for unhappiness because she was about to be transferred to a small branch of the institution outside the city. Other leftists in her department were also preparing to attack Lu. A big-character wall poster they signed was put up in the place at Beida where the Hundred Flowers posters had appeared ten years earlier. It accused Lu and two other senior officials of having failed to implement Mao's orders. Students and teachers, it added, should 'eliminate all demons and monsters, and all Khrushchev-type counter-revolutionary revisionists, and carry the socialist revolution through to the end'.*[6]

Students flocked to see Nie and her leftist comrades and to read the posters. Rallies were held to advance the cause, with fervent chanting, crashing cymbals and the beating of drums. As word spread, big-character posters went up everywhere, some defending Lu, most attacking him. At the other Beijing University, Qinghua, 65,000 posters appeared. In Shanghai, 2.7 million people were estimated to have joined the movement, writing 88,000 posters. In Xi'an, students plastered the walls of the Transport and Communications University with denunciations of the Party Committee – one girl who was writing twenty posters a day committed suicide under the strain. Suddenly, students were free to attack those in authority while, as Liu Shaoqi noted, security forces stood by and let them do as they wished.[7]

Middle-school pupils chatting in a Beijing park came up with a collec-

---

* Nie was still alive in Shanghai in 2006, having written a book about her experiences. According to the *New York Times*, she greeted visitors with a bright red business card carrying her portrait and constantly received mobile telephone calls during an interview on the fortieth anniversary of the Cultural Revolution (*NYT*, 10 June 2006).

tive name for the activists – Red Guards. As the unrest spread through colleges and schools across China, the government and Party suspended classes. This freed 103 million primary pupils, 13 million in secondary schools and half a million at university to join the struggle.

Not understanding what was going on, and reliving the official version of the Hundred Flowers, the minister of higher education thought the episode would be useful in luring destructive extremist student 'snakes' from their holes. But Mao, who was at his villa by the lake in Hangzhou, weighed in to back the big-character poster by Nie and her associates; carried on the shoulders of radical students at Beida, she exulted that 'Chairman Mao has said I am the first red banner – so anyone who opposes me opposes Chairman Mao.'[8]

The leader ordered his statement of support to be run by all newspapers and broadcast nationally. This was, he added, the start of a Beijing Commune that would be even more important than the Paris Commune of 1871. Liu Shaoqi only learned of the Chairman's move through a telephone call from Kang Sheng.[9]

Despite the Chairman's statement, Liu and Deng denounced the leftist tide as counter-revolutionary. They ordered Communist Youth League branches in universities to be suspended because they had become compromised by radicals – this created a vacuum into which grassroots Cultural Revolution committees moved. Work teams were sent in to restore order; one, which went to Qinghua, was led by Liu's wife.[10]

The teams used heavy-handed methods, dismissing activists and rationing paper and ink to try to stem the flood of posters. But the insurgents succeeded in painting them as 'black gangsters' who should be thrown off the campuses. Showing how little they realized what they were facing, Party leaders put Chen Boda in charge of a team meant to ensure order at the *People's Daily*; the newspaper promptly ran an editorial praising the original Beida poster under the headline 'Sweep Away All Freaks and Monsters'.[11]

Liu flew to Hangzhou to try to get the Chairman to return to Beijing. Mao was evasive and, on 18 June, Beida students escalated their action. Mimicking tactics the leader had described as being used by peasants against landlords in Hunan in 1927, they grabbed the university head, Lu, and a group of his colleagues* and stuck pointed dunces' caps or

---

* Different accounts speak of from forty to sixty other teachers.

wastepaper baskets on their heads. The teachers were made to kneel while they were kicked and punched, their faces spattered with black ink, their clothes ripped, their hair pulled, their arms bound. Wall posters were stuck to their bodies, and they were paraded around in disgrace. 'The privileges of the bastards who ruled Beida for decades came to an end like fallen flowers carried away by flowing water,' proclaimed a colleague of Nie Yuanzi. 'A red terror spread over the campus as the black gang trembled with fear and shook with fright, and the revolutionary teachers and students were filled with joy.'[12]

The Beida work team, which had been busy elsewhere when the incident started, moved in belatedly to break up the struggle session and free the teachers. Its report depicted the incident as an outbreak of adolescent hooliganism; it said one sixth-year student, a CCP member, had ripped open the clothes of a woman cadre to fondle her breasts and genitals. Liu Shaoqi approved the report and had it circulated as a guide to how to handle such disorders. But Mao ordered it to be withdrawn, and Tao Zhu, the propaganda chief who had replaced Peng Zhen in the Central Committee Secretariat, told students privately that the attack had been 'a terrific thing'. At another meeting, Chen Boda and Kang Sheng said that if the masses told them to 'piss off', the teams should withdraw.

Content to let the pot simmer and keeping himself closely informed through a flow of confidential news reports, Mao went to his home village of Shaoshan in Hunan, moving into a villa built for him at a place called Dishui Cave. Next to the family burial ground, it was in the heavy concrete and glass style he favoured, and was next to a reservoir where he could swim. From there, he pronounced the attempt to bring the Red Guard movement under control to be a mistake.

The Dishui Cave villa had no air conditioning and the only electric fan was ineffective, so the Chairman's party moved to Wuhan, where Mao took a much-publicized swim in the Yangzi; some reports said he had covered fifteen kilometres in sixty-five minutes, four times as fast as the world record. In reality, he appears to have spent most of his time floating on his back, his belly up in the air. No matter, the symbolism was evident. At seventy-three, the leader was still a life force for change and renewal. The media gave rapturous coverage. On 8 July, the Chairman wrote to Jiang Qing saying he would create 'great disorder under the heavens'. 'Great chaos will lead to great order,' he added. 'The demons and monsters will come out by themselves.'[13]

In Beijing, Liu admitted errors, but noted the lack of clarity from Mao as to what the new revolution meant. The number two appears to have attracted a good deal of sympathy from other members of the leadership, bewildered at what was going on. But they were forced on to the defensive when Mao returned to the capital in mid-July, immediately conferring with Chen Boda and Kang Sheng, but refusing to receive Liu.

The Chairman was in swingeing form when he attended a leadership session after his return. The attempt to restore order amounted to an act of suppression, terror and dictatorship, he said. Repeating his term of condemnation, he spied 'demons and monsters' in the room. As for the efforts of the work teams, 'all these restrictions must be smashed to pieces . . . we must not restrict the masses.'

Mao's words were transmitted across the country. On 24 July, he ordered the work teams to be withdrawn from universities; nobody argued with him. From now on, the movement in educational establishments was to be left to 'Cultural Revolution mass organizations' elected by teachers and students. Liu's daughter recalled that she had never seen her father so upset.

A meeting of 10,000 students and teachers was called in the Great Hall of the People to hear the decision. From the platform, Liu offered more self-criticism. Unbeknown to him, Mao was listening from behind a curtain. When Liu admitted that old revolutionaries like himself were facing new problems, the leader snorted: 'Old counter-revolutionaries is more like it.'

After Zhou Enlai had spoken, Mao suddenly stepped on to the stage. The audience roared approval as he walked back and forth, slowly waving his arms but remaining silent, his face impassive. He then went back to his suite in the Great Hall, the prime minister following him like a faithful dog. Throughout, he had not looked at Liu and Deng. The next day, he told the Red Guards he agreed with their view that rebellion against reactionaries was justified.[14]

Pressing on, Mao called a Central Committee Plenum on 1 August. It was presented with a document known as the Sixteen Points, calling for a great revolution to touch people's souls. This made plain the nature of the crusade by stating that 'the main target of the present movement is those within the Party who are in authority and are taking the capitalist road.' Red Guard methods were approved – 'Don't be afraid of disturbances,' the document urged. Adopted by the Plenum, the Points were read out on national radio and printed in the *People's Daily*. Four gramophone records of their being read out and of supportive speeches went on sale.[15]

During the Plenum, the Chairman had doodled 'Bombard the head-quarters – my big-character poster' on an old copy of the *Beijing Daily*. A secretary wrote up what he had in mind for mass circulation. An open declaration of war, the poster repeated the accusation that those who had been in charge in Beijing during Mao's absence had enforced a bourgeois dictatorship:

striking down the noisy and spectacular Great Proletarian Cultural Revolution. They have stood facts on their head, juggled black and white, encircled and suppressed revolutionaries, stifled opinions differing from their own, imposed a white terror, and felt very pleased with themselves. They have puffed up the arrogance of the bourgeoisie and deflated the morale of the proletariat. How vicious they are!

Mao pressed his assault on Liu by summoning Lin Biao from Man-churia, where he was resting and escaping the summer heat, to tell him he was to become the second-ranking figure in the regime. Lin wondered if his health would not be a problem – he must also have been aware of the extreme danger of the post. But the decision had been made for him. He was told to deliver a denunciation of Liu, which he did after being suitably briefed, reaching back to alleged 'right opportunist errors' in the 1940s. Expressing total support for Mao, he told the Cultural Revol-ution group that the movement should be so tempestuous that neither the bourgeoisie nor the proletariat would be able to sleep for six months.

The seventy-four full members of the Central Committee then elected a new Politburo. Lin took second place after Mao; Liu was relegated to eighth position. Despite being among four leaders who got unanimous support, Deng Xiaoping was placed only sixth. The rankings were decided not by the Party Organization Department, as they should have been, but by Mao, Lin and Jiang Qing. If Liu was the principal target, Deng was on probation.

Key departments, including those dealing with organization and propaganda, were thoroughly shaken up, provoking fresh suicides – killing oneself was taken as an admission of guilt. Huge demonstrations swelled in mid-August, and Mao appeared like a god at a rally of a million Red Guards in Tiananmen Square. Wearing an ill-fitting PLA uniform, he greeted the front ranks in person and had a Red Guard band pinned on his right arm by an eagerly smiling, bespectacled young woman. The speech-making was left to Lin Biao, who was described by a Red Guard taken to the platform as 'a small, thin, weak man, his face white as paper'. The marshal and Mao wore uniforms to stress the martial nature of the programme. Liu and Deng, who were placed off to one side, were told to wear civilian clothes. In comments on the pair, Chen Boda called them 'spearheads of the erroneous line'. Mao complained that they treated him like a corpse at a funeral. Liu was denounced as a 'bourgeois dictator', a Chinese Khrushchev.

The Chairman appeared at seven more rallies in the late summer and autumn of 1966, being seen by more than 10 million people. For the Guards, who were given free rail travel to the capital, the rallies were the apogee of their revolutionary experience, a delirious exultation in which the individual melded into the mass, living evidence that China had launched itself on a new path in all its might and that there were no bounds to what could be achieved.[16]

The demonstrations marked Jiang Qing's emergence as a leading public figure when she took over as mistress of ceremonies at a Tiananmen rally. A Red Guard found her stentorian tone of voice 'a bit weird' but was 'honestly inspired' by what she had to say. Her eyes shone and popped out as she exulted in the adulation of the biggest audiences any actor could hope for, her name emblazoned on the banners below the platform.[17]

To make sure that the Passionaria of the Cultural Revolution suffered no embarrassment from her past, agents of Kang Sheng and the Public Security Ministry went to work searching for records of her time in Shanghai in case any incriminating material remained. People who had known her were questioned and their homes searched. Many were arrested on spurious charges – the best man at her marriage to a screenwriter died in prison, as did a groom who had been wed in the joint ceremony. Boxes filled with papers were burned in her presence, but a record of her interrogation by the Nationalist political police could not be found – it may not have existed or may have been destroyed during the war or may have been taken to Taiwan. Her Shanghai husband was safe in Paris, running a restaurant.[18]

Red Guard activity followed a steady crescendo, much of it among pupils in middle and elementary schools. The names of streets were changed to more politically correct designations like Anti-Revisionism Road (by the Soviet embassy), though Mao baulked at designating Tiananmen as Red Square. Hong Kong, where Red Guards clashed with colonial police, was renamed 'Expel the Imperialists City'. In Shanghai the facades of colonial buildings were stripped of carvings, crests and bas-reliefs. Mao gave up the English lessons he had begun in 1963.

An attack was launched on 'Western' dress. Men in tapered trousers and pointed shoes were told to remove them. Women with stylish coiffures were escorted to hairdressers to have them cut off. Beijing middle-school students drew up a list of a hundred instructions on how to 'destroy the old and establish the new', including banning 'the bastards of the bourgeoisie' from using restaurants and laundries. Members of the exploiting classes were to 'collect their own feces and deposit them with the night-soil collector carts themselves'. Displays of magic and wrestling, use of poker cards, private shoe repairing and the purchase of snacks would be stopped while 'the family system shall be destroyed.'[19]

In Beijing, 4,000 centres were established for Guards arriving from the provinces – there were plenty of empty schools to use. The PLA drilled them on how to march through Tiananmen. Young men and women from the cities fanned out across the country to spread the message and visit sacred sites such as Mao's birthplace and the Jiangxi base. On packed trains, they crammed into the toilets or lay on luggage racks. This mass movement seriously disrupted train transport of goods – by the end of 1966, a backlog of 10 million tons had built up. There was another downside to the journeying – the travellers spread cerebral-spinal meningitis which affected 3 million people, of whom more than 160,000 died. Still, for many Red Guards, it was their Long March, opening up geographic horizons. But it also revealed to urban youths just how poor and backward much of the country was, and showed them the reality the peasants had lived through during the famine at the end of the Great Leap.[20]

The Guards were a law to themselves as terror escalated against real or imagined class enemies. This ranged from individual punishments to mass killings as in a district outside Beijing where more than 300 people were massacred, their bodies thrown down wells or into communal burial pits. In August and September 1966, 1,772 people were killed in the capital, while the death toll in Shanghai reached 1,238 – 704 of them suicides of people under attack. In Wuhan, nearly a hundred died in the autumn. In Tianjin, a writer recalled, people threw themselves to their deaths in the river almost every day – they were hauled out with iron hooks and laid out in rows on the bank.[21]

Less unfortunate class enemies were subjected to violent struggle sessions, and made to adopt the 'airplane position' for hours with their arms stretched out behind them. More than a hundred rallies were held in Beijing at which alleged rightists were humiliated and beaten in front of crowds of tens of thousands of screaming Guards.

Except for the Chairman and his immediate entourage, nobody was safe. The long-time PLA chief, Zhu De, was branded a 'black commander' and an 'old swine'. The former Beijing chief, Peng Zhen, was subjected to fifty-three denunciations. He Long, who had led an early Yangzi base, was accused of working against the regime. Peng Dehuai and his associate from the Lushan meeting, Zhang Wentian, were kicked and beaten at rallies and photographed bowing in humiliation on a platform. Still unable to walk after crippling himself in his suicide attempt, the former army chief of staff, Luo Ruiqing, was carried into sessions in a wicker basket, his legs hanging over the edge. The CCP first secretary in Tianjin killed himself under the criticism – Mao denounced his funeral, which was attended by 500,000 people, as 'using the dead to oppress the living'. On a more personal note, Jiang Qing exploited the campaign to vilify members of Mao's previous families, notably her stepdaughter-in-law, Zhang Shaohua, wife of the leader's mentally disturbed son, Anqing.[22]

Outside the capital, Party chiefs, administrators and military commanders were subjected to endless rounds of denunciatory rallies. Regions such as Tibet, Inner Mongolia and Xinjiang, where non-Han traditions remained strong, were ruthlessly subjected to one-size-fits-all Maoism. Any excuse for action sufficed. The governor of Heilongjiang province in Manchuria had his hair torn out for daring to wear it in a cut that looked like Mao's. In Harbin, Guards ransacked both the Russian Orthodox Church and the biggest Buddhist temple, where monks were made to hold up banners proclaiming 'To Hell with the scriptures: they are full of dog farts.' Children were turned against their parents – the writer Xinran recalls how she pricked her finger and wrote a one-sentence message in blood to her father, who was in jail: 'You must repay the blood of the Chinese people', after being told that, in the old days, he had helped his British employers to drink Chinese blood as if it was red wine.[23]

With Mao's approval, the Ministry of Public Security prohibited the police from interfering with student agitation. 'After all, bad persons are bad, so if they are beaten to death, it is no big deal,' the minister argued. Seeking to 'clarify' relations between the students and the security forces, Zhou limited himself to advising the first not to beat up the second or enter police premises.[24]

Few dared to dissent from the swelling movement. One who did, a student of German, Wang Rongfen, was appalled by what she saw as similarities with the Third Reich. In a letter addressed to Mao, she asked, 'What are you doing? Where are you leading China?' It concluded, 'The Cultural Revolution is not a mass movement, it is one man with a gun manipulating the people.' She went to the Soviet embassy, sat on the doorstep, drank four bottles of insecticide and deposited a note reading: 'Poor motherland, what have you become?' Her suicide attempt failed, and she was arrested. Her family members were persecuted and her college subjected to struggle sessions. Eventually, she was freed, and went to live in Germany in 1989.[25]

Any everyday action could become the basis for attack. A student recalled that his mother went to withdraw some money from a bank where her husband worked. Other clerks alerted the Guards that she might be up to something suspicious. A raiding party forced its way into their flat, smashing the contents. The mother was denounced. Her son spent the night walking the streets. In the morning, a sympathetic Red Guard let him go back to the apartment, where he saw his treasured stamp collection spread over the floor. He moved out; when he went back to see his parents, he found that the Guards had shaved his mother's head, and coloured it black and white.[26]

In all, sixty-five tons of gold were estimated to have been seized in the raids on homes across the country along with large quantities of silver, cash, valuables and antiques, some of which were sold abroad, and part of which found their way into the leadership's pockets – Jiang Qing was alleged to have paid seven yuan for some fine jewellery. Kang Sheng, a connoisseur of Chinese art, was said to have acquired fine pieces by placing his own agents among the Red Guard raiders with lists of what to grab for him. Mao got rare books which were sterilized and placed on his sitting room shelves.[27]

In Beijing, 4,922 out of 6,843 designated places of historical interest were trashed – the Forbidden City was protected because, hearing of a planned attack, Zhou sent in troops and ordered the gates closed. At the birthplace of Confucius in Shandong, Red Guards, acting with the tacit approval of Chen Boda, destroyed 6,618 registered cultural artefacts, including 2,700 books and 2,000 graves. Some reports say local inhabitants intervened to limit the damage.

In colleges and schools across China, teachers were attacked by pupils. Some were tortured and, in extreme cases, murdered, often in the most barbarous ways. One had a broom handle forced up his rectum after he had been beaten and had his feet lacerated by glass and thorns; others were made to sit on a box of explosives and set it alight – after the blast, their arms and legs hung from surrounding trees. Professors and scholars who escaped with their lives were sentenced to clean toilets. Almost 400,000 people branded as rightists were forced to leave cities and return to the villages from which they or their parents had come. The housing space they vacated was swiftly taken by revolutionaries and their supporters.[28]

Inevitably given the title of the movement, writers, artists and thinkers were prime targets, along with their works. Mao gave full vent to his suspicion of intellectuals, whom he compared to 'very adhesive soil' which the air could not penetrate and on which no plant would grow. Artistic works were subjected to Jiang Qing's edicts, which reduced output to political correctness devoid of originality. Everything had to celebrate the revolution. Conformity killed creativity.

In an echo of the First Emperor's destruction of non-utilitarian literature, great piles of books were burned. Exiled in the north-east, the writer Ding Ling was made to sleep in a cowshed and stand with her arms stretched behind her in the 'airplane' position in struggle sessions. The manuscript of a long novel she had been working on was taken from her and destroyed. She was separated from her husband, also a writer; but he managed to drop notes written on scraps of paper or rice husks when he passed her during their hours of hard labour. Despite her suffering, Ding thought that some of her captors were, in fact, protecting her from even worse treatment.[29]

In Shanghai, the opera star Yan Huizhu, who had married another celebrated performer, Yu Zhenfei, was targeted by Jiang Qing, who instructed: 'Tell her to stop performing. She should ponder her errors.'

Red Guards put up posters denouncing the couple, who were made to clean the lavatories at the drama school where they taught. Their house was broken into, the raiders taking off gold bars, cash and jewels hidden in vases and flowerpots. One day amid all this, Yan told her maid to buy good food and wine for the evening meal. Though the couple were estranged by then, her husband came to dinner. She asked him if they should kill themselves. 'We have nothing on our consciences, why should we die?' he replied. After the meal, he went to his room. Yan brought their eleven-year-old son to see him. They both prostrated themselves on the floor. At midnight, she hanged herself from a rail above the bath.[30]

In Beijing, the dramatist Tian Han, who had written the words of the national anthem, was taken to the courtyard of the Writers' Association with two other well-known authors. A Red Guard recalled seeing him there with his hair shaved and a placard round his neck denouncing him for counter-revolution. The tormenters were not young Guards, but men in their forties or fifties. They forced the 68-year-old Tian to kneel, his head lowered almost to the ground. On it were three razor cuts from the shaving. He was denounced for private misdemeanours, as well as political crimes. Two years later, he died in prison.[31]

Soon after the 18 August rally in Tiananmen Square, a group of thirty writers and artists was taken to the courtyard of a former temple in Beijing. Placards calling them 'demons and snake spirits' were hung round their necks, and they were made to kneel as they were beaten. Among them was Lao She, the great chronicler of the lives of the people of Beijing. Sixty-seven years old and in weak health, he was subjected to a struggle session at which he had to stand for hours in stifling summer heat holding up a placard denouncing his crimes. Some reports said he had been made to wear a dunce's cap. After being badly roughed up, he passed out. Then he was dragged to the headquarters of the Beijing Municipal Literary Federation, where screaming Red Guards spat at him, kicked and punched him, and pummelled him with leather belts.

When Lao was released and allowed to go home, the blood was so thickly congealed on his clothes that his wife had to cut them off. In his absence, his house had been ransacked and many of his books destroyed. He had been told to return to the Literary Federation building the next morning carrying a placard admitting that he was an 'active counter-revolutionary'. Instead, he went to Taiping Lake in the west of the city, and sat silently all day. That night, his body was found in the water; presumably he had committed suicide, unless his persecutors had come back and thrown him in. The authorities ordered an immediate cremation.

During this initial phase of his new revolution, Mao was restless, and seemed concerned about his safety. He had the security force in Beijing quadrupled to 100,000 men, as though he feared a coup attempt or that the violence might get out of hand. He was often on the move, finding comfort in the cocoon of his private train. When in the capital, he shuttled between the Zhongnanhai compound and his suite at the Great Hall of the People. According to his doctor, he even gave up women for a time, and cancelled his dance parties. This did not last for long.[32]

Though he clearly bore the prime responsibility for what was happening, the Chairman may well not have quite appreciated what he had unleashed. 'One big-character poster, the Red Guards, the great exchange of revolutionary experience, nobody – not even I – expected that all the provinces and cities would be thrown into confusion,' he remarked in October. 'I myself had not foreseen how that as soon as the Beijing University poster was broadcast the whole country would be thrown into turmoil,' he told a work session the same month.[33]

The truth was that, beyond the big slogans and generalities, he had no guidance to give the Guards on what was to follow their storming of the CCP citadels. Apart from Jiang Qing's activism in the arts, the Cultural Revolution offered only a few obiter dicta from on high. There was no positive programme, just the injunction of demolish the 'four olds'.

The movement took off, in large part, because – rhetoric aside – it was responding to social and human elements that had little to do with ideology, as such. By the mid-1960s, it was clear that 1949 had not brought paradise, but a deeply divided society. While the economy was recovering, the number of industrial jobs fell drastically after the failure of the Leap, just at a time when young people born in the first flush of the PRC were coming into the labour market – in the early 1960s, 2 million new people were looking for work each year, while retirement rates among those in employment were low. For the mass of people who did not belong to the elite or have insider contacts, life was dreary and harsh, hemmed in by restrictions. There could be resentment towards the CCP establishment which Mao was now attacking; as he observed, 'officials in China are a class, and one whose interests are antagonistic to those of the workers and the peasants.'[34]

Much of the countryside was still very poor and backward. Sent to take part in a campaign to foster the class struggle and fight against corruption in a village in rural Jiangxi, Mao's doctor had a first-hand view of just what conditions were like five years after the great famine. The peasants, he wrote, were 'poorer than poor'. Their clothes were threadbare and patched. Their food was meagre and almost indigestible – unhusked rice mixed with sand and bits of gravel, topped by a few paltry vegetables. Their homes were miserable, leaky huts without even rudimentary furniture, and the only roads were narrow dirt paths that turned into mud after rain.[35]

'There were no schools in the village, and I never saw any newspapers, magazines or books,' Dr Li went on. 'The overwhelming majority of adults in the village were illiterate, and illiteracy was being perpetuated in their children.' There were no farm machinery or draught animals, and few tools. The poorest, most overworked man in the village was the son of impoverished peasants who had got him adopted by a landlord, for which he still suffered decades later. When the doctor's team arranged a film show, people walked fifteen miles to see the first projection in their lives. One day, a villager patted Dr Li's jacket and said, 'If only I could have an overcoat like this; then I would know that Communism had arrived.'*

Despite having been in charge since the foundation of the PRC, Mao was not seen as the source of all the problems from which the country suffered. Given the hallowed status of the leader and his thoughts, the onus for the failure of the revolution must, therefore, lie with those around him. To have laid the blame at his door would have been to bring the whole edifice into question. So yet another lie was erected as the Chairman's new offering was presented as a vista of liberation – to students, women, peasants and workers. The sudden freedom to speak out against authority was intoxicating. In schools, pupils could criticize

* The doctor who looked after the Cultural Revolution leaders in Shanghai was also sent to work in the countryside. The village to which he went got its first telephone so that he could be taken back to the city if his eminent patients needed his care.

– and terrorize – teachers; in families, children could stand up to their fathers. 'In the wall posters, we can now write about things that have been forbidden for 20 years,' as a student remarked. 'Do you really want to know what the Cultural Revolution is? It is a feast of criticism.' There was also self-interest at play; the way in which junior staff at universities raided files for damaging material to use against their superiors in wall posters was not simply a matter of a political search for dirt; if the seniors were forced out, positions would fall vacant. A cadre from a factory reflected that it was an ideal opportunity for the incompetent to grab jobs.[36]

'Before the movement, I had been quiet, obedient, and almost shy in class, but only because my free and reckless nature had been suppressed,' An Wenjiang, a student son of a poor seaman who joined the radicals in Shanghai, recalled. 'Given the opportunity, I grew radical, daring and enthusiastic.'[37]

At the start of the movement, An found himself excluded from the Red Guard group at his Shanghai university. Its members, he recalled, were the children of high-ranking officials, student leaders and Party members. So he and like-minded outsiders set up a unit of their own. 'I can't deny there was a selfish element, a desire to show off, in my becoming a rebel leader,' he said. 'But it was mostly a conviction that the son of a working-class man should be allowed to participate in revolution.'

Following Mao's invitation to 'Bombard the headquarters', 1,400 members of An's group invaded the Shanghai drama academy for an all-night meeting. The establishment revolutionaries hit back with an article in a local newspaper attacking them. Troubled, An took advantage of the free rail travel on offer to go to Beijing to meet radicals, who reassured him. He attended a rally in Tiananmen, crying with joy as he saw the Chairman. Returning to Shanghai, An and his friends went to a big bookshop on Nanjing Road, bought photographs of Liu Shaoqi and burned them in the street, attracting a crowd of spectators. Suddenly, they felt free to express themselves, and play a part in society long denied by the straitjacket of the Party and the administration.

For young women in a male-dominated society, the Cultural Revolution offered a chance to step to the front, in the image of Jiang Qing and Nie Yuanzi. It was a young woman who presented Mao with his Red Guard armband in Tiananmen. The team that destroyed the relics at Confucius's birthplace was led by a female cadre. Reminiscences of the travels by the Guards to spread revolution speak of the discovery of love.

In the countryside, the weakening of old family patterns under land reform, collectivization and communal existence, along with the decline in the power of the clan chief and respect for elders, opened the way for new behaviour. Some teenage militants made a point of subjecting their own families to harsh treatment to show their allegiance to the movement as they beat the 'ox-monsters' and 'snake spirits' of reaction.[38]

As the first generation to have been brought up under Communism, the mythology of victory through violence on the Long March and in the civil war had been dinned into them. So 'violence and brutality were not negative words if used against class enemies,' as a Shanghai student leader put it. 'The more violent and brutal the better . . . Chairman Mao called on us to rebel, to bombard, to destroy, and we did so without hesitation. Just like a bunch of mad dogs, once angered each tries to be madder than the rest.' Or, as a woman who was at the most prestigious elementary school in Chengdu recalled, 'talking to friends about street fighting and deaths became like talking about food.'

The violence tapped into a long tradition of uprisings stretching back through Chinese history, and the habitual resentment felt by local people at newcomers dispatched by the central power to lord over them. The collapse of the CCP machine in many places facilitated the emergence, particularly in the countryside, of groups pursuing rivalries disguised by the rhetoric of the new revolutionary struggle. Whether the actors knew it or not, they drew on old symbols and practices. The sacred nature of the *Little Red Book* had less extreme parallels in the devotional reading out of Sun Yat-sen's will at morning ceremonies under the KMT. 'Loyalty dances' enforced by the Guards on officials had been used under the Tang dynasty. The way Red Guards took bottles of water from beneath the Gold Water Bridge by Tiananmen Square on trips to the provinces mirrored the way in which their ancestors had collected Holy Water from supposedly magic sources. The ritual, theatrical form of conflict in denunciation rallies had long antecedents; so did the demonization of opponents and use of extreme language, as when the head of state was dismissed as 'a heap of dog's dung' and his wife 'a bitch struggling in the water'. The eating of the flesh of enemies, which would be reported in Guangxi, was the latest manifestation of an old way of demonstrating mastery over adversaries.[39]

Like the Taiping and the Boxers before them, the Red Guards used the language of mythology. The bourgeois-capitalist counter-revolutionaries were the modern equivalent of malevolent figures of tradition, counterparts to the demonic Manchus and evil Christians targeted by the earlier movements. Like the old spectres, they were held to exist not only in a netherworld – the West or the USSR – but also to lurk among the population, threatening to devour and destroy people if they were not identified and exterminated. The old terms of devils, ghosts, snake spirits and tigers were employed once more. Enemies were locked up in what were known as 'cattle sheds' – the ox demon had been another major malignant force in mythology. In another echo of the Taiping and Boxers, a divine army consisting of the PLA and the Red Guards was marching under banners painted in auspicious red to defend their holy city of Beijing.[40]

On top of this was the legacy of two decades of rectification campaigns, denunciations, purges, the arbitrary exercise of power and lack of concern for human life. It all constituted a deep, poisonous well in which Mao fished adroitly. Killing became the mark of a true revolutionary. Musing in private on Hitler's ferocity, the Chairman asked, 'The more ferocious the better, don't you think? The more people you kill, the more revolutionary you are.'[41]

As 1966 drew to a close, the Cultural Revolution took on a broader and more complex character, and the cult of the man proclaimed to be China's Great Helmsman was boosted further. At their places of work, staff bowed three times before his portrait. The *Little Red Book* was held to cure illnesses and even, in one case, to have raised a man from the dead. Telephone operators answered calls by proclaiming, 'Long Live Chairman Mao.' Control was tightened. The only books, films and theatrical performances allowed were those approved by Jiang Qing; a total of just 124 novels were published during the Cultural Revolution. Any form of personal taste in clothing was out of bounds – women wore uniformly flat heels and most people donned Red Guard-style green uniform jackets, baggy trousers and caps, with a badge of the Chairman on the tunic pocket.[42]

The outside world hardly knew what to make of the events in China; foreign newspaper reports of the time record the huge numbers, and at least some of the violence, but grasping what was really going on was virtually impossible. The Mao cult, however, rose on the left internationally as it did among the faithful at home. Some intellectuals spied a new form of mass democracy and social engineering. For China, it was only natural that the ferment at home should be accompanied by a new push among revolutionary movements in the 'storm centres' of the Third World. Foreign militants trained in the PRC took the new doctrine and techniques home, among them Pol Pot, who returned to Cambodia around this time. 'The contradiction between the revolutionary peoples of Asia, Africa and Latin America and the imperialists headed by the United States is the principal contradiction in the contemporary world,' wrote Lin Biao.[43]

At home, the marshal granted cadets at military schools and academies the right to act as the Red Guards did, radicalizing the army from below. On the campuses of Beijing and Shanghai, the crusade split into factions. Young radicals challenged the more privileged students who had provided the initial leadership. Styling themselves 'rebels' in response to Mao's praise for opposition, the new men and women were linked to Jiang Qing and the Cultural Revolution Group, which was playing an ever more important role and heightening Mao worship.

The revolution was officially extended from education to industry and the rural world. Workers were allowed to set up 'revolutionary organizations', though they were expected not to let this interfere with production, while 'poor and lower-middle peasant youths' would form their own groups in the countryside. The degree to which either could be controlled was doubtful. Big-character posters at factories in Shanghai denounced the management; production was indeed affected. Managers who ceded to demands from the workers to get output going again were accused of 'economism' – that is, reducing social issues to matters of sheer economics.

The Leap slogan of 'More, Faster, Better, More Economical' resurfaced. Teams of Red Guards set off to build great projects, including dams that were put up so hastily that they had to be reconstructed within a couple of years. Guards in rural areas were told to focus on 'great contending and great blooming, big-character posters, debates on a grand scale and big democracy'.* In some communes, pigs were

---

* During the Hundred Flowers, Deng Xiaoping had warned against 'big democracy', likening it to the challenges to the Communist regimes in Poland and Hungary.

branded with the character for 'loyalty' to show that they were with the revolution. In villages of Guangdong, Red Guards burned 'yellow' books, including love stories, banned traditional weddings and funerals, and drove several officials to suicide.[44]

An agricultural brigade of the Dazhai commune in the mountains of Shanxi, which had pledged to boost output and build itself up after major flooding without any outside help, became the model rural unit. The *People's Daily* said it showed how revolutionary will could 'change the face of rivers and mountains'. 'We poor and middle-level peasants will hold even higher the great red banner of Mao Zedong Thought,' Dazhai's gravel-voiced, white-turbaned leader proclaimed as his unit was granted the honour of a visit from the Chairman.[45]

In industry, the oil town of Daqing, in Manchuria, was given similar hallowed status, embodying mass mobilization and will power – and freeing the PRC from reliance on Soviet fuel. 'Learn from Daqing' became the equivalent of 'Learn from Dazhai', as both were held to draw on the class struggle to promote a specifically Chinese model of development. While Daqing did, indeed, produce a lot of oil, model communes, like Dazhai, soaked up money that could have been better used elsewhere. As a model of self-reliance, it was a fraud, funded from outside – the bulldozer which was sighted levelling the top of a hillside would not usually have been available to such rural brigades. Land reclamation often employed huge amounts of forced labour for very little result, and much ecological damage – for instance, in reducing the number of lakes in Hubei from 1,066 to 326. To emulate the terrain of Dazhai, artificial hills were constructed on perfectly good arable land. The Chairman's long war against nature had found a new army of young champions espousing the military slogans of 'encircle the lakes', 'destroy the pastureland' and, in the supreme expression of the will, 'get grain from rocks'.[46]

Once more, farmers found themselves put under bosses ignorant of agricultural methods and intent on boosting output for political ends. A Sichuan county, which specialized in making paper from bamboo, was ordered to become self-sufficient in food; so the bamboo was cut down, and maize was planted on the hillsides. The uprooting of the bamboo eroded the soil, producing landslides that destroyed roads, bridges and the township headquarters. The cash from paper-making dried up. Before long, peasants at funerals burned imitation urban registration forms so that the dead might get the benefit of living in cities in the afterlife.[47]

In a southern county, the cadres ordered a peasant brigade to plant rice on hilly land which had been cleared of trees. The soil was dry and unsuitable, and the crop did not materialize. An irrigation system was built. Still no crop. So Japanese fertilizer was applied. Finally, the rice grew and the local CCP chief had a film made to demonstrate how the brigade had made itself a model for others with its triumph due to political mobilization, will and self-reliance. The imported fertilizer was not mentioned.[48]

In keeping with the accelerated tempo of the movement, the attack on Liu Shaoqi sharpened at the end of 1966. Mao accepted a suggestion from Jiang Qing and Kang Sheng that he should be accused of being the arch CCP renegade, as well as a capitalist-roader. The former number two appeared sad and nervy at a ceremony for Sun Yat-sen's birth on 12 November. A month later, as head of state, he signed a message of greetings to Kenya for its national day. Then he took Zhou's advice to drop out of sight at his home in the leadership compound.

Red Guards were set to comb files for evidence of his sins, and those of his wife, Wang Guangmei, a particular target of Jiang Qing, who resented her poise, upbringing and beauty. From a rich family, Wang had attended the American school in Beijing and interpreted for the US mission trying to bring the KMT and CCP together in the 1940s. She had wed her husband, twenty-three years older than her, in 1948, after he had gone through previous marriages and a string of affairs.[49]

Students and CCP workers produced posters vilifying Liu Shaoqi and Deng as 'China's Khrushchev'. Kang Sheng gave an outspoken student rebel 'black' material on the former number two. In the highest-level example of children denouncing their parents, Liu's daughter from an earlier marriage responded to Red Guard pressure by saying that she was 'of the opinion that my father is really the No 1 Party person in authority taking the capitalist road. For more than twenty years, he has all the time opposed Chairman Mao and Mao's Thought, carrying out not socialism but capitalism.'

Jiang Qing did not consider this enough. One of Liu's previous wives was lined up to deliver negative accounts of her life with him. After which, the daughter hardened her criticism of her father. The self-criticism the head of state had submitted in October was distributed to CCP branches across China – Mao's margin note at the time that it was 'basically, very well written and very serious' was omitted.[50]

On 1 January 1967, a small group from the Zhongnanhai leadership compound telephone exchange stuck up banners attacking 'China's Khrushchev' and warning that 'Opponents of Mao Zedong Thought will come to a no-good end.' A poster by two of Liu's children was put up inside the compound entitled 'Witness the Despicable Soul of Liu Shaoqi' – copies were made and sent all over China.

Two dozen clerical staff then burst into his house and for three quarters of an hour shouted at the man who was still nominally head of state, obliging him to read out passages from the *Little Red Book*. At dinnertime, they made him and his wife go outside to face fresh denunciations. Such action at the heart of power in the PRC was unthinkable without Mao's approval.[51]

Five days later, Wang got a telephone call telling her that her daughter by Liu, Pingping, was in hospital awaiting surgery on her legs after a road accident. The mother raced round. There was no sign of her daughter. But a group of students was waiting, and forced Wang to accompany them to another struggle meeting. The call had been a hoax. The students had not forgotten her role in leading the work team that had gone to Qinghua University to try to control radicals there.

In mid-January, 200 leftists delivered fresh denunciations in the court-yard of the Liu home. A film crew recorded the scene. Rebel Red Guards camped outside kept up a din to stop the president and his wife sleeping. Four hundred researchers were deputed to trawl through 2.5 million documents to look for evidence that Liu had betrayed the Party while under arrest in Manchuria in 1929. They found nothing, so an old CCP member from the region was forced to write a document that could be used to back up the accusation. Meanwhile, sixty-four people were lined up to accuse Wang of having been an American agent. Jiang Qing accused her of wearing a necklace on a state visit to Indonesia, and 'making herself a whore' with President Sukarno by donning a tight Chinese traditional dress.

The day after the latest courtyard demonstration, Mao invited Liu to call on him. Receiving his long-time deputy in the Hall of the Chrysanthemum Fragrance, the Chairman inquired about Pingping's health, showing he was aware of the hoax. Liu asked to be allowed to resign, and take his family to live in the countryside. A genuinely convinced, if blinkered and unimaginative Communist, he said he was ready to work as a peasant in a commune, and wanted to facilitate an early end to the Cultural Revolution to 'save the country some suffering'. Mao remained silent, drawing on a cigarette before advising the visitor to 'study well' and 'take good care of yourself'. Forty-five years after they had first come into contact in Hunan, and two decades after Mao had shared the cake that symbolized the marriage of Shaoqi and Guangmei in Yenan, the two parted for the last time.

Given its origins in that city, it was fitting that the next stage in the movement should take place in Shanghai. The Red Guards had lived up to the job given to them. But they were too anarchic to be the foundation for a new system of revolution. For that, the workers had to be enlisted under the control of the Cultural Revolution Group.

At the end of November 1966, a visit to Shanghai by the Beijing University poster writer, Nie Yuanzi, increased the militant temperature. Red Guards occupied the offices of the CCP newspaper, and, when they faced opposition from a crowd mustered by the local authorities, called for help from the Shanghai Rebels General Headquarters, made up of industrial workers.[52]

Its leading member, Wang Hongwen, had wandered around from his birthplace in Manchuria before rising to take charge of a security department at a Shanghai textile mill. An independent-minded, slim thirty-year-old, who looked younger than his age, he put up a big-character poster in June 1966, accusing the chiefs of his work unit of revisionism, failure to grasp class struggle and ignoring mass opinion. His resentment mounted when a work team sent in to the mill did not back him or give him the job of Cultural Revolution chairman at the plant. Showing once more the importance personal factors could have, he reflected later that 'If I had been allowed to serve as Cultural Revolution chair I would not have rebelled.'

Other prominent figures at the Rebel Headquarters included an illiterate, former KMT soldier with a reputation as a violent troublemaker and womanizer, a dandy lathe worker who was held back by the crimes of his opium-addicted father, a blacksmith petty hoodlum, and a former tea and cigarette stand operator turned steel mill worker, who was under suspicion from his bosses for his liaison with a young woman apprentice.

Wang Hongwen enjoyed highly placed backing from the city's propaganda official, Zhang Chunqiao, who had collaborated with Jiang Qing in the initial revolutionary salvoes before becoming deputy director of the Cultural Revolution Group in Beijing. By the turn of the year, the city was in uproar as the Rebel Headquarters fought a militia called the Scarlet Guards, set up by the city's establishment. At Christmas-time, after the rebels had briefly occupied the CCP building, Zhang told his wife, 'The peach of Shanghai is now ripe.' At a private dinner for his seventy-third birthday on 26 December, Mao spoke positively of 'revolutionary rebels rising up in Party and state organs' and raised a toast to 'the unfolding of nationwide all-round civil war'.[53]

Just before dawn on 30 December, 100,000 members of the Rebel Headquarters attacked 20,000 Scarlet Guards positioned round the main CCP building in Shanghai. After four hours of fighting, the Scarlet Guards gave in. Zhou Enlai telephoned the Party secretary, Chen Pixian, who was convalescing after surgery for nose and pharynx cancer, to tell him to sort things out.

A meeting which began at 5 a.m. on New Year's Day reached a compromise by drafting an open letter to the people of the city calling on them to 'grasp revolution, promote production and thoroughly smash the new attack by the bourgeois reactionary line'. The next day, Wang flew to Beijing to consult fellow radicals. On 4 January, Zhang Chunqiao and the leftist intellectual Yao Wenyuan took a plane to Shanghai from the capital, both wearing army greatcoats though neither belonged to the military.

If the official Shanghai leadership had hoped they would help the search for peace, it was mistaken. Zhang and Yao stirred up the media to attack the Scarlet Guards, and organized a rally at which 100,000 demonstrators approved motions dismissing the mayor, calling on the Party secretary to testify as to 'how he had opposed the Cultural Revolution', and advocating 'thoroughly re-organising the Municipal Party Committee', which, Yao informed Beijing, had completely collapsed.

The Scarlet Guards hit back, putting up posters to denounce Zhang as 'the Two-Faced Counter Revolutionary'. At a meeting held in a cinema, Zhang and Yao were subjected to a six-hour 'struggle session' of abuse, while two of their associates were kidnapped. But the Chairman had made his choice. The Party, government and armed forces all over the country should note what had been done in Shanghai and 'take concrete action', he said. In a formal act of recognition of the rebels, Zhou sent them a congratulatory message. After approving the text, the Chairman added the Cultural Revolution Group as a signatory – the first time it had been accorded such status.

Scarlet Guards were sent off to work in the countryside. One reflected later that 'it was time for the workers, peasants and soldiers to take over the movement. Mao's heart could not be at ease with these kids taking control of power.' Forty-five of the fifty-six members of the Shanghai Municipal Committee were expelled – four died subsequently from ill-treatment. On 16 January, Mao formally approved the transfer of power in the city. Three weeks later, the Shanghai People's Commune was proclaimed. It was a breathtaking example of the power shift taking place in China, showing just how far the Cultural Revolution might stretch.[54]

As what Chen Boda called 'a mighty revolutionary torrent' roared on, denunciations and struggle sessions were stepped up against other leading figures; and Jiang Qing added the names of wives she disliked to the list. A junior clerk, Chen Lining, who had been locked up in a mental hospital for having insisted some years earlier that Liu was a revisionist, was hauled out of detention to be sent on a tour of forty-eight lectures to more than 200,000 people. Kang Sheng exulted in the mobilization of the young shock troops. He recounted that, when he told them to drag out senior officials, 'within no more than an hour or two, they had organized a rally of 400,000 to 500,000 people. Discipline was excellent.' The numbers may have been bloated, but the scope and spirit of the offensive were clear.[55]

But some of those in the firing line refused to buckle. Bo Yibo, the economic planner and Mao's one-time swimming companion, resisted when hauled before a mass meeting at the Beijing Workers' Stadium, a heavy iron plaque round his neck detailing his alleged crimes. As he began to speak, Guards ran forward and grabbed him by his hair. Pressing his head to the ground, they shouted, 'Down with the big renegade!' Suddenly, Bo broke free to run to the microphone and declare, 'I am not a traitor! I am a member of the Communist Party!' Red Guards pulled him away by the hair, shouting, 'He is a dog, crawling out of the Kuomintang den for dogs.'[56]

Bo's wife was persecuted, too, and three of his four children rounded up. In the summer of 1967, he was taken with Peng Zhen to be held in the intense summer heat in a hut made of sheet metal at the Number 27 Rolling Stock Plant in a Beijing district. Deprived of food and water, they were struggled against and beaten with metal pipes and wooden cudgels wrapped in rubber, after which Bo could not sit or stand. When he asked for medical attention, the Guards told him, 'You are incredibly fortunate not to be dead yet.'[57]

Inside the leadership compound, communications at Liu Shaoqi's house were cut off. An article in the *People's Daily*, personally edited by Mao, denounced the head of state as 'the biggest capitalist-roader'. An eight-point condemnation stretched from the 1930s, when he was accused of having ordered Communists to surrender to the KMT, through his 'capitulationist line' in the civil war and his alleged opposition to socialist policies in industry and agriculture, to his current 'bourgeois reactionary line'. *How to be a Good Communist*, which had previously been a basic text, was dismissed as 'deceitful' and opposed to Marxism–Leninism and Mao Thought.[58]

One night, Liu's wife held up a bottle of sleeping pills to her husband, giving him a questioning look. Aware that their home was certainly bugged, he said nothing, but shook his head. Knowing the strength the couple drew from one another, Mao ordered them to be separated.

'Is it really goodbye?' Wang Guangmei recalls saying tearfully as, for the only time in their life together, her husband did the packing. Then they sat looking at one another. Liu said it was like waiting for a sedan chair to come to take his bride to the wedding. They both laughed. In their final embrace, he whispered, 'How fortunate that history is decided by the people.'

Deng Xiaoping was removed from the circulation list for documents coming from the Chairman, as was the propaganda chief, Tao Zhu. The Party secretary for Hubei and the deputy head of the PLA political department were purged. The foreign minister, Marshal Chen Yi, reacted robustly, but was forced to offer self-criticism at a struggle meeting in his ministry. Only Zhou Enlai's interventions saved the eighty-year-old Zhu De, who had joined Mao even before he got to the Jiangxi base. The premier also managed to get the old guerrilla leader He Long, who had been arrested for anti-Party activities and planning a military coup, moved to the Western Hills outside Beijing, but he was refused adequate medical treatment and died of diabetes in 1969.[59]

Revolutionaries beat to death the minister for coal. The first secretary of the CCP Committee in Yunnan killed himself after being verbally attacked by Chen Boda. When Kang Sheng's sister-in-law committed suicide, more than fifty people were arrested and charged with having conspired to murder her – a doctor who had tried to save her life in hospital was accused of having put poison in the stomach pump, and spent thirteen years in prison.[60]

The CCP's six regional bureaux were closed down, removing a powerful check on the activities of revolutionaries in the provinces. Ministerial departments were purged – Mao declared that 'you don't necessarily need ministries to make revolution.' Ministers who were not also vice-premiers were dismissed. Foreign diplomats began to be attacked; in all, incidents involved thirty-two countries. Chinese diplomats were called home. A few nations, among them Pakistan, Vietnam and Albania, were spared; but Kim Il-song of North Korea was attacked as a 'fat revisionist'. The Soviet embassy was besieged by a crowd for weeks; its diplomats who did get out were trapped in their cars for sixteen hours or so, the tyres slashed. Posters went up declaring, 'Hang Kosygin; smash Brezhnev's head'.

Other mobs surrounded the French, Yugoslav and Dutch missions. A crowd made the French trade counsellor stand for seven hours in the freezing cold while police watched without intervening. More than a million demonstrators filed past the British embassy, and Red Guards blocked access to the Queen's birthday party – the only guest was a Danish diplomat who climbed in over the wall. In Shanghai, Britain's consulate was closed down by the Chinese after a mob ransacked it and frogmarched the consul round his office; when he left, he was spat at, hit and smeared with glue.[61]

Yet, there were some discordant voices. A poster at Qinghua University criticized Lin Biao for having said that Mao stood higher than Marx, Engels, Lenin and Stalin. In what radicals denounced as a 'black wind', a group drawn from more conservative Red Guards – if one can use that term – asked, 'Who the hell is Lin Biao? Biao should step aside. Jiang Qing is a stinking old woman . . . Mao Zedong is being kept from the facts and he is a senile old fool!' The United Action Committee, which included sons and daughters of officials, advocated 'Fry Jiang Qing in shallow oil' and 'Oppose the arbitrary seizure of elderly revolutionaries.' They were said to have staged six attempts to 'assault' the Public Security

Ministry. In the last week of January, 139 of the group's members were arrested.[62]

On 10 February, Mao staged one of his abrupt, guerrilla-style sorties, starting with an unusual pair of targets – Chen Boda and his own wife. Summoning Zhou Enlai, Lin Biao, Politburo member Li Fuchun and senior members of the Cultural Revolution Group to a meeting, he attacked Chen for having infringed the unity of the Politburo by criticizing the propaganda chief, Tao Zhu – a highly hypocritical attitude since he had done the same himself. The nervy target of the Chairman's vituperation asked to be allowed to make an immediate self-criticism. That was refused, and Zhou Enlai had to dissuade Chen from suicide after the meeting.[63]

Mao then turned his fire on Jiang Qing as 'someone who has grandiose aims but puny abilities, great ambition but little talent'. 'Your eyes are aloft, your hands are at work down below,' he charged while also taking a swipe at Lin Biao for not keeping him properly informed. On the other hand, he praised Zhou for reporting everything important. The Cultural Revolution Group should meet to criticize Jiang and Chen, he added. Only five days after the proclamation of the Shanghai Commune, its two leading members, Zhang Chunqiao and Yao Wenyuan, were abruptly summoned to Beijing on Mao's orders to join in the soul-searching.

The leader was genuinely irritated by the shambolic, uncoordinated way in which the group operated, and wanted to be able to spread the blame if there was trouble when Tao Zhu was ousted. As a male chauvinist, and like Chiang Kai-shek after Meiling Soong's triumphal trip to the United States in 1943, he may also have felt it was time to bring his wife down a peg or two.

The Chairman ordered that nothing must be divulged about his attack, but the Politburo member Li Fuchun could not hold himself back from spreading the news. He called three colleagues to his house – Marshal Chen Yi and vice-premiers Tan Zhenlin and Li Xiannian. During the session with the Cultural Revolution Group, Mao had mentioned all three as men who should be included in similar discussions in the future. So Li Fuchun may have thought he was on safe ground in briefing them.

Mao's outburst led them and veteran PLA figures to hope that he had returned to his senses. So, wasting no time, they immediately called a larger meeting to confront the Cultural Revolution Group, whose member Zhang Chunqiao would dub them 'the February Counter-current'. Zhou Enlai was also invited.

The marshals and vice-premiers sat on one side of the conference table; facing them were Chen Boda, Kang Sheng and another group member, Wang Li. The meeting was meant to be about 'grasping revolution and promoting production', but Marshal Ye Jianying, the 69-year-old, thick-set secretary-general of the Military Affairs Commission who had participated in the Communist risings of 1927 and the Long March, started by laying in to Chen Boda and the group. Ye said they had made a mess of the Party, the government, the countryside and industry: now they wanted to make a mess of the army, too. 'What are you up to, going on like this?' he demanded.[64]

Another marshal, Xu Xiangqian, aged sixty-five, who had earned fame with his daring tactics to defeat the Model Governor in 1949, weighed in to say it was as if the Cultural Revolutionists did not want the PLA any more as a pillar of the PRC. Ye came back to attack the change in Shanghai, and the way it had been done without Politburo authorization. Chen Boda crumbled, saying he was covered in embarrassment. Zhou then brought the discussion to a close.

The following day, 12 February, the Chairman, who had moved to a house by his swimming pool in the leadership compound because he feared that his original home was being bugged, called in the Shanghai Commune's two chiefs, Zhang and Yao. If their example was followed all over China, he told them, there would be a problem; what would the country call itself? The People's Commune of China? This could cause diplomatic problems with foreign governments. So they should go away and decide on a new name. In any case, the Commune was proving too weak, Mao added.

The truth was that the Chairman had had second thoughts, and was putting up the feeble diplomatic excuse to mask his volte-face. He probably feared that the Commune would become self-governing, and set a pattern of regional autonomy. Whatever he said about handing power to the masses, he remained a through-going centralizing autocrat on imperial lines who wanted to be sure of being able to turn the revolution on and off as and when he decided.

On 16 February, Zhou convoked a fresh session of the marshals, vice-premiers and Cultural Revolution Group. Pleading illness, Jiang Qing stayed away.

The assault at the three-hour meeting began even before Zhou had formally opened the proceedings. Vice-premier Tan Zhenlin, sixty-four years old, who had been in charge of agriculture during the Great Leap, went into a diatribe about the way the group invoked the masses. 'What masses?' he asked. 'Always the masses, the masses. There's still the leadership of the Party! You don't want the leadership of the Party but keep talking from morning to late about the masses liberating themselves, educating themselves and making revolution by themselves. What is this stuff? It's metaphysics.'[65]

When the public security minister, Xie Fuzhi, remarked that his ally, Jiang Qing, was protecting Tan, the vice-premier replied indignantly, 'I don't want her protection! I work for the Party. I don't work for her!' He accused the group of wishing cadres with forty years of service to the Party to 'end up with a broken family, their wives and children separated from them'. After that, he got up, put on his coat, and gathered his papers to walk out. One account has him declaring, 'If I had known at the beginning that it would come to this, I would never have joined the revolution or the Communist Party. I should never have followed Chairman Mao for all those forty-one years.' Another version recounts that he told the meeting, 'Do as you like. I have had enough of you. I quit. Cut off my head. Put me in prison. Expel me from the Party. I will fight to the end.'

'Don't go,' the foreign minister, Chen Yi, victor of the great Huai-Hai battle of 1948–9, urged Tan. The vice-premier said he had cried for the first time in his life at what was happening. 'I've cried a lot too,' interjected the Politburo member Li Xiannian.

The man whose backing the old guard most needed declined to expose himself. Zhou parroted the line that the Cultural Revolution was being waged to expose Liu and Deng. Had he thrown his lot in with Chen and the others, even Mao would have had to take notice. But he preferred to take the cautious route, as usual.

The Chairman appeared to be continuing on his new revisionist path by approving an editorial printed in the *People's Daily* entitled 'Cadres Must be Treated Correctly'. But the two meetings had crossed the line of what he would tolerate. As so often, his apparent softening had encouraged dissenters to expose themselves, and so render themselves vulnerable to counter-attack. He called in Zhou, a representative of Lin Biao, Kang Sheng for the Cultural Revolution Group and four other officials. Kang recorded that he had never seen the Chairman so angry. Mao said the Cultural Revolution Group was carrying out the line laid down by the Party Plenum; its errors amounted to, at most, only 3 per cent of what it was doing. If anybody opposed it, he added, 'I will resolutely oppose him!'

Mao ordered that Chen Yi, Tan Zhenlin and Xu Xiangqian were to be told to ask for leaves of absence to work on self-criticisms. At seven meetings chaired by Zhou during the following three weeks, they were put under heavy pressure, while Jiang Qing warned that 'Signs of counter-revolutionary restoration are everywhere, beginning at the top all the way down to the bottom.'

The extreme left was back in the saddle. Though the Shanghai Commune body was renamed the Revolutionary Committee of the Shanghai Municipality in keeping with Mao's wishes, the Cultural Revolution Group members, Zhang and Yao, were confirmed as its chiefs, with the young enthusiast Wang Hongwen running things on the spot when they were attending to other duties in Beijing. A revolutionary committee was formed for the capital. Similar bodies were set up in Heilongjiang province in Manchuria and in Shanxi.

Having reasserted themselves, the radicals could go for one of their major targets. At 6.30 in the morning of 10 April, the Jinggangshan Regiment of Red Guards hauled Liu Shaoqi's wife to the seventh floor of a building in Qinghua University. Wang was not in good health, having run a fever for several days. The Red Guard record of what followed says she put up 'the ugly performance of a bitch struggling in the water'. As for her husband, the militants were advised to 'turn him into a heap of dog's dung spurned by mankind'.[66]

The interrogators produced the silk dress Wang had worn on the state visit to Indonesia, and demanded that she put it on. The First Lady, who was wearing a fur coat given to her by the Afghan government, refused, saying it was too cold to wear the thin dress. A group of Red Guards known as the Ghostbusters tried to force her to do as they wished. To frustrate them, Wang sat on the floor. They tugged her to her feet and pulled the dress over her head.

'You have violated Chairman Mao's instruction about not struggling against people by force,' she said.

The Red Guards met that by reading in unison a passage from the *Little Red Book* recording Mao's observation about a revolution not being a dinner party.

'You violate Chairman Mao's instruction . . .' Wang repeated. But she was forced to don silk stockings and high-heeled shoes, plus a necklace made of ping-pong balls.

'Down with the Three-Antis Element Wang Guangmei,' the Guards cried, attacking her for having lit a cigarette for President Sukarno at a banquet hosted by Liu. When Wang said this was in keeping with Indonesian customs, the interrogator shouted, 'To hell with you! We know nothing of those foreign conventions. You flirted with such a bad fellow as Sukarno.'

She was led away to be photographed in the incriminating dress with the mocking necklace. When the struggle began anew, Wang admitted to 'right-opportunism errors'. Her hands were shaking. She gasped for breath, and asked for a glass of water and two tranquillizers – she was given one. 'My nerves are no good,' she said. '[But] I am not afraid, and my mind is very calm.'

It was time for her to confront a mass meeting. As the Guards pulled her along, she dragged her feet, and asked for another tranquillizer.

'What have you in mind now?' the interrogator asked.

Pursing her lips, the veins standing out on the backs of her hands, Wang replied in a low voice, 'I am now ready to face the criticism, repudiation and struggle of the masses.'

At a subsequent 'trial', she was interrogated about her family background, her businessman father, her ten brothers and sisters, and an evening when she went to a dinner given by George Marshall's mission to China in 1946 and accepted a box of candy from an American. When she asked for medicine, the interrogator told her, 'Don't be afraid of death. You won't die yet.' To which Wang responded angrily, 'I regard death as going home.'[67]

23

All-Out Civil War

By the spring of 1967, Mao's young 'devils' were a problem that had to be dealt with more severely. A report from the north-east listed attacks on property, gang fighting, petty crime, hooliganism, bad language, attacks on girls; some young people, it added, 'mimic the behaviour of Teddy Boys'. Beijing's Qinghua University was a major focal point, with a firebrand student called Kuai Dafu leading the agitation. Radicals there formed the United Jinggangshan Regiment, named in honour of the base in Jiangxi, which fought with the more moderate Four One Four group, each using spears made from stainless steel pipes. Then rifles were brought in, and students manufactured grenades. A Regiment sniper gunned down a girl student as she ran across an open square; a fellow student dragged her into a building where she died in his arms, blood spewing from her wounds.[*][1]

In a bid to get education working, schools and colleges were reopened. Itinerant Red Guards were told to go home. At the same time, workers were instructed not to let political activities interrupt their eight-hour days. Peasants were urged to concentrate on the fields. Though Mao might praise disorder as a matter of principle, he knew the danger of letting the new revolution spiral out of control. To give muscle to the restraining measures, the PLA was called in. But the Chairman's wavering course in the following months suggested that he lacked a clear

* The postgraduate faculty at Qinghua included a 24-year-old hydraulic engineering researcher, Hu Jintao, who would become China's Communist Party leader four decades later. He was chosen by the head of the university to be a political counsellor. Radicals criticized him for being 'too individualistic' and belonging to a 'carefree clique', but he does not appear to have suffered. However, the tumult of the Cultural Revolution can only have buttressed the appetite for 'stability' (on Communist Party terms) which would mark Hu when he came to the top.

plan, as he moved alarmingly between using force to restore order and extolling 'trouble' as the way to pursue revolution.

A document issued by the Military Affairs Commission in March 1967 had given the PLA a leading role in imposing stability as well as helping to run ministries in Beijing. Discretion was left to local commanders to decide who were the 'rightists' they were told to suppress. As a result, soldiers found themselves in the unprecedented position of gunning down civilians shouting Communist slogans. There were clashes in Guangdong, Anhui, Henan, Hunan, Fujian, Inner Mongolia and Tibet. In Wuhan, where around fifty Red Guard factions competed with one another, the PLA took over the running of banks, granaries, warehouses, prisons and the broadcasting station as army commanders formed an outfit called the Million Heroes which attacked the radical Steel Tempered Workers Headquarters. In the north-western region of Qinghai, troops massacred militants occupying a newspaper office. In neighbouring Xinjiang, clashes between the PLA and radicals killed thirty-one people. After two mass organizations besieged the military headquarters in Chengdu for a week, the army arrested 100,000 people across Sichuan, crowding prisoners so tightly into underground cells that they had no room to lie down.

Mao and the Cultural Revolution Group then decided that the army had gone too far. Lin Biao ordered troops not to fire on mass organizations or to declare them reactionary – such labelling was now to be done at the centre. This emboldened leftists to hit back. In Wuhan, students marched to denounce the local commanders, and seized the broadcasting station. Mao showed where his sympathies lay by excluding the PLA commanders in the mid-Yangzi city from the May Day celebrations in Beijing. Jiang Qing put in an associate from the Cultural Revolution Group to run the army's political department. At the *Liberation Army Daily*, her daughter by Mao, who was a trainee, joined seven colleagues in a coup against the editor. They were recognized by the Military Affairs Commission as the 'mass supervisory group' at the paper. Lin sent congratulations, advising, 'do not fear "chaos" as only in the wake of chaos can there be order.'[2]

In keeping with the new line, Mao extolled 'trouble again and again, on and on' to a military group before leaving on a provincial tour that included Wuhan. In his absence, student protestors launched a fresh assault on Liu Shaoqi, camping in the street outside the leadership compound; Mao's doctor recalled that the 'smell, from thousands of sweaty bodies in the heat of July, the rotten food, and the open, make-shift toilets, was nauseating'. A group inside the walls led the president to the State Council auditorium. His wife was brought to watch.[3]

Red Guards ripped the 69-year-old's shirt and tugged at his hair. He was forced into the 'airplane' position, and his head pushed almost to the ground as his tormentors kicked and slapped him. His children were led in, as was Mao's daughter. Two weeks later, the performance was repeated, with both Liu and Wang forced into the 'airplane' position. Liu's leg was injured, and his face swollen. At one point, his wife broke free and clutched at her husband's clothes. For a brief moment, pummelled by kicks and punches, they held on to one another. Then they were separated for ever as he was marched back to his house.[4]

Wang was jailed, and their children sent to work as peasants. On 7 August, the head of state wrote to Mao to resign. He got no reply.

The commanders in Wuhan, Chen Zaido and Zhong Hanhua, were not at all minded to follow Mao's recipe of more 'trouble'. As fighting raged between the radical Steel Tempered Headquarters and the army-backed Million Heroes, the situation grew perilous for the Cultural Revolution-ists. Lin Biao sent in troops loyal to him along with five gunboats. Zhou flew to the mid-Yangzi with an ultimatum for the commanders. They were told to allow the Headquarters group to operate as a 'revolution-ary' organization, while their Heroes were branded as a 'conservative' group.[5]

Mao had, by then, reached Wuhan on his provincial tour, and Zhou took the recalcitrant generals Chen and Zhong to see him. The Chairman was emollient. If mistakes had been made, quick confessions by the two men would put things right, he said. Everybody seemed happy. Zhou flew back to Beijing.

On 19 July, Chen and Zhong offered self-criticisms to the Party committee at military headquarters. But then the situation was exacer-bated by the arrival in Wuhan of the public security minister, Xie Fuzhi, and a Cultural Revolution Group member, Wang Li, who told a rally that the commanders were no better than elementary-school pupils in understanding what was happening. An angry group of soldiers grabbed Wang, beating him up and breaking his leg. Truckloads of Million Heroes forces drove in. On the advice of Lin Biao and Jiang Qing, Mao flew to Shanghai – it has been suggested that there were fears of a rerun of the kidnapping of Chiang Kai-shek in Xi'an thirty years earlier.[6]

Zhou Enlai returned to Wuhan, and the release of Wang Li was arranged. The events in the Middle Yangzi were classed as a counter-revolutionary incident. The local commanders were ordered to come to Beijing to account for themselves. They were escorted to their plane by soldiers with fixed bayonets in the moonlight. After a rally of a million people in the capital to celebrate the revolutionary victory in Wuhan, they were sacked and replaced by more reliable figures. Behind them, 184,000 members of the Heroes were detained, beaten up or killed.

Mao made a return visit to Wuhan, riding through the city in the back of an open jeep. He spent a month in the city, keeping in touch with events in Beijing, but also taking time to read and relax. One day, he looked up from a story about a promiscuous maid who liked to make trouble for others. According to his doctor, he said that Lin Biao's wife was just like the character and added, 'so is Jiang Qing.'[7]

But he did nothing to rein in his wife or the extremists. Deng Xiaoping was made to kneel outside his home in the leadership compound in the 'airplane' position, though he was not beaten. He and his wife, who had been added to the 'struggle list' by Jiang Qing, were moved to a smaller house. His younger brother, working in Guizhou, was hounded by Red Guards until he killed himself. The Dengs' daughter and younger son were sent away to the countryside in Shaanxi. Their elder son, who was studying physics at Beijing University, was harassed by Red Guards. Caught by them on the roof of a building, he was pushed, or fell, to the ground below as he tried to escape. Refused admission to the university clinic, he was paralysed from the waist down, and spent the next four years in a home for the handicapped, weaving wire baskets while he lay on his back.

Taken to the Workers' Stadium to be struggled against at a mass meeting held to denounce the 'Liu–Deng–Peng–Bo Counter-Revolutionary Trust', the 59-year-old economist Bo Yibo was badly beaten, his body covered with wounds, his clothes left in tatters. At another of the recurrent sessions he endured that summer, his arms were twisted out of their sockets. He suffered severe pain in his stomach, and could barely move.[8]

After he wrote a 20,000-character statement denying the accusation that he had betrayed the Communists when held in a Nationalist jail in the 1930s, Bo was beaten again. A little while later, four Guards flung him in the air; his back was injured when he landed on the concrete. Kept awake all night, he was fed little. When he did get food, his hands shook so badly that he could not hold it on his chopsticks; the rice grains fell to the floor where he picked them up with his fingers. Water was limited to half a jar a day, which he saved for drinking, giving up washing or brushing his teeth.

One day, a Guard said sarcastically that Bo would probably want to know how his family was doing. His wife, the man added, had committed suicide – though other reports say she was beaten to death. Three of his children had been detained; the fourth, aged fourteen, had been sent on internal exile. Why didn't he consider their interests, the Guard asked. They had lost their mother. Things might be easier for them if their father confessed. Bo held out.

In all, he was detained for fifteen years. After his release, he came back into favour as one of the 'Eight Immortals' of the Communist Party, though he exercised little executive authority, increasingly occupying himself with calligraphy and chess. He survived until 2007, dying in Beijing a month short of his ninety-ninth birthday. His son, Bo Xilai, who had been imprisoned at the age of sixteen, rose to become mayor of Dalian and governor of the province of Liaoning in 2003. The following year, he was appointed minister of commerce, projecting the image of a modern-minded, media-savvy politician who speaks reasonable English, before being put in charge of the mega-city of Chongqing in 2008.

For Mao, the way the PLA in Wuhan and elsewhere had acted was a sign that more than a new military order was needed to ram through the revolution. He estimated that three quarters of army officers supported the right. The answer, he decided, was to give weapons to the people. 'Why can't we arm the workers and students?' he asked.

Responding to himself, he went on: 'I say we should arm them.' To Jiang Qing, he wrote to explain that arming the masses would prevent the advance of revisionism and reaction. She came up with the slogan, 'Attack with reason, defend with force.' Since the ideological enemy was said to be moving forward, violence was justified. At the end of July, battles broke out at factories in Kaifeng and Zhengzhou which killed thirty-seven people and wounded 290; two prisoners of the militants were buried alive.[9]

Pursuing his radical approach, Mao fell back on an earlier formulation to declare that what was needed was 'all-out civil war' headed by Revolutionary Committees. Once more, Shanghai took the lead. A unit was set up which, with the connivance of the police, kidnapped 800 people, killing three and crippling twenty-four with torture. Beijing then approved the formation of an armed force under the radical worker Wang Hongwen; it fought a ten-hour battle with a rival movement at the Diesel Engine Factory, in which eighteen died and 983 were wounded – production was halted for two months. A film of the event was shown to Mao in his secluded villa in the city, to his evident enjoyment. Many of the militia members in the city were women, who rode in motorcycle brigades, patrolled the waterways, and joined fire brigades and anti-aircraft detachments. Wang's most trusted associate among the cadres was a woman.[10]

Mao signed off on a statement that 'the revolutionary masses are to be armed.' Lin Biao knew the reservations of PLA commanders, but insisted that 'we must comply with Chairman Mao's instructions, arm the left and distribute rifles to the leftist masses.' In Beijing, there were clashes at schools and institutes after rifles were handed out. A fourteen-hour fight at the capital's Xidan market left eight dead and 390 wounded. There was heavy fighting in Hangzhou and the port of Wenzhou. In Guangzhou, hundreds were killed in street clashes between groups sporting such names as the Spring Thunder Fighters, the Doctrine Guards and the Poor and Lower-Middle Peasants' United Command; warehouses were looted, and rail and road transport disrupted. In Chongqing, 10,000 people took part in clashes, with 1,000 reported killed or wounded; it was said that one artillery shell was fired for each combatant. Battles for the city of Luzhou involved more than 30,000 people and killed more than 2,000. In one county in largely Muslim Ningxia, up to 400 died.[11]

In the Xinjiang capital of Urumqi, a radical force of 55,000, including 6,000 soldiers, attacked factories, government offices and colleges, and cut the railway line to the rest of the country – under attack, the local Party boss threatened to take over the nuclear test site at Lop Nor. Elsewhere, militants were said to be eyeing biochemical warfare establishments. In Manchuria, the Mao Zedong Combat Thought Regiment at the Geological Institute in Changchun claimed that it had tested two 'radioactive self-defence bombs'. There was particularly savage repression in Inner Mongolia as part of a campaign that stretched to 1969 to bring the enormous region into line. The death toll may have reached 100,000. The local leader, Ulanfu, had been dismissed in 1966 after a two-month struggle session in a Beijing hotel. Publications in the Mongol language were banned. Thirty years later, a Chinese historian wrote of Mongolians having their tongues torn out, and being branded with a hot iron or burned alive. Mao, himself, was reported to have remarked that 'excesses have been committed'.[12]

Tibet's traditions presented an all-too tempting target for the revolutionaries. There had been some relaxation of Chinese pressure in the early 1960s, but now it was time for a fresh campaign to eradicate local culture and customs. Red Guards harangued crowds of peasants, and some local youths joined them, from either conviction or fear. Thousands of monasteries were destroyed, artifacts demolished, and monks and nuns killed or imprisoned. Old ceremonies were repressed even more severely than before.

Red Guards in Guangdong inspired action by associates on the other side of the frontier fence in Hong Kong. There were bombings and shootings along the border. In the heart of the colony, fierce demonstrations broke out. Militants surrounded Government House, placarded buildings with anti-British slogans, harangued crowds from the terrace of the Bank of China offices and planted bombs. Fifty people were killed in street fighting, including eleven police, and 832 were injured. The PLA commander across the border proposed an armed invasion of the colony, but Zhou Enlai squashed the idea.[13]

In retaliation for the banning of pro-Beijing newspapers and the arrest of Chinese 'news workers' in Hong Kong, a mob stormed the Beijing home of the Reuters correspondent, Anthony Grey, beat him up, killed his cat and imprisoned him in a small room, an ordeal that would last for twenty-seven months. On the warm night of 22 August 1966, a 10,000-strong crowd gathered outside the British embassy in the Chinese capital as diplomats inside ate tinned sausages, peas and cheese, washed down with claret. After dinner, a Peter Sellers film, *The Wrong Arm of the Law*, was shown. Some of the men went to play bridge The chargé d'affaires had just bid three no trumps when the demonstrators attacked the building, setting fire to it as they advanced.[14]

Following an 'Armageddon' plan drawn up by the head of chancery, Percy Cradock, the diplomats fell back behind a series of grilles suppos-

edly protecting secure areas of the building, dragging across filing cabi-
nets to buttress the defences. It was no good. The mob swept on,
chanting, 'Kill! Kill!' The diplomats huddled in the dark behind the
metal door of the registry. Afraid of being trapped and trampled by
the crowd or burned to death or smothered by smoke from fires lit by
the attackers, the British walked out, holding their hands in the air. After
a moment's silence, they were dragged along by the hair, beaten with
bamboo poles and forced to kneel as their clothes were torn off. The
women, the chargé reported to London, 'were not spared lewd attention
from the prying fingers of the mob'. However, the portrait of the Queen
survived, slightly singed.

Beaten on the shoulders and back, Cradock was put on a soapbox
and held by two men while another punched him in the stomach. He
was told to say, 'Long live Chairman Mao!', which he did not do.
Together with three of his staff, the chargé was dragged across the road
and deposited outside the Albanian embassy; he recalled having quoted
Virgil to the Chinese. Eventually, the diplomats were driven home in
lorries. The Xinhua news agency explained that it had been 'a mighty
demonstration' against the 'frantic fascist persecution of patriotic
Chinese in Hong Kong'. Britain did not break off relations.

The missions of India, Indonesia and Burma were also assaulted.
Extreme leftists took control of the foreign ministry. Zhou Enlai, who
had authorized the demonstration outside the British embassy, was badly
shaken at how it had turned out, blaming his decision to give the
go-ahead on tiredness. Disaster loomed if things went on in the current
pattern, he told an associate, before suffering an angina attack that put
him out of action for a day and a half.

The economic costs of 'all-out civil war' were evident. Per capita growth
of national income dropped to 2.95 per cent in the second half of the
1960s. The number of fatal industrial accidents quadrupled in the same
period. The tax system broke down in many places. There was fighting
at mines and work stoppages at major plants. Employees ran amok at
the Daqing oil field in the north-east. Mass absenteeism cut coal output
dangerously – by the end of 1967, stocks were at their lowest ebb of the
decade. Steel production was barely a quarter of the planned total,
electricity generation was down 30 per cent. Chemicals and machine
tools were also hit. Street markets were trashed, and stall owners

paraded as enemies. In Harbin, only 800 of 12,600 individual enterprises set up since the Great Leap managed to survive.[15]

Still, according to official statistics, which are always subject to some doubt, China's economy managed to avoid the extreme disaster of the Great Leap. But there was fresh pressure to pay for what was known as the Third Front policy to develop industrial and military facilities and infrastructure deep in the interior provinces. With the United States stepping up its involvement in Vietnam, the Soviet Union antagonized and Taiwan posing a constant threat, the leadership felt it needed to prepare seriously for a major conflict, which would probably involve nuclear weapons. China should, it reasoned, draw on its huge geographical and population reserves to survive – in a reprise of the guerrilla tactics of retreat into terrain the enemy could not penetrate. 'We must build up the strategic rear,' the Chairman ordained. Zhou Enlai coined the slogan 'Prepare for War, Prepare for Famine, for the Sake of the People.'[16]

A vast programme was rolled out in supposedly safe mountainous regions of western China. In an echo of the transfer of plants from Shanghai to Chongqing during the Second World War, 380 factories and their labour forces were moved inland from coastal areas. New enterprises were built, operating on a self-contained basis cut off from towns and villages. At the same time an underground city was constructed below central Beijing with 30 kilometres of traffic tunnels and designed to shelter 300,000 people. As so often with Mao's sudden initiatives, everything had to be done at once, planning was rudimentary and costs soared as a result while projects fell further and further behind schedule, and spread severe ecological damage.[17]

This Third Front almost doubled spending on construction between 1966 and 1970 to 894 million yuan, with expenditure in the south-west leaping to nearly a quarter of the total. The new development ate up huge amounts of coal, power and steel. Pursuing this and 'all-out civil war' simultaneously, while keeping the general economy running and the country under some form of overall government, was beyond the bounds of fantasy. Reversing himself once more under the pressure of reality, the Chairman ordered an end to the distribution of arms to the leftists, and the return of those which had been handed out. He put Zhou in charge of the repression of the movement he had himself unleashed, with the army to revert to the role of restoring order and helping to staff the civilian administration.

To provide a pretext for action without invoking the true author – Mao – the prime minister and his aides reached back to a small-scale rebel movement, which had surfaced earlier in the year, known as the 16 May Conspiracy. Its members had put up posters and distributed handbills denouncing the prime minister as a 'backstage Black Wind boss' and disgraceful betrayer of Mao Zedongism. It had been suppressed in August. But now it was blown up into a huge conspiracy, with tentacles stretching through the Party, government and army. The criminals, the charge went, came from left and right; their unifying aim being to sabotage Mao, the PLA and the Cultural Revolution.[18]

Many of those hauled in for interrogation had no idea what they were being accused of, but eventually buckled and confessed to whatever they were told they had done. A prison was set up in the foreign ministry, where at least half the staff was charged. Wang Li, the man who had been kidnapped in Wuhan and had been a leading figure in the leftist surge, now found himself accused of being a member of the KMT and an agent for the Soviet KGB, while his family was stigmatized as 'black trash'. In all, several millions were detained under Zhou's aegis for involvement in a conspiracy that never existed.

The leftists had to swallow Mao's backing for the premier, but they were soon pressing a new campaign to 'cleanse the class ranks'. In Beijing, it took 3,731 lives, and was kept under fairly tight control. But, in the provinces, Revolutionary Committees enforced their authority, often choosing whatever methods they preferred; in Jiangxi, it was decided that using bullets was a waste, so people had their ears cut off and were left to bleed to death.

Hundreds of thousands were reported to have been involved in violent clashes in Sichuan. In Inner Mongolia, where soldiers went into action with framed portraits of Mao on their chests, the death toll was put at 22,900 with 120,000 maimed; an additional twist was added with a campaign to 'root out' potentially pro-Soviet nationalists among cadres and herdsmen. In Zhejiang, 9,198 people were killed. In the Guangxi capital of Nanning, 2,324 were executed after fighting between factions that left 50,000 people homeless. In Yunnan, where almost half a million people were detained, 6,979 perished from what was termed 'enforced suicide'.[19]

An estimated 650,000 people were killed in all in the violence that stretched on through 1968. Records for twenty-five counties reported more than 1,000 deaths in each. In one extreme case, 3,681 people were killed and thrown into a mass grave in a ten-day purge in a county in Guangxi; 639 were beaten to death in another district. A Guangdong county suffered 2,600 deaths. In an episode in Shaanxi, fighting involved more than 20,000 people. In at least two instances, in Guangxi and Yunnan, the executioners celebrated by eating the heart, brains, testicles, penis, flesh and liver of victims.[20]

Treatment of those sent to prison was harsh in the extreme. An inmate of Qincheng jail, an hour's drive from Beijing, described how convicts were fed drugs that induced hallucinations or terror or produced an overwhelming desire to talk. Loudspeakers blasted out twenty-four hours a day, sometimes announcing executions that were then called off at the last moment. The windows were pasted over so that one could not tell if it was night or day and, for five years, no reading matter was allowed. Another inmate said some doctors used prisoners as guinea pigs, subjecting the healthy to vaccinations that made them ill.

Sidney Rittenberg, an American who had lived in China for a quarter of a century and joined the CCP, but who had become yet another victim of the purges, recalled how he valued interrogations at the jail as the only time he had any human contact. When they stopped, he sat on his low-slung bunk staring at the grey walls, the grey floor, the dull red door, 'great spots and bands of colour floating and pulsating before my eyes, silence making my ears ring'.[21]

Amid all the turmoil, a group of scientists in their thirties beavered away on a project initiated in 1964 by Mao when he declared that China should have a hydrogen bomb as well as an atomic weapon. They had scant resources, but, after a hundred days of mathematical calculations, they made a vital breakthrough in September 1965, helped by information from an unidentified foreign source, and celebrated with a lunch of a bowl of noodles. A test area was established in the north-west, but there was no passenger train to reach it so the scientists travelled in a freight truck, and then boarded a lorry to the site, sitting on pickle jars.[22]

Their destination was a mining area, inhabited by people living in caves, and subsisting on a diet of barley and millet flour with a little oil; the newcomers preferred cabbage soup. The strong rays of the sun turned their skins dark; when they went home for a break, they pretended that they were working in the mines. On 17 June 1967, a fighter plane dropped a parachute. Three thousand metres above the ground, its payload exploded. A mushroom cloud erupted. China had a hydrogen bomb.

The Chairman now decided that the future lay in a 'great alliance' of the masses, cadres and soldiers. That meant dispensing with the Red Guards as shock troops. But this was easier said than done, as soldiers who tried to take over Beijing's Qinghua University found when they were stopped by barricades, explosive devices and barrages of stones which forced them to withdraw.[23]

Only one man could persuade the radical students to give up, so Mao invited students to a five-hour meeting in the Great Hall of the People. The guests tried to argue, one even saying that the Chairman's words could be subject to different interpretations. By his doctor's account, Mao was equable, but the message was plain. The 'voluntary disbandment' of Guard units was announced. Troops moved on to the campuses; this time they would not retreat.[24]

Twelve million young people were 'sent down' to the countryside and despatched to factories to gain experience from the proletariat and peasants. Among them, the future party chief, Hu Jintao, spent a year carrying bricks at a construction site in Guizhou. Millions of intellectuals, officials and Party cadres made the journey 'to learn from the masses'. 'Barefoot doctors' joined the movement from the cities, bringing a modicum of health care to peasants and seeing something of rural conditions for themselves. Workers were identified as Mao's new cutting edge, and a Party Plenum recognized the Cultural Revolution Group as superior to both the central state government and the Military Affairs Commission. A rewritten constitution named Lin Biao as the PRC's number two – the marshal said he had reservations about this but would 'submit to the organization'.[25]

Then it was time to deal with Liu Shaoqi. Mao's former deputy had lost all but seven of his teeth and caught pneumonia to add to his diabetes and high blood pressure. But Mao did not want him to die at least until the Party had pronounced on his case. The former number two, who had been leading major strikes while Mao was still a neophyte agitator, was deprived of his belt to prevent him from trying to hang himself. When he contracted a high fever in October, he was provided with medical treatment to keep him alive while, unknown to him, the Plenum debated his fate.[26]

Liu was condemned as a traitor, scab, 'highly venomous renegade' and 'exceptionally big bastard', expelled from the Party and dismissed from all his posts. One member of the group which examined the case said that Zhou Enlai remarked of his colleague of more than forty years, 'This one can be executed.' A single delegate to the Plenum failed to raise her hand in the voting, the vice-president of the All China Trade Union Confederation. She was spared from physical persecution because of her old age and bad health, but she lost her seat in the legislature and was expelled from the CCP.[27]

The author of *How to be a Good Communist* was not told of the verdict for a month. The news was held back to be delivered to him in his sick bed on his seventieth birthday. He vomited, became short of breath and broke into a sweat; his blood pressure and temperature shot up, and he was said never to have spoken again. Kept in solitary confinement, he was fed just enough to keep him alive – tea was refused. One of his legs was paralysed. Unable to get out of bed, he became covered in sores. He was deprived of the pills he needed to sleep, but he did get medicine for his other complaints, though he had to be drip-fed through his nose. Mao wanted him to remain a 'living target'.

Mao also used the Plenum to fire potshots at an assorted group of senior figures, and distribute some praise as well. He Long, the leader of an early Middle Yangzi base, could no longer be protected, he said – a team set up under the Cultural Revolution Group took on the case and arranged for the frail former base leader to receive the wrong medicine, leading to his death in hospital. Mao also went out of his way to praise Wang Hongwen, the radical leader of the Shanghai Revolutionary Committee, getting him to stand up to be identified as a model for younger comrades. Zhou rallied once more to his leader's cause; as well as denouncing the 'February Countercurrent' marshals, he attacked three vice-premiers who had done much of the economic work for him, and had a sideswipe at the old PLA chief, Zhu De, for not knowing how to fight a war.

The fate of Party secretaries in the regions often depended on Mao's imperial whims and mood shifts. In Zhejiang, for instance, the Chairman initially protected the CCP leader, Jiang Hua, who had been an ultra-loyalist since they first met in the Jiangxi base. As a long-time senior cadre, Jiang was an obvious target for Cultural Revolutionary attack and a 100,000-strong radical rally was held in the province to denounce him. But it was broken up by the secretary's supporters in the local 'Red Storm' movement who said they were following the Great Helmsman's instructions that Jiang should be defended and given a chance to correct his mistakes. Then Mao changed his mind, and an article by the Red Storm group announced that 'Jiang Hua cannot be protected'. In 1968, he was purged. The reason was probably an accusation raised by his opponents that he had bugged Mao's villa at Hangzhou. The charge was almost certainly groundless, but, in the paranoia of the times, it was enough to seal the fate of a comrade-in-arms of almost forty years.[28]

Deng Xiaoping was removed from all his posts, though Mao held back from giving him the full treatment meted out to Liu. The Chairman said he had reservations about expelling Deng from the CCP, calling him a man who had merely 'waved a goose feather' while the real danger came from elsewhere. Mao evidently harboured a fondness and respect for the Long Marcher, and may even have seen that he might need his services again another day. Later, Deng reflected that, had it not been for the Chairman's protection, Lin Biao and Jiang Qing would have had him killed.

He delivered his side of the bargain with a self-criticism running to 26,500 characters, traced his misdemeanours back to the 1920s and added, in a passage which might have been seen as ironic in other circumstances, that his only route forward lay in learning from Lin Biao how to school himself properly in the Chairman's works.[29]

In 1969, Deng was moved to Jiangxi as part of a scheme by Lin to disperse veterans from the capital at a time when there was sudden fear of a Soviet attack, for which they might form a fifth column. He and his family were given four rooms in a former military building. Now sixty-five, he grew vegetables, read copiously and went to work with his wife at a nearby tractor repair plant, a distant echo of his time at an engineering factory in France in the early 1920s. In 1971, their crippled son was allowed to join them, and they cared for him, lifting the stocky young man from his wheelchair to be washed, placed on the lavatory and put to bed.

In the dispersal of historic figures, Liu was taken from Beijing to Kaifeng, where he was incarcerated in an unheated building and was refused medicines. A request by doctors for him to get hospital treatment was turned down – this had to be on Mao's orders. His uncut hair grew to a foot in length. On 12 November 1969, Liu died of pneumonia.

His body was cremated under a false name. The death was not announced so long as Mao lived. Wang Guangmei learned of her husband's death only after their children met the leader and asked to be allowed to see their parents. 'Their father is dead, but they may see the mother,' the Chairman replied.

Liu's name continued to be vilified as his foes triumphed. A Party Congress in 1973 saw the introduction of the blanket condemnation of 'Liu and other swindlers'. A 'sham Marxist', he was blamed for everything from the poor quality of student essays to having advocated the development of an electronics industry, which was no better than 'a reactionary principle to oppose the principle of taking steel as the key link'.[30]

Finally, in 1980, Liu was rehabilitated; Wang, who had spent twelve years in jail, was allowed to go to Kaifeng to collect his ashes. She was subsequently given posts in the campaign against poverty, before dying in 2006 at the age of eighty-five. She always blamed Jiang Qing, not the Chairman, for the tragedy that befell her and her husband. A museum to commemorate Liu was opened in a 1930s bank building in Kaifeng. In 2007, the city's tourism guide recorded his 'brilliant contribution to the country . . . both in wartime and after the foundation of the People's Republic of China'. It said he had been 'prosecuted to death by the "Gang of Four"' during the Cultural Revolution. There was still no mention of Mao's role.

The Ninth CCP Congress in April 1969 was meant to mark the triumphal conclusion of the Cultural Revolution. But the official report of the Chairman's opening address to the 1,512 delegates acknowledged, in barely coded language, that much remained to be done – Mao hoped that 'still greater victories will be won throughout the country'.[31]

It was the first Party Congress for thirteen years; a formal session was needed to put the stamp of approval on the new leadership below Mao, to anoint Lin Biao as successor and to establish the leading role of the military – two thirds of the delegates wore uniform. Preparations were made in utmost secrecy, and the session was not announced in advance. No foreign guests were invited. Mao decided to allow some senior figures who were under attack to attend, remarking that they could constitute his 'opposition' but should 'not wag their tails'. Delegates were flown in on military planes at night and told to respect the 'five no's' – not to go out, not to receive visitors, not to make telephone calls, not to write letters and not to talk to anybody else about the congress.[32]

The rhetoric at the congress adopted the usual self-congratulatory tone, but, in the country as whole, things were getting even worse. Coal production fell further, steel output was halted at a big plant in Inner Mongolia and railway freight was affected by damage done to 2,000 wagons. Social breakdown led to a campaign entitled One Strike, Three Antis, aimed at 'bad people', corruption, profiteering, embezzlement, waste and extravagance; by the end of 1969, 284,800 people were reported to have been arrested. The CCP and government had both been ravaged; since 1966, 70–80 per cent of cadres had been purged at regional and provincial levels, and 60–70 per cent centrally. Four of six regional Party first secretaries had gone, as had twenty-three of twenty-nine provincial Party secretaries. Only nine of the twenty-three Politburo members survived in their posts, and only four of the thirteen Secretariat members. Half the vice-premiers had been deposed, along with two thirds of the Central Committee.[33]

Internationally, fighting a month before the congress between Soviet and Chinese forces on the Siberian frontier had shown the superiority of Soviet forces. The promulgation of the Brezhnev Doctrine, which proclaimed Moscow's right to intervene to protect Communism, could only be seen as an implied threat to a regime set on going its own way. The conclusion of a cultural exchange agreement between the US and USSR was a fresh reminder that Beijing faced both superpowers – the magazine *Chinese Literature* denounced a 'sinister deal' designed to give respite to 'reactionary, decadent and vicious' imperialist culture.[34]

Faced with such challenges, Mao was still lost for a coherent and constructive answer, while factionalism grew below him. In the new Poliburo, the biggest group numerically consisted of old revolutionaries and Zhou Enlai. But they were not organized, and some members were under attack. The Cultural Revolutionaries had seven representatives, and Kang and Chen Boda were elevated to the core Politburo Standing Committee beside Mao, Lin and Zhou. The PLA was the smallest group in the Politburo, with five seats, but military representation on the Central Committee rose from 19 to 45 per cent, and army influence grew steadily across the country – within two years of the congress, twenty-two of the twenty-nine CCP first secretaries and a majority of cadres running provincial CCP bodies came from the forces. PLA units' work teams operated at the grassroots in communes, factories and schools. Five of eight ministerial appointments between 1969 and 1971 went to military men. The Defence Ministry was reported to have formed special units to monitor government departments.[35]

The idea was that the PLA would assure stability and act as a vanguard of Communism while the Cultural Revolution Group looked after ideology, culture and education, and the old stagers and technocrats round Zhou kept the central administration running. On the surface, relations were good between the groups. Lin's wife went out of her way to make a show of friendliness to Jiang Qing, presenting her with gifts of watermelons from her husband, and an imported ionizer meant to cure her insomnia. In return, the former actress telephoned Ye Qun almost every day to ask after Lin's health.

But, as so often, the reality was very different, in terms of both power and people. Jiang and Ye saw one another as rivals – the Chairman's wife suspected that the marshal's wife was having her rooms bugged. Within the Cultural Revolution Group, itself, there was bad blood which led Chen Boda to shift his loyalty to Lin's faction, seeing the military as the dominant power bloc and the marshal as the future leader to whom he should hitch his destiny.

Chen's defection left what became known as the Gang of Four – Jiang Qing, Zhang Chunqiao and the writer of the first newspaper broadside, Yao Wenyuan, who were joined by the Shanghai activist Wang Hongwen. They had the backing of the public security minister, Xie Fuzhi, who sat on the Military Affairs Commission.

The first trial of factional strength came in late August 1970, at a leadership session in Lushan, where sparring began over the question of who should replace Liu Shaoqi as state president. Despite having been elevated to the number two slot, Lin Biao had not been offered the job, and the duties were carried out by an elderly figure put in for the time being. Lin suggested that Mao should take the post, as did Zhou Enlai, Chen Boda and Kang Sheng. But the Chairman declined, preferring to let it wither into a purely ceremonial role. However, if it was important in status, he said, it should go to Lin.

The muddle fuelled speculation. Despite Mao's reaction, Lin may have been seeking to 'work towards the Chairman', which meant buttering up Mao by going beyond his stated wishes. Or, if the Chairman persisted in his refusal, the marshal may have hoped to solidify his number two position by getting the job himself; his wife was rumoured to covet the position of First Lady.

With that issue left in the air, a debate opened up between the Cultural Revolutionaries and the military as to whether a reference to Mao having developed Marxism–Leninism 'with genius, creatively and comprehensively' should be written into the constitution. The words came from Lin, but Mao had vetoed their inclusion when the constitution was being reframed. Knowing this, the Shanghai godfather, Zhang Chunqiao, opposed their use, leading the air force chief, Wu Faxian, to attack Zhang for denying Mao's genius.

As Chen Boda and the military assaulted the Cultural Revolution Group for being running dogs of 'the imperialists, the revisionists and the counter-revolutionaries', Mao remained aloof, watching and waiting. Then, after Jiang, Zhang and Yao Wenyuan went to complain to him of the attacks on them, the Chairman launched one of his characteristic guerrilla strikes.

The growing strength of the military had aroused his suspicion. His doctor noticed that his patient was increasingly resentful of the number of soldiers surrounding him, and complained that the head of his security detail, Zhang Yaoci, was in thrall to the Lins – 'when [they] fart, Zhang acts like they're announcing an imperial edict!' he exclaimed. At Lushan, Mao had allowed the military faction to surge ahead in its criticism of the Cultural Revolutionaries like a KMT force chasing the Red Army. Now it was time to spring the ambush.[36]

Calling a Politburo session, the leader denounced Chen Boda as a false Marxist, a long-time KMT agent and a secret ally of his old foe, Wang Ming. Nobody spoke up. Mao ordered discussion of Lin's remarks on his genius to halt. Ye Qun and the commanders of the air force, the navy and the PLA logistics department were told to make self-criticisms. These were judged unsatisfactory, and they were instructed to have another go. Again the results were held to fall short of what was required as Mao kept them dangling.[37]

Having won his victory, the Helmsman could afford to take his time in following up. But the pressure was unmistakable over the following year. He placed trusted figures in the Military Affairs Commission to watch pro-Lin generals. He ordered the two top commanders of the Beijing military region to write self-confessions. The marshal was still number two in the regime and was 'shielded', as the leader put it; but his failure to offer pre-emptive abasement was a growing mark against him. Mao told Zhou they were facing a 'sinister affair' with a 'backstage boss'. Touring the Middle Yangzi, he warned a closed Party session that 'a certain person aims to become head of state, split the Party and grab power.' Ominously, he added that 'it is difficult for someone who has taken the lead in committing major errors . . . to reform.' His paranoia increased by repeated illnesses and a heavy diet of pills, the Chairman told Dr Li, 'Lin Biao wants my lungs to rot.'[38]

In 1971, the marshal and his wife spent a long summer break at their villa in the seaside resort of Beidaihe, where they occupied opposite ends of the grim building. Lin looked in even worse shape than usual, his face thin and pale, his eyes sunken. Ye swam in the pool, took history lessons, and read a biography of Nixon and a translation of Balzac's *Le Père Goriot*. She sought to retain the backing of Jiang Qing, telephoning her to pass on her husband's best regards and tell her to look after her health. Four fine watermelons were sent in the marshal's name to Mao's wife.[39]

With the Lins was their son, Lin Liguo, who was as active as his father was passive, a 25-year-old known in the family as 'Tiger'. Born in 1946, Liguo had enjoyed a stellar rise in the military, benefiting from the patronage of the air force commander Wu Faxian.* Strongly encouraged to assert himself by his mother, the young man had been at the Lushan meeting, where he joined in the attack on the Cultural Revolutionaries.

According to a document that was produced later, he and his clique of young officers drew up a plan called Outline of Project 571 – the number sounds like the term for a coup in Chinese. Until the archives are opened, it will be impossible to tell how genuine this was. It denounced a collapsing regime under a 'corrupt, muddled and incompetent' Trotskyite clique which had turned the state machine into 'a meat grinder for mutual slaughter and strife'. Mao, it added, was 'paranoid and a sadist'.[40]

Tiger's group wanted to stage a coup, if only to save Lin Biao, who, it argued, was about to go the way of Liu Shaoqi and Peng Dehuai.

---

* The air force was a favoured route ahead for sons of the powerful, including the offspring of Zhou Enlai, Zhu De and Mao's security chief, Wang Dongxing.

Better to 'risk everything on a single venture and wage a struggle than wait for our doom,' the young man told his sister Doudou. The rebels should form an alternative government in Guangzhou or wage guerrilla warfare in the mountains. Doudou, who was about to get married, was not impressed, considering Mao too powerful to be ousted.[41]

According to evidence given by one of the conspirators at his subsequent trial, whose value cannot be accurately judged, their ideas included attacking Mao's train with flamethrowers, bazooka or anti-aircraft guns, bombing a bridge, or hitting fuel tanks along the track and using the resulting confusion to get on board and shoot the leader. A piece of paper was produced by the conspirators said to be a vague handwritten order from Lin that could be interpreted as a call to action. Whether this was genuine is highly doubtful. Liguo had become adept at imitating his father's script, and, with her husband's approval, Ye had told several secretaries in her office to learn to do the same.[42]

Word that something was amiss must have reached Zhou Enlai because he suddenly ordered a check on the whereabouts of the Trident airliner that Tiger planned to use to spirit his father out of Beidaihe. This established that it was on the tarmac at the nearest airfield to the resort. When an instruction was issued for the plane to fly to Beijing, the base commander claimed it could not leave because of engine trouble.

In the Lin villa, the desperately worried Doudou confided in the bodyguards, who took no notice of her, and then went to the local commanders of Unit 8341, the security force that guarded the leadership from its building near the villa. Cautiously, they said they could do nothing until they had referred the matter to their bosses in Beijing.

Ye, meanwhile, told the family to get ready to move, giving Dalian as the destination. A bodyguard said she had, in fact, fixed on Guangzhou. Ye also called Zhou to say that Lin wanted to go to the north-east. Was there a plane at Beidaihe, the premier asked. No, Ye lied; she would call to ask for one.

Two cars arrived at the villa. Lin, Ye, their son and a bodyguard got into the first one. As it drove out, it passed the Unit 8341 building where Doudou still was, with her fiancé. Lin's bodyguard jumped out – he said later that he did so after hearing the marshal ask his son how far it was to Irkutsk, in eastern Siberia. This is the only piece of evidence that the marshal may have known that yet another destination was now planned, the Soviet Union.

The airfield guards did nothing to stop the Lins' car. A truckload of soldiers arrived, but did not intervene as the nine-strong party boarded the Trident. By the time other pursuers from Unit 8341 and Doudou and her fiancé arrived, the plane was high in the night sky. Told that her father, mother and brother had gone, Doudou looked in the direction their plane had taken and asked, 'Where can they go?'

The Trident flew west, then north. Other aircraft in Chinese air space were grounded. Zhou asked Mao if the plane should be shot down. 'Rain will fall, widows will remarry,' the Chairman replied. 'What can we do? Let him go.'

At 1.50 a.m. on 13 September, its fuel running low, the jet left Chinese air space and flew over Mongolia. In Beijing, Mao moved to the Great Hall of the People for a 3 a.m. meeting of the Politburo. He stayed there, considering it safer than Zhongnanhai in case there was a coup.

The following day, the Chinese ambassador in Ulan Bator was called to the Foreign Ministry to be told that a Chinese plane had crashed on the steppes after illegally entering Mongolian air space. All those on board had been killed.

Under Soviet influence, Mongolia was on bad terms with the PRC, and the embassy's direct communications with the Chinese capital had been cut off. So a diplomat had to go to the post office to send a cable to Beijing. At the crash site, the ambassador found nine bodies, seven pistols, two assault rifles, forty bullets and a woman's white leather shoe. The pilot had a copy of Mao's *Thoughts* in his pocket; Liguo had tucked a certificate from the Air Force College into his tunic. After the diplomats left, the bodies were buried, facing the morning sun. The crash was blamed on the plane running short of fuel, and the pilot making too abrupt a landing. Going to Beijing to report, the ambassador was taken to the Great Hall of the People to see Zhou, who surprised him by asking how far the crash site was from Irkutsk.[*][43]

The outline of the affair was circulated in a top-secret notice on 18 September. Six days later, four top generals who had worked with

---

* Naturally, other versions of Lin's end circulated. One had him, his wife and son machine-gunned to death in a restaurant. Another said they were killed by rockets fired at their car as they left a banquet with the Chairman (Yao Ming-le, *The Conspiracy and Death of Lin Biao* (New York: Kopf, 1983). A third had Lin planning to kidnap Mao and kill him with poison gas. On present evidence, the official version is right (*South China Morning Post*, 13 May 2006).

Lin were arrested and accused of being 'deeply involved in the factional activities of the Lin Biao and Chen Boda counter-revolutionary clique'; they were not tried for seven years, and then received prison terms ranging from sixteen to nineteen years. Because of the embarrassment of Lin's absence, National Day celebrations in Tiananmen Square on 1 October were cancelled, making plain that something important was going on. Though the press started to refer to the marshal as 'a swindler of the Liu Shaoqi kind', it was not until the Tenth Party Congress, in August 1973, that he was formally denounced in public and the constitution was rewritten, yet again, to remove the reference to him as Mao's closest follower and anointed successor.[44]

The episode had achieved Mao's aim of eliminating Lin, albeit by indirect means, but it raised the question of how the Chairman could have elevated this man now proclaimed as a traitor to the number two position. The aura of omniscience was pierced once more. The leader felt it, too. He fell into a depression, and lay in bed all day, saying little. 'When he did get up, he seemed to have aged,' his doctor recalled. 'His shoulders stooped, and he moved slowly. He walked with a shuffle and he could not sleep.' His blood pressure shot up; his lower legs and feet swelled; his lungs became congested; he developed a chronic cold and spat out large amounts of phlegm. His heartbeat became irregular. He rejected Dr Li's proposal for a full check-up and x-rays. When he eventually agreed to take pills, he stopped as soon as they began to have an effect. Television coverage of a meeting with the North Vietnamese prime minister showed a shuffling old man nearing eighty, with legs which looked like wobbly sticks.[45]

But the Helmsman could still rouse himself, and switch course once again. On 10 January 1972, he awakened at his usual late hour, in this case 1 p.m. Donning a silk robe and leather slippers, he ordered a car. He had not been due to attend the funeral of Marshal Chen Yi, of the 'February Countercurrent', but decided to go none the less. Worried about the effects of the cold wind, his doctor wrapped the Chairman in a coat and put a hat on his head.[46]

At the funeral home, Mao embraced Chen's widow, who had tears in her eyes. Zhou and Marshal Zhu De came in. 'Wails filled the room,' Dr Li recalled. But Mao was not really crying, he added; 'he was putting on a good show, blinking his eyes and making an effort to wail. His acting skills were still finely honed.'

The trip to the funeral was not simply a gesture to an old comrade-in-arms. It marked the start of the rehabilitation of some figures disgraced during the Cultural Revolution, including veteran military men. The Chairman authorized a memorial for the Red Base leader He Long, who had died under Red Guard persecution. Zhou delivered the eulogy and wept while embracing the widow, even though he had stood by while He was hounded to death.

A tribunal was established to examine individual cases from the old Peng Zhen administration in Beijing; thousands were released from detention. After Zhou Enlai had pointed out that foreigners were free to read classics forbidden to Chinese, the ban was lifted on works such as *The Dream of the Red Chamber* and Mao's favourite saga, *The Water Margin*.

The conditions of Deng Xiaoping's house arrest in Jiangxi were relaxed. After learning what had happened to Lin Biao, he wrote to Mao through the Unit 8341 commander in Beijing, Wang Dongxing, expressing support for the Chairman's 'brilliant leadership' and asking to be permitted to return to Beijing and resume work there. There was no reply, but two of his children were allowed to go to university, and his salary, which had been cut when he was sent away from Beijing, was restored to its original level. His crippled son was admitted to hospital.[47]

Zhou came up with the formulation that 'the right is bound to return unless we thoroughly denounce the left' and proposed a 'thorough denunciation of the ultra-leftist trend of thought and anarchism stirred up by the Lin Biao anti-Party clique'. Jiang Qing countered that Lin had been an 'ultra-rightist' – 'left in form but right in essence'. The gyrations on the tip of the ideological pin could not mask the increasingly bitter power struggle waiting to be fought after the elimination of the military faction.[48]

Mao had got rid of Liu, sidelined Deng and seen Lin destroyed; was he now to turn on his wife and her associates? He evidently found the issue one he did not wish to confront, dropping into another deep depression as he isolated himself in his bedroom with his companion Zhang Yufeng, a 27-year-old attendant on his private train to whom he had taken a fancy. During January 1972, he suffered heart failure and oedema. His oxygen level was dangerously low. He could not pass urine. But he still resisted taking the medicines Dr Li prescribed.

'I cannot make it,' he told Zhou wanly one day as he sat on a sofa with the premier in front of him on a chair. 'You take care of everything after my death. Let's say this is my will.'[49]

Jiang Qing, who was in the room, was horrified. According to Dr Li, who was also present, 'her eyes opened wide, her hands curled into fists.' Zhou put his hands on his knees, frozen.

'It's done now,' the Chairman said. 'You can all go.'

Jiang knew that, if Mao handed over to Zhou, she was finished. Her power stemmed from the Chairman. So, when they left Mao's room and went to a nearby duty office, she sprang into attack mode. Throwing her Red Guard cap to the floor, she announced that there was a 'spy ring' around them. 'Call a meeting of the Politburo immediately,' she told Zhou. He could have stood up to her but, characteristically, gave way.

The discussion of the Helmsman's health went on from 9 p.m. to 7 a.m. Jiang insisted that 'the Chairman is in good health.' Turning to Zhou, she asked, 'Why are you forcing him to transfer power to you?' Li and other doctors were called, and proved their case with medical evidence. Mao continued to deteriorate. His neck and forehead swelled up.

Finally, on 1 February 1972, the Chairman agreed to follow a treatment of antibiotics, diuretics and digitalis. As this started, there was a major scare. Mao began coughing and was so weak that he could not expel the phlegm in his throat. Unable to breathe, he collapsed. Li ran to get emergency equipment, put an oxygen mask on the Chairman and fitted an intravenous tube to his arm to pump medicine into the bloodstream. When he came round, Mao tried to pull the tube out. The doctor stopped him, explaining that it was keeping him alive. Informed of Mao's close call, according to Li, Zhou Enlai lost control of his bowels and soiled his trousers. He washed, changed his clothes and hurried to the leader's side.[50]

After that scare, things began to improve. An application of diuretics enabled the Chairman to pass 1,800cc of urine. 'It looks like I can recover,' he told the medical team. Then he unveiled the reason for his having agreed to the treatment and snapped out of his depression: 'America's President Nixon is coming.'

24

American Interlude

Amid all its internal turmoil, the People's Republic was conducting a serious re-evaluation of its foreign policy at the start of the 1970s. China had managed to add the hydrogen bomb and a satellite to its arsenal – the latter blared out 'The East is Red' in space. Beijing continued the crusade to spread Maoism in Africa, Latin America and Asia; 7 per cent of GDP went on funding Third World revolutionaries. The results were quite sparse. Movements backed by the PRC had kept the revolutionary pot simmering, and reinforced Mao's position as a global icon for the far left, but had not met with much practical success. Fidel Castro was solidly pro-Soviet. Hanoi needed aid from the USSR for the war in Vietnam, and North Korea was equally reluctant to side with Beijing against Moscow.

Though a meeting between Zhou Enlai and Kosygin suggested that neither side wanted war, Mao feared a pre-emptive Soviet attack, perhaps with nuclear weapons. October 1969 had been seen as a possible date for such an onslaught, and the Politburo agreed to a plan by the Chairman that all the senior leadership, except for Zhou Enlai and top military commanders, should be evacuated from Beijing in the middle of the month. Almost a million troops were mobilized. Though nothing happened, the effect had been to strengthen the PLA's position further, and to increase Mao's distrust of Lin Biao.[1]

In such a context, the Chairman was aware that a new look was needed, and four senior military men, led by Chen Yi, had been told to study China's foreign policy position. They saw that the country had to emerge from the straitjacket into which it had crammed itself. 'Why can't we play the American card?' they asked. The Soviet Union could not win the Cold War, they concluded. China's best interest was to pursue the contradictions between the two superpowers by opening up to the US. Mao did not react immediately. Zhou had simply said that the situation was changing. Then Lin Biao had stated that the Soviet Union was an enemy equal with the United States. If Beijing could build bridges to Washington, that would help to ward off any attack from the USSR and give the PRC greater flexibility in its foreign and strategic policies.[2]

Though the Chinese did not know it, a similar shift was taking place in Washington. Despite the doubts of his National Security Adviser, Henry Kissinger, the new president, Richard Nixon, saw China as a counter to the USSR, but his thinking went much further. A handwritten note in January 1969 read: 'Chinese Communists: Short range – no change. Long range – we do not want 800,000,000 living in angry isolation. We want contact.' He told Charles de Gaulle it was in America's long-term interest to recognize the PRC as a great power, and startled his Cabinet by asserting that Moscow was more aggressive than Beijing. For all his faults, Nixon had a genuine global vision, into which he wanted to fit the world's most populous country. Just as Roosevelt had seen in 1940 that the Soviet Union had to be brought into the international system, so Nixon recognized that America should deal with China – if only in its own interests.

Won over, Kissinger said at the end of 1969 that the US had no permanent enemies and that 'we will judge other countries, and specifically countries like Communist China, on the basis of their actions and not on the basis of their domestic ideology.' Having hinted earlier that it might remain aloof from a possible Sino-Soviet conflict if Moscow was helpful over North Vietnam, Washington now made clear to the Kremlin that it would regard an attack on China as a threat to world peace.[3]

The President and his adviser slotted reconciliation with Beijing into their strategy to link the different challenges their country faced, most immediately in Vietnam, on a broad scale against Moscow. There were obvious problems which would have to be marginalized or ignored. Hanging over everything was the gulf between a capitalist democracy that had fought Communism round the world and a nation in the throes of the Cultural Revolution, where anything Western was denounced. Nixon had begun his political career as a virulent anti-Communist, and it was only two decades since the two countries had fought in Korea. Mao had long denounced capitalist ways and made nationalism a foundation stone of his rise to power.

Then there was the more precise issue of Taiwan. Under the ageing Chiang Kai-shek, the island remained a dictatorship, but the Kuomintang had introduced land reform that was notably peaceful and popular in contrast to Mao's experiments. Though the Nationalists had massacred tens of thousands of the native population in 1947, and ruthlessly suppressed democracy advocates, there had been nothing like the purges and mass killing on the mainland.* Chiang's periodic suggestions of an invasion across the ninety-mile Strait were all rejected by Washington, but a US president could not turn his back on Taipei – in particular, not a Republican with a remnant China lobby in his party. Taiwanese troops were fighting as US allies in Vietnam. Nixon and Kissinger had to hope that Beijing would agree to soften its attitude to the island as part of any deal they might work out, enabling them to tell Chiang and his supporters in the United States that they had achieved a modus vivendi.

The idea of a breakthrough with Beijing was highly exciting for both men, coloured by the fascination of a mythical China – and the chance to meet the last of the towering figures of the century. Mao and Zhou were genuine first-generation revolutionaries, who had been on the Long March while Nixon was at law school in California and Kissinger was a schoolboy in Franconia in Germany. They represented History with a capital H and Power with a capital P, in contrast to the grey bureaucrats in the Kremlin. For the intensely ambitious National Security Adviser, a bargain with the PRC would be proof of his status as a master diplomatist; for the President, it would elevate him above the hurly-burly of politics with the mantle of a world statesman that he so craved.

For the Chinese leaders, engaging with the arch-capitalists would be, at the least, an interesting experience. Beijing could make sure it gave away nothing substantial, but contact might provide useful leverage between Moscow and Washington. The barbarians would certainly come bearing gifts that would help modernize China, and Mao's mastery was such that he did not have to worry about executing a sharp policy shift. Accordingly, there were attempts to send out friendly messages. The Chairman made a point of meeting Edgar Snow when he visited Beijing in 1970; he told the writer he was glad Nixon had won the

---

* Apropos the loss of the mainland, Chiang's son and successor, Ching-kuo, told the American journalist Robert Elegant in the early 1950s, 'We didn't kill enough people.' His subsequent opening of the door to democratization of the island should, however, balance this. (Private information.)

presidency – which may have surprised the left-winger. Mao believed the American was a CIA agent, and would pass on planted information about China's willingness to receive Nixon; he was wrong on both counts. But he repeated his view of Nixon to his doctor, telling him, 'I like to deal with rightists. They say what they mean.'[4]

With China-friendly Pakistan acting as go-between, a ballet of on-off contacts was initiated. Washington lifted travel and trade curbs; Beijing speedily released two Americans who had sailed by accident into its territorial waters. In April 1971, following a late-night decision by Mao, an American table tennis team, which had been playing in Japan, was invited to cross to China in what was immediately dubbed 'ping pong diplomacy'.[5]

In early June 1971, the call for Kissinger to visit Beijing came through. 'This is the most important communication that has come to an American President since the end of World War Two,' the National Security Adviser intoned; he later pushed the date back to the end of the Civil War. The President took out a bottle of fine brandy for a toast. 'Henry,' he said, '. . . Let us drink to generations to come who may have a better chance to live in peace because of what we have done.'

On 9 July 1971, the American landed in Beijing for secret talks with Zhou Enlai. Kissinger had set up an elaborate subterfuge to explain his absence during a visit to Pakistan, supposedly suffering from stomach trouble that forced him to go to rest in a hill station. He kept the State Department in the dark. This was the way that he and Nixon liked to operate – indeed, it added to the excitement of what they were doing. But it also had the important effect of keeping the approach to China out of American domestic politics; had this not been the case, and had the initiative become a subject of debate within the US – for instance through a leak from State – it would have been far harder to pull off.

Neither side in the Kissinger–Zhou discussions gave any real ground, but the desire to engage was evident, though a pattern was set by which the more powerful country played the role of suitor. America having entered their lair at its own volition, the Chinese dominated with a mix of imperial hauteur and Maoist guerrilla strategy. Glimpsing his greatest achievement, Kissinger could not allow the mission to fail. As for his hosts, they knew they had the upper hand. When they issued the prized invitation for Nixon to visit China, the phraseology made clear who was giving and who was receiving; the leader of the strongest nation on earth was being granted the fulfilment of his 'expressed desire' to visit the PRC. Kept in touch with the talks on a regular basis, Mao said the United States was evolving 'from a monkey into a man, not quite man yet, the tail is still there'. Later, Zhou would compare the President to 'a whore who would dress up elaborately and present herself at the door'.[6]

When Kissinger insisted that the US would refuse to join any anti-China front, Zhou did not respond by showing any interest in an anti-Soviet front with the United States. The premier refused to be drawn as the visitor indicated flexibility on Taiwan by saying Washington would set a timetable for withdrawal of its forces from the island and tried to link this to Chinese help over Vietnam. He would not budge from China's claim to the island, or rule out the use of force to achieve it.

So the communiqué remained ambiguous on the issue, saying Washington recognized that 'all Chinese on either side of the Taiwan Strait maintain that there is but one China, and that Taiwan is part of China. The United States does not challenge that position. It reaffirms its interest in a peaceful settlement of the Taiwan question by the Chinese themselves.' It was an ambiguity which continues to this day as Washington, and other countries, seek to avoid engaging with the true meaning of the 'One China' policy on which Beijing insists.

Still, Kissinger was euphoric as he left China, sending a telegram to the White House reading simply 'Eureka'. The conversations, he told Nixon, 'were the most intense, important and far-reaching of my White House experience'. On 15 July, the President revealed the Kissinger visit and his own impending trip on nationwide television. That night, he took his staff to dinner and ordered a $600 bottle of wine, which his aide, John Ehrlichman, bargained down to half the price.[7]

Richard Nixon would call his visit to China 'the week that changed the world', and hail it as the high point of his time in office. Dramatic as it was, the truth was rather more limited. The trip opened a vital door, leading to the most important global relationship of the twenty-first century. But, at the time, there was more symbolism and show than substance.[8]

Henry Kissinger had done the preparatory work on a follow-up visit shortly after the Lin Biao affair. One element in his approach, according to the US record, was to try to build up the perceived Soviet threat to

China to reinforce Beijing's interest in rapprochement with Washington. Other American envoys pushed the same theme; Kissinger's deputy, Alexander Haig, said the US would work against the Soviet attempt to encircle the PRC with unfriendly states. That brought a 'withering blast' from Zhou. He told Haig that China would never depend on external forces to maintain its independence because that would make it a 'protectorate or colony'.

As Kissinger was discussing the Nixon visit on his second China journey and trying to draft a communiqué in advance with Zhou, the issue of Taiwan's seat at the United Nations came up. The secretary of state, William Rogers, who had been excluded from the approach to China, had lobbied for the National Security Adviser to put off his trip because of the coincidence of timing with the Taiwan vote; so had the US ambassador to the world body, George Bush. For form's sake, the National Security Adviser said he would see if he could comply. But he and the President agreed that he should not delay. On 25 October, after a significant number of delegates had left the UN building to go home, the Assembly voted to 'expel forthwith the representatives of Chiang Kai-shek from the place which they unlawfully occupy at the United Nations and in all organizations related to it', recognizing the PRC as the only legitimate representative of China. Britain and Canada did not join the United States in opposing the motions.

The Taiwanese walked out slowly while African delegates danced in the aisles. In Beijing, Mao called in Zhou to say that a delegation should be sent immediately to New York – it was headed by the experienced ambassador to Canada and provided a valuable channel for Sino-US communications. The Chairman was delighted. The first Chinese speech at the UN, he said, must preach world revolution. Britain, Japan and other countries lined up to upgrade their relations with Beijing.

For public consumption, Nixon was outraged, sending aides to assure Ronald Reagan and other conservatives that he had done all he could to preserve the status quo. In fact, he was pleased. He reckoned that the conservatives in the Republican Party would not rebel. His China strategy was panning out. In Beijing, Kissinger was offering extraordinary incentives to win Chinese trust, still playing the role of the 'whore at the door'.

He supplied Beijing with secret intelligence on Soviet forces, and undertook to provide information on the SALT arms talks with

Moscow, while not telling the Kremlin anything about US negotiations with the PRC. In a further move to placate Beijing, Washington tilted towards Pakistan and against India when war broke out between the two in late 1971. Kissinger was convinced that Moscow was behind New Delhi, and expected gratitude from Beijing for backing Islamabad and standing up against an extension of Soviet influence in South Asia.[9]

However, the Chinese remained tough. After Alexander Haig said the US was concerned about China's 'viability', Zhou sent the interpreter to get dictionaries so that he could pin down the exact meaning of the word. The next day, he told the American the word was unacceptable. 'We do not like the way you use that kind of language to Chinese,' he said. 'China and the United States should be on an equal footing. Not one under the nuclear umbrella of the other.' At 3 a.m., Mao called the interpreter to his quarters to report on the Zhou–Haig talks. She mentioned the 'viability' matter. The Chairman said the premier had been correct.[10]

The PRC leaders, Kissinger wrote in a briefing paper for Nixon, were 'fanatic' and 'totally disagree with us where the world is going'. But he still thought them pragmatic, 'firm on principle [but] flexible on details'. Unlike the Soviets, they were not constantly pressing for petty gains, haggling over details or grudging. Kissinger found Zhou impressive. The premier and Chairman, he added, 'will make a truly imposing and formidable pair'.[11]

On 17 February 1972, Richard Nixon, his wife and Henry Kissinger set out on what the President called 'a journey for peace' to Beijing, stopping at Hawaii, Guam and Shanghai on the way. For all the preparations, it was a great gamble. There was no telling how the visitors would be received. Handed a map of the PRC with a CIA seal, Nixon made a rare joke: 'Do you think they'll let me in with this?'

As the Americans crossed the Pacific, Mao prepared himself by walking round his quarters to regain the use of his atrophied muscles. His heartbeat became more regular and his lung infection was under control, though oedema still swelled up his body so that he had to have a new suit and shoes made. Medical equipment sent in by the Americans in case the President fell ill was used for Mao. On the morning of 21 February, he was shaved and given his first haircut for five months, his attendant rubbing his scalp with a scented tonic. The medical equipment in his house was hidden away. The Chairman was kept informed of the progress of Nixon's plane, which landed first in Shanghai, where a Chinese crew took over. Dr Li found his patient as excited as he had ever seen him.[12]

Greeted at the airport by Zhou, the President was taken to a guesthouse to rest and have lunch. At 2.30, Mao telephoned the premier to say he could wait no longer. Nixon, Zhou, Kissinger and the adviser's assistant, Winston Lord, got into a car, with a secret-service agent.[13]

Arriving at Mao's residence in Zhongnanhai, the party walked along the hall to the book-lined study. The Chairman shuffled forward, supported by a young woman. The two leaders shook hands. Only Chinese photographers were on hand to record the scene. As had been evident during the Zhou–Kissinger talks, China was in the driving seat. The West had come to pay court and, abetted by the premier's adroitness, a pattern was set that continues to the present day as the heirs of the guerrilla fighters out-stare the superpower and the superpower takes it.

The meeting was held in a semi-circle of six armchairs. Mao sat in the centre, a white spittoon by his right leg. Across a table piled with books and papers was Nixon, dark-suited, hair slicked down. To Mao's right sat the sole interpreter, a bespectacled Chinese woman, who had been brought up in Brooklyn, and was adept at understanding the leader's slurred speech, with its strong Hunanese accent.

Kissinger was on the left of Nixon, flanked by Winston Lord, who was deleted from the official photograph because his boss feared that the presence of a junior official would be a red rag to the State Department, already up in arms at its exclusion from the China play and even more angry when the secretary of state realized that he had not been invited to meet Mao.*

The photograph can be read as a moment of intense satisfaction for Kissinger, who leans back in his chair smiling, hands crossed on his lap, the unworn sole of one shoe showing. Opposite him, Zhou concentrates his gaze on his leader. The Chairman was at ease, relishing the moment.

---

* Kissinger later wrote that he assumed there would be a second meeting with Mao, at which the secretary of state would be included. Maybe. Nixon was sufficiently concerned to instruct that William Rogers should be told that Zhou had arrived unexpectedly and had asked for just him and Kissinger to meet Mao before a plenary session later in the day. Rogers could not have been fooled.

A cameraman noticed that his pallor at the start was replaced by a rosy glow.

At times, Mao was unable to speak; at others, his words rushed out. Once, he leaned across to grasp Nixon's hand for a minute – 'the most moving moment,' the President recorded.

Nixon praised his host's writings. In return, Mao said that the President's book, *Six Crises*, was 'not bad'. Nixon recalled being impressed by Mao's 'remarkable sense of humour' and 'lightning' mind. Kissinger was even more bowled over. With the possible exception of Charles de Gaulle, he said on his return to Washington, he had met nobody who 'so distilled raw, concentrated will power'.

The conversation touched on the Soviet Union and Chiang Kai-shek, but when the President tried to get into substance, Mao said these subjects would be dealt with by Zhou. He would only concern himself with 'philosophical issues'. He waved aside Vietnam, Taiwan and Korea as 'troublesome issues I don't want to get into very much'. The meeting was an imperial audience, not a negotiation. When Nixon made a last effort to get down to specifics, the Chairman looked at his watch, turned to the premier and said, 'Don't you think we have covered enough today?' After an hour the visitors left; the meeting had lasted four times as long as scheduled. To his doctor, Mao spoke well of the President, but dismissed Kissinger as 'a funny little man ... shuddering with nerves'.

The Americans went on to visit the Great Wall, Shanghai and Hangzhou, continuing negotiations which led to a joint communiqué that papered over, or ignored, their great differences. To try to get the best deal, Kissinger – and, at times, Nixon – deployed high degrees of sycophancy, particularly towards Zhou. Whether it had any effect on the great survivor must be doubted. At the last moment, the Americans sought to ingratiate themselves further by handing over a fresh batch of top-secret military information on the Soviet Union; more would be passed through the UN ambassador, Kissinger promised, requesting that this service not be mentioned to US diplomats. Tellingly, he also asked the Chinese not to present the final statement as 'a major American defeat, or as any American defeat'.[14]

At a last tête-à-tête meeting with the premier, Nixon said he would keep the contents of the discussions secret even from members of his own administration. Zhou responded that their two countries should not attack one another in public unnecessarily – the kind of self-evident cliché which the Americans lapped up as a sign of progress. But he also pointed to the many areas where there was discord.

The Shanghai Communiqué which ended the visit was an adept piece of diplomatic work in which differences were recognized by each side putting forward its views separately before coming together in agreement that normalization of relations was in the interests of both, that each wanted to reduce the danger of military conflicts and that neither sought hegemony in Asia. The PRC asserted that Taiwan was a province and a matter of its internal affairs, while Kissinger repeated the statement that 'the United States acknowledge that all Chinese on either side of the Taiwan Strait maintain there is but one China and that Taiwan is part of China.'[15]

The Sino-US relationship would become enormously important, but the immediate fall-out from the trip was unimpressive, and the real change would have to wait for a decade, under another Chinese leader, who was repairing tractors in Jiangxi when Nixon met Mao. The visit did not shift the balance in the Cold War as the Americans had hoped. The Nixon–Kissinger theory that the China connection would bring them benefits of 'linkage', particularly in dealing with Moscow, proved illusory. The PRC declined to do anything to help in Vietnam; the Americans probably overestimated Beijing's leverage over Hanoi, in any case. There was a minor repercussion high in the Himalayas, where CIA backing for Tibetan rebels ended. But, having won at the UN, China did not soften on Taiwan. As Zhou made clear repeatedly, it was not going to have its foreign policy shaped by the interest of another power. Though they opened liaison offices in each other's capitals, the two countries would take another seven years to set up full diplomatic relations.

Still, a barrier of twenty-three years had been breached. For that alone, the trip was a historic moment which opened the way to visits to the PRC by US allies, notably by Prime Minister Kakuei Tanaka of Japan, which was followed by the establishment of diplomatic relations. When the visitor apologized for the invasion of China, the Chairman said that this had helped to make the Communist victory possible. Kissinger was outraged at the way in which the Japanese had jumped the gun to recognize Beijing ahead of the US, calling them 'treacherous sons of bitches'.[16]

Nixon got a hero's welcome when he got home, and Mao became a pop culture icon with Andy Warhol's silk screen portraits of him – the horrors of the famine, the Cultural Revolution and the rectification campaigns were either not known or were swept aside as the West adopted an image of the Chairman as a benevolent grandfatherly figure. The President's popularity rating jumped; nearly 70 per cent of those questioned in a poll thought the China trip would prove useful. But the way it would evolve was not grasped at the time by either side.

Seeking to toss a sop to the injured State Department, Kissinger had thrown it the issue of trade. In discussing the final communiqué, he advised the Chinese not to waste time on commerce which, even with great effort, could only be 'infinitesimal in terms of our total economy'. Trade merited one brief sentence in the statement. In 2007, the PRC had a $256 billion trade surplus with the United States. That would prove far more important than the search for 'linkage' or Cold War advantage.

Exactly a year after the presidential visit, Kissinger was back in Beijing for talks with Zhou Enlai which ranged widely over world affairs. At 11 p.m. on 17 February 1973, the Chinese premier told the visitor and his aide, Winston Lord, that they were invited to meet Mao at his home in the leadership compound. When the Americans arrived with Zhou, the Chairman was helped out of his chair by a young female assistant to greet them. 'I don't look bad, but God has sent me an invitation,' he said, according to the US record.' Mao smoked a cigar. He offered Kissinger one; he declined.*

'Let us not speak false words or engage in trickery,' said the Helmsman, reseated in a big armchair. 'We don't steal your documents. You can deliberately leave them somewhere and try us out. Nor do we engage in eavesdropping and bugging. There is no use in those small tricks . . . Your CIA is no good for major events.' Kissinger agreed that this was 'absolutely true'.

'So long as the objectives are the same, we would not harm you nor would you harm us,' the Chairman went on. 'And we can work together to commonly deal with a bastard.' That provoked laughter, after which the host continued: 'Actually, it would be that sometimes we want to

* Classified Top Secret; Sensitive; Exclusively Eyes Only.

criticize you for a while and you want to criticize us for a while. That, your President said, is the ideological influence. You say, away with you Communists. We say, away with you imperialists. Sometime we say things like that. It would not do not to do that.'

Turning to China's Communist rival, the Chairman said the world would be a better place if the Soviet Union attacked the PRC and was defeated. He noted that the level of Sino-American trade was 'very pitiful'. His country was poor, he went on, but 'what we have in excess is women.' Amid laughter, he offered tens of thousands to America. 'Let them go to your place. They will create disasters. That way you can lessen our burdens.' Returning to the theme later, he raised his offer to ten million women 'so we can let them flood your country with disaster and therefore impair your interests'.

It was after 1 a.m. when the meeting ended, Mao getting up unaided from his chair. He might be seriously ill, but he still had the strength to rise to the occasion, and retain the initiative.

25

Only Heaven Knows

On 28 August 1973, the Shanghai radical Wang Hongwen walked to the ballot box at the Communist Party's Tenth Congress in Beijing to post a crucial vote for the new Central Committee. The previous year, he had been called to Beijing, where he met Mao. He appears to have found the ideological reading list he was given intimidating, and was disconcerted by the routine followed by the Chairman, his wife and Zhou of going to bed at dawn and rising at lunchtime. In telephone calls with friends in Shanghai, he said he was bored and wanted to go home.

That was not to happen. A worker of peasant stock and a former soldier in his mid-thirties, Wang had been identified by Mao as a man for the future at the highest level. He was given a series of important jobs before the congress, including heading the selection committee which would pick members of the Central Committee. Along with another coming figure, Hua Guofeng, a CCP official from Hunan, he was invited to attend Politburo sessions. He still found time to oversee the expansion of radical forces in Shanghai, personally taking part in target practice on return visits to the city. Similar moves to strengthen militias were made in Manchuria, Tianjin, Guangzhou and Hangzhou, where detention centres were set up to hold alleged rightists. Wang and his fellow leftists wanted to be sure that, when Mao left the scene, they would be ready to withstand any move against them.[1]

The Chairman was too ill to take an active part in the congress. He had trouble breathing and walking. His eyesight was hazy, and he drooled. After a large loss of weight, the skin sagged on his stomach. Some speculated that he might be the father when his companion, Zhang Yufeng, became pregnant at the end of 1972. Dr Li knew this could not be on the cards; whether the progenitor was Zhang's husband or somebody else was not clear. Mao delegated the posting of his ballot to

Wang at the voting session on 28 August. The symbolism was clear to all. Liu and Lin had gone. Mao did not want to designate Zhou as his successor. So Wang, a genuine proletarian figure, became the chosen man.[2]

The main purpose of the Congress was to formalize the defeat of the PLA after the disappearance of Lin Biao. The number of military cadres on the Central Committee was almost halved. But, in the twisted logic that had become central to the CCP, the defeat of the 'Lin Clique' was portrayed as proving the correctness of the line taken at the previous congress in 1969. The marshal's name was removed from the constitution, which also dropped the post of state chairman – the functions of head of state went to the president of the National People's Congress, Zhu De.

With its youngest member enjoying the Chairman's favour, the Gang of Four lost no opportunity to strengthen its position. When Zhou had to lessen his workload because of the growth of the cancers that would kill him, Jiang Qing and Zhang Chunqiao were put in charge of propaganda and organization. Zhang wrote the premier's speech to the congress – he said later that he had just taken a string of quotations from Mao and put them together though he did not understand some. Wang delivered the report on the new constitution; that text was actually written for him by the Shanghai intellectual Yao Wenyuan. Zhang and Wang picked the members of the Central Committee from their home city – some were not even in Beijing and had to be woken in the middle of the night and flown to the capital to be present for their own election.[3]

But the congress also saw the return of the old guard, notably Deng Xiaoping. In early 1973, the Chairman allowed him to leave Jiangxi for Beijing. A visitor who called on Deng before he left found him reading an eleventh-century text, *The General Mirror for the Aid of Government*, compiled to tell emperors how their predecessors had ruled China. Restoring him to his post as vice-premier, the Chairman instructed him to focus on foreign affairs. So Deng travelled to New York to address a UN session on development, where he expounded Mao's theory of three worlds – the superpowers, the developed nations and the others, among which China loomed large. Deng's ideological line may have been impeccable, but it is interesting to wonder if the Manhattan he saw on his visit drummed home to him just how far the PRC lagged behind in the material world.

On his return to Beijing, Deng's status was underlined by the way in which most Politburo members went out to greet him at the airport. When Mao met the prime minister of Pakistan three weeks later, Deng occupied the seat traditionally taken by the Chairman's principal adviser, with Zhou relegated to the sidelines. At the Party Congress, he rejoined the Central Committee along with the economic planner Chen Yun and more than forty figures who had been criticized during the Cultural Revolution, including members of the 'February Counter-current'. But Deng was not allowed back in the Politburo, while Wang Hongwen was elevated to third place among its twenty-one members, behind only Mao and Zhou, who was increasingly ill with three separate cancers.

An unwritten rule laid down that Politburo members needed Mao's approval to undergo major surgery. Wielding this life-and-death power and also not believing in operations, the Chairman refused to permit the premier and others to get the full attention they needed. Subterfuges were required. Kang Sheng was also seriously ill, with bladder cancer, and his doctor had to pretend that he was only undergoing a 'minor' intervention. Zhou's surgeon also carried out a small operation, during which he removed a cancerous lump. But the premier was soon losing so much blood that he needed a transfusion twice a week, and Mao relented to allow a fuller operation, but with bad grace. With such inhumane and demeaning behaviour towards people who had served him for so long, the Helmsman sought malign solace in playing with their lives in the twilight of his own existence.

Zhou's growing weakness meant that the leadership of the Party and the government were both likely to fall vacant before long, while the PLA situation was confused after the purge of senior commanders fol-lowing the Lin Biao affair. The power vacuum that opened up as a result encouraged extreme factionalism which reached into the distant past, with the radicals identifying Zhou and Lin Biao with Confucianism while they extolled the harsh tradition of legalism applied by the First Emperor in his book-burning and repression of opposition in the third century BC.* Mao, who identified himself to a foreign visitor with his predecessor of twenty-two centuries, remarked that, whereas Confucianism 'blew away

* It was in this period that the farmers drilling for water outside Xi'an unearthed the First Emperor's terracotta warriors.

like chaff', the emperor's sons 'still remained', ignoring the way in which Confucianism had given China its main belief system over two millennia. But the Chairman was as ready to rewrite ancient history for his purposes as he was to distort more recent events as he wished – to suit any turn of fortune.

Jiang Qing resurrected another scary figure from the past, China's only woman emperor, Wu Zetian of the sixth century, who had combined advanced views of what a woman could achieve and some reforming ideas with extreme ruthlessness in eliminating opponents in the most brutal manner. Now Wu became an admirable unifier of the nation behind progressive policies. On one occasion, according to the hostile but well-informed Dr Li, the Chairman's wife ordered several imperial gowns to be run up for her in which to receive Imelda Marcos of the Philippines; she had second thoughts and did not put them on. Mao was told and disapproved.[4]

Still, Jiang clearly felt herself in the ascendant. She received foreign visitors in place of her husband. She enraged him by spending hours with an American, Roxane Witke, who wanted to write her biography, making what were, for the time and place, extremely unguarded remarks about her life in pre-war Shanghai, and signing her photographs for the visitor in imperial red ink.

While preaching extreme puritanism, Jiang had never entirely shed the more free-and-easy ways of her youth. Though she denounced Western music, she liked to dance with young men to modern tunes. While railing against pets, she kept some. Insisting on feeding the Chinese a diet of model operas and stilted ideological fare, she got her Western movies from the US Liaison Office in Beijing – her first was *The Day of the Jackal*. She played cards and rode horses in a park in central Beijing that was closed to the public. Sometimes she wore a scarlet blouse under her drab uniform, or a bright scarf over her Red Guard cap.[5]

This side of her character peeped out when she designed a new dress that appeared in stores throughout China – it had a tight bodice, a zipper, a Chinese collar, a tight waist and a full Western skirt. Since it cost the equivalent of several weeks' wages, there were few buyers. So Jiang decreed that a down-payment of a fifth of the purchase price would be enough to obtain one of her creations. She ordered cultural officials to buy large quantities to be worn by young ladies on ceremonial occasions. It was required garb for women television presenters, concert performers, staff at high-grade state establishments and representatives travelling abroad.[6]

At the same time, Jiang, who was living in the Spring Lotus Chamber in the Zhongnanhai compound, became obsessed by the idea that she might be the target of a helicopter attack in which a bomb would be dropped or she would be plucked up into the sky. After she made her fears known to her chief bodyguard, machine guns were mounted on the elegant tile roofs of her residence. She also suspected her staff of trying to kill her by giving her the wrong pills, and waged a constant fight with Mao's doctor, accusing him of mistaken diagnoses and of exaggerating the Chairman's health problems.[7]

Mao was growing increasingly irate with his wife, 'She is ignorant and ill-informed,' he raged. 'Drive her out of the Politburo immediately. We'll go our separate ways.' On his deathbed, Kang Sheng fell into line for the last time, writing a letter to the leader saying that Jiang and Zhang Chunqiao had been Kuomintang agents in the 1940s; it was never delivered.

In July 1974, Mao confronted Jiang to tell her that people were unhappy with her, but were 'too shy to tell you'. He advised the Politburo that she did not represent him – 'she represents herself . . . she belongs to the Shanghai gang.' Late in the year, he wrote on a letter she had sent him: 'Do not make too many appearances in public, refrain from commenting on too many documents, do not organise a cabinet behind the scenes. You have provoked too much enmity.' He may well have had her in mind when making his remarks to Kissinger the previous year about the trouble women caused, and offering to export 10 million to the United States.[8]

Meanwhile, Zhou's cancer had become so acute that State Council meetings had to be held at his hospital bedside. He managed to deliver a speech to the National People's Congress at the beginning of 1975 affirming the need for 'four modernizations' in agriculture, industry, defence and science–technology. But, as he grew steadily weaker, his deputies in the government were not up to the job of carrying out such a programme.

The economy required speedy and effective attention. Conditions in the countryside were bleak. Famine hit Sichuan. While industrial workers were better off, the self-reliance campaign had reduced the flow of goods, and migration to cities strained urban housing. Factories were short of money; some had to borrow heavily. The national mood was sour – at the end of October 1972, thousands of people staged an unusual protest in Beijing, digging up flowers round the Monument to the People's Heroes, and taking them home. What shook the regime was the ease with which they acted, despite the supposedly all-seeing security apparatus.

In October 1974, on a protracted visit to southern China, Mao showed that he had not lost all contact with reality by instructing that Deng Xiaoping be appointed the senior vice-premier. In the following months, the Chairman backed the returnee whenever the left tried to undermine him. At the end of the year, he praised Deng for his 'rare talent' and his political and ideological astuteness. He ordered the promotion of the man denounced seven years earlier as a capitalist-roader to become vice-chairman of the Party and the Military Affairs Commission, and made him chief of staff of the PLA while he retained responsibility for foreign affairs.

On 1 February 1975, with the Chairman's approval, Zhou Enlai, thin and shrunken, with a trace of grey in his neatly combed hair, called government ministers to his bedside to tell them that Deng would be 'running the State Council and sign off on major documents on behalf of the Premier'. He would also chair Politburo meetings. This meant that, under Mao's overall control, the little man was back with more power than anybody except Mao had enjoyed under the PRC.

Deng's return set the scene for the final, if protracted, power struggle of the era. The radicals, who had been weakened by the death of Kang Sheng, knew they had to regroup if they were to survive. As Mao had said, 'the little man scares some people', first among them the Cultural Revolution Group.

But the pressure on the leftists did not give up. Wang Hongwen's responsibilities for directing daily work at the Party Centre were transferred to Deng. Mao ordered Jiang Qing and her associates to offer self-criticism. On top of which, Deng's presence at Mao's meetings with foreign visitors meant he could produce real or alleged remarks from the leader to overawe the Politburo.

The Chairman's health was declining steadily. He had cataracts, and could hardly speak intelligibly. He no longer attended Central Committee sessions, and rarely went to Politburo meetings. A medical examination at the beginning of 1975 found that he was suffering from Lou Gehrig's disease or amyotrophic lateral sclerosis, which attacks muscles all over the body; the stage it had reached meant he was likely to die within two years. He also had coronary and pulmonary diseases, an infection in the lower half of both lungs, three bullae in the left lung, and bedsores on his left hip, as well as suffering a shortage of oxygen. At the time of the examination, he ran a fever and a bad cough. An eye operation was agreed. Tests were carried out on forty elderly men using different techniques. Mao chose one, and was soon able to read with spectacles.[9]

Gehrig's disease, and the other ailments, meant he had to spend most of his time lying on his side being fed by his companion, Zhang Yufeng, who had been appointed his confidential secretary and relished her position as the leader's gatekeeper. The only person who could make out what he was trying to say by reading his lips, she became a key figure, offering medical nostrums and overruling the doctors. Jiang Qing went out of her way to be nice, offering the young woman gifts that included foreign luxuries. Zhang was profoundly irritating to men such as the security boss, Wang Dongxing, not to mention Dr Li. Yet, as Wang put it, 'If we dismiss her, how will we be able to understand the Chairman?' Sometimes even Zhang could not make out Mao's grunts, and he had to scrawl characters on paper to be decrypted.

In April 1975, the leader learned of the death of his old opponent, Chiang Kai-shek. His reaction was not triumphant. He spent the day meditating and fasting, as if mortality had struck. He also rewrote an ancient poem to read:

> Go, let go, my honoured friend
> Do not look back.[10]

The deterioration in Mao's condition increased the latitude Deng enjoyed as he moved to implement the 'four modernizations' outlined by Zhou Enlai in agriculture, industry, defence, and science and technology. He ridiculed Jiang Qing's insistence on the role the class struggle should play in increasing grain output. In alliance with the rising CCP figure Hua Guofeng, Deng set out to get the education system working again, with a stress on science and technology. His no-nonsense working methods, and preference for action over talk went down badly with the ideologues, and could involve extreme use of force.

After ethnic violence broke out in a group of Muslim villages in Yunnan, Deng showed his repressive side by sending in the PLA, which killed more than 1,600 people, including 300 women, old folk and children trying to flee. His teams got rid of radical groups in the provinces. When there was trouble on the railways in early 1975, marked by looting and stoppages, the new boss declared disruption a crime – 11,700 workers were subjected to public denunciation, 3,000 were sent to prison, and eighty-five were executed. By April, all but one of the main lines were operating normally.

Deng also got to grips with the iron and steel industry, as well as the defence sector. He set tight deadlines for results, achieving increased output. In one highly symbolic move, he appointed as a vice-minister for machine-building the president of Beijing University, who had been the target of the first big-character poster in 1966. In his role as PLA chief of staff, he denounced the forces for 'bloating, laxity, conceit, extravagance and inertia', and introduced cuts of 13.6 per cent in the 6-million-strong army. He instructed the daughter of the purged former Yangzi base commander, He Long, to conduct a secret investigation of Jiang Qing's work in art and literature.[11]

Mao recognized the need for Deng's new course, but he could not admit his own error over the Cultural Revolution, and held back from the final step of abandoning the radicals ideologically. Revisionism, he declared, remained an essential target for attack. He ordered Zhang Chunqiao and Yao Wenyuan, who was running the propaganda machine, to comb Lenin's works for suitable quotations and write appropriate articles. Needing no further encouragement, they produced calls for class struggle, warning of the danger of material improvements breeding embourgeoisification. A new enemy was conjured up – dubbed 'empiricism', meaning Deng's policies. This, Jiang told a meeting in the Great Hall of the People, 'is the great enemy, the accomplice of revisionism, and . . . has to be struck down'.[12]

Once more, Mao backed Deng in the ensuing debate. Rebuffed again, the Gang of Four avoided seeing one another for three months, as if this would remove the idea that they constituted a faction. On her husband's instructions, Jiang Qing paid a visit to Deng at his home; he was not impressed – he told his children that she 'blew her usual trumpet. Pretty low quality stuff.' On another occasion, he referred to her taste for rhetoric rather than positive action by saying, 'she sits on the toilet but does not manage a shit.' The Gang tried to link Deng's policies with 'capitulationism', which Mao had condemned in a comment on one of his favourite sagas, *The Water Margin*. This backfired when the Chairman blocked the distribution of a speech made by his wife on these lines, and wrote in the margin: 'Shit! Wide of the mark.'[13]

Still, there were currents flowing in the other direction. Mao's nephew, Yuanxin, who had been ousted from a big factory in Manchuria, moved into the leadership compound in Beijing, and saw a lot of his uncle. Yuanxin bore a grudge against Deng for the loss of his job, and fed his uncle with negative information. More important, as so often before, Mao was growing to resent the authority of a subordinate he had raised to power. In this case, Deng gave him cause for concern as he acted without reporting to his leader or consulting the Politburo. The senior vice-premier stepped over the ideological line by identifying statements by the Chairman on promoting stability, unity and economic development as the 'key link' for policy. The only key link Mao wanted to recognize was class struggle. Building his case, the leader declared that the man he had brought back had reverted to the pragmatism he had preached in the early 1960s, and made no distinction between imperialism and Marxism. In the past, Deng had been ready to offer self-criticism to such assaults, but now, in changed circumstances, he declined to do so. In the face of such *lèse-majesté*, Mao called a Politburo meeting to evaluate the Cultural Revolution. He had already decided that it had been 70 per cent positive; Deng could not agree. Suddenly, everything was up for grabs.[14]

The radicals leaped at the chance this opened up for them. Zhang launched a campaign against a leading Deng ally, the education minister, staging repeated struggle meetings and inserting into his ministry a work group headed by the leader of the militia in a Shanghai steel plant. After many struggle sessions, the minister died. More than a thousand big-character posters went up at Qinghua University denouncing those who dared 'to negate the Great Proletarian Cultural Revolution'. Almost 400,000 people from all over the country visited the campus to read them. Yao Wenyuan warned of a new bourgeoisie emerging in the CCP that had to be uprooted. In Manchuria, Zhang Zhixin, a woman member of the propaganda department in Liaoning province, was arrested and sentenced to death for having expressed doubts about the Party to a friend: before she was led to her death, her vocal cords were cut to stop her making any protest at the execution ground. At the end of 1975, Deng bent to an extent with a partial self-criticism, though Mao judged it insufficient.

Though their young contender, Wang Hongwen, was a fading star by now, the radicals were further strengthened by the death of Zhou Enlai on 8 January 1976. While this provoked genuine national mourning, Mao did all he could to prevent the dead man being lionized. There was no lying in state. Press coverage was kept to a minimum. Workers were told not to hold memorial meetings, and staff at the leadership compound not to wear mourning armbands. Deng delivered the eulogy at the funeral; Mao was too ill to have to decide whether to attend. Those present and the television viewers noted that, when she passed the bier, Jiang Qing did not remove her cap; a crowd watching a communal television in Canton chanted, 'Beat her up! Beat her up!'[15]

Three weeks later, Mao passed the cold, dark night of Chinese New Year alone with his companion, Zhang Yufeng, who fed him with a spoon. He had difficulty opening his mouth or swallowing. Afterwards, she settled him in the sitting room, where he rested his head on the back of a sofa, remaining silent. Suddenly, firecrackers exploded in the distance. In a low, hoarse voice, the Chairman asked her to get some and set them off. When she arranged for this in the courtyard outside, a faint smile crept over his old and weary face. Outside, guards rushed up, fearing an attack.[16]

Despite his deteriorating condition, Mao continued to receive foreign visitors, even if the encounters often had to be kept short. He enjoyed these events as evidence of his global status, often playing the potentate regardless of political correctness. The guests were overawed by this historic figure; none questioned him about what had really taken place in China since 1949.

Relations with the United States were jarred by disagreements over Taiwan and Tibet – the head of the US representative office in Beijing, George Bush, warned the White House of the domestic dangers of being seen to give way on the Taiwan issue. But both sides wanted to build on the relationship launched in 1972 by Richard Nixon, who had subsequently been forced to resign from the presidency by the Watergate affair, which was simply incomprehensible to the Chinese leadership.

In December 1975, Nixon's successor, Gerald Ford, visited China and met Mao. Ford proclaimed his desire to normalize relations with the PRC and there was talk of an anti-Soviet alliance stretching from Beijing and Tokyo through Pakistan, Iran and Turkey to Nato. But Beijing was cool towards the new president. It was all too clear to the Chinese that they were just part of the jigsaw Washington was putting together; that was not the role they saw for themselves.[17]

Ford's party found dealing with Deng tougher than negotiating with Zhou – they were also surprised by his habit of using a spittoon – as he explained, 'I'm just a country boy.' Kissinger, now secretary of state, called him a 'nasty little man'. The tension was only broken when a PLA band broke into 'The Yellow Rose of Texas'.

Ford was taken aback by Mao's condition. 'It was as if the Communist leader had lost control of his tongue,' he told the journalist Roy Rowan, who covered the trip. When his companion Zhang and the interpreters could no longer read his lips, Mao held a soft lead pencil in his shaky right hand and wrote a few characters. But, for all his infirmity, the Chairman was firm in dismissing America's strategic arms negotiations with Moscow as 'futile'. Ford came away convinced that his host's mind was still clear. China followed the relatively cool meeting with Ford by giving Nixon a lavish welcome when he came back on a private visit in February 1976, including a session with the Chairman. The former president found the meeting painful as Mao issued a 'series of monosyllabic grunts and groans'.

The Qingming grave-sweeping festival in the spring of 1976 produced an outpouring of emotion in Beijing for Zhou Enlai, and provoked the showdown between Deng and the left. By early April, there were 2,073 memorials to the late premier in Tiananmen Square, and the number was rising by the day. Some made scarcely veiled attacks on Mao in proclaiming that the day of the First Emperor was gone. But the main target was the Gang of Four, and especially the woman who had not raised her cap in memory of Zhou. The Gang was denounced as 'wolves and jackals', a phrase that found its way into the official media under the guise of being condemned – Yao scented a counter-revolutionary plot. There were tributes to Mao's previous wife, and references to an emperor mistakenly bewitched by a concubine. One poem warned:

Lady X, indeed you are insane.
To be empress is your ambition . . .
Yet for types like you
Good times won't last long.[18]

Passing through the square, Dr Li saw tens of thousands of people singing, making speeches and reading poems. Thousands of banners flapped in the breeze. The wreaths ran from the centre of the huge square right up to the Tiananmen Gate of the Forbidden City.

For a regime which had sought to impose absolute control, the out-pouring of emotion was deeply worrying. Mao's nephew told his uncle that it was all a bid to split the Party Centre and attack the Chairman. Grief about the passing of Zhou was being used as a cover to whip up support for Deng, he added. It was the work of a secret conspiracy and action was needed.

On the grave festival day, 5 April, hundreds of thousands of people joined in. The mayor of Beijing said there had been no such spontaneous outburst of feeling since 1949. It was time for a crackdown. After midnight, troops on 200 lorries rolled into the square to take away the wreaths and memorials. The following day, scuffles broke out between mourners and police. Ten thousand people demonstrated outside the Great Hall. They overturned a loudspeaker truck sent in to tell them to disperse and warn of sabotage by class enemies. As the protest gathered steam, an official car, two jeeps and a minibus were burned, as was a security post.

In the Great Hall of the People, the leaders watched the scene through binoculars. Mao's new protégé, Hua Guofeng, ran meetings to discuss the crisis. The Cultural Revolution radicals decided to blame it all on their enemy, Deng. Zhang Chunqiao cursed him as 'an ugly traitor', and compared him to Imre Nagy, the leader of the 1956 revolt in Hungary. 'He stuck to his odious attitude, but had no choice but to nod his head in silence,' Zhang wrote to his son.

At 6 p.m., the head of the Beijing Revolutionary Committee broadcast a message to those on the square, calling for the crowd to disperse and denouncing 'a tiny handful of bad elements, unrepentant capitalist-roaders promoting "the right deviationist wind"'. All but 200 did so. At 9.30 p.m., floodlights were turned on, and 10,000 club-wielding militiamen, backed by thousands of troops, beat up the remaining demonstrators. Fifty-nine were sentenced to prison terms. There was talk of people having been killed – the reformist speechwriter Ruan Ming wrote that he knew of 'ten outstanding young people' who died. Foreign correspondents who visited the square the next day saw no trace of blood, but, one wrote, 'the place was a shambles, with burned-out cars and charred pine trees, a gutted building and sundry debris lying around.'

Attempts to arouse support for the leadership and denounce Deng fell flat. People paid no attention, or turned away, as trucks drove through the street carrying drummers, cymbal players and red bunting praising the 'wise decisions' of the Party. The propaganda magic the regime had once been able to deploy was, by now, being shown up as a Wizard of Oz trick.

Still, the radicals were overjoyed. The Shanghai writer Yao Wenyuan could not sleep for excitement at the way 'this counter-revolutionary coup d'état' had been crushed 'in the interests of the proletariat'. 'Good! Good!' Mao said when his nephew told him that the enemy had exposed itself and that the action against it had boosted the revolutionary morale of the masses. The following morning, he expressed approval of Zhang's comparison of Deng to Nagy. 'Throw him out!' he told his nephew. Hearing this, Jiang Qing celebrated with a meal of roast pork and peanuts washed down with the fiery liquor *maotai*. 'We are victorious,' she toasted. 'Drink up! I will become a bludgeon, ready to strike.'[19]

The next day, the Politburo formally appointed the Chairman's latest choice to be his successor as premier and first vice-chairman of the Party, Hua Guofeng. Born in 1921 into a very poor peasant family, he had joined the Red Army at the age of fifteen and made his mark organizing collectives as a county CCP secretary in Hunan. His work came to the attention of Mao, who had him made the province's Party boss and head of the Revolutionary Committee. Amiable and phlegmatic, shambling and with a soft manner some found sinister, the plump-cheeked Hua was an efficient administrator, and got on with colleagues. Mao could see him as a compromise between the radicals and the pragmatists, a man who might rise above the raging factionalism at the top.

On a proposal from 'our great leader, Chairman Mao Zedong', the Politburo decided to strip Deng of all his posts, though he was allowed to remain a member of the Party, 'so as to see how he will behave in the future'. His economic policies were branded 'dangerous weeds' that had to be rooted out. However, radical suggestions that he should be 'dragged out' were not acted upon, and, with Mao's approval, the leadership security chief had Deng and his wife installed secretly in a house in the old legation quarter. From there, he wrote to the Party Centre to express approval of Hua's appointment and his gratitude at having been permitted to retain Party membership. As a bridge player, he knew when to pass on a bad hand.

The dispersion of the Tiananmen mourners set off yet another wave of repression. How many people were targeted is unknown, figures varying from the official 1,662 detainees to a Taiwanese claim that nearly 10,000 lost their lives and a Hong Kong estimate that millions were affected. While the radicals were having their fling and Jiang Qing was warning that the true danger stemmed from 'persons in power inside the Party walking the capitalist road, big officials', Hua strove to establish himself.[20]

This was a difficult task. For the realists, he was no substitute for Deng, who had taken off for Guangdong, where he hid in hot springs and was driven about in a wagon with its windows blacked out so that he could not be spotted as he mustered support. Crucially, he enjoyed the backing of the influential defence minister, Marshal Ye Jianying, who organized resistance to the Gang of Four in Beijing.

For the radicals, Hua was an outsider who lacked the true faith. But he got a boost when Mao, increasingly unable to speak, scrawled: 'With you in charge, I am at ease' on a piece of paper at one of their rare meetings. It might have been merely a passing endorsement, but Hua could use it as an expression of general belief in him from the Great Helmsman.

However, the figure on whom all depended was sinking steadily. At his home in the leadership compound, films, including *The Sound of Music* and *Love Story*, were projected to keep Mao entertained. Though she thought the cinema might be bad for his eyes, Jiang Qing insisted that there was nothing seriously wrong with her husband; Dr Li began to wonder if she wanted him not to get proper treatment so that he would die quickly and she could stage a takeover. Zhang Yufeng said injections of glucose would cure the Chairman. The security chief, Wang Dongxing, came up with a remedy made of crushed pearls. Hua Guofeng volunteered to act as a guinea pig for a nasal feeding tube the doctors wanted to use; he found it uncomfortable but not painful. However, the

Chairman would not accept it. All he would agree to was to have his pulse taken.

In May, Mao had a heart attack during a row with his companion and then received his last official foreign visitor, Prime Minister Bhutto of Pakistan; his eyes were half closed, his face blank. In June, he had a second, more serious, attack. Calling Hua Guofeng, his wife and four other radicals to his bedside, he was said to have made a statement in which he remarked on his longevity and added that he had done two things in his life:[21]

I have fought Chiang Kai-shek for a few decades and I have driven him to a few islands. After eight years of war against the Japanese, they were sent home. We fought our way to Beijing and, at last, to the Forbidden City. The second thing you know. It was to initiate the Cultural Revolution which is now supported by few and opposed by many. But this matter is not finished yet. It is a legacy which has to be handed down to the next generation. How to hand it down? If not in peace, then in turmoil. If this is not properly handled, there will be bloodshed. Only Heaven knows what you are going to do.

On 6 July, Mao's old comrade-in-arms, Zhu De, died at the age of ninety. On the 28th, two huge earthquakes shook north China; according to official figures, more than 242,000 people were killed. Despite the decades of eradicating superstition, this could only be seen as a portent of disaster at the top. After the first quake, Mao was wheeled to an extra-solid building, where the second tremor was hardly felt. The Gang of Four sent a message to the people of the city of Tangshan, which had been worst hit by the disaster, calling on them to 'deepen and broaden' their criticism of Deng Xiaoping.

On 2 September, the Chairman had another major heart attack. His lung infection worsened. He produced hardly any urine. Three days later, Hua asked Jiang Qing, who was at the model commune of Dazhai, to return to Beijing. She paid a brief call on her husband, then ensconced herself in the Spring Lotus Chamber. Two days elapsed before she made another visit. Mao was asleep when she arrived; according to Dr Li, she insisted on massaging his back and moving his limbs, rubbing powder into the skin, though the dust was bad for his lungs. The next morning, she returned, overruling the duty doctor to get her husband moved from his usual position on his left side, where he breathed most easily. It was as if she could not wait for him to expire.

Late on 8 September, members of the Politburo were called to the leader's home. Mao lay under a white sheet. Led by Marshal Ye Jianying, the visitors filed past his bed. As Ye was about to leave, he was called back. The dying leader tried to speak. Only a hoarse sound emerged.

At ten minutes past midnight, the Great Helmsman died of heart failure. 'Doctors! Quickly!' Jiang Qing cried. 'Save the Chairman! Why don't you save him?'

Mao's death deprived the Gang of Four of its only real source of support. It would now have to survive or die on its own. The bulk of the Party had been thoroughly alienated by the depredations of the Cultural Revolution and the factionalism of Jiang Qing and her colleagues. The radicals enjoyed little support in the PLA, whose chiefs wanted an end to the disorder and uncertainty. The country, as a whole, needed stability. In the first Politburo meeting after the Chairman's passing, according to Dr Li, the old signs of deference paid to Mao's wife vanished; nobody stood up when she entered, and other members chatted among themselves when she spoke.[22]

Her wreath, which the press said she had put together with her own hands while weeping for her husband, called him 'revered master teacher' and herself his 'student and comrade in arms'. At the funeral, attended by a million in Tiananmen Square, she appeared in a smartly cut Sun Yat-sen suit, staring ahead as Hua read the eulogy agreed by the Politburo.

Jiang, the oldest of the group at the age of sixty-two – to Zhang's fifty-nine, Yao's forty-five and Wang's forty – made unsuccessful bids to get hold of the Chairman's papers, as did Mao's nephew; this would have given them control over his words for posterity. The widow insisted that the anti-rightist campaign must not be interrupted by her husband's death. A mass letter drive was organized to call for her to take over the leadership of the CCP. Jiang also unsuccessfully proposed at the Politburo that Deng should be expelled from the Party.

Wang launched a heavy-handed effort to get provincial officials to report directly to him through his secretary – this was undone when the Hunan Party chief telephoned Hua Guofeng to ask who this secretary was, and Hua told him not to obey the instruction. The Gang used its media control to get the *People's Daily* to run an item saying that Mao had ordered that all must 'abide by set principles'. Hua insisted that the late leader had used the term 'past principles'. The first would set the Cultural Revolution in stone, the second could open the way for change.

Meanwhile, an old establishment coup bid which had started to take shape before Mao's death moved ahead fast under the direction of Marshal Ye, and with the obvious backing of Deng. The plotters were mostly senior military men, joined by a few civilian officials. Deng reckoned that they could count on the PLA in Guangzhou, Fuzhou and Nanjing. Crucially, the plot was joined by the leadership security chief, Wang Dongxing, who offered to provide troops in the capital; he had discussed the idea of arresting Jiang Qing with Hua Guofeng in the last weeks of Mao's life.

Clearly aware of what was going on, and caught in the middle, Hua hesitated. In his memorial speech for Mao, he had stuck to the claim that the Cultural Revolution had 'smashed the schemes of Liu Shaoqi, Lin Biao and Deng Xiaoping'. But he could only fear that it would be the schemes of Jiang Qing and her associates which would either overthrow him or reduce him to a figurehead. In early October, he decided to join the Ye plot.

A meeting of the Politburo Standing Committee was called for the night of 6 October, ostensibly to discuss Mao's works. As they arrived, Zhang and Wang were detained by soldiers stepping from behind a screen across the middle of the room to take them in. 'You have entered into an anti-Party and anti-Socialist alliance . . . in a vain attempt to usurp the leadership of the Party and seize power,' Hua read to them from a text.

When Wang tried to resist, he was wrestled down and handcuffed. 'Didn't think it would happen this quickly,' he muttered as he was led away. 'What's going on?' Zhang Chunqiao asked, wiping his glasses. Yao had not turned up and was arrested at home.

Troops from Unit 8341 drove to Jiang Qing's home in the Spring Lotus Chamber of the Zhongnanhai compound. She was in bed. After jumping up, she fell to the floor, weeping. 'The chairman's body is barely cold,' she cried. 'And you have the gall to mount a coup!' After being allowed to go to the bathroom, she was taken with the other three to solitary confinement in an underground complex, where it so happened that the Chairman's body was being stored. Popular mythology has it that one of her servants spat at her as she left the Spring Lotus Chamber.

Prominent Gang supporters were detained, including Mao's nephew.

By Chinese tradition, family members were victimized, including Jiang Qing's daughter and half-sister. The army was solidly behind the move. Those who could afford it celebrated the fall of the Gang by ordering a dish of four crabs – three male and one female. Photographs of Mao's funeral developed a strange hole in the middle – where the Gang of Four had been airbrushed out.

Radical leaders in Shanghai were tipped off that things had gone wrong in the capital by a coded message reading 'Mother's operation has been unsuccessful'. Shocked, they went into emergency session, drawing parallels between what had happened in Beijing and Chiang Kai-shek's move against the Communists in their city in 1927. The spirit of the Paris Commune was evoked. A battle cry was prepared: 'Heads may roll, blood may flow: Mao Zedong Thought must not go!' But the PLA swiftly seized the militia's weapons, and took control of factories and trade union premises.

Elsewhere, there was some fighting between army units and local revolutionary militia, in part a rearguard action by Gang supporters and in part a bid by local leaders to maintain their autonomy. In Tianjin, clashes continued till the end of the year. But there was no threat of a rising that could restore Jiang Qing and her comrades. The Gang of Four was gone. Just under a month after Mao's death, the Cultural Revolution was over, at an economic cost estimated at the equivalent of $34 billion and incalculable human losses.[23]

The crab dinners symbolized hopes that a mad period of personal and ideological adventure had ended. Though others were blamed, the upheaval since 1966 had been the doing of the Chairman, who gave every sign of relishing the insanity. At times, he had glimpsed the need to restore order but, given the way he had destroyed other organs of state, the only way of doing that had been to give the PLA a dangerous degree of power. He had never been ready to call a final halt. Each temporary stabilization had been followed by a fresh plunge towards extremism, making the Cultural Revolution either one of the most ideologically sustained epochs in modern China or simply a massive exercise in personal irresponsibility.

That was also the case for the whole experience since the foundation of the PRC, when Mao had been Stalin, Lenin, Marx and the First Emperor rolled into one, a figure from the past who was set on being a resolutely modern revolutionary with Chinese characteristics. Though unable to regain Taiwan, he had enjoyed great successes, reunifying the mainland and making it into a major, nuclear-armed global player, which punched above its real weight as it inspired would-be emulators round the world and allowed the leaders of the greatest superpower to come to pay court.

Backed by the immense cult of his personality, the charismatic, narcissistic Son of Heaven, who thought himself capable of changing human nature through his mass campaigns, could demand complete loyalty to the cause of revolution as he chose to define it. Nobody and nothing could be excused from utter dedication and readiness to contribute whatever was demanded. Private life meant nothing. People were a blank sheet of paper, mere numbers to be used as the leader saw fit. Maoist autocracy reached heights of totalitarianism unparalleled by Hitler or Stalin, accompanied by massive hypocrisy as the leader who preached simplicity, morality and proletarian values had his favourite fish flown up from Wuhan, dallied with a succession of young ladies, had rarely used villas built for him at great cost, and raked in the royalties from his *Little Red Book*. A potent terror organization ensured obedience, a huge gulag swallowed up real or imagined opponents, and a massive propaganda machine fed the myths. Yet it is hard to argue that Mao did not inspire adulation. He was a monster, but a monster whom people revered as the symbol of a new China that would wipe away all the suffering and weakness of the hundred years before 1949 and who offered at least a promise of an 'iron rice bowl' of food and welfare, however much it was contradicted by his actions.

The Great Helmsman could have been content with all that, but he felt a constant need to change and to attack. Though he wrote voluminously and claimed a monopoly on ideology, what he produced was rarely clear and was always subject to alteration – the officially sanctioned meaning of 'socialism' changed seven times in the first four decades of the PRC. The unrelenting drive that had brought him to power after two decades of struggle remained his prime motive force. Having defeated the KMT, he turned on the very bodies that underpinned the new state – the Party, the government and the army. As a result, Maoism lost any coherence it had once possessed, and China was subject to fresh trials to equal, or surpass, those of the past.[24]

On a personal level, he was vengeful towards anybody he saw as a real or potential opponent, bringing down men and women who had spent their lives in the service of the Party, subjecting them to death or awful treatment and always, as the supreme egoist, assuming that those who survived would come back to serve him. Which they did, thereby heightening the leader's self-esteem and disdain for others, a frame of mind that could only be strengthened by the way in which his leading subordinates were ready to fall in line to persecute old comrades.

There was nothing unknown or untold about the methods he used, even if the details might be kept under wraps. Indeed, the Chairman extolled them. Even if most foreigners chose to avert their eyes, the Chinese were well aware of how the system worked. Authoritarianism was the Maoist way, drawing on a long tradition as the ruler extolled the harsh methods of the First Emperor; Qin Shi Huangdi, the Helmsman once remarked, had buried 460 scholars alive but 'we have buried 460,000'. Revolutionary violence was the means to pursue that way, and anybody considered likely to step out of line was automatically a counter-revolutionary. The 'bad people' pursued by the Cultural Revolutionaries were in a long line of sinister forces that run through Chinese mythology. Who they were was no more precisely defined than the identification of witches in medieval Europe. Reason and words had lost their meaning under a leader who described himself, in an old Buddhist phrase, as a lone monk wandering under a leaky umbrella, denoting not humility but that he was a free spirit who had risen above any control. Now that the People's Republic was going to have to outlive its Helmsman, the question was whether China would continue on the erratic, self-destructive path Mao had ended up setting for it, or whether his successor could find a new course.

PART 5

The Age of Deng

Like emperors before him, Mao sought to designate a successor who would carry on his work. He failed. The result was a power struggle which ended with the accession of the pretender whom the Chairman had spared and esteemed, but had never named as the next ruler. Deng Xiaoping set a course that diverged wildly from Maoism in major respects, but stayed fundamentally true to its central political chord.

The outcome was a nation which roared ahead economically and underwent huge social transformations, but remained subject to the rule of a party that, increasingly, lost its ideological moorings because of the very changes Deng brought. Neon lights shone in place of drabness, and televisions and modern household appliances became common, in cities, at least. Tens of millions moved from the countryside to urban industries, injecting a low-cost labour force into the global economy as China engaged with the world as never before, drawing in foreign investment, spewing out exports and amassing an enormous treasury of foreign reserves.

Growth came with a high price in inequality, environmental damage, corruption, social tension, imbalances and economic strain arising from the scale and speed of expansion. Sheer momentum drove China forward, but the process launched by Deng raised deep questions of whether the Communist Party could run a country whose character veered increasingly away from its tenets and which threatened to get beyond control.

This was not all the work of one man. Many millions contributed. What Deng did was to unleash a transforming economic motor on to the world. But he was also hidebound by the straitjacket political system and unready to risk the threat freedom posed to the Communist Party he had served all his life. The result, three decades after he launched China's transformation, is a country marked by contradictions even greater than those celebrated by Mao.

26

Little Peace Plays His Trumps

A chain-smoker who made liberal use of his spittoon, a soccer enthusiast who played bridge twice a week and had a taste for pomelos, Deng Xiaoping stood just under five feet tall.* While working underground for the Communist Party during the Nationalist repression of the 1920s, he had shown his sense of humour and a certain recklessness by adopting the pseudonym that remained for the rest of his life, Xiaoping, meaning 'little peace'. In later life, he made much of being a family man, accompanied everywhere by his daughter, Deng Rong, who acted as his interpreter as his hearing went and his speech slurred. In a biography of her father, she described him as 'an introvert and a man of few words. He is unpretentious and prefers to keep his experiences to himself.' Even more than with Mao, those experiences encompassed the story of Chinese Communism in the twentieth century.[1]

Deng was born in 1904 into a small landowning family in Sichuan, his father a member of the late imperial railway rights recovery movement who also led a local militia. In 1918, he told his son of a newspaper advertisement announcing a school in Chongqing to prepare young people to go to France. In August 1920, at the age of sixteen, Deng began the journey by taking a steamer down the Yangzi at the start of the passage to Paris. 'We felt China was weak, and we wanted to make it strong,' he recalled much later in an interview. 'We thought the way to do it was through modernization. So we went to the West to learn.'[2]

A year later, the scheme collapsed for lack of funds; the young Chinese were left to fend for themselves. Deng's family was going through a difficult patch and could not send him money. Jobs in France were hard

---

* He smoked Panda cigarettes, the most up-market Chinese brand, which became generally available only in 2004, when long queues formed to buy packs.

to find, but he survived until 1926, working in factories and, most important, joining the Communist Party of Chinese Youth in Europe, which operated from the Paris hotel bedroom of another young Chinese, Zhou Enlai.

Deng ran the group's mimeographed fortnightly newsletter, *Red Light*, leading to his nickname, Doctor of Mimeography. He subsisted for a time on a diet of milk and croissants, for which he developed such a taste that he ordered a boxful to be delivered to his plane when it stopped over in Paris on a trip in 1974. Joining the senior Chinese Communist Party in Europe in 1924, he helped to organize protests against the 30 May Incident in Shanghai, in which British police had shot Chinese demonstrators – the action in Paris included storming the Chinese legation, and forcing the minister to sign a statement attacking foreign rights in China. French police surveillance increased, and Deng decided it was time to go to Moscow, where he studied at Sun Yat-sen University. At the end of 1926, he returned to China on the staff of the Christian General, with whom Moscow was dallying. He was still only twenty-two.

From then on, Deng was plunged into Chinese revolutionary politics. But his time in France had opened wider horizons for him – and for Zhou – than Mao ever enjoyed. He had learned to speak French, and operate in a foreign context. He demonstrated his survival skills when he slipped away as the warlord joined Chiang Kai-shek in turning on the Communists in 1927. Appointed chief secretary to the Central Committee in Shanghai, he returned to clandestinity. Now married, he was sent to work with the Guangxi generals in one of their recurrent risings.

As political commissar of the Chinese Red Army of Workers and Peasants in Guangxi, Deng organized revolts, grabbed arms from government arsenals, declared Soviets and formed pacts with non-Communist commanders. He returned from time to time to visit the underground headquarters in Shanghai, he and his wife staying at Zhou Enlai's home. During one visit in 1930, his wife died after giving birth. Back in Guangxi, Deng was ordered by the CCP leader Li Lishan to attack cities as part of the over-ambitious military campaign of 1930. His army suffered heavy losses at the hands of his former allies, the Guangxi warlords, and set off on a long march across southern China to join Mao's base in Jiangxi.[3]

Deng did not go all the way with it. He was instructed to head to

CCP headquarters in Shanghai. But, in the late summer of 1931, he travelled to the Jiangxi base, where he got married again and moved steadily up the ladder. Like Mao, he came under attack from the Returned Bolsheviks when they settled in the base in 1931; his wife left him for one of his main accusers. At the price of self-criticism, he survived to edit the weekly newspaper, *Red Star*, and join the Long March, where he played a major role in the propaganda machine. In Yenan during the war with Japan, he anticipated the changes he would bring to China four decades later by seeking to boost production by 'rewarding the hardworking and punishing the lazy' through payment of bonuses to those who performed well, and by allowing farmers to keep output above the quotas set for them. A US military adviser who met him at this time recalled him as 'physically tough and with a mind as keen as mustard'.[4]

The civil war saw Deng in Shandong and in the mountains behind Nanjing and Wuhan – at one point, pursued by a 200,000-strong force led by the Guangxi general Bai Chongxi, his unit was reduced to 500 men. Surviving, he acted as political commissar and organizer during the great Huai-Hai battle of 1948–9 that sealed the fate of the Nationalists. His front-line experience gave him connections and cachet with PLA commanders. He had a high opinion of his own military skills and achievements in the civil war; speaking to Lin Biao, he made clear that he regarded the Huai-Hai and the crossing of the Yangzi as more significant than the victories in the north.[5]

Though he worked closely with Liu Shaoqi, notably in the recovery from the Great Leap, Deng emerged as the ultimate survivor, a loyalist who had gone along with the purge of Peng Dehuai and delivered grovelling self-criticism when necessary, a man whose loyalty and abilities could not be seriously doubted, but who knew, in times of trouble, how to sway with the tide like a rocking doll. He deployed enormous energy and determination, intent on maintaining a monopoly of power for the CCP, and ready to use daring means to achieve this, but circumscribed by political inhibitions, dedicated to, as he put it, crossing the river by feeling the stones.

Though the Gang of Four had been arrested on 6 October 1976, the cards were stacked against Deng after Mao's death. In his memorial address for the Helmsman, Hua Guofeng set him with the arch-traitors

Liu Shaoqi and Lin Biao, and forecast many more movements like the Cultural Revolution. The former security chief, Wang Dongxing, who had taken charge of ideological matters and become Hua's right-hand man, bracketed Deng with the Gang of Four, accusing him of opposing Mao's thought and revolutionary line; 'Deng can't hold a candle to Hua,' he added. 'We've already tried Deng out. He's no good.'[6]

Deng began by making the necessary obeisance, writing to say that he supported Hua's promotion to head the Party and government 'with all my heart'. Referring to himself as a 'capitalist-roader', he repeated his backing when the two men met while visiting an old comrade in hospital. Asked by Hua what he thought should be done, the septuagenarian laid out ideas of combining economic liberalization with political control. In keeping with the Sichuan proverb he had quoted at the Seven Thousand Cadres Conference in 1962, he did not care about the colour of the cat so long as it caught the economic mouse.

Apart from Hua's men, the second major power group was the 'survivors faction', led by Marshal Ye Jianying, organizer of the coup against the Gang of Four. It included two senior PLA figures and two important vice-premiers. Though loyal to Hua, Ye was ready to see Deng return in some kind of role. A third group, the 'rehabilitated cadres' faction, made up of men who had been attacked in the Cultural Revolution but had then been allowed to attend Mao's funeral, lined up behind Little Peace. Its most prominent member was the economic planner Chen Yun, who was resentful of the way he had not been reinstated to the Politburo. Others included the one-time finance minister Bo Yibo and three early victims of the Cultural Revolution, the former Beijing boss, Peng Zhen, the crippled PLA chief of staff, Luo Ruiqing, and the ex-head of the CCP Central Committee General Office, Yang Shangkun.[7]

Deng's supporters opened the struggle with wall posters calling for the reversal of the Tiananmen verdict against him, and criticizing Wang Dongxing and his ally, Wu De, boss of Beijing and a fellow Politburo member. In February 1977, the *People's Daily*, *Liberation Daily* and *Red Flag* hit back with editorials insisting that 'whatever policies Chairman Mao decided, we shall resolutely defend; whatever instructions he issued, we shall steadfastly obey.' This line, known as the 'two whatevers', would provide the central platform for Hua and Wang in contrast to Deng's more supple interpretation of loyalty to the legacy.

Though support grew steadily in the Party and the PLA for Deng's restoration and the correction of the Tiananmen verdict, Hua tried to dig in. In March 1977, he absurdly told a Central Work Committee that the pro-Deng agitation was really a cover for a bid to restore the Gang of Four. 'To let Deng Xiaoping resume work now would be to forget Mao,' Wang Dongxing declared. 'Aren't we supposed to carry out Chairman Mao's instructions?'[8]

Deng gained an important and highly active supporter in the person of the new vice-president of the Communist Party School (Hua was the president), Hu Yaobang, a 62-year-old from Hunan, who was as short as Deng, but a good deal less barrel-like. Hu, who was part of Deng's bridge group, had joined the revolution at the age of thirteen and gone to the Jiangxi base. A Long Marcher, he was a great believer in travelling round the country to see for himself what was going on, and a voracious reader of foreign works, as well as Chinese ones. Open-minded, he liked to talk to intellectuals. On one occasion, Wang Juntao, a twenty-year-old undergraduate at Beida University who had been imprisoned for participating in the Tiananmen Square demonstrations after Zhou's death, knocked at the door of his house, unannounced; Hu spent four hours discussing politics and reform with the young man and a mechanic who accompanied him. His manner was animated, enlivened by gestures unusual for an official. Mao had remarked caustically of him: 'Only focuses on the surface, likes to talk and make grandiose statements.'[9]

A former chairman of the Communist League, Hu was sacked twice by radicals during the Cultural Revolution, and sent to work in a commune. He survived to be put in charge of the Party School in western Beijing in 1977. There, he pressed the doctrine of 'seeking truth from facts', and of the need to break the 'two whatevers'. He also formed an association with the early Cultural Revolution victim General Luo Ruiqing.

Deng worked with small groups of trusted people, including former associates from the civil war in the military. This could bring together disparate supporters who had little in common except for the leader's conviction that they could do the job for him. Support rose far enough to force Hua to agree to a deal to acknowledge that Deng's work when he was recalled in 1975 contained successes as well as shortcomings, and that the mourning for Zhou Enlai had started out as a reasonable expression of grief. In return, Deng promised support for the new Chairman, and pledged to obey any decision the Central Committee made about him. But he also hit out at the 'two whatevers', arguing, in effect, that specific policies laid down by Mao might be questioned or ignored, so long as Maoism as a whole was respected. The Helmsman, he recalled, had, himself, admitted to making mistakes.[10]

The weakness of the Hua camp was signalled when the *People's Daily* ran a Dengist article arguing that it was not necessarily wrong to update Mao Thought to meet changing reality. Another article exhumed a previously unpublished speech by the late leader in which he acknowledged personal responsibility for some errors during the Great Leap Forward. The *Liberation Daily* joined in by endorsing Deng's policy of seeking truth from reality. Faced with this bandwagon, Hua struck a deal. Deng was allowed to address a Party Plenum in July 1977. The following month, the Eleventh CCP Congress, which formally declared the end of the Cultural Revolution, elected him as the third-ranking member of the five-man Standing Committee of the Politburo.

At the age of seventy-three, Deng was back for the third time. He was, however, still inferior to Hua, who headed the Party, government and military. While Deng became a CCP vice-president at a Party conference in August 1977, Ye, Wang and another Hua loyalist were appointed to the same rank. Still, the returnee made his view of the younger leader plain enough when, in contrast to Ye's reference to 'our wise leader Chairman Hua Guofeng', Deng referred to him merely as 'Comrade'. In the autumn of 1977, Dengists were steadily promoted to important posts. Hu Yaobang became chief of the Party Organization Department. The economist Hu Qiaomu, Mao's former secretary who had drafted Deng's 1975 policies, was named to head the new Chinese Academy of Social Sciences (CASS). In November, an influential PLA figure, Marshal Nie Rongzhen, published an article backing 'seeking truth from facts'. A Party Plenum proclaimed that, while Mao's feats were indelible, 'it would not be Marxist to demand that a revolutionary leader be free of all shortcomings.'[11]

Giving ground, Hua adopted some Dengist phraseology, and professed himself an exponent of modernization, though, in agriculture, he remained true to the Dazhai model of mass communal action in opposition to the older man's advocacy of encouraging individual initiatives. In February 1978, Hua pushed through a highly ambitious Ten-Year Plan which, contrary to Deng's advice, focused on heavy industry.

Nearly 40 per cent of the state budget was allocated to capital investment. Scientific research, the adoption of foreign techniques and a degree of intellectual liberalization were encouraged; all recent ills were blamed on the Gang of Four. Hua also sought to build up his own personality cult by stressing the late leader's faith in him. Huge posters showed the two men together, quoting a remarkably fit-looking Chairman as asserting his ease at seeing the younger man take charge. Hua even changed his hairstyle to resemble Mao's.[12]

Unfortunately for him, he also aped Mao in seeking to do everything at the same time. His overambitious economic plan created chaos on a massive scale. Heavy investment spending sent the budget deficit to a record 15.5 per cent of state revenue. Huge bottlenecks built up. Wage increases fuelled inflation. Imports soared. A planned expansion in oil extraction and exports failed to materialize; faith in the so-called Petroleum Clique of the heavy industry and energy minister evaporated after an oil rig in the Bohai Gulf collapsed and killed seventy-two of those on board.

In 1979, the rehabilitated planner Chen Yun launched a successful attack on the 'flying leap' of the Ten-Year Plan, calling for three years of retrenchment under the slogan 'readjustment, reform, correction and improvement'. Appointed vice-premier with overall responsibility for economic planning, Chen worked with Bo Yibo and a Deng associate, Yao Yilin, to have hundreds of projects cancelled. At the same time, an experiment to return to the pre-collectivization system to allow individual initiative in the countryside was producing far greater output than the Cultural Revolution communal model, which Hua still supported. The leader of the Dazhai movement, who had become a vice-premier and Politburo member, was held under house arrest in Beijing. Provincial leaders who resisted Deng's policies found it increasingly hard to ignore reality.[13]

To try to check criticism, Wang Dongxing closed down a publication which ran poems by Tiananmen demonstrators of 1976 and that urged a reversal of the negative verdict on them. Refusing to yield, the editorial staff took the page proofs of their magazine and put them up on the Democracy Wall in Beijing used during the Hundred Flowers. That set off an explosion of big-character posters calling for democracy and the rehabilitation of Cultural Revolution victims, attacking the bureaucracy and then, as in 1957, Mao himself. 'The people want to speak,' Deng told an American journalist. 'Let them!' 'We do not have the right to deny or criticise the blossoming of democracy and the posters,' he said to a Japanese delegation. 'If the people are angry, we have to let them blow off steam.'[14]

A poster put up by a factory accountant called Ren Wanding called for the establishment of a China Human Rights League; a gathering to start organizing one was held at Ren's plant, attended by twenty people who met by candlelight for fear of being discovered if they turned on the lights. A garment worker, Huang Xiang, published fierce poems and posters denouncing the excesses of the Mao era. Four new publications were launched to cover politics, fiction and poetry.

An electrician at Beijing zoo, Wei Jingsheng, emerged as the leading dissident figure of the time, running a magazine, *Explorations*. Son of an ardent Maoist from Anhui, he had attended the Chairman's first Red Guard rally in Tiananmen Square before falling foul of the Cultural Revolution. Joining the PLA, he was horrified by what he saw as he travelled across the country – naked, starving peasants, parents selling children, people eating dumplings stuffed with human flesh. A chain-smoker, with lean features, Wei had a magnetic effect on all who met him as he called for a fifth modernization – true democracy. Without that, he argued, what was being done was no more than a 'new-fangled lie'. When it was suggested that he might meet Deng, he snapped back, 'Why? He has no legal status to talk to me. He wasn't elected by the people.'[15]

Urged on by Hu Yaobang's network in the Party School and Youth League, the democracy campaign attacked the 'two whatevers'· and pushed the use of practical, scientific methods. Hu Qiaomu of the Social Science Academy addressed the State Council on the benefits of giving managers of enterprises more autonomy, and of relaxing administrative controls. The way in which the Gang of Four had been able to operate for so long was held up as an example of weaknesses in the political system, pointing to the need to safeguard socialist democracy.

Press articles called for legal reforms and freedom of speech, and referred to the 'blood-soaked legacy' of the Cultural Revolution. Tiananmen Square detainees got enthusiastic welcomes when they were released. The pressure began to tell when Wu De, the boss of Beijing and a key Hua associate, lost his job. At a work conference in November 1978, Chen Yun gained wide support for advocating the rehabilitation of Peng Zhen, Bo Yibo and Peng Dehuai, and the reversal of the condemnation of the Tiananmen demonstrations. The Pachen Lama was released and given the task of resurrecting Buddhism after its travails during the Cultural Revolution.

The cataclysms of the past two decades had shown that Mao's search for a specifically Chinese, ideologically dominated road to modernization led only to disaster. Instead, Deng offered a new path of learning from the outside world, and applying this to propel China forward. He strongly backed a scheme to send 10,000 students abroad, 80 per cent of them scientists; 'If a few run away, it doesn't matter,' he wrote. What counted was to join the progress other nations enjoyed. The world had changed. As Deng observed, 'Engels did not ride in an aeroplane; Stalin did not wear Dacron.'[16]

It was the argument the Self-Strengtheners had deployed in the 1870s, a means of boosting the nation by absorbing lessons from overseas and, eventually, using barbarian methods to defeat the barbarians. Though, in both cases, critics would accuse those responsible of selling out to the foreigners, the motivation was the contrary, a deeply nationalistic desire to save China from the decline created by the dead end of the imperial and Maoist systems. Pressed by Deng's supporters, Hua and his associates caved in on the Tiananmen issue. The Party also decided to rehabilitate victims of both the Cultural Revolution and the 1957 anti-rightist campaign, which had followed the Hundred Flowers and which, in one of the many ironies of the times, had been led by Deng. In all, three quarters of a million were pardoned. At the end of 1978, a commemoration was held in Beijing for Peng Dehuai. In some places, officials guilty of oppression were criticized, but the Party often protected its own, limiting proceedings against them.[17]

The Third Plenum of the Eleventh Central Committee, held in Beijing in December 1978, marked the triumph of Deng's ideas, though for his protection the great survivor was reported to have carried a pistol in his pocket. 'Socialist modernization' became the watchword, with decentralization, rationalization, performance-linked rewards and management responsibility at its core. Mass movements were to be abandoned, and collective leadership adopted, along with legality and Communist-style democracy. Chen Yun, Hu Yaobang and two Deng allies joined the Politburo. A new disciplinary outfit was established.

As he accrued power, Deng and his senior colleagues kept returning to the question of democracy and popular sentiment. In a discussion at the end of January 1979, he said that proletarian democracy must outdo capitalist democracy to carry forward the good aspects of bourgeois democracy. 'We want the people to be the rulers,' Deng told one meeting, according to the speechwriter Ruan Ming, who was present. Speaking to a Central Work Conference, Marshal Ye identified the Democracy Wall as 'yet another model of people's democracy' (though these words were struck out when his text was circulated). Chen Yun said people were 'impatient and tired of waiting ... They say, you cadres have already been rewarded for your suffering. Why must we the people go on suffering without end?'[18]

But there was an inescapable underlying contradiction between democracy, as expressed in the big-character posters, and maintaining sole Communist Party rule. The Democracy Wall and the articles attacking the 'two whatevers' were useful political tools. But the embrace of democracy and free speech carried with it a much more fundamental question for a political movement that had always insisted on a monopoly hold on power.

On the other side of the world, Jimmy Carter had come to office dedicated to jettisoning the Nixon approach to politics and administration. But he followed in the old pattern in one respect – China. The Kissinger model of seeing China as the counter to the Soviet Union, so that it had to be courted, still held sway over American policy. Enough, certainly, to encourage the Chinese to make the most of the opportunities open to them.

Diplomatic relations had not followed Nixon's 1972 visit, in large part because of the complication of Taiwan. The Carter administration and its National Security Adviser, Zbigniew Brzezinski, wanted to put that right. As Kissinger had done, Brzezinski played the dominant role, marginalizing the State Department under Cyrus Vance.* The Chinese sensed who was their best friend in Washington. When Vance visited the PRC, he got a cool reception. Brzezinski's was warmer, and he

---

* As Brzezinski himself noted, it was a 'strange coincidence' that the two advisers, who conducted crucial negotiations with Beijing hidden from the State Department, were both sons of immigrants from Europe who came from an academic, not diplomatic, background. (Brzezinski, p. 209. The ensuing material in the book gives his account of the negotiations with the Chinese.)

worked out an ingenious arrangement on the contentious matter of arms sales under which the US would maintain its own embargo on China, but would encourage its European allies to sell weapons to the PRC. The administration could thus deny arming the Communist power, while ensuring that Beijing got what it wanted. On Taiwan, a formula was found to acknowledge Beijing's position that there was only one China, which included the island, and that the PRC administration was China's sole legal government. The US would maintain trade, cultural and other non-official relations with Taiwan but would sever diplomatic ties and withdraw its forces. The Taiwan Relations Act passed by the US Congress said that Washington would regard any non-peaceful attempt to determine the island's future as a matter of 'grave concern', but did not oblige America to intervene in such an eventuality.[19]

On 13 December 1978, agreement was reached to establish embassies the following 1 March. Vance, who was on a trip to the Middle East at the time, was only told at the last moment. The Soviets were furious; the SALT arms talks between America and the USSR ran into the ground; a Carter–Brezhnev summit was postponed. The reaction in Taiwan was predictably fierce. When the deputy secretary of state, Warren Christopher, went to explain the decision there, he was met by a senior official at Taipei Airport who spoke of 'disastrous damage wrought by this mistake'. As the American party drove into town, a mob broke a window of its main car and poked bamboo poles inside, while police looked the other way.

However, Washington had reserved its position, though this only became known twenty-nine years later, when Jimmy Carter read from his diary of the time. Deng, he had recorded, 'agreed that our statement to settle the Taiwan issue peacefully would not be contradicted publicly by China and he understood that we would sell defensive weapons to Taiwan after [a US–Taiwan defence] treaty expired. Publicly they are going to disapprove of this action, but privately they have acknowledged that it will be done.' Thus the patriarch admitted that America could supply Taiwan with sufficient weapons to defend itself against attack from the PLA, as it continued to do in the following decades.[20]

Deng had kept up Mao's habit of supervising foreign affairs, visiting Burma, Nepal, Thailand, Malaysia, Singapore and Korea. In March 1979, he discussed the future of Hong Kong with the visiting British governor of the colony. London was concerned at what would happen when its leases on the New Territories across the bay from the island expired in 1997. It has been suggested that this was a mistake, and that Beijing would have ignored the expiry date and allowed the status quo to continue into the twenty-first century. That hardly seems likely. Perhaps caught unprepared by the way the British raised the issue without warning, Deng set down the basic line that the colony must return to PRC sovereignty, at which point, it would be granted special status within China. The smaller Portuguese colony of Macau would surely follow suit.[21]

At the end of 1979, it was time for Deng to visit the United States. The trip was a great success. The pint-sized Communist appeared at a rodeo in a ten-gallon hat, visited the New York Stock Exchange, toured a Ford plant in Georgia and worked the controls of a space shuttle simulator. He won the applause of conservative Texan oilmen, and was photographed staring up at members of the Harlem Globetrotters. The visit opened the way to a series of subsequent accords.

The two countries agreed to intelligence co-operation, and the US set up monitoring stations on Chinese territory to replace those it had lost in Iran after the fall of the Shah. There was also an agreement on educational exchanges, which led to a flood of young Chinese applying to study in the United States. In a step that was to have huge consequences, the administration extended most-favoured-nation status to China in trade. As he hardened the US stance towards Moscow, Carter allowed 'non-lethal' military equipment to be sold to the PRC, including reconnaissance technology. Successive CIA directors travelled to China, maintaining the secrecy that had marked Washington's approach to China since the first Kissinger visit. The first Agency chief to make the journey, Stansfield Turner, did not go to the US embassy and kept away from places where he might be recognized. He also grew a moustache.[22]

Meeting the president in the White House, Deng asked for the room to be cleared because he had something confidential to raise. Only Carter, Vance, Brzezinski and the vice-president, Walter Mondale, remained. The Chinese leader then outlined a plan to attack Vietnam. The next morning, the president handed the visitor a note advising restraint. That was all. No threat of freezing relations. It was all Deng could have hoped for. The barbarians would stand aside while he conducted a war aimed at humiliating Vietnam for having kept up its Soviet links, damaging Moscow's standing in Asia and demonstrating that the PLA had achieved China's fourth modernization.[23]

A series of frontier clashes provided the immediate pretext, but other factors were at play, exacerbating the centuries-old rivalry between the two nations. Hanoi had annoyed Beijing by signing a friendship treaty with the USSR, and joining the Kremlin-led Comecon economic grouping. Vietnam's invasion of Cambodia to overthrow the Khmer Rouge was a considerable irritant, both for having ousted Beijing's favoured regime and for having shown that China could not save it. Deng decided that the PRC had to 'shrink the swollen heads' of the Vietnamese.

On 17 February, 80,000 PLA troops backed by 200 tanks crossed into North Vietnam. More than 100,000 Chinese soldiers were mobilized as reinforcements; the total deployment during the war was estimated at 300,000. Deng appears to have thought that the campaign would be as swift and successful as the foray into India in 1962. But the advance was slow through the mountainous jungle, while the legacy of the Cultural Revolution still affected the PLA. When the British ambassador asked a minister if the army was not losing a lot of young men, the official gave a high-pitched laugh and replied, 'We have a lot more.'[24]

Though Hanoi was heavily committed in Cambodia, it deployed militia units, as well as the regular forces, to outnumber the invaders. Vietnam was confident – the North had beaten France, the United States and South Vietnam, whereas in the quarter-century since Korea the PLA could only count its easy campaign against India in the Himalayas and the suppression of Tibetan guerrillas. Hanoi also had more modern weapons; like the Chinese Communists during the later stages of the civil war, its units used US arms captured in the war in the South, as well as up-to-date Soviet guns denied to the PRC by the split with Moscow.

In the middle of March, the Chinese withdrew, implementing a scorched-earth policy. Figures on each side are disputed. Senior Chinese officials spoke later of 25 per cent PLA casualties, and a similar 20,000 figure for the Vietnamese army; the Vietnamese said the Chinese had killed 100,000 civilians but Beijing insisted they were militia. The PRC admitted to the loss of half its tanks. The fighting had shown the backwardness of China's command, logistics and communications systems, and an inability to deploy the air force effectively. Maps were seventy-five years old. Runners were used for lack of secure radio links. Tactics amounted to human wave attacks against entrenched positions.

The years of being used as a political tool under Mao had blunted the military effectiveness of the army which conquered China in 1949. The PLA was, clearly, in need of serious modernization.

The only plus point was a negative one – that Moscow had not intervened to help Hanoi, showing the limits of Soviet support. On the other hand, the Kremlin may have felt that the Vietnamese were doing quite well enough on their own. The war was followed by recurrent frontier clashes, which did not end till the implementation of an agreement in 2001. The Chinese in Vietnam were persecuted, many leaving as boat people. But, at the start of the twenty-first century, Hanoi dropped the number of civilians it said had died to 10,000, and abandoned its earlier demand for an apology for the invasion as relations grew warmer after the collapse of the USSR and as Vietnam set out to imitate China economically.

The setback was clearly galling for Deng, particularly given his own view of his military capabilities. His mood may well have contributed to his lashing out at the Democracy Wall activists, particularly when they began to home in on the war and criticize him personally, crossing the line as the Hundred Flowers protestors had done with Mao – the person of the emperor was to remain sacred. Conservatives mobilized. The NPC Standing Committee vice-chairman, Tan Zhenlin, denounced calls for democracy as the work of people who 'specialize in making trouble', while the People's Daily warned of instability and attacks on cadres. 'Such actions will be vigorously suppressed,' it declared. The Beijing municipal authorities introduced restrictions on meetings, and limited protests to an area round the Democracy Wall.

After Wei Jingsheng called the leader a 'new dictator' and a 'dictatorial fascist' in the model of the Gang of Four, Deng swung behind the hardliners. 'These counter-revolutionaries and bad elements must be dealt with sternly,' he said. Attacking members of the free-speech movement as collaborators with Taiwan and associates of remnants of the Gang of Four, he added that, 'to talk about democracy in the abstract will inevitably lead to the unchecked spread of ultra-democracy and anarchism, to the complete disruption of political stability and unity, and to the total failure of our modernization programme.' It was a spectre that would become a leitmotif of the regime and its leader, conjuring up the recent experience of the Cultural Revolution and positing democracy as the enemy of material progress.

The Beijing Democracy Wall was shut down. Magazines were closed. Wei Jingsheng was arrested, supposedly for having told a foreigner the name of the Chinese commander in the war in Vietnam, together with troop strength and casualty figures. How he could have been in possession of details on the last two subjects was unclear. When the accountant Ren Wanding tried to stage a protest at Wei's detention, he was taken in, too. At his trial, at which the charges were broadened into a general accusation of counter-revolution, Wei mounted a stout, well-argued defence. 'I cannot agree with this debasing of the concept of revolution,' he added, invoking his constitutional rights. He was sentenced to fifteen years in jail. The news was broadcast over factory loudspeaker systems to scare others.[25]

Ren Wanding was given a four-year sentence, which was reported to have been lengthened when he refused to confess to crimes. A 32-year-old woman called Fu Yuehua, who said she had been sacked after complaining about rape by a male cadre and who organized mass petitioning protests in Beijing against hunger, oppression and unemployment, was investigated for a year, and sent to jail, the judge calling her 'a moral degenerate'. The *People's Daily* warned 'all counter-revolutionaries that, no matter how fashionable your banner is, no matter how cunning your ways, in the end you will not escape the net of the people's justice'.[26]

Despite its declaration of concern for human rights elsewhere, the Carter administration turned a blind eye to the PRC. References to China in the annual State Department report were watered down. Briefing Congress, the deputy assistant secretary of state, John Negroponte, said that 'an encouraging trend has begun to emerge in the direction of liberalization [in China]'. Visiting Beijing in 1987, Carter was asked about Wei Jingsheng. 'I'm personally not familiar with the case you described,' he replied of China's best-known dissident, who, by then, had been in jail for eight years.[27]

As Deng ordered the crackdown and swung to a more conservative course, he also intensified the campaign against Hua Guofeng and his associates. Hua was still nominally the superior of the two, but the difference in their authority was evident – among other things, Deng had made the trip to the most important superpower while Hua had to be content with visiting Britain.

Deng's camp won over provincial leaders by offering them greater financial and administrative autonomy, and encouraged the promotion of younger PLA officers to replace conservatives. To press his campaign, Deng had more Cultural Revolution victims brought back, and new men promoted. The former Beijing Party leader, Peng Zhen, the first top-level victim of 1966, returned to the Politburo, with responsibility for security and intelligence. The Inner Mongolian leader, Ulanfu, was appointed as a vice-premier. A younger man, the economic pragmatist Zhao Ziyang, who had made his mark in Sichuan, emerged as a leader for the next generation.

Son of a landowning family in Henan, broad-faced and slow-speaking, Zhao had joined the Party in 1938, and risen to head its apparatus in Guangdong at the age of forty-two – during the Cultural Revolution, he was paraded through the streets of Guangzhou in a dunce's cap. Restored in the early 1970s, he was sent to run Sichuan, where he experimented with letting farmers sell anything not required by their quotas. Successful in that, he was marked for fast promotion, a clearly focused technocrat in horn-rimmed spectacles.[28]

In February 1980, Zhao and Hu Yaobang ascended to the Politburo Standing Committee. Hua's main allies, including Wang Dongxing, Wu De of Beijing and the capital region's military commander, were forced to resign their CCP and state posts – this softer form of exit was adopted to mark a difference with the brutality of the Cultural Revolution, and because it was favoured by Marshal Ye Jianying and other senior figures.

In August, Zhao replaced Hua as premier, and then Hu Yaobang took over as head of the CCP. With Ye lining up behind the new order, Hua was blamed for inflation, which reached 11 per cent a year, and for waste, pollution, poor control of wages, population growth and the failures of the Ten-Year Plan. At the National People's Congress (NPC) in the autumn, there were damning, and well-publicized, disclosures of attempts to hush up the oil rig disaster in the Bohai Gulf, and a case in which a government minister had tried to stop a police probe into a kidnap, rape and murder allegedly carried out by his driver.[29]

The men in charge launched a programme known as the 'Gengshen Reforms' (after the lunar calendar designation for 1980), to promote specialization, accountability, responsiveness and, in the regime's terms, democracy – Deng was ready to go along with this so long as it was a means of increasing the internal efficiency of the CCP, not of opening the way to a return of the Democracy Wall experience. For all his clampdown on Wei and his peers, the leader knew that the Party needed to modernize to strengthen its grip on power. Personally, he had to mediate between reformers and conservatives, using both for his purpose, but also preventing either from gaining such strength that it could threaten his supremacy, his stance often changing as events unfolded.

Thus, the Solidarity Movement strikes by Polish workers that began in the summer of 1980 were initially welcomed in Beijing for showing up the dangers of old-style Communist economics, bureaucratism and corruption; Hu Yaobang thought the news from Gdansk illustrated how a measure of democracy might pre-empt a similar challenge in China. In October, his associate, Liao Gailong, put forward a programme for a strong legislature, independent judiciary and trade unions, a free press, peasant associations, internal democracy in enterprises, and separation of the Party and government.

But, at the same time, Peng Zhen got the NPC to adopt a proposal to eliminate the guarantee of 'four big freedoms' enacted after Mao's death that laid down the right of citizens to 'speak out freely, air their views fully, engage in great debates and write big-character posters'. These were blamed for opening the door to Cultural Revolution-style chaos – which was how conservatives characterized the Democracy Wall. Chen Yun called for enhanced financial and economic discipline under the slogan 'Oppose Bourgeois Liberalization'. Though tightly controlled, local elections had produced a scattering of voices critical of the system that could only be seen by conservatives as a threat of renewed dissidence. Events in Poland now came to be regarded as a matter for concern. A fresh attack was launched on writers who strayed too far from the Party line. Amid this opening tug-of-war around Deng, there was a major show – the trial of the Gang of Four.[30]

On 20 November 1980, cortège of cars and buses cut through the wintry smog of Beijing to take thirty-five judges and 880 'representatives of the masses' to the Public Security compound in Zhengyi ('Justice') Road near Tiananmen Square. The defendants sat in a row behind slatted barriers in the large, brightly lighted courtroom. Zhang Chunqiao wore a black costume. Wang Hongwen looked like a model student. Yao Wenyuan had his lips turned down in bad temper. Despite having deserted the Gang for Lin Biao, Mao's scriptwriter, Chen Boda, was also in the dock; now seventy-six, he had to be helped to his seat by two guards and stared at the courtroom through big circular spectacles as if he could not quite understand what was going on.

Jiang Qing was defiant, her right arm resting on the barrier in front of her, left hand to her mouth, waiting to play her role. 'Her jet-black hair was pulled severely back behind her ears,' a watching journalist wrote. 'She marched into the courtroom with her head regally erect and then alternately smirked and yawned during the reading of the indictment, apparently to show contempt for the proceedings. She swiftly dismissed the lawyers assigned to defend her, taking on the job herself.'[31]

Collectively, the Gang members were charged with persecuting 727,420 people and causing the deaths of 34,274. They were accused of having been linked with the alleged Lin Biao plot to overthrow Mao and, in Jiang Qing's case, of having persecuted artists and sought to cover up incriminating material on her past. The verdicts were in no doubt. 'We're going to nail them to history's pillar of shame,' proclaimed the *People's Daily*. Jiang was the target of a flood of mocking cartoons and jokes. She was cast as a snake and a fox – that is, an immoral woman depicted in a wig from Japan and false teeth from France.[32]

As the trial got underway, Zhang Chunqiao remained obstinately silent while the other two male Gang members cut poor figures. Yao was ridiculed for his bald head and pop eyes, Wang for his vanity and self-indulgence. Facing the serried ranks of the judges and observers, Jiang Qing developed the argument that she had only carried out her husband's orders, and alluded to the way others had gone along with the Cultural Revolution. 'There are many issues from within the Party that you people simply don't know about,' she told the court. 'In those years, the Communist Party did the things you complain about . . . You put everything on my back. It seems I was a giant with three heads and six arms who worked miracles . . . I was the one who stood by Chairman Mao Zedong! Arresting me and bringing me to trial is a defamation of Chairman Mao!'[33]

Her superior attitude cracked, however, when an aged writer from Shanghai, who had been jailed for eight years during the Cultural Revolution, took the witness stand.[34]

'You and your kind committed countless crimes of all kinds,' he said, wiping the tears from his spectacles. 'They are more numerous than the hairs on a human head.'

'No more of your lies,' Jiang yelled, jumping to her feet.

'Sit down!' the principal judge ordered.

Jiang took no notice.

'You shut up!' the writer shouted at Jiang.

'Spy revisionist!' Mao's widow fired back.

The judge told her he objected to her behaviour.

'Go ahead and object; I'm already talking! What can you do about that?' Jiang cried.

A female judge shouted that Jiang was committing new crimes.

'What the hell do you mean by crimes?' the accused shouted back. 'You bitch!'

Two burly women bailiffs took hold of her. Jiang hit them. They locked her arms behind her back, and frog-marched her out.

At the end of January 1981, the Gang was convicted of crimes ranging from slandering officials to plotting to assassinate Mao. Jiang and Zhang were handed death sentences, but with a two-year suspension to allow them to reform. Wang got life, Yao twenty years, Chen Boda nineteen, though he was soon released because of his age and ill-health. At the same time, six other defendants, including former top military officers accused of the Lin Biao plot, received from sixteen to nineteen years in prison. Handcuffed when her sentence was read out, Jiang, now sixty-seven, shouted, 'Revolution is no crime! To rebel is justified! Down with revisionism!' She refused to walk out of the courtroom, seemingly wanting to drop to the floor like a tragic heroine. Three bailiffs grabbed her by the scruff of the neck and took her away.[35]

The Chairman's widow was held in Qincheng prison outside Beijing, where many of her victims had suffered. The rehabilitated Peng Zhen, who had been given the job of questioning Jiang before the trial, went to visit her. She asked to be allowed to talk to Deng and Hua, who did not agree. For compulsory manual labour, she made cloth dolls, listening to the radio and humming to herself as she sewed. She developed throat cancer, and, in May 1991, hanged herself in hospital.[36]

Plans to hold similar trials at provincial and lower levels were abandoned. The Cultural Revolution had been too widespread and complex to be settled in courtrooms. Many of those still in power had been implicated. As one magazine put it, 'Some people fixed others; some were fixed by others; and some fixed others and were in turn fixed by still others ... To settle all the scores accumulated in those ten years might be impossible, even with the aid of a computer.' There were also reports of young people watching the proceedings on television cheering Jiang Qing for exposing the hypocrisy of what was going on. Nor did the PLA want any investigations into its conduct during the great upheaval.

By the time the sentences were delivered on the Gang, Hua Guofeng had been subjected to humiliation. In December 1980, Mao's last designated successor was attacked remorselessly at Politburo sessions, which ended with the conclusion that he 'lacks the political and organisational ability to be the Chairman of the Party'. 'That he should never have been appointed Chairman of the Military Commission, everybody knows,' it added. Hua asked to be allowed to resign from his CCP posts. This was agreed, though the announcement was put off for seven months since, formally, the decision had to be taken by the Central Committee, which was not due to meet till June. In the interim, the job was done by Deng and Hu Yaobang, with the younger man fully taking over in the summer. Hua lingered on as a powerless vice-chairman till September 1982. In 2002, he lost his last post, as a member of the Central Committee. In 2007, he was photographed, obese and asleep, at the Party Congress, before dying the following year.[37]

With Zhao in charge of the government and Hu as Party boss – the title of chairman was replaced with that of general secretary – Deng's only formal position was as Chair of the Military Affairs Commission, showing the importance he always gave to controlling the PLA. In theory, he ranked in the CCP below not only Hu Yaobang, but also Marshal Ye, who held second place in the Politburo. But, as Hu himself said, the old man was 'the supreme decision-maker in the CCP'. The personal nature of power was thus perpetuated. During the past century, China had been ruled by the Dowager Empress from behind a screen, by Yuan Shikai, by the disparate collection of warlords who followed, by Chiang Kai-shek and by Mao. The personality of the ruler had always outweighed the institutions of state, even if their power had been limited by circumstances and by the need to balance factions. The result, continuing into the late twentieth century, was a stunted political system subject to sudden shifts at the decision of the man on top.

Returning to Beijing for negotiations on Hong Kong, the British diplomat Percy Cradock found a 'short, barrel-like figure, with bruised face and dismissive gestures and almost limitless authority, chain-smoking and spitting'. In terms of history, which always counted for a lot, Deng was supreme. His revolutionary credentials were unique, stretching back to his years in France.[38]

At that point, it might have been better for China if he had elevated himself to the role of an elder statesman, allowing Hu and Zhao to get on with the modernization of the nation. But there were at least three problems. One was personal ambition; Deng had not fought the struggle for six decades to kick himself upstairs now that he had finally achieved supreme power. Then there was the succession issue. Hu's appointment to head the Party meant that he appeared to be the first choice, but he was short on top-level experience, impetuous and outspoken, and did not impress veterans such as Marshal Ye or the PLA. He also faced latent rivalry from Zhao, five years his junior, who would ally with him against the conservatives but could see himself as a leadership contender.

The third snag arose from the continuing presence of old colleagues, including Chen Yun and Peng Zhen, who were reluctant to step back and could invoke credentials that outshone those of Hu and Zhao. A Central Advisory Committee (CAC) was created which was meant to move them into an advisory, upper-house role. But they declined to be sidelined. Photographs of the leaders in what was meant to be an era of rejuvenation show lines of aged men, some with geriatric smiles for the camera.

In the circumstances, Deng remained the ultimate guide and arbiter, the supreme glue of the machine. By design or accident, or both, he was essential. The resulting recipe would bring spectacular material progress to China, but block political advance, and perpetuate the pattern of supreme power resting in the hands of one man. As the pro-Communist newspaper in Hong Kong, *Wen Wei Po*, put it with rare honesty, 'Deng Xiaoping knows quite well that the value of his existence does not lie in acting as "the great standard bearer" but is based on balancing the strengths of all sides. Should one side win complete victory, and the other side suffer complete loss, the value of his existence would thereupon be lost.' Thus, after 1898, 1912, 1927, 1929 and 1949, China was deprived once more of a chance to become a normal political state for its people.[39]

27

To Get Rich is No Sin

In the late 1970s, China was a very poor country. The rising population, which reached 962 million in 1978, put a severe strain on food supplies. Average calorie intake was only marginally above the minimum survival requirement, particularly in rural areas. Some 250 million people lived in absolute poverty. Transport and infrastructure were primitive. Steel production was still low.[1]

China lagged behind its East Asia neighbours, not just Japan but also South Korea. Most galling was the progress of Taiwan. Helped by American backing and finance, the island's government had overseen the distribution of 864,583 acres of public and private land to 217,653 households in the 1950s. Rents were cut. Landlords were compensated for loss of property with bonds and shares in state companies; some moved into business, and invested the money in new firms.[2]

From a predominantly agricultural economy, the Republic of China became an exporter of industrial goods, textiles and chemicals. As it evolved up the added value chain of manufacturing, annual growth hit 11 per cent between 1964 and 1973, with small and medium-sized enterprises playing a major role. By the 1970s, when expansion slowed but remained at a strong 7 per cent, the island was able to dispense with American aid. It built modern roads, railways, dams and electricity networks. National income per capita doubled in two decades. Services grew. Foreign investment flowed in.[3]

Politically, Chiang Kai-shek had kept a tight grip on power under martial law, backing the oppression of the native Taiwanese by the newcomers from the mainland. Manipulation of Kuomintang factions ensured the succession of the Generalissimo's son, Ching-kuo, when the old man died in 1975. Chiang's widow was kept at arm's length by the new ruler, and some relaxation was permitted. An unofficial opposition made up of a network of associated personality-based groups was tolerated, and the share of seats in provincial assemblies won by non-KMT parties rose from 6 to 27 per cent at elections in 1977, while such groups took 16–20 per cent of the vote for county seats and the Taipei City Council.[4]

Deng felt he had to reject the political pattern across the strait, which would lead to full electoral democracy by the end of the twentieth century. But the economic message was unmistakable, as was the example of the booming British colony of Hong Kong beside Guangdong on the Pearl River delta. After the Cultural Revolution and the Great Leap, it was impossible to argue for a continuation of Maoist economics.

The first priority was the countryside, where 795 million lived. In 1976, the average annual cash distribution to each member of agricultural communes was 12 per cent less than it had been in 1973. Agricultural output had declined to account for only a third of GDP, compared to 50 per cent for industry. To stem the decline, policies were needed which would encourage the farmers to grow more. Private enterprise was introduced in Anhui, Henan, Shandong and Sichuan. Under the 'household responsibility system', land was contracted out to farmers, who were required to hand over a certain amount of output and to pay taxes, but could sell whatever was left over.[5]

To boost the rural revolution, state expenditure allocated to farming was increased to make it double the tax from the countryside. The concentration on rice and wheat was reduced where other crops were more suitable, including those which earned bigger cash rewards. Grassland was turned to pasturage. The state payment for grain was raised by 20 per cent, and the official price for private sales went up 50 per cent. Prices for vegetable oil, meat and fish rose. This all fuelled inflation, but that was a cost the rulers were ready to pay to jump-start the heart of the nation.[6]

In the past, a peasant had been part of a huge, amorphous commune or collective run by cadres, who might know nothing of farming, and subject to orders from political bosses. Now, individuals could better themselves by their own effort and skills. It was the greatest change seen since the early Communist land reforms, and a frontal attack on everything done since the early 1950s. It was also stunningly successful.

There was initial resistance in some places, and in Hebei a reminder of how natural disasters could impede progress: drought between 1980 and 1982 brought big crop losses, and 14 million people needed emergency rations as some ate tree bark to survive. But by 1984 98 per cent of agricultural households had adopted the new system. In the once-model commune of Dazhai in Shanxi, a woman cadre recalled how, in the past, she had intervened to stop people selling produce, but now 'you can do anything you like, raise pigs to eat or sell, make cloth tigers and sell them at market.' Progress in the countryside brought new transport links; bus routes overcame the traditional village isolation while rural railway station platforms were piled with goods waiting to be taken to market. The change was not only in the fields. Doctors, teachers and lawyers set up village practices.[7]

Farm output rose by 8–10 per cent a year, with a record harvest in 1984. Grain yields went from 2.5 tonnes per hectare in 1978 to 3.5 in the mid-1980s. Rural incomes increased by an average of almost 18 per cent a year between 1978 and 1984. In agricultural Guangdong, incomes doubled between 1978 and 1982 – and doubled again in the following six years. In Dazhai, the cadre and her husband were able to buy a Panda television set, which they thought was 'magic with its sounds and images'.[8]

Piece rates were reintroduced after being dropped in the name of Cultural Revolution egalitarianism. Bonus payments also became more common. Under-employed workers, particularly in the state sector, found second jobs to supplement their income. To compensate for increased food prices, the wages of urban inhabitants were raised. Cities saw the growth of individual enterprises, often consisting of only one person or a couple. To absorb more than 25 million unemployed school leavers and youths returning after having been 'sent down' to the country during the Cultural Revolution, urban collectives were organized, making everything from furniture to zip fasteners, or offering catering and undertaking services. They set the wages of members and distributed any profits after paying taxes. In the Hunan capital of Changsha, almost half the 23,000 school graduates went into such groups.[9]

The *danwei* work units remained in place in urban areas, allocating housing, jobs and benefits to their members. But greater labour mobility was allowed, even if this ran into opposition from units which did not want to lose members or their authority over them – they could exert pressure by withholding the dossiers officially required to gain a job elsewhere, though other employers might simply take on people without papers, whatever the regulations. China was still far from having a free labour market, with the *haikou* system of local registration officially tying people to their home districts. But, increasingly, workers were allowed to move as temporary migrants: by the end of the 1970s, there were estimated to be 10 million such 'non-fixed' workers; they had fewer rights than settled staff in state-owned enterprises, but they could seek employment in new and expanding sectors.

Despite all this change, public sector factories remained predominant for the moment, with CCP committees in plants having the last word. 'The critical issue of giving enterprises decision-making power has not been dealt with,' as an official document noted in 1984. Still, state enterprises began to seek profits, and appointed managers who might achieve that, though observers found the pace of work slow, with much standing around and cigarette smoking. Unions, which had been disbanded from 1966 to 1973, were re-established but acted as arms of the Party and management – the right to strike was contained in the constitution; however, it was stipulated that this must not interfere with production.

Cities began to lose their drabness. In Beijing, a two-year programme starting in 1980 built 150,000 flats while two ring roads were constructed to handle the growing volume of traffic. Consumerism started to return. By 1980, advertising was common. Some foreign goods could be found, though very few people could afford them. Overseas Chinese began to invest, earning patriotic points from the regime; Deng went in person to preside at the opening of a Beijing hotel built by a shipping tycoon from Hong Kong, and wrote the calligraphy for its neon sign. In Nanjing, a hotel financed with foreign money towered over low-rise buildings surrounding it.[10]

Markets thrived. The experience of the capital during a shortage caused by bad weather in 1979 was indicative of how things were changing – while the shelves of official shops were half empty, the thirteen officially permitted markets were filled with food on sale at higher prices. The Qianmenwei area was lined with stalls selling porcelain, crab apples, roasted duck, musical instruments, lapel badges, brightly coloured tablecloths, plus pictures of Western film stars and bathing beauties showing off their legs.

Fortune tellers reappeared on the streets, as did peddlers of fake medicines. Hawkers in Tianjin became celebrated for clearing shops out of clothes, shoes and quilts as soon as they appeared, and selling them on at a profit. In Kaifeng, a Western visitor, who had last been in China during the Maoist era of austerity, was taken aback at the array of fresh vegetables for sale on the pavements, and by the way in which managers at the local cigarette factory paid bonuses to the most productive workers.[11]

Life became more relaxed, and enjoyable, within the limits of what was available. As class warfare waned, 'capitalist-roaders' and 'big landlords' were able to reintegrate into society. In cities, family discipline lessened, and the number of divorce cases rose by 50 per cent in the first half of the 1980s, to 46 per 10,000 population. A Beijing resident wrote indignantly to a newspaper of gangs which traded jackets, trousers, watches, cameras, bicycles, gold and currency, as well as 'photos of nude women and foreign sex magazines'.

Percy Cradock, who had returned to Beijing as the British ambassador, recalled seeing 'louche young men in T-shirts and sunglasses [who] belonged to a new, non-revolutionary world. The girls had taken to high heels, smart dresses, curls and make-up. Even the PLA were out of their workmanlike fatigues and arrayed in elaborate uniforms, with much gold braid. There was Western-style dancing, Taiwan and Hong Kong hit-tunes, portable radios and ghetto-blasters . . . There were privately-run restaurants and inns and even agencies providing cooks and nannies for better-off families.'[12]

Shortages were still frequent for everything from bicycle tyres and matches to sewing machines and plastic shoes; a saying had it that China's light industry was 'like a train entering a station, making a lot of noise but moving very slowly'. Big centres such as Beijing, Shanghai and Guangzhou were best supplied. Luxuries were generally unavailable; women's stockings were coarse – most wore socks. The closest thing to a glossy magazine, the monthly *China Pictorial*, was aimed at foreigners.

But, in one area of life, state intervention was stepped up as the regime tried to impose a one-child policy. China already had a high legal minimum age for marriage – twenty for women and twenty-two for men. Permits were required to give birth. There had been sterilization drives. But the population still rose. In 1979, a one-child limit was implemented in cities – a second child was allowed in the countryside after a gap of five years. The urban restriction was backed by an array of fines and punishments, and a mass movement conducted in the manner of Maoist days. A propaganda barrage was launched, with 'struggle sessions' against parents who had two or more infants, and the despatch of medical teams to conduct abortions and sterilizations, and fit contraceptive devices.[13]

The limitation led to an emphasis on having boys. For farming families, in particular, girls were unwelcome. They were regarded as less fitted for work in the fields; they would marry outside the family and support their families-in-law, rather than their own parents. So there was an upsurge in abortions of female foetuses and female infanticide. In 1981, when the population reached a billion, there were 108.5 males for every 100 females in China; by 1985, this had risen to 111 and to 114 by 1989

As foreigners began to arrive to assess the new market that was opening up in China, the victory of the reformers appeared complete. But there were divisions in their ranks. For the planner Chen Yun, the economy should be like a birdcage, the state sector forming the structure within which the bird of private enterprise was allowed to flutter, and setting limits to its freedom. Chen, who reached his seventy-fifth birthday in 1980, advocated 'a high degree of centralism and unification' to stop regions pursuing autonomous economic policies. More ambitious figures such as Premier Zhao Ziyang saw the bird flying freely, but there was an inbuilt tension between the two leading reformers, Hu Yaobang and Zhao, as candidates to succeed the ageing Paramount Leader.

By temperament, Hu was always the more impulsive, and his prime area of operations – the CCP – was always open to counter-moves by political conservatives, while Deng had shown the limits he placed on democratization. Zhao's economic reform portfolio was, on the other hand, strongly backed by the chief. Despite their differences on the 'birdcage', Chen Yun saw Zhao as a man he could work with – 'Ziyang and I, we speak the Beijingese of the capital,' he remarked to Hu. 'You, you prefer local dialects.'[14]

Deng championed Special Economic Zones (SEZs) on a pattern begun in Taiwan, South Korea and Ireland (officials from Shanghai visited the zone at Shannon). The idea was said to have taken shape in his mind after he heard of an executive from a Hong Kong company who had gone to Guangdong to look for a site at which to break up old ships for scrap. After all, the leader remarked, hadn't the Yenan base been a special zone?[15]

The idea of development zones and export bases had emerged in the early 1960s, without much result. The new zones adopted foreign technology and investment and were entirely export-orientated. In a policy that Zhao Ziyang dubbed 'placing two heads outside', the PRC saw the developed world both as a source of technology and investment, and as a market. Exports were boosted by a steady devaluation of the yuan, whose value almost halved against the US dollar between 1980 and 1985.[16]

China's foreign trade duly jumped by between 50 and 100 per cent in the first half of the 1980s, depending on which data is used, with imports and exports tracking one another. In 1985, exports reached $25 billion, compared to $10 billion in 1978. In the second half of the decade, imports surged ahead of sales abroad for a time as machinery and materials were bought, but from 1990, helped by continuing devaluation, the PRC again enjoyed an expanding surplus.[17]

The SEZs were granted special privileges, tax breaks and subsidies to attract foreign investment, technology and expertise. Since they did not produce for the domestic market, they did not threaten existing firms, while their goods would earn the foreign exchange needed to fund national growth. Guangdong, home of the Taiping, the ideologues of the Hundred Days and Sun Yat-sen, played a leading role in this new change.

Despite the centralizing policies pursued since 1949, the province had retained much of its special character, including its links with Overseas Chinese, whose investments played a key role in economic modernization. In May 1980, its fishing village of Shenzhen was declared the first SEZ, chosen for its position just across the border from Hong Kong. It was followed by zones at Zhuhai, near Macau, and the old treaty city of Shantou, in east Guangdong. A fourth SEZ was opened in the one-time tea port of Xiamen in Fujian, on the Strait opposite Taiwan, which, political differences notwithstanding, was to be a big source of investment and trade.

The incomes of SEZ workers had a strong multiplier effect, not only locally but through remittances of migrant employees back to their home villages. Before the zones, crude oil and refined-petroleum products were major Chinese exports; manufacturing now became steadily more important. This encouraged a shift away from the big monopolist state enterprises towards collectives and joint ventures, with a large role played by small to medium-sized undertakings established under official control in rural towns and villages and known as Commune and Brigade Enterprises (CBEs). In some cases, these grew out of the local groupings which had emerged during the Cultural Revolution and now turned their attention to a new form of upheaval, drawing on community roots that stretched back for centuries. Guangdong, once again, took a leading role – its CBEs tripled their total income between 1978 and 1983. Though the enterprises were meant to operate as collectives, peasants who had obtained their own land began to branch out individually.[18]

Successful as it was in its own terms, the economic relaxation aroused political tensions and produced an upsurge in corruption, leading Deng to consider where China was heading. He noted how cadres were becoming imbued with 'bourgeois life-styles' in the coastal provinces where they met foreigners and where the children of high officials used their contacts to extract bribes from overseas businesses. 'It is quite a problem to decide how far we should go in stimulating the economy,' he told a Military Commission. 'We are determined to open up and so stimulate the economy. But in order to ensure that this policy really benefits our modernization and does not take us off the socialist path, we must at the same time fight economic crime. Otherwise things will get out of hand.'[19]

In the remaining years of the century, he added, there were four main aims – to restructure the administration and economy with younger, better-educated, more competent and more revolutionary cadres; 'to strive to build a socialist civilisation which is culturally and ideologically advanced; to combat economic and other crimes that undermine social- ism; and to rectify the Party's style of work and consolidate its organiz- ation.' In a major address to the Twelfth National Congress of the Party on 1 September 1982, he insisted on the need to pursue modernization on the basis of 'Chinese realities'. While the country should learn from foreigners, mere mechanical copying of their methods would lead no- where, he argued. Ending with a phrase that was to become the hallmark of his era, he went on: 'We must integrate the universal truth of Marxism with the concrete realities of China, blaze a path of our own and build socialism with Chinese characteristics.'

As always with such formulations, what precisely was meant was open to interpretation. That was part of the point. But some developments were plain. Cadres who had suffered since 1957 were rehabilitated by the hundreds of thousands, bringing back a corps of officials who might not always be as reform-minded as Deng and his immediate comrades, but who put a new complexion on the regime.

A CCP Plenum rehabilitated Liu Shaoqi; his wife was now allowed to collect his ashes, and a memorial ceremony was held at which Deng delivered the eulogy. A Party resolution, which Deng revised nine times, judged that the Cultural Revolution had caused the most severe setback and heaviest losses since 1949. It pinned responsibility for the 'grave "left" error' squarely on Mao, saying that, for all his achievements, he made 'gross mistakes' in the last ten years of his life. Still, overall, 'his merits are primary and his errors secondary.' Lin Biao and Jiang Qing were excoriated for counter-revolutionary sabotage and plotting. Zhou Enlai was praised for his devotion to the Party and the people, and for having done all he could to keep things running during the upheaval.

While far franker than anything that had appeared before, the resolution did not mention the Great Leap famine and did not explain why the Party had done nothing to stop Mao launching the Cultural Revolution, or why the chaos had lasted for so long – or touch on the equivocal role of the PLA. Though hundreds of millions had their memories and the 1966–76 period remains an acutely sensitive matter in today's China, the resolution was thought to have done enough to draw an official line under the past. No further official re-evaluation has been undertaken since.

Neither Hu nor Zhao – nor, above all, Deng – had any interest in further inquiry into the episode during which they had all suffered. Papering over the past was the best way of moving on to the future. By early 1983, the two younger men were focused on their own relationship, with a debate about how to handle profits of state enterprises providing the battleground. The premier favoured a centralizing approach while the Party leader wanted to delegate, and leave part of the cash at the disposal of local managers. The row was aggravated when Hu promoted his approach while Zhao was away on a tour of Africa. Chen Yun rounded on the Party chief at a Politburo meeting for 'making a mess of the economy'. On Zhao's return, the old economist produced a ten-point indictment of the CCP secretary based on investigations by the propaganda boss, Deng Liqun.

The strong growth risked over-heating, the conservatives warned. It was all Hu's fault for having talked to Party branches about GDP quadrupling by the end of the century. Zhao insisted that everything had been in perfect shape when he left for Africa; if there were any worries about excessive expansion, these must, indeed, be the fault of Hu and his uncalled-for intervention in economic matters. Chen pressed the campaign by proposing a meeting of provincial chiefs to criticize Hu further. Meanwhile they were told of the attacks on the Party secretary.[20]

Deng Xiaoping did not commit himself, listening silently to the debate; but he reportedly took Hu aside afterwards to advise him to stick to politics, and leave the economy to Zhao and Chen. The supreme leader consulted Marshal Ye, who counselled against sacking Hu. To lose another CCP boss so soon after the demolition of Hua Guofeng would be dangerous. So Hu kept his job, but was put outside the vital economic sector and had suffered an obvious rebuff. In the ruthless world of leadership politics, it was time for the conservatives to stage a fresh attack.

The lead was taken by Deng Liqun, a tough and opinionated operator born in 1914 who was known as 'Little Deng'. Another of the Hunan natives who took leading posts in the PRC, Little Deng had helped put down Muslim resistance to Communist rule in Xinjiang and had then become Liu Shaoqi's secretary. After suffering in the Cultural Revolution, he bounced back to head the Policy Research Office and, as propaganda chief, waged a protracted battle against liberalization in all its forms, lining up with Peng Zhen, Chen Yun and the head of the Party School, Wang Zhen, who had commanded the garrison in Yenan and then 'pacified' Xinjiang with Little Deng before surviving the Cultural Revolution as minister for farms.[21]

Deng chose 'spiritual pollution' as his target, easily linking it to the economic reforms. He warned against:

Spreading things that are obscene, barbarous, treacherous, or reactionary;

Vulgar taste in artistic performances;

Efforts to seek personal gain and indulgence in anarchism and liberalism;

Writing articles or making speeches that run counter to the country's socialist system.[22]

Western hair-dos and high heels, moustaches and whiskers were attacked, along with 'decadent music' and 'Hong Kong-style' advertising, 'worship of individualism' and 'looking to make money in everything'.

A notice outside the headquarters of the Beijing Municipal Party Committee declared: 'No admittance to persons with hair too long, skirts too short, slacks too tight, or face powdered and rouged.' Nothing in the Shenzhen SEZ was socialist except for its five-starred red flag, Little Deng thundered.

In a debate about 'socialist humanism', Deng Xiaoping backed an assault on the liberals. A campaign was waged against economic criminals which, while valid enough in itself, played into the hands of the conservatives – between 6,000 and 10,000 people were reported to have been executed in the second half of 1983.[23]

But Little Deng had gone too far. Hu and Zhao could see the campaign bringing all reform to a halt. So, in November 1983, they joined forces in self-defence. They denounced the drive against 'spiritual pollution' as a 'false show of force' and detected a dangerous leftist tendency that aimed to overthrow progress made in the period since Mao's death, which Hu characterized as 'one of the best periods since Liberation'. Little Deng shouted at the top of his voice during a session of the Central Party Secretariat that 'spiritual pollution threatens the life of the Party'. At which Zhao noted that Japanese businesses were postponing agreements because of the campaign. 'If things go on like this, I shall be Prime Minister no longer,' he added.[24]

Fearful for the economic reform programme, Deng Xiaoping intervened to halt the conservative crusade. Soon afterwards, Hu appeared in public in a Western suit, and Zhao did the same on a visit to the United States. At the end of 1983, a Politburo member, Yu Qiuli, explained to senior PLA cadres that 'it is not right to speak of wearing high-heeled shoes, getting permanent waves, wearing sunglasses, wearing new styles of clothing and smoking filtered cigarettes as manifestations of spiritual pollution ... There will be chaos in our thinking if everything is regarded as spiritual pollution.'

Despite his victory, Hu's position was still fragile. He had expected Little Deng to be sacked but, when word of this leaked out and was broadcast by the Voice of America, Xiaoping was so annoyed that he kept the leftist on. The Party chief had to agree to the dismissal of two of his leading reformist colleagues as part of the settlement to end the campaign against 'spiritual pollution'. An anti-leftist campaign he mounted expelled only 40,000 CCP members, instead of the target of 3 million. Though the PLA was rejuvenated and reorganized, this was largely Deng Xiaoping's doing; the army had little time for Hu and turned down a suggestion by Deng that he should take over the chair of the Military Affairs Commission. At the National Day march-past in Tiananmen Square, Hu wore civilian clothes and had to be content with clapping his hands while Deng was in PLA uniform and saluted.[25]

The rejuvenation of the top army ranks led to the resignation from the Politburo in 1985 of its six military members, including Ye Jianying. Among the new members on the full Politburo were two rising younger men, both aged fifty-six – Vice-Premier Li Peng, who had been trained as a hydraulic engineer in the USSR and spoke Russian, and Hu Qili, a liberal associate of Hu Yaobang who had been purged in the Cultural Revolution but returned to head the General Office of the CCP. The other new members were a reform economist, Tian Jiyuan, the foreign minister, Wu Xueqian, vice-premier Yao Yilin, a planner with close ties to Chen Yun, and Qiao Shi, a Shanghai student leader from the 1940s who directed the Party Organization Department.

The Politburo changes coincided with a major shift in the Central Committee as Deng pursued his quest for rejuvenation. Old stagers were replaced by younger, better-educated members, known as 'the third echelon'. But, in the Politburo, the veterans Chen Yun, eighty, and Peng Zhen, eighty-three, retained their posts, as did the 76-year-old Li Xiannian, who had remained in the body throughout the Cultural Revolution and had become head of state in 1983, a largely ceremonial job but recognition for his long career. Little Deng also held on in the Central Secretariat, though he would lose his propaganda portfolio in 1986.

Marshal Ye's departure meant that one seat on the core Standing Committee was vacant. The conservatives wanted Peng Zhen to take it. The liberals backed the newly arrived Hu Qili. Deng declined to break the deadlock. The post was left unfilled. Though his power and prestige were at their zenith, it was a metaphor for the leader's abiding desire not to commit himself politically between the factions around him, if only to retain his own pivotal position.[26]

Still, he was ready for a new initiative in the economic area, by calling for further development of the SEZs, which he had visited in January 1984. 'We cannot curl up on ourselves; we have to go on opening up,' he wrote. He attributed the success of the fastest growing area in Shenzhen to the devolving of expenditure decisions, the use of the contract system and the attribution of rewards and punishment. Whereas urban construction elsewhere was often slow and of low quality, Deng noted that, in Shenzhen, migrant workers put up one storey in a day and finished a whole building in a couple of weeks. The zones, he added, would 'extend the positive impact of our country on the world'.[27]

Hainan Island, covering 13,000 tropical square miles in the South China Sea, became a SEZ, adding factories to its rice, sugar-cane and tobacco fields, timber and mineral deposits. Guangdong was declared a 'comprehensive reform experiment zone', opening the way to further development of private enterprise there. Fourteen Economically Opened Coastal Areas and Cities were established, including Qingdao, Ningbo, Fuzhou and Dalian. Shanghai was allowed to attract foreign investment.

The following year, three big Coastal Economic Zones were set up, in the Yangzi Delta round Shanghai, in the Pearl River round Guangzhou, and in South Fujian round Xiamen. In 1987, coastal southern Manchuria and Shandong followed. Jumping on the bandwagon without official approval, local governments launched schemes to attract foreign investment and build up export industries. By the end of the decade, an estimated 50,000 Chinese managers were running factories for investors from abroad, constituting a new technological class in touch with foreign methods, and sometimes using the skills they acquired to branch out on their own.

The SEZs grew at an average of 30 per cent annually – that is doubling in three years – as they pumped out exports. Investment poured in through Hong Kong and Taiwan. Companies in the British colony moved manufacturing over the border, employing millions; as a result, Hong Kong developed into an advanced services centre, while its factory owners made second fortunes from property development of their sites. By 1990, Guangdong would account for a fifth of all China's exports, and almost two fifths of its growth came from export industries, its private companies amassing more capital than its state and collective sectors. To show his disapproval, Chen Yun never visited a SEZ.[28]

The policy meant that the Chinese economy was, in effect, split in two – the booming coastal zones and the far larger and backward interior. In industry, the new areas were financed with foreign money, used foreign technology, drew in millions of migrant workers, engaged in fierce competition with foreign firms and with one another, and orientated themselves exclusively towards the outside world. On the other hand were the old state factories, to which little attention was paid as they grew into rustbelt dinosaurs, particularly in the north-east.

Zhao Ziyang dreamed of a great information technology revolution, spurred by the ideas of the American futurologist Alvin Toffler, who had lectured in China in 1983. After visiting the United States, the premier became even more enthusiastic. Two thousand senior cadres were summoned to lectures on the subject. The World Bank provided a $200 million loan to import microcomputers. Western technology firms offered free samples to the government, universities and research institutes to get a toehold in what could prove an enormous market.[29]

Away from the cities and the SEZs, another hugely important change was taking place in rural towns and villages. In 1984, the CBE brigades that had started small-scale industry in the countryside were replaced by Town and Village Enterprises (TVEs). Some were collectives, but restrictions on ownership were greatly relaxed. The CBEs had been officially limited to making things that served agriculture; TVEs could turn out anything they liked. Geographical limitations were done away with, enabling them to sell outside their home districts. They were allowed to take out loans from state banks, and collectively owned TVEs got tax relief.

In 1980, there had been around 1.5 million CBEs; twelve years later, 20 million TVEs employed 100 million people (and 140 million in 2007). Their average output rose by 30 per cent a year to account for a quarter of China's total production at the end of the decade. More and more TVEs were owned by individuals or families, or by local groups. In coastal provinces, they poured out exports. Spearhead Guangdong had 1.1 million by the mid-1980s, with 6.5 million workers.[30]

The TVEs added to the pressure on the old state firms whose share of output fell sharply. Per capita income in the new enterprises rose at an average of 7 per cent a year, three and a half times as fast as in the previous twenty-one years. In the fields, quotas for crops were replaced by a system under which the central government set national targets and then negotiated supply with producers. Accumulated household savings rocketed, boosting the pool of cheap capital available for investment.[31]

The influence of the new economics was felt in at least some public sector factories, where managers were given more authority over staffing, marketing and procurement. Planning was reduced. Three levels of industrial prices were established – one was fixed to assure guaranteed supply, another was allowed to move between set limits while the third was completely free to encourage as much production as possible. Ten billion dollars were invested in the Shengli oilfield at the mouth of the Yellow River, a huge integrated complex covering 18,000 square miles. It had 153,000 workers, a 30,000-acre farm, 152 schools, China's biggest computer and 15,000 vehicles. Technical advice came from a Texan oil company. Though Shengli was a state firm, it applied contracts, profit incentives and internal competition to boost output on the Deng model. But it retained at least one characteristic of the old approach: in military style, workers were organized under a General Battle Headquarters.[32]

Shengli was still protected by its state status, but the new private and semi-private businesses operated by market rules in what were often cut-throat conditions. Their exports had to compete with global products. They lacked property rights, clear commercial laws, proper accounting procedures or a stock market. Local authorities often took a slice of the action in return for letting entrepreneurs get on with the job without interference. There were no independent courts to which to appeal. When raw materials ran short, private businesses could find it hard to ensure supplies, while state banks preferred to channel money into public sector firms. Many of the new businesses operated on the margins of legality – the Finance Ministry estimated at one point that 70–80 per cent of private enterprises evaded taxes; keeping honest books was of little use at tax-time since it was assumed that they were cooked. Not that state firms were all that much more honest – the estimate was that half of them dodged taxes.[33]

A new class was being born, which would spawn the bourgeoisie Mao had so feared. Its members were tough operators, able to navigate the system, spot openings and amass the labour and capital needed to fill the market gap. Initially, at least, they were likely to come from outside official channels, since cadres were loath to abandon their privileges to take risks and could cash in by exploiting their positions to gain perks in return for favours. Overseas Chinese who embarked on joint ventures on the mainland could find the ground swampy – an early entrant into the new world of China recalled being swindled twice by well-connected local partners, and then finding that a hotel he had opened on Hainan was trashed by the PLA, which ran its own establishment nearby.[34]

Still, material improvement on a scale not seen since 1949 was now available for those who grasped the chance. Whether Deng ever actually said that it was glorious to grow rich is uncertain. But in an American television interview in September 1986 he made his basic position plain:[35]

There can be no Communism with pauperism, or Socialism with pauperism. So to get rich is no sin. However, what we mean by getting rich is different from what you mean. Wealth in a socialist society belongs to the people. To get rich in a socialist society means prosperity for the entire people. The principles of socialism are: first, development of production and second, common prosperity. We permit some people and some regions to become prosperous first, for the purpose of achieving common prosperity faster. That is why our policy will not lead to polarization, to a situation where the rich get richer while the poor get poorer.

To take examples of the entrepreneurship that flourished in addition to the bigger organized manufacturing firms of the economic zones:

Because of his 'bad' family background, Zong Qinghou was sent to the countryside at the age of seventeen, working on a tea plantation for fifteen years. He then joined his mother, who was teaching at an urban school, and set up a small business peddling iced lollipops, which he and two associates sold round Hangzhou from their bicycles. Two decades later, his company, Wahaha, was the biggest Chinese soft drinks firm, with sales of more than $1 billion a year. He even began exporting its 'Future Cola' to the USA. Zong became a delegate to the National People's Congress and got involved in a rancorous lawsuit with his French joint venture partner, Danone. 'Highly-educated people aren't fit to be entrepreneurs,' he said. 'If you know too much, you might hesitate and not take a chance.'[36]

The four brothers Liu from Deng's home province of Sichuan were also sent to the countryside during the Cultural Revolution. Afterwards, they stayed on and raised money to start a business by selling their bicycles, watches and other personal belongings. They began by buying quail eggs from farmers and marketing them in the city of Chongqing. Before long they bred quails; by the end of the 1980s, their farms had more than 10 million birds. From that, they went into pig and bird feed, fish powder and worms for poultry. Their Hope Group, which subsequently split into separate companies, became one of China's biggest business success stories, with 107 factories. In 2008, the eldest of the Liu clan topped the China Rich List drawn up by *Forbes* magazine and one of his siblings ranked fourth.[37]

Zhou Peikun, a radical Nanjing factory worker during the Cultural Revolution, got a one-month loan of 400 yuan from a friend of his father in 1984. He set up an enterprise selling 'hatched eggs' – those from which the chick does not emerge – which were a prized delicacy in his home city. Getting up at midnight, he rode thirty miles on a borrowed tricycle to a chicken farm to collect them. Reaching home with the eggs, he and his wife sold a third of them to peddlers, and boiled the rest to offer at street corners. He grew so tired from the cycling that, on one trip, he fell asleep and crashed into a tree, but he would not spend the money on hospital treatment.

With the profits from the eggs, he and his wife bought a sugar cane crusher and added juice to their wares. They opened a fruit shop that stayed open later than state stores and allowed customers to pick and chose. Having prospered in the first businesses, they gave the enterprises to their daughter and her husband, and went into fashion underwear retailing, still working seven days a week, 365 days a year. Was he grateful to Deng, he asked himself in the late 1990s. 'In public places, I know the right thing to say,' he replied. 'But deep in my heart, I don't feel the need to be grateful. Before China was not normal. Now, China is more or less normal, where people get rewarded for their hard work.'[38]

After her soldier father was jailed as a capitalist-roader in the Cultural Revolution, Cheung Yan went to work in a textile mill as a teenager to support her mother and seven brothers and sisters. She then got a job in a paper firm in southern China and realized that, as Chinese production of goods rose, the demand for packaging would increase. In 1985, Chinese paper companies dispatched her to Hong Kong with 4,000 US dollars to start a business collecting good-quality waste paper for recycling over the border. From there, she went to America. Despite speaking very little English, she saw the potential for a business collecting the packaging of Chinese exports, and sending it home to be used again. Within five years, she was the biggest US exporter of waste paper. Returning to the PRC, she set up a network of paper plants which, by 2006, made her Nine Dragons group one of the three biggest paper makers in the world, and the one-time textile worker the richest self-made woman on earth.[39]

Or take a chubby man from the coast who had been exiled to Sichuan during the Cultural Revolution and who was visited in the early reform period by the British journalist David Bonavia. The local township had let him establish a metalwork shop with twenty staff. Using the enterprise's earnings and bank lending, he developed a firm specializing in making reinforcing bars for construction work. Within a decade, it employed 18,000 people, its plant spread over acres, with two electric-arc blast furnaces. The visitor likened him and his peers to the robber barons of the nineteenth-century United States or the Victorian mill owners of Britain, men who forged ahead with little regard for legalities or the niceties of business in a rapidly changing economic context.[40]

Internationally, the Deng revolution required peace. The Mao-era effort to fan global revolution had to be most firmly shelved. The links with the USA established under Nixon, Ford and Carter were expanded further under Ronald Reagan, who abandoned his earlier jeremiads against 'a statist monopoly founded on violence and propaganda, and destructive of the humane tradition of the Chinese people themselves'. Zhao Ziyang was received at the White House, and the Republican president went to China, musing on the way home about the 'so-called Communist country' he had just visited. Business contacts thrived. The Plaza accords which increased the value of the Japanese yen made China's exports more competitive in currency terms and stimulated the upward path of PRC exports to the US.

Beijing's relations with Moscow began to improve. China still objected to the stationing of Soviet troops along the border and in Mongolia, as well as to the invasion of Afghanistan. But, between 1982 and 1986, contacts were resumed to seek normalization. As preconditions, Beijing insisted that Moscow pull its forces out from Mongolia, the border area and Afghanistan and put pressure on Vietnam to do the same from Cambodia. There was no immediate agreement, but an anti-Soviet reference in Reagan's speech at the Great Hall of the People was deleted from the version broadcast by Chinese television. Washington could no longer automatically count on China as a reliable partner against Moscow.

The PRC had held back from direct action to regain Hong Kong – the colony was valuable as a bridge to the rest of the world and a source of trade, and marching in across the border would have upset the peaceful relations Deng wanted. It took second place in Beijing's overall priorities to the recovery of Taiwan, for which the formula 'one country, two systems' was evolved. But the expiry of the land leases in the New Territories in 1997 necessitated a decision on whether they would be renewed or reverted to China.* Margaret Thatcher visited Beijing in 1982 to discuss the issue. Deng seemed ill at ease negotiating with a woman, while the British leader remarked to Percy Cradock, who had become her adviser, on how 'cruel' she found the Chinese leader.[41]

The talks were tough, as the British sought to put conditions on the insistence by Deng and Zhao that Beijing had an absolute right to act as it wished on what would once more become Chinese territory. The Paramount Leader told the prime minister that the PLA could walk in and take the whole colony in an afternoon. 'There is nothing I could do to stop you,' she replied. 'But the eyes of the world would know what China is like.' A senior Chinese official revealed in 2007 that Beijing had been ready to 'requisition by force' the territory if the negotiations had sparked unrest there.[42]

Nor were matters helped when the prime minister developed a cold, and slipped on the steps of the Great Hall of the People. The smoked salmon her party brought for a banquet it gave in the Hall sat oddly with the sea slugs served up by the Chinese kitchen, as did regimental silver decorating the table. Cradock found the immediate outcome bleak, but comforted himself that at least agreement had been achieved to conduct further talks during which the British might, as he put it, 'instruct the Chinese in the economic realities of Hong Kong . . . we still had everything to play for.'

In 1984, the two countries agreed a Joint Declaration that accepted a change of sovereignty in 1997 but guaranteed that the territory's way of life would continue under the application of the 'one country, two systems' formula. Democracy advocates in Hong Kong were, and would remain, unhappy, but the colony was not a democracy and the British and Chinese ensured that electoral politics would not disturb the handover.

For all China's economic progress, problems which had been inherent in modernization from the start grew ever larger. Corruption soared,

---

* The leases expired ninety-nine years after Britain had been granted the concessions. Hong Kong island had been taken in perpetuity, but was unviable without the New Territories – or the water supply from Guangdong.

much of it petty graft, but also large-scale smuggling, speculation and currency manipulation in the new economic zones. The economist Bo Yibo, who had returned to the front line, listed practices such as the establishment of dummy 'briefcase companies', black market dealing in foreign currency, unauthorized sale of lottery tickets, distribution of state money under false pretexts, plus feasts, gifts, nepotism and cronyism.

In the most spectacular of a series of smuggling cases, officials in Hainan used bank loans, allocations of foreign exchange, currency from exports by state firms and black market cash to import 90,000 motor vehicles, 120,000 motor cycles, 250,000 video recorders and almost 3 million television sets worth $600 million in all. These were then shipped to the mainland to be sold at a big profit. When the ring was uncovered, the only punishment was the demotion of those involved. The combined effect of such dodges was to reduce China's foreign exchange reserves by more than a third – $6 billion – in the first half of 1985.

Some 'princeling' children of high figures made the most of the status of their parents either to exploit their contacts or claim immunity from the police. The son of Hu Qiaomu, a long-time Central Committee member who had been Mao's secretary and was now honorary president of the Academy of Social Sciences, was alleged to have skimmed millions of yuan from fees at a correspondence school he ran, and to have supplied pornographic videos to PLA sex parties. When Hu Yaobang proposed to charge the young man, his father threw himself on Deng's mercy. The case was quietly dropped, and the son given a mild rebuke. Children of the conservatives Chen Yun and Wang Zhen were reported to be profiteering, and were investigated; but, again, nothing happened. Though Zhao Ziyang would later acknowledge the uninhibited entrepreneurship of his two sons, they were not troubled by the authorities.[*43]

Deng had accepted that the pace of growth would be uneven; 'it doesn't matter if some areas get rich first,' he said. But regional disparities became an inherent destabilizing element in the new China, adding to other strains produced by change. Inflation rose fast, ahead of the official rate of 9 per cent, and hit those on fixed official salaries. The system of different price levels boosted production but also encouraged manufacturers to shift to the third category of freely priced products,

---

* Zhao offered in 1989 to have them hauled up in front of a tribunal; his leadership colleagues declined to take him up on this. It might have set an awkward precedent.

creating shortages of guaranteed goods and fostering more corruption, a booming black market and further inflation. The increased money supply to pay for reforms primed the pump. Provinces made the most of weaknesses in central planning to set their own agendas, encouraging local industries which were not always competitive with those elsewhere but were protected by barriers to trade with other regions.[44]

TVEs distracted peasants from the land. With remunerative work for the young prized above education, the number of school pupils dropped from 168 million to 123 million during the 1980s. The flow of migrant workers soared by 140 per cent to 24 million between 1978 and 1988. As well as providing abundant cheap labour, particularly for exporting plants, they helped to fund their home villages through the remittances. But they lacked rights, and suffered discrimination.[45]

Birth control, including the one-child policy, was largely ineffective in rural areas. A survey in 1988 reported that 93 per cent of women in the countryside who had one child gave birth to another, that 47 per cent with two children gave birth to a third, and that 28 per cent of those with three had a fourth. After ten years of the programme, slightly over half the newborn babies were not first children. The population rose by 156 million during the 1980s.[46]

Greater intellectual liberty as preached by Hu Yaobang and his associates meant that criticism of the regime began to be heard more freely. Beijing students protested at their living conditions, corruption and privileges granted to foreigners, with Japanese businesses as particular targets. Still, there were limits – the long-haired singer and guitarist Cui Jian, who melded rock 'n' roll with folk melodies and became the voice of the younger generation with his anthem 'Nothing to My Name', was banned from giving public performances. A watch was kept on independent film makers. While Hu's fellow liberal Hu Qili urged intellectuals to 'break through' outdated Marxist concepts and scholars and writers called for the freeing of arts and culture from political control, Deng went into a familiar conservative crouch. 'It seems that anti-liberalism must be emphasised at the present and for the next twenty years,' he said. 'If we don't fight against this ideological trend and oppose all the messy stuff that is entering the nation as a result of the open door policy, these two things could destroy our socialist Four Modernizations.'

Hardliners made sure that these remarks were widely distributed despite an attempt by Hu Yaobang to restrict their circulation. But dissidence was in the air among students and scholars who, in Chinese tradition, felt a special duty to ensure correct behaviour among the rulers. Fang Lizhi, an astrophysicist from Anhui, argued that everybody was born with human rights, including democratic rights, and that political legitimacy was bestowed by citizens on the regime, not the other way round. He pointed a finger at men like a thoroughly unscientific vice-mayor of Beijing, who had enjoyed the perk of joining a delegation to a US conference on high-energy physics. Becoming a student hero, Fang toured campuses. Recordings of his explosive claims were circulated.

Students in a score of cities demonstrated in November 1987 against corruption and for democracy – they were also being hit by the effects of inflation, just as their teachers were suffering because of their fixed salaries. In Shanghai, they marched on the city hall and demanded a meeting with the mayor, Jiang Zemin. He sent out a deputy, who failed to get them to leave. At dawn, police dispersed them. In December, there were fresh student rallies in more than a dozen cities, those in Shanghai and Beijing attracting 30,000 people.

Despite occasional use of force, the official reaction was relatively mild. But Deng was on the watch politically. No liberalization should be allowed, he told senior officials. The door to ideological change was as firmly shut as ever. For all his courage and spirit, the Paramount Leader was, politically, the man of his past. That would lead to a great tragedy as others imagined a China whose evolution went beyond bounding growth figures.

28

Gathering Storm

On 27 December 1986, Deng Xiaoping was visited at his home in a side street behind the leadership compound by five old conservatives – Wang Zhen, Peng Zhen, Hu Qiaomu, Bo Yibo and Deng Liqun. They wanted Hu Yaobang dismissed. Given his expression of support for the Party chief in the past, this would involve loss of face for the patriarch. Nor was there an obvious successor. Whatever his doubts about political reform, Deng did not want to see the appointment of one of the old guard, who might try to put a brake on economic change.

Still, the Paramount Leader had grown exasperated by the student agitation, its questioning of the regime, and what he saw as the failure of his younger colleagues to deal with the problem. It was time to crack down; in Beijing, regulations were being brought in to ban parades and some agitators were arrested. At 10 a.m. on 30 December 1986, Deng called in a small group of senior figures, including Hu and Zhao Ziyang. He was in a cantankerous mood.

He began by attacking leaders 'in various places' for having failed to take a firm attitude towards bourgeois liberalization. The Party should expel the scientist Fang Lizhi and two prominent liberal writers, Liu Binyan, who blamed China's problems on the left, and Wang Ruowang, who had just published an article in Hong Kong depicting Deng's nomination of the 'third echelon' of leaders as 'feudal'.[1]

'We must adopt dictatorial measures that must not only be talked about, but used when necessary,' Deng stormed. 'If we don't take any measures and if we retreat, we'll only be confronted with more troubles later.' Modernization needed leadership, stability and unity, he went on. Bourgeois liberalism would bring only turmoil, and the CCP would lose the will to fight.[2]

Having initially taken a benign view of the Solidarity strikes in Poland, he now backed the repressive action of the authorities in Warsaw. As for foreign reactions if the regime clamped down on protests, Deng recalled that the jailing of Wei Jingsheng at the time of the Democracy Wall had done the country no real harm in the world. 'We must show foreigners that the political situation in China is stable,' he added.[3]

In a speech at the Party School on 31 December, the old conservative bruiser Wang Zhen grew so agitated that he severed the wires to the microphone as he declared of the protestors: 'They have three million college students, but I can marshal three million PLA troops. I am going to cut off heads! These sons of whores!' Harassed by police and security forces, the students gave up their struggle. Fang, Liu and Wang were thrown out of the CCP; the scientist was moved from his prestigious post in Anhui to a minor job in the capital. But, though the outbreak of free speech was easily quashed, the causes remained. A survey in Beijing showed that 92 per cent of graduates and 62 per cent of undergraduates saw CCP corruption and lack of democracy as the root of the protests; only 10 per cent were 'very confident' things would improve.

On 2 January 1987, Hu Yaobang submitted his resignation, admitting 'serious mistakes'. Rather than pleading the liberal case, he wrote that 'some villainous people dare to make me their protective umbrella in order to stir up people's hearts, poison the youth, create chaos, and threaten stability and unity.' Later, the liberal speechwriter Ruan Ming reported, Hu regretted his failure to fight his corner.

Deng considered Hu's letter at home, cutting himself off from his family as he did so – his injured son was pro-liberal. On 16 January, the axe fell at a meeting of the enlarged Politburo, attended by seventeen senior figures. Speaker after speaker condemned Hu. Among them, according to sources quoted later, was Zhao, though he was moderate compared with the hardliners. An old soldier, Xi Zhongxun, was said to have been the only one to have spoken up against what was happening. Xi had been an associate of Mao's victim Peng Dehuai, and had disappeared from view after the purging of his friend before returning to reach the heights of the Politburo. 'What are you guys doing here?' he asked. 'Don't repeat what Mao did to us.'[4]*

The meeting took no notice. At 7 p.m. that night, the state television network, CCTV, broadcast the news of Hu's departure. A six-point

---

* In 2007, Xi's son, Xi Jinping, emerged as Hu Jintao's putative successor as CCP leader.

charge sheet was drafted by the Cultural Revolution victim Bo Yibo. It parroted the conservative line in accusing Hu of not having fought 'spiritual pollution', and having opposed only leftism, not rightism, while contributing to 'total Westernisation' and encouragement of consumer demand. There were also vague charges that he had spoken about government legislative work in a way that was not serious, had said 'things that should not be said' in foreign affairs, and expressed ideas without Central Committee authorization.

Hu offered self-criticism, though he did not bow on the crucial point of ideological laxism which was alleged to have permitted spiritual pollution. His submission was enough for him to be allowed to retain his Politburo place. Compared to Mao's victims, he was treated extremely leniently, demoted but not cast out. That was not only a sign of changing times, but also politically sensible since Hu still enjoyed wide support. Though he had to curtail his activities when he suffered a heart attack, he continued his provincial visits, read history books and walked a lot, following a '10,000 steps a day' routine.[5]

Named as the new Party boss, Zhao Ziyang was, for the moment, the big winner, and lost little time in heaping opprobrium on his predecessor. At the end of January, he told a meeting of more than 200 senior cadres in the Zhongnanhai leadership compound that, though not everything Hu had done had been bad, he had shown 'timidity in the struggle against liberalism', and his case had been 'dealt with in the most perfect way'.

Still, as he moved in to his new job, Zhao was careful to seek to limit the fight against bourgeois liberalism to the Party; he did not want it to become a broad political movement or get in the way of economic policy. He won a tussle with Little Deng, who suffered when the number of candidates for posts voted on at the Party Congress was set above the number of jobs available, introducing a measure of carefully controlled competition. The ideologue scored so badly that he was obliged to relinquish his place on the Central Committee. Hu Yaobang, on the other hand, did well in the polling, and remained in the much more important Politburo.

Zhao wanted to reconcile economic reform with continued Communist rule, but took a more subtle approach than most of his colleagues. 'China's existing political structure was born out of the war years,' he noted. 'It fails to suit the economic, political and cultural modernization

Victory: Mao Zedong, the army and the people celebrate the new order in 1949.

The new leaders: (*top*) Mao with Liu Shaoqi (*right*) and Zhou Enlai (*left*). An unusually tall Deng Xiaoping stands on the far left; (*bottom*) Marshal Lin Biao, who would become Mao's chosen successor and then die mysteriously.

Before the storm: Mao indulges in his only exercise, swimming, before launching a purge of former associates at Lushan in 1959.

Changing the world: Mao meets Richard Nixon in Beijing in 1972, with Zhou Enlai (*left*) and Henry Kissinger (*right*).

Backyard steel: home furnaces propel the Great Leap Forward – badly.

Arouse the masses: the Cultural Revolution unleashed a huge anarchic movement
from 1966 to 1976.

Demons and monsters: anybody could be the target of savage Red Guard attacks, like these alleged class enemies paraded in typical dunces' hats.

The Helmsman passes: Mao's corpse viewed by his widow and her associates in the Gang of Four in 1976.

Hope and blood: (*top*) demonstrator exults in Tiananmen Square during the protests in the spring of 1989; (*middle left*) Party secretary Zhao Ziyang (*with loudhailer*) goes to Tiananmen Square to tell students 'we have come too late' – behind him (*in black*) is Wen Jiabao, who would become prime minister in 2002; (*middle right*) dead in the streets as the army advances; (*bottom*) tanks rolling over the protestors' tents in the square.

Architect of change: Deng Xiaoping radically reformed China economically, but left it in a political straitjacket.

The next generations: (*left*) prime ministers Zhu Rongji (*left*) and Li Peng (*right*); and (*right*) Communist Party leaders Hu Jintao (*left*) and Jiang Zemin (*right*).

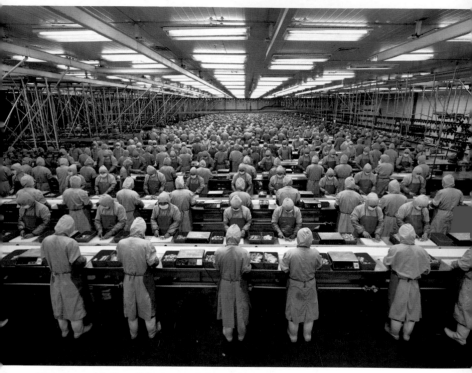

Global assembly line: China's mix of cheap labour, capital and productivity transformed the nation – and the world. Here, a chicken-processing plant in the north-east.

under peacetime conditions or the development of a socialist commodity economy.' Power needed to be redistributed within the system. 'We should not require unanimity in everything,' he added.[6]

Zhao also enunciated a doctrine that China had to use whatever means it could find to move through the first stage of its development. 'The state regulates the market; the market guides the enterprise,' he proclaimed. Private markets should be established for property, labour, funds, technology and information. He showed the seriousness of his intentions by closing down the leftist ideological journal Red Flag, and pushing through a plan to remove portraits of Marx, Engels, Lenin and Stalin from Tiananmen after the PRC's fortieth anniversary in 1989. In advance, two Mao statues were hauled away from the Beijing University campus in the middle of the night.[7]

The new Party secretary's authority appeared to be enhanced when nine old members of the twenty-man Politburo announced that they would retire; among them were Chen Yun, Li Xiannian, Peng Zhen – and Deng Xiaoping himself. Younger men, including Li Peng, moved up. At the same time, the Central Committee was reduced from 385 full and alternate members to 285, 42 per cent of whom were new. Deng said he wanted to pass the chairmanship of the Military Affairs Commission to Zhao, but the PLA refused to agree as it had with Hu. Deng did not want an army nominee. So he stayed on.

Zhao would have liked to have been able to run both the Party and the government, establishing himself as the clear successor to the Paramount Leader. But the old men, some of whom had reacted badly to the eclipse of Little Deng, mustered for yet another stand. They had reason to be apprehensive. Not only was Zhao in the ascendant, but the new voting system in the Party, with its internal competition, posed a new threat – as well as Little Deng's discomfiture, Chen Yun's son failed to win a place on the Beijing Party Committee.

So the conservatives dug in their feet when it came to the question of the premiership. Deng favoured the economic reformer Wan Li, who had made his mark in Anhui and filled in for Zhao in his absences. Zhao favoured his close associate Tian Jiyun. The old guard settled on Zhou Enlai's foster son, Li Peng, who had joined the Standing Committee of the Politburo in 1987. Given the stand-off between Wan and Tian, Deng concluded that 'Li is the only candidate acceptable to all sides.' According to the reformist Ruan Ming, Zhao thought that Li was 'not very capable or very quick, and that he would be easy to handle', particularly with Tian as a vice-premier.[8]

But the dour Soviet-trained technocrat, both of whose parents had been killed by the Nationalists, steadily accrued power. Nobody could doubt his devotion to the Party, or his strict orthodoxy. After returning from the Moscow Power Institute in 1954, he had worked in the energy sector in China, also becoming a municipal politician in Beijing, and then moving on to the national stage as minister of power, where he championed the construction of the massive dam across the Three Gorges on the Yangzi. Li personified order, a master of the bureaucracy who found it impossible to relax in public and filled his speeches with routine rhetoric. Fifty-nine at the time of his elevation to the premiership, he might not be a shooting star, but would prove a tough obstacle to Zhao's liberalizing instincts with backing from the old Party leaders.

Zhao's authority was, in any case, circumscribed by a move agreed behind the scenes, which was kept secret for two years. On stepping down from the Politburo, Chen, Bo Yibo and other Elders moved to the Central Advisory Committee Deng had set up as a place to park his old comrades. In fact, it provided them with a forum from which to watch the activities of the new generation. Their potential to influence events was underlined by the secret provision that they could 'control and supervise leaders at the highest levels in Party and Government'.*

This was unconstitutional. Deng, himself, did not hold any senior Party or government posts so had no formal authority to make such a decision. Most of the Elders were no longer in office. The move might have been merely a matter of recognizing reality as far as the supreme leader, himself, was concerned, but it also served to reassure Chen and his associates that they would be able to have a continuing say in policy.

The Elders, who included a sole woman, Zhou Enlai's widow, Deng Yingchao, had belonged to different groups, and had followed different trajectories; but they were a solidly anti-progressive bloc devoted to defending the achievements of the revolution as they defined them, drawing on the past that they represented to ensure that it shaped the future. The Advisory Committee could be seen as a ploy to dissuade them from factional agitation against Deng's policies. But it was also a

---

* The other old comrade, Ye Jianying, died in October 1986.

sign that, even at the height of his power, the leader felt the need to balance out those around him in search of unity.

If they wanted immediate ammunition, the economic conservatives could point to the effects of reform. By the end of 1987, inflation and the money supply were spiralling out of control. People got significantly better off as a whole during the second half of the 1980s – average annual cash incomes in cities and rural areas rose significantly. But demand in urban areas was rising even faster.[9]

In the first quarter of 1988, fresh-vegetable prices rose by almost 50 per cent. Rationing was introduced for pork, eggs and sugar as real incomes fell. A poll in thirty-three cities showed that prices were the main concern of 70 per cent of those questioned. Corruption and the black market thrived. A vignette in the first issue of *China Consumer News* showed how the new system worked at grassroots level. It reported from a town in which street vendors were tipped off when consignments of cigarettes arrived. They bought all the supply, and sold it at a profit, insisting that buyers also purchase a packet of otherwise unsaleable smokes. The reporter asked one of the sellers why the state bureau was not dealing with the matter; 'his whispered reply – after a few moments of hesitation – was that the vendors were all relatives of cadres at the bureau and the state-run shops.' The shops won prizes for the speed with which they sold their stocks.[10]

The scale of profiteering was such that an announcement of the expulsion of 150,000 CCP members, most for corruption, did not make the intended impact. Only 97 of the total were at or above provincial level. A survey of 600,000 workers reported that just 7 per cent thought the clean-up campaigns had produced a better spirit in the Party, while another poll ranked cadres in the bottom third of professionals. The official theoretical journal, *Seeking Truth*, described graft by cadres as an ulcer feeding off a 'sick system'.

A fresh campaign against corrupt firms hit mainly little enterprises that could not defend themselves, and left the major players unscathed. Officials who were charged usually had their trials postponed indefinitely, or the accusations were dropped. The four biggest conglomerates, which had appointed senior former Party and government bosses to lucrative posts, went on with business as usual – one was reported to have a branch producing erotica. As so often in China's modern history, it was a case of the centre proclaiming that 'something must be done' and those responsible for implementation on the ground turning a blind eye, and often actually drawing profit from the graft.[11]

In the cities, factory reform led to hundreds of thousands of workers being laid off. Under the pressure of rising prices for supplies, a growing number of TVEs went under, while half of all state enterprises did not pay full taxes. China was booming and imploding at the same time under a system that could not cope with its own growth.

Rising crime and outbreaks of mass violence – including a soccer riot in Sichuan – shook society. Gangs held up buses and trains, like the bandits of old. Factory managers were attacked. The press of serious cases was such that the power to hand down death sentences was delegated from the central judicial authority in Beijing to provincial courts.

Conservatives could point to the crime rate as a sign that everything was going rotten. They also took offence at a widely watched six-part television documentary, *River Elegy*, which used the slow-moving waters of the Yellow River as a metaphor for the country. The programmes set off a debate in the leadership, with Zhao said to approve of them. When a ban was eventually imposed, the discussion had gone on for so long that the whole series had been aired.

There were also problems with some development projects which were pushed ahead in the early stages of reform and proved to have been badly constructed. A survey reported that many were in a dangerous state. Investment in water control and irrigation had fallen. So had pest control. The amount of arable land declined steadily through erosion and as farmers concentrated on only the most productive fields or built on terrain they had taken into their own ownership; the total was said to have dropped by 1.25 million hectares a year. The momentum seemed to be going out of rural progress; one journal wrote of a 'silent crisis' looming in the countryside.[12]

A regular visitor to the city of Guangzhou noted the changes there, for good and bad. In 1980, hardly anyone appeared overweight; by the end of the decade, obesity was officially recognized as a health issue. In 1980, plastic bags were a highly prized commodity; now they constituted a waste problem. Then, the Nanfang Department Store offered only basic goods; now, it had a section for video games and cassettes. Living space had doubled; there were no longer quality problems with cups whose handles came off or drinking glasses that disintegrated in one's hand – or leaky bicycle tyres. That was all very good for the inhabitants of Guangzhou, but in many areas conditions were still closer to those of 1980, and news of material progress in growth zones fostered resentment in villages that consisted of mud huts without running water or electricity. The two-speed society which was to mark contemporary China was being steadily forged.[13]

Students staged fresh demonstrations against prices and grants that did not keep pace with inflation. In the first six months of 1988, there were rallies on seventy-seven campuses in twenty-five cities. Weekly sessions were held to discuss the future of China and promote democratic ideas. At Beida University in the capital, Wang Dan, a thin first-year history undergraduate with thick glasses and lanky hair, emerged as a major voice, quoted by the foreign reporters who attended the meetings.

In the leadership, an argument broke out about price liberalization. Li Peng worried about its inflationary effect, but Deng was in favour and Zhao fell into line with him. When news of the impending policy became known, people rushed to the shops to buy everything they could while controls were still in effect. Interest rates were raised to 13 per cent, but that was still seven points below inflation. A run on the banks began. Older people recalled the hyper-inflation of the late Nationalist years.[14]

Recognizing reality, Deng switched course, and the scheme was shelved. Zhao shouldered the blame, making a self-criticism in front of the Politburo and State Council. At the end of 1988, the conservatives were sufficiently emboldened for Chen Yun to issue the first of eight critiques of Zhao's leadership, accusing him of having allowed 'almost all proletarian ideological bridgeheads [to be] occupied by bourgeois ideologies'. 'It is time for us to counter-attack,' Chen was reported to have told his associates.[15]

The context looked promising for the conservatives given the problems the new economic policy was throwing up. Inflation remained high. Farmers who had stayed with grain were doing less well than those who had diversified into higher cash crops or joined TVEs. State sector industrial workers, civil servants, intellectuals and scholars were left behind financially, and felt resentful. The gap widened steadily between the coastal provinces and the interior. Despite warnings from Deng to watch their step, independent-minded provinces set local economic policies, varying taxes and offering incentives to foreign investors. In a sign of the pace of change, 360,000 new trading companies were set up between 1986 and 1988. For the bulk of the population, there was the psychological challenge of seeing old certainties swept away. But little had been done to prepare a people bred and beaten into accepting the post-1949 system for something so radically different in economic and social terms.[16]

Deng's insistence on combating bourgeois liberalism reflected the ideological void at the heart of the regime. Maoism had been ditched, but the Four Cardinal Principles he had put in its place as the guiding light for the future were redolent of the past. The first bracketed Mao Zedong Thought with Marxism and Leninism as the doctrine to pursue. Then came adherence to Socialism, the dictatorship of the proletariat and the leadership of the Communist Party. It was an uninspiring mix, at odds with the leader's radicalism in economic matters, and meant that, when challenges came, the only answer could be force, as so often in China's history.

Some of Zhao's supporters sought a way out of the Party's political–economic conundrum by adopting the theory of 'neo-authoritarianism' enunciated by the American political scientist Samuel Huntingdon – though the author denied it applied to China. Looking to South Korea and Singapore, this argued that a strong central power was needed to break down the barriers of bureaucracy and ensure the implementation of a reform agenda. As one young economist put it, in terms that might have come from the Hundred Days of the late Qing, the policy should be to use 'liberal totalitarianism to maintain stability and eradicate the obstacles to freedom'. Modernization of a country like China had to go through a phase in which 'strong, authoritarian leaders . . . serve as the motivating force for change,' Zhao explained to Deng.[17]

'I quite agree with this notion,' the leader replied. 'But the specific phrasing has to be refined.'

Zhao's notions repelled intellectuals who favoured democracy, and deprived him of wholehearted support from that quarter. His approach was hardly helped when Dai Qing, a missile scientist who was the adopted daughter of Marshal Ye Jianying, praised Chiang Kai-shek's son, Chiang Ching-kuo, for having used his authoritarian power to open the way for democracy in Taiwan, where the post-1949 martial law had been lifted and opponents of the KMT proclaimed the foundation of the Democratic Progressive Party in September 1986.

China already had a strong leader, and, however much he shed official positions, Deng had no intention of stepping back in favour of Zhao in fundamental matters. At the same time, he grew concerned at the signs of the unravelling of the Soviet empire in Eastern Europe and the course the USSR was taking under Mikhail Gorbachev. This came at a time of renewed activity by Chinese liberals and students: posters at a Sichuan university blamed the CCP for inequality, inflation and deteriorating living conditions. A series of polls showed widespread alienation from the system and declining support for economic reform among the young. Most of those questioned in one youth survey believed that 'social ethics are worse this year than last.' This, the report warned, could 'lead to aberrant political behaviour'.[18]

The one political initiative of the time came far from the universities and centres of urban liberalism, in the countryside. Elections of village councils, held every three years, began in 1988. The aim was to give local inhabitants greater control over daily affairs, reducing the influence of provincial authorities. The outcome was much disputed. In some places, farmers did make their feelings felt, but, in most, Communist cadres dominated the process, and went on ruling as before. Though there was some screening out of Party candidates, no real political competition to the CCP was allowed. A few elected officials stood up to township cadres; many others simply played along with the superior power structure. The village elections would continue, aided by the Carter Foundation of the United States; yet they were, at best, only a small step towards democracy, and certainly not intended to weaken the Communist hold on power. In the next century, the lack of grassroots electoral democracy and the continuing power of officials and of provincial administrations would be shown in tens of thousands of annual protests and severe shortcomings in health, education and welfare provision in the countryside.[19]

At the end of 1988, liberals launched a campaign on behalf of political prisoners and in favour of democracy. Ren Wanding, the worker who had been imprisoned after Democracy Wall and had been released in 1983, directed a four-page appeal to the United Nations, Amnesty International and the Hong Kong Commission for Human Rights calling for them to investigate the conditions of democracy advocates who were still in prison. In an open letter to Deng, the scientist Fang Lizhi added his voice to the appeal for the release of detainees, including Wei

Jingsheng. In early 1989, thirty-three scholars and writers, including the makers of the programme *River Elegy*, signed a petition organized by the poet Bei Dao backing up Fang's call, followed by a similar appeal by forty-four academics and scientists to the Standing Committee of the Politburo and other leaders.[20]

At a conference sponsored by the CCP Propaganda Department and the Chinese Academy of Social Sciences (CASS), a senior theoretician, Su Shaozhi, criticized the campaign against spiritual pollution and bourgeois liberalism, and called for the reexamination of the cases of two editors at the *People's Daily* who had suffered under Little Deng's onslaughts. The department tried to prevent the speech being reported, but it appeared in the reform-minded *World Economic Herald* in Shanghai. The leading intellectual newspaper, the *Guangming Daily*, ran editorials arguing that China needed to draw lessons from Western democracy.

A further incident which attracted international attention occurred when, at the suggestion of the US embassy in Beijing, Fang Lizhi was invited to a banquet given at the Great Wall Sheraton Hotel by President George Bush during a brief visit to Beijing. Bush had headed the US liaison office in Beijing from 1974 to 1976, and, in the White House, maintained the good relations with the PRC established by his predecessors, despite controversy over China's supply of missiles to Iran and Saudi Arabia. Washington felt obliged to impose economic sanctions, but they were mild – certainly not enough to disrupt the Bush visit.

Though his briefing papers noted Fang's dissident status, the president does not appear to have been aware of the trouble the invitation could cause, even after it had been reported in the *Los Angeles Times*. But the Chinese Foreign Ministry warned the ambassador, Winston Lord, that, if Fang turned up at the dinner, the Chinese leaders present would boycott the occasion. Told of this on *Air Force One* as he headed for China, Bush is said to have shouted at his advisers 'Who is Fang Lizhi?'

Lord, who had been part of Kissinger's team in the initial contacts with the PRC, negotiated a compromise by which Fang would attend the dinner, but would be placed inconspicuously at the back of the room, where the leaders would not see him. Bush would not make the usual round of the tables with a toast, so that there would be no chance of him and the scientist coming face to face. While these points were being worked out, the president met Li Peng, presenting him with a pair of black leather cowboy boots with a US flag on one and a Chinese flag on the other; the premier responded with Flying Pigeon bicycles for the visitor and his wife. When Bush tried to get an undertaking from Li not to send missiles to the Middle East, the reply was meaninglessly vague.[21]

On the night of 26 February 1989, Fang Lizhi and his wife set out for the hotel in the car of an American academic, Perry Link. After two blocks, police stopped the vehicle for a supposed traffic violation. Fang and his companions began to walk towards the Sheraton. Police halted them. The scientist showed his invitation. That did no good. They got into a taxi, which was stopped. Fang tried to board a bus; security officers told the driver not to let him on. The group walked to a flat from where they telephoned the US embassy, only to be told the dinner was over.[22]

Fang held a press conference at which he said that the trouble the regime had taken to stop him showed its weakness. As he left China, the president expressed 'regret' over the barring of Fang, but, when the party got back to Washington, Brent Scowcroft, the National Security Adviser, held an off-the-record briefing that blamed the episode on Lord, who objected with an angry note to the White House. Less than three weeks later, he was replaced as ambassador by a Bush confidant and former CIA station chief in Beijing, James Lilley.

Washington had another cause for concern in the steady warming of relations between Beijing and Moscow as Mikhail Gorbachev made placatory noises on frontier issues and announced partial troop withdrawals from Mongolia and Afghanistan. The USSR understood and respected China's modernization goals, Gorbachev added. In an interview with the US television journalist Mike Wallace, Deng said that, if the obstacles to Sino-Soviet relations were removed, 'I shall be ready to . . . go to any place in the Soviet Union to meet with Gorbachev.' As it turned out, it was the Russian who would make the trip; May 1989 was fixed as the date for him to go to the PRC.[23]

The fuss over Fang Lizhi enabled conservatives to argue that the Americans were trying to use political liberals to interfere in China's internal affairs. Needing to buttress his position, and probably genuinely concerned at the incident, Zhao attacked Western criticism of his country's human rights record. The publisher of the liberal Shanghai newspaper World Economic Herald was summoned to Beijing, where he promised to wait for six months before printing anything by any of the signatories of the petition calling for release of political prisoners. A dissident, Chen Jun, who had joined in the campaign, was expelled to Hong Kong. When one of the editors of the Democracy Wall journal, *April Fifth Forum*, was freed after eight years in jail, he was ordered not to write for three years – for part of his time in jail, he had been kept alone in a six-foot-square cell with the light on twenty-four hours a day for having passed a note to another prisoner. Both his two co-editors remained inside; one had been in solitary with no visits since 1985.[24]

Still, three of the Elders – Bo Yibo, Wang Zhen and Li Xiannian – launched an attack on Zhao, suggesting to Deng that he should be forced to resign at a Party Plenum in March 1989. Deng declined, as he had before, again reportedly on the grounds that he had already lost one Party chief in the person of Hu and had no replacement to hand.

There was also evidence of the regime's repressive force when unrest broke out in Tibet after the death of the second-highest-ranking spiritual figure, the Panchen Lama. Beijing arranged to have a suitable boy candidate picked as his successor, but the Tibetans preferred another. There had been disturbances in both 1987 and 1988 after the PRC rejected a peace plan advanced by the Dalai Lama and turned down his suggestion that a 'one country, two systems' policy similar to that proposed for Hong Kong should be applied to his homeland.

Now, a rising in Lhasa in March 1989 led Beijing to declare martial law at the suggestion of the new CCP chief in Tibet, the 46-year-old former Qinghua University student Hu Jintao, who had survived the Cultural Revolution to become a Party functionary and had been sent to the remote territory after blotting his copybook by refusing to join in full-blooded criticism of Hu Yaobang. He handled the situation there to maximum personal advantage, donning a helmet and anti-riot gear to show his toughness while leaving himself a political escape route in case things went wrong. An estimated 200 protestors were killed, and thousands arrested, but, for Beijing, the operation was a great success. Among those impressed was Deng, though Hu Jintao soon put a distance between himself and Tibet for health reasons – he suffered from altitude sickness and did his job by remote control from Beijing.[25]

By the spring of 1989, therefore, a high level of tension had built up in the leadership, and among important sections of the population. As always, much of China was not directly affected. But the spread of mass media and greater personal mobility meant that information was distributed far more than before. The problems thrown up by growth were widespread, and unmistakable. Cities suffered from power cuts due to inadequate grid supplies. Factories in Shanghai went on a three- to four-day week and those in Jiangxi cut back to two days. The lights even went out sometimes in Tiananmen Square.

General crime shot up; at 560,000, the number of cases in the first quarter of 1989 was greater than for the whole of 1985. Convictions for corruption and bribery were 27 per cent higher than the previous year. In Hunan, the Party Committee reported many complaints of bandits, robbery and lawlessness – 'even murder seems no more serious than slaughtering a chicken.' Prostitution had returned, the report went on, while gambling, clan battles, and fights over land and water had reached levels unprecedented since 1949. There was even trouble in the prison camps. Eleven major riots broke out at such establishments in Xinjiang in 1988–9; in one, in the desert, prisoners armed with knives and hammers killed guards, took hostages and burned buildings.[26]

The fault lines – particularly the gap between market economic growth and political immobilism, and the lack of safety valves – created an ever-growing potential for confrontation. The regime still held back from seeking greater political legitimacy. A showdown of some kind was inevitable. All that was needed was a spark, which came from an unexpected event in the spring of 1989.

29
Beijing Spring

On the morning of 8 April 1989, the Politburo met for what appeared to be a routine session, with Zhao Ziyang in the chair. Down the table sat his predecessor as Party chief, Hu Yaobang, demoted but not cast out. The chairman of the Education Commission, Li Tieying, whose mother had become Deng Xiaoping's wife, delivered a briefing. As he did so, according to the secret official account, others present noticed that Hu looked unwell, his face pinched and ashen. A rumour that he had been engaged in a fierce argument with Bo Yibo does not figure in the internal report. Nor does a story that the Wei Jingsheng case was on the agenda, and that Hu became upset at the intolerance of his colleagues. The report simply says that, after some forty-five minutes, the former Party chief rose to his feet to ask permission to leave, but then collapsed back into his chair.[1]

'Comrade Ziyang,' he said, his voice trailing as he gestured in the air.

Everybody else stood up and stared at Hu, somebody saying he had probably had a recurrence of an earlier heart attack.

Zhao asked if anybody present had nitro-glycerine to deal with such a case; one did, and Hu was fed two pills. Medical staff arrived from a nearby hospital in ten minutes and he was taken off for treatment. His condition stabilized, but, a week later during a visit by his family, he suffered another massive attack, dying on 15 April. Told the news, Deng Xiaoping ground out his cigarette and crossed his hands weakly on his chest. Then he lit another cigarette and puffed at it fiercely.[2]

Zhao Ziyang summoned another Politburo session, at which his assessment of Hu was adopted. It described the dead man as 'a loyal, tried and tested Communist fighter, a great proletarian revolutionary and politician, an outstanding political worker for our army and a prominent leader' – no mention of his ousting or the errors with which he had been charged.

According to the inside account of the period contained in the *Tiananmen Papers*, some members of the leadership were immediately concerned that mourning for Hu might spill over into protests, with senior vice-premier Yao Yilin warning of rising prices and the growing gap between rich and poor, while Li Peng said a close eye should be kept on universities since 'college students are always the most sensitive.' The education boss, Li Tieying, was reassuring: 'Things are good at the universities,' he told the meeting. 'It's not very likely there'll be any trouble.' Qiao Shi, who had taken over from Peng Zhen in charge of security matters, advised that 'Society's in pretty good shape. Things are fairly stable.'[3]

The mourning soon began in Tiananmen Square, Shanghai, Nanjing, Tianjin and Xi'an. Hu was remembered and venerated not so much for what he had done, but for what he represented. Like Sun Yat-sen, he was transformed in death into an icon. His admirer, the intellectual and speechwriter Ruan Ming, regarded him as 'the last reformer in the Party . . . a sacrificial lamb to the hypocritical and corrupt palatial totalitarian politics'. On the Beijing University campus, a poem was posted:

> The honest man is dead.
> The hypocrites live on:
> The enthusiasm is dead;
> Indifference buried him
> Hollow words, futility, mah-jong, bridge.[4]

The protests feared by conservatives began to take shape as students marched into Tiananmen Square bearing banners and shouting slogans in favour of democracy, freedom and the rule of law. By mid-afternoon on 17 April, their numbers had reached 10,000. 'Hu Yaobang's death made it possible for a crowd to gather in a public place, and gave them something to discuss,' the labour activist Han Dongfang observed. 'And that led to discussions of all kinds of other issues . . . In a crowd, [people] felt it was safe to let off steam. Often, someone would rant and rave and then quickly disappear back into the crowd.' Or, as another participant told the correspondent of the London *Times*: 'That is really a pretext. We came here because we have something to say. I don't think we'll achieve anything, but it's better to do something than nothing.'[5]

Growing less sanguine, Li Tieying told Zhao Ziyang and Li Peng that he was hearing about worrying trends. Zhao replied that the students were patriotic; reason should be the leadership's watchword. But Li Peng telephoned the mayor of Beijing, Chen Xitong, to ask what was going on in Tiananmen. The municipal government reported that some demonstrators were 'highly emotional'. Among more than 700 posters that had gone up on university campuses were 'inflammatory attacks on the current state of society'. Vice-premier Yao Yilin warned that advocates of bourgeois liberalism would exploit the student movement for their own ends. The Education Commission issued a national order for university officials to 'carry out painstaking thought work to strengthen the guidance of students . . . [and] keep a clear head in dealing with certain people with ulterior motives'.[6]

Thus, from the start, conservatives in the leadership were reacting to popular feeling by detecting the presence of 'black hand' conspirators, and envisaging repressive measures rather than dialogue. It was a tradition which stretched back to the purges in the Jiangxi base and which, however great the relaxation since Mao's death, was still central to the mindset of those running the PRC. Not that they were mistaken at the challenge they faced. The elementary rights and freedoms being called for in Tiananmen were a visceral threat to the regime, and to the leaders' purchase on power. So a confrontation was inevitable. The question was whether it would take a soft form, as favoured by Zhao, or whether a combination of entrenched hardline power at the centre and the insistence of the student leadership on maximum demands would bring tragedy.

The students, as they were well aware, were heirs to a long tradition. They enjoyed a special place in society, their dissent generally regarded more indulgently than that of workers or peasants. Under the empire, they had been trained to act as watchdogs of the Mandate of Heaven, set apart by their learning. In 1895, they had staged the first mass demonstration in Beijing in protest at the treaty with Japan. In 1919, they had set off the May Fourth movement, the seventieth anniversary of which was looming. In the warlord era and under the Republic, they had spearheaded Nationalist demonstrations, and at the end of the KMT period, universities had been a major focus for opposition. From 1966 to 1976, they were the shock troops of the Cultural Revolution, Mao's 'little devils'.

As the original student leaders, including Wang Dan from Beijing

University, discussed the situation, more demonstrators from various colleges in the capital arrived in the square during the evening and night of 17 April. They marched behind a big banner in white – the Chinese colour of mourning – and festooned the imposing Heroes' Monument in the square with wreaths.[7]

At dawn on 18 April, several hundred undergraduates mounted a sit-in in front of the Great Hall of the People. They demanded that the leadership back Hu's views on freedom and democracy, admit that the campaigns against spiritual pollution and bourgeois liberalization had been wrong, publish information on the incomes of state leaders and their families, allow private newspapers and freedom of speech, raise funding for education and the pay of intellectuals, lift restrictions on demonstrations in Beijing and hold democratic elections to replace those who made bad decisions. Low-ranking officials came out from the Hall to talk to student leaders. But the protestors were not satisfied, and stayed put, joined by thousands of others flooding into the square.

Zhao remained cool. When the 82-year-old president, Yang Shangkun, asked by telephone what he thought about the student action, the Party chief replied, 'On the whole, I think we should affirm the students' patriotism.'

Some of the demonstrators advanced from Tiananmen Square to the Xinhua Gate of the Zhongnanhai leadership compound. Zhao ordered the guard to be stepped up to ensure security, but told the soldiers to remove their bayonets and avoid physical contact with the students. His aide, Wen Jiabao, the director of the Central Party Office, went to the gate to oversee operations.

At noon on 19 April, more than a thousand students marched into the square shouting 'Yaobang will not die!', 'Be done with dictatorship!' During the day other students joined them. A banner reading 'the Soul of China' was hung on the Heroes' Monument, and undergraduates at the Central Academy of Fine Arts placed a giant portrait of Hu beneath it, with a sign asking, 'How can we revive his spirit?' Despite the rain, a huge crowd stayed in the square to listen to speeches by student leaders.

That night, demonstrators moved once more to the Xinhua gate, where they sang the Internationale and scuffled with police, watched by a crowd of 10,000. 'What's going on?' former president Li Xiannian asked Li Peng by telephone. 'Is someone orchestrating this from behind the scenes?' A report from the Beijing Municipal Party Committee warned that events were taking a new course, with demonstrators 'slipping political ideas into mourning activities', using 'reactionary language', and shouting slogans attacking the leadership. These included 'Down with corrupt government!' and 'Down with the Communist Party!' and even 'Attack Zhongnanhai! Torch Zhongnanhai!' Wall posters urged students to go to factories, shops and the countryside to mobilize the masses.[8]

On 20 April, autonomous student associations were established to take the place of the official bodies, with the Beida undergraduate Wang Dan among those on a seven-person leadership committee. One of the initial demands was the liberation of Wei Jingsheng. Class boycotts began. A Beijing Workers' Autonomous Federation was set up. It backed the students and blamed 'dictatorial bureaucrats' for inflation, falling living standards and misappropriation of funds. Its manifesto called on police to stand on the side of the people and justice. The workers' movement was, as yet, small, but it would grow, as would the involvement of the citizens of the capital.

In the first crackdown that same day, 20 April, police detained more than 400 students in a residential area near the Beijing University campus, and beat unconscious a student as he walked away from the Great Hall of the People to take the underground back to college. Hundreds more continued to move into Tiananmen through the rain, some wearing white flowers and carrying banners reading 'Summon the spirit of democracy and freedom' and 'Root out corrupt officials.'

Late that night, students from the Central Academy of Drama joined the demonstrators, carrying helium balloons marked with the words 'Yaobang will never die' – police confiscated them. At the same time, 2,000–3,000 students gathered at the Xinhua Gate, watched by a crowd of Beijing citizens. 'Li Peng, come out!' they shouted as they made six attempts to break through the security line guarding the entrance. Shortly after midnight, police shepherded the onlookers several hundred yards away. The Beijing municipality declared temporary martial law, ordering the students to be taken back to their campuses in buses. A hundred or so refused to be moved, fighting with security forces before they were pushed on to the vehicles.

Conservatives in the leadership were thoroughly alarmed by now, and looked for 'black hands' to explain the revolt since they could not admit that it was the system itself which was at fault. 'With Beijing in chaos like this, we've got to guard against a second Cultural Revolution,' Peng

Zhen, the one-time boss of the capital, warned his successor in charge of the city, Chen Xitong. 'These students are in rebellion,' 'Big Cannon' Wang Zhen told Deng Xiaoping: 'We've got to do something right away!' 'We should approve of the students' patriotism, but must expose the people with ulterior motives who are prodding them to cause trouble,' Zhou Enlai's widow advised her husband's adopted son, Li Peng.[9]

The movement spread out to other cities. Students boycotted classes in Wuhan, Nanjing, Tianjin and Shanghai. In Changsha, vandals took advantage of demonstrations to loot. In Xi'an, a 10,000-strong crowd set fire to part of the provincial government building and its car park. A crowd of similar size in Nanjing interfered with traffic, and shouted slogans outside the provincial CCP headquarters such as 'Shedding blood doesn't matter; freedom is the most valuable thing.' In Wuhan, the Party Committee noted how political the protests were, with strong attacks on the government and Party.[10]

In the first report by state media, the television broadcast an official statement deploring the unrest. Reacting to the attempted breakthrough at the Xinhua Gate, the *People's Daily* ran an editorial headlined 'Maintenance of Social Stability is the Prime Concern'. Students burned copies of the newspaper. On Deng's orders, 9,000 soldiers from the 38th Army stationed outside the capital moved into the city to reinforce the police and escort Hu's hearse to the cemetery.

In a play on Deng's name, Beijing University students smashed bottles – a homonym of *ping* means 'bottle'. They called for proper press coverage of what was going on, and demanded 'severe punishment of those responsible'. At the Political Science and Law College, the bloody clothes of the student who had been beaten on his way to the underground were put on display. Leaflets asked if the laws allowed the police to behave in such a manner – 'Have they no brothers and sisters of their own?'

An official report noted 'four major disturbances' in Tiananmen on 21 April.* In the most serious, several thousand people broke through the police cordon round the Great Hall and mounted the steps before being driven back. The report described the crowd as 'onlookers' who had blindly rushed after foreign correspondents and students, indicating that Beijing citizens were taking an active part in the protests.[11]

---

* The official reports cited and accounts of leadership meetings that follow are taken from the *Tiananmen Papers* as noted.

No sooner had the demonstrators been pushed back than students who had just arrived by train from Tianjin paraded from the station to the square with a huge portrait of Hu, handing out copies of a petition demanding competitive elections, freedom of the press, reform of the selection of members of the National People's Congress, and clear separation of the legislature from the CCP. The official report noted that they attracted a crowd of 40,000–50,000 people, whose emotions rose to 'fever pitch'. The Democracy Wall activist Ren Wanding appeared in the square to proclaim that 'The people are praying for the country to wake up to the rule of law.' Police tried to detain him but were blocked by demonstrators.

That night, nearly 10,000 students staged a fresh march to Tiananmen, shouting, 'Down with official profiteering!', 'Long live democracy!', 'Oppose dictatorship!' and 'Patriotism is no crime.' The official report noted that they were stimulated by applause from crowds on the pavements, and began to shout, 'Long live the people!' and 'What are we doing? We're telling the truth.' The onlookers provided cups of hot water for the students to drink.

Up to 100,000 people gathered in silence in the square outside the Great Hall for the memorial service to Hu Yaobang, which was held inside the huge, squat building on the morning of 22 April. Police began to move into place at 5 a.m. Deng looked 'grey, bloated and stunned', in the words of a Western reporter. Big Cannon Wang Zhen urged him to tell the police to chase the protestors away. Deng demurred.[12]

As the leaders left, with the security chief Qiao Shi and Standing Committee ideologue Hu Qili accompanying the coffin to the cemetery, students chanted, 'Dialogue, dialogue, we demand dialogue' and 'Li Peng, come out.' At the door, Zhao Ziyang reminded Deng that he was leaving for North Korea the following day, and suggested how to handle the protests. The students should be got back to classes immediately, and legal proceedings should be used to 'punish severely all who indulge in beating,* smashing and robbing'. The core approach should be persuasion, and 'multi-level dialogues'. 'Good,' Deng replied. Zhao relayed

---

* By this, he meant demonstrators who fought police, not the other way round. The phraseology Zhao used was that applied to Red Guard activity in the Cultural Revolution, and so was additionally pejorative.

this to colleagues. In his absence, he added, Li Peng would take charge of the Party Centre.[13]

Word spread among the students that they would get an audience with the leadership, but they were kept waiting, and it is not clear whether any such undertaking was actually given. Three of the demonstrators mounted the steps of the Great Hall, and went on their knees in the fashion of imperial petitioners. One held up their demands on a scroll. Behind them, rows of police sat on the ground. Some people in the crowd threw their shoes in protest. In the early afternoon, complaining at not having been received, angry students surged towards the Great Hall, but were driven back. Only one newspaper, the *Science and Technology Daily*, reported the protests – its editor was sacked and the publication was shut down. From the provinces came news of more violence in Xi'an and Changsha, where ninety-eight people were arrested; Xinhua news agency said most were workers or farmers. In Shanghai, an edition of the liberal *World Economic Herald* which criticized the treatment of Hu was banned.[14]

Later in the day, the Politburo decided to end the mourning period for Hu, not to reverse the verdict on him and to insist on the correctness of the campaign against bourgeois liberalism. Zhao was reported to have dissented from this decision, but he was outvoted. Though Deng's paramount position was unchallenged, the leadership was increasingly factionalized, like an old imperial court.

In the Politburo, hardline conservatives headed by Chen Yun and the propaganda director, Wang Renzhi, had Li Peng as their man for the future. Dogmatists such as Little Deng lurked on the sidelines. The military faction included Wang Zhen and President Yang Shangkun, Deng's representative in the Standing Committee of the Politburo. Yang's cousin was a member of the Central Military Commission, and some foresaw the emergence of a Yang clan aiming for even greater authority.

The president, one of the 'Eight Immortals' of the Communist regime, was already as powerful as anybody below Deng. Both from Sichuan, the two men had grown close during their time at Yenan. Yang had been imprisoned and struggled against repeatedly during the Cultural Revolution. After Deng's ascension to power, he held a series of senior posts and was installed as number two on the Military Commission, outranking Zhao Ziyang.

Enjoying a personal friendship with Deng, the old soldier could go to the leader's home at will. He was likely to be the figure most able to influence the Paramount Leader, if he wished to. His attitude towards Zhao is a matter of dispute. Though the reformer Ruan Ming described him and Wang as staring at the Party chief during the memorial for Hu like 'vicious tigers stalking their prey', other historians see him as having been closer to Zhao than other members of the Politburo Standing Committee, and the record shows him seeking to act as a mediator at several key moments.[15]

The Party secretary's sole firm backing was from the 'new authoritarian' group who saw him as the only man who could handle both the economic task and the challenges presented by the protests. Political reformers were even more isolated, divided between maximalists and those ready to compromise to gain central support. The fall and death of Hu Yaobang, and Zhao's need to play a cautious political game if he was to continue economic change, greatly weakened those who argued for relaxation. Ruan Ming likened them to 'a wandering nomadic tribe fighting in isolation on a narrow battlefront . . . their position in the CCP so marginal that they no longer carried any weight'.[16]

As a result, the torch of agitating for political reform was taken up by very different people far from the leadership, who would not be bound by the parameters of the Communist regime, as Hu had been. That enabled them to draw on a deep and broad well of support, since the discontent that mounted in 1989 came from outside the system, and could not be dealt with by any of the techniques honed by the CCP over the decades. The Party was isolated and unfitted to comprehend, but those who emerged to lead the new forces pressing for political change lacked any hold on the organs of power or the force at the disposal of the regime, or a clear and unified message of their own.

The day after the memorial to Hu, Zhao Ziyang departed on his scheduled week's trip to North Korea. His close aide, vice-premier Tian Jiyun, urged him not to leave the country at such a crucial moment, but Zhao replied that postponing the visit would lead foreigners to speculate that the political situation was shaky. So he took the train to Pyongyang on the afternoon of 23 April after instructing that newspapers were to emphasize the 'positive' side of the demonstrations.

At the first Politburo meeting called by Li Peng after Zhao's departure, a distinct change of tone was evident and was to persist, as recounted in the accounts published in the *Tiananmen Papers*. Deng had called the demonstrations 'disturbances'; now, Politburo members used the tougher term 'turmoil'. The mayor of Beijing, Chen Xitong, warned that student emissaries wanted to call a nationwide strike in schools and universities, and were seeking support from factory workers. 'No country can permit unruly freedom or irresponsible freedom,' Qiao Shi said. 'We are deep into a struggle with bourgeois liberalism,' Li warned.

A Small Group to Halt the Turmoil was formed, made up primarily of hardliners and with Li in the chair. It decided to circulate a list of counter-measures, and instruct the Beijing Municipal Committee to mobilize the masses. The students were organizing, too. Twenty-one universities formed a joint committee, and elected as its president one of the three young men who had knelt on the steps of the Great Hall, Zhou Yongjun of the Political Science and Law College in Beijing. This strengthened the autonomous movement and destroyed the government's hope of working through official university unions. At the founding meeting, Wang Dan said it was the greatest student movement since May Fourth, 1919, and showed the strength of the people. 'We're going to take back the power of democracy and freedom from that gang of old men who've grabbed power away from us,' he added.[17]

Demonstrations were reported from more than twenty large and medium-sized cities. Broadcasts by the Voice of America carried news of the latest events. Activists from the capital travelled to the provinces to spread the word. In Tianjin, 10,000 people marched in a procession stretching for a mile after being urged on by young people who had gone to Beijing for the Hu Yaobang memorial service. Police cleared the way for them. In Changsha, where posters reading 'Down with Deng Xiaoping' appeared, another outbreak of violence led to 138 arrests, mainly of non-students. In Xi'an, provincial authorities reported that 270 people had been detained for 'beating, smashing, robbing and burning' – two thirds of them were farmers, workers and the unemployed. In reaction, officials launched a Patriotism and Hygiene Month to clean posters from university walls.

To assess the situation, Li Peng, Chen Xitong, Qiao Shi and President Yang went to a meeting at Deng's home on the morning of 25 April. In Zhao's absence, his close aide, Bao Tong, was not told of the session. The premier personalized the threat by warning the Paramount Leader that 'the spear is now pointed directly at you and the others of the older generation of proletarian revolutionaries.'[18]

Deng was in an irascible mood. He complained about a suggestion from the dead man's family and liberals that Hu Yaobang should be officially described as 'a great Marxist'. 'Even when I die, they will not call me a great Marxist,' he groused. 'Who do they think that turtle egg* Yaobang was? . . . Hu Yaobang was irresolute and made concessions in combating bourgeois liberalism.'[19]

'We must take a clear-cut stand and forceful measures to oppose and stop the turmoil,' he declared. 'Don't be afraid of students, because we still have several million troops.' Citing the example of Poland, he added that the greater the concessions by government, the stronger the opposition became. 'This is no ordinary student movement,' Deng summed up. 'This is a well-planned plot whose real aim is to reject the Chinese Communist Party and the socialist system at the most fundamental level.'[20]

Li suggested that an editorial should be drafted for the *People's Daily* setting out the leader's line. The drafting was entrusted to Hu Qili, a one-time aide to Hu Yaobang, who was the Standing Committee member in charge of ideology but was a reformer. The result was regarded as insufficiently tough, calling the protests simply 'demonstrations'. It was reportedly Deng who substituted the killer word, 'turmoil'.

The article, which appeared on 26 April, would become a key point of conflict between the leadership and the demonstrators. Under the headline 'It is Necessary to Take a Clear-Cut Stand to Oppose Turmoil', it denounced a planned conspiracy by 'a small number of people with ulterior motives . . . to sow dissension among the people, plunge the entire country into chaos and sabotage the political situation of stability and unity'. They were fabricating rumours 'in an attempt to create greater unrest which in essence aims at negating the leadership of the Party and the Socialist system,' it added. 'This is a most serious political struggle that concerns the whole Party and nation.' From Pyongyang, Zhao sent a message expressing his 'complete support' when he was told of Deng's position, though he subsequently said he disavowed the article's thrust.[21]

The editorial was broadcast nationally and put out repeatedly on the

---

* A particularly offensive term in Chinese.

radio. Li told the Politburo it was 'an alarm bell against turmoil in the minds of all the people'. State television warned that protests would not be tolerated, and told workers not to participate. The Shanghai Party under the city's boss, Jiang Zemin, sacked the liberal editor of the *World Economic Herald*, which had just published an appeal for a re-evaluation of Hu and was preparing to run a full account of his dismissal. In Tiananmen, the wreaths for Hu were removed under cover of darkness.

Rather than inducing the students to buckle under, the editorial galvanized them into fresh action. The government line was attacked as being too harsh, the term 'turmoil' as unjustified and the switch away from the previous largely tolerant line as too sharp. All that was needed, the students argued, was for the authorities to open a dialogue with them. A major demonstration was staged which, to the surprise of the authorities, went straight past Tiananmen – 'we want to march around Beijing and let everyone know what we want,' a student explained. At one point, a police officer and his 400 men were engulfed – he gave a slight sign and the men melted into the crowd.[22]

Demonstrations against the editorial also took place in Changchun, Shanghai, Tianjin, Nanjing, Hangzhou, Xi'an, Changsha, Hefei, Shenyang, Dalian, Nanning, Kunming and Shenzhen. Three thousand students staged a sit-in in front of the Party Office in Jilin. Dissenting from the *People's Daily* line, authorities in Heilongjiang, Liaoning, Henan, Fujian, Jiangxi and Xinjiang said the climate in their provinces did not amount to turmoil, while some PLA reports noted that officers were hoping for the continuation of reform and the resolution of problems highlighted by students.[23]

In Beijing, another rally brought out 50,000 students, who called out to onlookers, 'Mama, we haven't done anything wrong.' 'Down with corrupt officials!' they chanted. 'Patriotism is not a crime!', 'Justice will prevail!', 'The press must tell the truth!' The people of the capital were on their side, and the use of Tiananmen Square, the PRC's symbolic centre, provided a unique platform both nationally and internationally as foreign correspondents fascinated by this turn in China's history reported with none of the inhibitions of the domestic media.[24]

The failure of the *People's Daily* editorial to end the protests brought criticism of Li Peng within the leadership. The Party had spoken; it had not been heeded. Searching for an explanation, Bo Yibo talked on

28 April of an attempt by foreigners 'to encourage the students and to throw our Party and our national spirit into confusion'. Li Peng ordered up another editorial headlined 'Defend the big picture, defend stability', which warned students against being exploited by 'dragons ... with hidden intentions'. In an evident reference to the Cultural Revolution, it concluded: 'If you believe the insult, slander and attack on the Party and state leaders in all the protest posters that appear everywhere, if you buy all the rumours about "seizing power" and "taking over", if you skip classes and go networking, our country could well fall into total chaos again.'[25]

On 29 April, the leadership finally agreed that Yuan Mu, the State Council spokesman, and He Dongchang, the vice-minister for education, should meet forty-five student representatives, mainly from official unions. The two men simply repeated the official line that the demonstrators were being manipulated. Despite all the evidence to the contrary, they denied that there was a serious corruption problem in the CCP or that censorship was being exercised. The tape of the meeting was played on television, provoking student demonstrations in twenty-three cities.

When Zhao Ziyang returned from North Korea on 30 April, the situation appeared calmer on the Beijing campuses, but there were official reports of 'rebelliousness' from Hebei and Shanxi provinces and from Tianjin, where the number of wall posters increased and up to half the mid-level cadres were estimated to be showing sympathy with the demonstrators. Almost three quarters of government ministers and vice-ministers were said to take the same position, while 800 senior military officers were reported to believe that troops should not be used. In some provinces, officials and demonstrators were co-operating – in Guangzhou, students complied with an official request for rallies to be arranged so that they did not interfere with workers going to their factories, and the authorities laid on buses to take demonstrators back to their campuses after late-night sit-ins in the city.[26]

In an address commemorating May Fourth and a speech to a meeting of the Asian Development Bank, Zhao said reason and restraint should be used towards the protestors. They did not reject the system, he argued, only its malpractices. Their demands should be dealt with through democracy and legal means. However, conservatives held a majority in the Politburo, and Zhao could not organize effective support for reform below the top level.

So the Party secretary found himself fighting a rearguard action. When he criticized the Shanghai leadership for 'bungling' in closing the *World Economic Herald*, the city's boss, Jiang Zemin, entered a stout defence of his action and gained the private backing of Deng and Yang Shang-kun. The hardline Politburo member Li Xiannian and the Elder Chen Yun telephoned Deng to express reservations about the Asian Development Bank speech. When Zhao suggested a *People's Daily* editorial to distinguish between the mass of students and a minority that was making trouble, and proposed using 'the policies of persuasion and guidance and avoiding the sharpening of conflict', Li Peng said simply, 'I disagree, Comrade Ziyang.'[27]

In the circumstances, Zhao temporized, allowing Li to hold the initiative. A conspiracy theory has it that he did this in the belief that the premier would fail and be dropped by Deng. Rather, his behaviour in the spring of 1989 suggests an honest, well-meaning man who did not know what to do, and was hemmed in by the forceful figures around him, in particular the lurking presence of the Elders and of the Paramount Leader sitting behind the walls of his home as he calculated what needed to be done to avoid his economic revolution tipping over into political change that could mean the end of Communism in China.

30

Three Weeks in May

On the seventieth anniversary of the May Fourth movement of 1919, 150,000 people crowded into Tiananmen Square. They sang a patriotic song from the 1930s:

> Today we are blossoming,
> Tomorrow we will be pillars of society.
> Today we are singing together,
> Tomorrow we will rise in a powerful wave
> To defend our country.
> Fellow students, be strong,
> Shoulder the fate of our nation.[1]

In the following fortnight, an estimated 1.5 million students and the staff of 500 higher-education institutes in eighty cities took to the streets to support the protestors in the capital. The organizers used modern communications, including fax machines, to outflank the authorities. Backed by the Beijing Workers' Autonomous Federation and 500 journalists, the students in Tiananmen called for the reassessment of bourgeois liberalism, freedom of the press, and the publication of the salaries and benefits of senior officials and their children. However, a division was to emerge between the early leaders such as Wang Dan, and more radical figures, such as the graduate student Chai Ling. The heads of the main reformist think-tank, Chen Ziming and Wang Juntao, sought to act as mediators, but found themselves overtaken by extreme elements.[2]

On 9 May, a petition was published signed by 1,031 journalists calling for freedom to report the protest and evoking the suppression of the *World Economic Herald* in Shanghai. 'We don't want to lie any more,' read the banner borne by staff from the *People's Daily*. The next morning, as 10,000 students toured Beijing on bicycles distributing petitions and pamphlets, Zhao Ziyang suggested to the Politburo that 'maybe we can turn a bad situation to our advantage by leading the patriotic students and people into a new order that is both socialist and democratic.' He hoped that a partial rectification of the *People's Daily* editorial of 26 April would divide the majority of students from 'the tiny minority of anti-Communist troublemakers'. But, in the Standing Committee of the Politburo, he could count only on the reformer Hu Qili, though he thought the security chief, Qiao Shi, might rally to him. But Li Peng and Senior Vice-Premier Yao Yilin were bound to oppose his ideas.

The concern of the leadership was heightened by a report from the Beijing Party secretary, Li Ximing, about the participation of workers in the protests – 'if the workers rise up, we're in big trouble,' President Yang observed. The situation was all the more worrying because of the impending arrival of Mikhail Gorbachev for his summit with Deng. 'We have to have order in Tiananmen,' Deng insisted. 'Our international image depends on it. What do we look like if the Square's a mess?'[3]

The control by which the Communist Party set such store was breaking down. The student demonstrations were emboldening others to make their complaints heard. Tens of thousands of Muslims in Beijing, Qinghai, Inner Mongolia and the city of Lanzhou demonstrated against a book called *Sexual Customs* that they considered defamatory. In Lanzhou, they injured 115 paramilitary police in clashes, burned a truck and demanded the execution of the author; elsewhere the protests were peaceful. In Xinjiang, former uranium miners staged a sit-in to complain about radiation sickness. In the Inner Mongolian capital of Huhehot, demonstrators protested at poor education funding.

The refusal of the authorities to open talks and the *People's Daily* editorial remained major bones of contention. Demonstrators, led by the 23-year-old student activist Chai Ling, gathered outside the Party newspaper office to chant:

> Full of nonsense!
> Lying to the people!
> Where's your conscience?
> You may think you're safe!
> But your time will come!
> When the time is here,
> The people will have their day![4]

Meeting on 11 May, six student leaders worried that the movement might run out of momentum, allowing the authorities to arrest demonstrators at will and disband the independent unions. So, as Wang Dan recalled, 'it was necessary to escalate the movement, to use more radical methods and apply more pressure to force the government to concede to our demands. Since demonstrations and sit-down strikes no longer bothered the government, we felt the next step should be a hunger strike.'

The following day, Wang and Chai Ling spoke to the students in Tiananmen. Crying, Chai said the authorities were forcing them to put their lives on the line. 'We are staging a hunger strike in order to reveal the true face of the government and the true face of the people,' she went on. 'We want to see whether the Chinese have any conscience, whether there is any hope for China . . . We are prepared to face death for the sake of true life. The oath written by our lives will brighten the skies of our country.'[5]

The hunger strike began the following day after a ceremonial last lunch. The State Security Bureau reported that 1,000 protestors joined in, including Wang and Chai. The watching crowd swelled to 100,000.

Originally conceived as a short-term protest, the strike was soon extended to last 'to the bitter end' in pursuit of dialogue with the government and an end to official 'name-calling'. It marked a radicalization and escalation of the political theatre at which the students were showing themselves to be experts, drawing on rituals and traditional themes of innocent virtue confronting aged, self-interested tyrants, as young idealists bravely pursued their crusade in public while the oppressors huddled behind the walls of their palace. Claiming the heritage of May Fourth, they could present themselves as representatives of intellectual rigour that encapsulated the essence of China – and which the rulers feared might produce martyrs to sully their reputation.[6]

Zhao sent his close aide, Bao Tong, to try to initiate talks, but he was rejected as an unacceptable 'neo-authoritarian'. When the reformist head of the CCP United Front Work Department, Yan Mingfu, held a meeting with some demonstration leaders, the students demanded a live television relay so that those outside could see what was going on; an official refusal to agree to this led the protestors to rush into the hall and disrupt the session. The hunger strikers adopted increasingly strong, emotional language; 'Farewell, fellow students, take care!' read one manifesto. 'Our pledge, written at the cost of our lives, will surely illuminate the skies of the Republic.' Some declarations were written in blood. Posters were put up in English for foreign reporters.

As public sympathy for the students escalated, Deng, Yang and Zhao met at the leader's home, where the Party secretary repeated his argument that what was needed was to isolate a tiny minority who were 'fishing in troubled waters' from the mass of the students. He gained tacit support from Yang, who said a separation had to be drawn between legitimate demands for democracy (as defined by the CCP) and bourgeois liberalization. Summarizing the dilemma, the president told Deng and Zhao, 'We can't let people promote bourgeois liberalisation under the banner of democracy; and, on the other hand, when we crack down on bourgeois liberalisation, we have to be sure we don't squash democracy.' For the hardliners, however, the two were synonymous.

Deng seemed at a loss. For all his tactical political skills, he was caught between the equally unyielding forces of the demonstrators and the Elders. 'Dialogue is fine,' he told Yang and Zhao. 'But the point is to solve the problem. We can't be led round by the nose . . . Senior comrades are getting worried. Chen Yun, Peng Zhen, Li Xiannian, Wang Zhen and Sister Deng* – and me too – are all worried. We have to be decisive. I've said over and over again that we need stability if we're going to develop. How can we progress when things are in an utter mess?' On 14 May, the Paramount Leader told the hardliner Li Xiannian that the situation was 'grim'.†[7]

While the constituency of the demonstrators expanded among the people of the capital, the Elders retreated into the cavern of their mindset formed by long years of struggle and their image of the Party as being under constant attack from adversaries. The past vitally affected the present by means of the mythology constructed for the CCP from the Jiangxi base through the Long March and the wars with Japan and the KMT. Though they did not invoke it directly, the recent example of what happened when 'young devils' of the Cultural Revolution were given their head was certainly in their minds, particularly among those who had suffered so much between 1966 and 1976.

Attempts by older intellectuals to mediate got nowhere, one protest

---

* As he referred to Zhou Enlai's widow.

† Again, I have drawn on the *Tiananmen Papers* for accounts of leadership meetings in May–June 1989 in this and the next chapter.

leader, Wuerkaixi, accusing them of treating the demonstrators as children. As the author Dai Qing recalled, 'We failed completely ... we intellectuals were caught between a totally irrational government and totally irrational students. What could we do?' The radical student leaders felt they had the wind in their sails, and voices of reason would have less and less impact as the confrontation escalated.

Mikhail Gorbachev arrived in Beijing on 15 May 1989, for one of the more unusual of visits. Marches to Tiananmen staged during his stay attracted anywhere from 300,000 to a million people from all walks of life – artists, journalists, teachers, historians, representatives of the Fashion Institute, the Foreign Language Institute, the Landscape Gardening Institute and the Earthquake Administration. Protestors at one rally bore placards declaring 'Deng Xiaoping, you made a mistake' and 'The people's government, where are you now?' Police sitting on the steps of the Great Hall, their trousers rolled up as they played cards in the sun, rose to clap them.[8]

The loss of face for the regime was enormous. A large official ceremony for the visitor in the square had to be cancelled. When Gorbachev went to the Great Hall to meet Deng, he used a side entrance. International reporters covering the summit turned their attention to the protestors. 'What a place, what a time, what a story!' Dan Rather told viewers of CBS news. 'It's the people's square, all right. More than a million Chinese demanding democracy and freedom, and proclaiming the new revolution.'[9]

Not surprisingly, the exchanges Gorbachev had with China's leaders were little more than symbolic. Deng said merely that old disputes between Beijing and Moscow had blown away. But it was noted that, whereas he had given the East German leader, Eric Honecker, a bear hug on his visit shortly before, he contented himself with a formal handshake for the Russian.[10]

On the evening of 16 May, Zhao called on Gorbachev to express satisfaction at the restoration of relations with Moscow. Some young people had doubts about socialism which could only be dealt with through reform, he remarked. The Party chief also unwittingly handed his adversaries a weapon that would be turned against him when he mentioned that, although Deng held no formal Party or government posts, he would still make the final decision in major matters.[11]

In search of agreement with the demonstrators, Zhao sent the United

Front Work chief, Yan Mingfu, to try for dialogue. Yan assured the students that they represented the future, were essential to the reform process, and had stirred the nation – before telling them to look after their health. On the verge of tears, he promised that the problem of the *People's Daily* editorial would be resolved, and that activists would not be persecuted, adding, 'If you don't believe me, you can take me hostage.' As Wang Dan recalled, 'the atmosphere was so highly emotional, it was impossible for either of us to continue.' Yan left with empty hands. Nor did the broadcast of a letter from Zhao in which he personally, in effect, reversed the 26 April editorial do any good. It was too late.[12]

The number of hunger strikers had risen to 3,100. Two hundred, who fainted, returned to the square after being revived by medical teams. There was agreement that any end to the protest would have to be unanimous, which meant that a radical minority could call the tune.

Within the leadership, Li Peng countered Zhao's call for a new editorial to rectify the harsh line of 26 April by pointing out that this would mean correcting Deng's words. At an emergency meeting of the Politburo Standing Committee to which Zhao drove after seeing Gorbachev, Bo Yibo denounced the protestors as not showing 'an ounce of human decency', and Li painted a picture of a conspiracy to topple the CCP, the government and 'the people's democratic dictatorship'. Yang Shangkun abandoned his earlier advocacy of dialogue to describe the situation in the capital as 'something like anarchy'.

The liberals seemed discomforted. Zhao foresaw 'a real nightmare' if things went on as they were, while Hu Qili thought the demonstrations had stopped being an ordinary student movement and had become 'turmoil created by those who hope to gain from it'. Adopting an inter-mediate position which marked his approach, Qiao Shi warned that, if things were not turned around, the whole reform process would be very much in danger. 'Our side can't give any more ground now, but we also haven't found any good way out of the mess,' he added. 'We should still do what we can to avoid confrontation of course.'[13]

Unable to resolve their differences, the leaders agreed on one thing – to go to see Deng the following day after Zhao had delivered a written speech to the students assuring them that their opinions were taken seriously, urging them to end the hunger strike and promising that there would be 'no retribution once peace is restored'.

The meeting in Deng's home on 17 May was a crucial moment. Li

Peng pressed his offensive, saying that Zhao bore the main responsibility for the escalation of the protest movement and for the difficulty of controlling it. Vice-Premier Yao Yilin said the Party chief's speech to the Asian Development Bank had 'fanned the flames of the student movement' by revealing differences within the leadership. Then he brought out the Gorbachev charge. He did not understand why Zhao had mentioned Deng's ultimate authority to the visitor. 'This can only have been intended to saddle Comrade Xiaoping with all the responsibility and to get the students to target Comrade Xiaoping to attack. This made the whole mess a lot worse.'[14]

Zhao said his speech had been mild and had been praised at the time by colleagues, including Li. As for his remark to Gorbachev, he had merely wanted to explain that any action Deng took was quite legal. He had said the same thing to Kim Il-sung on his trip to North Korea – the only difference this time was that it had been reported.

When Deng intervened, it was clear that he had made up his mind. The Asian Development Bank speech had been a turning point, he said; since then, things had got steadily worse. As recorded in the *Tiananmen Papers*, he went on to set out the concept that would become the regime's leitmotif to this day, and so can stand as the political summation of the Deng era and what has followed.

Of course we want to build socialist democracy, but we can't possibly do it in a hurry, and still less do we want that Western-style stuff. If our one billion people jumped into multi-party elections, we'd get chaos like the 'all-out civil war' we saw during the Cultural Revolution. You don't have to have guns and cannon to have a civil war; fists and clubs will do just fine. Democracy is our goal, but we'll never get there without national stability.

The true threat came not from the students but from 'people with ulterior motives [whose] goal is to set up a bourgeois republic on the Western model,' he added. 'We have no room for retreat,' Bo Yibo said, while President Yang warned: 'Our backs are to the wall. If we retreat any further, we are done for.'

After which, Deng delivered his final judgement. He had decided that the army should be brought in and martial law declared.

'It's always better to have a decision than not to have one,' Zhao responded. 'But, Comrade Xiaoping, it will be hard for me to carry out this plan. I have difficulties with it.'

'The minority yields to the majority,' the supreme leader reminded him.

'I will submit to Party discipline,' Zhao replied. 'The minority does yield to the majority.'

When the others had left, Deng telephoned Chen Yun, Li Xiannian and Peng Zhen to tell them of the decision and had messages sent to other Elders. Li Peng called in the Beijing city bosses and other associates to make preparations, but also asked for inquiries to be made about the possibility of visiting hunger strikers in hospital before the PLA moved.

During the day, demonstrations erupted from Shenyang in the northeast, where 100,000 people massed outside the Party headquarters, to the SEZ of Shenzhen in the south, where 3,000 students marched. Ordinary people were participating in ever-greater numbers, including workers. In the Sichuan capital of Chengdu, where heavy-handed police tactics produced popular anger, students announced that they would begin a hunger strike. In Hefei, in Anhui, more than 10,000 people marched through the streets chanting, 'We don't want old-man government' and 'Enough behind-the-scenes government.'

Beijing, as always, was the focal point. 'Why are the leaders so uncaring?' was the common complaint. 'All of a sudden,' remarked one retired official, 'the people's smouldering resentment of the government has found an opportunity to flare up.' In all, 1.2 million people were estimated to have demonstrated in the city on 17 May, including journalists from the *People's Daily*, carrying banners denouncing their own newspaper's editorial. The next day huge rallies continued, with more and more non-students, including industrial workers and farmers from the surrounding countryside. A celebrated restaurant sent a van with 'Delivering duck soup' written on the side. A uniformed group from the police school joined the demonstration, as did some soldiers who put on civilian clothes, but carried banners identifying them with the army. In three days, 57,000 students arrived by train from the provinces.[15]

At a Politburo Standing Committee session on 17 May, Zhao was outspoken in his opposition to martial law, arguing that it would only aggravate matters. 'One more big political mistake might well cost us all our remaining legitimacy,' he warned. 'So I see martial law as extremely dangerous. The Chinese people cannot take any more huge policy blunders.'[16]

Hu Qili backed him, fearing that martial law could set off mass resistance. Qiao Shi, a man known for his reserve, equivocated – there could be no more concessions, but a way to resolve the situation had not been found, so it was hard to come out for or against the proposal.

Bo Yibo and President Yang also attended. Though Bo noted that he and Yang did not have the right to vote, he said they both backed Deng's plan. A vote was taken. It was two–two, with Qiao abstaining.

Yang suggested seeking a final decision from Deng and the Elders – there could be no doubt what the outcome would be.

'My duties must end here today,' Zhao said. 'I cannot continue to serve . . . so I'm asking to resign.'

'Don't bring up this question,' Bo interjected. 'Didn't you agree at the morning meeting with Comrade Xiaoping that the minority should yield to the majority?'

Yang weighed in to tell Zhao that his attitude was not right – 'How can you bail out right now, when we most need unity?'

The Party secretary replied that his health was not good. He was suffering from dizziness and had low blood pressure.

Bo repeated Yang's proposal that the matter should be taken to Deng and the Elders in the morning. That was agreed. At 5 a.m. Zhao, Li Peng and other leaders went to visit fasting students who had been taken to Beijing hospitals. Nothing changed as a result. Zhao went on to his office, where he composed a letter to Deng and the Standing Committee. Knowing what would happen when the Elders met, he wrote that: 'After much thought, I have concluded that, given my current level of awareness and my state of mind, I simply cannot carry out the decision on implementing martial law in Beijing that you have decided on. I still maintain my original opinion. Accordingly, I ask to resign as General Secretary of the Communist Party of China and as First Vice-Chair of the Military Affairs Commission.'[17]

He sent the letter, marked 'extra urgent', to Yang for the president to read before it was circulated to the others. Yang telephoned to dissuade him on the grounds that resignation would have a polarizing effect, and damage Deng's prestige. Pointedly, he asked, 'Are you for him or against him?'

'I'll think it all over once more,' Zhao conceded. 'Right now, my chest feels stuffy and my head a bit dizzy. I won't be going to the meeting in the morning. Please tell the others I'm ill.' A little later, he sent Yang another missive. 'Thank you for your criticism,' it read. 'In respect of your opinions, I will not send my letter. But I still maintain my views, and hence my work will be very difficult. I cannot carry out this policy.'

Though remaining closeted, Zhao wrote to Deng, urging him to change his decision and drop the martial law plan. He also asked Yang to intercede to try to achieve a shift in the leader's view of the students, but the president said that would bring them all crashing down.

At 8.30 on the morning of 18 May, Deng and the other seven Elders met at his house, with the four members of the Standing Committee and three men from the Military Affairs Commission. Speaker after speaker backed martial law, and inveighed against the growing anarchy. Zhao's ally in the Standing Committee, Hu Qili, said he had to think things through, but would follow Party discipline. The abstainer of the previous day, Qiao Shi, said he supported martial law in some parts of Beijing. The decision was made to declare it at midnight on 21 May. Yang Shangkun would take charge of the action plan.[18]

That night, Zhao walked out into Tiananmen with Li Peng, who looked nervous. 'We have come too late,' he told the students tearfully. Deng reacted angrily to Zhao's visit to the square and accused him of lacking discipline. On 19 May, he signed the martial law order. One commander said he could not carry out the instruction; at Yang's prompting, he was stripped of his rank and, as the military record put it, sent to a hospital 'to recover his health'. There was also opposition from eight generals.[19]

But the die was cast. Zhao had given up the fight. The Standing Committee of the Politburo had relinquished its constitutional authority to the Elders. If there had been any hope of political modernization accompanying the economic reform, it was killed by the decisions taken on 18–19 May. As the writer Jonathan Mirsky put it, the veterans saw themselves as the 'Founding Members of the Firm'. They had survived the struggles for power and the vicissitudes of the Maoist era and were not going to be bested by a bunch of students. Continuing mass demonstrations in Beijing and across the country, including a march by a crowd of 100,000 in Shanghai, could only stoke their concern as a growing number of banners attacked the leadership personally; adapting the Paramount Leader's celebrated phrase, some posters read: 'It doesn't matter if a cat is black or white so long as it resigns.' The rulers might have to be helped around by nurses and might be caught by television staring vacantly ahead, but their own power and position came first. China has lived under the shadow of that ever since.[20]

In a dialogue of the deaf, Li Peng held a session with student leaders in the Great Hall, on the afternoon of 18 May, also attended by the education chief Li Tieying and the Beijing mayor and Party bosses. Sitting in a maroon, velvet-covered armchair with white antimacassar, the dark-suited premier said the meeting, which was broadcast live, should confine itself to seeking means of curtailing the fast. His paternalist tone was met by defiance from the start. The student leaders, pale, drawn and hollow-eyed from fasting, wore white headbands. Wuerkaixi had come from his sickbed; he was in pyjamas and had an oxygen tube up his nose. It was all quite genuine, but it also made superb political theatre.[21]

Wuerkaixi told Li that the students had initiated the meeting, so they would decide the agenda. After that frosty start, Wang Dan offered that, if the protests were recognized as being patriotic and a dialogue between the students and officials was televised, the demonstration leaders would try to persuade their colleagues to clear the square. But Wuerkaixi explained that there had to be unanimity, so 0.1 per cent of the protestors could block evacuation. The *People's Daily*, he added, should publish an editorial admitting its mistake on 26 April.

Unused to the lack of deference, Li grew exasperated as other student leaders piled in with demands. 'Are you people finished yet?' he asked. One participant recalled that his face turned red and then white. Beijing officials expressed concern for the health of the hunger strikers. The premier inquired if the protestors could imagine what the outcome of the current unrest might be. He was only interested in ending the hunger strike; other issues could wait. To which Wuerkaixi said the way of resolving the matter was for the government to agree to the student demands. Wang Dan added that, if turmoil increased, the demonstrators would blame it on the government. Another Beijing student, who addressed the premier as 'dear Comrade Li', said that there was no connection between the demonstrations and turmoil.

As the students got up to leave, Wuerkaixi collapsed in a faint. Li rose and extended his hand to the visitors. It was brushed aside. 'You've gone too far,' the premier muttered. Visibly angry, he walked from the room. Because of leaks, the timing of the imposition of martial law was brought forward to the morning of 20 May as the demonstrators braced themselves for an attack. On the night of 19 May, a session of the Party Centre and the State Council was called, also attended by civilian and military officials. Li and Yang explained why action had to be taken. One of the six chairs on the platform was empty – Zhao's. Protests were reported in 116 cities that day, with more than 10,000 people in the street in Shanghai, Tianjin, Harbin, Changsha, Nanjing, Xi'an and a dozen other big centres.

The criticism was becoming increasingly personal, singling out leaders by name. The disquiet of even official media was evident when the announcer who read the proclamation of martial law on China Central Television – wearing a black suit he was said to have borrowed for the occasion – did not look up once from the paper in front of him and used a tone of voice that viewers would connect to a funeral.[22]

Official loudspeakers broadcast the order to Tiananmen. Troops from twenty-three divisions of ten PLA armies were already moving into the city. Helicopters hovered over the square. But the people of Beijing and the students halted the army's advance, setting up blockades with buses and trucks, surrounding the vehicles, and calling on the soldiers not to act against the population. Some put newspapers over the windscreens so that the drivers had to stop. Long columns of military trucks were immobilized on the roads into the capital. 'Flying Tiger' motorcyclists sped past acting as liaison agents, weaving to avoid the crowds, their wives on the back waving V signs.[23]

The troops were nonplussed, dazed, as ordinary people argued with them and offered food and water. They were facing not the reactionary elements they had been told about or wild student agitators, but ordinary folk, workers, shopkeepers, women, intellectuals and students. An estimated 2 million *shimin* – city people – stood in their way. 'Only the old people and the children are asleep,' a mother told a journalist. As the clear dawn broke, a long column of marchers arrived in Tiananmen, headed by factory workers wearing headbands proclaiming 'Dare to Die' – a phrase associated with a reformer executed in the late imperial period and taken up by the revolutionaries of 1911.

In all, 300,000 people massed in the square. An appeal by Li Peng to 'stop the turmoil and stabilize the situation' was met with jeers. In the western suburbs, troops waited in front of the roadblocks looking sheepish and unsure of what to do. In places, demonstrators lay on the road to stop the armed forces. 'This is not chaos,' workers shouted. 'This is the voice of the people. We want democracy. We want Deng to go.'

It was a stunning victory over the martial law forces. The students remained at the core of the protests, but the nature of the challenge to the regime altered with the massive involvement of the *shimin*, in particular the workers and at least some of those who had benefited as individuals from the economic changes. For all the bounding growth figures, the depth of discontent with the regime was breaking out as never before. Some reports had it that the hunger-striking students seemed indifferent to their new supporters. This may have been, in part, because of their exhaustion, but they also appeared to take the support of the people as their due, perpetuating the superiority complex of intellectuals inherited from the imperial era.[24]

As the troops retreated to their bases, foreign reporters spread the news round the world. At one point, CBS in the US delayed the transmission of the last episode of the soap opera *Dallas* in favour of live coverage from Beijing that showed people handing soldiers flowers; after a valiant rearguard rhetorical action by the anchorman Dan Rather, the authorities shut down the network's satellite link. In Hong Kong, 600,000 people demonstrated, stimulating the pro-democracy movement in the colony eight years before the scheduled handover to the PRC. The students' cause appeared to get high-level backing when the Politburo member Wan Li, who had pressed early reforms in Anhui, spoke out against martial law during a visit to the United States. He said he wanted to 'firmly protect the patriotic enthusiasm of the young people in China'.

It was time for the Elders to plan their fight-back. Deng told a meeting of the veterans at his home that the reason for the failure lay in internal CCP problems, which he laid at the door of Zhao's 'intransigence' that had revealed divisions others should not know about. 'Our Party and state face a life-and-death crisis,' he added. Zhao and his ideological ally, Hu Qili, should be sacked from the Politburo, it was agreed. But who should lead the Party?[25]

Though the constitution gave it no such powers, the group of veterans began to discuss the succession. Jiang Zemin of Shanghai was mentioned as one possibility, but he had no experience at the centre. Wan Li, who was chairman of the Standing Committee of the National People's Congress, was thought well of, but considered a bit old at seventy-three

– his remarks in the US could not help him, either. It was decided that he should return home anyway; he pleaded ill-health to his hosts as a reason for cutting short his visit. Deng praised the Party boss in Tianjin, Li Ruihuan, as 'energetic, effective and thoughtful'. One name was mentioned only by Wang Zhen – Li Peng. The premier might have been the faithful executor of the hard line, but his evident unpopularity was seen as disqualifying him from taking on a job which would require much bridge-building.

Not knowing of the decision by the Elders, Zhao returned to his office on 22 May after his three-day break to recuperate. He found he had no papers, no work and no news of what was going on. His close aide, Bao Tong, secretary to the Politburo, who had collaborated with the reformist heads of the Beijing Social and Economic Sciences Research Institute (SERI) to try to find a solution to the impasse in the square, was being investigated by the State Security Ministry.*

More politically liberal than Zhao, Bao had been under increasing pressure. In April, he was barred from meetings of the Central Committee, refused access to documents and put under surveillance. When Li Peng read the resulting report, he wrote a note on it in large characters so the Elders would have no trouble reading it. Bao, he judged, had 'leaked top-level secrets about martial law to confuse people's minds. I suggest he immediately be punished according to the law.' The hardliner Li Xiannian denounced him as a man who wore blue jeans and gaudy jackets within the leadership compound, his head 'full of bourgeois liberalisation'.[26]

On the evening of Zhao's return to unemployment, Li Peng called a meeting of the Politburo, without Zhao but including Jiang Zemin and Li Ruihuan, along with a swathe of other senior officials. Except for Qiao Shi, whose associates were lobbying for him to take over the CCP leadership, all those who spoke criticized Zhao.[27]

For the people and the students, the elation of victory in the streets soon gave way to apprehension of a fresh advance as PLA helicopters circled above the city. New barriers were erected with coal trucks, buses, dustbins and steel cables. People gathered on the flyovers and intersections on the way to Tiananmen, watching for troops. At one

* Bao also had contacts with the human rights body set up in China by the financier George Soros.

checkpoint, a group of police on bicycles was forced to retreat, to cheers from the crowd. 'Down with Li Peng, down with Deng Xiaoping,' workers chanted from the back of trucks. Outside Beijing's main station, a contingent of soldiers was stuck on the tracks by a crowd that surrounded their train.[28]

South of the city, a convoy of tanks stretched out near a military airport. A crowd gathered round to stare at them. The crews sat on top of their machines, smoking. Children eating ice creams were lifted up to sit beside the machine guns.

'You weren't going to use these against us, were you?' asked a girl.

'No, we were just on manoeuvres,' a soldier replied.

It had been a rare exhibition of people power in a country which was, nominally, run for the people. But it had been a fragile victory and there was no agreement on what to do next, no leader who could pull the whole thing together. The protestors called for democracy and dialogue, but those were vague concepts. The main motivations were negative – against Li and Deng, against the Elders, against corruption, against profiteering cadres, against inflation, against the uncertainties of economic reform. The breadth of their claims and complaints gave them wide appeal but meant they lacked a coherent message.

Reformers and students hoped that there might be progress when Wan Li, the Politburo member who had spoken out against martial law, returned from the United States. As head of the National People's Congress, he would decide whether to agree to a request by a prominent liberal, Hu Jiwei, and fifty-seven others for a special meeting of the Standing Committee of the legislature to consider the situation. This would be a riposte to the closed-door meeting of the Elders, and might promote some relaxation of the tension. In theory, the NPC had the power to declare martial law illegal.

When Wan got back to Shanghai on 25 May, he was taken to be briefed by Jiang Zemin on what had happened in his absence. Two days later, he emerged from seclusion to announce that he now supported martial law, following the line that disorder, fomented by a small conspiratorial group, was undermining national progress. Though he continued to refer to the students as patriots, he had decided to bend with the wind.[29]

In a television address, Chen Yun alluded to Zhao's connections with a 'treacherous anti-Party clique'. As well as Bao Tong, other associates of the deposed CCP leader, including the Politburo member Hu Qili, were attacked by hardliners at a Central Committee session. On 27 May, the Elders met again to decide who should take over from Zhao and on the composition of the Politburo Standing Committee. On Deng's recommendation, Jiang Zemin, a Russian-trained electrical engineer who had shown both firmness and a taste for economic modernization in Shanghai, was chosen as Party secretary. His victory was a narrow one since Li Peng, Qiao Shi and the conservative Yao Yilin all had their backers. But Deng's support for the Shanghai chief was decisive. Li Ruihuan from Tianjin and a Chen Yun associate, the planner Song Ping, joined the Politburo Standing Committee alongside Jiang, Li Peng, Qiao and Yao.[30]

Once again, the veterans asserted their power over China's constitutional organs. This ensured that the future political path would be a conservative one. Reformers, liberals, students, workers, *shimin* people of Beijing and all others who wanted a new start politically forty years after the establishment of the People's Republic were to be relegated to second place behind the interests of the monolith of the Party as defined by the small circle of the leadership.

Massacre in Beijing

In the later days of May 1989 the protest in Tiananmen Square seemed to be on the verge of winding down. Some students were starting to return to classes, leaving behind accumulated garbage, the air fouled by stinking, unemptied portable toilets. There was dissension in the ranks between those like Wang Dan and Wuerkaixi who wanted to evacuate the square, for safety's sake and because they considered it good tactics, and the more militant group, the Tiananmen Square Command Headquarters, led by Chai Ling and her associates, who rejected any withdrawal. The radicals were strengthened by provincial protestors arriving to join the sit-in and wishing to continue the demonstration. Chai's personal suspicions of leaders such as Wang had not dissipated, either.[1]

On the morning of 27 May, a liaison group of demonstrators and liberals met at the Academy of Social Sciences, among them the liberal think-tankers Chen Ziming and Wang Juntao, who were trying to steer the protestors to a positive, peaceful, solution. The initial statement under consideration called for an emergency session of the National People's Congress, with its theoretical power to overturn martial law. If this was not agreed, the draft added, the occupation of the square would continue until 20 June, when the legislature was due to hold its next regular session.

Representatives of the autonomous students' association then said that it had just decided to withdraw from Tiananmen after a final monster demonstration on 28 May. With support rallies planned abroad for that day, the students would be able to end their action on the moral high ground, and bloodshed could be avoided. Having won the backing of the *shimin* of Beijing and widespread support in cities across China, the students would have laid down a huge marker for the future to a regime which had been unable to cope and had seen its prime weapon, the PLA, halted by unarmed civilians.

It was all that could have been hoped for by Chen and Wang, who had been in discussions with Zhao Ziyang's embattled reform associate, Bao Tong. The hope was that the resolution proposed by Wang Dan and his colleagues could discomfort CCP hardliners and usher in a new political climate.

However, the evacuation had not been approved by the Command Headquarters. At this point, Chai Ling, the General Commander of the Headquarters, arrived at the meeting, with her husband Feng Congde. She said she was exhausted and confused. Students were leaving the protest, supplies were short, ordinary citizens might stop blocking the PLA. Despite the desire of her comrades to stay put, evacuation could be the right course, she admitted. When a vote was taken, Chai raised her hand in support of withdrawal. This made the vote unanimous. A peaceful outcome appeared to have been achieved.

Returning to Tiananmen, Chai told her lieutenant, Li Lu, that they were pulling out.

'What are you talking about?' he replied, recalling that the group had voted two days earlier to stay.

They could not hold out until 20 June, she responded.[2]

'It's too dangerous,' the agitated Li yelled back. 'If we leave, they'll stop the NPC. Beijing will be under army control. We won't be able to demonstrate. They'll surround the colleges and block the exits. They'll throw us in jail. You're talking defeat. They've given us nothing we asked for. All our hopes will be gone!'

Chai broke into tears. Students grabbed the statement brought back from the meeting and scribbled new wording on it. That evening, Wang Dan read out the declaration at a press conference. When he reached the point on evacuation, he paused for a moment, then said softly, 'It has been proposed to the Capital Joint Liaison Group that the students evacuate Tiananmen Square on 30 May.' That was not accepted. Instead, a new version was read out: 'Unless a special meeting of the National People's Congress is convened in the next few days, the occupation of the square will continue until 20 June.'

Chai later accused those who had wanted to withdraw of having 'a very negative effect on the movement' and said she had not realized how harmful their decision would be when she had initially gone along with it. If the square stronghold was lost, she warned, 'the conservatives will overrun China!' Wang Dan said he felt he could not compete with the emotional appeal of those who wanted to stay. Walking from the microphone, he submitted his resignation, and returned to his campus to do what he could there. On both sides, the hardliners were in control.[3]

'I've come to the end of my strength, both physically and mentally,' Chai Ling told those in the square as she too resigned her post. The movement was going off the rails, she added. Money was being stolen from the protest strongbox; the original leadership was finished; she asked Li Lu to try to work things out.

However, spirits were boosted by the appearance of a 30-foot-high Styrofoam statue of the Goddess of Democracy made at the Central Academy of Fine Arts. It was placed to look at the giant portrait of Mao gazing out at the square. A manifesto proclaimed the statue to be 'sacred, inviolable' and pledged that 'the people will never tolerate any destructive behaviour towards it.' As it was being put up, a voice over the official loudspeaker in the square warned: 'Your movement is bound to fail. It is foreign. This is China, not America.'[4]

The rubbish was cleared away and the stinking toilets removed. Money and a consignment of brightly coloured nylon tents arrived from sympathizers in Hong Kong, where large marches supported the students and the Beijing-backed newspaper *Wen Wei Po* cleared its editorial column after the proclamation of martial law to run four characters saying simply: 'With grief and sorrow.'[5]

Taken to a hotel by a visitor from the colony, Chai had a shower, put on new clothes and returned to the square, saying she was ready to rejoin the struggle. 'We will mobilize Chinese people around the world to protest martial law!' she declared. 'Martial law won't succeed in ten days, in a year, in a hundred years! Those who lose the hearts of the people will perish! Overthrow the illegal government headed by Li Peng!'

Clearly distraught, she gave a remarkable filmed interview to an American journalist, Philip Cunningham, in which she said she could not help thinking sometimes:

you, the Chinese, you are not worth my struggle! You are not worth my sacrifice! But then I can also see that in this movement there are many people who do have a conscience. There are many decent people among the students, workers, citizens, and intellectuals ... The students keep asking, 'What should we do next? What can we accomplish?' I feel so sad, because how can I tell them that what we are actually hoping for is bloodshed, for the moment when the government has no choice but to brazenly butcher the people. Only when the square is awash with blood will the people of China open their eyes. Only then will they really be united. But how can I explain any of this to my fellow students?[6]

Laying bare the divisions within the student movement, she said it was 'truly sad' that:

some students, and some famous, well-connected people, are working hard to help the government, to prevent it from taking such measures. For the sake of their selfish interests and their private dealings they are trying to cause our movement to collapse and get us out of the square before the government becomes so desperate that it takes action . . . I feel so sad, because I can't say all this to my fellow students. I can't tell them straight out that we must use our blood and our lives to call on the people to rise up. Of course, the students will be willing. But they are still such young children!

Others might have to shed their blood for the cause, but she told Cunningham she would not remain in the square:

because my situation is different. My name is on the government's hit list. I'm not going to let myself be destroyed by this government. I want to live. Anyway, that's how I feel about it. I don't know if people will say I'm selfish. I believe that others have to continue the work I have started. A democracy movement can't succeed with only one person!

Chai said she had to leave Beijing to go underground. In the event, she stayed till almost the end.

Meanwhile, four young men began a new hunger strike at the Heroes' Monument. One was a 32-year-old, Taiwanese-born rock star, Hou Dejian, who had moved to the mainland to 'choose liberty' and had had an up-and-down career – he was now in a good phase, driving a red Mercedes and singing his hit song, 'Descendants of the Dragon', which wondered why a country with as rich a history as China was so poor and weak. Joining the protest, he explained that he could only stay for forty-eight hours because of a recording commitment in Hong Kong.

Reflecting on the elitism which too often permeated the student leaders and the refusal of some to compromise, a fellow hunger-striker, a teacher and critic, Liu Xiaobo, told the crowd that 'a major problem with the student movement is that it is obsessed with opposing the government, but unconcerned with practising democratic principles in its own ranks. To replace a military dictatorship with a student dictatorship would hardly be a victory; it would be a failure, a tragic failure.' But the four, Hou in particular, found it hard to remain cool; the atmosphere was too strong. 'I felt that my words could sway the fate of the nation,' the star recalled.[7]

In the festive climate, crowds flocked to see the Goddess. The workers' leader, Han Dongfang, told a foreign journalist he believed the Communist Party would be 'able to overcome its difficulties, that it will accept the people's suggestions and keep its officials honest and uncorrupted'. But the end was approaching. The rifts between the moderates in the square and radicals were widening; at one point, a group of provincials tried to kidnap Chai Ling and her student leader husband, Feng Congde, after hearing stories about money being misappropriated. Her associate, Li Lu, accused student guards of getting drunk and allowing government agents to sabotage equipment. 'It's over,' a more realistic reformer who had sat in the square told the journalist Jonathan Mirsky, after going to his hotel room and gesturing to him to turn on the television to drown the bugging device. 'I'm not sorry about what I've done, but many of my colleagues are already planning how to confess and inform on others.'[8]

Having been humiliated by ordinary unarmed people stopping its supposedly invincible army, the leadership could not permit this to happen again; nor could it let the students continue their defiance without appearing like a paper tiger. Looking back to more than six decades as a revolutionary with Chinese Communist characteristics, his role in the victories of the civil war, his long switchback course under Mao, his victory over the Gang of Four, Hua Guofeng and all the others, Deng Xiaoping was not going to allow himself to be beaten by the students in the square or, more threateningly, by the workers and citizens who had blocked the PLA and were seen as being manipulated by outsiders intent on destroying the Communist Party as he knew it. His whole career, notably in the anti-rightist purge of the late 1950s, his suppression of the Democracy Wall movement two decades later and his failure to encourage political reform, meant that neither he nor the regime he headed had laid the groundwork for the kind of dialogue which might have averted brutal confrontation.

In keeping with Chinese tradition, the students could still draw on a residual well of sympathy even from a hardliner such as Chen Yun, who spoke of their 'good, pure, kind hearted and constructive motives'. Tradition made them the standard-bearers of truth and virtue. The workers and the ordinary people of Beijing enjoyed no such understanding, all the less so given the fear that they might stage a movement similar to Solidarity in Poland, with figures such as Han Dongfang acting as a Chinese Lech Walesa. There had been talk of a general strike, which would pose an even greater test of army loyalty.[9]

On 2 June, the Elders met in belligerent mood. 'Those goddamn bastards,' Wang Zhen exploded, typically. 'Who do they think they are, trampling on sacred ground like Tiananmen for so long? They are really asking for it.' Li Peng and Li Xiannian both pointed at subversive foreign influences; Deng agreed. The previously equivocal Qiao Shi said clearing the square was the only option. 'As soon as possible,' Yao Yilin added. After which, Deng summed up that martial law forces should end the occupation of Tiananmen by the protestors within two days.[10]

As they began to move into the city again, the troops tried to avoid being noticed. Some were unarmed, their weapons having been brought in separately – a few of the buses and trucks carrying arms were surrounded by citizens and their contents seized, though student leaders ordered the guns to be handed back.

Shortly before midnight on 2 June, a jeep from the People's Armed Police, travelling at high speed, went out of control and killed two cyclists and a pedestrian. A crowd surrounded the vehicle, broke its windscreen and slapped the driver before he was rescued by three men travelling with him. Police intervened to escort the four away. The jeep had no numberplate and, when they searched the vehicle, onlookers found military uniforms, maps and mobile telephones.

This incident heightened the tension and, in the early hours of 3 June, the autonomous associations of students and workers broadcast warnings over their loudspeakers that the army was coming. Once again, crowds surrounded military vehicles and buses, puncturing their tyres and isolating the soldiers inside. Thousands of students rode bicycles down Chang'an Boulevard running along the top of Tiananmen and in front of the Forbidden City and the leadership compound. 'We have won!' the protest loudspeakers in the square announced at 5 a.m.

Just before dawn on 3 June, a crowd of unarmed soldiers in short-sleeved white shirts, olive-coloured trousers, rucksacks and running shoes jogged towards the square. Though the exact reason for their appearance has not been explained, they were probably heading for a weapons dump near Tiananmen and were hoping that their jogging garb would enable them to get through. But they were stopped by a roadblock and a large group of *shimin*. Isolated in small groups, the young men were lectured for hours on democracy, human rights, and relations between the PLA and civilians. Eventually, one lot broke out and fled. The others were then allowed to leave, without their shoes, rations and rucksacks, pursued by shouts and insults.[11]

During the morning, the confrontations became more violent as citizens threw stones, beat soldiers and kidnapped a few wounded PLA men when they headed for hospital. Students seized weapons and climbed on top of buses containing soldiers, grabbing helmets and raising them on the end of bayonets in triumph. In the early afternoon, troops and armed police fired tear gas to try to disperse crowds outside Zhongnanhai; the demonstrators surged back, and obliged the security forces to break up or take refuge in the compound.[12]

Inside, Yang Shangkun summoned an emergency meeting attended, among others, by Li Peng, Qiao Shi and the Beijing city and Party chiefs. The prime minister spoke of 'a counter-revolutionary riot' which called for 'resolute' measures. Yang relayed Deng's instruction that the problem had to be solved by dawn – everything possible should be done to avoid spilling blood, but, in the last resort, the soldiers should use 'all means necessary'. It was agreed that troops and police would start their operation at 9 p.m. that night, and clear Tiananmen by 6 a.m. on 4 June.[13]

In the late afternoon, the crowd on brightly lit Chang'an Boulevard was so thick that cyclists could not get through it. Some parents brought their children to witness the historic event. Young men rode by with their girlfriends on the pillions of their motorcycles. There were even a few invalids in wheelchairs.[14]

The workers' association issued its members with clubs, meat cleavers, metal chains and sharpened bamboo poles. A thousand people were mobilized to knock down a wall on a construction site to provide bricks and steel beams as weapons. Overhead, helicopter crews gathered information about the situation on the ground. Soldiers in plain clothes slipped into the square. Others took up position in and around the Great Hall, though they were held back by the size of the crowd. After the authorities issued an announcement telling people to 'stay at home to safeguard their lives', the throng began to disperse. At around 10 p.m., students at the Heroes' Monument took an oath: 'We swear to protect the cause of Chinese democracy. We are not afraid to die. We do not wish to continue living in a troubled country. We are here to protect Tiananmen to the death. Down with Li Peng's military government!'[15]

The PLA began to move in through the suburbs, encountering the familiar resistance from civilians who believed the troops would not open fire on them and that they could repeat their earlier successes. Though the ensuing events would become known as the Tiananmen Massacre, most of the killing that night took place several miles west of the square, round the big Gongzhufen intersection, where armoured vehicles crashed through buses blocking the road, firing into the crowd and crushing people to death, and then, further into the city at Muxidi crossroads, where a bridge spanned a fetid canal on the boulevard leading to Chang'an and the city centre. The victims were ordinary citizens of Beijing, not the students in the square.[16]

At Muxidi, the 38th Group Army ran into determined opposition from civilians blocking its path. Students wearing red headbands arrived from Tiananmen to help organize them. Buses had been pulled across the bridge to block the troops. An anti-riot squad fired rubber bullets and tear gas. The crowd retreated and then regrouped, flinging stones and bottles, broken pavement slabs and bricks brought in on lorries and tricycle flatbeds. A detachment of troops that advanced on to the bridge was forced back. Then armoured vehicles moved up to dislodge the barrier. People in the crowd threw flaming projectiles to set the buses alight.[17]

By 10.10 p.m., according to the army report, tens of thousands of people formed a human wall twenty to thirty metres from the front line of the troops. Using a loudhailer, the commanding officer urged them to give way. When they refused to do so, soldiers fired in the air. Then the troops took up position, the first two rows kneeling, those behind standing. Rocks cascaded on them. At 10.30, they opened fire, showering sparks in the air. Chanting, 'If nobody attacks me, I attack no one; but if people attack me, I must attack them', soldiers and armed police surged on to the bridge, doing what the protestors thought they never would, shooting the people whose security they were meant to safeguard.

As demonstrators fell to the ground, dead or wounded, the crowd broke, but continued to pelt the soldiers with missiles, shouting, 'Fascists!', 'Murderers!', 'Bandits!' The obstacles they had set up in the road hampered their escape. Under the barrage of rocks and bottles, some soldiers fired indiscriminately. Others sprayed nearby blocks of flats, from which they were also being bombarded with projectiles. The official report noted that 'bullets ricocheted off buildings up and down the five hundred metres [from] Muxidi.'[18]

The troops advanced remorselessly down the avenue towards Tiananmen. Armoured vehicles rolled along the boulevard which Peng Zhen had ordered in 1958 should be made strong enough to support the heaviest tanks. Helicopters hovered overhead. 'There were no more lulls in the shooting,' the State Security Ministry account reproduced in the *Tiananmen Papers* went on. 'Soldiers on the trucks fired into the air continuously until people hurled rocks or verbal insults, and then they fired into the crowd.' When the soldiers had passed, civilians returned to the street and pulled buses back into place as barricades against any reinforcement, setting them on fire once they were in position. The toll of dead in this phase of the confrontation has never been established, but certainly ran into hundreds as against the figure given in the official internal report of about twenty with 2,000 wounded.

The soldiers were on edge, in a hostile city, without clear bearings – a police unit which had been meant to act as guide had been blocked by protestors. Some armoured vehicles were caught in obstacles lain across the road. People jumped up on top, yanked open the canopies and pulled the soldiers out, beating them and, in one case made much of by officialdom, disembowelling an officer and putting his cap back on his head at a jaunty angle.

Wounded civilians were rushed to nearby Fuxing hospital, where doctors performed mouth-to-mouth resuscitation, their faces red from the blood. The frank Ministry report concluded:

To the east of the bridge, near the subway station, lay twelve lumps of flesh, blood and debris. The bodies of the dead and wounded were being delivered continuously to Fuxing Hospital. Some arrived on three-wheeled flat-bed carts, others were carried on wooden doors, and some came in on the back of motorcycles . . . Virtually everyone at Fuxing Hospital was cursing 'Fascists!' 'Animals!'

'Bloody massacre!'. At 1.30 a.m., Fuxingmenwai Boulevard in the area of Muxidi was deserted and shrouded in deathly silence.

Some of the wounded were taken to Tiananmen, where they were treated in the demonstrators' medical facility. Six weeks after Hu Yaobang's death had set off the protests, the students could have no doubt what was about to happen to them. Parents hurried to the square to take their children home. Hou Dejian sang a song:

> Freedom-loving people,
> Let's spread our wings.
> People with a conscience,
> Let's open our hearts.
> Today we are beautiful.
> Everything can be changed.
> Everything is within our reach.

At the entrance to the square, a concrete road divider, two blazing buses and a military vehicle, which had also been set on fire, stood as their only defence at the end of Chang'an Boulevard. At 11.30 p.m., an armoured car drove up. The concrete divider blocked its progress, and students threw Molotov cocktails, forcing it to turn and drive away, in flames. At the Xinhua Gate to Zhongnanhai, helmeted soldiers stood impassively, with metal batons held across their chests, while people cursed them and flung stones.

A second armoured car ventured into the square with three soldiers inside, and was surrounded by a crowd that pelted it with Molotov cocktails. As the vehicle burned, a soldier emerged. He was swiftly beaten to death. A second soldier peered out. He was grabbed by the hair, ears and face. His skin was ripped off. Somebody beat his skull till it split. The third soldier was pulled out. Watching, the British journalist John Simpson described the members of the crowd as 'like dogs', their mouths open and panting, their eyes expressionless. Students drove up in a bus and tried to get the trooper away from the crowd, but it held on to him. A man beat at the soldier's head with a half-brick. Shouting obscenities, Simpson, a large man, threw himself at the attacker, who dropped the brick. In the space that the journalist's intervention created, the students got hold of the soldier and drove off with him in the bus.[19]

By 1 a.m., the troops had flooded into the vast square, built by Mao to signal his country's greatness. A proclamation broadcast repeatedly by the Beijing Municipal Government and the Martial Law Command warned that 'a severe counter-revolutionary riot has broken out in the capital' and ordered that Tiananmen be evacuated immediately. 'The People's Liberation Army is the friend of the people,' went a mantra over the official loudspeakers. 'No good person need fear it.' As students pleaded to the troops to put down their weapons, there were outbreaks of gunfire. A girl was carried away, her face smashed; a young man was taken off, his chest a bloody mess. Ambulances raced through the night. Some victims were removed on tricycle pedicabs. A commandeered jeep sped off with a man lying on the roof, several others sprawled inside. The north-western corner of the square was full of burning vehicles which set up an orange glow. Under the trees on one side of the square, large soldiers stood with clubs. Armoured troop carriers moved up so slowly that they seemed like cardboard models against the night sky.[20]

The last-hour hunger-strikers, including the singer Hou, who had been given a big padded coat and a helmet by students, urged a pull-out. 'Blood is being spilled all over the city,' they said. 'More than enough blood has already been shed to awaken the people. We know you're not afraid of dying, but leaving now doesn't mean that you're cowards.' To which Chai Ling replied, 'Those who wish to leave may leave. But those who don't may stay.'

The four men got into an ambulance and drove across to a troop position on the east side of the square. They said they would undertake to get all the students out of Tiananmen if the army would not shoot. The political commissar said he would have to consult his superiors. As he did so, the lights were put out on a pre-arranged schedule at 4 a.m. This caused momentary panic. But the commissar returned to say that the deal was on. 'We will now begin clearing the square, and we accept your appeal to evacuate,' the loudspeakers boomed.

At the Heroes' Monument, demonstrators lit a bonfire, and did not move. Soldiers of a 'shock brigade' advanced, their weapons glinting, their assault rifles pointed alternately in the air and at the students. A hasty voice-vote was held – one witness said the 'Stay' voices were 'much, much stronger' than those shouting 'Leave', but Chai Ling's husband, who had taken on the leadership, declared that the 'Leave' group was in the majority. As Hou Dejian observed, 'Those who wanted to leave would be ashamed to shout very loud, while those who wanted to stay would shout with all their might.' Feng Congde said simply, 'Because of this situation, I felt that when the two sides sounded about the same, most likely more people voted to leave. So I announced the decision to leave.'[21]

At 4.30, the lights were turned on. The sight that greeted the demonstrators was daunting – ranks of heavily armed troops, backed by tanks and armoured cars. The soldiers and riot police moved steadily forward, hemming in the students until only twenty metres separated them. A military vehicle knocked down the Goddess of Democracy. Others rolled over tents. The voice from the official loudspeakers warned of 'disorderly times' and, bizarrely, of pickpockets as it insisted that 'the People's Liberation Army loves the people; the people love the PLA. Only bad people do not love the Army.'[22]

The students fell back to the south-eastern corner of the square, threading their way between the tanks and armoured cars. They sang the Communist anthem, the 'Internationale', waving their college flags. Some spat at the soldiers. Others shouted, 'Bandits! Bandits!', 'Fucking Animals!' and 'Down with Fascism!'

When dawn broke at 5.20, only a few hundred students remained. Tanks advanced towards them, and they, too, left the square, shouting insults at the troops. In reply, the soldiers fired into the air and cried their PLA motto in unison: 'If no one attacks me, I attack no one.' By 5.40 a.m., the square was clear.

The official account insists that nobody was killed by gunfire in Tiananmen, or run over by a tank. But eyewitnesses told a very different story, of demonstrators shot point blank and armoured vehicles crushing civilians, some of them still in the student tents. Arriving by bicycle in the square after witnessing the battle on Fuxingmenwai Boulevard, an American journalist, John Pomfret, saw 'a lot of shooting. A lot of young people were running towards the military, being shot or falling, and then running away. Fellows on these flatbed pedicabs were bicycling into that area to try to pick up wounded people; some of them were shot as well.' As most of the students left the square, they heard fresh gunfire behind them. An hour later, a tank ran over students on a nearby avenue, and troops pursued civilians through the side streets.

At Muxidi, meanwhile, the crowd regrouped to stage a counteroffensive. Their new roadblocks were strong enough to immobilize trucks, tanks and armoured vehicles. Soldiers sat in the back of their lorries while people cursed them. A young man threw a gas bomb into an armoured car, forcing the men inside to get out, clutching their throats in agony. Dozens of other military vehicles were set alight. At Fuxing hospital a crowd gathered to ask if relatives were among the dead and wounded. The names of forty-two of those who had been killed were posted on the wall of the bicycle shed. In the afternoon, the mortuary was opened for identification of the corpses, which were laid out on straw mats or white cloth on the concrete floor. Outside, family members burned paper spirit money for the dead.[23]

The clampdown spread through the city. Some protestors who approached the army lines to remonstrate with the soldiers were shot. Trucks roamed the streets, soldiers firing from the back. Doctors were killed as they tended the wounded. As a State Security Ministry report noted, the soldiers sitting on tank turrets opened fire whenever somebody jeered. People caught throwing stones and bottles at the troops risked summary execution. Troops in a convoy passing the International Hotel opened fire on a crowd in the early morning of 4 June; among the victims was a boy with schoolbooks strapped to his bicycle. According to the Ministry report, enraged civilians beat to death a military truck driver, burned six soldiers alive in another lorry, flung a soldier from an overpass and doused his body in petrol to set it alight before hanging it from the railings above.[24]

Tanks rolled through daytime streets – provoking the intervention of the white-shirted, black-trousered 'Tank Man' with a plastic shopping bag who halted one, dodging and weaving in front of it like a matador before being led away. At Beijing University, corpses from the night of 3–4 June were paraded around – five were laid out on a table surrounded by ice. White paper mourning flowers were put in the trees. A bloodstained greatcoat hung in a gateway. The autonomous students' association denounced 'this fascist massacre [which] pushes the people of the entire nation beyond the outer limits of toleration'. Thousands were arrested, and many beaten up or maltreated; some were killed and some of those shown on television as 'counter-revolutionary turmoil elements' could hardly stand. The Beijing mayor, Chen Xitong, broadcast a speech castigating 'a small handful of rioters' who had forced the Party and government to take extraordinary measures. It did not go down well.[25]

Precise casualty figures will never be known; the government said nearly 300 died in all the fighting, including several dozen soldiers.

Independent observers put the death toll in the low thousands, with at least 3,000 hurt.[26]

Demonstrations flared in sixty-three cities across the country during the day of 4 June, underlining how widespread was the call for change. By the following day, the number had swollen to 181. In Shanghai, more than 30,000 demonstrators brought traffic to a halt, and two thirds of factory workers stayed away from their plants. When police cleared 120 road blocks, another 145 were set up. In Wuhan, a sit-down protest closed the bridge across the Yangzi, forcing the steel mill to shut down; when unarmed troops tried to move them away, people resisted and spat at the soldiers. In Chengdu, police used electric prods to beat back demonstrators, who set fire to a shopping mall, a restaurant, a cinema and two police stations.[27]

In Manchuria, tens of thousands marched in the main four cities, bearing banners proclaiming 'Why don't you shoot us, too?' and 'Put down your butcher's knife, Li Peng'. In Lanzhou, in the north-west and Hangzhou on the east coast, protestors blocked the main railway lines by lying down on the tracks. In Guangzhou, the crowd of demonstrators was estimated at 50,000, and local residents stocked up on rice, salt, sugar, eggs and pork in case of trouble. In the SEZ of Shenzhen, 20,000 turned out. In Nanjing, 5,000 students marched in the rain, playing solemn music on tape recorders and carrying banners reading 'Blood debts must be repaid in blood'. In the prefecture of Shijiazhuang in Hebei, home of the 27th Army, which had taken part in the repression in the capital, 8,000 demonstrators laid wreaths at the military head-quarters on 5 June; the following day, more than 3,000 students attacked the building shouting '27th Army butchers!' A newsreader on the English-language service of Radio Beijing spoke of thousands of casualties, 'most of them innocent civilians' – the broadcast was immediately cut off.

Foreign governments issued condemnations. President Bush announced a suspension of weapons sales to the PRC, as did the European Union. The World Bank said it was stopping loans to China. In Hong Kong, 5 billion local dollars were withdrawn from the Bank of China. But no nation broke off diplomatic relations. Apart from some firing at a hotel occupied by foreigners, this had been an entirely internal affair. For the leadership, the criticism was a minor price to pay. 'In China, even one million people can be considered a small sum,' an official in Li Xiannian's office quoted Deng as saying.[28]

On 6 June, the leaders in Beijing met to assess the situation. 'If we hadn't been firm with these counter-revolutionary riots – if we hadn't come down hard – who knows what might have happened,' Deng began. He said a 'forgiving' attitude should be adopted towards the students – there was no such care for the *shimin* of Beijing or the workers. The only officially designated 'martyrs' were PLA soldiers. Making his first appearance on television since Gorbachev's visit, the patriarch was shown at martial law headquarters on 9 June, where he asked for a minute's silence in honour of the military dead.

There has been speculation that Deng was angry at the way in which the operation had been conducted on 3–4 June. A Party source was reported to have said that the leader told Yang Shangkun and Li Peng that they had bungled things. But he also denounced 'the cruelty of our enemies for whom we must show no mercy or forgiveness'.[29]

Once more, China's leadership was faced with a fact of history with which it could not engage properly, for its own sake. The demonstrations of the spring and early summer of 1989 are still set down officially as a counter-revolutionary action nipped in the bud by the resolution of Deng, Li Peng and their colleagues before it could destabilize the People's Republic. Though mothers of students who had died kept up a campaign for recognition of what had happened, it was only on the anniversary in 2007 that one was allowed to lay flowers on the spot where her son was killed – she was followed by plainclothes police. There was no re-examination of the event which had shocked the world. For the leadership it remains a taboo subject.

Fifteen years later, a doctor who treated victims at Beijing Army Hospital said that, when he reported on the carnage to Yang Shangkun, the president said the massacre had been the most serious mistake in the CCP's history. But he added that he could not do anything to put this right, though 'mistakes would be corrected in the future'. Asked for his observations on the tenth anniversary of the killings, the prime minister, Zhu Rongji, said the date meant nothing to him. At the end of 2007, police clamped down on the funeral of the dissident intellectual Bao Zhunin, whose pro-democracy ideas had been influential in the Beijing Spring and who had been imprisoned for five years. Up to a dozen security men were deployed to stop a single person leaving his or her home for the occasion, while a strong police force at the funeral home videoed those who managed to attend.[30]

Abroad, supporters of Beijing shy away from the very use of the word 'massacre'. At home, official control of the media has fostered amnesia; at the start of the twenty-first century, when a foreigner showed Beijing University students a photograph of the man confronting the tank, they did not recognize it. An episode in Chengdu on the anniversary of the massacre in 2007 showed both sides of the coin. A short classified advertisement was placed with the local evening paper reading 'Saluting the strong mothers of the victims of 64' – the numerals standing for 4 June. The clerk who handled the advertisement did not know what they meant. She telephoned her superior, who said it was the date of a mining disaster. The advertisement appeared, and was picked up by observant websites. Alerted, the authorities ordered copies of the paper to be withdrawn from sale. The deputy editor-in-chief and two colleagues were sacked.[31]

At a Party Plenum on 23–4 June, Zhao Ziyang faced his critics. The deposed Party chief was allowed to offer a self-defence to the condemnation of him that had been drawn up by Li Peng and endorsed by the Elders. Zhao admitted some minor errors, but did not deliver the kind of self-criticism which others, including Deng, had served up in the past. In particular, he denied the two main accusations – that he had heightened the turmoil of the demonstrations and had split the CCP. That brought charges that he was 'incorrigibly stubborn' and 'adamantly unrepentant'; but it also burnished his reputation as an honest man. Like Hu Yaobang in death, his standing grew as a symbol of what might have been.

Though some hardliners wanted to pursue Zhao, Deng ordered that no further action should be taken against him: 'Let us not get tangled up in who is responsible,' the leader said. The former Party boss was put under house arrest but was allowed to travel from time to time under official supervision and was sighted playing golf. A few photographs of him appeared, thinner-faced and grey-haired. His name remained closely associated with reform. The regime, under Deng and his successors, showed great nervousness about any of his thoughts being circulated. He wrote at least two letters to the authorities proposing a re-examination of the Tiananmen verdict; there was no response and they were not published.

When Zhao died in 2005, apparently of pneumonia and a series of strokes, minimum publicity was given in official media, which did not note the posts he had held and limited themselves to a fifty-nine-word obituary. Websites which discussed his life were shut down. In Hong Kong, a candlelight vigil attracted up to 15,000 people. When the question of a state funeral came up, Beijing said that such occasions were no longer held. Zhao was cremated at the Babaoshan Revolution Cemetery outside the capital. The 2,000 vetted mourners were forbidden to bring flowers. A disagreement between the authorities and the family meant there was no eulogy. State television mentioned his death for the first time that day, saying he had made serious mistakes in 1989. His ashes were denied a place at the cemetery, so his family took them home.

The liberal Politburo Standing Committee member Hu Qili, who had opposed martial law, lost all his posts. Bao Tong was sentenced to seven years in jail and expelled from the Party. The culture minister, the writer Wang Meng, whose short story had been quarrelled over during the Hundred Flowers two decades earlier, was forced to resign for his sympathy with the students. Two pro-Zhao members of the Central Secretariat and several supportive editors lost their jobs. Another bright younger figure, the economic planner of Tianjin, Wei Zhang, was put under 'hotel arrest' after resigning his official posts in protest at martial law, before going to teach at Harvard and Cambridge in Britain; he was not allowed back to China.

Wang Dan, who had left Beijing for Nanjing, returned stoically to the capital to meet his fate. He was imprisoned twice, for a total of seven years. On being released, he left for the United States. At the end of a show trial, the liberal think-tankers Chen Ziming and Wang Juntao, now castigated as 'black hands behind the black hands', received thirteen years each. The labour organizer Han Dongfang went to the police after hearing his name on the list of wanted people to tell them, 'I've come here because you've got your facts wrong'; he was held for twenty-two months without trial and then released, seriously ill with tuberculosis, and went to live in Hong Kong, where he continued to promote workers' rights. The singer Hou got away, but his fellow hunger-striker, the teacher Liu Xiaobo, was imprisoned for twenty-two months as an 'evil mastermind [who] conspired with reactionary forces at home and abroad to manipulate the students and instigate turmoil'. The writer Dai Qing, who had sought to get the students to leave the square early on, was sent to prison for ten months for having shown sympathy towards them.

Others hid in the countryside or were smuggled away by sympathizers, sometimes with help from associates in Hong Kong. Wuerkaixi, who had slipped out of Tiananmen in time, got to France before moving to Taiwan. The scientists Fang Lizhi and his wife were given sanctuary in the US embassy, where they remained for a year before being flown out on an American air force plane to England and then on to the USA.

Chai Ling escaped, too, leaving behind a taped message declaring, 'The more frenzied the fascists become in their brutal suppression, the closer we are to the birth of a true people's, democratic republic! The final moment has come for the survival of our nation! Compatriots, awaken! Down with fascists! Down with military rule! The people will be victorious!' Like her associate Li Lu, she reached America, where she would later start a software firm, its publicity saying that a woman who had stood up to the Communist regime could get the better of Bill Gates. Her husband, Feng Congde, also escaped abroad.[32]

There was persecution of anybody who questioned the official version of events. A 42-year-old laid-off worker, who asked in an interview with the American ABC television network, 'Is this what the people's government does? Using tanks to crush people?', was jailed for ten years as a 'vicious counter-revolutionary instigator'; neighbours had denounced him after Chinese television showed his picture.[33]

A dozen provinces reported the arrest of 10,147 'turmoil elements' and the liquidation of 417 illegal organizations. In Beijing, 4,386 people were detained and 546 groups broken up. In Shanghai, there were only 273 arrests, but the Public Security Ministry was told that two Taiwanese-Kuomintang spy rings had been cracked. An internal Xinhua news agency story said that a fifth of all students remained defiant. Classroom graffiti proclaimed 'China is dead!', 'The truth will out some day' and 'Where is justice?' When the lights went out in dormitories, the report added, young male students 'vent their rage with wild yelps and cries'. But most ignored current events, it said, concentrating rather on romance, amusements and mahjong. 'The campuses had calmed down, but had also turned as silent as a graveyard,' the report concluded. Some students who had taken part in the demonstrations were given poor grades as punishment. In places, they were rejected as troublemakers, turned away from hotels and disqualified from jobs.[34]

*

As had been the case repeatedly since the Hundred Days of 1898, pressure for reform had been met by repression. Deng joined the Dowager Empress, Yuan Shikai, Chiang Kai-shek and Mao Zedong as a man who clamped down on freedom if it appeared to threaten the form of regime he headed, and, thereby, his own position. The reasoned search for political progress was still not part of the Chinese system. Hu Yaobang and Zhao Ziyang had been upstaged by Li Peng and Wang Zhen, Wang Dan by Chai Ling.

The monolith held for a variety of reasons. Despite its internal factions and arguments, the pervasive authority established by the Communist Party over Chinese society since 1949 gave it great strength in depth, and meant that independent bodies paled in comparison. The leadership could take comfort from the way in which the urban protests had not aroused an echo in the countryside; as the Party secretary of Shanxi put it, 'at this crucial moment, peasants have been siding with the Party and the government . . . thereby contributing in a special way to the stabilization of the situation and setting the people's minds at rest. The Party and government are indebted to you.'[35]

Though there had been demonstrations in cities such as Guangzhou and Shenzhen, the coastal zones where economic progress was greatest had remained relatively quiet. The discipline of the CCP had been in marked contrast to the divisions and uncertainties among its opponents, their lack of a common positive message that could engage the nation, and the absence of an effective united front between citizens, workers and students. Despite the initial blocking of the army, the army also had brute force at its disposal. On top of which, it was easy for the authorities to play on fears of instability, particularly given recent memories of the Cultural Revolution, and thus to present itself as the guarantor of the nation, in possession of the Mandate of Heaven in a tradition stretching back through the centuries.

In this mode, at the meeting on 6 June, Deng set the tone for the future:

We Chinese have self-confidence; inferiority complexes get you nowhere. For more than a century, we were made to feel inferior, but then, under the leadership of the Communist Party, we stood up. No behemoth out there can scare us. We fought the Japanese for eight years and fought the Americans in Korea for three. We have a tradition of winning even when we are outnumbered and under-armed.

Our people are not going to cower before foreign invasions or threats, and neither will our children or our grand-children.

A stable domestic situation was, he added, indispensable if China was to meet its development goals:

We don't care what others say about us; all we care about is a peaceful environment for our own development . . . If people demonstrate 365 days a year and don't want to do anything else, reform and opening will get nowhere. We've got to make it understood both inside and outside China that we're tightening control for the sake of stability, which means for the sake of reform and opening and modern construction.

Nearly two decades later, in 2007, the reformer Bao Tong wrote in an essay:

If indeed it is the case that the great and glorious victory of the Chinese Communist Party was really only that it substituted for the one-party rule of the Nationalist Party the one-party rule of the Communist Party, then it certainly won't be enough to change the system of ownership, or to change society.

Throughout the whole of Chinese history, all the characters, great and small, who believe in the superstition of the barrel of the gun – from Mao Zedong to Chiang Kai-shek, to the Northern Warlords and the Boxer Rebellion . . . not one of them has succeeded in changing the pattern of their forefathers. Instead, they have been condemned to repeating version after version, amid cycles of violence and bloodshed, of the same drama, enacting without change the rise and fall of kings and bandits.[36]

PART 6

Jiang Zemin and Hu Jintao

The crushing of dissent in 1989 marked a fundamental choice by the Chinese leadership which endured into the twenty-first century. If there is such a thing as historic inevitability, the record going back not just to 1949 but to 1898 made the repression inevitable. Deng ensured that economic reform would be preserved. But, as under the empire, politics and the running of the state were to be subject to a monopoly regime claiming to hold the keys to truth. Though the new leaders, Jiang Zemin and then Hu Jintao, lacked the historic weight of their predecessors, they presided over economic growth that outdid anything achieved before, while confirming China's re-emergence as a major global player. With Hu, the leadership entered the managerial age. Senior cadres wore dark, Western-style suits instead of Mao jackets. The spitoons used by the Helmsman and Deng disappeared, replaced by mobile telephones and PowerPoint presentations. But the decisions of the 1980s, culminating in the use of troops to put down the students and people in the capital on 3–4 June 1989, ensured that China would be trapped in a political cocoon, going through ideological gyrations to try to reconcile extreme economic mobility with the preservation of the statist system that had died in Europe with the end of the Soviet Union. In true Dengish tradition, talk of political reform under Jiang and Hu did not mean sharing power, but finding ways of making the rule of the CCP more effective – or, at least, to provide for its survival.

A century and a half after the Qing dynasty confronted the rising challenges to the empire of two millennia, its Communist heirs faced a not dissimilar array of tests. At the heart of them was the ability of the regime to cope with broad-based changes, and to live up to its own claims to monopoly power. The overarching question for the twenty-first century was whether the new generation of rulers could rise above the past, or whether the nature of 21st-century China – for all its vast economic success – made it a country-continent whose political and social fault lines would always be threatening its material achievements, this time with global implications.

32

The New–Old Generations

Once the protests had been repressed in early June 1989, the Party embarked on the task of reasserting itself under a leadership that was both new and old. With Jiang Zemin installed as CCP chief at the head of the Third Generation of Communist leaders, three hold-overs remained on the Standing Committee of the Politburo – the security chief Qiao Shi, who might have hoped for the top job himself, the premier, Li Peng, who was seen as too unpopular to have been promoted, and the conservative Yao Yilin. The two new men appointed to the committee constituted a balancing act.

One, the boss of Tianjin, Li Ruihuan, was a man of many parts who had kept his city relatively quiet during the upheaval – some attributed this, in part, to the way in which he allowed demonstrators to take the train to Beijing. Deng thought highly of Li as an economic reformer and an energetic operator who got things done. The other new appointee, Song Ping, was a boring conservative apparatchik who was rewarded for his work in maintaining Party unity as head of the CCP Organization Department. Li was fifty-five, Song seventy-two.

A rectification campaign was launched in which all urban CCP members were investigated. Li Peng promulgated a law prohibiting demonstrations that questioned CCP leadership, or threatened stability in any manner. At the same time, a crackdown on corruption was ordered along with austerity at the top: children of officials were banned from business, and top figures were to forgo personal cars and foreign food.

On 29 September 1989, Jiang Zemin gave the official verdict on what had happened earlier in the year. 'The turmoil and rebellion that occurred in the late spring and early summer of this year was the result of the combination of the international climate and the domestic climate,' he told a meeting.

Hostile forces at home and abroad created this turmoil to overthrow the leadership of the CCP, subvert the socialist system, and turn China into a bourgeois republic and into an appendage of big Western capitalist powers once again ... We have won this struggle ... We should educate and unite with the overwhelming majority of people, isolate and deal blows to an extremely small number of hostile elements, thoroughly investigate all counter-revolutionary activity, eliminate any hidden perils, and draw profound lessons from all this.[1]

At a CCP Plenum six weeks later, Deng stressed the need to put the summer events to rest, overruling the desire of hardliners to subject Zhao Ziyang to the harsh punishment meted out to ideological transgressors in the past. Rather, the Paramount Leader used the meeting to announce his withdrawal from active involvement in running the country, subject to the proviso that 'if I have any useful ideas and suggestions, I will gladly convey them to the new leadership.' He also remarked to officials that they should not pay attention if he started to say 'crazy things' as he aged. To show he was serious about stepping back, Deng handed the chairmanship of the Military Affairs Commission (MAC) to Jiang Zemin.

This undoubtedly disappointed President Yang Shangkun, who saw himself in the job. But the head of state became first vice-chairman and his brother was named as general secretary of the commission, creating a strong family power base at the top of the military, further buttressed by Jiang's lack of army credentials. The fall of the Ceauşescu dictatorship in Romania in December after it had lost the support of the army was seen in Beijing as evidence of the need to ensure PLA loyalty; as a result, several thousand officers had their conduct investigated, resulting in some court martials and dismissals. An indoctrination campaign was launched among the troops against bourgeois liberalization and 'peaceful evolution' – meaning the spread of Western capitalist democracy to the PRC. The military budget for 1990 was increased by 15 per cent. To sweeten it further, the PLA was allowed to join in the economic boom by expanding its business interests.[2]

As well as the specific case of Romania, Mikhail Gorbachev's policies of liberalization in the USSR and Eastern Europe were a wider cause for concern. Jiang denounced the Soviet leader as 'basically of the same ilk' as Trotsky. As the Soviet empire disintegrated, the Chinese leadership made much of the resulting instability. The Plenum reasserted Deng's policies of opening up economically, attracting foreign investment, and seeking to 'reform and perfect' industry, but conservative policies long advocated by Chen Yun took precedence. Demand was to be held back by limiting wage rises; growth was to be halved from the 14 per cent reached in 1988; macro-economic controls were to be strengthened, and priority given to state enterprises. The trading companies that had flourished under reform would be brought to heel, with fines and, in the case of one of the biggest conglomerates, break-up.

Jiang's priority was to establish himself politically as the 'core' of the CCP, the role Deng had designated for him in the summer of 1989. His arrival at the top had been facilitated by the way that more powerful figures regarded him as a transitory leader, but his personal ambition melded completely with strengthening the CCP after the shock of 1989, and enabled him to build up his own position through favours, tactical alliances, the appointment of associates from Shanghai in the centre, and the adroit use of his expansive personality in contrast to the dour Li Peng.

Born in 1926 in Jiangsu province, Jiang was the adopted son of a revolutionary hero who died fighting the Japanese. He went to the USSR as a young man to work at the Stalin Automobile Factory in Moscow before returning to apply his expertise in the Shanghai area. Politically cautious, he avoided trouble during the Cultural Revolution. After spells heading the Machine Building and Electronics ministries, he became mayor of Shanghai in 1985 and entered the Politburo two years later. Though his city had seen its share of demonstrations in 1989, Jiang's handling was held by the leadership to have shown strength while avoiding the bloodshed seen in Beijing.

A gregarious polyglot and rounded personality who could speak at least some English, Russian, Japanese and Romanian as well as the Cantonese dialect, Jiang gave every impression of enjoying his rising status to the full. Known for his liking of Chinese poetry and music, he also showed a taste for Western melodies, from Beethoven and 'O Sole Mio' to karaoke Elvis Presley. Stout and with the regulation dyed-black hair, he relished the wider world stage, even if he appeared like a chubby wind-up doll on state occasions and was once caught embarrassingly by a photographer combing himself in an ante-room before meeting the king of Spain.

Though he would draw up ideological lists of the Twelve Relationships or the Seven Differentials, the secretary's doctrinal influence was confused, confusing and minimal, until, at the end of his period in power, he came up with a formula to reconcile business and the CCP. His favourite exhortation to 'talk more about politics' could be read in different ways – as a call for cadres to spend more time studying the sacred texts of the regime, as a warning to pay attention to what the leadership ordained or as an injunction to find truth by applying the truths of Marxism–Leninism–Mao Zedong Thought as interpreted by the Party secretary. Easy to write off as a lightweight, particularly when compared to Mao and Deng, he showed acute political skills appropriate to a calmer era in which the emphasis came to be on extending the material progress set in train in the 1980s without putting the CCP-directed status quo at risk.[3]

Though Deng had announced his withdrawal from day-to-day affairs and was showing his age, the first two and a half years after the Beijing showdown were dominated by a major power struggle between economic conservatives and the heritage of the changes launched by the Paramount Leader in 1978. The clock could not be turned back to before 1978; market-driven measures were taken such as the opening of the Shanghai stock exchange at the end of 1990 (located in the hotel where Zhou Enlai had hidden after the White Terror purge was launched in 1927). But the faction headed by Chen Yun in the Central Advisory Committee, grouping the Party Elders, adopted an increasingly confrontational attitude towards reform, singling out the new Standing Committee member, Li Ruihuan, as a particular target. In a frontal attack, Li Peng said that 'reform and opening up should not be taken as the guiding principle. Instead, sustained, steady and co-ordinated development should be taken as the guiding principle.' Wang Zhen decried the way in which economic change was ushering in 'western religion, capitalism and clans', with fewer and fewer young people joining the CCP – a poll showed that the main motivation for membership was to achieve a position that could be exploited for gain. In one conversation with Peng Zhen, Big Cannon Wang became so heated about what was going awry that he fell over and broke his pelvis.[4]

The debate on economic ideology was accompanied by one on agriculture, with some conservatives pressing for a revival of collectivization. The pressure was such that, in some places, peasants sold their livestock in case they were seized for new communes. But the reformers stood their ground, arguing that collectivization would lead to 'a severe deterioration in relations between the peasantry and the Party and government' bringing severe damage to rural output.[5]

Deng's policy of friendship towards the United States came in for criticism from those who thought the PRC should take a more assertive international role. The discontent broke through when a group of 116 PLA officers wrote to Jiang in 1993 complaining that concessions to Washington had 'impaired the dignity of the Chinese people, damaged the image of the Chinese nation, undermined the glorious tradition of the People's Liberation Army, and dampened the army's morale and combat effectiveness'. This fronde, which found an echo among some political conservatives, did not shift policy, and civilian control of the PLA remained intact – militarily the army's position had been weakened by the revelation of its backwardness compared to the performance of US forces in the Gulf War. But it was a warning of the growth of nationalism.[6]

The conservatives also made much of the corruption spawned by reforms, not just in business but also among the police and judges; between 1989 and 1991, more than 42,000 cadres were prosecuted for economic crimes, nearly all of them 'small potatoes' occupying positions below provincial government level. At the same time, a tough, centralized authoritarian doctrine emerged, aimed at keeping bourgeois liberalism at bay and preventing the Chinese Communist Party from collapsing as in Eastern Europe and the USSR.

However, after the victory of 1989, full-throated political repression was not in vogue. Deng's insistence on limiting the persecution of liberals held. Hardline efforts to get the 1989 protests classified as 'counter-revolutionary rebellion' were unsuccessful. Chen Yun was said to have disapproved of the use of force in June 1989. Several liberal officials who had suffered then were rehabilitated, though to lower positions than they had held before. The rectification campaign launched after the suppression of the demonstrations resulted in the punishment of only 1,179 cadres out of an estimated 800,000 officials who backed the students.[7]

The regime showed no compunction, however, when faced with protests and autonomist demonstrations in both Tibet and Xinjiang in 1990. The brutality used against the Tibetans pushed the Dalai Lama to take a much tougher stand against Chinese occupation as security forces unleashed a wave of arrests, beatings and killings in Lhasa. A group of Uyghurs, meanwhile, prepared for a jihad to free their territory; twenty-two were killed and 200 arrested when they were put down.

In poor health, Deng had trouble countering the challenge to his key policy. 'Nobody takes any notice of me,' he complained in an interview. As a weathervane, Jiang Zemin moved closer to the Chen Yun camp. His speech on the seventieth anniversary of the founding of the CCP in July 1991 took such a hard line that the Paramount Leader was reported to have called it 'one-sided'. His successor as mayor of Shanghai, Zhu Rongji, who had been promoted to vice-premier charged with supervising industrial restructuring, came under conservative attack. Chen Yun proposed a leading position in the Party for Little Deng, who warned of 'extremely dangerous' sprouts of liberalism appearing in the CCP. An article in the *People's Daily*, from the Chen camp, echoed the Mao-era 'Better Red Than Expert' line in arguing that politics should be more important than ability in determining promotions. Bo Yibo pointed to the chaotic effect of liberalism in the former USSR. Big Cannon Wang attacked the Wenzhou area of Zhejiang, a model for private-sector, market-driven economic development, as a 'quasi capitalist enclave' outside CCP control. Chen Yun decried the way in which Western ideology was spreading in from the coast, and could lead to 'a huge price' being paid.[8]

Deng used his influence at a Party Plenum at the end of 1991 to finesse the issues by avoiding most of them. The following month, Little Deng was reported to have met five other conservatives, including Wang Zhen and the new Standing Committee member, Song Ping, to discuss writing an emergency report saying that the PRC risked undergoing a capitalist restoration. In reaction, Li Ruihuan, attacked 'dry and empty sermons and ... formalistic propaganda'. Undeterred, the conservatives proposed changes in the SEZs to rid them of their capitalist elements.

On 15 January 1992, though in weak health, Deng launched his counter-offensive, the last major action of his life and one which would set his decisive stamp on the evolution of China into the twenty-first century. The hallowed status that he was accorded subsequently masks how severe the attack on the Paramount Leader's core policy had become, forcing him to throw his full personal weight into the battle to prevent a roll-back.

Deng's Southern Tour of 1992 took him in his private train from Wuhan to the special zones of Shenzhen* and Zhuhai, to give the economic

---

* A massive mural of Deng stands in the centre of Shenzhen to mark the trip.

reform process its vital second wind. He also went to Shanghai, which had been overshadowed by the development zones but was now given the mission of making the Yangzi Delta into a new growth pole, greatly aided by the presence in Beijing of its former mayor and his associates in the 'Shanghai Faction', which ensured that the city reclaimed its role as a commercial and industrial centre.

On his tour, the Paramount Leader insisted on the need to put fresh muscle behind the opening-up process and industrial modernization using foreign technology and capital. 'We should be bolder in carrying out reforms and opening up to the outside world and in making experimentation; we should not act like a woman with bound feet,' he said, echoing one of the phrases Mao had used to mock adversaries. 'For what we regard as correct, just try it and go ahead daringly.' Deng drew an explicit link between economic reform and stability, saying that, without material progress, 4 June would have led to chaos and civil war. To achieve the victory of socialism, he argued, 'we must boldly absorb and draw on all fruits of civilisation created by the society of mankind . . . including advanced capitalist countries.'[9]

Though the Paramount Leader was still the major actor in the PRC, reporting of the tour was minimal to start with. But, led by Li Ruihuan, the pro-Dengists eventually got the Party and state media to write about the trip, and the attack on leftism rose steadily. Thirty-five conservatives, including Chen Yun, drew up a paper urging Deng to cleave tightly to socialism, oppose 'peaceful evolution' and change the policy direction. But the sortie to the south was proving irresistible in its vision of a fast development for which the CCP would be able to claim credit. The SEZs boomed. Foreign money poured in. Western firms saw the cost benefits of using Chinese labour. Modern machinery was imported. Tens of millions of migrant workers crowded into the development zones. Annual growth soared. The seeds of a middle class began to emerge, made up of entrepreneurs and well-connected businessmen who could use their political contacts to move ahead. The generally peaceful international climate provided the essential context for rising exports and inward investment. China's role as assembly shop for the world became irreversible.

Deng's victory also ensured that there would be no new collectivization in the countryside. The household responsibility system which had revolutionized rural life in the 1980s was maintained, and, in 1994, regulations were issued to give farmers thirty-year leases on their land. There was a recognition in the leadership that the stress on industry had penalized agriculture, and legislation was introduced to protect farmers and boost investment in the countryside above revenue taken out in taxation. But government investigations in the mid-1990s found that rural investment was still low, and that farmers were hit by high taxes and rising prices for inputs. Land under cultivation shrank, and irrigation works became antiquated. Rural protests against taxes erupted in several provinces, as they had done back to imperial times. In inner-Party elections, urban areas had eight times as many votes as the countryside. Officials kept a tighter grip on state land rights in rural areas than in cities.[10]

Having incurred some displeasure from the Paramount Leader for leaning towards the Chen Yun camp at the start of the economic debate, Jiang Zemin swiftly trimmed his sails to gain Deng's backing, though the patriarch brought a younger man, Hu Jintao, into the Standing Committee of the Politburo as his chosen candidate for the succession when Jiang stepped down in 2002. (He also had an octogenarian general, Liu Huaqing, promoted to the Committee to 'balance' Jiang further – he was the last Long Marcher on the top CCP body.)

Getting back into line, the Party secretary went out of his way to warn against leftism, and insist on the need to do everything to 'liberate productive forces'. President Yang also came out in support. 'It is normal to have differences of opinion, but opposition in action is not allowed,' Jiang decreed. 'Anybody who fails to realise this point is no Communist.' The supreme authority of 'one centre' – that is of Deng and his policy – was asserted.

Vice-premier Tian Jiyun laid on the sarcasm with a trowel when he proposed establishing a zone where leftist policies would be applied through total state planning, rationing and queuing for food, where foreign investment and foreigners would be banned, and inhabitants would not be allowed to travel or send their children abroad. Would leftist leaders be ready to move to such a place, he asked, before attacking the 'wind faction' of leaders who shifted their position according to prevailing conditions; he mentioned no names, but Jiang Zemin and the security chief Qiao Shi were obvious candidates.

Though Chen Yun remained semi-detached, and would continue his argument with Deng as they advanced into their dotage, other conservatives and fence-sitters fell into line. Qiao urged intense study of Deng Thought to achieve wisdom. Though he still advocated cutting annual growth to 6 per cent, Li Peng told ministries to 'grasp the current favourable opportunity to step up economic and political reforms'.

The premier had good reason to seek favour; a vote at the National People's Congress in 1992 on his pet project for the Three Gorges Dam had resulted in the unusually high proportion of one third of delegates either voting against the idea or abstaining. Jiang's fellow Shanghainese, Zhu Rongji, who was described by Deng as 'one of the few cadres who really understands how the economy works', loomed as a potential replacement when the prime minister's term expired in 1993.

Zhu was a somewhat mournful-looking figure given to outbursts of temper; his early career as a promising young economist had been interrupted by a period in disgrace after being branded as a rightist in the repression that followed the Hundred Flowers. But, in the 1980s, he made it back to the State Economic Commission, where he attracted Deng's attention. From 1988 to 1991, he served as mayor and then CCP secretary in Shanghai, gaining the nickname of 'One-Chop Zhou' for the way he cut through the bureaucracy with his tough management style. When he moved to Beijing in Jiang's wake, there could be no doubt that he was the man best placed to push through economic reform, attack corruption and rationalize the state sector. He urged local leaders to 'storm the heavily fortified position' of loss-making state firms. His driving, hard-working style led to the saying that 'once Rongji takes charge, he can do the work of two.' But he lacked a strong political base – and had many enemies in the establishment which still held ultimate control.[11]

Deng underlined his encouragement for 'accelerated market reform' during a well-publicized visit to the Capital Iron and Steel Plant in Beijing in May 1992. The plant's role as a major polluter, situated in the middle of the city, was of no importance beside its adoption of market management methods which the Paramount Leader praised. Meanwhile, the economic restructuring agency answered Li Peng's call for 6 per cent growth by advocating 10 per cent expansion. Adopting Zhu Rongji's suggestion, the State Council issued a fifty-four-point decree to increase the freedom of enterprises to run themselves and render it easier to shut down loss-making state companies. The vice-premier had already made his mark with a campaign to render state-owned enterprises (SOEs) less reliant on subsidies and more alive to the need to make profits, in the process trying to dismantle the complex chain of debts between them.[12]

China's uneconomic coal mines were a prime target for rationalization; the Five-Year Plan for 1991–5 provided for 400,000 of the 7 million workers in the heavily loss-making industry to be laid off. Visiting a huge coal mine in Shanxi in 1992, Zhu was filmed upbraiding the managers to their faces about how they should cut the labour force, with plenty of details to back up his argument. Acknowledging his abrasiveness, the vice-premier wondered why people would not do their jobs properly until he lost his temper with them.[13]

At the Party Centre, Li Ruihuan got the upper hand over hardliners in the information apparatus, notably with the departure of the highly conservative propaganda director. There was some relaxation in the arts as films by leading director Zhang Yimou such as *Raise the Red Lantern* were cleared to be shown for the first time. Li recognized the place of non-political entertainment, and said there should be no censorship of works which did not violate the constitution. In this easier attitude, China's first gay 'salon' opened in Beijing, though homosexuality was still officially regarded as a mental ailment. 'Men's World' lasted for only six months before being shut down by the Public Health Ministry. Still, a symposium held at a leading hotel in the capital heard speakers argue that heterosexuals and homosexuals should be treated equally.[14]

The success of Deng's Southern Tour in relaunching economic change came with a considerable price. Growth got out of hand, registering a 16 per cent year-on-year spurt in the six months after he ended his trip. Industrial output was up by 19 per cent in the same period. Investment in plant and other fixed assets soared by 30 per cent, fuelled by cheap loans from state banks encouraged by officials who put politics, crude output growth and cronyism ahead of a proper assessment of the credit risks involved. A huge stock market bubble inflated as inexperienced investors piled in to the exchanges in Shanghai and Shenzhen, where limitations on the availability of shares provoked rioting. Deng had praised the launch of the two exchanges. Conservatives saw them as capitalist poison. When the indexes on the two markets fell by two thirds, get-rich-quick punters were taught a savage lesson in the way shares could plunge as well as soar.

Using the 1989 condemnatory term of 'turmoil' to describe the stock market ride, Chen Yun issued another lengthy critique of the path Deng was following, warning of the social and political dangers being created, which he pointedly compared to the threat posed by leftist policies in the past. But the Fourteenth CCP Congress, held in October 1992, ratified the pursuit of a 'socialist market economy' and 'socialism with Chinese characteristics'. Jiang's report to the meeting called on comrades to 'break the shackles of traditional conceptions and subjective prejudices and overcome our habit of following the beaten track and rejecting new things'. The Party secretary had nothing new to offer politically, however – in that, he was simply reflecting the barrenness of Deng's outlook, as when the Paramount Leader declared flatly that 'the status of the Chinese Communist Party must never be challenged; China cannot adopt a multi-party system.'[15]

Though Deng was reported to be discontented from time to time, Jiang enjoyed his general backing. But he was still subject to sniping from some who thought Qiao Shi or Li Ruihuan should get his job, and played his habitual game of trying to attract all the support he could get to place himself at the core of the regime. So, while he adopted Deng's dictum to 'watch out for the Right, but mainly defend against the Left', he also stressed the need to strengthen the dictatorship of the people against 'hostile forces' and continued to refer to the 1989 demonstrations as 'counter-revolutionary rebellion'.[16]

The Party Congress in 1992, which saw an upsurge in praise for the Paramount Leader and his 'brilliant' economic policies, was the occasion for Deng to execute changes at the top of the regime which he had held back from since the upheaval of 1989. It thus marked a significant point, with the promotion of men who would ensure that there was no turning back from the reforms initiated in 1978.

A batch of younger technocrats was elected to the Central Committee, most of them university-educated. PLA representation also rose. In keeping with the rejuvenation Deng had always sought below him, eight senior members of the fourteen-strong Politburo resigned or did not stand for reappointment. Among them were three hardliners and two reformers. The head of state, Yang Shangkun, finally stepped down from the Politburo at the age of eighty-five, only to be replaced by his 72-year-old brother. However, the younger brother was dropped from the Military Affairs Commission because of opposition from the PLA, and, no doubt, Deng's desire to cut the 'Yang Family Party' down to size. When Yang relinquished the state presidency the following spring, the job went to Jiang.

Zhu Rongji was one of seven supporters of reform who joined the Politburo, alongside Party secretaries from Shanghai, Guangdong, Tianjin and Shandong. Four more appointees were either centrists or former conservatives who could be classed in the 'wind faction'. Vice-premier Zhu, now sixty-four, was elected to the Standing Committee at the apex of the regime, alongside the PLA general Liu Huaqing, a Deng associate who would assure the army its voice was being heard, and the rising young technocrat Hu Jintao, who had been singled out by Deng as the likely chief of the next generation of leaders for the twenty-first century and who had shown an adroitness at maintaining links with different CCP factions.

Born in 1942 in Jiangsu,* Hu appeared very different from Jiang, serious and reserved in contrast to the Party secretary's outgoing bonhomie. Though his parents were both modest teachers, his grandfather had been a tea merchant. But this capitalist ancestry did not stand in his way as he progressed to study hydraulic engineering at Qinghua University in Beijing where he was inducted into the Communist Youth League. After being sent to 'learn from the masses' during the Cultural Revolution, he spent fourteen years in all in poverty-stricken Gansu, where he got married and rose to run infrastructure projects, attracting the attention of the province's Party secretary, future Politburo member Song Ping. Going to the Party School in Beijing in 1981, he got to know the son of Hu Yaobang, a fellow student, who introduced him to his father, who made him secretary of the Youth League, first in Gansu and then nationally.[17]

By the time Deng Xiaoping decided to drop Hu Yaobang, Hu Jintao was on another poor-province assignment, as Party chief in Guizhou, where he escaped the fall-out from his patron's eviction. He was well known by then in CCP circles as a polite, hard-working, youngish man with a photographic memory, and good connections both in the Youth League and among rising cadres who worked in poor regions. But his

* A certain confusion was purposely created over Hu's birthplace with references to his family coming from Anhui. This was because his real birthplace, Taizhou in Jiangsu, was close to the hometown of Jiang Zemin and another Politburo Standing Committee member. This might have led to suggestions that a clique from Jiangsu had gathered excessive power at the top of the CCP so the place was obfuscated (Lam, *Hu*, p. 5).

refusal to join in the denunciations of Hu Yaobang brought a semi-demotion when he was assigned to troublesome Tibet. Once again, however, being sent to a backward area turned out to be to Hu's advantage as he master-minded the repression of anti-Beijing, anti-Han rallies in March 1989.

In 1992, Jiang planned to name Hu as minister for water resources or education minister, but Deng insisted on his promotion to the Politburo and a leap-frog jump to the top echelon of the Standing Committee. 'It would be a mistake to waste such a big talent,' the Paramount Leader told the Party secretary. The younger man had shown himself to be both 'red and expert', and 'tough with both fists' – in pushing economic reform but also in dealing with opponents of the Party. As a further sign of his ascension, he was named to head the six-person Central Party Secretariat, which was also joined by the fifty-year-old official Wen Jiabao, a former aide of both Zhao Ziyang and Zhu Rongji, who would accompany him when the time came for the new generation to assume power and who, like Hu, had worked in Gansu.

In the top rank, Zhu, Hu and Li Ruihuan were firmly in the economic reform camp, which now included both Jiang Zemin and Qiao Shi. For the PLA, General Liu was likely to go along with the majority. That left Li Peng isolated if he tried to follow a conservative course – in voting for the Central Committee, he was reported to have received the lowest tally of any Standing Committee member, while Zhu got the highest. As age set in and his health declined (he had to be supported by his daughter on the Southern Tour and during his visit to the Beijing iron and steel plant), Deng had thus set in place both a successor and a leadership team he could count on to pursue his policies.

Conservatives did poorly in the voting for the Central Committee at the 1992 congress – Little Deng Liqun was not even nominated as a candidate. They had been weakened by the deaths of several aged hard-liners, and would lose a strident voice when Big Cannon Wang died the following March. Though they launched a fresh offensive during the winter of 1992–3, their defeat was underlined by the abolition of the Central Advisory Committee, which Chen Yun had used as his spring-board to criticize economic reform. Li Peng raised his recommendation for the growth rate from 6 to 9 per cent, still well below the actual 13 per cent but a sign of how the conservatives were being forced to recognize that Deng's revolution had come to stay.

Though prominent associates of Zhao Ziyang were dropped from the Central Committee, a bid by hardliners to get the 1992 Congress to pass a formal condemnation of the ousted Party chief failed, in line with the Paramount Leader's policy of avoiding a show trial. The prison sentence on his lieutenant, Bao Tong, was held to be enough. A full-scale ideological trial of Zhao would have been awkward on several counts now that reform was roaring ahead once more. It would have raised the question of whether Deng was as fallible as Mao had been in choosing putative successors. Party unity could have been harmed. Conservatives would have had a field day. However, Deng also firmly opposed any attempt to reconsider what had happened in 1989, let alone issue a formal amnesty for those sentenced for their activities then. Better for Bao to be the sacrifice, for Zhao to be shut up under house arrest, for the wisdom of the CCP in suppressing the 'turmoil' to be upheld, and for the prestige of the Party to be preserved as June Fourth was set down in the official texts as a necessary defence of the stability that was enabling the world's biggest population to get steadily richer.[18]

However, despite the victory of Deng and his supporters, there was no escaping the need to get the economy under control. A Leading Group on Finance and the Economy was formed in late 1992; Zhu Rongji was appointed the body's deputy alongside Li Peng, immediately below Jiang. He headed the Leading Group on Agriculture and took charge of the Central Bank as he was entrusted with the job of reconciling economic reform and stability. Though he had initially had some doubts about the new path, Zhu applied all his famed drive to cooling down the economy, ruffling many feathers on top of the hostility his clean-up of state-owned firms had already created; he remarked that he would have 100 coffins made – 99 for those he pursued and one for himself when one of his quarry killed him. He was on an inevitable collision course with Li Peng. In April 1993, the premier suffered a heart attack. His recovery was difficult and, in July, his economic responsibilities were moved wholesale to Zhu. Cadres began to talk of a 'Jiang–Zhu axis' and a joke in Beijing had it that Li had been advised to take a long rest by 'Dr Deng'.[19]

The problems facing China were, however, not restricted to economic over-heating, though many were linked to it. As would be the case into the twenty-first century, the PRC had a particular combination of difficulties spawned by the combination of very high growth with a static political system in a country that was still relatively backward and was marked by significant social troubles and its historical legacy. Illiteracy rose. The wealth gap widened between booming coastal provinces and the far larger interior. Fuelled primarily by local industries, output from the three eastern provinces of Jiangsu, Zhejiang and Shandong in the early 1990s was ten times the combined total of nine provinces and autonomous regions in the west while the income disparity between the two areas doubled.

Provinces asserted their quasi-independence in pursuing growth, and – as in the late imperial or Republican periods – resisted attempts by the centre to get them to contribute more in tax revenue. Further down the scale, the decentralization that sprang from Deng's encouragement of local initiative led towns and villages to go their own way. The most notorious was Daqiu, on the edge of Tianjin, which was lauded in state media as a model – the reform-era equivalent of the Dazhai commune. In 1992, the village had 280 enterprises, sixty of them foreign-funded. Its Party secretary rode round in a Mercedes and wore Pierre Cardin suits. It then turned out that he had been running the village as a personal fiefdom, terrorizing local inhabitants if they crossed him and drawing on his links with senior figures in Beijing. Eventually, paramilitary police moved in. Fierce fighting erupted. The secretary was arrested and jailed for twenty years. Daqiu was an extreme example, but, across China, the lure of access to wealth tempted cadres, and created a connection between officialdom and business that undermined policies formulated at the centre which would not be applied locally if they threatened the incomes and growth targets of local government and individual officials.[20]

As new factories sprouted, conditions were often primitive and oppressive, with workers toiling for very long hours, and sometimes locked into the plants and the dormitories at night – there were several cases of fatal fires as they could not escape. Environmental controls were non-existent, accelerating the ecological degradation under Mao. Provinces put overwhelming emphasis on industrial development; not only did this hurt agriculture, but it also led to uncoordinated expansion and overproduction. The rise in exports was not accompanied by the growth in consumption needed to balance the economy: large-scale fixed asset projects in industry and infrastructure became excessively important as economic drivers. The tragic cost of the rush to get richer was symbolized by a major scandal in Henan, where 180,000 farmers sold their blood in a money-making scheme mounted by provincial officials, and many contracted HIV/AIDS from unsterilized equipment.

Alienation from the system grew, particularly among the young. The 'spiritual pollution' against which Little Deng had thundered was evident particularly in the fast-growing cities of the east coast. Sex, drugs and rock 'n' roll replaced the austerity still preached by the CCP. Pledges by Jiang to reform the Party, eliminate placemen and toughen discipline in the bureaucracy carried little weight as the Party secretary refrained, in fact, from doing anything that might bring him into confrontation with the allies on which he depended.

Violent crime and juvenile delinquency rose, with more girls among the offenders. Corruption soared. Despite repeated warnings from the top, the 'princeling' sons and daughters of senior officials continued to make more and more money from their connections, among them Deng's own children. The PLA used its position to run lucrative monopolies and got into arms exports to rogue regimes. In the summer of 1993, Jiang acknowledged that 'Corruption is a virus that had infected the Party's healthy body. If we just ignore this phenomenon, it will bring down our Party and our system.' The snag was that the opportunity for graft was a major incentive for joining the CCP. While old norms were breaking down, new ones had not yet been consolidated, a Beijing professor explained at a seminar in July 1993. 'Money and commodity worship have corroded people's minds and affected people's behaviour,' he added. As a remark attributed to Little Deng put it, if the Party did not manage to eliminate corruption, it was done for; but, if it succeeded, it was equally doomed.[21]

Bandit gangs resurfaced in the countryside. In 1995, there were reckoned to be nearly 11,000 of them, with a total of a million members – the number was said to double annually. Some used old rites of passage, such as drinking chicken's blood. Others were led by low-level cadres. A few had political agendas, reminiscent of the anti-Manchu movements of the nineteenth century, such as the Plum Flower Group in Hunan or the Black Dragon Gang in Guangxi, which wanted an end to Communist rule. The drug trade increased, both internally and with China's neighbours; a rally of 40,000 people in the Yunnan capital of Kunming specifically linked the fight against narcotics with economic progress in a slogan on huge banners reading 'Wage a Struggle against Drugs to Ensure Smooth Progress in Reform'.[22]

Smugglers made the most of the opening up of the coast. Guangdong, across from Hong Kong and containing booming Shenzhen, was home to a proliferation of gangs that robbed, kidnapped, murdered, fought gun battles with police and nurtured links with Triads in the colony – a joint fifty-day crackdown by police in Guangdong, Hong Kong and Macau in 1995 reported breaking up 418 criminal organizations. The growth of prostitution and the kidnapping and sale of women and children provoked official concern at 'these vile social phenomena'.[23]

The resurfacing of clans in the countryside contributed further to the disruption of social order. In 1994, the *Legal Daily* reported 600 clan feuds the previous year, some spilling over into violence that killed more than a hundred people and injured 2,000. 'At present, village Party branches and village committees in some rural areas are basically paralysed,' the newspaper went on. 'There are no authorities in the villages, the masses are as disorganised as a plate of sand . . . Villages are powerless against local thugs and village brutes, and the evil tendency grows unchecked.' Another official report warned of revived patriarchal clans, superstitions and secret societies. In Hunan, thousands of peasants from rival groups fought pitched battles with home-made guns mounted on the balconies of flats, schools and hospitals. In the north of the province, they resisted cadres, beat police and chased away family planning agents.[24]

This last aspect of the disorder in Hunan reflected resistance to a renewed government drive to keep down the rise in the population, which reached 1.15 billion in the early 1990s. The one-child policy was strengthened, the population minister urging 'fewer but better babies'. If women pregnant with a second or third child declined to have an abortion, the minister went on, they must be persuaded at 'ideological work sessions'. Mentally handicapped women should be sterilized to prevent men taking advantage of them, she added – a report from Gansu told of this being done to 6,271 'child-bearing mentally retarded adults', and there were indications of wider application of the practice.[25]

At the centre, Deng retreated into the shadows of old age, suffering from Parkinson's disease and lung infections. He gave up playing bridge. He communicated through his daughter, who could understand his mumbling, and convey messages to him. He was said to be able to sit at table for family meals, and to watch television.

In Deng's absence, Jiang enhanced his status as Party chief, and won support from the PLA by reversing the patriarch's policy of holding down military spending. In 1995, he used the corruption issue to move against the boss of Beijing – Chen Xitong, a hardliner of 1989, who was now implicated in a big scandal that led to the suicide of one of his deputies, who was accused of having embezzled the equivalent of US $37 million. Forced to resign, Chen was expelled from the Politburo and sentenced to sixteen years in jail. Jiang thus eliminated a potential rival and could claim to be striking at the very top in pursuing graft, though, as always, the choice of target was dictated by politics. Still, the campaign for greater purity in the CCP was continued – 'all levels of leaders should . . . exercise self-scrutiny,' the CCP secretary declared. Though the masses might go to nightclubs, senior cadres should shun them, he added. But Chen was reported to have delivered a telling shot as he went down. He might bear the blame for graft in the capital, he said, 'but who is responsible for corruption in the entire CCP?'[26]

In place of any new political ideas, Jiang encouraged nationalism, as he claimed to be protecting the nation from foreign infiltration. A Patriotic Education campaign was launched, with Japan as the main target – despite Tokyo providing the PRC with $30 billion in cheap loans over thirty years as development aid and as quasi-reparations for the 1931–45 invasion that did not dare to speak their name, given Japanese domestic politics. A visit to Tokyo by Jiang in 1998 was marked by friction which Beijing blamed on 'right wing forces in Japan'. Relations were then marred by visits by senior Japanese officials, including the prime minister, to the Yasukuni shrine in Tokyo that honours, among others, convicted war criminals. Anti-Japanese demonstrations became a means for the regime of arousing Chinese nationalism, which, given the past and the temperature of East Asian relations, could easily be uncorked. Chinese arts and culture were extolled so that the PRC would not become the 'vassal' of Western values. A nationalist book entitled *China Can Say No* became a bestseller in 1996. 'We must prevent and obliterate the spread of Western rubbish,' proclaimed a CCP Plenum, while the Party secretary declared that the interests of the Chinese race towered above everything, with himself clearly cast as its main defender. However great the appeal of foreign popular culture might be (Jiang loved the film *Titanic* and sang 'Love Me Tender'), the old warnings against 'spiritual pollution' still lurked in the CCP's vocabulary.[27]

On the economic front, Jiang sounded an increasingly strong reformist tone, pointing to the antiquated equipment of many state-owned enterprises (SOEs). 'We must have a sense of urgency,' he declared in 1995. 'We must be bolder. It won't do if we do not bear some risks.' The ownership structure was not the problem, he said. All that was needed was deeper reform, better management and subsidies. 'It is true that SOEs have problems,' he noted at the same time. 'Yet they also have advantages and potentials. We must look on the bright side.' The Party leader was, after all, the product of the state sector. For most of his first ten years in power, his sympathy for private enterprise was limited.[28]

Though inflation still ran at 22 per cent in 1994, and Li Peng sniped from the sidelines, Zhu Rongji managed to get the economy off the boil little by little. He limited fixed investments, cut back on the plethora of loss-making projects, promoted agriculture and reined in state bank lending. Growth fell to 10 per cent, high enough to ensure continuing strong expansion, but back under some kind of control as inflation declined. The currency was tied to the US dollar at a rate that ensured the competitiveness of sales abroad. Cheap domestic capital and foreign direct investment powered export industries. State-owned enterprises were reformed, though this led to high, if officially unacknowledged, unemployment.

Guangdong became the outsourcing home for Hong Kong manufacturing firms, while Shanghai found a new life as the standard-bearer for modernity, with its gleaming tower blocks and the development of a business centre on the swampland of Pudong across the Huangpo River from the Bund, where foreigners began to return to their pre-war playground. By refusing to devalue during the Asian economic crisis that broke in 1997, the PRC cut its growth rate but buttressed its reputation for serious economic management, and Zhu became an unlikely pin-up boy of international finance. Talks began for its entry into the World Trade Organization (WTO). In 1998, the 'economic tsar', as Zhu had become known, was appointed prime minister; Li Peng became chair of the National People's Congress. A huge programme of infrastructure spending, accompanied by the easing of bank lending restrictions was launched to modernise the country and counter the effects of the Asian crisis on exports. Private housing was allowed, leading to construction of 30 million homes in ten years.

Fundamental issues remained, and were growing in importance, among them the coastal–interior divide, the ecological cost of industry and Beijing's sometimes tenuous hold over provincial governments set on maximizing growth. Despite repeated campaigns, corruption continued to have a life of its own; HCCs (High Cadres' Children) exploited the positions of their parents for profit, and 'princelings' rose up the political and business ladders. At the heart of the system, the monopoly of the Communist Party hampered efficient decision-making as factions and provincial chieftains jockeyed for power and influence – defending 'the interests of the Party' took over from defending 'the interests of the people'. Seen from outside, China's economy might appear unsustainable, but Zhu had given it a chance of reaching the combination of stability and growth it needed to become a superpower for the twenty-first century, despite all the constraints inherent in the top-down authoritarian regime that mirrored China's past in its imperfections.

Deng Xiaoping died on 19 February 1997, at the age of ninety-two. Six days of mourning followed, supervised by a committee from which his kin insisted on excluding Little Deng. On 24 February, the evening television programmes showed the family paying their final respects to the corpse lying in an open coffin at a military hospital in Beijing. The route to the Babaoshan crematorium was lined by 100,000 people, but the final ceremony was private. The ashes were taken in an urn to the Great Hall of the People and then, in line with the Paramount Leader's wishes, scattered at sea.

Since the 1920s, Deng had shown himself to be perhaps the greatest survivor of twentieth-century history, an acute realist with a keen appreciation of power, and an ability to absorb reverses without admitting defeat. He had ended up putting China on a path which ran counter to the received Western wisdom that economic progress would lead inevitably to political freedom. Having grown up at a time of China's great weakness, he had identified a path to national strength at odds with that charted by the man who had led the Communists to power. Into his eighties, he had defended his vision, and given the world a new nascent superpower as a result. But the process had spawned a host of major fault lines that ran through the PRC as it neared the end of the twentieth century. How those were addressed would be a major global issue for the coming decades.

Deng left no road map. His recipe – economic growth which would buttress the position of the Communist Party – was both brilliantly simple and myopic in its refusal to admit the seriousness of the imbalances that resulted, the scale of corruption and ecological devastation, or the divisiveness of the two-speed nation that was created. The 'little man' had changed China, and, through it, the world, but the broader and deeper effects of that change would be for other, less historic, figures to manage.

Among the members of the funeral committee for Deng was the heir to a Hong Kong shipping fortune, Tung Chee-hwa. Five and a half months later, the avuncular Tung was sworn in as the first chief executive of the newly declared Special Administrative Region (SAR) of Hong Kong when Britain's richest colony returned to the sovereignty of China in the early hours of 1 July 1997. Jiang Zemin beamed as the PRC flag replaced the Union Flag, the PLA moved in to the modern barracks by the harbour, and the Prince of Wales sailed off into the rainy night after representing the outgoing power at the handover ceremony.

The handover had been inevitable since Deng's initial meeting with the colonial governor in 1979. The Paramount Leader had been intent on reclaiming this example of China's pre-Communist weakness on the expiry of the land leases in the New Territories in 1997. In 1984, the Joint Declaration between Britain and China sealed the agreement, followed by the Basic Law for the territory drawn up in 1990. The deal was straightforward. Britain was not going to try to hold on, and negotiated what it considered the best accord available in keeping with Deng's formulation that the handover would result in 'one country, two systems'.

Hong Kong would remain as it had been materially and socially for fifty years, and the PRC would be able to prevent any developments, such as democracy, that might be seen to threaten its own one-party rule. There was a promise of elections, but what these would consist of was left vague. The House of Commons could bask in the assumption that they would be on British lines, while, as a senior official was reported to have put it, 'the Chinese have nothing against elections; they just rather like to know the result before voting takes place.' As the chief mainland negotiator, Lu Ping, acknowledged subsequently, Beijing focused on keeping the colony's Chinese tycoons happy, reassuring them that they would not lose anything from the handover.[29]

The carefully choreographed script laid down by Whitehall and Beijing was upset when the last governor, Chris Patten, appointed in 1992, unveiled a programme to install the democracy the British had always refused in the past. This initiative unleashed a burst of real politics in the colony, and infuriated the Chinese, who feared that the 'Hong Kong virus' of freedom could infect the mainland. Denounced by Beijing as 'a sinner for a thousand years', Patten stuck to his guns, but faced the unrelenting opposition of the bulk of the Chinese and Western business class that, in many ways, really ran Hong Kong and had no desire to alienate the PRC. After a century and a half of being politically muzzled, the colony's articulate middle class was finally given a voice; but every step forward the last governor took made it even more certain that the PRC, with Tung as its chosen agent, would move back to the status quo ante when sovereignty changed hands.

The handover turned out to be a peaceful affair. The PLA kept to its barracks, and the direct mainland presence was minimal. But, from the moment that Jiang had publicly singled him out at a gathering as Beijing's man, there was no doubt that Tung Chee-hwa answered to the PRC's dictates, trying to gauge what might please Beijing rather than representing Hong Kong's interests. When a key supreme court ruling went against the SAR administration, the executive applied to Beijing to get the National People's Congress to 'reinterpret' the constitution to make sure it got its way. There were popular elections for part of the Legislative Council, but a system that gave more seats to representatives of professional groups and members picked by a committee approved by Beijing ensured that a 70 per cent vote for pro-democracy parties left them in a minority in the chamber. As dictatorships fell in Indonesia and the Philippines, people there were allowed to chose their rulers; but the people of Hong Kong were told they would have to wait till 2017.

Still, in line with the agreements, the SAR kept its way of life. Its people enjoyed freedoms denied to mainlanders – freedom of movement, freedom of speech, freedom to move their money in and out at will. Those who were able to do so had obtained foreign passports in the years before the handover – the least useful of these were a special class of documents issued by the British which bore little weight. Though the passport hunt and the buying of property abroad reflected the uncertainty that hovered over the return to Chinese rule, they ended up by providing an element of stability since people knew they could get out to a new home if things went wrong.

Democrats continued to be extremely frustrated as the high vote tally they received at the carefully arranged elections were not translated into authority. Mass demonstrations made popular sentiment felt on such key issues as an anti-subversion law. Yet things did not turn as sour as pessimists had forecast. The run-up to the handover saw a boom, and Hong Kong surfed the Asian financial crisis of 1997 and a property slump at the start of the new millennium.

Little by little, the PRC eased entry restrictions for mainlanders, bringing in visitors who pumped up the retail and property businesses. A scheme was mooted to bring the SAR and Shenzhen together in a mega-city. Hong Kong remained a global commercial and financial centre. Its people thought of themselves as in a special category – a survey at the end of 2007 reported that the number who saw themselves as purely Hongkongers, not Chinese, had risen from 13 to 21 per cent in a year, while the proportion who said they were both Hongkongers and Chinese rose from 53 to 56 per cent and those who regarded themselves as purely Chinese fell from 33 to 22 per cent. The inhabitants of Lord Palmerston's 'barren rock' had built a great metropolis from nothing under one colonial power; the question for the future was whether they would be able to perpetuate their special place in the world under what was, in many ways, another outside ruler.[30]

The return of Hong Kong to China, followed two years later by that of the Portuguese colony of Macau across the Pearl River delta, wiped out two sources of national shame at the legacy of the 'unequal treaties' of the imperial era. Jiang could draw satisfaction from having completed the job begun by Deng. But, when it came to the third territory Beijing wanted to reclaim, he met with less success.

After four decades of heavy-handed KMT rule, marked by oppression of native Taiwanese, rampant corruption and a steadily declining international presence as nation after nation shifted recognition to the PRC, Chiang Kai-shek's son, Ching-kuo, loosened up the political system in Taiwan in the eighteen months before his death in 1988. When the split of 1949 occurred, the Communists and the KMT had had a number of similarities – Leninist organizations, leadership cults and militarization – but the Nationalist machine had unravelled on the island, making political liberalization easier than it was on the mainland. Ching-kuo lifted martial law. The press was freed. An opposition group, the

Democratic Progressive Party (DPP), was allowed to contest elections, and began by making its mark at local level.

One thing had united Chiang and the leaders across the Strait – the belief that there was only one China, be it the People's Republic based in Beijing or the Republic of China in exile in Taiwan. As its global influence rose, Beijing imposed its version on any country which wanted relations with it. Taiwan, it insisted, was an errant province that should be brought back into the fold and at which it aimed hundreds of missiles. For a growing number of inhabitants of the island who pointed out the non-Chinese nature of their forebears, this was a false argument, and the concept of 'Taiwanese identity' gained ground.

Talks between representatives of Beijing and Taipei danced around forms of words, but achieved no concrete results. Jiang Zemin tried various formulas, without success. At one point, Ching-kuo's successor, Lee Teng-hui, refused to attend a secret summit with Jiang for fear of impeding the democratization of the island. The reality was that, by the 1990s and apart from KMT diehards, Taiwanese increasingly felt that they belonged to an entity which was different from the PRC, having been under direct mainland rule for only four of the previous hundred years. Its economy made it one of the four Asian 'tigers' and, as democracy took root, the idea of a separate 'Taiwanese identity' grew, fostered by the DPP and its associates, while Lee Teng-hui ended the Chiang family's long mastery of the KMT. (Having failed to make her influence felt, Madame Chiang went to the US, where she lived to 2003, dying at the age of 106 in New York City.)

Though from the KMT, Lee was a native of Taiwan, born to a Hakka family near Taipei. He had grown up under Japan's occupation, and mainland sources sometimes painted him as an agent of Tokyo who woke from snoozes at banquets speaking Japanese. Pressing on with democratization, he reflected the new consciousness on the island by speaking of Taiwan as a 'state' and making a visit to the United States during which he acted as if he was head of a government, rather than the administrator of a Chinese province. In retaliation, the PRC staged missile tests in the Strait in 1996, leading President Clinton to mobilize the US fleet in the area to prevent the hostilities escalating. Beijing backed down. America's precise commitment to Taiwan was open to various interpretations, but Washington could clearly not stand by if China made an all-out attack.

Things got worse for Jiang and his colleagues when the opposition DPP's candidate, Chen Shui-bian, won the presidential election of 2000 emphasizing 'Taiwanese identity'. The victors presented a clean new face to voters in contrast to the ageing, factionalized, corrupt KMT. That was enough to get 39 per cent of the vote to finish ahead of 36 per cent for an independent candidate and 23 per cent for the KMT. Though the DPP did not entirely live up to its promise and Taiwanese politics became mired in infighting, Chen was re-elected in 2004.

Despite talk of constitutional revision and of renaming the Republic of China as the Republic of Taiwan, the DPP did not pursue formal independence, but it constantly asserted the island's separate identity. Jiang (and his successors) were thus left with a conundrum. They could not give up the claim to Taiwan even if they had wished to do so. The PLA still declared the reunification of the island with the mainland to be its sacred duty, and had its missiles pointing across the ninety-mile Strait. But though direct travel links were barred by Taipei, economic ties grew: by the early twenty-first century, some 300,000 Taiwanese were working in the Yangzi Delta area. The island was a major source of investment funds into the mainland, either from Taiwanese or from foreigners using it as a conduit.

Under Jiang and his successor, Beijing might hope that economic links would bring Taiwan increasingly into the PRC's ambit. Though Taipei was still recognized by only two dozen small states round the world as it and Beijing waged chequebook diplomacy in Africa, Central America and the South Pacific, the international desire not to get on the wrong side of the PRC was not yet big enough to enable Beijing to get away with a forcible takeover of the only entity with 'China' in its name to have practised full-scale democracy. Economic sanctions would come with a significant cost for the mainland. Military action, which could bring in the United States, would shatter the stability necessary for the economic growth that underpinned CCP rule. The development of democracy on the island made it ever less likely that it would accept the 'one country, two systems' formula. So the Republic remained a potential flashpoint and a living reproach to the PRC leadership, a challenge for which there might be no resolution so long as neither side let rhetoric and nationalism overcome the status quo.

*

The death of Deng, the recovery of Hong Kong, the economic management of Zhu Rongji, the sidelining of rivals and, above all, the relentless economic growth of the PRC all induced a certain degree of complacency in the Jiang Zemin regime at the turn of the century. The Party chief and president had sidelined rivals such as Li Peng and Qiao Shi. By a mixture of favours and politics, he had assured himself of the backing of the PLA, which had plunged so deeply into business that one estimate had half its ground forces working in its companies. Deng's heir was establishing an international profile, visiting the United States in 1997 and beaming at Asian summits. The world paid court to a reviving China. President Chirac of France and Chancellor Schröder of Germany were eager visitors. US and EU arms embargoes imposed after the Beijing massacre remained in place, but foreign investment in the PRC boomed.[31]

Though Bill Clinton made a pointed remark about the PRC being 'on the wrong side of history' when Jiang visited the US, human rights became a declining concern of Western powers. Dissidents were still persecuted. Wei Jingsheng was freed, rearrested and expelled to the United States. Harry Hongda Wu, who had left China for America in 1985 and devoted himself to exposing the PRC's gulag of labour camps, was arrested on a secret trip to the mainland, sentenced to fifteen years in prison and then sent back to the USA. Most foreign governments gave commerce precedence. Having seen its previous bid for the Olympic Games fail because of its human rights record, the PRC won the 2001 vote for the 2008 event. When Jiang went on a state visit to London, Wei and a few other dissidents who tried to demonstrate were kept well away from the guest as he was driven to Buckingham Palace.

China was identified as the coming superpower, a country which might rival the USA in the twenty-first century. Visiting the PRC in 1998, Clinton hailed a strategic partnership between China and the US. Despite tension after American planes bombed China's embassy in Belgrade during the Nato attack on Serbia, in 1999, killing three diplomats,* and the continuing residual threat of a confrontation over Taiwan, the relationship between the US and the PRC had become too important to both sides to let ideological differences intrude. The Bush administration began by viewing China as a competitor, but economic

---

* The US insistence that this was accidental was not believed in China.

realities soon intervened, with the PRC's heavy buying of securities to fund the federal deficit and its cheap imports keeping down American inflation and interest rates. A potential crisis over a US spy plane that was forced down over Hainan Island in 2001 was solved amicably.

China gained confidence as growth stabilised at 7 per cent and then rose to 9 per cent in 2002 and its trade surplus soared, particularly with the United States, boosting the foreign exchange reserves. Western business visitors returned home amazed by the development. Under Jiang, recognition in the constitution of the evolution of the 'socialist market economy' led to the private sector being dubbed 'an important component' alongside state enterprises. In 2001, the PRC entered the World Trade Organization. As well as making basic cheap goods, the country became a factory line for the world: shipping partly assembled goods to be put together there was cheaper than doing the job at home in Europe, the United States or Japan. Politically, Beijing was increasingly influential in East Asia, in some ways re-creating the tribute system of the empire and developing its armed forces to weigh against American military domination in the Far East.

As his time in office neared its end, Jiang sought to leave an ideological legacy with a theory known as the 'Three Represents', which proclaimed that the CCP represented 'advanced productive forces', advanced culture and the fundamental interests of the majority. The first formulation signified that the business people who were powering China's growth were now recognized as playing a politically acceptable role. Communist China was to come to terms with its entrepreneurs. Posters hailing Jiang's theory showed computers and satellites, bullet trains and the television tower spiralling over the Shanghai waterfront. If economic expansion had been the proof of Deng's reforms, it became the overwhelming priority for the Jiang regime.[32]

In this, as the 1989 reformer Bao Tong pointed out, Chinese society grew ever more unequal. 'As long as the principle stands that the CCP leads everything, civil and political rights will not be realised,' he wrote in an essay. If the regime held out an olive branch to 'red capitalists', this did not imply the loosening of the principle of one-party rule, he added. 'On the contrary, it implies that it is now time for the CCP, which controls all, to admit the unspoken truth and formally declare that it has become China's Party for the Rich, the Noble and the Powerful. It is that simple, and should come as no surprise. The theory of Three

Represents will not begin a new era of democracy. Nor will those red-capitalists attracted by absolute power become the engine for political reform.'[33]

How Jiang and his colleagues reacted to anything regarded as an organized challenge was made evident when a deep-breathing movement, the Falun Gong, staged protests against police treatment of some of its members. The first of these, outside the leadership compound in Beijing in 1999, spooked the regime by the way in which it suddenly materialized in the heart of the capital without the authorities having had any idea of what was happening. Using mobile telephones and the internet, the Falun Gong practitioners continued to demonstrate, and were relentlessly repressed. The government denounced them for 'illegal activities, advocating superstition and spreading fallacies, hoodwinking people, inciting and creating disturbances, and jeopardizing social stability'.[34]

The movement, based on the writings of a former grain clerk, denied that it was an organized sect, instead offering a system of cultivation of mind and body on the 'Great Law of the Wheel of Law' drawn from Buddhist teachings to encourage virtue, moral standards and character. Intense practice was said to lead to superhuman abilities as consciousness was raised to mystical levels. It could be seen as the latest in a long line of semi-mystical groups using rituals, and certainly inspired devotion among a growing number of people, particularly among those who had been brought up under Maoism but had then been deprived of the certainties of the 'iron rice bowl' by the economic reforms. Mounting an international campaign, which included publication of an English-language newspaper and a permanent protest site opposite the PRC embassy in London, the Falun Gong alleged that its practitioners were being murdered in concentration camps, or having their organs removed for sale.

For the Communist leadership, the Falun Gong was not only a set of superstitions that should be eradicated but, more potently, a movement which had shown a worrying ability to come together and persevere in a manner that might recall the early days of Chinese Communism. The treatment it received said much about the persistent insecurity of the regime. In a different domain, the crisis caused by the outbreak of Severe Acute Respiratory Syndrome (SARS) in China in 2002–3, with 8,000 cases and 774 deaths, showed the difficulty the system had in reacting to a sudden crisis, and the secrecy that the government and Party still sought to impose. There was a similar cover-up over the major scandal involving blood-trafficking in Henan province which infected recipients as well as donors with the HIV virus. When a fire in a theatre in Xinjiang killed 325, the head of state television decided not to report the disaster on the day and the government then issued a notice banning coverage.[35]

As the time came for Jiang to hand over to the 'Fourth Generation' of leaders under Hu Jintao at the Sixteenth Party Congress, in 2002, another aspect of the regime emerged: factionalism. The outgoing CCP chief had built up the position of his Shanghai Faction, and wished to retain a degree of power – if not as much as Deng Xiaoping had done after 1989 then certainly more than the formal arrangements gave him. Five of the Shanghai group held senior Politburo positions, and Jiang retained the chair of the Military Affairs Commission. As a result, Hu had to devote attention during his first years in power to establishing his own influence, gradually moving his own people into important provincial posts, and seeking to increase his clout in the Politburo over figures from the Jiang years.

In 2004, the new leader scored a significant victory when he lined up sufficient support to oblige Jiang to pass the chairmanship of the Military Affairs Commission to him. At the same time, Shanghai's leading property tycoon, who had incarnated the close links between business and politics, was arrested and sentenced to three years in jail for stock market fraud and falsifying documents. Two years later, the president's camp moved against the Party secretary in the city, who took little notice of instructions from the centre and was said to have openly defied the premier, Wen Jiabao. He lost his job amid major corruption allegations involving a municipal fund that had invested large sums in an obscure investment company in which his associates had stakes; up to fifty other prominent members of the city's establishment were also targeted. In 2007, a new man took over as the local CCP boss. Then a senior member of the Politburo promoted by Jiang, Huang Ju, died, and another, Vice-President Zeng Qinghong, reached an accommodation with the number one.

As economic growth roared ahead at 11 per cent a year, the trade surplus rose to $262 billion in 2007. China built up foreign reserves heading to $2 trillion; a middle class emerged, individual liberty increased; tens of millions of Chinese travelled abroad, and big cities such as Shanghai and Beijing flaunted their material modernity, the capital making the most of the 2008 Olympic Games. Hu paid state visits to the United States, Europe, Africa, Latin America and the Middle East. At the White House he lectured George W. Bush on democracy as the PRC established itself as the great beneficiary of globalization. Its economic influence was felt in everything from the manufactured and assembled goods flooding out of the mainland to the effects of its demand on raw material prices and the world supply chain.

Internationally, under Hu, China propagated a theory of its 'peaceful rise' and a 'harmonious world', insisting that it posed no threat to other nations, despite the fast-expanding military budget, the development of the navy and the shooting down of a communications satellite in 2007 which demonstrated a space capability that worried the American military. A 'soft power' drive was launched to win hearts and minds round the world; as America's reputation dipped after the invasion of Iraq, the PRC came to be seen by some, at least, as offering a different kind of model, its repression put to one side by those seeking an alternative to the Western consensus. Beijing courted African countries with large loans and investments, and, closer to home, dropped its anti-Japanese nationalism to explore a political relationship with Tokyo to accompany the burgeoning economic links between the two countries.

Beijing ploughed its own furrow over the upward revaluation of its currency despite repeated calls from the United States and Europe to move faster. It dismissed criticism of its policy in Sudan after the film director Stephen Spielberg pulled out as an adviser to the opening ceremony of the 2008 Olympics to protest at the PRC's implicit connection to the genocide in Darfur. The American president and British prime minister, among other leaders, drew a distinction between the sporting event and politics, which could only gladden Hu Jintao's heart. Beijing's links with unsavoury regimes was undeniable, as was its repression of domestic dissidence and its clampdown in Tibet, but its global status was such that it could get away with it.

However, Taiwan remained beyond the PRC's grasp, wedded to democracy and to charting its own course, though the poor domestic performance of the DPP led to its defeat in the 2008 presidential elections by a revived Kuomintang. While political tension did not prevent the development of economic ties, with agreement reached at the end of 2008 on direct shipping, air and postal links, Beijing's attempts to court anti-autonomy politicians fell flat. Polls showed the number of people on the island who defined themselves as 'Taiwanese' as having risen from 17 per cent in 1992 to 46 per cent in 2005, with another 42 per cent saying they were 'Taiwanese and Chinese'. Only 7 per cent said they were simply Chinese. PLA sabre-rattling and Hu Jintao's insistence on the One China policy were met with warnings that Taipei had missiles which could hit Shanghai. Washington, which Taipei promised to consult before firing such weapons, urged the Taiwanese not to rock the status quo, and the United Nations snubbed the island when it sought recognition. But the strength of 'Taiwanese identity' politics in the 2008 presidential election obliged the victorious Kuomintang to reinvent itself as a party that acknowledged Taiwan's separateness while promising to defuse tension with Beijing and increase economic links with the mainland, which grew in importance as the island's exports slumped at the end of 2008.

Hu proclaimed his doctrine of a 'harmonious society' to lessen the inequalities of growth as it soared above 11 per cent in both 2006 and 2007. Land tax was abolished along with rural school fees. The ratio of voting weights within the CCP was cut from eight to one in favour of urban areas to four to one. The government promised increased spending on farmers while sharp food inflation in 2007 boosted agricultural incomes. Around the CCP Congress of 2007, there was talk of greater democracy – but only within the Communist Party, which Hu could view as a way of sidelining old cadres and promoting a new efficient generation as Deng Xiaoping had sought to do in the 1980s.

Scholars at the Central Party School warned in a report in 2008 that China risked dangerous instability unless it embraced democratic reforms to limit the power of the CCP, fostered competitive voting and allowed more freedom of expression. The aim should be a 'modern civil society' by 2020, it added. A 'mature democracy and rule of law' would follow.

China's Communist leaders had shown a Darwinian ability to adapt since Mao's death, but they had no intention of taking the final evolutionary step and relinquishing power. The Party School report still said the CCP must retain overall control while the leadership insisted that the nation was only in the first stage of socialist development, so one-party rule should continue for decades to come. The media remained tightly controlled; human rights activists were harassed; and 'cyber cops' patrolled the Internet for websites that might threaten the CCP's definition of order. Secrecy shrouded the regime. Land grabs and other arbitrary action by officials, environmental degradation that could be life-threatening and simple frustration fuelled protests. But the law was at the service of political power and the prospect of the Communist Party submitting to independent judgement was as far away as ever.

However, that power was not what it had been under earlier Communist rulers. The CCP no longer had a commanding figure in the Mao or Deng mould. At the Seventeenth Communist Party Congress in October 2007, Hu Jintao defended the Party's monopoly, though, as the economy turned down a year later, he acknowledged that its capacity to rule was being tested. He was given a second five years in office in 2007, and his doctrine of 'scientific socialism' was adopted to 'unleash the vitality of socialism' while broadening and deepening reforms to combine prosperity and social harmony. But, when it came to top-level power politics, he was unable to impose his chosen successor, the Party secretary of Liaoning province, Li Keqiang.

Instead, the strength of other groups in the Politburo forced him to accept the Shanghai Party secretary, Xi Jinping, as the putative next head of the Party, with Li, who ranked one place behind Xi in the new nine-man Standing Committee of the Politburo, likely to take the subordinate post of prime minister in 2012. Xi was further advanced by being given the job of overseeing the Beijing Olympics. A significant number of 'princelings' joined the wider Politburo; they might not form a cohesive group of their own, but neither did they constitute a united cohort behind Hu and Wen.

The official line was that the PRC could only benefit from a more collective leadership (one senior diplomat went as far as to claim to the author that the PRC had always been run collectively, even under Mao). It was not that there was an organized opposition among the leadership. Rather, Hu appeared to be unable to exercise the requisite degree of dynastic authority to impose himself. Though this might prove healthy in some ways by diluting the central dictatorship, it risked impeding policy formulation and implementation at a time when the leadership badly needed to get to grips with the economic, social and political fault lines that had built up since 1978.

The following year was meant to be a celebration of what the official news agency called China's 'renaissance', symbolised by the 2008

Olympics. Things turned out rather differently before and after the grand spectacle of the Games, at which China topped the gold medals table, with 51. The stock market lost more than 60 per cent of its value from its peak in 2007, while property prices wobbled. Inflation rose to four times its normal rate, fuelled by explosive food prices and excessive liquidity. January and February saw a major freeze in southern and central China. In March, riots in Tibet focussed world attention on resistance to Chinese rule. In May, an earthquake in Sichuan killed 75,000 people. Violence broke out in Xinjiang. In the autumn, the global financial crisis deepened China's economic problems in a double-whammy effect. Coupled with the impact of monetary tightening to fight inflation, rising labour costs and appreciation of the currency, this took growth down to the lowest level since 2003 as thousands of factories closed and migrant workers losing their jobs raised the threat of social instability.

The Hu–Wen team showed considerable managerial aptitude in dealing with these challenges. The prime minister flew immediately to the earthquake zone and became portrayed as caring 'grandfather Wen'. He appeared on Facebook and also became known as a student of the stoic philosopher Marcus Aurelius. A 4 trillion yuan stimulus package focussed on infrastructure was announced in November along with measures to protect export industries, cut interest rates, help the property market, boost rural incomes and give farmers the right to rent out land they leased from the state. Currency appreciation was halted.

What was lacking was any description of how the regime's leaders intended to reinvent the Communist Party as a movement capable of directing a society that increasingly escaped it while rebalancing the economy through domestic consumption and technological modernis-ation. The contradictions built into the expansion launched by Deng within a constrained political structure were coming home to roost. The challenges the regime faced were thus both new, born from the growth process, and old, reprising elements of central weakness in the face of an evolving society that had appeared during the decline of the Qing and had been perpetuated under the Kuomintang. The outcome of this latest test would determine China's future, and whether economic revival could bring a new path out of the tumult of the previous 150 years, or whether the People's Republic would remain caught on the cusp between political rigidity and explosive economic and social evolution.

Epilogue

For twenty-one centuries, China lived under the template set by the First Emperor, Qin Shi Huangdi. It contained the oldest continuous civilization on earth, and possessed a self-confidence which would easily be caricatured by foreigners as imperial rule declined in the nineteenth century, but which rested on a real belief that the Middle Kingdom was unique, standing apart from, and above, all other regimes. The theory of the Mandate of Heaven, which the gods could withdraw for bad behaviour and hand to the next ruling house, allowed for changes of dynasties without shaking the foundations of the system. There were times when the model broke down, notably during the Period of Disunion that stretched from AD 265 to 589, but, even then, claimants to the throne insisted that they were worthy of the mandate. Through the centuries, a cycle of dynastic rise and fall asserted itself, as strong rulers gave way to weaker successors, courts were riven by factionalism, excessive expenditure sapped the imperial treasury, rural leaders raised revolts and nomadic armies swept down from the north.

The overthrow of the empire and the establishment of the republic in 1912 altered the political system, but in no way brought the social transformation the country needed. The anarchy of the warlord period was followed by a fragile central government and the ultimately debilitating fourteen years of Japanese aggression. Despite the initial successes of the Nationalists against the Communists when civil war broke out in 1945, their claim to the mandate to rule was fatally undermined by their inability to offer a convincing new form of national government. But, if China was ready for revolution in 1949, the Communist victory was largely a military achievement, won on the battlefields of Manchuria and central China, and a consequence of the Kuomintang's failure, which the CCP's efficient machine, forged in the Yenan base, was able to exploit to the full. The far-reaching upheaval that followed came at the price of an autocracy every bit as domineering as the toughest years of imperial rule, marked by the traumas of mass repression, the Great Leap Forward, the ensuing famine and the Cultural Revolution.

Deng Xiaoping's reforms demonstrated a belated recognition of the need for China to better itself materially and join the world. Economically, the outcome has been stunningly successful, despite the continuing imbalances and challenges, notably the impact of the global downturn in 2008–9 with its threat to social stability and the regime's claim to legitmacy through strong growth.

Still, politically, the PRC remains in a systemic time warp stretching back to 221 BC. As intellectuals of left and right debate the way ahead, the leadership appears to recognize the need for evolution, but it shrinks from initiating real change, bogged down by history, fear, competing interest groups – and its own weakness. As a result, the PRC does not fit into a conventional global category any more than it did under the empire. The Middle Kingdom of our day has reverted to uniqueness.

Is China still socialist, as Hu Jintao proclaims? The predominance of market economics, lack of social care, pollution, recurrent food scandals, growing wealth disparities and illiteracy that is estimated to have risen by 30 million people in five years argue otherwise. At the end of 2008, new high school history textbooks in Shanghai cut the text on socialism to one short chapter out of 52 while giving a single sentence to pre-1978 Chinese Communism and making one reference to Mao. The workers in whose name the CCP claims to rule have lost out. Encouraging output through market mechanisms has proved a lot easier for this authoritarian system than defending its citizens from the adverse effects of growth. The Maoist 'iron rice bowl' welfare safety net is gone. The World Bank estimates that the share of wages in the PRC's gross domestic product dropped from 53 per cent in 1998 to 41 per cent in 2005 (compared to 56 per cent in the USA).

China's leaders still call themselves Communists, but what does this mean for them? Is the state atop which they sit the purest expression of capitalism on earth in the early twenty-first century world in which the application of savings to investment at low interest rates has fuelled an economy which has grown fourteenfold in real terms since reform was launched in 1978? How can followers of Communism privatize on an enormous scale, throw millions out of work at state enterprises, pass laws to defend private property and introduce bankruptcy regulations that recognize shareholders and relegate the rights of workers?

And what kind of movement is the CCP, in any case? Jiang Zemin's 'Three Represents' is put forward as having marked the shift from its being a revolutionary party to a ruling party. But it is wildly unrepresentative of the population as a whole, drawing 75 per cent of its membership from urban areas while a majority of the population remains in the countryside. This imbalance is accentuated by tilted procedures in carefully controlled internal CCP elections which give city members four times the weight of those from the rural world. The proportion of industrial and farm workers in the membership has fallen from 65 per cent in 1978 to 43 per cent in the mid-2000s, compared to 21 per cent of white collar workers, 19 per cent of retirees and 5 per cent from the private sector.* Members of the first group were notable by their absence at the Party Congress of 2007, and have never figured much in the leadership. Is it simply the case that, as the son of the economist Chen Yun once put it: 'we are the Communists, and we define what Communism is'?[1]

But, if this is a system whose deep flaws may give capitalism a bad name, how does one account for the continuing presence of the Party at all levels, with branches in more than 400,000 private enterprises and insisting, as did its imperial and republican predecessors, on its sole right to run the country, marginalizing or suppressing dissent, discussion and heterodoxy, and absorbing intermediate layers in society? The CCP's role means that comparing today's China to the Britain of the Industrial Revolution or the United States of the robber baron era is too facile given the political context within which the economy and society are evolving. Best to settle for the description of China's system as one of bureaucratic capitalism, underpinned by force and marked by exploitation, with little time for fostering human happiness in anything other than material terms; as the last major Leninist state, only with Chinese characteristics; as a nation whose impact is changing the world but which remains deeply unfathomable as its own rulers grapple with problems of unprecedented size.

Though Hu Jintao pledges that 'power will be exercised in daylight', the Seventeenth Party Congress in October 2007 was anything but

---

* Of the 73 million members, 20 per cent were women.

transparent, and appointments at central and provincial level for his second five-year term reflected the balancing of factions in the tradition set under the empire and the Kuomintang. Hu's target, of 'harmony within the Party', sounds very like the creed of a chief who has had to accept that he cannot impose himself.[2]

Autocracy on imperial lines remains the regime's leitmotif, but, to perpetuate its rule, the leadership has to negotiate on a regular basis with political and economic interest groups, provinces and regions. The hermetic nature of the structure increases the inner tension, and works against more effective governance. The separation of the CCP and the government suggested by Deng in the mid-1980s has been reversed under Jiang and Hu. Despite the presence of extremely competent technocrats in state bodies, success as a Communist Party apparatchik is the surest way to the top. Hence, a protégé of Jiang Zemin held the key Politburo portfolio for financial reform until his death in 2007 despite being unfitted for the job. Hu Jintao's 'clone', Li Keqiang, has an unimpressive record as a provincial Party secretary, but is still likely to become prime minister in due course. Yet, whatever weaknesses this breeds and whatever the logic for political opening-up, it does not mean that the system is going to change in any significant manner.

Predictions that economic progress would bring democratization have proved mistaken; elections which have been held at village level have often been carefully controlled and the experiment has been delayed in townships. When Hu Jintao and other leaders speak of the need for democracy, they mean mechanisms within the Communist Party to make it more effective, just as talk of modernization at the end of the Qing era was intended to bolster the ruling house. The essential bulwarks of democracy are still missing. China has, at most, the rule *by* law, as promulgated by the legalist First Emperor, not rule *of* law. Arbitrary action by the police and authorities remains common; measures were announced in 2007 to 'modernize' the penal regime of 'reform through labour', but the punishment camps stay in place. Accountability is, at best, an internal affair for those in authority. High-level anti-corruption campaigns tend to be politically targeted. As over the previous centuries, networks of influence are crucial. The 'princelings' are well on their way to constituting a hereditary aristocracy. Rather than promoting the cause of general liberty and democracy, the new rich and the emerging middle class appear keener on playing the system to their advantage, while a poll in 2007 showed that 70 per cent of those questioned think the new rich are immoral and unworthy of respect.[3]

The regime can claim three principal reasons for its rule six decades on from the victory of 1949. The first is the material improvement over which it has presided, unequally distributed to be sure, but unquestionable in its effects since 1978. But the economy is still only one-third of America's in value, and much of China remains poor. Officials like to quote Deng Xiaoping's observation that the PRC is both strong and weak, rich and poor. But the transformation of cities and of everyday life for hundreds of millions has moved China towards the material, social revolution it missed in 1912. People recognize that – a poll published in 2008 showed that 84 per cent of Chinese perceived improvement in domestic economic conditions, the highest in the ten countries surveyed. This advance provides a new Mandate of Heaven, with Hu promoting his doctrine of 'scientific socialism' by telling the Party Congress of 2007 that only the CCP could assure growth and 'emancipate the mind [as] a magic instrument for developing socialism with Chinese characteristics, reform and opening up'.[4]

The Communist Party's second claim to legitimacy rests on its record of national stability. After the turmoil reaching from the mid nineteenth century to the Cultural Revolution, the years since 1978 can be portrayed as a time when the country came to rest – the Beijing massacre of 1989 being classified officially as a necessary ingredient in that process as the regime warded off the threat of disruption. The grassroots protests that have totalled up to 80,000 in a year are localized, one-issue affairs, not the expression of a generalized challenge to the regime. The continuing colonialization of Tibet and Xinjiang is taken for granted on the mainland as a security issue and as part of China's civilizing mission. If Taiwan is beyond Beijing's grasp, Hong Kong and Macau have been recovered. For anybody who questions whether this stability justifies the continuation of the one-party dictatorship China has always known, backed by the army and a heavy repressive apparatus, the leaders have only to invoke the past.

Thirdly, China has gained its proper place in the world, drawing on its generally peaceful international relations to provide the context for its booming trade. The country which once suffered under the unequal treaties imposed by foreign powers now helps to fund the US federal deficit. Hu Jintao is welcomed by Washington as an ally in the 'war on terror', giving Beijing backing for its crackdown on separatists in Xinjiang. The economic importance of the People's Republic is such that most more-developed countries will find just about any excuse to avoid crossing it. So Hu feels free to lecture the Americans on democracy, the PRC maintains its links with rogue regimes across the globe, and foreign leaders who meet the Dalai Lama find themselves the target of Beijing's anger as France did at the end of 2008.

When financial crisis rolled across western nations in 2008, one response was to look for succour from China's $2 trillion foreign exchange reserves. But Hu Jintao made it clear that he considered the best contribution his country could make to global recovery was to focus on the health of its own economy with a huge rolling stimulus package while ministers ticked off the US for its profligacy and planned industrial restructuring to make the PRC even more competitive. Surveying sixty years, a posting that shot round Chinese websites noted:

1949: only socialism could save China
1979: only capitalism could change China
1989: only China could save socialism after the fall of the Soviet Union
2009: only China could save capitalism

Though the flaws and imbalances in the economy mean that major dislocations are always possible, the sheer momentum bred since 1978 has been able to absorb pressures that might tear another nation asunder. In part, at least, this must be due to the historical heritage. China's experience between the mid nineteenth century and Mao's death was one from which any population would want to escape. The initial years of Communist rule may have aroused enthusiasm, but it has been in the period of economic reform that far more people have acquired a direct stake in the continuation of the economic and social system than ever before. Nobody except Manchu loyalists and Nationalist diehards wept over the disappearance of the empire or the republic; many would feel threatened if the present regime gave way either to a reversion to the past or to an even more uncertain future.

This book has argued that, for all the manifestations of modernity, China's history is not another country. Now, the cumulative effects of the process launched by Deng Xiaoping are leading to a phase that could be plucked right out of imperial dynasties or from the republic. If Mao was the strong, wilful dynastic founder and Deng the consolidator who saw a way of renewing the mandate, Hu Jintao can be taken as a successor who holds the keys to power but cannot turn them as his predecessors did. True, there is no organized opposition to confront the Communist dynasty, no Red Army lurking in the backwoods, no political movement marshalling resistance in the countryside. But the regime faces a different kind of risk, which again has its roots in China's early history. Since the First Emperor in AD 221, rulers have feared losing control of major forces in society, whether they take the form of questioning officials and scholars, military commanders, or, in the last decades of empire, the modernizing gentry. Today, those impelled by the rush to the market and material self-improvement march increasingly to their own drum. Interest groups, individuals and competing power centres proliferate within the overall supposedly unitary structure. State-owned enterprises join private firms in playing the stock exchange and using their positions to maximize profits. The result is an authoritarian state which increasingly lacks authority, an empire without an emperor.

At the top, the leadership proclaims goals which, on their own, are often well-thought-out answers to the problems confronting China. But implementing them is quite another matter. Contradictions abound – for example, between maintaining growth and fighting environmental destruction, or between seeking a 'harmonious society' but failing to launch a proper welfare system. For all the talk of 'inner democracy', the Communist Party still needs to reward its members with at least some of the pickings. In such circumstances, the 'dynamic forces' in society move into an ambit of their own. They do not challenge the structure, which serves them well. But they exist within it on their own terms as the economy shows diminishing respect for the political and ideological centre in good times while in the more strained circumstances of 2008–9, the centre felt obliged to pour in trillions of yuan to try to sustain growth.

At the provincial level, authority can be equally difused. Guangdong, leader of reform in the 1980s, lobbied for greater autonomy in formulating policy. Experiments in modifying the household registration system (*hukov*) were set in motion in Wuhen Hunen and Sichuan. Beijing, meanwhile, remains acutely aware of the limitations on its control over how its transfers of money to provinces that are strapped for cash are used by local officials. In 2007, a provincial deputy governor disclosed in an unusually frank speech that, to combat pollution, his administration ordered 150 factories to close. By the autumn, twenty-five had done so. Five cities simply took no notice of the instruction.

As under the ancient regime, local power holders offer allegiance to the emperor, so long as he remains on the other side of the mountain. Hu Jintao pursues a harmonious society, but China has many of the attributes of nineteenth-century Europe or America. The social price is evident to anybody who wandered from the bright lights of Beijing during the 2008 Olympics or from Shanghai's gleaming centre as it prepared for the 2010 World Expo to the back streets or visits the poorer rural regions. Up to 150 million migrant workers continue to live hard existences without protection or welfare. The cost of medical care can eat up the bulk of a farmer's annual income. Slave labour conditions were exposed in coal mines in 2007. Product and industrial safety standards are often low.

For all the material improvements since 1978 and the increase in individual freedom, huge disparities remain, bringing warnings that echo laments from the late period of the Qing dynasty. The nineteenth-century scholar Zong Zizhen wrote of the way in which 'the wealthy vie with each other in splendour and display while the poor squeeze each other to death'; this would stoke hatred and 'fill the space between heaven and earth with darkness', he forecast. In early 2008, the Xinhua news agency warned that wealth inequality had gone well beyond the critical level, after rising by 35 per cent in a generation. The 1989 reformer Bao Tong asks:

How is it that the workers and the peasants who are named in the Constitution as 'the basis of the country' have nothing left to depend on, turned into a voiceless group of colonized weaklings, who are routinely bullied and humiliated by those with power and money? . . . How come power and money have replaced free competition in almost every major transaction.[5]

With tears in his eyes, a member of the upper house of the legislature read a doggerel to the prime minister at a meeting on rural strategy in 2007:

Hoodwinking starts from the villages;
Then the lies are copied by township officials without changes which roll all
    the way from county officials to the State Council,
Whose orders are heralded word for word in an inverted pyramid of rank,
    but only end in receptions that make messengers drunk.[6]

The central authorities inveigh against 'money worship and hedonism' and 'moral erosion which usually starts with small things like drinking, dining and vulgar entertainment in which sex is often involved'. Campaigns are launched against officials who keep strings of mistresses, and the Party leader and prime minister make a point of being photographed during national holidays fraternizing with workers and peasants. But there is little sign that anybody is paying heed to the calls for moderation in an increasingly volatile society which described itself in a survey in 2006 as a 'stir fry nation'. 'The key issue,' commented the *People's Daily*, 'is to maintain the right temperature.'[7]

Given the enormous dynamism which the economic reform process had released, and the sheer exercise of hard work by hundreds of millions of people, the first three decades since the late 1970s may have been the easy part. Transforming this into a long-term, viable social and political system is likely to prove much tougher, particularly because of the highly complex heritage bequeathed to the Fourth Generation of leaders by events since the mid nineteenth century. China's future will be built on that deeply flawed past. Behind the booming statistics and the enormous challenges, this is the basic issue facing a country that has taken on a core global role without having sorted out its own evolution from the history that still prevails.

Notes

Introduction

1. Southern News Online, 27 November 2007.
2. (Businessman) Ye, pp. 24–5.
3. Elizabeth Economy, *The Nation*, 7 May 2007.
4. (Yangzi) BBC News, 16 April 2007.
5. This and next paragraph, (Illiteracy) *China Daily*, 3 April 2007. (Retirees) *NYT/Observer*, 1 April 2007. (Gender imbalance) *The Times*, 12 January 2007.
6. (Food) *FT*, 30 May 2007. (Counterfeiting) International Data Corp., *WSJ*, 16 May 2007. (Pirate) Sang Ye, pp. 163–4.
7. 'Limited transmission' document made privately available to the author.
8. (Land grabs) *SCMP*, 22 March 2007.
9. (Yu Dan book on Confucius) *Economist*, 19 May 2007.
10. (Poll) www.chinaelections.org, 7 February 2007.
11. (Ghost brides) http://www.forbes.com/2007/06/15/china-ghost-bride-face-markets-cx_jc_0614autofacescan01.html?partner=alerts. (Births) *WP*, 1 March 2007.
12. (Official tongue) BBC-Xinhua, 7 March 2007. (Rail) *China Economic Quarterly*, quoted at ft.com, 23 April 2007, Xinhua, 20 June 2007, *Economist*, 19 May 2007, *SCMP*, 25 January 2008.

Introduction to Part 1

1. Li Ruzhen, *Destiny of Flowers in the Mirror* (Berkeley: University of California Press, 1965). (Governor) Nichols, pp. 101–2, 196.

Chapter 1: Sons of Heaven

1. Hershatter et al., pp. 156, 79.
2. Pelissier, p. 86.
3. (Infanticide) Cumming, p. 195. (Fujian) Perry, *Mandate*, p. 5. (Veneration) Yang Lien-sheng, quoted in Li Yu-ning, pp. 16–17.
4. (Eunuchs) Rawski, pp. 163, 165.
5. (Runners) Ch'ü, chapter 4.
6. Ch'ü, chapter 3. (Clerks) Mary Wright, pp. 93–4. (Henan) Perry, *Rebels*, p. 113.
7. (Qing), Rawski, p. 191.
8. Spence, *Search*, p. 147.
9. Schurmann and Schell, *Imperial China*, pp. 139–40; Pelissier, pp. 90, 86–7; Fairbank, *Revolution*, p. 106.

10. Tun Li-ch'en, pp. 11, 55, 100. (Foxes) Xiaofeng Kang, *The Cult of Foxes* (New York: Columbia University Press, 2006).
11. Anderson, pp. 98–9.
12. Kwan Man Bun, p. 75.
13. Spence, *Roundabout*, p. 245. (Zhidong) Zelin. The argument for the beneficial nature of opium is made in Dikötter, Laamann and Zhou Xun.
14. Anderson, pp. 92, 94, 100. (60–80 per cent) Feuerwerker, *Studies*, p. 15.
15. John Stuart Thomson, p. 322. Borst-Smith, p. 18.
16. Myers, pp. 241, 182.
17. Knapp, p. 8. Pelissier, p. 230. Esherick, *Boxer*, p. 261. Spence, *Roundabout*, p. 171.
18. Esherick, *Boxer*, p. 21. Reynolds, p. 137. Philip Kuhn, pp. 118–19. Michael, quoted in Spector, p. xxxiv. Pelissier, p. 104.

Chapter 2: Upheavals

1. Perry, *Rebels*, p. 140.
2. Ibid., p. 46.
3. The Nien story is told in ibid.; Teng; Spector.
4. Spence, *God's Chinese Son*, pp. 82–3, 111. (Guangxi) Mary Wright, p. 118.
5. The Yunnan revolt is covered in Atwill.
6. Spence, *God's Chinese Son*, p. 161.
7. Lutz and Rolland, pp. 171–3. Jen, chapter 3, gives details of preparations.
8. Callery and Yvan, pp. 204–5.
9. (Taiping, Wuhan) Rowe, *Hankow*, pp. 244–9.
10. Michael, quoted in Spector, p. xxxix.
11. (Sincerity) Spector, p. 19; Zeng quoted in Spector, p. 14. (Behaviour) Jen, p. 233, note 30. (Zeng methods) Philip Kuhn, pp. 146–8. (Officers) Spector, table, p. 21. (Suicide bid) Jen, pp. 236–7.
12. Spector, table, p. 21.
13. Van de Ven, p. 427.
14. Pelissier, p. 97.
15. Wakeman, *Strangers*, pp. 174–6.
16. Kwan Man Bun, pp. 97–8.
17. Mary Wright, pp. 12–13. (Gordon) Spence, *China Helpers*, p. 74.
18. Seagrave, *Dragon Lady*, gives a vivid account of these events, pp. 70–83.
19. Ibid., p. 63.
20. Kwong, pp. 21–2. Hedin, pp. 268–9.
21. Haldane, p. 26.
22. Rawski, pp. 127, 133, 134–7. See Seagrave, Warner, for biographies of Cixi.
23. See Trevor Roper for Backhouse's tales and forgeries, which were used by correspondents in China, notably reporters for the *Times* of London, as the basis for news reports.
24. Rawski, pp. 169–70. Kwong, p. 39; Bland, *Events*, p. 66.
25. (Zeng) Kwong, p. 36.
26. See Kwong, pp. 34–40.
27. (Shanghai trade) Spector, p. 27.
28. (Zeng, Li and Shanghai) Spector, pp. 33–50. Jen, pp. 544, 513. Jen's book was based on half a century of research and is particularly valuable for the insights it gives into the Taiping, in contrast to earlier accounts which drew, rather, on the version given by their opponents.
29. (Shi) Jen, pp. 317–19.
30. Philip Kuhn in Fairbank, *Cambridge, Vol. 10*, p. 317.
31. Perry, *Nien*, p. 147.
32. Atwill, pp. 181–4.
33. Pelissier, p. 157. Cheng and Lestz, pp. 142ff. Laura Newby in Liu and Faure, pp. 71,

73–4, 76. For Xinjiang under the Qing, see Millward. (Sinicization) Millward in Hershatter et al., pp. 127–8.

34. Quoted in Mary Wright, p. 122.

35. (Tax, currency) Mary Wright, pp. 152–3. (Zeng) Ibid., p. 154.

36. This and following, Dong Shouyi and Wang Yanjing in Reynolds, pp. 17, 18–19. (Opium) Nichols, p. 65.

Chapter 3: Strength and Weakness

1. (Poem) Spector, p. 3. (Li) Biographies by Little, *Li*, Bland, *Li*, Spector; Paine, pp. 46–53; Spence, *Search*, pp. 217–22; Hsü, *Rise*, pp. 246–8, 278–87, 336–48, 396–403; J. A. G. Roberts, pp. 69–81, 85–8; W. A. P. Martin, pp. 349, 350, 353; Foster, *Memoirs*, pp. 125, 93; Hutchings, pp. 184, 225, 400. Peter Ditmanson at www.aasianst.org/absts/1996abst/china/c100.htm.

2. See Samuel Chu, chapter 13 in Chu and Liu, for assessment of Li's career and p. 268 on modernization.

3. Spector, p. 236. Carlson, chapter 1. (Li in Zhili) Kwang-ching Liu, chapter 3 in ibid. (Shanghai) Yuen-sang Leung, chapter 5 in ibid. (Shanghai–Tianjin telegraph) Chu and Liu, pp. 110, 111.

4. (Memorial) Bland, *Events*, pp. 84–7.

5. Spector, pp. 287–96.

6. Bland, *Events*, gives a contemporary view of this, pp. 133–4.

7. This and next paragraph, Little, *Li*, pp. 109, 302; Pelissier, p. 184. Hsu, p. 284. Fairbank et al., p. 10. (Christ) Little, *Li*, p. 184. (Chinese) Ibid., p. 268.

8. Beresford, pp. 271–3.

9. (Projects) Fairbank, *Revolution*, p. 117. (Sleep) Little, *Li*, pp. 110, 117–18. (Annoying) Mesny, *Progress in China*, vol. I.

10. Little, *Li*, pp. 112–17.

11. Mesny, *Progress in China*, vol. I. (Hanyang) Feuerwerker, *Studies*, Ch. 6.

12. (Guizhou) Alexander Hosie, pp. 33–4, 46.

13. Hsü, *Rise*, pp. 282–91. The institutional argument was set out by Albert Feuerwerker in his major work on China's early industrialization.

14. (Hart) Fairbank, Bruner and Matheson, p. 10.

15. (Funding) Spector, p. 245. (Purists, weak) Chu and Liu, pp. 276–8. Bays, p. 15. Haldane, pp. 68–9. (Yen) Teng and Fairbank, p. 151.

16. (Censors) CE, 8 March 1889, p. 126. (Governor) Nichols, p. 193.

17. Fairbank, *Revolution*, p. 119. (Zhang) Schurmann and Schell, *Imperial China*, pp. 232–3.

18. Schurmann and Schell, *Imperial China*, p. 225.

19. Fairbank, *Revolution*, p. 118.

20. *NYT*, quoted in Seagrave, *Dragon Lady*, p. 142.

21. This and revolt, Rowe, *Hankow*, pp. 316, 322, 326–330.

22. (Procession) CE, 8 March 1889; NCH, 15 March 1889.

23. Report by French Legation physician, Dr Dethève, 1898; Seagrave, *Dragon Lady*, pp. 253–4.

24. (Concubines) Kwong, pp. 9–60; Haldane, p. 109; Seagrave, *Dragon Lady*, pp. 173–4. (Cousin) Kwong, pp. 60–61.

25. (Edict) Haldane, pp. 111–12.

26. (Eunuch) Ibid., p. 112.

27. CE, 3 March, 29 March and 19 April 1889.

28. (Budget) Kwong, p. 56. (Eunuch punishment) Ibid. pp. 48–9.

29. (Trains) Haldane, p. 130; NCH, 11 July 1898.

30. This and next paragraph, NCH, compilation for second half of 1894, pp. 589, 569, 570.

31. Beasley, *Japanese Imperialism*, p. 55.

32. (Outbreak of war) Paine, p. 124; *NCH*, 21 September 1894, and in compilation for second half of 1894, p. 567.
33. Schurmann and Schell, *Imperial China*, pp. 243–4. Little, *Li*, pp. 219–20. Imperial decree of 1 August in *NCH* compilation for second half of 1894, pp. 776–9.
34. (Hart) Paine, p. 127.
35. (Numbers) Du Boulay, pp. 10, 13.
36. Vladimir, pp. 161–2. Du Boulay, pp. 234–6. *NCH*, 21 September 1894, and in compilation for second half of 1894, p. 477.
37. *NCH* compilation for second half of 1894, p. 478.
38. (Eyewitness) Little, *Li*, pp. 226–7.
39. This and following, Allan, pp. 66–7, 79–91. Some writers have questioned Allan's account of events in Port Arthur, but, while the writing may have been heightened in the retelling, there seems no reason to doubt its central story.
40. This and next paragraph, *New York World*, 17–19 December 1894. Also Creelman, chapter 5. *New York World*, 19 December 1894.
41. (Censor) *NCH*, 12 October 1894. Little, *Li*, pp. 228–9.
42. (Coats, pay, looting) imperial decrees of 25 and 27 November 1894, in *NCH* compilation for first half of 1895, p. 81.
43. (Chile) *NCH*, 12 October 1894.
44. *NCH* compilation for second half of 1894, p. 1015. (Memorial) Bland, *Dragon Empress*, pp. 103–7.
45. (Talks) Paine, pp. 260–61; Little, *Li*, pp. 238–45.
46. This and next paragraph, Paine, pp. 262–6.
47. (Reactions) Duus et al., *Informal Empire*, p. 66. Little, *Li*, p. 247; Kwong, p. 73. Lone, p. 180. Schurmann and Schell, *Imperial China*, pp. 244–5; *NCH*, 29 March 1895; *NCH*, 28 December 1894, and in compilation for second half of 1894, p. 1037.
48. (Gladstone, Devonshire) Little, *Li*, p. 262.

Chapter 4: Reform and Reaction

1. This and next paragraph, Dun J. Li, pp. 68–77. Beresford, pp. 368–9. Vigneron, p. 3. (Hunan) *NCH*, 4 July 1898. (Nanjing) *NCH*, 11 July 1898. (Jiangsu) *NCH*, 2 August 1898. (Tianjin) *NCH*, 25 July 1898. Esherick, *Origins*, p. 167.
2. (Corruption, flour, rice) Beresford, pp, 356, 397, 368–9. (Suzhou) Bernhardt, p. 143. (Cotton) Alexander Hosie, p. xxx. Dun J. Li, pp. 68–77.
3. (Cow) Wehrle, p. 96.
4. (New enterprises) Feuerwerker quoted in Fairbank and Liu, pp. 28–9. Beasley, *Japanese Imperialism*, pp. 61–2. (Trade) Beasley, p. 127. (Investment) Beasley, p. 133.
5. Halcombe, p. 55.
6. Fairbank, Bruner and Matheson, *IG*, pp. 28–9. (Break) Dupée, p. 126.
7. (Hart) NCH compilation for second half of 1894, pp. 449–50; Spence, *Helpers*, pp. 122, 124, 128.
8. (Li) Little, *Li*, p. 276.
9. Hsü, *Rise*, pp. 347–8. (Li, Singapore and attack) Little, *Li*, pp. 278–9.
10. *NCH*, 5 September, 4 November, 18 July 1898.
11. Lü Xiaobo in Reynolds, pp. 50–51.
12. This and next paragraph, Andrea Janku and T'aoung Pa, *International Journal*, vol. xc (Leiden, 2004). Beresford, pp. 163, 273. Kwong, pp. 74–5. (English) *NCH*, 4 July 1898; Reynolds, p. 54. For Zhang, see contributions by Seungjoo Yoon and Tse-ki Hon in Karl and Zarrow.
13. Hao Chang, 'Introduction', provides a good summary analysis of the ferment and ideas. (Hart) Fairbank, Bruner and Matheson, p. 25.
14. Lü Xiaobo in Reynolds, chapter 3, pp. 49 ff.
15. This and following, ibid. pp. 56–60.

16. Shanghai Post Office Museum exhibition.
17. Linsun Cheng, pp. 24ff. (Bonds) Kwong, p. 156. (Sheng companies) Feuerwerker, *Studies*, Ch. 7.
18. Decree, 20 August 1895 (Edicts file). (Horses) Shanghai Post Office Museum exhibition.
19. Lü Xiaobo in Reynolds, pp. 60–61. (Sheng) Esherick, *Reform*, p. 70. Wang Jianhua in Reynolds, pp. 80, 77.
20. (Memorials) Kwong, p. 178. (Pill) *NCH*, 15 August 1898.
21. This and next paragraph, list of reforms, Hsü, *Rise*, pp. 375–6. (Hollow, calligraphy, schools, opium) *NCH*, 22 August 1898. (English) *NCH*, 19 September 1898. (University) Imperial Decree, 11 June 1898 in *Peking Gazette*. (Rooms) *NCH*, 5 September 1898. (Army) *NCH*, 8 August 1898. (Navy) *NCH*, 15 August 1898. (Militia) *NCH*, 22 August and 12 September 1898. (Mausers) *NCH*, 29 August 1898.
22. *NCH*, 15 August 1898. (Rites) *NCH*, 12 September 1898.
23. *NCH*, 29 August 1898.
24. *NCH*, 29 August, 5 September, 12 September, 15 September, 19 September and 3 October 1898.
25. Kwong, pp. 160–65, 241–2. Hart letter to George Morrison, 18 June 1898, in Morrison, *Correspondence* (Cambridge University Press, 1976).
26. Hart letter to George Morrison, 18 June 1898, in Morrison, *Correspondence* (Cambridge University Press, 1976).
27. For a contemporary, damaging, but nuanced, assessment of Kang-i, see Wen Ching, pp. 331–7.
28. Kang is examined critically in Kwong. See also Hao Chang, pp. 22–3, 25; Fairbank, *Revolution*, p. 131; Seagrave, *Dragon Lady*.
29. Kwong, pp. 85–6, 138.
30. Hsü, *Rise*, p. 370.
31. *NCH*, 18 July 1898, and Liang in Hsü, *Rise*, pp. 371–2.
32. Teng and Fairbank, Document 46. (Summary) Hsü, *Rise*, pp. 371–2.
33. Hao Chang, pp. 66–8, 75, 81, 91, 99, 101.
34. Kwong, chapter 9, puts Kang in perspective and is the source for much of the information here.
35. Seagrave, *Dragon Lady*, pp. 228, 233–4.
36. Ch'en, *Yuan*, p. 55. (Jung) Little, *Li*, p. 274. (Mine) *NCH*, 1 August 1898.
37. (Yuan movements) Ch'en, *Yuan*, p. 55.
38. Haldane, pp. 144–6, quoting Der Ling, *Old Buddha* (London: John Lane, 1919).
39. Der Ling, *Old Buddha*, chapter 9.
40. (Books, robes) Little, *Li*, p. 294.
41. Little, *Li*, pp. 285–6. (Health) Seagrave, *Dragon Lady*, p. 434 and note, p. 553.
42. *NCH*, 24 October 1898.
43. Zhang Kaiyuan in Eto and Schiffrin, pp. 79, 81, 86.
44. (Education) Article by Timothy Weston in Karl and Zarrow. Little, *Li*, p. 283. Hao Chang, p. 75.

Chapter 5: On the Ropes

1. Esherick, *Boxer*, pp. 299–300.
2. (Cross) Hsü in Fairbank and Liu, p. 78; Eddy, p. 92
3. Wehrle, p. 50. Esherick, *Boxer*, pp. 75, 78.
4. (Women, Swedes) Wehrle, pp. 60, 57–8.
5. (Weed) Esherick, *Boxer*, p. 133.
6. *NCH*, 16 August 1895. (Massacre) Wehrle, pp. 86, 108, 90.
7. Esherick, *Boxer*, pp. 299–300.
8. Perry, *Rebels*, p. 102.
9. Esherick, *Boxer*, p. 214.

10. For this and following, Esherick, *Boxer*, pp. 293, 295.
11. Ibid., pp. 297–8.
12. Ibid., p. 244. Hsü in Fairbank and Liu, p. 118.
13. (Buried) Nichols, p. 14.
14. Wehrle, p. 152.
15. For this and next paragraph, Esherick, *Boxer*, pp. 289, 302.
16. Wehrle, p. 175.
17. (Fun) FO 17.1413, MacDonald to Salisbury.
18. Brandt gives the fullest account of the Shanxi events: *Massacre*, pp. 231ff.
19. (Li) Little, *Li*, p. 302; Bland, *Dragon Empress*, pp. 305–8.
20. (Rising) Bays, pp. 78–100.
21. Preston, chapter 13 gives an account of conditions in the legation quarter.
22. (Siege, letters) Wehrle, pp. 184, 186–7. (Jung-lu) Wen Ching, p. 337. (Hart) Seagrave, *Dragon Lady*, p. 382. (Cathedral) Esherick, *Boxer*, pp. 278–9.
23. Mather, p. 381.
24. Steel, p. 20.
25. Steel, p. 54. (Baoding) Nichols, p. 15. (Russians) Cohen, *Three Keys*, p. 279.
26. Prince Su in the *NYT*, 8 January 1902.
27. (Famine) Nichols, pp. 228, 233, 234, 242.
28. Hsü, *Rise*, pp. 400–401, gives details of the settlement and the breakdown of the indemnity payments.
29. (Shanxi official) Nichols, pp. 81–2.

Chapter 6: Final Act

1. Fairbank, Bruner and Matheson, letters 1231 and 1232. Photograph in Spence, *Chinese Century*, pp. 28–9.
2. Townley, pp. 285–6.
3. Bastid, pp. 45, 56. Pitcher, p. 86.
4. Beahan in Guisso and Johannesen, p. 232.
5. Brown, pp. 214–18.
6. The Fujian campaign is dealt with in Mandancy.
7. Hsü, *Rise*, p. 409; pp. 410–11 gives a list of the reforms. (Zhang) Spence, *Roundabout*, p. 195.
8. (Women's groups) Chang, Beahan in Guisso and Johannesen, pp. 215ff. (Chen) Karl and Zarrow, p. 227.
9. Beahan in Guisso and Johannesen, p. 227.
10. Bastid, pp. 78, 70–73, 75.
11. Esherick, *Reform*, p. 120.
12. This and following, Zhu Ying in Reynolds, pp. 107ff.
13. Wellington Chan in Fairbank and Liu, p. 416; Bays, pp. 207–10. (Tianjin) Kwan Man Bun, p. 106. Bastid in Fairbank and Liu, pp. 556, 558. Qin Shao's book describes Nantong in detail, including its intended role of a showpiece city.
14. This and next paragraph, Linsun Cheng, pp. 27ff.
15. (Concentration) Rhoads, p. 267. Xiong Yuezhi in Liu and Faure, pp. 100–110.
16. Ramon Myers in Duus et al., *Empire*, pp. 101–2, 104–5, 107, 115, 126.
17. Beahan in Guisso and Johannesen, pp. 233–5.
18. (Protests) Bastid, p. 94, and in Fairbank and Liu, pp. 587–8.
19. Tai Hsüan-chih, p. 11.
20. This and following, Esherick, *Reform*, pp. 123–42.
21. Bastid-Bruguière, pp, 60, 61–2, 65. (Hankou, Wuchang) Esherick, *Reform*, p. 121.
22. Zhang in Schurmann and Schell, *Imperial China*, p. 227.
23. Zhu Ying in Reynolds, pp. 120–21.
24. This and next paragraph, He Yimin in Reynolds, pp. 146–8, 149–53. Stapleton, chapter 3.

25. (Cartoon) Felder in Eto and Schiffrin, p. 106.
26. Bastid-Bruguière in Fairbank and Liu, pp. 543–4.
27. (Sichuan) He Yimin in Reynolds, p. 138.
28. (Guangdong) Rhoads, pp. 91–4.
29. Beahan in Guisso and Johannesen, p. 226.
30. ($6.75m) Rhoads, p. 268. Esherick, *Reform*, p. 80.
31. (Courtesan handbooks) Catherine Yeh in Liu and Faure. (Secretary) Ku Hung-ming, pp. v, 34, 47. (Pamphlet) Esherick, *Reform*, p. 47.
32. Rankin, p. 18.
33. Ibid., pp. 174–5.
34. (Horse) Karl and Zarrow, p. 202. (Photographs) Rankin, pp. 42–3.
35. (Rising and Qiu) Rankin, pp. 4–6, 174, 182–4, 184–7. (Xu) Rhoads in Eto and Schiffrin, pp. 6–7.
36. Rankin, p. 189.
37. (Insurrections) Bastid-Bruguière in Fairbank and Liu, pp. 594, 197.
38. This and next paragraphs, Haldane, pp. 256–9; Seagrave, *Dragon Lady*, p. 434.
39. For the racial aspects of the anti-Manchu movement and its link with secret societies in particular, see Duara, chapter 4.
40. (Assemblies make-up) Chang P'eng-yuan in Eto and Schiffrin, p. 66. Esherick, *Reform*, p. 99.
41. Esherick, *Reform*, p. 112. Li Kan in Eto and Schiffrin, pp. 45, 48.
42. Esherick, *Reform*, p. 116.
43. Kwan Man Bun, pp. 141–52.
44. Stapleton, pp. 159–60.
45. This and following, ibid., pp. 170–76.
46. This and following, ibid., pp. 177–9.

Chapter 7: A Very Young Baby

1. (Choice of Li) Jin Chongji in Eto and Schiffrin, pp. 59–62.
2. Esherick, *Reform*, p. 202.
3. This and next paragraph, Rhoads, chapter 9.
4. Ch'en, *Yuan*, pp. 118–19.
5. Ibid, p. 121.
6. Anschel details Lea's career. Also, exhibition at presidential palace, Nanking.
7. (Eggs) Ho Hsiang-ning quoted in Li Yu-ning, pp. 138–9.
8. Laitinen, pp. 148, 165. Dittmer and Kim, pp. 77–9.
9. Sun, *Memoirs*, p. 184. (Republic) Lary, *China's Republic*, p. 1.
10. This and following, Esherick in Eto and Schiffrin, pp. 142–6.
11. *NCH*, 6 January 1912.
12. Harrison, pp. 99–101.
13. This and next paragraph, Bergère, *Sun*, p. 218.
14. Guisso and Johannesen, pp. 260, 236, 230.
15. (Discussion) Fung, p. 225.
16. Kidd, p. 68.
17. Ch'en, *Yuan*, pp. 129–30.
18. (Cable) Li Kan in Eto and Schiffrin, p. 51. (Broken) Christie, p. 264.
19. Selle, p. 129.
20. (Sun, one member) *NCH*, 5 April 1912.
21. (Famine, flooding) *NCH*, 6 April 1912.
22. (Duan) *NCH*, 6 April 1912. (Poem) Hsüeh, p. 221. Reinsch, pp. 1–3. Bergère, *Sun*, p. 229.
23. (Sun railways) Eto and Schiffrin, p. 83. Selle, pp. 133–8.
24. Eto and Schiffrin, pp. 90–98. Feuerwerker in Fairbank and Twitchett, chapter 2.

25. (Hunan) Esherick, *Reform*, pp. 247–9. Ernest Young, p. 277, note 70.
26. This and next paragraph, Rhoads, pp. 251–9.
27. Ch'en, *Yuan*, pp. 148–50.
28. (Song) Dittmer and Kim, p. 68.
29. Reinsch, p. 11.
30. Rhoads, pp. 260–65.
31. Fenby, p. 36.
32. Selle, pp. 144–5.
33. Ernest Young, pp. 139–45.
34. Hobsbawm, chapter 30. Perry, *Mandate*, chapter 4.
35. Guisso and Johannesen, p. 237.
36. *NCH*, 31 December 1915.
37. Ernest Young, pp. 228–9, 242.
38. (Provinces) Ch'en, *Yuan*, pp. 169–70.
39. (Loans) Ch'en, pp. 182–4
40. (Killing) *NCH*, 27 May 1915, *Proceedings of Conference*, vol. II, pp. 32, 24–5. (Chiang) Ch'en Chieh-ju, pp. 81, 79 ff. *NCH*, 13 November 1915.
41. This and following *re* Donald, Selle, pp. 178–9.

Chapter 8: Warlords

1. (Li reception) La Motte, chapter XIII.
2. Ch'i, *Warlord Politics*, p. 18.
3. This and following, Selle, pp. 207–9.
4. (Arms) Ch'i, *Warlord Politics*, p. 24, footnote.
5. Mitter, *Revolution*, is the best account. (Japanese troops) Sheridan in Fairbank and Twitchett, p. 281.
6. Mitter, *Revolution*, pp. 3–10.
7. Mao, *Selected Works*, vol. 1, p. 129. Chang and Halliday, p. 17. (Women) Schram, *Road*, vol. 1, pp. 421–38, 442–4.
8. Spence, *Gate*, pp. 217–18. Mitter, *Revolution*, pp. 57–60.
9. Chang and Halliday, p. 27.
10. (Zou) Mitter, *Revolution*, pp. 54–7, 80–88.
11. For warlords, Ch'i Hsi-sheng's *Warlord Politics* is an authoritative survey. Biographies of individual militarists by Gillin, McCormack, Sheridan, *Chinese Warlord*, and Wou, as well as Pye and article by McCord. Fenby chapter VI. Ransome, pp. 128–33, for contemporary account.
12. (International relations) Ch'i, *Warlord Politics*, pp. 8–9. (Relationship charts) Ibid., pp. 68–71.
13. Pelissier, p. 293.
14. (Gambling) Ch'i, *Warlord Politics*, p. 254.
15. Ibid., pp. 253, 258 note 1.
16. (Forest) Powell, p. 88. (Tanaka) Duus, p. 288. Christie, p. 279.
17. (Concubines) Abend, *Life in China*, p. 64. (Ruffian) *NCH*, 27 September 1928.
18. (Journalist) Gunther, p. 201.
19. Powell, pp. 84–5.
20. Levich, pp. 7–15, has fuller pen portraits.
21. (Yang) Forbes, pp. 12–21.
22. (Ma) Ibid., pp. 21–8; photograph of his body, p. 26. Skrine, pp. 86–8.
23. Bergère, *L'Age d'or*, is the classic study of this expansion, particularly in Shanghai.
24. Hershatter et al., p. 225.
25. Ch'i, *Warlord Politics*, tables on pp. 129–30.
26. Tai Hsüan-chih, pp. 17–25. *NCH*, 4 September 1926. Wou, pp. 77–8.
27. Fenby, p. 104. Wou, p. 79.

28. Fairbank and Feuerwerker, p. 262.
29. Peking United International Famine Relief Committee, pp. 11–13. Ch'ien Tuan-sheng, p. 12. Fenby, p. 106.
30. (Numbers) Perry, *Mandate*, p. 17. (Women) Perry, *Rebels*, p. 71.
31. (Song) Perry, *Rebels*, p. 22.
32. Tai Hsüan-chih, pp. 26–8.
33. Powell, chapter XI. French, pp. 115ff.
34. Tai Hsüan-chih, p. 10. Perry, *Rebels*, intro, p. xiv.
35. Fairbank and Feuerwerker, p. 291. Tai Hsüan-chih, p. 113.
36. This and following, Tai Hsüan-chih: pp. 59ff.; (limitless) pp. 73–4; (United Village) p. 83.
37. Ibid., pp. 68–73.

Chapter 9: Ice and Ancient Charcoal

1. Fenby, *Generalissimo*, pp. 50–54.
2. Ming Chan in Hershatter et al., p. 234.
3. (Troops) Lary, *Warlord Soldiers*, p. 72. (Customs) PRO, London, FO 371–12440/9156; FO 94/87/10. Wilbur and How, Document 3. (American) Francke, p. 266.
4. Loh, *Débâcle*, pp. 76–7, 80–81, mainly quoting Chiang's 'diary'.
5. Ransome, p. 81.
6. See also Wilbur and How, pp. 88–9.
7. (Chiang–Sun correspondence), Furuya, p. 117.
8. Borodin's life and his time in China are expertly covered in Dan Jacobs's biography.
9. Jacobs, pp. 115–16.
10. Hershatter et al., p. 233. See Chan's essay here for an overview of the Canton Decade.
11. Chang and Halliday, pp. 33, 38.
12. Abend, *Life*, p. 24.
13. Wilbur and How, pp. 523ff. Bennett, pp. 124–5. Cherepanov, p. 104.
14. Loh, *Débâcle*, pp. 94–5.
15. *CWR*, 12 June 1924, p. 82.
16. Ch'en Chieh-ju, p. 148.
17. *CET*, 23 October 1924. Swisher, pp. 2–3. *NCH*, 15 November 1924. *CET*, 23 October 1924.
18. This and next paragraph, *NCH*, 29 November and 9 December 1924.
19. *NCH*, 5 September 1925. Ch'en Chieh-ju. p. 158.
20. Wilbur, *Frustrated Patriot*, p. 290. (Family) Reuters, 27 March 1925. (Coffin) Ibid., 2 April 1925. Zhang interview with Japanese journalists, *CET*, 19 March 1925.
21. Harrison, pp. 144–51. Ransome, p. 66.
22. Fitzgerald, *Nationalists*, p. 38.
23. Wilbur and How, p. 698. (Interpreter: Vera Vishnyakova), Ibid., p. 219.
24. Ch'en Chieh-ju, p. 155.
25. Furuya, p. 153. Ch'en Chieh-ju, p. 168. Reuters, 4, 6 and 9 June 1925. Swisher, p. 7.
26. *NCH*, June–July 1925. Abend, *Life*, p. 17.
27. Cherepanov, p. 158. T'ang, p. 115.
28. Jordan, *Northern Expedition*, p. 304. Furuya, p. 165. *NCH*, 28 November 1925. Wilbur and How, p. 698. Han Suyin, p. 75.
29. Cherepanov, p. 226. Wilbur and How, p. 51. Ibid., p. 525, document 26. Botjer, p. 56. Abend, *Life*, p. 33.
30. Wou, p. 133.
31. Botjer, p. 5. Jordan, *Northern Expedition*, p. 18. (Soong) Abend, *Life*, p. 19.
32. Wilbur and How, pp. 318–19.
33. Powell, p. 85.
34. *NCH*, 31 August and 11 September 1926. Reuters, 27 August 1926.

35. *NCH*, 11 September 1926.
36. Jordan, *Northern Expedition*, pp. 240–41, 212.
37. Mowrer, pp. 80–81. FBI Memorandum to the Director Jan. 9, 1943. Seagrave, *Dragon Lady*, p. 261.
38. Ch'en Chieh-ju, chapter 25. Tyson Li, p. 74.
39. Ch'en Chieh-ju, p. 187. The dismissing is from chapter 19. (Proposal) Snow, *Star*, p. 85. Hahn, p. 86.
40. *NCH*, 26 February 1927.
41. Ransome, p. 70. (Chiang) Ch'en Chieh-ju, pp. 226–7.
42. Jordan, *Northern Expedition*, pp. 283–4. Chen Li-fu, p. 53.
43. *NCH*, 26 March 1927.
44. (Fessenden) Powell, p. 326.
45. Ibid., pp. 150–52. Misselwitz, pp. 25, 27. *NCH*, 24 March 1927.
46. Powell, p. 143.
47. Ibid., pp. 145, 146–7, 166–8. *NCH*, 2 April 1927.
48. Brian Martin, pp. 91–3. Frazier. Chen Li-fu, p. 63. Brian Martin, pp. 104–5. (Gangsters) Pan, *Old Shanghai*, pp. 48–51. Chen Li-fu, p. 60. Faligot and Kauffer, p. 40.
49. Chen Li-fu, p. 62.
50. *NCH*, April 1927. Powell, pp. 148–60. Tien-wei Wu, 'Chiang Kai-Shek's April 12 Coup', in Chan and Etzold. Wilbur, *Revolution*, pp. 99–113. Seagrave, *Soong*, pp. 228–9. Fewsmith, *Elites*, chapter 5. Author visit, 2006.
51. Chiang, *Soviet Russia*, p. 48. Stella Dong, pp. 184–5. *NCH*, 30 April 1927. Wilbur, *Revolution*, pp. 110–11. *NCH*, 23 April 1927. diary, 24 April and 29 May 1927, in Swisher. Sheean, p. 227. (Hunan) McDonald, p. 316.
52. Coble, *Shanghai Capitalists*, pp. 34 and 40. *NYT*, 4 May 1927. Chapman, pp. 231–2. (Ransoms) Coble, *Shanghai Capitalists*, pp. 34–5. *NCH*, 30 April, 21 May and 4 June 1927. Brian Martin, p. 197. (Chiang approval, company handover) Coble, *Shanghai Capitalists*, p. 33.
53. *NCH*, 16–30 April 1927.
54. Coble, *Shanghai Capitalists*, p. 38. Abend, *Tortured China*, pp. 176–7. *NCH*, 11 June 1927. Misselwitz, p. 123. Lu Lan quoted in Li Yu-ning, pp. 176–7.

Chapter 10: Divided We Stand

1. Zhang, *Trail of the Century*, part two.
2. *NCH*, 4 March 1927.
3. Ransome, p. 75.
4. (Closures, inflation) Powell, pp. 135–6.
5. (Sikhs) Ibid., pp. 137–8.
6. Bryna Goodman in Leutner and Spakowski, pp. 351–75.
7. Hershatter et al., p. 216.
8. (Chen) Perry, *Mandate*, p. 174. Hershatter et al., pp. 83–4.
9. Sternberg, pp. 82–3.
10. Sheean, p. 267.
11. Tong and Li, pp. 216–17.
12. Misselwitz, p. 118.
13. North and Eudin, pp. 107, 111, 123, 127 and chapter 6. Misselwitz, p. 126. Sheean, p. 240. Jacobs, p. 279. Short, *Mao*, pp. 190–91. T'ang, p. 155.
14. Sheean, p. 268.
15. Ibid., p. 302.
16. (Water, Zhou) Chang and Halliday, pp. 52–3, 73.
17. This and next paragraph: Reuters in *NCH*, 13 August 1927. Chiang, *Soviet Russia*, pp. 51–2. (Galen's post-China career) Wilbur and How, p. 427. Davies, p. 183.
18. Tong and Li, pp. 219–20, p. 222.

19. *NCH*, 20 August 1927.
20. Misselwitz, pp. 138–9.
21. Chang, *Madame Sun Yat-sen*, p. 66.
22. The letter was subsequently published by a Catholic newspaper in Tianjin: Crozier, p. 116.
23. Klein and Clark, vol. II, p. 1014. *SCMP*, 14 December 1927. *NCH*, 24 December 1927. Swisher, pp. 115, 91.
24. (Canton) *NCH*, 17–24 December 1927. Wilbur, *Revolution*, pp. 164ff. Chang and Halliday, p. 63.
25. Crozier, p. 123. Furuya, p. 236.
26. This and the next paragraph: Abend, *Life*, pp. 78–80. Abend, *Tortured China*, pp. 90ff. Reuters, 21 May 1928. Furuya, p. 247. *NCH*, 5 May 1927.
27. *NCH*, 12 May 1928. Reuters, 7 May 1928. Kuo Min, 8 May 1928; Toho, 14–15 May 1928. Chiang, *China's Destiny*, p. 123
28. (Interviewer) Snow, *Front*, p. 65. (Donald) Selle, p. 256.
29. *China Year Book*, 1928, pp. 1373–4. Hedin, pp. 27–8. (Toynbee) Mackerras, p. 122.
30. Ch'ien Tuan-sheng gives detailed description and analysis of the Yuan in chapters XI, XIII, XVI, XVIII.
31. (Tariff) Abend, *Life*, pp. 94–5; Hahn, p. 138.
32. (Beijing) Madeleine Yue Dong, p. 78. (Nanjing) Reuters, 13 December 1929. Yorke, p. 53. Lipkin's account gives details of the attempts to modernize Nanjing.
33. (Congress) *NCH*, 16 March 1929. Wang Ke-wen, pp. 258, 250. Kuo Min, 23 March 1929. Faligot and Kauffer, p. 78. Chen Li-fu, p. 65. Eastman, *Revolution*, pp. 74–5.
34. Liang, p. 50. *NCH*, 14 April 1929.
35. (Casualties) Reuters, 13 October 1930. Sheridan, *China in Disintegration*, p. 186. (Finance) Coble, *Shanghai Capitalists*, p. 87.
36. *NCH*, 8 July 1930.
37. Powell, pp. 175–6.
38. (Visitor) Abend, *Life*, p. 118.
39. *NCH*, 31 December 1926. Rengo news agency, 7 May 1930. Leung, *Dictionary*, pp. 54–5.
40. See Lao She stories such as 'Camel Xuangzi'.
41. (Trade, tea) Yorke, pp. 294, 315.
42. (Investment, traditional sectors) King, pp. 126–7, 132. (Beijing) M. Y. Dong, pp. 116–18. (Strikes and Shanghai labour) Perry, *Mandate*, chapter 5. (Coal) Tim Wright, pp. 171–4. Feuerwerker, *Studies*, Ch. 5, particularly pp. 156–8.
43. (Zhejiang, pigs) Yorke, p. 308.
44. Figures in this and the next paragraph, Ch'ien Tuan-sheng, pp. 212–13.
45. (Statistics) Fenby, pp. 232–3. Chin, p. 98. (Teacher) Fu I-hsing quoted in Li Yu-ning, pp. 183–4.
46. Yutang, p. 182. Eastman, *Revolution*, pp. 14–17, for this and the next two paragraphs.
47. (Rent reform) Lin Chu-ching in Tawney, pp. 144–9.
48. Myers, pp. 292–3. Brandt in Wakeman and Edmonds, p. 53. *NCH*, 24 January 1934. (Statistics) Eastman, *Family*, p. 70. Gaoyang, *CQ*, November 2007.
49. (Health) *NCH*, 1 July 1936. (Fertilizers) Brodie, p. 120.
50. (Tea) Chang Yu-sui in Tawney, p. 2. Shih Ko in Tawney, p. 234.
51. Kuo Shih-tze in Tawney, pp. 167–71.
52. (Shaanxi) Chang Chiao-fu in Tawney, pp. 199–204.
53. Ku Nung in Tawney, pp. 184–8.
54. Tobacco reports by Hsu Yung-sui and Min Chi in Tawney, pp. 171–9.
55. (Gansu) Chang Kiang in Tawney, pp. 129–30. (Highway) Pai Yua-yuan in Tawney, pp. 110–12.
56. (Weaving) Lo Chun and Chen Nyi-kuan in Tawney, pp. 239–47.
57. Lo Kuo-hsian in Tawney, pp. 188–93. (Sichuan) Lee Kuo-ch'un in Tawney, pp. 193–9. (Flooding) Yorke, p. 72.

58. Brandt in Wakeman and Edmonds, p. 53. *NCH*, 24 January 1934. Spence, *Gate*, p. 273.
59. (Opium, remedy) Dikötter et al., pp. 332–3. Wakeman and Edmonds, *Re-appraising*, pp. 264–6. Brook and Wakabayashi, pp. 286–9. Anhui, ibid., p. 312.
60. (Yunnan) Tawney, pp. 118–22, 122–6.
61. (Du) Nellist, p. 110. Leith-Ross, pp. 207–8. Sues, pp. 88–90, 92–4.
62. Bergère, *L'Age d'or*, pp. 279–92.
63. (Unions) Perry, *Mandate*, chapter 6. *NCH*, 4 August 1931.
64. Kuo Min, 4 December 1929. *CWR*, 20 June 1931.
65. Wakeman, *Spymaster*, is the outstanding biography. Description on p. 1.
66. Eastman, *Revolution*, pp. 25–6.
67. Chiang, *China's Destiny*, p. 98.
68. Meiling Soong, *New Life for Jiangxi*, pp. iii–v. Kuo Min, 28 November 1932. (Pigs) *NCH*, 29 April 1936.
69. (List of New Life rules) Cheng and Lestz, pp. 298ff. (Best chance) *NCH*, 4 January 1934.
70. *NCH*, 16 September 1936. Fenby, p. 249.
71. Theodore White, p. 117.

Chapter 11: Enemy of the Heart

1. Ch'en in Eastman et al., p. 53.
2. Eastman et al., pp. 56, 65, 76, 300.
3. Rowe, *Crimson Rain*, p. 255.
4. Base details taken from McColl, E. L. Dreyer, Ch'en in Eastman et al., p. 72.
5. Ch'en in Eastman et al., pp. 72, 64.
6. (Dinner party) *Guide Weekly*, no. 191, pp. 2063–4. Ch'en, map, p. 87.
7. Terrill, *Mao*, pp. 97, 113. Schram, *Thought*, 'Introduction'. Chang and Halliday, pp. 41–2, 56.
8. Chang and Halliday, pp. 60–61. Terrill, *Mao*, pp. 131–2 including song.
9. Terrill, *Mao*, pp. 133–4.
10. Short, *Mao*, chapters 7–9. Hutchings, pp. 246–7. Chang and Halliday, chapter 6.
11. Chang and Halliday, pp. 83–91.
12. *NCH*, 27 January 1931. E. L. Dreyer, pp. 160–61. Short, *Mao*, pp. 256–7. Figures for the number of troops Chiang put into the field in the five campaigns against the Communists vary considerably because of discrepancies between the strength of units on paper and their actual numbers: I have taken those given in Ch'i, *Nationalist China*, p. 246, quoting from Kuo-fang-pu, *Chiao-feichan-shih* (Taipei 1962).
13. The purge is best told in Short, *Mao*, chapter 8, and Chang and Halliday, pp. 96–101.
14. (Zhang) Ch'en in Eastman et al., pp. 64, 67. (Armed force) Short, *Mao*, p. 188.
15. Rowe, *Crimson Rain*, pp. 309–16.
16. (Plot) McColl, p. 53. (He Long base) Sun, *Memoirs*, p. 92.
17. E. L. Dreyer, pp. 163–4. Short, *Mao*, pp. 258–60, 286–7. *NCH*, 1 March 1931. Kuo Min, 3 July and 7 September 1931.
18. (Zhu De) Short, *Mao*, p. 261.
19. Short, *Mao*, p. 287.
20. (Gu) Faligot and Kauffer, pp. 36, 39, 41–2, 46–7; subsequent events, ibid., pp. 63ff. Wakeman, *Spymaster*, pp. 138–41, 151–60.
21. Faligot and Kauffer, pp. 67–8. (Arrest, defection) Warren Kuo, vol. 2, pp. 313–19.
22. *NCH*, 1 December 1931. (Rumours) Faligot and Kauffer, p. 79.
23. (Shot on bus) Schoppa, *Blood Road*. (Deng) Eastman, *Revolution*, pp. 93–6.
24. (Chiang) Taylor, p. 59, quoting *Nanking Diaries*, 15 and 16 December 1931, and p. 60 for diary of 27 December 1931.

Chapter 12: Enemy of the Skin

1. Abend, *Life*, pp. 152–3.
2. (Mukden take-over) *NCH*, 18–30 September 1931; Snow, *Front*, p. 74; Fenby, *Generalissimo*, pp. 200–203. Mitter, *Myth*, explores the ramifications of the incident in depth.
3. (Zhang) Ibid., p. 73.
4. This and following: Ienaga, pp. 6–12; Iris Chang, p. 218; Bix, pp. 276, 176; Furuya in *Manshu Nichinichi Shimbun*, p. 309; Duus, pp. 290–95.
5. Snow, *Front*, p. 80.
6. This and following: ibid., pp. 86–8.
7. Abend, *Life*, pp. 167–8.
8. This and following on Jinzhou: Powell, pp. 186–8.
9. Mitter, *Myth*, p. 40. Harries and Harries, p. 131.
10. Snow, *Front*, pp. 114–17.
11. Jerome Ch'en, *China*, p. 412. (Song) *NCH*, 3 November 1930.
12. Reuters, 28 September 1931.
13. (Association) Snow, *Front*, p. 168.
14. Beasley, *Japanese Imperialism*, p. 261.
15. Furuya, pp. 348–51. Jordan, *Trial*, pp. 7, 11–12. Selle, pp. 270–72. Sergeant, pp. 184–5.
16. Abend, *Life*, pp. 186–91.
17. Sergeant, pp. 185–6. Snow, *Front*, pp. 191–2. Fenby, p. 211.
18. Snow, *Front*, p. 203.
19. Jordan, *Trial*, p. 223.
20. Ibid., pp. 146–8.
21. Henriot, *Shanghai 1927–1937*, pp. 94–5. Snow, *Front*, p. 207.
22. *NCH*, 22 March 1932. Henriot, *Shanghai 1927–1937*, pp. 92–5. Abend, *Life*, p. 193. Fogel, *Journal of Asian Studies*, vol. 59/4. *NCH*, 22 March 1932. Fenby, *Generalissimo*, pp. 213–14. Snow, *Front*, p. 216.
23. Manchukuo is excellently analysed and described in Yamamuro, and frontier fighting figures evocatively in Haruki Murakami's 'Lieutenant Mamiya's Long Story' in *The Wind-Up Bird Chronicle* (Vintage Books, 2004).
24. Kuo Min, 22 September 1931. Reuters, 25–6 September 1931.
25. (Colonial management) Y. Tak Matsusaka in Duus, Myers and Peattie, chapter 4. (Massacre) Mitter, *Myth*, p. 112; Powell, p. 195. (Hamlets) Harries and Harries, p. 216.
26. This and following: Mitter, Myth, 112. Powell, p. 195. (Hamlets) Harries, p. 216. (Companies, planes, railways) *Daily News*, 'Japanchukuo' in this and the next paragraph, Snow, *Front*, pp. 263, 266, 269, 271, 272, 274. (Harbin) Clausen and Thøgersen, photograph after p. 108. Tim Wright, p. 85. Ito, pp. 123 9. (Economy) Myers in Duus, Myers and Peattie, chapter 5. Harries and Harries, pp. 207–8.
27. Powell, pp. 196–8.
28. (Communists) Mitter, *Myth*, pp. 194–6. (Headquarters) Clausen and Thøgersen, photograph after p. 108.
29. Powell, pp. 198–201.
30. Abend, *Life*, pp. 170–71. Powell, pp. 200–201.
31. *NCH*, 19 October 1932. Reuters, 14–15 July 1932. Kuo Min, 19 December and 8 October 1932. Rowe, *Crimson Rain*, p. 319.
32. E. L. Dreyer, p. 186.
33. (Meeting) Short, *Mao*, p. 288. (Wait) Terrill, *Mao*, p. 150.
34. This and following: Fenby, *Generalissimo*, pp. 221–2. Kuo Min, 6 August 1932. Reuters, 9–11 August 1932.
35. Fleming, pp. 35–6. *NCH*, 16 October 1935. (Weeds) *NCH*, 24 January 1934.
36. (Bo Gu) Short, *Mao*, pp. 2–3. Terrill, *Mao*, p. 139. Chang and Halliday, p. 122.
37. (This and following account of Jehol) Hedin, pp. 16, 83, 128. (Artillery) Yorke, p. 109,

83. Selle, pp. 280–81. Reuters, 4 March 1932. *NCH*, 1–8 March 1933. (Korean girls) Fleming, p. 92. Yorke, pp. 103–4.
38. (Chiang–Zhang meeting) *NCH*, 22 March 1933. Selle, p. 281.
39. *NCH*, 22 March 1932. Fenby, p. 222.
40. Abend, *Life*, p. 204.
41. Song is covered in Dryburgh.
42. *NCH*, 24 May 1933.
43. (Soong) *NCH*, 1 November 1933.
44. This and next paragraph: Snow, *Front*, p. 279. Puyi, pp. 285, 292–5; Li Yü-ch'in quoted in Li Yu-ning, pp. 228–9, 241–4.
45. Terrill, *Mao*, pp. 146–7.
46. Kuo Min, 29 April 1934. Short, *Mao*, p. 313. Mao, *Selected Works*, vol. 1, p. 231.
47. Kuo Min, 6 June 1934. *NCH*, 20 June 1934. Reuters, 1 July 1934. *NCH*, 4 July 1934.
48. Reuters, 12 October 1934.
49. Short, *Mao*, pp. 316–17. Chang and Halliday, p. 157.

Chapter 13: Mao's March

1. The Long March is covered in detail in Sun, Short, *Mao*, Wilson, Salisbury, and Jocelyn and McEwen. Chang and Halliday's debunking is not always convincing, as shown in this chapter.
2. (Ages) Terrill, *Mao*, p. 152.
3. Xinhua, http://news.xinhuanet.com/english/2006-10/21/content_5232264.htm.
4. Sun Shuyun, *March*. (Reds for son) Chang and Halliday, chapter 12.
5. (Battle) Salisbury, *March*, pp. 92–104; Short, *Mao*, p. 4; Wilson, *March*, pp. 77–9.
6. Short, *Mao* pp. 9–10.
7. (Meeting) Ibid., pp. 11–14. Chang and Halliday, pp. 000.
8. Short, *Mao*, p. 13.
9. (Chiang campaign) *NCH*, 10–17 April and 5 June 1935. Reuters, 6 April 1935. Wakeman, *Spymaster*, p. 242. (Wife) Short, *Mao*, p. 328.
10. Hall, p. 175. (Bloomers) Lacam, p. 158.
11. (Dadu) Short, *Mao*, p. 326; Chang and Halliday, pp. 159–60; Sun, pp. 156–64; Tsang and Benton, p. 4.
12. Powell, pp. 283–4.
13. This and the next two paragraphs: Fenby, pp. 273–4.
14. Powell, pp. 284–9.
15. (League) Harries and Harries, p. 210.
16. Abend, *Life*, pp. 212–15.
17. (Darkest) Snow, *Star*, p. 432. Terrill, *Mao*, pp. 162–3.
18. Description by survivors to Agnes Smedley, in Wilson, *March*, p. 204.
19. Sun, chapter 12.
20. (Bodyguard) Wang Dongxiang quoted by Michael Schoenhals, SOAS lecture, London, 30 November 2006.
21. Snow, *Star*, pp. 79–80.
22. This characteristic of Mao's thoughts comes out most clearly in MacFarquhar and Schoenhals's masterly work on the Cultural Revolution and is well summarized and commented on in the review by Jonathan Mirsky, *Times Literary Supplement*, 20 October 2006.

Chapter 14: Total War

1. Van de Ven, pp. 151–63.
2. (Matsuoka) Harries and Harries, p. 163.
3. (Chen Lifu, negotiations) Van de Ven, pp. 173–4.

4. Abend, *Life*, p. 225.
5. (Dai Li) Wakeman, *Spymaster*, p. 232.
6. James Thomson, pp. 138–42.
7. (Centralization) Vermeer, pp. 73–4.
8. The site can be visited; there is a bullet hole in the window of Chiang's room, circled in red. (Incident) Fenby, Prologue.
9. Van de Ven, p. 187.
10. (Dai Li) Wakeman, *Spymaster*, p. 236. (Meiling arrival) Photograph at Zhang museum, Xi'an.
11. (Meeting) Fenby, *Generalissimo*, pp. 10–11.
12. Central News Agency, 28 December 1936. Selle, p. 334. Fenby, *Generalissimo*, p. 12.
13. Zhang Xueliang, part three; *China Post*, 7 June 2002.
14. (Lin Sen) Kuo Min, 10 April 1937.
15. Gibson, pp. 362–3, chapter 1; (war) pp. 43–9.
16. Harries and Harries, pp. 175–6.

Chapter 15: The Great Retreat

1. (Troop strengths) Eastman et al., p. 119.
2. Van de Ven, p. 213.
3. Ibid., p. 195.
4. This account of the battle is based on contemporary accounts notably from the *NCH* and by Farmer, Abend, the *Manchester Guardian* correspondent Harold Timperley and Donald, plus histories of the city by Dong, Henriot, Pan, Sergeant and Wakeman, military studies by Edward L. Dreyer and Ch'i, and Bix's biography of Hirohito. Abend, *Life*, pp. 256–8, gives eyewitness accounts.
5. This and the next paragraph: Selle, pp. 339–40.
6. Ashihei Hino, pp. 38, 78, 85, 90, 107.
7. Farmer, p. 85. *NCH*, 25 September 1937.
8. Pelissier, pp. 382–3. Bix, p. 333. Farmer, pp. 86, 97.
9. (Retreat) Harries and Harries, p. 184. Van de Ven, pp. 212–13.
10. This account draws on Iris Chang's account of the massacre; Rabe; the *NCH* for December and January 1937–8; John Powell memoirs; Bix; Farmer; the collection of evidence from missionaries in the Yale Divinity School archive edited by Zhang Kaiyuan. In particular, Iris Chang, pp. 44–53, 109–22, Rabe, diary in *Good Man*. Powell, pp. 306–8. Farmer, pp. 101–2. Higashinakano, particularly Preface and Conclusion. Bix, pp. 326, 343–5. (Number killed) David Askew, in Wakabayashi, and 'The Nanjing Incident', http://www.japanesestudies.org.uk/articles/Askew.html.
12. Auden and Isherwood, p. 102.
13. (Account of battle) Van de Ven, pp. 221–4. Edward L. Dreyer, pp. 225–8; Auden and Isherwood, pp. 102, 112; Farmer, p. 150; I Feng, pp. 21–3; Tong and Li, pp. 356, 372–3.
14. Tong and Li, pp. 353–4, 417. Domei, 4 April 1937; Auden and Isherwood, p. 151. Van de Ven, pp. 221–4. I Feng, pp. 80, 84.
15. Selle, p. 342. (Ambassador) Central News, 5 October 1937. Chen Li-fu, pp. 135–6.
16. (Chiang on KMT) Eastman, *Seeds*, pp. 89–90. Farmer, pp. 168–9.
17. (Ambulance) Oliver, photograph opposite p. 96. Mowrer, pp. 78–80. Auden and Isherwood, pp. 64–5.
18. This and the following paragraph: *NCH*, 1 June 1938. (Leaflets) Furuya, p. 603. (Kaifeng) Oliver, p. 211.
19. Han Suyin, *Destination*, p. 58. White, pp. 90–91. Eastman et al., pp. 207–8. Harries and Harries, p. 193. Farmer, pp. 136–7.
20. I Feng, chapters 4, 7 and 9 give an eyewitness account of conditions in the wartime countryside and refugees.
21. See map in Eastman et al., p. 117.

22. (Zhu) Bertram, *Unconquered*, pp. 163–4, 444.
23. Farmer, p. 130. (Orang-utans) *NCH*, 5 October 1938. (Losses) Edward L. Dreyer, p. 233; Bix, p. 346.
24. (Wang defection and regime) Boyle, pp. 230–31. Van de Ven, p. 230. (Assassination attempt) Boyle, pp. 228–30. (Peace call) *Proceedings of Conference*, vol. II, Chiang yung-ching, p. 665. Reuters, 2 January 1939. Han-sheng Lin in Coox and Conroy, pp. 211–41. *NCH*, 16 August 1939. Domei, 10 October 1939.
25. (Chiang) *Proceedings of Conference*, vol. III, p. 421; vol. II, pp. 653–4.
26. Description from Esherick, *War*, chapter 11. Farmer, pp. 207–11. Fairbank, *Chinabound*, p. 243. Theodore White, pp. 66–76. Han Suyin, *Destination*, p. 162. Peck, p. 143.
27. This and the next paragraph: Wasserstein, p. 20; Boyle, pp. 278, 281–5. (Mayor) *NCH* 16 October 1940. (Foreign minister) *NCH*, 19 February 1939. (Poisoning) Domei, 11 June 1939. Powell, pp. 335–6.
28. This and following: Wakeman, *Spymaster*, pp. 1, 15, 17, 242–6, 253, 256, 272.
29. (Donald leaves) Selle, p. 350. (To die) Selle, p. 367. (Funeral) *Shen Pao* newspaper, Shanghai, 11 November 1946.
30. White and Jacoby pp. 56–7. Eastman et al., *Nationalist Era*, pp. 130–33. *Proceedings of Conference*, vol. III, p. 649.
31. (Military weakness) Ch'i, *Nationalist China*, chapter 2. Farmer, p. 204. Eastman et al., p. 140. Van de Ven, p. 233.
32. (Changsha) Reuters, 18 and 21 November 1938.
33. (Winter offensive) Ch'i, *Nationalist China*, pp. 590ff. Van de Ven, pp. 239–43.
34. *NCH*, 16 August 1939. (Aspirant dictator) Domei, 10 October 1939.
35. Edward L. Dreyer, p. 253. Van Slyke, *Modern Asian Studies*, vol. 30(4), October 1996, pp. 979ff.
36. (Fourth Army) Benton, *Fourth Army*, pp. 515–16, pp. 545–6, 563–4, 567, 572–8. White and Jacoby, p. 76. Theodore White, pp. 115–17.
37. (Wang regime) Barrett and Shyu, chapter 5, gives an excellent summary of continuities.
38. (Combat effectiveness) Ch'i, *Nationalist China*, pp. 62–3, 58.
39. (FDR) Safe Files.

Chapter 16: Tangled Alliance

1. Furaya, p. 725. Payne, *Diary*, pp. 44–50. Information from Fu Bingchang's granddaughter, Dr Yee-Wah-Foo.
2. (Team report) Bachrack, p. 18. Koen, p. 27.
3. Theodore White, p. 134.
4. Alanbrooke, entry for 23 November 1943.
5. Williams and Wallace, pp. 65, 69–70.
6. 'Secret' memo in FDR library.marist.edu/psf/box2/a16001. Stilwell, p. 158 – the US report was by Colonel David Dean Barrett, the military attaché.
7. (Memo) Romanus and Sunderland, p. 154. Liang, pp. 66–7, 59–60.
8. (Three Demands) E. L. Dreyer, pp. 272–3.
9. Eastman et al., p. 252.
10. Saich and Van de Ven, pp. 275ff. Vladimirov, pp. 83, 84, 134. Fenby, *Generalissimo*, pp. 442–3.
11. Vladimirov, p. 58. Van de Ven, p. 425.
12. (Campaigns) Eastman et al., p. 248, table.
13. Short, *Mao*, pp. 376–85.
14. (Wang) Ibid., pp. 385–7.
15. (Acknowledgement, applause) Ibid., p. 394. (Southern China) Van de Ven, p. 425.
16. (Liu, pupils) Short, *Mao*, p. 392.
17. White and Jacoby, pp. 229–34 for visit.

18. Fenby, *Generalissimo*, p. 4. Tyson Li, p. 226. Eastman et al., pp. 285–6, 290.
19. Theodore White, p. 146. Peck, p. 393. Belden, p. 62.
20. Cowles, pp. 88–9. Fenby, pp. 390–92.
21. (Cairo) Fenby, *Generalissimo*, pp. 408–15. Stilwell, pp. 246, 251–6.
22. Fenby, *Generalissimo*, pp. 414–16. Stilwell, pp. 273ff. For Stilwell's views on Chiang, see ibid., pp. 33–4.
23. Davies, p. 299.
24. (Ichigo) Van de Ven, pp. 74–7, 80–82. E. L. Dreyer, pp. 284ff. Fenby, pp. 416–22, 431–2. Tuchman, pp. 470–72. White and Jacoby, chapter 12. Chennault, pp. 300–301. Stilwell, pp. 326–30.
25. Peck, pp. 588–90.
26. Tuchman, p. 470. Fenby, *Generalissimo*, pp. 423–5.
27. Fenby, *Generalissimo*, p. 424.
28. (Message and Stilwell withdrawn) Ibid., pp. 426–8.
29. (Hurley and negotiations) Carter, pp. 106–8, 116–33. Fenby, *Generalissimo*, pp. 437–40, 453–9.
30. Hart, pp. 59–60. Fenby, *Generalissimo*, p. 4–5.
31. Harries and Harries, pp. 385–6.

Chapter 17: The Last Battle

1. (Resent) Chang and Halliday, p. 296; and following paragraph. Fenby, *Generalissimo*, p. 453ff.
2. Campbell, private papers.
3. Ibid.
4. Short, *Mao*, p. 400.
5. (Yellow Rifles) Li Xiaotao in Clausen and Thøgersen, pp. 174–7.
6. This and following: Belden, pp. 6, 39, 224–6; Arthur Young, p. 76ff.
7. Eastman et al., pp. 311–13. King, p. 161. Lynch, p. 141.
8. Belden, p. 404.
9. Miller, pp. 288–9. Seagrave, *Soong*, pp. 426–7.
10. (Constitution) John Fitzgerald in Draguhn and Goodman, pp. 79–80.
11. Eastman et al., p. 323.
12. This passage draws particularly on chapter 4 of Levine.
13. Chang and Halliday, pp. 308–9.
14. Xiong Xianghui obituary, *Guardian*, 26 September 2005.
15. *Pictorial History*, vol. II, pp. 265–8. Lynch, p. 139. Rittenberg and Benett, pp. 118–19. (Wear and tear) Mao, *Selected Works*, vol. 4, p. 133.
16. Buck, pp. 198–9.
17. (100,000) Chang and Halliday, p. 317.
18. (River) Belden, pp. 354–7.
19. *Japan Times*, 25 February 2002. Hutchings, p. 248. Levine, p. 124. (Flesh) *Time*, 1 April 1948.
20. Eyewitness account of fall of Mukden, Rowan, photographs in chapter 7. Birns, pp. 43–55.
21. Interview with *New York Herald Tribune*, in Levine, p. 237.
22. Rowan, pp. 152, 148. *Times*, 2 December 1948. (Fires) *Times*, 4 December 1948.
23. (Ching-kuo) Taylor, pp. 154–61. (Du) Perry, *Mandate*, p. 126. (Kong) Stella Dong, pp. 288–9. Taylor, pp. 153–4.
24. Eastman et al., pp. 311–13. Lynch, p. 141. (Saying) Howe, p. 38.
25. (Pilot, Gettysburg, agency) Rowan, pp. 154, 147, 158.
26. (Drink) Morwood, p. 369. (*Time*) Rowan, p. 155.
27. (Resign) Chiang Ching-kuo, p. 152. (Sun memorial) Topping, p. 52. (PLA) Bodde, p. 100. (Truman) Rowan, p. 162.

28. Chiang Ching-kuo, pp. 154 ff.

29. Bodde, pp. 100–101.

30. This and the next paragraph, Rowan, pp. 121–32.

31. Report of US minister-counselor, Nanjing, 21 April 1947. Chiang's official diary for 7 March 1947; I am indebted to Professor Stephen Tsang for this.

32. Rowan, pp. 116–18.

33. (Barr, Truman) Ibid., p. 158.

34. Guillermaz, p. 197; Topping, chapter 4. Also Belden, p. 456; Rowan, p. 199. (Newspaper) *Chung Yang Jih-pao.*

35. (Secretary) Belden, p. 440. (Shanghai visit) Chiang Ching-kuo, pp. 207, 214–15.

36. Refugees and other Shanghai scenes from Birns.

37. Details from Rowan, chapter 13.

38. Ibid., pp. 214–16. (Yan) John Gittings in *China Review* (London, February 2007).

39. Stuart to secretary of state, 24 May 1949: Rea and Brewer, p. 326.

40. Hayford, pp. 223–5. Benson, chapter 7.

41. Short, *Mao*, pp. 419–20.

42. Vogel, pp. 43–4. Chiang Ching-kuo, p. 283. Taylor, p. 184.

43. (Executions) Kuo Kwan-ying, part four. Also for following paragraph.

44. Mao, *Selected Works*, vol. 4, p. 374, as amended by Short, *Mao.*

Chapter 18: The Winner

1. Howe, pp. 48, 56. (Store) Bonavia, p. 29.

2. (Mao) Barnouin and Yu, *Zhou*, p. 150.

3. MacFarquhar and Schoenhals, p. 1.

4. (Guangdong) Vogel, pp. 41–6, 54–5.

5. Hinton, *Fanshen*, gives an account of village life.

6. Teiwes, *Politics and Purges*, pp. 104–5. Vogel, pp. 104–5.

7. (Emblem) Information from Prof. Arne Westad.

8. Bodde, pp. 225–6. MacFarquhar, *Politics*, pp. 24–5.

9. Hayford, pp. 222, 227. Mary Mazur in Cheek and Saich, chapter 2. Teiwes, *Politics and Purges*, p. 208.

10. Shambaugh in Cheek and Saich, pp. 128–9. Short, *Mao*, p. 435. Vogel, p. 64.

11. (Mao) Short, *Mao*, p. 440.

12. Lieberthal, *Revolution*, chapter 3.

13. Vermeer, p. 88. James Gao, p. 76. Taire, pp. 4–6. (Zhou) Zhang and Macleod, pp. 8–12. (75 per cent) Perry, *CQ*, March 1994. (Yan) Gittings, *China Review* (London, February 2007).

14. Hua-yu Li, p. 189.

15. (Health) Banister, p. 52. For *danwei* see Lü & Perry, particularly Introduction.

16. Bachman in *CQ*, December 2006. Wang Zheng in *CQ*, December 2006. Draguhn and Goodman, p. 109. (Beggars) Bodde, p. 180. (Button factory) Kidd, p. 132. (Opium) Faligot and Kauffer, p. 269.

17. Banister, pp. 53–5, 58–9. (Water holes) Smith, *CQ*, December 2006.

18. (*People's Daily*, suicides) James Gao, p. 156. (Rape) Bachman, *CQ*, December 2006.

19. Fairbank, *New History*, p. 349. (Opium) Faligot and Kauffer, p. 269. (Mao) Cheek and Saich, p. 27. (Black gates) Kidd, p. 139. (Buns) Cheek and Saich, p. 320, note 33. Gates, pp. 246–7.

20. Gladney, *Muslim*, pp. 89–90. Sara Davis discusses the ethnic identification issue; I am grateful to the author for information on this point.

21. Banister, pp. 53–5, 58–9. (Sects) Perry, *Mandate*, pp. 281, 278–9.

22. John Garver, *CJ*, January 2003.

23. (Staggered) Short, *Mao*, p. 422.

24. This and the next two paragraphs: ibid., pp. 424–5.

25. John Garver, *CJ*, January, 2003.
26. This and the next paragraph: Lynch, pp. 147–8. Chang and Halliday, pp. 368–9.
27. (Stalin) John Garver, *CJ*, January 2003. Gancharov, Lewis and Xue Litai, p. 145.
28. Li, Millett and Yu, p. 1.
29. Ibid., pp. 31–2.
30. Chang and Halliday, pp. 445–7.
31. This and the next paragraph, Lynch, p. 153; Short, *Mao*, p. 434.
32. Starr, p. 902.
33. James Gao, p. 253.
34. (Xi'an) Vermeer, p. 89. Teiwes, *Politics and Purges*, pp. 114–15. (Shanghai) Faligot and Kauffer, pp. 205–9.
35. James Gao, p. 167.
36. This and the next paragraph: ibid., pp. 160–61.
37. Cheek and Saich, pp. 28–9.
38. (Statistics) Selden in Draguhn and Goodman, p. 86. (800,000) Saich, *Governance*, p. 29.
39. Potter and Potter, pp. 43ff. (Teacher) Mobo Gao, p. 15.
40. Potter and Potter, pp. 37–40.
41. Ibid., pp. 49–50.
42. Faligot and Kauffer, pp. 215–17.
43. Barber, chapter 14.
44. (Missionaries) De Jong, p. 336.

Chapter 19: Plots and Plans

1. MacFarquhar, *Politics*, p. 32.
2. (Mistresses) Li Zhisui, p. 150.
3. King, pp. 172, 181. Harding, *Organizing China*, p. 65. Hua-yu Li, pp. 166–7.
4. (Statistics) J. A. G. Roberts, p. 226. (Factory) Laughlin, pp. 248–55.
5. Teiwes, *Politics and Purges*, pp. xvi–xxii. Also Teiwes, *Politics at Mao's Court*.
6. (Health) Teiwes, *Politics and Purges*, p. 161.
7. (Sex) Li Zhisui, p. 150.
8. Bandwagon politics is the theme of Goldstein's book.
9. MacFarquhar, *Origins*, vol. 1, p. 5.
10. Teiwes, *Politics and Purges*, pp. xv, xvii. (Leader) MacFarquhar, *Origins*, vol. 1, p. 7.
11. Roux, p. 88.
12. Faligot and Kauffer, pp. 274–5.
13. (Liu) Schram, *Mao*, p. 254.
14. Chang and Halliday, pp. 413–15. Short, *Mao*, pp. 489–90.
15. (Jobs) Whyte and Parish, p. 30.
16. Huaijin Li, *CQ*, March 2006.
17. Lieberthal, *Governing*, pp. 94–5. Selden, p. 71. (Mao) J. A. G. Roberts, p. 231.
18. (Henan) Domenach, p. 44. (Guangdong) Potter and Potter, p. 68.
19. Robert Ash, *CQ*, December 2006.
20. Teiwes, *Politics and Purges*, pp. 276–7.
21. MacFarquhar, *Origins*, vol. 1, pp. 90–91, 129.
22. Elizabeth Perry, *CQ*, March 1994, p. 18.
23. MacFarquhar, *Origins*, vol. 1, chapter 6. (Henan) Domenach, pp. 42–5.
24. This and the next paragraphs: MacFarquhar, *Origins*, vol. 1, pp. 86–8.
25. This and the next paragraphs: ibid., vol. 2. Harding, *Organizing China*, pp. 118–29. Teiwes, *Politics and Purges*, pp. 177–80. Frederick Teiwes, *CJ*, January 2006.
26. (Peng) MacFarquhar, *Origins*, vol. 1, p. 147.
27. (Mao speeches) MacFarquhar, Cheek and Wu, part 2, texts 1 and 3.
28. (Chen Yang) MacFarquhar, *Origins*, vol. 1, p. 219.
29. (Reporter) Zhang and MacLeod, p. 66.

30. This and details of Hundred Flowers, MacFarquhar, *Origins*, vol. 1, chapter 16. Teiwes, *Politics and Purges*, chapter 6. Short, *Mao*, pp. 464–7. Harding, *Organizing China*, chapter 5. MacFarquhar, Cheek and Wu, chapter 1. Chang and Halliday, p. 436. Lynch, pp. 160–64. (League) Harding, *Organizing China*, p. 144. (70 per cent) Teiwes, p. 233 note. (Early posters) Leijonhufvud, p. 48. (Sects) Perry, *Mandate*, p. 284.

31. This and the next paragraph: MacFarquhar, Cheek and Wu, p. 51.

32. Teiwes, *Politics and Purges*, pp. 197–9. Evans, p. 138. Teiwes, *Politics and Purges*, p. 200. MacFarquhar, *Origins*, vol. 1, pp. 216–17.

33. Teiwes, *Politics and Purges*, pp. 207, 232.

34. Ibid., pp. 232–3. (Deputy Secretary) MacFarquhar, Cheek and Wu, p. 146.

35. Harding, *Organizing China*, p. 144.

36. Elizabeth Perry, 'The Shanghai Strike Wave of 1957', *CQ*, March 1994. (Mao) MacFarquhar, Cheek and Wu, pp. 161, 174–5.

37. (Queer) Teiwes, *Politics and Purges*, p. 257.

38. (Numbers) Ibid., p. 228 note. MacFarquhar, *Origins*, vol. 1, p. 314. (Courts) Bachmann, *CQ*, December 2006.

39. This and the next two paragraphs: Zhang and MacLeod, pp. 66–70.

40. Gittings, *China Review* (London, February 2007). (Lavatories) Schram, *Mao*, pp. 289–90.

41. (Liu) MacFarquhar, *Origins*, vol. 1, p. 311.

42. Teiwes, *Politics and Purges*, p. 234.

43. (Wind) *Peking Review*, 6 September 1963.

Chapter 20: Leaping to Disaster

1. Schram, *Mao*, pp. 292–3.

2. MacFarqhuar, Cheek and Wu, pp. 378ff.

3. What followed in the Great Leap is covered by Alfred Chan. See also MacFarquhar, *Origins*, vol. 1; Bachman and Lieberthal in MacFarquhar and Fairbank.

4. Oksenberg in Lindbeck, p. 85.

5. Ibid., p. 94. Alfred Chan, pp. 47–8.

6. Li Zhisui, p. 230. (Mao) Evans, p. 146.

7. Alfred Chan, pp. 64, 66.

8. Ibid., p. 171. John Gittings, *Guardian*, 24 January 2007.

9. Alfred Chan, pp. 72–4.

10. http://www.danwei.org/guest_contributor/new_years_past_other_spring_fe_1.php#note3. (Mao, Liu) Alfred Chan, p. 69.

11. (More you collected) Zhang and MacLeod, p. 75.

12. Alfred Chan, pp. 181, 201, 202, 217.

13. Shapiro, pp. 86–9.

14. Sheldon Lou, pp. 38–42.

15. (Shopkeeper) Professor Zhang Letian at London School of Economics, 5 December 2006.

16. This and the next paragraph: Li Zhisui, pp. 261–2.

17. (Submarines) John Garver in *CJ*, January 2003.

18. (Eisenhower) http://www.time.com/time/magazine/article/0,9171,863863,00.html?promoid=googlep

19. (Requisitioning) Ash, *CQ*, December 2006.

20. Potter and Potter, p. 73.

21. (Forest) Shapiro, pp. 82–3, 88.

22. This and the next paragraph, Goldstein, p. 124.

23. Alfred Chan, pp. 215–16 footnote.

24. Goldstein, p. 127. Evans, p. 149. Alfred Chan, p. 214. Shapiro, p. 76.

25. (Mao) Goldstein, p. 126.

26. (Photographs) MacFarquhar, *Origins*, vol. II, after p. 238. (Doctor) Li Zhisui, p. 270; chapters 31–2 describe Mao's trips and his joy in detail.
27. (Dissimulation) Alfred Chan, p. 101.
28. Ibid., pp. 105–6.
29. MacFarquhar, *Origins*, vol. II, pp. 207–12.
30. Ibid., pp. 204ff. develops the manipulation theory.
31. Li Zhisui, pp. 313–14.
32. MacFarquhar, *Origins*, vol. II, pp. 217–18.
33. Nolan, p. vi.
34. (Mao's dominance) Teiwes and Sun, *Road*, pp. 179–88.
35. Li Zhisui, p. 317.
36. This and following, MacFarquhar, *Origins*, vol. II, pp. 223–51.
37. Bernstein, *CQ*, June 2006.
38. (Fertilizer) Bonavia, p. 25.
39. (Redness) MacFarquhar, *Origins*, vol. I, p. 306.
40. Ibid., vol. II, pp. 320, 250.
41. (Statistics) Bachman, pp. 4–7.

Chapter 21: Famine and Retreat

1. (Death rates) MacFarquhar, *Origins*, vol. III, p. 8. Bernstein, *CQ*, June 2006.
2. Becker, *Hungry Ghosts*, remains the prime source on the famine; see also Kane, Dali Yang, MacFarquhar, *Origins*, vol. II, pp. 1–7. Thomas Bernstein, in *Theory & Society*, May 1984.
3. *CJ*, July 2003, p. 43.
4. Zhang and MacLeod, pp. 81ff.
5. Domanech, pp. 145–7.
6. Zhang and MacLeod, p. 74. Becker, *Hungry Ghosts*, pp. 206–7. (Suffer, abundance) Stefan Feuchtwang talk, SOAS, London, 28 October 2008.
7. (Suchuan, dinner) Li Zhisui, pp. 307, 330–32.
8. (Articles) MacFarquhar, *Origins*, vol. III, p. 72.
9. This and next paragraph, Li Zhisui, pp. 378–84.
10. Ruan Ming, p. 5.
11. Short, *Mao*, pp. 510–11.
12. This and the next paragraph, MacFarquhar, *Origins*, vol. III, pp. 274–81.
13. (One third) Saich, *Governance*, p. 39.
14. (Sino-Soviet split) Whiting in MacFarquhar and Fairbank, chapter 11.
15. (Ghosts) MacFarquhar, *Origins*, vol. III, pp. 21–2.
16. Operations described in Knaus.
17. Gittings, *World*, p. 214.
18. (Measures, Rusk) Etzold, pp. 148–9. (Johnson) http://www.lbjlib.utexas.edu/johnson/archives.hom/speeches.hom/650407.asp.
19. (Policy) MacFarquhar, *Origins*, vol. III, pp. 374–5.
20. Chang and Halliday, pp. 505–6.
21. This and the next paragraph, Lü and Perry, p. 174; Lardy in MacFarquhar and Fairbank, pp. 392–5. MacFarquhar, *Origins*, vol. III, tables, pp. 28–9. Evans, pp. 163–4.
22. Tyrene White, pp. 48–54.
23. (Temples) Perry, *Mandate*, pp. 288–9. Spence, *Gate*, p. 389.
24. MacFarquhar, *Origins*, vol. III, pp. 112–14.
25. Li Zhisui, pp. 392–3.
26. MacFarquhar, *Origins*, vol. III, p. 408.
27. Andrew Nathan, *New Republic*, 27 November–4 December 2006, p. 36.
28. (Hospital) Li Zhisui, pp. 413–15.

29. MacFarquhar, *Origins*, vol. II, pp. 419–27.
30. Chang and Halliday, pp. 513–14. MacFarquhar, *Origins*, vol. III, p. 423.
31. The intersection of the personal and the political is a major theme of Jin Qiu's highly revealing book, *The Culture of Power*.
32. (Politicization) Ellis Joffe in Lindbeck.
33. Li Zhisui, p. 453. Chang and Halliday, pp. 524–5.
34. Jin Qiu, p. 146.
35. As well as biographical material in Jin Qiu's book, I am indebted to Dr Wei Zhang for information and clarification on the Lin family.
36. MacFarquhar, *Origins*, vol. III, p. 409.
37. (Chen Boda) Li Zhisui, p. 390. MacFarquhar and Schoenhals, p. 33. Short, *Mao*, p. 513. Chang and Halliday, pp. 514–15. His son wrote a book presenting him in a more favourable light as a true defender of the masses; see Christopher Hughes, *CQ*, January 2006.
38. (Special Case) Short, *Mao*, pp. 521–2.
39. Hutchings, p. 250. MacFarquhar and Schoenhals, p. 33. Kang's career is dealt with in Faligot and Kauffer – chain smoking etc., p. 259.
40. Terrill, *Demon*, chapter 4, covers her time in Yenan.
41. Ibid., p. 135.
42. Ibid., p. 243.
43. Dr Li makes a string of references to her behaviour in this vein
44. Jin Qiu, p. 148.
45. (Dog) Short, *Mao*, p. 521.
46. MacFarquhar, *Origins*, vol. II, pp. 381–2; vol. III, pp. 385–7. (Shanghai) Terrill, *Demon*, p. 228.
47. MacFarquhar and Schoenhals, pp. 19–20.
48. This and the next paragraphs: ibid., pp. 20–24; Li Zhisui, pp. 413, 435–6, 439, 442; Chang and Halliday, p. 525; MacFarquhar, *Origins*, vol. III, pp. 449–50.
49. Li Zhisui, pp. 446–9.
50. Terrill, *Demon*, p. 230. Li Zhisui, pp. 451–2.
51. This and following, MacFarquhar and Schoenhals, pp. 32–40. (Tense) Li Zhisui, p. 455.
52. (*Liberation Army Daily*) MacFarquhar and Schoenhals, p. 53.

Chapter 22: Demons and Monsters

1. (Biography) Lifton. (Poem) 'Yearning' in *Poems of Mao Zedong* (Beijing: Intercontinental Press, 2006–7), p. 142. Li Zhisui, p. 459. (Devils) Schram in Goldman and Ou-Fan Lee, p. 301.
2. (Hero to himself, identification, revolution) Gittings, *Face*, pp. 43–4, 60–62.
3. Oksenberg chapter in Lindbeck discusses this aspect, pp. 107–8.
4. MacFarquhar and Schoenhals, pp. 100–101. (Kang) Faligot and Kauffer, p. 336.
5. (Nie, Party) *New York Times*, 10 June 2006.
6. This and following, Short, *Mao*, pp. 535ff.; Lynch, pp. 184–8. (Nie) Walder, *CQ*, December 2006.
7. Leijonhufvud, pp. 62–3.
8. (Meeting, Nie) Gittings, *Face*, p. 69.
9. MacFarquhar and Schoenhals, p. 58.
10. Leijonhufvud, p. 61.
11. MacFarquhar and Schoenhals, pp. 67–77. Dittmer, *Liu*, p. 66. Harding, *Organizing China*, p. 238. Dittmer, *Liu*, p. 64. Andrew Walder and Tan Lifu, *CQ*, December 2004.
12. This and next paragraph, MacFarquhar and Schoenhals, pp. 73–5.
13. This and next two paragraphs, Li Zhisui, pp. 459–63; MacFarquhar and Schoenhals, pp. 84–5. (Record) Cradock, p. 37.
14. This and the next paragraph, Li Zhisui, pp. 470–71.
15. This and the next two paragraphs, MacFarquhar and Schoenhals, pp. 90–93.

16. Spence, *Gate*, pp. 396–7.
17. Terrill, *Demon*, p. 229.
18. Feng Jicai, p. 84. (Jiang) Faligot and Kauffer, p. 338. Terrill, *Demon*, pp. 240–42.
19. *Far Eastern Economic Review*, 8 September 1966. Schoenhals, pp. 210–11, 212–22.
20. (Meningitis) MacFarquhar and Schoenhals, p. 113.
21. (Toll) Ibid., p. 124.
22. (Tianjin) Ibid., p. 172. Zhang and MacLeod, p. 165.
23. (Harbin) *China Journal*, July 2004. (Xin Ran) *Guardian*, 17 September 2004.
24. MacFarquhar and Schoenhals, p. 125.
25. *New York Times*, 10 June 2006.
26. Feng Jicai, pp. 158–60.
27. MacFarquhar and Schoenhals, pp. 118–21. Chang and Halliday, pp. 540–41.
28. (Rectum, explosives) Short, *Mao*, p. 545.
29. (Mao) Barnouin and Yu, *Ten Years*, p. 173. Spence, *Gate*, pp. 393–4.
30. This and following, John Gittings, *China Review* (London, February 2007).
31. Feng Jicai, p. 85.
32. Li Zhisui, chapter 63.
33. Chong, p. 70.
34. (Jobs) Whyte and Parish, p. 36. (Mao) Jack Grey, *CQ*, September 2006.
35. Li Zhisui, chapter 55.
36. Leijonhufvud, p. 67. Feng Jicai, p. 35.
37. (An) Zhang and MacLeod, pp. 118–26.
38. Potter and Potter, p. 88. Poster quoted in Schoenhals, p. 146.
39. (Water) Steve Smith, *CQ*, December 2006. (Insults) Elegant, p. 347.
40. Haar, chapter 2.
41. (Hitler) MacFarquhar and Schoenhals, p. 102.
42. Short, *Mao*, p. 550.
43. (Lin) Gittings, *World*, p. 261.
44. This and following, Potter and Potter, pp. 84–91.
45. Shapiro, pp. 96–9.
46. (Slogans) Ibid., p. 107.
47. Jacob Eyferth, *CQ*, March 2003.
48. Zweig, p. 40.
49. Schoenhals.
50. (Daughter, self-criticism) Dittmer, *Liu*, p. 83.
51. This and following on Lius in this chapter, Short, *Mao*, p. 554; Barnouin and Yu, *Ten Years*, pp. 88–9; Dittmer, *Liu*, p.83; MacFarquhar and Schoenhals, p. 147; Chang and Halliday, chapter 49.
52. Perry, *Mandate*, pp. 340–54.
53. (Mao) MacFarquhar and Schoenhals, pp. 155, 164.
54. (Scarlet Guard) Zhang and MacLeod, pp. 124–6.
55. (Chen Lining) Gittings, *Face*, pp. 58–9. MacFarquhar and Schoenhals, p. 148.
56. Barnouin and Yu, *Ten Years*, pp. 185–6.
57. Schoenhals, pp. 122–4.
58. Barnouin and Yu, *Ten Years*, pp. 89–90.
59. Cradock, p. 55.
60. (Suicide) Li Zhisui, pp. 571–2.
61. MacFarquhar and Schoenhals, pp. 156–160. (Diplomats) Schoenhals, pp. 169–70. (British) Cradock, p. 57.
62. Faligot and Kauffer, pp. 337–8. MacFarquhar and Schoenhals, pp. 197–8.
63. This and following on meetings, Barnouin and Yu, *Ten Years*, pp. 116–20; MacFarquhar and Schoenhals, pp. 188–9; Terrill, *Demon*, p. 235.
64. (January–February meetings and military counter-attack) Barnouin and Yu, *Ten Years*, pp. 115–20; MacFarquhar and Schoenhals, pp. 192–7.

65. Barnouin and Yu, *Ten Years*, p. 117. MacFarquhar and Schoenhals, p. 193.
66. Elegant, pp. 347–67, has the fullest text of the interrogations.
67. (Subsequent session) Ibid., pp. 359–67.

Chapter 23: All-Out Civil War

1. Schoenhals, pp. 176–8. (Girl) Sheldon Lou, pp. 199–201.
2. (Lin) MacFarquhar and Schoenhals, p. 183.
3. Ibid., p. 206. Li Zhisui, p. 489.
4. Li Zhisui, pp. 489–90. Short, *Mao*, p. 569.
5. MacFarquhar and Schoenhals, pp. 208–14.
6. Li Zhisui, p. 491.
7. (Maid) Ibid., p. 493.
8. Schoenhals, pp. 122–35. See also John Gittings obituary, *Guardian*, 24 January 2007.
9. This and following on 'civil war', Michael Schoenhals, *CQ*, June 2005, which establishes Mao's direct responsibility. MacFarquhar and Schoenhals, p. 214.
10. Perry, pp. 216–17, 219–20, 223–5.
11. (Guangzhou) Vogel, pp. 330–32. (Xinjiang Lop Nor) Starr, pp. 95–8. Feng Jicai pp. 224–42.
12. MacFarquhar and Schoenhals, pp. 217–18. (Inner Mongolia) Kerry Brown, *Asian Affairs*, 2007, pp. 176–7.
13. (Invasion) Lu Ping quoted in *Sunday Times*, 25 June 2007.
14. Cradock, chapter 6.
15. Draguhn and Goodman, chapter 6. (Harbin) Clausen and Thøgersen, pp. 190–91. Yeung and Chu, p. 47.
16. Shapiro has an excellent summary and case study, pp. 145ff.
17. (Shaanxi) Lü and Perry, p. 11.
18. (16 May) Barnouin and Yu, *Ten Years*, pp. 192–8. MacFarquhar and Schoenhals, pp. 221–38.
19. (Mao, Sichuan) Barnouin and Yu, *Ten Years*, p. 172. (Mongolia) Schoenhals, photograph in section after p. 184, and pp. 315–16. (Tolls) MacFarquhar and Schoenhals, pp. 243, 247–9. For Inner Mongolia, I am indebted to Dr Kerry Brown.
20. Schoenhals, pp. 315–16.
21. MacFarquhar and Schoenhals, pp. 342–5. Rittenberg and Bennett, pp. 414–15.
22. *People's Daily*, 20 June 2007.
23. Li Zhisui, p. 503.
24. Ibid., pp. 501–3. MacFarquhar and Schoenhals, chapter 14. Dittmer, *Liu*, p. 134. Barnouin and Yu, *Ten Years*, p. 179. Dr Wei Zhang, private information.
25. Barnouin and Yu, *Ten Years*, p. 172. (Lin) MacFarquhar and Schoenhals, pp. 278–9.
26. Dittmer, *Liu*, pp. 86–2. Barnouin and Yu, *Ten Years*, pp. 171–5. MacFarquhar and Schoenhals, chapter 16.
27. (Plenum) Dittmer, pp. 91–2. MacFarquhar and Schoenhals, p. 277. (Woman) Barnouin and Yu, *Ten Years*, pp. 174–5.
28. (Zhou) MacFarquhar and Schoenhals, p. 275. Forster in Law, pp. 137–41.
29. (Deng) Evans, pp. 180–85. MacFarquhar and Schoenhals, pp. 279–80.
30. (Congress) Dittmer, *Liu*, p. 279.
31. (Congress) Barnouin and Yu, pp. 175–8. MacFarquhar and Schoenhals, chapter 17.
32. (Tails) Barnouin and Yu, p. 174. (Delegates) MacFarquhar and Schoenhals, p. 288.
33. Harding in MacFarquhar, *Politics of China*, pp. 242–3.
34. Schoenhals, pp. 269–71.
35. Harding, *Organizing China*, pp. 300–301.
36. Li Zhisui, pp. 518–19.
37. Ibid., p. 531.
38. Short, *Mao*, p. 595.

39. (Jiang Lins) Terrill, *Demon*, p. 269.
40. (Liguo) Jin Qiu, pp. 155–162. (Outline) Ibid., pp. 160–61.
41. Ibid., pp. 164–5.
42. Ibid., pp. 169–70, evidence at trial of Jiang Tengjiao, Document, Jin Qiu, p. 172.
43. (Lins flight) Short, *Mao*, pp. 597–8, MacFarquhar; *Origins*, vol. III, pp. 271–5.
44. *SCMP*, 13 May 2006, based on memoirs of the diplomat Sun Yixian, *There in the Great Desert* (Beijing: China Youth Publishing House, 2006).
45. Li Zhisui, pp. 542–5.
46. This and the next paragraph, ibid., chapter 77.
47. MacFarquhar and Schoenhals, p. 359.
48. (Left) MacFarquhar and Schoenhals, pp. 354–6.
49. Li Zhisui, chapter 79.
50. This and following, Li Zhisui, chapter 80.

Chapter 24: American Interlude

1. MacFarquhar, *New York Review of Books*, 28 June 2007, p. 70.
2. Macmillan, pp. 142 4.
3. Macmillan provides the authoritative account of the visit and negotiations. See also James Mann, and Pollack in MacFarquhar and Fairbank. US archive at http://www.gwu.edu/)nsarchiv/NSAEBB/NSAEBB70/. (Nixon) *Foreign Relations of the United States*, 1969–76, vol. XVII, docs. 7 and 20.
4. Li Zhisui, pp. 532, 542. See also documents in MacFarquhar, *Sino-Soviet Relations*.
5. (Invitation) Chang and Halliday, p. 602.
6. Macmillan, p. 196. Chang and Halliday, p. 605.
7. Macmillan, pp. 197–8.
8. Ibid., p. 6.
9. (War) http://www.gwu.edu/~nsarchiv/NSAEBB/NSAEBB70/. Macmillan, pp. 217–19.
10. (Viability) Zhang and MacLeod, pp. 161–2.
11. (Kissinger note) http://www.gwu.edu/~nsarchiv/NSAEBB/NSAEBB70/.
12. Macmillan, chapter 5. Li Zhisui, chapter 81.
13. Macmillan, pp. 70–77.
14. Ibid., pp. 305–7.
15. (Communiqué) Ibid., pp. 330–34.
16. (Tanaka) Li Zhisui, p. 568. (Kissinger) William Burr of the National Security Archives, Washington, quoted by Agence France Presse, 27 May, 2006.
17. *Foreign Relations of the United States*, China, 1973–1976, pp. 123ff.

Chapter 25: Only Heaven Knows

1. Barnouin and Yu, *Ten Years*, p. 249.
2. Perry, *Patrolling*, pp. 243–9. MacFarquhar and Schoenhals, pp. 360–65. Li Zhisui, pp. 569, 571.
3. MacFarquhar and Schoenhals, pp. 361, 362–3.
4. Barnouin and Yu, *Ten Years*, p. 256. Short, *Mao*, p. 612. Li Zhisui, p. 586.
5. Chang and Halliday, p. 624.
6. Terrill, *Demon*, pp. 294–5.
7. Ibid., p. 279. Short, *Mao*, p. 618.
8. Barnouin and Yu, *Ten Years*, p. 272; Kissinger, p. 68.
9. Li Zhisui, pp. 581, 592.
10. Chang and Halliday, p. 653.
11. MacFarquhar and Schoenhals, pp. 386, 388–9. Dittmer, *Continuous Revolution*, p. 204.
12. MacFarquhar and Schoenhals, pp. 394–5.

13. Terrill, *Demon*, p. 293. (*Water Margin*) Short, *Mao*, p. 618.
14. MacFarquhar and Schoenhals, pp. 411–12.
15. Short, *Mao*, p. 620. (Beat) Terrill, *Demon*, p. 316.
16. Barnouin and Yu, *Ten Years*, p. 290.
17. (Ford, Nixon visits) Rowan, pp. 228–9. Short, *Mao*, p. 621.
18. (Tiananmen) MacFarquhar and Schoenhals, pp. 422–30; Terrill, *Demon*, pp. 316–17; Evans, p. 211; Li Zhisui, p. 611; Gittings, *Face*, p. 96; Bonavia, pp. 100–101; Ruan Ming, p. 22.
19. Terrill, *Demon*, p. 318.
20. (Repression, Hua) MacFarquhar and Schoenhals, pp. 434–43; Li Zhisui, pp. 614, 616, chapter 91.
21. Short, *Mao*, pp. 622–6; Barnouin and Yu, *Ten Years*, p. 291; Evans, p. 214; Li Zhusui, p. 629; Chang and Halliday, p. 654.
22. This and following: Terrill, *Demon*, pp. 325, 328–9; Barnouin and Yu, *Ten Years*, pp. 294–5; Terrill, *Demon*, p. 327. (Wang) Perry, *Patrolling*, p. 254; Baum, p. 27; Short, *Mao*, p. 627.
23. (Cost) MacFarquhar and Schoenhals, p. 608, note 24.
24. (Socialism) Stefan Polter, *Asian Affairs*, November 2006.

Chapter 26: Little Peace Plays His Trumps

1. Hutchings, p. 109.
2. Maomao Deng, p. 4. This and the next paragraph: Evans, chapter 1. http://www.time.com/time/magazine/article/0,9171,1074880-6,00.html.
3. Evans, pp. 48–57.
4. Evans, chapter 4. http://www.time.com/time/magazine/article/0,9171,1074880-6,00.html.
5. (Deng-Lin) Ruan Ming, p. 56.
6. Evans, pp. 218–19.
7. Baum, pp. 27–8, 45–7.
8. Ruan Ming, p. 21.
9. (Wang) Black and Munro, pp. 54–5.
10. This and following: Goldman and MacFarquhar, p. 53; Ruan Ming, pp. 29–30; Baum, pp. 56–61.
11. Baum, pp. 48–51.
12. Ibid., pp. 51–4.
13. Friedman, Pickowicz and Selden, *Resistance*, p. 238.
14. This and following: Black and Munro, p. 49ff.; MacFarquhar and Schoenhals, Conclusion. (Deng, Democracy Wall) Zhang and MacLeod, pp. 179–82; Ruan Ming, p. 40; Baum, pp. 60–61.
15. (Wei) Black and Munro, pp. 49–50.
16. (Run away) Cradock, p. 101. (Engels) Baum, p. 63.
17. Friedman, Pickowicz and Selden, *Resistance*, p. 236.
18. This and next two paragraphs: Baum, pp. 78–81.
19. US–China relations under Carter are excellently covered in James Mann, chapter 4.
20. AFP, 5 December 2007.
21. (Deng visits) Evans, p. 246. (Hong Kong) Cradock, pp. 163–8.
22. James Mann, pp. 113–14.
23. Ibid., pp. 98–100.
24. (Ambassador) Cradock, p. 140.
25. Bonavia, pp. 252–6. Baum, p. 82.
26. (Fu, *People's Daily*) Spence, *Gate*, pp. 414–15; Baum, pp. 76–7, 82.
27. James Mann, pp. 102–3.
28. Baum, p. 88.
29. (NPC and aftermath) Baum, pp. 104–8, 111–13.

30. In line with his severe criticism of Chen Yun, Ruan Ming gives an account of 'Chen and his clique' manoeuvring against Hu in alliance with Zhao at this point, pp. 97ff.
31. http://www.time.com/time/printout/0,8816,924552,00.html.
32. (Cartoon) Gittings, *Face*, p. 95.
33. Terrill, *Demon*, p. 343.
34. This and following, ibid., p. 340.
35. http://www.time.com/time/magazine/article/0,9171,920973,00.html.
36. (Dolls) Terrill, *Demon*, pp. 346–7.
37. MacFarquhar, *Politics*, pp. 326–7.
38. Cradock, p. 179.
39. Baum, p. 168.

Chapter 27: To Get Rich is No Sin

1. I am indebted to Professor Robert Ash for this and other statistics. Ash and Kueh, p. 253. Jingquan Yu in Bui et al., p. 34.
2. Gates, pp. 218–21.
3. Sih and Selya give comprehensive accounts of Taiwan, post-1949. Nathan, p. 132. Yongping Wu, 'Rethinking the Taiwanese Development State', in *CQ*, March 2004.
4. Jeremy Taylor, 'The Production of the Chiang Kai-shek Personality Cult 1929–75', *CQ*, March 2006.
5. Ash and Kueh, p. 13. Tang Tsou, pp. 193–8. Ruan Ming, chapter 5.
6. Ash, *CQ*, December 2006.
7. Friedman, Pickowicz and Sedden, *Resistance*, pp. 245, 249, 258. (Dazhai) Zhang and MacLeod, pp. 189–93.
8. Rohwer, p. 127. (Guangdong) Yefei Yang in Bui et al., p. 80. (Dazhai) Zhang and MacLeod, pp. 189–93. (Yields) Yabuki and Harner, p. 59, chart.
9. Nolan, p. 215. Ikels, pp. 210–14. Bonavia, p. 9.
10. *China Daily Archive*, 7 June 2007.
11. Bonavia, chapter 12. (Visitor) Rowan, p. 229; Joseph Cheng, p. 599.
12. Evans, p. 257. Cradock. pp. 151–2.
13. Delia Davin, *Times Higher Education Supplement*, 16 March 2007. Tyrene White, pp. 1–4.
14. Ruan Ming, p. 165.
15. Tyrene White, pp. 44, 61–2. Baum, p. 67.
16. Ash and Kueh, p. 233.
17. Ash and Kueh, p. 220, table. Rohwer, p. 134, table. Jingchao Geng in Bui et al., p. 112.
18. Ikels, pp. 18–19.
19. Deng Xiaoping, pp. 386–97.
20. This and the next paragraph: Ruan Ming, pp. 129–30; Baum, pp. 150–53.
21. (Deng, Wang in Xinjiang) Starr, pp. 86–7, 149–50.
22. Cradock, p. 156.
23. Baum, pp. 160–61, 156.
24. Ibid., pp. 161–2.
25. Ibid., pp. 167–8, 183–5. Ruan Ming, p. 142. Evans, p. 273.
26. Baum, pp. 185–6.
27. Ruan Ming, p. 134.
28. Rohwer, pp. 135–6. Baum, p. 165.
29. Baum, p. 166.
30. Rohwer, p. 130. Jingchao Geng in Bui et al., pp. 112–17.
31. Joseph Chai in Ash and Kueh, p. 247. Yeh in ibid., pp. 19, 24. Field in ibid., p. 100.
32. (Shengli) Salisbury, *Emperors*, pp. 407–9.
33. (Tax) Ikels, p. 182.
34. (Cadres) Clausen and Thøgersen, pp. 194–5.

35. (Glorious) *Financial Times*, 'Creative Business', 21 September 2004. Deng interview with Mike Wallace, CBS, 2 September 1986, http://english.people.com.cn/dengxp/vol3/text/c1560.html.
36. *New York Times*, 20 June 2004.
37. Zhang and MacLeod, pp. 241–7.
38. Ibid., pp. 209–15.
39. *Economist*, 9 June 2007, http://www.cnn.com/2007/WORLD/asiapcf/06/03/talkasia.cheungyan/index.html?eref-rss_latest.
40. Rohwer, pp. 130–31.
41. Cradock, pp. 179–82.
42. Lu Ping, *Sunday Times*, 25 June 2007.
43. Baum, pp. 176–9.
44. Evans, pp. 255–6.
45. Yeh in Ash and Kueh, pp. 20–21, 43, 46. (Migrant numbers) Nolan, p. 215.
46. This and next two paras, Yeh in Ash and Kueh, pp. 16–19. Cradock, pp. 135–6. Evans, pp. 278–9. Baum. pp. 200–201.

Chapter 28: Gathering Storm

1. (Wang) Ruan Ming, p. 147.
2. Ibid., p. 167
3. Ibid. Baum, p. 230.
4. Baum, pp. 207–8.
5. '10,000 steps', *Times* obituary, 17 April 1989.
6. Dassu and Saich, p. 51.
7. Baum, pp. 215–20. Ruan Ming, p. 187.
8. Ruan Ming, p. 192.
9. (Incomes) NBS, Robert Ash information.
10. Gittings, *Face*, p. 114.
11. Baum, pp. 230, 236–7.
12. Gittings, *Face*, pp. 134–5.
13. (Guangzhou) Ikels, p. 55.
14. Evans, pp. 286–7.
15. (Chen) Baum, p. 239.
16. (360,000) Ibid., p. 236.
17. Black and Munro, pp. 134–5.
18. Black and Munro, p. 132. Nathan and Link, pp. 12–14, 17–18.
19. Lianjiang Li and Kevin O'Brien in Goldman and MacFarquhar. Robert Pastor and Qingshan Tan, *CQ*, June 2000. See also Carter Foundation website.
20. Black and Munro, p. 143.
21. James Mann, pp. 173–4, 179.
22. The Fang–Bush story is in ibid., pp. 178–83; newspaper report, *New York Times*, 3 March 1989.
23. Wallace interview, http://english.people.com.cn/dengxp/vol3/text/c1560.html.
24. (Prisoners) *Times*, 13 April 1989.
25. Lam, *Hu*, pp. 8–9. Hutchings, p. 205.
26. This and the next paragraph, Nathan and Link, p. 6.

Chapter 29: Beijing Spring

1. This account is from Nathan and Link, pp. 20–21. It is based, in part, on an account by a rising official, Wen Jiabao, who would become prime minister at the start of the next century. (Reports) Black and Munro, pp. 143–4.

2. Nathan and Link, p. 23. This is from material provided by the compiler of the Tiananmen Papers, from which much of the detail of the following account of the tragedy of the early summer of 1989 is drawn. While there has been some questioning of this material, it appears to be a reliable, and unique, account of events from the inside which is of enormous value in charting this episode of Chinese history.

3. Nathan and Link, p. 22.

4. Ruan Ming, pp. 211–12.

5. (Han) *Gate of Heavenly Peace* documentary, http://www.tsquare.tv/film/transhu.html. *Times*, 18 April 1989. This is another key source.

6. Nathan and Link, pp. 27–8.

7. The following account of the first stage of the demonstrations is taken mainly from: Nathan and Link, pp. 2–100; Baum, chapter 11; Gittings, *Face*, chapter 12; *Gate of Heavenly Peace*; and the London *Times*, *Guardian* and *Observer* for the relevant period. Barmé and Minford contains valuable material on the demonstrators and dissidents.

8. Nathan and Link, pp. 33–5.

9. Ibid., p. 46.

10. (Protests) Ibid., pp. 44–5.

11. Report of Beijing Municipal Party Committee and Municipal Government, in Nathan and Link, p. 42.

12. (Reporter) Jonathan Mirsky, London *Observer*, 23 April 1989.

13. (Students) Ibid.

14. Baum, pp. 248–51. (Newspapers) *Guardian*, 24 April 1989.

15. Ruan Ming, pp. 218–19. (Others) Nathan and Link, pp. 140–41.

16. Ruan Ming, pp. 220–21.

17. State Security Ministry Report, in Nathan and Link, pp. 62–6.

18. (Bao) Evans, p. 291.

19. Baum, pp. 249–50.

20. Baum, p. 251.

21. This and the next paragraph: *Times*, 26 April 1987; Baum, p. 251.

22. *Observer*, 30 April 1989.

23. Nathan and Link, pp. 77–8.

24. *Gate of Heavenly Peace*, http://www.tsquare.tv/film/transapril.html.

25. Nathan and Link, p. 83.

26. (Guangzhou) Ikels, p. 175.

27. Nathan and Link, p. 118.

Chapter 30: Three Weeks in May

1. *Gate of Heavenly Peace*, http://www.tsquare.tv/film/transmay4.html.

2. Baum, p. 253.

3. (Meeting) Nathan and Link, pp. 131–8.

4. *Gate of Heavenly Peace*, http://www.tsquare.tv/film/transmay4.html.

5. Ibid., http://www.tsquare.tv/film/transhs.html.

6. (Virtue) Bergère in Dassu and Saich, p. 137. (Theatre) Esherick and Wasserstrom in Wasserstrom and Perry, chapter 2; Baum, p. 256.

7. Nathan and Link, pp. 145, 147–152.

8. *Guardian*, 16–17 April 1989. *Observer*, 21 May 1989.

9. CBS Evening News, 16 May 1989.

10. (Deng) *Guardian*, 17 April 1989.

11. Nathan and Link, pp. 176–7.

12. *Gate of Heavenly Peace*, http://www.tsquare.tv/film/transhs.html. Baum, p. 258.

13. Nathan and Link, pp. 177–81.

14. (Meeting) Ibid., pp. 184–90.

15. Oksenberg, Sullivan and Lambert, pp. 282–4, for statements. (Journalists) Liu Binyan, p. 33. Nathan and Link, p. 214.
16. (Standing Committee) Nathan and Link, pp. 191–3.
17. Ibid., p. 200.
18. (Meeting) Ibid., pp. 204–11.
19. (Commander, generals) Ibid., pp. 213, 239, 265.
20. Mirsky, *Observer*, 11 June 1989.
21. (Meeting) Ibid., 21 May 1989; Oksenberg, Sullivan and Lambert, pp. 269–82; Baum, pp. 260–61; Nathan and Link. pp. 202–3. Chaohua Wong, in *London Review of Books*, 5 July 2007.
22. (Television) Esherick and Wasserstrom in Wasserstrom and Perry, p. 35.
23. *Guardian*, 20 May 1989. Black and Munro, p. 198. Baum, pp. 262–9.
24. (Indifference) Black and Munro, p. 199.
25. (Wan Li) Baum, p. 368. Nathan and Link, pp. 257–64.
26. Black and Munro, pp. 189–90. Nathan and Link, pp. 307–8.
27. Oksenberg, Sullivan and Lambert, pp. 317–20.
28. *Guardian*, 20 May 1989.
29. *Observer*, 28 May 1989. Baum, pp. 268, 270.
30. Baum, p. 296.

Chapter 31: Massacre in Beijing

1. (Chai) *Gate of Heavenly Peace*, http://www.tsquare.tv/film/transml.html.
2. Black and Munro, pp. 211–20.
3. *Gate of Heavenly Peace*, http://www.tsquare.tv/film/transmay27.html.
4. *Observer*, 11 June 1989.
5. Ogden et al., pp. 342–3. (*Wen Wei Po*) *Observer*, 28 May 1989.
6. *Gate of Heavenly Peace*, http://www.tsquare.tv/film/transmay27.html.
7. Black and Munro, p. 235. *Gate of Heavenly Peace*, http://www.tsquare.tv/film/transjune2.html.
8. Calhoun, p. 115. Black and Munro, pp. 231–2. (Mirsky) *Observer*, 28 May 1989.
9. (Chen Yun) Black and Munro, p. 220.
10. Nathan and Link, pp. 354–62.
11. (Joggers) Baum, pp. 278–9.
12. Black and Munro, pp. 232–3. Nathan and Link, pp. 366–7.
13. Nathan and Link, pp. 368–70.
14. *Guardian*, 5 June 1989.
15. (Oath) *Guardian*, 5 June 1989.
16. Jay Matthews, *Columbia Journalism Review*, Sept–Oct 1998. See also *NYT*, 13 June 1989.
17. (Muxidi battle) Martial Law Command and State Security Ministry reports in Nathan and Link, pp. 372–7; John Pomfret, http://www.pbs.org/wgbh/pages/frontline/tankman/interviews/pomfret.html; Baum, pp. 282–3; *Observer*, 4 June 1989.
18. State Security Ministry report in Nathan and Link, pp. 373–5.
19. *Granta Book of Reportage* (London: Granta, 1993), pp. 245–7.
20. This and following: Beijing Municipal Government, Martial Law Command, State Security Ministry statements in Nathan and Link, pp. 379–82; Jonathan Mirsky, *Observer*, 4 and 11 June 1989; Gittings, *Face*, pp. 241–4; reports by Gittings and Jasper Becker in the *Guardian*, 5–8 and 26 June 1989; *Times*, 5–8 June 1989; Baum, pp. 285–8; Black and Munro, pp. 244–8, takes strong issue with 'student massacre'.
21. (Witness) John Pomfret, http://www.pbs.org/wgbh/pages/frontline/tankman/interviews/pomfret.html. (Hou, Feng) *Gate of Heavenly Peace*, http://www.tsquare.tv/film/transjune4.html.
22. (Loudspeaker) *Observer*, 11 June 1989.

23. State Security Ministry report in Nathan and Link, pp. 376–7.
24. Gittings, *Face*, pp. 223–4.
25. (Students) *Times*, 6 June 1989; Nathan and Link, pp. 385–6; Gittings, *Face*, p. 246. (Chen Xitong) Nathan and Link, pp. 387–8.
26. See, for instance, Gittings, *Face*, p. 244.
27. Nathan and Link, pp. 398–416. *Times*, 6 June 1989. Friedman et al., p. 269.
28. (Deng) *Times*, 5 June 1989.
29. Evans, p. 299.
30. (Yang) Jonathan Mirsky, *International Herald Tribune*, 25 August 2004.
31. *SCMP*, 7 June 2007. *Guardian*, 8 June 2007.
32. *Gate of Heavenly Peace*, http://www.tsquare.tv/film/transend.html.
33. (Worker) *Gate of Heavenly Peace*, http://www.tsquare.tv/film/transend.html.
34. Nathan and Link, pp. 450–54. (Grades) Zhang and Macleod, p. 230.
35. Goldman and MacFarquhar, pp. 212–13.
36. http://rfaunplugged.wordpress.com/2007/03/31/bao-tong-of-kings-and-bandits/.

Chapter 32: The New–Old Generations

1. Sullivan, pp. 21–2.
2. Baum, pp. 304–7.
3. Lam, *Jiang*, chapter 2.
4. (Wang) *SCMP*, 12 March 1991; Baum, pp. 320–21.
5. Bernstein in Goldman and MacFarquhar, pp. 214–15.
6. Evans, pp. 310–11.
7. (Punishments) Baum, p. 316.
8. Ibid., pp. 333–6.
9. Xinhua, 5 November 1993.
10. Bernstein in Goldman and MacFarquhar, pp. 215–16.
11. (Deng on Zhu) Baum, p. 350.
12. (Debts, Zhu) Miles, pp. 284–5.
13. Sullivan, p. 190. (Coal) *CD*, 16 August 1993. (Zhu) Miles, p. 286.
14. *Ming Pao*, Hong Kong, 19 May 1993.
15. (Deng) Evans, p. 311.
16. (Congress) Baum, pp. 360–62.
17. (Hu) Lam, *Hu*, pp. 4–10.
18. Baum, pp. 362–3.
19. (Dr Deng) Ibid., p. 375.
20. Miles, pp. 304–5.
21. (Jiang) Baum, p. 379. (Professor) Sullivan, pp. 219–20.
22. (Kunming) Sullivan, p. 234.
23. (Crime, corruption) Elizabeth Perry in Goldman and MacFarquhar, chapter 14. (Prostitution), Xinhua, 20 December 1999. (Women), *CD*, 24 August, 1991.
24. Miles, pp. 182–3.
25. AFP, *Hong Kong*, 9 June 1991. Ming Pao, Hong Kong, 31 January 1992.
26. (Self-scrutiny, nightclubs) Lam, *Jiang*, p. 50. (Chen) ibid., p. 77.
27. (Nationalism) Ibid., pp. 52–3.
28. Ibid., pp. 61–6, 80.
29. *SCMP*, 21 May 2007.
30. *SCMP*, 28 November 2007. Fenby, *Dealing*, gives journal of post-handover Hong Kong. Discussion of ten years after 1997, http://www.time.com./time/specials/2007/article/0,28804,1630244–1630282–1630197,00.html.
31. (PLA estimate) Lam, *Jiang*, p. 196.
32. (Posters) http://www.iisg.nl/~landsberger/jzmt.html. (Rich) *Forbes*, 24 November 2003.
33. (Bao) *FEER*, 5 September 2002.

34. (Illegal activities) *PD*, 14 June 2006.
35. (Fire) *Southern Weekend*, 26 November 2007.

Epilogue

1. Prof. Yongnian Zhang, Chatham House, London, 16 November 2007.
2. Lam, *China Brief*, 31 October 2007, sums up the Congress.
3. Willy Lam, *Wall Street Journal Asia*, 19 October 2007.
4. Hu speech, 31 October 2007, p. 2. Poll, *CD*, 12 September 2007.
5. Bao Tong, Radio Free Asia, 24 October 2007.
6. Lam, *Hu*, pp. 254–5. See also *China Quarterly* on inequality, September 2008.
7. *PD online*, 23 April 2007.

Bibliography

Newspapers, Agencies and Periodicals

Celestial Empire (CE)
China Daily (CD)
China Express and Telegraph (CET)
China Journal (CJ)
China Quarterly (CQ)
China Weekly Review (CWR)
Domei Japanese news agency (Domei)
Far Eastern Economic Review (FEER)
Journal of Asian Affairs (JA)
Kuo Min KMT news agency (Kuo Min)
Republican China (RC)
North China Herald (NCH)
People's Daily (PD)
South China Morning Post (SCMP)
Toho Japanese news agency (Toho)

Abend, Hallett, *My Life in China 1926–1941* (New York: Harcourt, Brace and Company, 1943)
—, *Tortured China* (New York: Washburn, 1932)
Alanbrooke, Field Marshal Lord (eds. Alex Danchev and Dan Todman), *War Diaries* (London: Weidenfeld and Nicolson, 2001)
Allan, James, *Under the Dragon Flag* (London: Heinemann, 1898)
Anderson, E. N., *The Food of China* (Cambridge, Mass.: Yale University Press, 1988)
Anschel, Eugene and Homer Lea, *Sun Yat-sen and the Chinese Revolution* (New York: Praeger, 1984)
Anthony, Robert and Jane Kate Leonard (eds.), *Dragons, Tigers and Dogs: Qing Crisis Management* (Ithaca, NY: Cornell University Press, 2002)
Ash, Robert and Y. Y. Kueh, *The Chinese Economy under Deng Xiaoping* (Oxford: Clarendon Press, 1997)
Ashihei, Hino, *Wheat and Soldiers* (New York: Farrar and Rhineheart, 1939)
Atwill, David G., *The Chinese Sultanate* (Stanford University Press, 2005)
Auden, W. H. and Christopher Isherwood, *Journey to a War* (London: Faber and Faber, 1938)
Austin, Alvin, *China's Millions* (Grand Rapids: Eerdman, 2007)
Bachman, David Mark, *To Leap Forward: Chinese Policy-Making, 1956–1957* (Ann Arbor: University Microfilms International, 1984)
Bachrack, Stanley, *The Committee of One Million* (New York: Columbia University Press, 1976)
Baker, Barbara, *Shanghai* (Oxford University Press, 1998)

Banister, Judith, *China's Changing Population* (Stanford University Press, 1991)

Barber, Noel, *The Fall of Shanghai* (New York: Coward McCann and Geoghegan, 1979)

Bard, Émile (adapted from the French by H. Twitchell), *The Chinese at Home* (London: George Newnes Ltd, 1907)

Barmé, Geremie and John Minford, *Seeds of Fire* (New York: Hill and Wang, 1988)

Barnes, Linda, *Needles, Herbs, Gods and Ghosts* (Cambridge, Mass.: Harvard University Press, 2005)

Barnett, A. Doak, *Cadres, Bureaucracy and Political Power in Communist China* (New York: Columbia University Press, 1967)

—, *China on the Eve of the Communist Takeover* (London: Thames and Hudson, 1963)

—, *China's Far West* (Boulder, Colo.: Westview, 1993)

Barnouin, Barbara and Changgen Yu, *Ten Years of Turbulence* (London: Kegan Paul, 1993)

—, *Zhou Enlai* (Hong Kong: Chinese University Press, 2006)

Barrett, David, *Dixie Mission* (Berkeley: University of California Press, 1970)

Barrett, David and Lawrence N. Shyu (eds.), *China in the Anti-Japanese War* (New York: Peter Lang, 2001)

— (eds.), *Chinese Collaboration with Japan, 1932–1945* (Stanford University Press, 2001)

Bastid-Bruguière, Marianne, *L'Evolution de la société chinoise à la fin de la dynastie des Qing 1973–1911* (Paris: Les Cahiers du Centre Chine, 1979)

Baum, Richard, *Burying Mao* (Princeton University Press, 1994)

Bays, Daniel H., *China Enters the Twentieth Century* (Ann Arbor: University of Michigan Press, 1978)

Beal, John Robinson, *Marshall in China* (Toronto: Doubleday, 1970)

Beasley, W. G., *Japanese Imperialism 1894–1945* (Oxford: Clarendon Press, 1999)

—, *The Modern History of Japan* (Tokyo: Charles E. Tuttle, 1982)

Becker, Jasper, *The Chinese* (London: John Murray, 2000)

—, *Hungry Ghosts* (London: John Murray, 1996)

Bedeski, Robert, *State-Building in Modern China* (Berkeley: University of California Press, 1981)

Behr, Edward, *Pu Yi le dernier empereur* (Paris: Robert Laffont, 1987)

Béja, Jean-Philippe, Michel Bonin and Alain Peyraube, *Le Tremblement de terre de Pékin* (Paris: Gallimard, 1991)

Belden, Jack, *China Shakes the World* (New York: Modern Reader Press, 1949)

Benewick, Robert and Paul Wingrove (eds.), *China in the 1990s* (Basingstoke: Macmillan Press Ltd, 1999)

Bennett, Milly (ed. Tom Grunfeld), *On Her Own* (New York: M. E. Sharpe, 1993)

Benson, Linda, *The Ili Rebellion* (Armonk, NY: M. E. Sharpe, 1990)

Benton, Gregor, *Mountain Fires* (Berkeley: University of California Press, 1992)

—, *New Fourth Army* (Berkeley: University of California Press, 1999)

Beresford, Charles, *The Break-Up of China* (London: Harper, 1905)

Bergère, Marie Claire, *L'Age d'or de la bourgeoisie chinoise 1911–1937* (Paris: Flammarion, 1986)

—, *Sun Yat-sen* (Stanford University Press, 1998)

Bernhardt, Kathryn, *Rents, Taxes, and Peasant Resistance* (Stanford University Press, 1992)

Bertram, James, *First Act in China: The Story of the Sian Mutiny* (New York: Viking, 1938)

—, *Unconquered: A Journal of a Year's Adventure among the Fighting Peasants of North China* (New York: John Day, 1939; reissue, New York: Da Capo Press, 1975)

Bianco, Lucien, *Origins of the Chinese Revolution 1915–1949* (Stanford University Press, 1971)

Bickers, Robert, *Empire Made Me: An Englishman Adrift in Shanghai* (London: Allen Lane, 2004)

— and Christian Henriot, *New Frontiers: Imperialism's New Communities in East Asia 1842–1953* (Manchester University Press, 2000)

Birns, Jack, *Assignment Shanghai* (Berkeley: University of California Press, 2003)

Bix, Herbert, *Hirohito* (New York: HarperCollins, 2000)

Black, C. E., *The Dynamics of Modernization* (Columbus, Ohio: Ohio State University Press, 1972)

Black, George and Robin Munro, *Black Hands of Beijing* (New York: John Wiley, 1993)

Bland, J. O. P., *Li Hung-chang* (Freeport, NY: Books for Libraries Press, 1971)

—, *Recent Events and Present Policies in China* (London: Heinemann, 1912)

— and E. Backhouse, *China under the Dragon Empress* (Beijing: Henry Vetch, 1936)

Bland, Larry (ed.), *George Marshall's Mediation Mission to China* (Lexington, Ky: George C. Marshall Foundation, 1998)

Blecher, Marc, *China against the Tides* (London: Continuum, 2003)

Bodde, Derk, *Peking Diary* (New York: Henry Schuman, Inc., 1950)

Bonavia, David, *Verdict in Beijing* (London: Burnett Books, 1984)

Bonnard, Abel, *In China* (London: Routledge, 1926)

Boorman, Howard (ed.), *Biographical Dictionary of Republican China* (New York: Columbia University Press, 1967–71)

Borg, Dorothy, *The United States and the Far Eastern Crisis of 1933–38* (Cambridge, Mass.: Harvard University Press, 1964)

Borst-Smith, Ernest, *Caught in the Chinese Revolution* (London: T. Fisher Unwin, 1912)

Bosshardt, R. A., *The Restraining Hand* (London: Hodder and Stoughton, 1936)

Botjer, George, *A Short History of Nationalist China 1919–1949* (New York: G. P. Putnam's Sons, 1979)

Boyle, John Hunter, *China and Japan at War, 1937–45* (Stanford University Press, 1972)

Bramall, Chris, *Living Standards in Sichuan, 1931–78* (London: SOAS, 1989)

Brandt, Conrad, *Stalin's Failure in China* (New York: W. W. Norton, 1958)

—, Benjamin Schwartz and John King Fairbank, *A Documentary History of Chinese Communism* (London: George Allen and Unwin, 1952)

Brandt, Nat, *Massacre in Shansi* (Syracuse University Press, 1994)

Brodie, Patrick, *Crescent Over Cathay* (Oxford University Press, 1990)

Brook, Timothy and Bob Tadashi Wakabayashi (eds.), *Opium Regimes* (Berkeley: University of California Press, 2000)

Brooks, Barbara, *The Japanese Foreign Ministry and China Affairs: Loss of Control 1895–1938* (Ann Arbor: University of Michigan Press, 1991)

Brown, Frederick, *China's Dayspring after Thirty Years* (London: Murray and Evenden, Ltd, 1914)

Brown, Kerry, *Struggling Giant* (London: Anthem Press, 2007)

Buck, David, *Urban Change in China* (Madison: University of Wisconsin Press, 1978)

Bui, Tung X., David C. Yang, Wayne D. Jones and Joanna Z. Li, *China's Economic Powerhouse* (Basingstoke: Palgrave Macmillan, 2003)

Buruma, Ian, *Bad Elements* (London: Weidenfeld and Nicolson, 2002)

Byron, John and Robert Peck, *The Claws of the Dragon* (New York: Simon and Schuster, 1992)

Caldwell, Oliver, *A Secret War* (Carbondale: Southern Illinois University Press, 1972)

Calhoun, Craig, *Neither Gods nor Emperors* (Berkeley: University of California Press, 1994)

Callery, J. M. and Melchior Yvan, *History of the Insurrection in China* (London: Smith, Elder & Co, 1853)

Cameron, Meribeth, *The Reform Movement in China 1898–1912* (Stanford University Press, 1931)

Cameron, Nigel, *Old Peking Revisited* (Hong Kong: FormAsia Books Limited, 2004)

Carlson, Ellsworth, *The Kaiping Mines* (Cambridge, Mass.: Harvard East Asian Monographs, 1997)

Carroll, John, *Edge of Empires* (Cambridge, Mass.: Harvard University Press, 2005)

Carter, Carolle, *Mission to Yenan* (Lexington: University Press of Kentucky, 1997)

Chan, Alfred, *Mao's Crusade: Politics and Policy Implementation in China's Great Leap Forward* (Oxford University Press, 2001)

Chan, F. Gilbert (ed.), *China at the Crossroads* (Boulder: Westview, 1980)
— and Thomas H. Etzold (eds.), *China in the 1920s* (New York: New Viewpoints, 1976)
Chan Ming Kou, *Labor and Empire: The Chinese Labor Movement in the Canton Delta, 1895–1927* (Ann Arbor: University Microfilms International, 1984)
Chang Chen, Fu-mei and Jerome Cohen, *Essays on China's Legal Tradition* (Princeton University Press, 1981)
Chang, Gordon G., *The Coming Collapse of China* (New York: Random House, 2001)
Chang, Hao, *Chinese Intellectuals in Crisis* (Berkeley: University of California Press, 1987)
Chang, Iris, *The Rape of Nanking* (Harmondsworth: Penguin Books, 1997)
Chang, Jung, *Madame Sun Yat-sen* (Harmondsworth: Penguin Books, 1986)
—, *Wild Swans* (London: HarperCollins, 1991)
— and Jon Halliday, *Mao, the Unknown Story* (London: Jonathan Cape, 2005)
Chang, Kia-ngau, *The Inflationary Spiral: The Experience in China 1939–1950* (New York: John Wiley, 1958)
Chang, Maria Hsia, *The Chinese Blue Shirt Society* (Berkeley: University of California Press, 1985)
Chang, Sydney and Leonard Gordon, *Sun Yat-sen and His Revolutionary Thought* (Stanford University Press, 1991)
Chapman, H. Owen, *The Chinese Revolution, 1926–27* (London: Constable, 1928)
Cheek, Timothy and Tony Saich (eds.), *New Perspectives on State Socialism in China* (Armonk, NY: M. E. Sharpe, 1997)
Ch'en, Chieh-ju (Chen Jieru or Jennie Chen) (ed. Lloyd E. Eastman), *Chiang Kai-shek's Secret Past* (Boulder, Colo. Westview Press, 1993)
Chen Guidi and Wu Chantao, *Will the Boat Sink the Water?* (New York: Public Affairs, 2007)
Ch'en, Jerome, *China and the West* (London: Hutchinson, 1979)
—, (ed.), *Mao* (Englewood Cliffs, NJ: Prentice-Hall, Inc., 1969)
—, *Mao and the Chinese Revolution* (Oxford University Press, 1965)
—, *Yuan Shih-k'ai 1850–1916* (London: George Allen & Unwin, 1961)
Chen, Jian, *Mao's China and the Cold War* (University of North Carolina Press, 2001)
Chen, Leslie, 'Chen Jiongming and the Chinese Federalist Movement', *Republican China* (November 1991)
Chen Li-fu, *The Storm Clouds Clear over China* (Stanford University Press, 1994)
Chen Tung-his, Wang An-tsiang and Wang I-ting, *General Chiang Kai-shek: The Builder of New China* (Shanghai: Commercial Press, 1929)
Chen Yung-fa, John Israel and Donald Klein, *Rebels and Bureaucrats* (Berkeley: University of California Press, 1976)
Cheng, Chu-yuan, *Behind the Tiananmen Massacre* (Boulder, Colo.: Westview Press, 1990)
Cheng, Joseph Y. S. (ed.), *China in the Post-Deng Era* (Hong Kong: Chinese University Press, 1963)
Cheng, J. C., *The Taiping Rebellion* (Hong Kong University Press, 1963)
Cheng, Li (ed.), *China's Changing Political Landscape* (Washington: Brookings, 2008).
Cheng, Linsun, *Banking in Modern China* (Cambridge University Press, 2003)
Cheng, Pei-kai and Michael Lestz, with Jonathan Spence, *The Search for Modern China: A Documentary Collection* (New York: W. W. Norton, 1999)
Chennault, Claire, *Way of a Fighter* (New York: Putman, 1949)
Cherepanov, A. I., *As Military Adviser in China* (Moscow: Progress Publishers, 1982)
Chesneaux, Jean, *The Chinese Labour Movement, 1919–27* (Standford University Press, 1968)
—, *Secret Societies in China* (London: Hutchinson, 1972)
—, Françoise Le Barbier and Marie-Claire Bergère, *China from the 1911 Revolution to Liberation* (Hassocks: Harvester Press, 1977)
Ch'i, Hsi-sheng, *Warlord Politics in China 1916–1928* (Stanford University Press, 1976)
—, *Nationalist China at War* (Ann Arbor: University of Michigan Press, 1982)
Chiang Ching-kuo, *My Father* (Taipei: Ming Hwa Publications, n.d.)

Chiang Kai-shek, *China at the Crossroads* (London: Faber, 1937)

—, *China's Destiny* (London: Dobson, 1947)

—, *Selected Speeches* (Taipei: China Cultural Service, n.d.)

—, *Soviet Russia in China* (New York: Farrar, Straus and Cudahy, 1965)

Ch'ien Tuan-sheng, *The Government and Politics of China 1912–1949* (Stanford University Press, 1970)

Chin, Annping, *Four Sisters of Hofei* (London: Bloomsbury, 2003)

China Year Book (Shanghai: published annually to 1949)

Chong, Woei Lien (ed.), *China's Great Proletarian Cultural Revolution* (Lanham, Md: Rowman & Littlefield, 2002)

Christie, Dugdale, *Thirty Years in Moukden* (London: Constable, 1914)

Chu, Samuel C. and Kwang-Ching Liu, *Li Hung Chang and China's Early Modernization* (Armonk, NY: M. E. Sharpe, 1994)

Chu Shao-jang, *On Chiang Kai-shek's Position on Resisting Japan* (thesis submitted to University of British Columbia, 1999)

Ch'ü, T'ung-tsu, *Local Government in China under the Ch'ing* (Cambridge, Mass.: Harvard University Press, 1962)

Claudel, Paul, *Sous le signe du dragon* (Paris: La Table Ronde, 1948)

Clausen, Søren and Stig Thøgersen, *The Making of a Chinese City* (Armonk, NY: M. E. Sharpe, 1995)

Clissold, Tim, *Mr. China* (London: Robinson, 2004)

Clubb, Edmund, *Twentieth-Century China* (New York: Columbia University Press, 1964)

Coble, Parks, *Chinese Capitalists in Japan's New Order* (Berkeley: University of California Press, 2003)

—, *Facing Japan* (Cambridge, Mass.: Harvard University Press, 1991)

—, *The Shanghai Capitalists and the Nationalist Government, 1927–37* (Cambridge, Mass.: Harvard University Press, 1980)

Cohen, Jerome and Randle Edwards, *The Criminal Process in the People's Republic of China* (Cambridge, Mass.: Harvard University Press, 1968)

Cohen, Paul, *China Unbound* (London: Routledge Curzon, 2003)

—, *Discovering History in China* (New York: Columbia University Press, 1986)

—, *History in Three Keys* (New York: Columbia University Press, 1997)

Coox, Alvin and Hilary Conroy (eds.), *China and Japan* (Santa Barbara, Calif.: ABC-Clio, 1978)

Cornelius, Wanda and Thayne Hort, *Ding Hao: America's Air War in China, 1937–45* (Gretna, La: Pelican Publishing, 1980)

Cowles, Gardner, *Mike Looks Back* (New York: Gardner Cowles, 1985)

Cradock, Percy, *Experiences of China* (London: John Murray, 1999)

Creelman, James, *On the Great Highway* (New York: Lothrop, 1901)

Croll, Elisabeth, *China's New Consumers* (Abingdon: Routledge, 2006)

Crossley, Pamela, *The Manchus* (Oxford: Blackwell, 1997)

Crow, Carl, *Foreign Devils in the Flowery Kingdom* (New York: Harper, 1940)

Crozier, Brian, *The Man Who Lost China* (London: Angus & Robertson, 1976)

Cumming, Gordon, *Wanderings in China* (Edinburgh and London: William Blackwood and Sons, 1886)

Curtis, Richard, *Chiang Kai-shek* (New York: Hawthorn, 1969)

Cuthbertson, Ken, *Nobody Said Not to Go: The Life, Loves, and Adventures of Emily Hahn* (Winchester: Faber and Faber, 1998)

Darmon, Reed, *Made in China* (San Francisco: Chronicle Books, 2004)

Dassu, Marta and Tony Saich, *The Reform Decade in China* (London: Kegan Paul, 1992)

Davidson, Robert and Isaac Mason, *Life in West China* (London: Headley Brothers, 1905)

Davies Jr, John Paton, *Dragon by the Tail* (London: Robson Books, 1974)

Davin, Delia, *Women-Work: Women and the Party in Revolutionary China* (Oxford University Press, 1976)

Davis, Sarah, *Song and Silence* (New York: Columbia University Press, 2005)

De Burgh, Hugo, *China: Friend or Foe* (Cambridge: Icon Books, 2006)

De Jong, Gerald, *The Reformed Church in China 1942–1951* (Grand Rapids, Mich.: Eerdmans, 1992)

Deng, Maomao, *My Father* (New York: Basic Books, 1995)

Deng, Rong, *Deng Xiaoping and the Cultural Revolution* (Beijing: Foreign Languages Press, 2003)

Deng Xiaoping, *Speeches and Writings* (Oxford: Pergamon, 1987)

Der Ling, *Two Years in the Forbidden City* (New York: 1st World Library, 2004)

D'Huriel, Tristan (ed.), *La Chine vue par les ecrivains français* (Paris: Bartillat, 2004)

Dikötter, Frank, *Crime, Punishment and Prison in Modern China* (London: Hurst, 2002)

—, Lars, Laarmann and Zhou Xun, *Narcotic Culture* (London: Centre for Crime and Justice Studies, 2002)

Dirlik, Arif, *The Origins of Chinese Communism* (Oxford University Press, 1989)

Dittmer, Lowell, *China's Continuous Revolution* (Berkeley: University of California Press, 1987)

—, *Liu Shao-ch'i and the Chinese Cultural Revolution* (Berkeley: University of California Press, 1974)

— and Samuel Kim, *China's Quest for National Identity* (Ithaca, NY: Cornell University Press, 1993)

Dolan, Sean, *Chiang Kai-shek* (New York: Chelsea House, 1988)

Domenach, Jean-Luc, *The Origins of the Great Leap Forward* (Boulder, Colo.: Westview Press, 1995)

Dong, Madeleine Yue, *Republican Beijing* (Berkeley: University of California Press, 2003)

Dong, Stella, *Shanghai 1842–1949* (New York: HarperCollins, 2000)

Dorn, Frank, *The Sino-Japanese War, 1937–41* (New York: Macmillan, 1974)

Draguhn, Werner and David Goodman (eds.), *China's Communist Revolutions* (London: Routledge Curzon, 2002)

Dreyer, Edward L., *China at War, 1901–1949* (London: Longman, 1995)

Dreyer, Jane Teufel, *China's Political System* (New York: Paragon House, 1993)

Dryburgh, Marjorie, *North China and Japanese Expansion* (London: Curzon, 2000)

Duara, Prasenjit, *Rescuing History from the Nation* (University of Chicago Press, 1995)

Dubarbier, Georges, *La Chine contemporaine* (Paris: Librairie Orientaliste, 1926)

Du Boulay, N. W. H., *An Epitome of the Chino-Japanese War, 1894–95* (London: Stationery Office, 1896)

Dupée, Jeffrey N., *British Travel Writers in China – Writing Home to a British Public, 1890–1914* (Lampeter: Edwin Mellen Press, 2004)

Duus, Peter, (ed.) *The Cambridge History of Japan*, vol. 6 (Cambridge University Press, 1988)

—, Ramon H. Myers and Mark R. Peattie (eds.), *The Japanese Informal Empire in China 1895–1937* (Princeton University Press, 1989)

—, Ramon H. Myers, and Mark R. Peattie (eds.), *The Japanese Wartime Empire* (Princeton University Press, 1996)

Eastman, Lloyd E., *The Abortive Revolution* (Cambridge, Mass.: Harvard University Press, 1990)

—, 'China's Democratic Parties and the Temptation of Political Power', *Republican China* (November 1991)

—, *Family, Fields, and Ancestors* (Oxford University Press, 1988)

—, *Seeds of Destruction: Nationalist China, 1937–49* (Stanford University Press, 1984)

—, et al., *The Nationalist Era in China* (Cambridge, Mass.: Harvard University Press, 1991)

Eberhard, Wolfram, *A History of China* (London: Routledge, 2005)

Economy, Elizabeth C., *The River Runs Black* (Ithaca, NY: Cornell University Press, 2004)

Eddy, Sherwood, *I Have Seen God Work in China* (New York: Association Press, 1944)

Edmonds, Robert Louis (ed.), *The People's Republic of China after 50 Years* (Oxford University, Press, 2000)

Elegant, Robert, *Mao's Great Revolution* (London: Weidenfeld and Nicolson, 1971)

Elliott, Mark, *The Manchu Way* (Stanford University Press, 2001)

Elvin, Mark, *The Patterns of the Chinese Past* (Stanford University Press, 1973)

—, *The Retreat of the Elephants* (New Haven, Conn.: Yale University Press, 2004)

Epstein, Israel, *The People's War* (London: Gollancz, 1939)

—, *The Unfinished Revolution in China* (Boston: Little, Brown, 1947)

Esherick, Joseph W., *The Origins of the Boxer Uprising* (Berkeley: University of California Press, 1988)

—, *Reform and Revolution in China: The 1911 Revolution in Hunan and Hubei* (Berkeley: University of California Press, 1976)

—, 'War and Revolution: Chinese Society during the 1940s', *20th Century China* (November 2001)

Eto, Shinkichi and Harold Schiffrin (eds.), *China's Republican Revolution* (University of Tokyo Press, 1994)

Etzold, Thomas H., *Aspects of Sino-American Relations since 1784* (New York: New Viewpoints, 1978)

Evans, Richard, *Deng Xiaoping* (London: Hamish Hamilton, 1993)

Fairbank, John King (ed.), *The Cambridge History of China, Vol. 10: Late Ch'ing, Part 1* (Cambridge University Press, 1978)

—, *China: A New History* (Cambridge, Mass.: Belknap Press, 1992)

—, *Chinabound* (New York: Harper & Row, 1982)

—, *The Great Chinese Revolution, 1800–1985* (New York: Harper & Row, 1986)

— and Albert Feuerwerker (eds.), *The Cambridge History of China, Vol. 13: Republican China, Part 2* (Cambridge University Press, 1986)

— and Kwang Ching Liu (ed.), *The Cambridge History of China, Vol. 11: Late Ch'ing, Part 2* (Cambridge University Press, 1980)

—, Edwin Reischauer and Albert Craig, *East Asia: Tradition and Transformation* (Boston: Houghton Mifflin, 1989)

— and Denis Twitchett (eds.), *The Cambridge History of China, Vol. 12: Republican China, Part 1* (Cambridge: University Press 1983)

Faligot, Roger and Remi Kauffer, *The Chinese Secret Service* (New York: William Morrow, 1989)

Fan Shen, *Gang of One* (Lincoln: University of Nebraska Press, 2004)

Farmer, Rhodes, *Shanghai Harvest* (London: Museum Press, 1945)

Feis, Herbert, *The China Tangle* (Princeton University Press, 1953)

Fenby, Jonathan, *China's Journey* (Hong Kong: Forum Asia, 2008)

—, *Dealing with the Dragon* (London: Little, Brown, 2000)

—, *Dragon Throne* (London: Quercus, 2008)

—, *Generalissimo* (London: Free Press, 2003)

—, *The Seventy Wonders of China* (London: Thames and Hudson, 2007)

Feng Chongxi and David Goodman, *North China at War* (Lanham, Md: Rowman & Littlefield, 2000)

Feng Jicai, *Chrysanthenums and Other Stories* (San Diego: Harcourt, Brace, Jovanovich, 1985)

Feuerwerker, Albert, *China's Early Industrialization: Sheng Hsuan-huai (1844–1916) and Mandarin Enterprise* (Cambridge, Mass.: Harvard University Press, 1958)

—, *The Chinese Economy, Part I: 1870–1911* (Ann Arbor: University of Michigan Press, 1981)

—, *The Chinese Economy, Part II: 1912–49* (Ann Arbor: University of Michigan Press, 1981)

Fewsmith, Joseph, *China Since Tiananmen* (Cambridge University Press, 2001)

—, *Party, State and Local Elites in Republican China* (Honolulu: University of Hawaii Press, 1984)

Fitzgerald, C. P., *The Birth of Communist China* (Harmondsworth: Penguin Books, 1964)

—, *A Concise History of East Asia* (Harmondsworth: Penguin Books, 1978)

—, *Why China?* (Melbourne University Press, 1985)

Fitzgerald, John, *Awakening China* (Stanford University Press, 1996)

— (ed.), *The Nationalists and Chinese Society* (Melbourne University Press, 1989)

Fleming, Peter, *One's Company* (London: Jonathan Cape, 1934)

Folsom, Kenneth, *Friends, Guests and Colleagues* (Berkeley: University of California Press, 1968)

Forbes, Andrew D. W., *Warlords and Muslims in Chinese Central Asia* (Cambridge University Press, 1986)

Foreign Languages Press, *The Reform Movement of 1898* (Peking, 1976)

Forman, Harrison, *Report from Red China* (London: Robert Hale, 1946)

Foster, John Watson, *American Diplomacy in the Orient* (Boston: Houghton Mifflin, 1903)

—, *Diplomatic Memoirs* (Boston: Houghton Mifflin, 1909)

Francke, Harry, *Roving through Southern China* (New York: The Century Co., 1925)

Frazier, Martin W., 'Mobilizing a Movement: Cotton Mill Foremen in the Shanghai Strikes of 1925', *Republican China* (November 1994)

French, Paul, *Carl Crow – A Tough Old China Hand* (Hong Kong University Press, 2006)

Friedman, Edward, *Backwards Towards Revolution: The Chinese Revolutionary Party* (Berkeley: University of California Press, 1974)

—, Paul Pickowicz and Mark Selden, *Chinese Village, Soviet State* (New Haven, Conn.: Yale University Press, 1991)

—, Paul Pickowicz and Mark Selden, *Revolution, Resistance and Reform in Village China* (New Haven, Conn.: Yale University Press, 2005)

Fung, Edmund S. K., *In Search of Chinese Democracy* (Cambridge University Press, 2000)

Furuya, Keiji, *Chiang Kai-shek* (New York: St John's University Press, 1981)

Gamble, Sidney D., *Peking: A Social Survey* (London: H. Milford, 1921)

—, (eds. Nancy Jervis and Jonathan D. Spence), *Sidney Gamble's China Revisited* (New York: China Institute, 2004)

Gancharov, Sergei, John Lewis and Xue Litai, *Uncertain Partners: Stalin, Mao and the Korean War* (Stanford University Press, 1993)

Gao, James, *The Communist Takeover of Hangzhou* (Honolulu: University of Hawaii Press, 2004)

Gao, Mobo, *Gao Village* (London: Hurst, 1999)

—, *The Battle for China's Past* (London, Pluto Press, 2008).

Gates, Hill, *China's Motor. A Thousand Years of Petty Capitalism* (Ithaca, NY: Cornell University Press, 1996)

Gentzler, Mason, *Changing China* (New York: Praeger Publishers, 1977)

Gernet, Jacques, *A History of Chinese Civilization* (Cambridge University Press, 1982)

Gibson, Michael, *Chiang Kai-shek's Central Army, 1924–38* (dissertation, George Washington University, 1985)

Gifford, Rob, *China Road* (London: Bloomsbury, 2007)

Gilbert, Rodney, *What's Wrong with China* (New York: Frederick A. Stokes, 1932)

Gilley, Brice, *Tiger on the Brink* (Berkeley: University of California Press, 1998)

Gillin, Donald, *Warlord: Yen Hsi-ghan in Shanxi Province 1911–1949* (Princeton University Press, 1967)

Ginsbourg, Sam, *My First Sixty Years in China* (Beijing: New World Press, 1982)

Gipouloux, François, *Les Cents Fleurs à l'usine* (Paris: Ecole des Hautes Etudes en Sciences Sociales, 1986)

Gittings, John, *The Changing Face of China* (Oxford University Press, 2005)

—, *China through the Sliding Door* (London: Simon & Schuster, 1999)

—, *The Real China: From Cannibalism to Karaoke* (London: Simon & Schuster, 1996)

—, *The World and China 1922–1972* (London: Eyre Methuen, 1974)

Gladney, Dru, *Dislocating China* (London: Hurst & Company, 2004)

—, *Muslim China* (Cambridge, Mass.: Harvard University Press, 1991)

Goh, Evelyn, *Constructing the US Rapprochement with China, 1961–74* (Cambridge University Press, 2005)

Goldman, Merle and Leo Ou-Fan Lee (eds.), *An Intellectual History of Modern China* (New York: Cambridge University Press, 2001)

— and Roderick MacFarquhar (eds.), *The Paradox of China's Post-Mao Reforms* (Cambridge, Mass:: Harvard University Press, 1999)

Goldstein, Avery, *From Bandwagon to Balance-of-Power Politics* (Standford University Press, 1991)

Gottschang, Thomas, 'Incomes in the Chinese Rural Economy, 1885–1945', *Republican China* (November 1992)

Gray, Jack, *Rebellions and Revolutions* (Oxford University Press, 2002)

Gray, John Henry, *Walks in the City of Canton* (San Francisco: Chinese Materials Center, Inc., 1974)

Grieder, Jerome, *Intellectuals and the State in Modern China* (New York: Free Press, 1981)

Guisso, Richard and Stanley Johannesen (eds.), *Women in China* (New York: Philo Press, 1981)

Ha, Dongping, *The Unknown Cultural Revolution* (New York: Garland Publishing, 2000)

Haar, B. J. ter, *Telling Stories* (Boston: Brill, 2006)

Hadfield, Charles and Jill, *Watching the Dragon* (London: Impact Books, 1986)

Halberstam, David, *The Coldest Winter: America and the Korean War* (New York: Hyperion, 2007)

Halcombe, Charles, *The Mystic Flowery Land* (London: Luzac & Co., 1896)

Haldane, Charlotte, *The Last Great Empress of China* (London: Constable, 1965)

Hall, J. C. S., *The Yunnan Provincial Faction, 1927–37* (Canberra: Australian National University Press, 1976)

Han Suyin, *China, 1890–1938* (Vaduz: Jeunesse Verlagsanstalt, 1989)

—, *Destination Chungking* (London: Jonathan Cape, 1943)

Hao Chang, *Chinese Intellectuals in Crisis* (Berkeley: University of California Press, 1987)

Harding, Harry, *China's Second Revolution* (Washington; Brookings, 1987)

—, *Organizing China* (Stanford, University Press, 1981)

Harries, Meirion and Susie, *Soldiers of the Sun* (London: Heinemann, 1991)

Harrison, Henrietta, *The Making of a Republican Citizen* (Oxford University Press, 2000)

Hart, John, *The Making of an Army Old China Hand* (Berkeley: Institute of East Asian Studies, 1985)

Hart, Robert (eds. John King Fairbank, Katherine Frost Bruner and Elisabeth MacLeod Matheson), *The I.G. in Peking: Letters of Robert Hart* (Cambridge, Mass.: Belknap Press, 1975)

Hauser, Ernest, *Shanghai: City for Sale* (New York: Harcourt Brace, 1940)

Hayford, Charles, *To the People* (New York: Columbia University Press, 1990)

Hedin, Sven, *Jehol* (London: Kegan Paul, 1931)

Henriot, Christian, *Prostitution and Sexuality in Shanghai* (Cambridge University Press, 2001)

—, *Shanghai 1927–1937* (Berkeley: University of California Press, 1993)

— and Alain Roux, *Shanghai années 30* (Paris: Editions Autrement, 1998)

— and Wen-hsin Yeh (eds.), *In the Shadow of the Rising Sun* (Cambridge University Press, 2004)

Hershatter, Gail, Emily Honig, Jonathan Liman and Randall Stross (eds.), *Remapping China* (Stanford University Press, 1996)

Hewlett, Meyrick, *Forty Years in China* (London: Macmillan, 1943)

Higashinakano, Shudo, *The Nanking Massacre* (Tokyo: Sekai Shuppan, 1998)

Hinton, William, *Fanshen: A Documentary of Revolution in a Chinese Village* (Berkeley: University of California Press, 1997)

Holcombe, A. N., *The Chinese Revolution* (New York: Alfred A. Knopf, 1930)

Hoo, Mona Yung-Ning, *Painting the Shadows* (London: Eldridge & Co., 1998)

Hosie, Alexander, *Three Years in Western China* (London: George Philip & Son, 1890)

Hosie, Lady, *Brave New China* (London: Hodder and Stoughton, 1938)

Howe, Christopher, *Shanghai, Revolution and Development in an Asian Metropolis* (Cambridge University Press, 1981)

Hsiang, James and Steve Levine (eds.), *China's Bitter Victory* (Armonk, NY: East Gate, 1991)

Hsiao, Kung-chuan, *Rural China, Imperial Control in the Nineteenth Century* (Seattle: University of Washington Press, 1960)

Hsü, Immanuel (ed.), *Readings in Modern Chinese History* (Oxford University Press, 1971)

—, *The Rise of Modern China*, (Oxford University Press, 2000)

Hsüeh, Chün-tu (ed.), *The Chinese Revolution of 1911: New Perspectives* (Hong Kong: Joint Publishing Co., 1986)

Hu Sheng, Liu Danian et al., *The 1911 Revolution* (Beijing: New World Press, 1983)

Huang, Philip, 'The Study of Rural China's Economic History', *Republican China* (November 1992)

Huang, Ray, *China, A Macro History* (Armonk, NY: M. E. Sharpe, 1997)

Huang, Yasheng, *Capitalism with Chinese Characteristics: Entrepreneurship and the State* (Cambridge University Press, 2008)

Hudson, G. F., Richard Lowenthal and Roderick MacFarquhar, *The Sino-Soviet Dispute* (New York: Frederick A. Praeger, 1961)

Hughes, Christopher, *Chinese Nationalism in the Global Era* (London: Routledge, 2006)

Hunt, Michael H., *The Genesis of Chinese Communist Foreign Policy* (New York: Columbia University Press, 1996)

—, *The Making of a Special Relationship* (New York: Columbia University Press, 1983)

Hutchings, Graham, *Modern China* (London: Penguin Books, 2000)

Hutton, Will, *The Writing on the Wall* (London: Little, Brown, 2007)

Idema, W. L. (ed.) *Leyden Studies in Sinology* (Leiden: E. J. Brill, 1981)

Ienaga, Saburo, *The Pacific War, 1931–45* (New York: Pantheon, 1978)

I Feng, *Give Back My Rivers and Hills* (London: Macmillan & Co., 1945)

Ikels, Charlotte, *The Return of the God of Wealth* (Stanford University Press, 1996)

Iriye, Akira, *The Chinese and the Japanese* (Princeton University Press, 1980)

Isaacs, Harold R., *The Tragedy of the Chinese Revolution* (Stanford University Press, 1961)

Israel, John and Donald Klein, *Rebels and Bureaucrats* (Berkeley: University of California Press, 1976)

Ito, Takeo, *Life along the South Manchurian Railway* (Armonk, NY: M. E. Sharpe, 1988)

Jacobs, Dan, *Borodin* (Cambridge, Mass.: Harvard University Press, 1981)

Jeans, Roger, 'The Third Force', *Republican China* (November 1993)

Jen, Yu-wen, *The Taiping Revolutionary Movement* (New Haven, Conn.: Yale University Press, 1973)

Jenner, W. J. F., *The Tyranny of History* (London: Allen Lane, 1992)

Jiang, Yarong and Donald Ashley, *Mao's Children in the New China* (London: Routledge, 2000)

Jin Qiu, *The Culture of Power* (Stanford University Press, 1999)

Jing Tsu, *Failure, Nationalism and Identity* (Stanford University Press, 2005)

Jocelyn, Ed and Andrew McEwen, *The Long March* (London: Constable and Robinson, 2006)

Johnson, Chalmers, *Peasant Nationalism and Communist Power* (Stanford University Press, 1963)

Johnson, Linda Cooke, *Cities of Jiangnan in Late Imperial China* (Albany: State University of New York Press, 1993)

Jones, F. W., *Changing China* (Kilmarnock: Christian Literature Publications, 1946)

Jordan, Donald, *China's Trial by Fire* (Ann Arbor: University of Michigan Press, 2002)

—, *Chinese Boycotts v Japanese Bombs* (Ann Arbor: University of Michigan Press, 1991)

—, *The Northern Expedition* (Honolulu: University of Hawaii Press, 1978)

Kane, Penny, *Famine in China* (Basingstoke, Macmillan, 1988)

Kaplan, David E., *Fires of the Dragon* (New York: Macmillan Publishing Company, 1992)

Kapp, Robert, *Szechwan and the Chinese Republic, 1911–38* (New Haven, Conn.: Yale University Press, 1973)

Karl, Rebecca, *Global Connections: Liang Qichao and the 'Second World' at the Turn of the 20th Century* (Durham, NC: Duke University Press, 1993)

— and Peter Zarrow (eds.), *Rethinking the 1898 Reform Period* (Cambridge, Mass.: Harvard Asia Center, 2002)

Kataoka, Tetsuya, *Resistance and Revolution in China* (Berkeley: University of California Press, 1974)

Kates, George, *The Years That were Fat* (Oxford University Press, 1988)

Kau, Michael (ed.), *The Lin Piao Affair* (Armonk, NY: M. E. Sharpe, 1975)

— and John Leung (eds.), *The Writings of Mao Zedong, 1949–76* (Armonk, NY: M. E. Sharpe, 1986)

Kemenade, Willem van, *China, Hong Kong, Taiwan, Inc.* (New York: Alfred A. Knopf, 1997)

Kidd, David, *Peking Story* (London: Eland, 1988)

King, Frank H. H., *A Concise Economic History of Modern China* (London: Praeger, 1969)

Kirby, William, 'Engineering China: Birth of the Developmental State 1928–1937', in Yeh, *Becoming Chinese.*

—, 'Joint Ventures: Technology Transfer and Technocratic Organization in Nationalist China', *Republican China* (April 1987)

—, *State and Economy in Republican China* (Cambridge, Mass.: Harvard University Press, 2001)

Kissinger, Henry, *Years of Upheaval* (Boston: Little, Brown, 1982)

Klein, David and Anne Clark, *Biographic Dictionary of Chinese Communism 1921–65*, 2 vols. (Cambridge, Mass.: Harvard University Press, 1971)

Knapp, Robert (ed.), *Chinese Landscapes* (Honolulu: University of Hawaii Press, 1992)

Knaus, John Kenneth, *Orphans of the Cold War* (New York: Public Affairs, 1999)

Ko, Dorothy, *Cinderella's Sisters* (Berkeley: University of California Press, 2005)

Koen, Ross, *China Lobby* (New York: Harper and Row, 1974)

Ku Hung-ming, *Papers from a Viceroy's Yamen* (Shanghai: Mercury, 1901)

Kuhn, Philip, *Rebellion and Its Enemies in Late Imperial China* (Cambridge, Mass.: Harvard University Press, 1970)

Kuhn, Robert Lawrence, *The Man Who Changed China: The Life and Legacy of Jiang Zemin* (New York: Crown, 2005)

Kuo Chang-ming, *Labour and Empire: The Chinese Labour Movement in the Canton Delta, 1895–1927* (doctoral dissertation, Stanford University, 1975)

Kuo, Helena, *Westward to Chungking* (London: Hutchinson, 1943)

Kuo Kwan-ying, *A Century Walked Through* (four-part video documentary and interview with the Young Marshal) (Taipei: 1993)

Kuo, Warren, *Analytical History of the Chinese Communist Party* (Taipei: Institute of International Relations, 1969)

Kurlantzick, Joshua, *Charm Offensive* (New Haven, Conn.: Yale University Press, 2007)

Kwan Man Bun, *The Salt Merchants of Tianjin* (Honolulu: University of Hawaii Press, 2001)

Kwei Chung-shu et al., *Japan's Undeclared War* (Shanghai: Chinese Chamber of Commerce, 1932)

Kwong, Luke, *A Mosaic of the Hundred Days* (Cambridge, Mass.: Harvard University Press, 1984)

Kynge, James, *China Shakes the World* (London: Weidenfeld and Nicolson, 2006)

La Motte, Ellen, *Peking Dust* (New York: The Century, 1919)

Lacam, Guy, *Un banquier au Yunnan dans les années 1930* (Paris: L'Harmattan, 1994)

Ladany, Lazlo, *The Communist Party of China and Marxism* (London: Hurst, 1988).

Laitinen, Kauko, *Chinese Nationalism in the Late Qing Dynasty* (Copenhagen: Nordic Institute of Asian Studies, 1990)

Lam, Willy Wo-Lap, *Chinese Politics in the Hu Jintao Era* (Armonk, NY: M. E. Sharpe, 2006)

—, *The Era of Jiang Zemin* (New York: Prentice Hall, 1999)

Lan, Hua and Vanessa Fong (eds.), *Women in Republican China* (New York: M. E. Sharpe, 1999)

Langer, William, *The Diplomacy of Imperialism* (New York: Random House, 1950)

Lardy, Nicholas R., *China's Unfinished Economic Revolution* (Washington: Brookings Institution Press, 1998)

—, *Economic Growth and Distribution in China* (Cambridge University Press, 2004)

—, *Integrating China into the Global Economy* (Washington: Brookings Institution Press, 2002)

Lary, Diana, *China's Republic* (Cambridge University Press, 2007)

—, *Region and Nation: The Kwangsi Clique* (Cambridge University Press, 1974)

—, *Warlord Soldiers* (New York: Columbia University Press, 1985)

Lattimore, Owen, *China Memoirs* (University of Tokyo Press, 1990)

Laughlin, Charles, *Chinese Reportage* (Durham, NC: Duke University Press, 2002)

Law, Kam-yee (ed.), *The Chinese Cultural Revolution Reconsidered* (Basingstoke: Palgrave Macmillan, 2003)

Lawrance, Alan, *China Since 1919* (London: Routledge, 2003)

Lederer, André, *La Mission du Commandant A. Wittamer en Chine (1898–1901)* (Brussels: Académie Royale des Sciences d'Outre-Mer, 1978)

Lee, James Hsioung, *A Half-Century of Memories* (Hong Kong: South China Printing, n.d.)

Lee, Leo Ou-fan, *Shanghai Modern* (Cambridge, Mass.: Harvard University Press, 1999)

Leijonhufvud, Göran, *Going against the Tide* (London: Curzon, 1990)

Leith-Ross, Sir Frederick, *Money Talks* (London: Hutchinson, 1968)

Leonard, Mark, *What Does China Think?* (London: Fourth Estate, 2008)

Leung, Edwin Pak-wah, *Historical Dictionary of Revolutionary China* (New York: Greenwood Press, 1992)

—, *Political Leaders of Modern China* (Westport, Conn.: Greenwood Press, 2002)

Leutner, Mechthild and Nicola Spakowski (eds.), *Women in China* (Münster: Lit Verlag, 2005)

Levenson, Joseph, *Confucian China and Its Modern Fate* (Berkeley: University of California Press, 1968)

Levich, Eugene William, *The Kwangsi Way in Kuomintang China, 1931–1939* (Armonk, NY: M. E. Sharpe, 1993)

Levine, Stephen, *Anvil of Victory* (New York: Columbia University Press, 1987)

Leys, Simon, *Broken Images* (London: Allison & Busby, 1979)

—, *The Chairman's New Clothes* (London: Allison & Busby, 1997)

—, *Chinese Shadows* (New York: Vintage, 1974)

—, *La Fôret en feu* (Paris: Hermann, 1983)

Li, Cheng, *China's Leaders* (Lanham, Md: Rowman & Littlefield, 2001)

Li, Dun J., *Modern China: From Mandarin to Commissar* (New York: Charles Scribner's Sons, 1978)

Li, Hua-yu, *Mao and the Economic Stalinization of China, 1948–1953* (Lanham, M: Rowman & Littlefield, 2006)

Li, Laura Tyson, *Madame Chiang Kai-shek* (New York: Atlantic, 2006)

Li, Lincoln, *The Japanese Army in North China 1937–1941* (Oxford University Press, 1975)

—, *Student Nationalism in China 1924–1949* (State University of New York Press, 1994)

Li, Tien-min, *Mao's First Heir-Apparent: Liu Shao-Ch'i* (Taipei: Institute of International Relations, 1975)

Li, Xiaobing, Allan R. Millett and Bin Yu (eds.), *Mao's Generals Remember Korea* (Lawrence: University Press of Kansas, 2001)

Li Yu-ning (ed.), *Chinese Women through Chinese Eyes* (Armonk, NY: M. E. Sharpe, 1992)

Li, Zhensheng, *Red-Color News Soldier* (London: Phaidon Press, 2003)

Li, Zhisui, *The Private Life of Chairman Mao* (New York: Random House, 1994)

Liang, Chin-tung, *General Stilwell in China* (New York: St John's University Press, 1972)

Library of America, *Reporting World War II* (New York: Literary Classics, 1995)

Lieberthal, Kenneth, *Governing China* (New York: W. W. Norton, 1995)

—, *Revolution and Tradition in Tientsin, 1949–1952* (Stanford University Press, 1980)

— and Michel Oksenberg, *Policy Making in China* (Princeton University Press, 1988)

Lifton, Robert Jay, *Revolutionary Immortality* (New York: Random House, 1968)

Lilley, James and Jeffrey Lilley, *China Hands* (New York: Public Affairs, 2004)

Lin, Gang and Xiaobo Hu (eds.), *China After Jiang* (Washington: Woodrow Wilson Center Press, 2003)

Lindbeak, John (ed.), *China: Management of a Revolutionary Society* (London: Allen and Unwin, 1972)

Linebarger, Paul, *The China of Chiang Kai-shek* (Boston: World Peace Foundation, 1941)

Ling Fei, *Les Chinois* (Paris: Editions Autrement, 1997)

Link, Perry, *Evening Chats in Beijing* (New York: W. W. Norton, 1994)

Lipkin, Zwia, *Useless to the State* (Cambridge, Mass.: Harvard University Press, 2006)

Little, Mrs Archibald, *In the Land of the Blue Gown* (London: Cassell, 1903)

—, *Li Hung-chang* (London: Cassell, 1903)

Liu Binyan, *Tell the World* (New York: Pantheon Books, 1989)

Liu, F. F., *A Military History of Modern China* (Princeton University Press, 1956)

Liu, Po-cheng et al., *Recalling the Long March* (Peking: Foreign Language Press, 1999)

Liu, Tao and David Faure (eds.), *Unity and Diversity* (Hong Kong University Press, 1996)

Loh, Pichon, P. Y. (eds.), *The Early Chiang Kai-shek* (New York: Columbia University Press, 1971)

—, *The Kuomintang Débâcle of 1949* (Boston: Heath, 1965)

Lone, Stewart, *Japan's First Modern War* (New York: St Martin's Press, 1994)

Lötvet, Trygve, *Chinese Communism 1931–1934* (Copenhagen: Nordic Institute of Asian Studies, 1973)

Lou Ruiqing et al., *Zhou Enlai and the Xian Incident* (Beijing: n.p., 1963)

Lou, Sheldon, *Sparrows, Bedbugs and Body Shadows* (Honolulu: University of Hawaii Press, 2005)

Lovell, Julia, *The Great Wall* (London: Atlantic Books, 2006)

Lu Han-chao, *Beyond the Neon Lights* (Berkeley: University of California Press, 1999)

Lü, Xiaoho and Elizabeth Perry, *Danwei* (Armonk, NY: M. E. Sharpe, 1997)

Lubman, Stanley, *Bird in a Cage* (Stanford University Press, 2000)

Lutz, Jessie and Ray Rolland, *Hakka Chinese Confront Protestant Christianity, 1950–1900* (Armonk, NY: M. E. Sharpe, 1998)

Lumley, F. A., *The Republic of China under Chiang Kai-shek* (London: Barrie & Jenkins, 1976)

Lynch, Michael, *Mao* (London: Routledge, 2004)

Ma Jianzhong, *Strengthen the Country and Enrich the People* (Richmond: Curzon, 1998)

McColl, Robert, 'The Oyüwan Soviet Area 1927–32', *Journal of Asian Studies* (November 1967)

McCord, Edward A., *The Power of the Gun: The Emergence of Chinese Warlordism* (Berkeley: University of California Press, 1993)

—, 'Warlordism at Bay', *Republican China* (November 1991)

McCormack, Gavan, *Chang Tso-lin in Northeast China* (Folkestone: Dawson, 1977)

McDonald, Angus, *Urban Origins of Rural Revolution* (Berkeley: University of California Press, 1978)

McElderry, Andrea, 'Robber Barons or National Capitalists: Shanghai Bankers in Republican China', *Republican China* (November 1985)

MacFarquhar, Roderick, (ed.) *China Under Mao: Politics Takes Command* (Cambridge: Massachusetts Institute of Technology, 1966)

—, *The Hundred Days Campaign and the Chinese Intellectuals* (New York: Praeger, 1960)

—, *The Origins of the Cultural Revolution*, 3 vols. (Oxford University Press and New York: Columbia University Press, 1974, 1997, 1999)

— (ed.), *The Politics of China 1949–1989* (Cambridge University Press, 1994)

—, Timothy Cheek and Eugene Wu (eds.), *The Secret Speeches of Chairman Mao* (Cambridge, Mass.: Council of East Asian Studies, 1989)

— and John K. Fairbank (eds.), *The Cambridge History of China, Vol. 14: The People's Republic, Part 1* (Cambridge University Press, 1987)

— and John K. Fairbank (eds.) *The Cambridge History of China, Vol. 15: The People's Republic, Part 2* (Cambridge University Press, 1991)

— and Michael Schoenhals, *Mao's Last Revolution* (Cambridge, Mass.: Belknap Press, 2006)

Mackerras, Colin, *Sinophiles and Sinophobes* (Oxford University Press, 2000)

—, Pradeep Taneja and Graham Young, *China Since 1978* (Melbourne: Longman Cheshire, 1994)

MacKinnon, Stephen and Oris Friesen, *China Reporting* (Berkeley: University of California Press, 1987)

McLane, Charles, *The Soviet Union and the Chinese Communists, 1920–42* (New York: Columbia University Press, 1958)

Macmillan, Margaret, *Seize the Hour* (London: John Murray, 2006)

MacNair, Harley Farnsworth, *China in Revolution: An Analysis of Politics and Militarism under the Republic* (University of Chicago Press, 1931)

Ma Jian, *Beijing Coma* (London: Chatto & Windus, 2008)

Mallory, Walter, *China, Land of Famine* (New York: American Geographical Society, 1926)

Malraux, André, *La Condition humaine* (Paris: Gallimard, 1946)

—, *Les Conquérants* (Paris: Bernard Grasset, 1976)

Manchoukou Yearbook, 1934 (Tokyo: 1934)

Mandancy, Joyce, *The Troublesome Legacy of Commissioner Lin* (Cambridge, Mass.: Harvard University Press, 2003)

Mann, James, *About Face* (New York: Knopf, 1999)

Mann, Susan, *Local Merchants and the Chinese Bureaucracy* (Stanford University Press, 1987)

Mao Zedong, *On New Democracy* (Beijing: Foreign Languages Press, 1967)

—, *Selected Works* (Beijing: Foreign Languages Press, 1967)

Marshall, David, *Letters From Mao's China* (Singapore Heritage Society)

Marshall, George, *Marshall's Mission to China*, 2 vols. (Arlington, Va: University Publications of America, 1970)

Martin, Brian, *The Shanghai Green Gang* (Berkeley: University of California Press, 1996)

Martin, W. A. P., *A Cycle of Cathay* (New York: Fleming H. Revell, 1900)

Mather, A. H., *Siege Days* (New York: Fleming H. Revell, 1903)

Maurer, Herrymon, *The End is Not Yet* (London: William Heinemann Ltd, 1942)

Maynard, Isabelle, *China Dreams* (Iowa City: University of Iowa Press, 1966)

Meisner, Maurice, *The Deng Xiaoping Era* (New York: Hill and Wang, 1996)

Meng Chengshun, *Mistress & Maid* (New York: Columbia University Press, 2001)

Meng, Yue, *Shanghai on the Edge of Empire* (University of Minneapolis Press, 2006)

Mesny, William, *China Stories*, www.mesny.com

Metzger, Thomas W., *Escape From Predicament* (New York: Columbia University Press, 1977)

Michael, Franz, 'Regionalism in Nineteenth-Century China', Introduction to Stanley Spector, *Li Hing-chang and the Hui Army* (Seattle: University of Washington Press, 1964)

—, *The Taiping Rebellion* (Seattle: University of Washington Press, 1988, 1971)

Miles, A. R., *The Legacy of Tiananmen* (Ann Arbor: University of Michigan Press, 1996)

Miller, Merle, *Plain Speaking* (New York: Putnam's, 1973)

Millward, James, *Eurasian Crossroad: Xinjiang* (London: Hurst, 2007)

Ming Pao, *June Four* (Fayetville: University of Arkansas Press, 1989)

de Miribel, Jean and Léon Vandermeersch, *Sagesses Chinoises* (Paris: Dominos Flammarion 1997)

Misselwitz, Henry Francis, *The Dragon Stirs* (New York: Harbinger Books, 1941; Ann Arbor: University Microfilms International, 1978)

Mitter, Rana, *A Bitter Revolution* (Oxford University Press, 2004)

—, *The Manchurian Myth* (Berkeley: University of California Press, 2000)

Moorad, George, *Lost Peace in China* (New York: Dutton, 1949)

Morse, H. B., *The Trade and Administration of the Chinese Empire* (Shanghai: Kelly & Walsh, 1908)

Morwood, William, *Duel for the Middle Kingdom* (New York: Everest House, 1980)

Mowrer, Edgar Ansel, *Mowrer in China* (Harmondsworth: Penguin Books, 1938)

Munemitsu, Mutsu, *Kenkenroku* (University of Tokyo Press, 1982)

Myers, Ramon, *The Chinese Peasant Economy* (Cambridge, Mass.: Harvard University Press, 1970)

—, Michel Oksenberg and David Shambaugh (eds.), *Making China Policy* (Lanham, Md: Rowman & Littlefield, 2001)

Nathan, Andrew, *China's Crisis: Dilemma of Reform and Prospects for Democracy* (New York: Columbia University Press, 1990)

— and Bruce Gilley, *China's New Rulers: The Secret Files* (*The New York Review of Books*, 2002)

— and Perry Link (eds.), *The Tiananmen Papers* (London: Little, Brown, 2001)

Nellist, George, *Men of Shanghai and North China* (Shanghai: n.p., 1933)

Nichols, Francis H., *Through Hidden Shensi* (London: George Newnes, 1902)

Nien Cheng, *Life and Death in Shanghai* (London: Flamingo, 1995)

Nolan, Peter, *China's Rise, Russia's Fall* (London: Macmillan, 1995)

North, Robert and Xenia Eudin, *M. N. Roy's Mission to China* (Berkeley: University of California Press, 1963)

O'Brien, Kevin J. and Lianjiang Li, *Rightful Resistance in Rural China* (Cambridge University Press, 2006)

O'Dowd, Edward, *Chinese Military Strategy in the Third Indochina War* (London: Routledge, 2007)

Ogden, Suzanne, *China's Unresolved Issues* (Englewood Cliffs: Prentice Hall, 1995)

—, Kathleen Hartford, Lawrence Sullivan and David Zweig, *China's Search for Democracy* (Armonk, NY: M. E. Sharpe, 1992)

Oksenberg, Michael and Robert B. Oxnam, *China and America, Past and Future* (New York: Foreign Policy Association, 1977)

—, Lawrence Sullivan and Marc Lambert (eds.) *Beijing Spring, Confrontation and Conflict: The Basic Documents* (Armonk, NY: M. E. Sharpe, 1990)

Oliver, Frank, *Special Undeclared War* (London: Jonathan Cape, 1939)

Ono, Giichi, *Expenditures of the Sino-Japanese War* (Oxford University Press, 1922)

Paine, S. C. M., *The Sino-Japanese War of 1894–1895* (Cambridge University Press, 2003)

Paludan, Ann, *Chronicle of the Chinese Emperors* (London: Thames and Hudson, 1998)

Pan Lynn (Lin Pann), *China's Sorrow* (London: Century Publishing, 1985)

—, *In Search of Old Shanghai* (Hong Kong: Joint Publishing Co., 1997)

—, *Shanghai: A Century of Change in Photographs 1843–1949* (Hong Kong: Hai Feng Publishing Co., 1994)

—, *Sons of the Yellow Emperor* (London: Mandarin, 1996)

Payne, Robert, *Chiang Kai-shek* (New York: Weybridge and Talley, 1969)

—, *Chinese Diaries* (New York: Weybridge and Talley, 1945, 1947, 1950)

—, *Chungking Diary* (London: William Heinemann, 1945)

Peck, Graham, *Two Kinds of Time* (Boston: Houghton Mifflin, 1950)

Peerenboom, Randall, *China Modernizes* (Oxford University Press, 2007)

Pei, Minxin, *China's Trapped Transition* (Cambridge, Mass.: Harvard University Press, 2006)

Peking United International Famine Relief Committee, *The North China Famine of 1920–1921* (Taipei: Ch'eng Wen Publishing Company, 1971)

Pelissier, Roger, *The Awakening of China* (London: Secker and Warburg, 1967)

Pepper, Suzanne, *Civil War in China* (Lanham, Md: Rowman & Littlefield, 1999)

Perry, Elizabeth, *Challenging the Mandate of Heaven* (Armonk, NY: M. E. Sharpe, 2002)
—, *Chinese Perspectives on the Nien Rebellion* (Armonk, NY: M. E. Sharpe, 1981)
—, *Patrolling the Revolution* (Lanham, Md: Rowman and Littlefield, 2005)
—, *Rebels and Revolutionaries in North China, 1845-1945* (Stanford University Press, 1980)
—, *Shanghai on Strike* (Stanford University Press, 1993)
Phillips, Richard, *China Since 1911* (London: Macmillan, 1996)
Pictorial History of the Republic of China, 2 vols. (Taipei: Modern China Press, 1981)
Pieke, Frank (ed.), *People's Republic of China, Vols.* I and II (Aldershot: Ashgate, 2002)
Pitcher, Philip Wilson, *In and About Amoy* (Shanghai and Foochow: The Methodist Publishing House in China, 1912)
Polachek, James, *The Inner Opium War* (Cambridge, Mass.: Harvard University Press, 1992)
Pomerantz, Kenneth, *The Great Divergence* (Princeton University Press, 2000)
Pong, David, *Shen Pao-chen and China's Modernization* (Cambridge University Press, 1994)
Potter, Pitman, *From Leninist Discipline to Socialist Legalism* (Stanford University Press, 2003)
Potter, Sulamith Heins and Jack M. Potter, *China's Peasants* (Cambridge University Press, 1990)
Powell, John, *My Twenty-Five Years in China* (New York: Macmillan, 1945)
Preston, Diana, *The Boxer Rebellion* (New York: Walker & Company, 1999)
Price, Eva Jane, *China Journal 1889-1900* (New York: Charles Scribner's Sons, 1989)
Price, Ruth, *The Lives of Agnes Smedley* (Oxford University Press, 2005)
Pringle, J. M. D., *China Struggles for Unity* (Harmondsworth: Penguin Books, 1939)
Proceedings of Conference on Chiang Kai-shek (5 vols.) (Taipei: 1987)
Pruen, Mrs, *The Provinces of Western China* (London: Alfred Holness. Glasgow: R. L. Allan & Son, 1906)
Pu Yi, Aisin-Gioro, *From Emperor to Citizen* (Beijing: Foreign Languages Press, 1989)
Putnam Weale, B. L., *The Fight for the Republic in China* (London: Hurst & Blackett, 1918)
Pye, Lucian W., *Warlord Politics* (New York: Praeger, 1971)
Rabe, John (ed. Erwin Wickert), *The Good Man of Nanking* (New York: Alfred A. Knopf, 1998)
Rand, Peter, *China Hands* (New York: Simon & Schuster, 1995)
Rankin, Mary, *Early Chinese Revolutionaries* (Cambridge, Mass.: Harvard University Press, 1971)
Ransome, Arthur, *Chinese Puzzle* (London: Allen & Unwin, 1927)
Rawski, Evelyn, *The Last Emperors* (Berkeley: University of California Press, 1998)
Rea, Kenneth and John Brewer (eds.), *The Forgotten Ambassador* (Boulders, Colo.: Westview Press, 1981)
Reardon, Lawrence, *The Reluctant Dragon* (Seattle: University of Washington Press, 2002)
Reinsch, Paul, *An American Diplomat in China* (New York: Doubleday, 1922)
Reynolds, Douglas (ed.), *China 1895-1912: State-Sponsored Reforms and China's Late-Qing Revolution* (Armonk, NY: M. E. Sharpe, 1995)
Rhoads, Edward J. M., *China's Republican Revolution* (Cambridge, Mass.: Harvard University Press, 1975)
Ristaino, Marcia Reynders, *Port of Last Resort* (Stanford University Press, 2001)
Rittenberg, Sidney and Amanda Bennett, *The Man Who Stayed Behind* (Durham, NC: Duke University Press, 2001)
Roberts, Claire (ed.), *Evolution and Revolution: Chinese Dress 1700s-1990s* (Sydney: Powerhouse Publishing, 1997)
Roberts, J. A. G., *Modern China* (Stroud: Sutton, 2000)
Rodzinski, Witold, *The Walled Kingdom* (London: Fontana, 1991)
Rohwer, Jim, *Asia Rising* (New York: Simon & Schuster, 1995)
Romanus, Charles F. and Riley Sunderland, *Stilwell's Mission to China* (Washington DC: Department of the Army, 1953)

Rose, Caroline, *Sino-Japanese Relations* (Abingdon: Routledge, 2005)

Ross, Robert S. and Jiang Changbin (eds.), *Re-Examining the Cold War* (Cambridge, Mass.: Harvard University Press, 2001)

Roux, Alain, *La Chine au XXème siècle* (Paris: Armand Colin, 2006)

Rowan, Roy, *Chasing the Dragon* (Guilford, Conn.: The Lyons Press, 2004)

Rowe, William, *Crimson Rain* (Stanford University Press, 2007)

—, *Hankow, 1796–1895* (Stanford University Press, 1989)

Rozman, Gilbert, *The Modernization of China* (New York: Free Press, 1982)

Ruan Ming, *Deng Xiaoping: Chronicle of an Empire* (Oxford: Westview Press, 1994)

Saich, Tony, *Governance and Politics of China* (Basingstoke: Palgrave, 2001)

—, *The Origins of the First United Front in China: The Role of Sneevliet*, 2 vols. (Leiden: Brill, 1991)

—, and Hans Van de Ven, *New Perspectives on the Chinese Communist Revolution* (Armonk, NY: M. E. Sharpe, 1995)

Salisbury, Harrison, *The Long March* (London: HarperCollins, 1985)

—, *The New Emperors* (Boston: Little, Brown, 1992)

—, *Tiananmen Diary* (London: Unwin, 1989)

—, *To Peking and Beyond* (London: Hutchinson, 1973)

Saunders Candlin, Enid, *The Breach in the Wall* (London: Cassell, 1974)

Scharping, Thomas, *Birth Control in China 1949–2000* (London: Routledge Curzon, 2003)

Schell, Orville, *Discos & Democracy: China in the Throes of Reform* (New York: Pantheon, 1988)

—, *Mandate of Heaven* (London: Little, Brown, 1995)

Schiffrin, Harold, *Sun Yat-sen and the Origins of the Chinese Revolution* (Berkeley: University of California Press, 1968)

Schoenhals, Michael, *China's Cultural Revolution* (Armonk, NY: M. E. Sharpe, 1996)

Schoppa, R. Keith, *The Columbia Guide to Modern Chinese History* (New York: Columbia University Press, 2000)

—, *Twentieth Century China* (Oxford University Press, 2004)

Schram, Stuart, *Mao Tse-tung* (Harmondsworth: Penguin Books, 1975)

—, *The Thought of Mao Tse-tung* (Cambridge University Press, 1989)

— (ed.), *Authority, Participation and Cultural Change in China* (Introduction) (Cambridge University Press, 1973)

— (ed.), *Mao's Road to Power: Revolutionary Writings 1912–49*, 5 vols. (Armonk, NY: M. E. Sharpe, 1989–97)

Schurmann, Franz, *Ideology & Organization in Communist China* (Berkeley: University of California Press, 1966)

— and Orville Schell (eds.), *Imperial China* (Harmondsworth: Penguin Books, 1977)

— and Orville Schell (eds.), *Republican China* (Harmondsworth: Penguin, 1967)

Schwartz, Benjamin (ed.), *Reflections on the May Fourth Movement* (Cambridge, Mass.: Harvard University Press, 1973)

Seagrave, Sterling, *Dragon Lady* (New York: Vintage, 1993)

—, *Lords of the Rim* (London: Bantam Press, 1995)

—, *The Soong Dynasty* (London: Sidgwick & Jackson, 1985)

Selden, Mark, *The Political Economy of Chinese Development* (Armonk, NY: M. E. Sharpe, 1993)

Selle, Earl Albert, *Donald of China* (New York: Harper & Brothers, 1948)

Selya, Roger Mark, *Development and Demographic Change in Taiwan* (Singapore: World Scientific Publishing, 2004)

Sergeant, Harriet, *Shanghai* (London: John Murray, 1998)

Shakya, Tsering, *The Dragon in the Land of Snows* (London: Penguin Books, 2000)

Shao, Qin, *Cultural Modernity: The Nantong Model 1890–1930* (Stanford University Press, 2004)

Shapiro, Judith, *Mao's War against Nature* (Cambridge University Press, 2001)

Sheean, Vincent, *In Search of History* (London: Hamish Hamilton, 1935)
Shen, Han-yin Chen, 'Tseng Kuo-fan in Peking', *Journal of Asian Studies* (November 1967)
Shen Tong, *Almost a Revolution* (Boston: Houghton Mifflin, 1990)
Sheridan, James E., *China in Disintegration* (New York: Free Press, 1977)
—, *Chinese Warlord: The Career of Feng Yü-hsiang* (Stanford University Press, 1966)
Shirk, Susan L., *China: Fragile Superpower* (Oxford University Press, 2007)
Short, Philip, *The Dragon and the Bear* (London: Abacus, 1982)
—, *Mao, a Life* (London: Hodder and Stoughton, 1999)
Sih, Paul, *Taiwan in Modern Times* (New York: St John's University Press, 1973)
Simmie, Scott and Bob Nixon, *Tiananmen Square* (Vancouver: Douglas and McIntyre, 1989)
Skrine, C. P., *Chinese Central Asia* (London: Methuen, 1926)
Smith, Richard L., 'The Reform of Military Education in Late Ch'ing China 1842–1895', *Journal of the Hong Kong Branch of the Royal Asiatic Society*, vol. 18 (1978).
Smith, Sara R., *The Manchurian Crisis, 1931–1932* (New York: Columbia University Press, 1948)
Snow, Edgar, *Far Eastern Front* (London: Jarrolds Publishers, 1934)
—, *Red Star over China* (London: Gollancz, 1937)
Soong, Meiling, *New Life for Jiangxi* (Shanghai: no publisher cited, 1935)
Spector, Stanley, *Li Hung-chang and the Huai Army* (Seattle: University of Washington Press, 1964)
Spence, Jonathan, *The China Helpers* (London: Bodley Head, 1969)
—, *The Chinese Century* (New York: Random House, 1996)
—, *Chinese Roundabout* (New York: W. W. Norton, 1993)
—, *The Gate of Heavenly Peace* (Harmondsworth: Penguin Books, 1981)
—, *God's Chinese Son* (London: Harper Collins, 1997)
—, *Mao* (London: Weidenfeld and Nicolson, 1999)
—, *The Search for Modern China* (New York: W. W. Norton, 1990)
Stapleton, Kristin, *Civilising Chengdu* (Cambridge, Mass.: Harvard University Asia Center, 2000)
Starr, Frederick (ed.), *Xinjiang* (Armonk, NY: M. E. Sharpe, 2004)
Steel, Richard, *Through Peking's Sewer Gate* (New York: Vantage Press, 1985)
Sternberg, Josef von, *Fun in a Chinese Laundry* (New York: Mercury House, 1988)
Stone, Albert and Hammond Reed (eds.), *Historic Lushan* (Hankow: Arthington Press, 1921)
Strauss, Julia (ed.), *The History of the PRC* (Cambridge University Press, 2007)
Studwell, Joe, *The China Dream* (New York: Atlantic Monthly Press, 2002)
Stuttard, John B., *The New Silk Road* (New York: John Wiley & Sons, 2000)
Sues, Ilona Ralf, *Shark's Fins and Millet* (Boston: Little, Brown, 1944)
Sullivan, Lawrence (ed.), *China Since Tiananmen* (Armonk, NY: M. E. Sharpe, 1995)
Sun Shuyun, *The Long March* (London: HarperCollins, 2006)
Sun Tzu, *The Art of War* (Oxford University Press, 1971)
Sun Yat-sen, *Memoirs of a Revolutionary* (London: 1918)
Sutter, Robert, *China's Rise in Asia* (Lanham, Md: Rowman & Littlefield, 2005)
Swisher, Earl, *Canton in Revolution 1925–1928* (Boulder, Colo.: Westview Press, 1977)
Tai Hsüan-chih, *The Red Spears, 1916–1949* (Ann Arbor: Center for Chinese Studies, University of Michigan, 1985)
Taire, Lucian, *Shanghai Episode* (Hong Kong: Rainbow Press, 1960)
T'ang Leang-li, *The Inner History of the Revolution* (London: Routledge, 1930)
Tang Tsou, *The Cultural Revolution and Post-Mao Reforms* (University of Chicago Press, 1988)
Tang, Xiaobing, *Global Space and the Nationalist Discourse of Modernity: The Historical Thinking of Liang Qichao* (Stanford University Press, 1966)
Tawney, R. H. (ed.), *Agrarian China* (London: George Allen & Unwin, 1939)
Taylor, Jay, *The Generalissimo's Son* (Cambridge, Mass.: Harvard University Press, 2000)

Teiwes, Frederick, *Politics and Purges in China* (Armonk, NY: M. E. Sharpe, 1993)
—, *Politics at Mao's Court* (Armonk, NY: M. E. Sharpe, 1999)
—, *Provincial Leadership in China* (Ithaca, NY: Cornell University Press, 1974)
— and Warren Sun, *China's Road to Disaster* (Armonk, NY: M. E. Sharpe, 1999)
— and Warren Sun, *The End of the Maoist Era* (Armonk, NY: M. E. Sharpe, 2007)
Teng, S. Y., *The Nien Army and Their Guerrilla Warfare* (The Hague: Mouton & Co., 1961)
— and John King Fairbank, *China's Response to the West* (Cambridge, Mass.: Harvard University Press, 1979)
Terrill, Ross, *Madame Mao, the White-Boned Demon* (Stanford University Press, 1999)
—, *Mao, a Biography* (Stanford University Press, 1999)
Thomson, James, 'Communist Policy and the United Front in China 1935-6', *Papers on China*, Vol. 11 (December 1977)
Thomson, John Stuart, *The Chinese* (London: T. Werner Laurie, 1910)
Thornton, Richard, *China: A Political History, 1917–1980* (Boulder, Colo.: Westview Press, 1967)
Tian, Chenshan, *Chinese Dialectics* (Lanham, Md: Lexington Books, 2005)
Tien, Hung-mao, *Government and Politics in Kuomintang China, 1927–1937* (Stanford University Press, 1972)
— and Yun-han Chu (eds.), *China under Jiang Zemin* (Boulder, coto.: Lynne Rienner, 2000)
Tong, Te-kong and Li Tsung-jen [Zongren], *The Memoirs of Li Zongren* (Boulder, Colo.: Westview Press, 1979)
Topping, Seymour, *Journey between Two Chinas* (New York: Harper & Row, 1972)
Townley, Susan, *My Chinese Note Book* (London: Methuen, 1904)
Tregar, Mary, *Chinese Art* (London: Thames & Hudson, 1980)
Tretiakov, S. (ed.), *Chinese Testament: The Autobiography of Tan Shih-hua* (London: Gollancz, 1934)
Trevor-Roper, Hugh, *The Hermit of Peking* (London: Eland, 1993)
Tsang, Stephen and Gregor Benton, 'Opportunism, Betrayal, and Manipulation in Mao's Rise to Power', *CJ* (spring 2007)
Tsui, Kai-Yuen, Tien-tung Hsueh and Thomas Rawski (eds.), *Productivity, Efficiency and Reform in China's Economy* (Hong Kong: The Chinese University, 1995)
Tubilewicz, Czeslaw (ed.), *Critical Issues in Contemporary China* (London: Routledge, 2006)
Tuchman, Barbara, *Stilwell and the American Experience in China* (New York: Macmillan, 1970)
Tun Li-ch'en, *Annual Customs and Festivals in Peking* (Hong Kong University Press, 1965)
Tyler, Patrick, *A Great Wall* (New York: Century Foundation, 1999)
Tyson Li, Laura, *Madame Chiang Kai-shek* (New York: Atlantic Monthly Press, 2006)
Uli, Franz, *Deng Xiaoping* (Boston: Harcourt, Brace, Jovanovich, 1988)
Van de Ven, Hans, *War and Nationalism in China 1925–1945* (London: Routledge Curzon, 2003)
Vassal, Gabrielle, *In and around Yunnan Fou* (London: William Heinemann, 1922)
Vermeer, Eduard, *Economic Development in Provincial China* (Cambridge University Press, 1988)
Vigneron, Lucien, *Deux ans au Se-Tchouan* (Paris: Bray et Retaux, 1881)
Vladimir, *The China–Japan War* (London: Sampson, Low, Marston, 1896)
Vogel, Ezra, *Canton Under Communism* (Cambridge, Mass.: Harvard University Press, 1969)
Wakabayashi, Bob Tadashi (ed.), *The Nanking Atrocity 1937–38* (New York: Berghahn Books, 2007)
Wakeman Jr, Frederic, *Policing Shanghai 1927–1937* (Berkeley: University of California Press, 1996)
—, *Spymaster* (Berkeley: University of California Press, 2003)
—, *Strangers at the Gate* (Berkeley: University of California Press, 1966)

— and Richard Louis Edmonds (eds.), *Re-appraising Republican China* (Oxford University Press, 2000)

Walder, Andrew G., Joseph Esherick and Paul Pickowicz, *The Chinese Cultural Revolution as History* (Stanford University Press, 2006)

Wang Gungwu, *China and the Chinese Overseas* (Singapore: Times Academic Press, 1994)

Wang, Hui, *China's New Order* (Cambridge, Mass.: Harvard University Press, 2003)

Wang Ke-wen, 'After the United Front', *Republican China* (April 1993)

Wang Ming, *Mao's Betrayal* (Moscow: Progress Publishers, 1979)

Wasserstein, Bernard, *Secret War in Shanghai* (London: Profile Books, 1999)

Wassertrom, Jeffrey and Elizabeth Perry, *Popular Protests and Political Culture in Modern China* (Boulder, Colo.: Westview, 1992)

Weber, Maria, *Welfare, Environment and Changing US–Chinese Relations* (Cheltenham: Edward Elgar Publishing, 2004)

Wehrle, Edmund S., *Britain, China, and the Antimissionary Riots 1891–1900* (Minneapolis: University of Minnesota Press, 1966)

Weidenbaum, Murray and Samuel Hughes, *The Bamboo Network* (New York: Free Press, 1996)

Welch, Denton, *Maiden Voyage* (Harmondsworth: Penguin Books, 1983)

Wen Ching (pseudonym of Lim Boon Keng), *The Chinese Crisis from Within* (London: Grant Richards, 1901)

Westad, Odd Arne and Sophie Quinn-Judge (eds.), *The Third Indochina War* (London: Routledge, 2006)

White, Theodore, *In Search of History* (London: Jonathan Cape, 1978)

— and Annalee Jacoby, *Thunder out of China* (New York: Da Capo, 1974)

White, Tyrene, *China's Longest Campaign* (Ithaca, NY: Cornell University Press, 2006)

Whyte, Martin King and William L. Parish, *Urban Life in Contemporary China* (University of Chicago Press, 1985)

Wilbur, C. Martin, *The Nationalist Revolution in China 1923–1928* (Cambridge University Press, 1983)

—, *Sun Yat-sen, Frustrated Patriot* (New York: Columbia University Press, 1976)

— and Julie Lien-ying How, *Missionaries of Revolution* (Cambridge, Mass.: Harvard University Press, 1989)

Williams, Peter and David Wallace, *Unit 731* (London: Hodder and Stoughtan, 1989)

Wilson, Dick, *China, the Big Tiger* (London: Little, Brown, 1996)

—, *The Long March* (London: Penguin Books, 1982)

Wou, Odoric, *Militarism in Modern China* (Canberra: Australian National University Press, 1978)

Wright, Mary, *The Last Stand of Chinese Conservatism* (Stanford University Press, 1957)

Wright, Tim, *Coal Mining in China's Economy and Society, 1895–1937* (Cambridge University Press, 1984)

Wu, Tien-wei, 'The March 20 Incident', *Journal of Asian Studies* (November 1967)

—, *The Sian Incident: A Pivotal Point in Modern Chinese History* (Ann Arbor: Michigan Centre for Chinese Studies, 1976)

Wylie, Raymond F., *The Emergence of Maoism* (Stanford University Press, 1980)

Xing Lu, *Rhetoric of the Chinese Cultural Revolution* (University of South Carolina, 2004)

Yabuki, Susumu and Stephen Harner, *China's New Political Economy* (Boulder, Colo.: Westview, 1999)

Yamamuro, Shin'ichi (trans. Joshua Fogel), *Manchuria under Japanese Domination* (Philadelphia: University of Pennsylvania Press, 2006)

Yan Yunxiang, *Private Life under Socialism* (Stanford University Press, 2003)

Yang, Dali, *Calamity and Reform in China* (Stanford University Press, 1996)

Yang, Rae, *China: Fifty Years inside the People's Republic* (New York: Aperture, 1999)

Yao, Ming-le, *The Conspiracy and Death of Lin Biao* (New York: Knopf, 1983)

Yardley, Herbert, *The Chinese Black Chamber* (New York: Houghton Mifflin, 1983)

Ye, Sang, *China Candid* (Berkeley: University of California Press, 2006)

Yeh, Wen-hsin (ed.), *Becoming Chinese* (Berkeley: University of California Press, 2000)

Yen Mah, Adeline, *Falling Leaves* (London: Michael Joseph, 1997)

Yeung, Y. M. and David Chu, *Fujian* (Hong Kong: Chinese University Press, 2000)

Yorke, Gerald, *China Changes* (London: Jonathan Cape, 1935)

Young, C. W. H., *New Life for Kiangsi* (Shanghai: 1935)

Young, Ernest, *The Presidency of Yuan Shih-k'ai* (Ann Arbor: University of Michigan Press, 1977)

Yu, Maochun, *OSS in China* (New Haven, Conn.: Yale University Press, 1996)

Yutang Lin, *My Country and My People* (New York: Reynal and Hitchcock, 1935)

Zarrow, Peter, *China in War and Revolution 1895–1949* (London: Routledge, 2005)

—, *Creating Chinese Modernity* (ed.), (Bern: Peter Lang Publishing, 2006)

Zelin, Madeleine, *The Merchants of Zigong* (New York: Columbia University Press, 2006)

Zhang Kaiyuan (ed.), *Eyewitnesses to Massacre* (Armonk NY: M. E. Sharpe, 2001)

Zhang, Lijia and Calum MacLeod, *China Remembers* (Oxford University Press, 1999)

Zhang, Shu Guang, *Economic Cold War: America's Embargo against China and the Sino-Soviet Alliance, 1949–1963* (Stanford University Press and Washington, DC: Woodrow Wilson Center Press, 2001)

—, *Mao's Military Romanticism: China and the Korean War 1950–1953* (Lawrence: University of Kansas Press, 2006)

Zheng Yangwen, *The Social Life of Opium in China* (Cambridge University Press, 2005)

Zweig, David, *Freeing China's Farmers* (Armonk, NY: M. E. Sharpe, 1997)

Appendices

WHO'S WHO IN MODERN CHINA

CCP	Chinese Communist Party
Chiang	Chiang Kai-shek
CPPCC	Chinese People's Political Consultative Conference
CR	Cultural Revolution
Deng	Deng Xiaoping
GLF	Great Leap Forward
Immortal	One of the Eight Immortals of the PRC
KMT	Kuomintang
LM	Long March
Mao	Mao Zedong
NPC	National People's Congress
PLA	People's Liberation Army
PRC	People's Republic of China

Bai Chongxi (1893–1966) Muslim general in Guangxi Clique and leading Nationalist strategist.

Bao Tong (1932–) Close aide to CCP Secretary Zhao Ziyang in 1980s. Sent to jail for seven years in 1989 for sympathy for student protestors. After release, continued to criticize the regime.

Bo Gu (1907–46) Moscow-aligned head of the CCP 1931–5. Forced out by Mao on LM. Died in plane crash.

Bo Yibo (1908–2007) CCP economist. Purged in CR. Rehabilitated under Deng. Immortal.

Borodin (Mikhail Gruzenberg) (1884–1951) Soviet adviser to KMT in Canton who reorganized it as a Leninist party. Left China after Chiang's purge of left in 1927. Died in Siberian gulag.

Braun, Otto (1900–1974) German CCP adviser ousted by Mao during LM.

Cai Tingkai (1892–1968) Commmander of 19th Route Army in Battle of Shanghai in 1932. Rebelled against KMT the next year. Supported the CCP in final stages of civil war.

Chai Ling (1966–) Leading figure in Tiananmen protests of 1989. Escaped to US, where she founded a software firm.

Chen Boda (1904–89) CCP theoretician and Mao speechwriter. Allied with left and army in CR. Sentenced to eighteen years in jail, but released because of his ill-health.

Chen Duxiu (1879–1942) First CCP chairman. Intellectual pushed aside by Party in-fighting.

Chen Guofu (1892–1951) With brother, prominent KMT politician and Chiang aide.

Chen Jieru (Ch'en Chieh-ju, Jennie Chen) (1906–71) Second wife of Chiang, who disowned her in 1927 to marry Soong Meiling. Later wrote an account of her life with Chiang, which was suppressed in the USA.

Chen Jiongming (1878–1933) Reformist leader in southern China who ran progressive regionalist regime in Guangdong, but clashed with Sun Yat-sen and Chiang, who defeated him and forced him to flee to Hong Kong, where he died of typhus.

Chen Lifu (1900–2001) With brother, close Chiang aide. Leading KMT ideological enforcer.

Chen Shui-bian (1950–) Elected president of Taiwan in 2000 at head of Democratic Progressive Party, ending KMT dominance of the island and stressing 'Taiwanese identity'. Re-elected 2004.

Chen Yi (1901–72) PLA commander, mayor of Shanghai, vice-premier and foreign minister. Target of attack by Gang of Four and Red Guards.

Chen Yun (1905–95) Conservative CCP economist who clashed with Mao and Deng. Immortal.

Chennault, Claire (1893–1958) American airforce strategist for Nationalists and chief of the 'Flying Tigers', who fought running battle with Joseph Stilwell

Chiang Ching-kuo (1910–88) Son of Chiang. Succeeded his father as president of Republic of China in Taiwan 1978–88. Began democratization to go with economic growth.

Chiang Kai-shek (1887–1975) Leader of Nationalist China as head of the KMT after victory of Northern Expedition in 1926–8. Unable to resist Japanese invasion. Defeated by Communists in 1949. Fled to Taiwan to head Republic of China there.

Chun (Prince) (1883–1951). Regent from 1908 to 1911 as father of the last emperor.

Cixi, Dowager Empress (1835–1908) Former concubine, she was the main power at court from the 1860s to her death.

Dai Li (1897–1946) Nationalist political police chief who headed a huge security apparatus. Killed in plane crash on way to meet his mistress.

Deng Liqun (Little Deng) (1914–) Conservative CCP crusader against liberalism and 'spiritual pollution'.

Deng Xiaoping (1904–97) Revolutionary survivor who opened door to market economy in 1978. LM veteran, purged under Mao, he came back to win supreme power and change China. Immortal.

Ding Ling (1904–86) Leading author and feminist who joined the Communists in Yenan. Denounced as 'rightist' in CR and sent to work on farm before being rehabilitated in 1978.

Donald, William Henry (1875–1946) Australian journalist and adviser to Sun Yat-sen, Zhang Xueliang and Madame Chiang.

Du Yuesheng (Big Ears Du) (1887–1951) Head of Green Gang in Shanghai. Allied with KMT right. Godfather drug baron and an opium addict.

Duan Qirui (1864–1936) Major faction leader in early years of Republic.

Fang Lizhi (1936–) Scientist and leading reformist advocate in 1980s.

Feng Yuxiang (The Christian General or Betraying General) (1882–1948) Major warlord of 1920s who rebelled repeatedly against KMT.

Galen (Vasilii Konstantinovich Blyukher) (1889–1938) Soviet KMT adviser who masterminded military successes in 1925–7. In USSR, he held senior commands before dying in Stalin's purges.

Gang of Four (1966–76) CR leading group, tried and sentenced in 1971. See Jiang Qing, Wang Hongwen, Yao Wenyuan, Zhang Chunqiao.

Gao Gang (1905–54) Communist boss in Manchuria after 1949 before being promoted to Politburo. Lost Mao's support and was purged, killing himself in jail.

Gong, Prince (1833–1898) Regent in the 1860–70s outmanoeuvred by Dowager Cixi.

Gordon, Charles (Chinese Gordon) (1833–85) British mercenary who took part in attack on Beijing in 1860 and led Chinese army against Taiping rebels.

Han Dongfang (1963–) Leader of first independent trade union in 1989. Imprisoned and expelled to Hong Kong.

He Long (1896–1969) Commander of early CCP base on Yangzi. Joined LM. PLA marshal. Purged during the CR, and deprived of medicines, causing his death.

He Yingqin (1890–1987) Long-time KMT war minister. China's senior lay Catholic.

Hong Xiuquan (1814–64) Teacher from the south who led Taiping Rebellion in mid nineteenth century, ruling over the 'Heavenly Kingdom' in Nanjing.

Hu Hanmin (1879–1936) Prominent KMT politician who allied with Chiang, and then fell out with him.

Hu Jintao (1942–) CCP general secretary since 2002 as well as president and head of military. Designated as future leader by Deng after masterminding suppression of unrest in Tibet in 1989.

Hu Yaobang (1915–89) CCP general secretary and reform advocate unseated by conservatives in 1987. His death in 1989 led to demonstrations that grew into the Tiananmen protests.

Hu Zongnan (The Eagle of the North-West) (1896–1962) KMT general who suffered series of defeats at hands of PLA before becoming the last commander to cross to Taiwan in 1950.

Hua Guofeng (1921–) CCP chairman 1976–81. Mao's designated successor, trumped by Deng.

Huang Jinrong (Pockmarked Huang) (1867/8–1951) Green Gang boss in Shanghai while also senior Chinese detective in French Concession. Executed under the Communists.

Huang Xing (1874–1916) Leading late-Qing revolutionary. Sun Yat-sen's deputy in 1912.

Hurley, Patrick (1883–1963) US ambassador who brought Chiang and Mao together in 1945.

Jiang Qing (Madame Mao) (1914–1991) Leading figure in Gang of Four during CR. Arrested after Mao's death, she hanged herself fifteen years later.

Jiang Zemin (1926–) CCP general secretary (1989–2002), state president and head of the military. Presided over China's boom.

Jung-lu (1836–1903) Manchu military commander. Had been betrothed to Dowager Empress.

Kang Sheng (1898–1975) CCP secret police chief and member of the Gang of Four in CR.

Kang Youwei (1858–1927) Reform propagandist of the Hundred Days of 1898 who was less important than he made out subsequently.

Kong Xiangxi (H. H. Kung) (1881–1967) Nationalist prime minister, finance minister, banker. Husband of Ailing Soong.

Kuai Dafu (1945–) Beijing student and Red Guard leader.

Lao She (1899–1966) Leading Beijing writer. Tortured by Red Guards, he was either murdered by them or committed suicide because of the harassment.

Lee Teng-hui (1923–) President of Taiwan and KMT chairman 1988–2000. Implemented democratic reforms and backed the island's autonomy.

Li Hongzhang (1823–1901) Leading 'Self-Strengthener'. Pioneered industry and acted as Qing negotiator with foreigners.

Li Lisan (1899–1967) CCP leader 1930–31. Labour minister in PRC. Tortured and died in CR.

Li Peng (1928–) Prime minister 1987–98. Conservative who backed use of force against 1989 protests.

Li Xiannian (1909–92) Early economic reformer. PRC president 1983–8. Then CPPCC president. Immortal.

Li Yuanhong (1864–1928) Gentry general. President of the Republic 1916–17 and 1922–3 after heading revolution in Hubei in 1911.

Li Zhisui (1919–95) Mao's doctor. Wrote warts-and-all portrait of the Chairman after moving to US.

Li Zongren (1890–1969) Leader of Guangxi Clique who feuded over two decades with Chiang. Briefly president of the Republic before fall of KMT regime.

Liang Qichao (1873–1929) Reformer and writer in Hundred Days of 1898.

Lin Biao (1907–71) PLA general who led civil war campaign in the north. Promoted to number two in PRC during CR. Killed in plane crash fleeing China.

Liu Bocheng (1892–1986) One-eyed PLA marshal and LM chief of staff. In 1948–9, his army helped win the key Huai-Hai battle. Deng's saying about the colour of a cat not mattering came from Liu.

Liu Shaoqi (1898–1969) Mao Zedong's deputy in the PRC till hounded to death in CR.

Long Yun (1884–1962) Warlord of Yunnan 1927–45. Later held posts under Communists.

Lu Xun (1881–1936) One of China's greatest twentieth-century writers. His *Story of Ah Q* stands as a telling allegory for the state of the nation.

Mao Zedong (1893–1976) CCP leader who gained supremacy on LM. Founder of PRC. Responsible for tens of millions of deaths.

Marshall, George (1880–1959) US Army chief of staff in Second World War sent on fruitless mission to resolve China's divisions in 1946. Future secretary of state.

Nie Yuanzi (1921–) Beijing University official who put up first big-character poster of CR.

Peng Dehuai (1898–1974) Communist commander, LM veteran and PRC defence minister. Purged by Mao after opposing GLF.

Peng Zhen (1902–97). CCP boss of Beijing before being purged by Mao. Immortal. Rehabilitated under Deng.

Puyi (1906–67). Last emperor of China. Made puppet ruler of Manchukuo by Japanese and underwent re-education under the PRC, ending life as a gardener.

Qiao Shi (1924–) Prominent CCP politician in 1980s and 1990s. Head of security apparatus, and then chairman of NPC.

Qiu Jin (1875–1907) Revolutionary heroine against late Qing. Executed after failed rising.

Snow, Edgar (1905–72) American journalist chosen to have first interview with Mao and put the CCP on the map with book *Red Star over China*.

Song Jiaoren (1882–1913) KMT politician. Masterminded election victory in 1912–13 but was assassinated before he could claim premiership.

Song Renqiong (1909–2005) PLA commander and Central Committee member. Vice-chair of CPPCC. Immortal.

Soong Ailing (1890–1973) Eldest Soong sister. Wife of H. H. Kong, known for her love of money.

Soong Meiling (Madame Chiang Kai-shek) (1897–2003) Youngest Soong sister. Married Chiang in 1927, and became main foreign spokesperson for KMT regime.

Soong Qingling (Madame Sun Yat-sen) (1893–1981) Middle Soong sister. Married Sun Yat-sen. Backed the left and held state post in PRC.

Soong Tzu-wen (T. V. Soong) (1894–1971) Senior member of Soong dynasty. Businessman, banker, prime minister, finance minister and foreign minister under Nationalists.

Stilwell, Joseph (Vinegar Joe) (1883–1946) US adviser to Nationalists in Second World War. Recalled after violent disagreements.

Sun Zhuanfeng (1885–1935) East China warlord in 1920s. Defeated by Nationalists.

Sun Yat-sen (1866–1925) Revolutionary and first president of the Republic. 'Father of the Republic' and KMT founder. Political philosophy was based on the Three Principles of the People – nationalism, democracy and the people's livelihood.

Tan Sitong (1865–1898) Reformist martyr. After joining the Hundred Days of 1898, he refused to flee and was executed.

Tan Yankai (1876–1930) Revolutionary chief of Hunan and early KMT ally who became prominent figure in Nationalist governments.

Tang Enbo (1898–1954) KMT general and Chiang loyalist badly defeated by Japanese. Commander in Shanghai in 1949, he organized the removal of troops and treasure to Taiwan.

Tang Shengzhi (1889–1970) Hunan warlord who joined KMT on Northern Expedition. Named to defend Nanjing in 1937, he fled before the massacre.

Tung Chee-hwa (C. H. Tung) (1937–) First chief executive of Hong Kong after its return to China in 1997. Avuncular shipping magnate, he failed to win popularity and resigned in 2005.

Wang Dan (1969–) Leading student activist in Tiananmen protest of 1989. Imprisoned before being exiled to the US in 1998.

Wang Guangmei (1921–2006) Wife of Liu Shaoqi, detested by Madame Mao. Persecuted by Red Guards and imprisoned. Released in 1979, she headed bodies to fight poverty and help mothers.

Wang Hongwen (1936–1992). Youngest member of the Gang of Four. Shanghai labour organizer favoured by Mao for a time as his successor. Sentenced to life imprisonment after fall of Gang.

Wang Jingwei (1883–1944) Sinuous, pomaded KMT politician. Lost out repeatedly to Chiang. Ended up heading collaborationist regime with Japanese.

Wang Ming (1904–74) Moscow-aligned CCP leader bested by Mao.

Wang Zhen (Big Cannon) (1908–93) Hardline CCP elder and scourge of 'bourgeois liberalization'. Immortal.

Wei Jingsheng (1950–) Leading democracy activist. Imprisoned for treason 1979–93 and again until 1997 before being deported to the United States.

Wen Jiabao (1942–) Prime minister since 2003. Visited Tiananmen students with Zhao Ziyang but saved from retribution by administrative skills. Went on to work with Zhu Rongji.

Weng Tonghe (1830–1904) Imperial tutor and major official at court before being abruptly dismissed by emperor during Hundred Days reform in 1898.

Wu Peifu (The Philosopher General) (c.1874–1939) Warlord in Central China in 1920s. Drank heavily. Defeated by KMT Northern Expedition.

Wuerkaixi (1968–) Student leader in 1989. Escaped after Massacre to settle in Taiwan.

Xiang Ying (c.1895–1941) Political leader of Communist New Fourth Army killed by a member of his staff after showdown with Nationalists.

Xue Yue (1896–1998) Leading Nationalist general who fought successfully against CCP and Japanese.

Yakub Beg (1820–77) Muslim nineteenth-century rebel. Set up independent state in Xinjiang. Defeated by Chinese army, he committed suicide.

Yan Xishan (The Model Governor) (1883–1960) Warlord of Shanxi. Survived for more than two decades before fleeing in 1949 to Taiwan, where he became prime minister.

Yang Hucheng (1893–1949) Shaanxi warlord. With Zhang Xueliang, detained Chiang in Xi'an in 1936. Imprisoned, he was executed as KMT regime fell in 1949.

Yang Shangkun (1907–98) PRC president 1988–93. Immortal. Close to Deng.

Yao Wenyuan (1931–2005) Writer and member of Gang of Four. Jailed for twenty years in 1981.

Ye Jianying (1897–1986) PLA general and defence minister. Led coup against Gang of Four.

Ye Ting (1896–1946) Head of Communist regiment on Northern Expedition who became commander of New Fourth Army. Jailed by Nationalists in 1941. Died in plane crash.

Yuan Shikai (1859–1916) Ambitious, able late imperial general. Forced the Qing to abdicate in 1912, and took power in the early republic, briefly proclaiming himself emperor.

Zeng Guofan (1811–72) Confucian organizer of resistance to the Taiping who reflected shift of power from dynasty to gentry.

Zhang Chunqiao (1917–2005) Member of Gang of Four. Organized Shanghai Commune in 1967. Sentenced to death in 1981, but this was commuted to life imprisonment.

Zhang Guotao (1897–1979) Founding CCP member and leader of big base. His army joined up with Mao's on the LM. The two fell out, and Zhang defected to the Nationalists, before going to Canada, where he died.

Zhang Wentian (1900–1976) LM veteran. CCP general secretary 1935–45. Persecuted in LM and CR.

Zhang Xueliang (The Young Marshal) (1901–2001) Drug addict, he succeeded his father as warlord of Manchuria, allied with KMT, only to be driven out by Japanese. Kidnapped Chiang at Xi'an in 1936, and spent next fifty years as political prisoner.

Zhang Xun (1854–1923) Qing loyalist general who tried to restore the empire.

Zhang Zongchang (The Dogmeat General) (1881–1932) Shandong warlord known for his violence and wanton ways. Defeated by Nationalists, he was killed by the son of one of his many victims.

Zhang Zuolin (The Old Marshal) (1873–1928) Epitome of old-style warlord. Ran Manchuria in 1920s and expanded across north China. Assassinated by Japanese.

Zhao Ziyang (1919–2005) Reformist prime minister 1980–87 and CCP general secretary 1987–9. Deposed for sympathies towards 1989 protestors. Under house arrest for last fifteen years of his life.

Zhou Enlai (1898–1976) Mao's urbane servitor. Prime minister and foreign minister under PRC. The regime's main negotiator with the West.

Zhu De (1886–1976) Military commander at Jiangxi base before undertaking LM. PLA chief. Attacked in CR.

Zhu Rongji (1928–) Prime minister and 'economic tsar' 1998–2003.

THE LATE-QING EMPERORS

Daoguang	1821–50
Xianfeng	1851–61
Tongzhi	1862–74
Guangxu	1875–1908
Puyi	1909–12

CHINA'S GROWTH 1976–2006

	1976	1986	1996	2006
Population (million)	937	1,075	1,223	1,307
GDP (billion Rmb, current prices)	294.4	1,020.2	6,788.5	21,100
Average per capita GDP (Rmb, at current prices)	316	963	5,846	14,040
Household consumption (Rmb, current prices)	171	497	2,789	5,439
Retail sales (million Rmb, current prices)	133,940	495,000	2,836,020	7,641,000
Merchandise trade (million US$)	13,430	73,850	289,880	1,760,700
Exports (million US$)	685	30,940	151,050	969,100
Imports (million US$)	658	42,910	138,830	791,600
Foreign direct investment used (million US$)	1,769 (1979–82)	2,244	41,726	63,000

Sources: National Bureau of Statistics; *Chinese Compendium of Statistics; China Statistical Yearbook*

COMMUNIST PARTY LEADERS IN THE PEOPLE'S REPUBLIC

Chairmen of the CCP

Mao Zedong	1949–76
Hua Guofeng	1976–81
Hu Yaobang	1981–2

General secretaries of the Secretariat*

Deng Xiaoping   1954–66†
Hu Yaobang   1978–87
Zhao Ziyang   1987–9
Jiang Zemin   1989–2002
Hu Jintao   2002–

* The general secretary was called chief secretary from April 1954 to September 1956 and from December 1978 to September 1982.
† De facto, as the Secretariat ceased to function during the Cultural Revolution, which began in 1966.

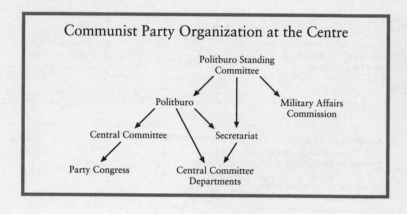

Communist Party Organization at the Centre

Index

Subheadings are arranged in chronological order.

Communist Party – *contd.*
Nanchang Uprising,
189–90
Canton uprising, 192–3
dominance of USSR, 217
rural bases, 218–19
Jiangxi base, 219, 220–21
urban campaigns failed,
221–2
KMT's encirclement
campaigns, 222–3,
224–5, 226, 228
internal purge, 223–5
Chinese Soviet Republic
established, 226
Shanghai CCP loss, 226–7
loses E-yu-wan base, 243
holds Jiangxi base, 244–5
loses Jiangxi base, 250–51
forms Shaan-Gan-Ning
base, 273
Hundred Regiments
Offensive, 296–7
conflict with KMT, 297–9
'Three Alls' attack, 301
hardship and opium trade,
308–9
less fightings with Japan,
309
purges in Yenan, 309–11
'Dixie Mission', 311
centralizes authority,
312
agreement with Hurley,
325
links up with Soviets, 328
class struggles, 370–74
power over government,
379
conflict after Great Leap,
419–21
members attacked in
Cultural Revolution,
449
leaders attacked in
Cultural Revolution,
465–6, 473–4, 475–6,
483–7
corruption, 557, 568–9,
577, 654, 657–8
reaction to student
demonstration, 590–91,
593–6

agrees talk with student
demonstrators, 603
martial law, 605–7, 609,
611
dialogue with students,
610
elders takes control,
612–13, 614–15
clears up Tiananmen
Square, 620–21, 622
verdict on Tiananmen
demonstration, 630–31,
639–40
conservatives' policies on
reform, 640–41
reformists under attack,
642–4
leftists under attack,
644–6
accelerated market
reform, 647–9
younger technocrats joins
Politburo, 649, 650,
651
conservatives beaten,
651–2
Three Represents, 665
denounces Falun Gong,
666
factionalism, 667
harmonious society, 669
collective leadership,
669–70
challenges for, 670–71
privileges, xxxiv–xxxv
autocracy, xxxviii–xxxix,
xlii–xliii, 674–5
membership imbalance,
xliv, 674
legitimacy claim, 676–7
lack of authority, 677–80
Chinese Soviet Republic, 226
Chongqing, 291–4, 349–50,
477
Christian missionaries, 79,
80–82 *see also* Boxer
Rising
Christianity, revival, xlv
Christopher, W., 539
Chun, Prince, 43
Civil War
peace talk, 329–31
outbreak, 331–2

Marshall's ceasefire effort,
332–3
PLA and KMT force,
333–4
economic and political
problems, 334–5
Zhangjiakou taken by
KMT, 336
PLA modernized, 337
E-yu-wan battles, 338–9
Manchuria battles, 338
KMT loses Manchuria,
339–40
Huai-Hai Battle, 340–41
KMT economic reform,
341–2
US aid suspended, 342
PLA takes Tianjin, 343
PLA takes Beijing and
Taiyuan, 344
KMT retreats to Taiwan,
344–5
PLA takes Nanjing,
345–6
PLA takes Shanghai,
347–8
PLA takes Chongqing,
349–50
People's Republic formed,
349
end of KMT era, 350
Cixi *see* Dowager Empress
climate, 12
Clinton, B., 662, 664
coal mines, 648
Coastal Economic Zones,
562
Commercial Press, 237
Commune and Brigade
Enterprises (CBEs), 557,
563
Communist International,
143
Confucius, revival, xliv–xlv
Convention of Chefoo
(1878), 33
Cowles, G., 315–16
Cradock, P, 478–9, 549,
554, 568
Creelman, J., 50
Cui Jian, 570
Cultural Revolution *see also*
Gang of Four

PENGUIN HISTORY

AFTER TAMERLANE: THE GLOBAL HISTORY OF EMPIRE
JOHN DARWIN

'*After Tamerlane* is a deeply significant book ... It is rather wonderful to doff one's hat to a historian who can range across time and space, giving the reader continual cause for pause, in the way that Darwin has done'
Paul Kennedy, *Sunday Times*

After Tamerlane takes a fresh look at our global past. Our idea of world history is still dominated by the view from the West: it is Europe's expansion that takes centre-stage. But for much of the 600-year span of this book, Asia's great empires seemed more than a match for the intruders from Europe. It took a revolution in Eurasia to change this balance of power, although it never did so completely. The Chinese empire, against all the odds, has survived to this day. The British empire came and went. The Nazi empire was crushed almost at once. The rise, fall and endurance of empires – and the causes behind them – remain one of the most fascinating puzzles in world history.

At the heart of this book is the story of the dramatic shifts and unpredictable changes in the relations between the West, the states and empires of the Islamic world and the great civilizations of East Asia. It forms the historical perspective in which we can see more clearly the great resurgence of Asia, the central feature of our modern 'globalized' world. If we are to make sense of our future, we need also to make sense of our Eurasian past.

After Tamerlane deals with the most famous and exciting events in Europe and Asia's history – and makes them fresh and surprising once more.

PENGUIN HISTORY

FORGOTTEN WARS
CHRISTOPHER BAYLY AND TIM HARPER

'[A] tragic and bloody story ... a brilliant, devastatingly honest analysis of the last years of Britain's Asian Empire' *Daily Telegraph*

The Second World War ended officially in 1945, yet for Asia the conflict was far from over. Britain's Asian Empire was engulfed in a new series of diverse, intense and bloody wars, which raged throughout Indonesia, India, Burma, Malaya and Vietnam as an unstoppable wave of nationalism swept the old colonial ways aside. This is the story of the struggles of military commanders and revolutionary leaders, but also of ordinary people caught up in the insurgency, rioting and turmoil that heralded the birth of a new Asia.

'An outstanding narrative account ... If there are lessons from history they are surely to be found in this book' Richard Overy

'They have done a marvellous job in recovering [this] largely forgotten history ... a delight to read' *Independent*

'Bayly and Harper's strength, apart from lucid, inexhaustible scholarship, is to show us what a mazy, murderous path both Asians and their colonial occupiers were forced to walk' *Observer*

'Destined to be indispensable for many years to come' *Asian Review of Books*

Penguin History

EMPIRE: HOW BRITAIN MADE THE MODERN WORLD
NIALL FERGUSON

Once, vast swathes of the globe were coloured imperial red and Britannia ruled not just the waves, but the prairies of America, the plains of Asia, the jungles of Africa and the deserts of Arabia. Just how did a small, rainy island in the North Atlantic achieve all this? And why did the empire on which the sun literally never set finally decline and fall? Niall Ferguson's acclaimed *Empire* brilliantly unfolds the imperial story in all its splendours and its miseries, showing how a gang of buccaneers and gold-diggers planted the seed of the biggest empire in history – and set the world on the road to modernity.

'The most brilliant British historian of his generation ... Ferguson examines the roles of "pirates, planters, missionaries, mandarins, bankers and bankrupts" in the creation of history's largest empire ... he writes with splendid panache ... and a seemingly effortless, debonair wit' Andrew Roberts, *The Times*

'Thrilling ... an extraordinary story' *Daily Mail*

'A brilliant book ... full of energy, imagination and curiosity' *Evening Standard*

'A remarkably readable précis of the whole British imperial story – triumphs, deceits, decencies, kindnesses, cruelties and all' Jan Morris

'Dazzling ... wonderfully readable' *New York Review of Books*

'An enormous saga ... crammed with the kind of anecdotes that leave the reader wanting more' *Sunday Herald*

Penguin History

EMPIRE MADE ME: AN ENGLISHMAN ADRIFT IN SHANGHAI
ROBERT BICKERS

The highly charged, evocative story of one ordinary man's life and death as a servant of the British Empire.

Shanghai in the wake of the First World War was one of the world's most dynamic, brutal and exciting cities, rivalled only by New York and Berlin. Its waterfront crammed with ocean freighters, gunboats, junks and a myriad coastal craft, it was the great focus for trade between China and the world, creating for Chinese and foreigner alike immense if precarious opportunities. Shanghai's great panorama of nightclubs, opium-dens, brothels, racetracks and casinos was intertwined with this industrial powerhouse to create a uniquely seductive but also terrifying metropolis.

Into this maelstrom stepped a tough and resourceful ex-veteran Englishman to join the Shanghai police. It is his story, told in part through his rediscovered photo albums and letters, that Robert Bickers tells here. Aggressive, bullying, racist, self-aggrandizing, Maurice Tinkler was in many ways a typical Briton-on-the-make in an empire world that gave authority to its citizens purely through their skin colour. But Tinkler was also very much more than this – for all his bravado, he could not know that the history that packed him off to Shanghai could just as readily crush him.

A detective story, a recreation of a lost world and a meditation on loss, *Empire Made Me* is both a moving account of one man's life and a fascinating insight into how the British Empire *really* worked.

'A fascinating and dispassionate portrait of how the British Empire kept afloat for so long. In the process he vividly brings to life the forgotten multitude of ordinary British who oiled its wheels, arrested its enemies, fed off its fat, and sometimes died for its cause' Matthew Kneale

'Bickers' detailed recovery of an obscure and "unimportant" policeman's life gives a valuable street-level view of a complex scene. A fascinating book' *FT Magazine*

'Superb' Giles Foden

He just wanted a decent book to read ...

Not too much to ask, is it? It was in 1935 when Allen Lane, Managing Director of Bodley Head Publishers, stood on a platform at Exeter railway station looking for something good to read on his journey back to London. His choice was limited to popular magazines and poor-quality paperbacks – the same choice faced every day by the vast majority of readers, few of whom could afford hardbacks. Lane's disappointment and subsequent anger at the range of books generally available led him to found a company – and change the world.

'We believed in the existence in this country of a vast reading public for intelligent books at a low price, and staked everything on it'
Sir Allen Lane, 1902–1970, founder of Penguin Books

The quality paperback had arrived – and not just in bookshops. Lane was adamant that his Penguins should appear in chain stores and tobacconists, and should cost no more than a packet of cigarettes.

Reading habits (and cigarette prices) have changed since 1935, but Penguin still believes in publishing the best books for everybody to enjoy. We still believe that good design costs no more than bad design, and we still believe that quality books published passionately and responsibly make the world a better place.

So wherever you see the little bird – whether it's on a piece of prize-winning literary fiction or a celebrity autobiography, political tour de force or historical masterpiece, a serial-killer thriller, reference book, world classic or a piece of pure escapism – you can bet that it represents the very best that the genre has to offer.

Whatever you like to read – trust Penguin.